Reserve Collection

Telephone : 01 - 340 3343

HIGHGATE LITERARY & SCIENTIFIC INSTITUTION
11, SOUTH GROVE, N.6

14193

Time allowed FOURTEEN Days

Date Issued	Date Issued	Date Issued
3 OCT 1974	27 SEP 1975	
12 OCT 1974	- 8 SEP 1984	
26 OCT 1974	18 JUN 1987	
20 JAN 1975	26 NOV 1988	
13 FEB 1975	20 OCT 1989	
- 8 MAR 1975	- 8 DEC 1989	
21 MAR 1975	19 JUN 1990	
10 APR 1975	22 FEB 1992	
- 1 MAY 1975		
28 MAY 1975		
25 JUN 1975		
10 JUL 1975		
- 1 AUG 1975		

TIMES
TO
REMEMBER

TIMES
TO
REMEMBER

An Autobiography

ROSE FITZGERALD KENNEDY

COLLINS
St James's Place, London
1974

William Collins Sons & Co Ltd
London · Glasgow · Sydney · Auckland
Toronto · Johannesburg

14193
—————
920

First published 1974
© 1974 by The Joseph P. Kennedy Jr Foundation
ISBN 0 00 216761 1
Set in Monotype Garamond
Made and Printed in Great Britain by
William Collins Sons & Co Ltd Glasgow

ILLUSTRATIONS

ILLUSTRATION
ACKNOWLEDGMENTS

Wide World Photos: 1a, 1c, 5a, 14a, 15a, 22b
Kennedy Family Collection: 1b, 1d, 2a, 2c, 3a, 3b, 3c, 4a, 4b, 4c, 4d, 5b, 5c, 6b, 9a, 9b, 10b, 12a, 12b, 13a, 13b, 13c, 15b, 16a, 17a, 17b, 18, 20a, 21b, 22a, 24a, 26a, 27a, 27c, 28a, 28c, 29a, 29b, 31a
Vose: 2b
Acme Newspictures Inc.: 6a
Keystone Press Agency Ltd: 7a, 12c
Peter Hunter, Press Features, Amsterdam: 8
International News Photo: 10a
Bristol Evening Post: 10c
Harcourt-Harris, NYC: 14b, 14c, 14d
Toni Frissell Collection, Library of Congress: 14 inset
Lisa Larsen, Time-Life Picture Agency: 15c
US Navy Photograph: 16b, 16c
Christian Science Publishing Society: 17c
Miller Studio, Hyannis, Mass.: 19a
Boston Record: 19b
Paul Schnutzer, Time-Life Picture Agency: 20b
Hans Knopf, Pix Inc.: 21a
Robert Knudson, The White House: 22c, 23b
Pierre Boulat, Time-Life Picture Agency: 23a
UPI: 24b
Mort Kaye Studios: 25
Van Durand: 26b
Jacques Lowe: 27b
Bert and Richard Morgan: 28b
Toronto Star Syndicate: 30a
Gilbert A. Michie & Co. Ltd: 30b
Roland Andersson: 31b
Ron Mosati, *Buffalo Courier-Express*: 31c
Lane: 32

ACKNOWLEDGEMENT

I am most grateful to my children – Eunice Shriver, Patricia Lawford, Jean Smith, and Senator Edward Kennedy – and to my daughters-in-law – Joan Kennedy, Ethel Kennedy, and Jacqueline Onassis – and to my sons-in-law – Sargent Shriver and Stephen Smith – for their advice and counsel in all of the stages of this book. Without their thoughts, memories, anecdotes and other contributions, my book would never have become a faithful portrait and history of our family. Robert Coughlan also deserves special thanks for his research, his editorial skills and his fidelity to the main purpose of my endeavour. I also want to express my thanks to Sandy Richardson for his sensitive guidance, advice and support. To many others, who are quoted in these pages, my warm appreciation.

'Never let success hide its emptiness from you,
achievement its nothingness, toil its desolation. And
so . . .
Keep alive the incentive to push on further, that pain in
the soul which drives us beyond ourselves.

'Do not look back. And do not dream about the future,
either. It will neither give you back the past, nor satisfy
your other daydreams. Your duty, your reward – your
destiny – are *here* and *now*.'

DAG HAMMARSKJÖLD

'All things have their season, and in their times all
things pass under heaven.
A time to be born and a time to die. A time to plant,
and a time to pluck up that which is planted.
A time to kill, and a time to heal. A time to destroy,
and a time to build.
A time to weep, and a time to laugh. A time to mourn,
and a time to dance.
A time to scatter stones, and a time to gather. A time
to embrace, and a time to be far from embraces.
A time to get, and a time to lose. A time to keep,
and a time to cast away.
A time to rend, and a time to sew. A time to keep
silence, and a time to speak . . .
And I have known that there was no better thing than
to rejoice, and to do well in this life.
For every man that eateth and drinketh, and seeth good
of his labour, this is the gift of God . . .
And I have found that nothing is better than for a man
to rejoice in his work, and that this is his portion.
For who shall bring him to know the things that shall
be after him?'

Ecclesiastes is one of my favourite Books of the Old
Testament, as it was also for my son, President John F. Kennedy.
Some of these lines were read during his funeral services in 1963.

ROSE FITZGERALD KENNEDY

This book is dedicated to my daughter Rosemary and
others like her, retarded in mind but blessed in spirit.
My vision is a world where mental retardation will
be overcome, where we no longer mourn with mothers
of retarded children; but exult and rejoice with parents
of healthy, happy youngsters. Then, and only then,
can we say, in the words of St Paul: 'I have fought
the good fight. I have finished the course. I have
kept the faith.'

I

There have been times when I felt I was one of the more fortunate people in the world, almost as if Providence, or Fate or Destiny, as you like, had chosen me for special favours.

Now I am in my eighties, and I have seen the worst of times as well as the best. I can neither forget nor ever reconcile myself to the tragedies. Age, however, has its privileges. One is to reminisce and another is to reminisce selectively. I prefer to remember the good times, and that is how this book begins.

Before I began to write what follows, I had to ask myself some hard questions, and the first was, 'Why do it?' And the second was, 'Well, supposing I do, then How? What is the best way?' I think that anyone who reads the book is entitled to have my answers to myself.

Surely anyone who writes a memoir or autobiography must either believe that he or she is someway a rather special person with a special wisdom or body of experience, or has a contribution of some unique and valuable kind to make. If this were not so, history and literature would be lacking all that great body of valuable (and less valuable) works that give us insights into times past and people and societies gone.

Yet my reason for writing this book – and in my own mind the over-riding one – is that I want to set the record straight. Millions and millions of words have been written about my family, collectively and individually, and if I were to make a guess about the contents of this mountain of print, I would reckon that most of it has, at best, been flawed by inaccuracies, misunderstandings, misinterpretations, and the worst has been mendacious and deceitful or even totally untrue stories that sound like pulp fiction and are often confused with history. For a great many years I tried to ignore everything, from the honest errors to the pure trash, for if I had allowed myself to care I would have been driven to distraction. There was too much; the flow was too heavy. I suppose it will continue at least awhile, so long as there are Kennedys in politics or somehow in the public eye; and I can do nothing about the

errors and falsehoods that come off the presses. Nor can I possibly cope
with all those that came off in the past. But at least, in this book, I can
deal with the major ones, and thus perform a service both to my family
and to historians.

As for the second question, the best way to do the book, I was
uncertain until, wonderfully enough, the question began to answer
itself. I had diary notes that I had been keeping with some faithfulness
since the years of the Ambassadorship, and from these and various
memorabilia I had worked up a thick sheaf of manuscript pages, some
of which I thought were quite good. There were other resources, such
as the black leather-bound 'Commonplace Books' in which, for many
years, I had been collecting quotations (Emerson's and Euripides', used
above, came from this trove), interesting words, apt phrases, homilies,
ideas and philosophical jottings and aphorisms, on all sorts of subjects,
for potential uses in campaigning, other public speaking, and goodness
knows what. There were other things, scrap books, clippings, notes,
photographs, and so forth, along with a library of Kennedy books,
some written by Kennedys. Still, somehow, with all these tools at
hand, there did not seem to be enough resources to do justice to the
theme. Neither my husband nor any of the children had written any
substantial memoirs of the family; therefore this book would be – so
far – the only book about the Kennedys written by a Kennedy, a large
responsibility.

I will amend that now to take account of a rumour about the
Kennedys that is quite true, and to supply what seems to me a happy
ending for this first chapter. The true rumour is that the Kennedys
co-operate with one another and that an individual's project is likely to
become a family project, with everyone pitching in to help the common
cause. I have been helped, with time and energy and painstaking
research, and attention and concern and encouragement and everything
else that love and loyalty can inspire – and all this because I let them
know of the project and the problems I felt; asked them if there were
some intra-family letters, notes or other artifacts that might help fill
gaps and add variety and a sense of life as it was for one or another of
us at some particular time; and asked further if they would mind
talking about me, and the life of our family, and how things really
were in all weathers, with a tape-recorder nearby.

I was getting on in years, I said, and memories of long ago were
hard to recapture, but I needed to do so. ('Good Lord!' said my
daughter-in-law Ethel. 'Twenty, thirty years ago? Remembering? Half
the time I can't even remember half the things that happened yesterday
afternoon! Who can?')

Extraordinary and beautiful things began to happen. Were there surviving letters? Hundreds and hundreds of them began to flow in, along with dozens of bits of childhood memorabilia, valentines, Christmas cards, second-grade scrawls and fourth-grade poetic efforts, most of which I had long since forgotten, however much delight they had given me at the time.

Would they mind recording their memories of me and our life on tape? They did not mind, or at least mind excessively, and so now there are many tapes with printed transcripts and I find them invaluable, not only in helping me remember but also as what might be called 'contra-memoirs'. I have my own, special memories of family and friends, of me in a landscape of Kennedys as it were, and invariably their memories differ in some ways from my own. Useful, corrective, instructive, fascinating; and so, even though I don't agree with everything, large portions of these 'contra-memoirs' are inserted in this book as and when the context indicates – along with many, many of the letters, in brief portions or in full. All these add new dimensions, values, and insights to these memoirs. The letters and tape-recordings were the missing elements, I now think, to the kind of book, historically true but with the full breath of life in it, that I had wanted to write.

Again Emerson: 'Properly there is no such thing as history, only biography.' This, then, to the degree that I have succeeded, is a book about Joseph and Rose Kennedy, with something about their parents and a great deal about their children; in their settings, their humanity, their natures and destinies.

With all the help I have received from so many people, and with all my thanks in many directions, this remains my own book, stuffed with my memories, especially memories of my children, and with my own thoughts and precepts and goals when I was raising them.

What I was able to pass on to them was, of course, in an indefinable but substantial degree, what I had received from my parents, and they in turn from theirs.

2

As with so many other American families of Irish descent, we begin with the famines that swept Ireland during the middle of the last century. Thousands of people died. Other thousands, younger and stronger and luckier, emigrated, most of them to the United States and a large share of these to the city and hinterlands of Boston. I have read that the fare, including food, was about $20, and that the voyage sometimes took as long as two months. With overcrowding, disease, and miserable and debilitating conditions perhaps one passenger in ten died on the voyage. An Irish immigrant had to be both hardy and lucky to set foot at last in America.

My paternal grandparents, Thomas Fitzgerald and Rose Mary Murray, made that grim voyage in the 1840s. They both came from County Wexford, but they met and were married in Boston. Later another son of Wexford, Patrick Kennedy, arrived in Boston. There he, too, met and married an Irish immigrant girl, Bridget Murphy. I have no direct memories of these four brave souls because each had passed away before I was born. But I know they arrived with scarcely more than determination and faith, that they worked hard, and raised their children in the love and care of God.

The Fitzgeralds had eleven children, nine of them survived infancy, among these was John Francis Fitzgerald. He married Mary Josephine Hannon and they had six children – of whom I was the eldest. The Kennedys had four children, including an only son called Patrick Joseph (known later in Boston political annals as 'P.J.'). He married Mary Hickey and they had three children – one of them, again an only son, was Joseph Patrick Kennedy.

The two family lines joined when Joseph Patrick Kennedy and I were married.

Grandfather Thomas Fitzgerald had worked for a while as a farm hand at South Acton, a village 25 miles or so from Boston, just beyond Lexington and Concord, but later came back to Boston's 'North

End', where he spent most of the rest of his life as a grocer. Thus it was in the North End (in a modest flat in an eight-family dwelling) that my father was born, raised, and felt most at home. And so in turn, after he and my mother married and had saved enough to set up housekeeping (a modest house also). It was there that I was born, on July 22, 1890, christened Rose Elizabeth.

The North End had been the centre of Colonial Boston: of all those mercantile, religious, cultural and political activities that made the city the hub of Massachusetts colony and much of New England. In fact it encompassed most of the city, which in those years had a population of only about 17,000. As every schoolchild knows, many of the causes, ideas, ideals of the American Revolution originated and were nurtured in Boston, and many of the first decisive acts of the Revolution happened there. So the old North End is full of historical buildings and sites – Faneuil Hall, the old North Church, and Paul Revere's house.

By the time he was in his late teens, my father was a fascinated amateur expert on Boston's history and was even conducting guided tours, with his own lectures. I remember as a child and as a young girl that it was a rare outing in Boston or anywhere in the area that did not inspire a discourse on historical names, dates and incidents, delivered in a style that was informative yet also marvellously interesting and entertaining. He made history come to life. Sometimes, a scene or event would remind him of Irish history and the migrations. He knew a great deal about them as well, mostly from listening to his own father. His conversation was wide-ranging. From Boston's history to America's, Ireland's to England's, from these to the world's. From history to current events and from current events to their causes, which he would analyse and interpret and prognosticate about in a rush of thoughts and words, something like spontaneous combustion.

He talked to me incessantly when I was a child and young girl growing up: about everything in sight, but since so much in sight had some association with American history that is what I heard about more often than not. Naturally this had an influence on me. Evidently, in fact, it was especially noticeable when it came to raising my own children. I believed they should know history and especially the history of their own country and, when they grew old enough to understand, I used to take them to the landmarks in Boston and the countryside, explaining what had happened there and discussing events with them so they would remember them.

I was determined about this, and I may have overdone it a little since there can be too much even of a good thing. My daughter Eunice says it seemed to her I was always dragging them off to Bunker Hill or

Concord Bridge and there were times when she thought of me as a schoolteacher. In any case they did learn, their interest developed with the years, and I suspect that this may be one reason why as adults they wanted to serve the country in public life. Jack, especially, was fascinated by history; he read it, wrote it, and lived it, and I think his sense of history guided his whole career and gave his Presidency a quality of its own.

There is another family characteristic that I think derives from my father. This is a mixture of abundant energy, vitality, physique, quick reflexes and a psychological or endocrinological x-factor. I refer not only to the touch football games, for instance, that became famous, but to the strenuous activities that were always going on. Of course, Jack's Presidency is remembered, among many things, for its encouragement of increased physical fitness in the nation and calls for 'vigour'.

The influences of heredity and environment being as elusive and incalculable as they are, there is no way to assign shares, but it is clear to me that our children inherited these traits from both sides of the family. Joe was a superb athlete, and few men ever had such energy and stamina. And then there was my father.

He was an extraordinary athlete. Although he was only about 5 ft 7 ins, he was tremendously strong and agile. As he once recalled, speaking of his boyhood, 'In those days we used to run on the sidewalks and cobblestones of Hanover Street, and I could always beat any of the boys.' At the Boston Latin School – the oldest and, at least in those days, perhaps the most prestigious public high school in the country – he managed and played in the baseball team, played football, and was team captain for two years. He also edited the school magazine. There was no interscholastic athletic organization in Boston in those days; so, shortly after he graduated, he founded one and became its first president. Later, he developed a great fondness for riding. I should add that he also loved to dance as long as the music played, charming and beguiling his partners and talking a mile a minute, between numbers.

My father also had ability to think and speak precisely and rapidly, and I dare say it served him well in business and politics. This was the era before radio, television and public address systems and all the other modern media (and a far more sophisticated public) when it was necessary to speak directly and succinctly and with time enough between sentences so that whatever one is attempting to communicate will soak in.

Many times I saw my father walk into a room – a parlour, ballroom, the main lounge of an ocean liner – full of somnolent, inhibited people bored stiff with one another, and within five minutes have them smiling, attentive, active, having fun, perhaps even singing. He took charge of them and they loved it. And he did, too. I think he felt it was a challenge to wake them up. Yet he also truly liked people and liked to see them happy.

As for his scholastic abilities, there was never reason to doubt them. The Boston Latin School had high academic standards and he had done well there. He was accepted at Harvard Medical School and was already in his first year when Fate intervened to change his life.

His mother, Rose Mary Fitzgerald, had died three years earlier. Now his father, Thomas Fitzgerald, died. Both had been in their thirties. They left nine surviving children, all sons, of whom my father (then aged eighteen) was third eldest; which of course left six more down the line from him, from teen-agers to toddlers. Thomas Fitzgerald had left a small amount of money but nowhere near enough to keep this large brood fed and sheltered very long, and obviously nothing could be spared for my father's expenses at medical school. He could have made his way through entirely on his own, I expect, but he felt a deep obligation to the memory of his parents and to what would have been their dearest wish, that the family stay together, despite the practical advice of the parish priest that the younger brothers be placed in foster homes. Consequently, he left school, took a civil service examination and landed a steady job as a clerk in the Boston Custom House. (Incidentally, his top boss, the Collector in charge of the Custom House, was the future distinguished Senator from Massachusetts, Leverett Saltonstall). I never learned why the two older brothers didn't take more responsibility, but the fact was that my father became the mainstay of the family and continued to be so until the youngest boys were ready to take care of themselves.

This marked the end of my father's formal education. I'm sure he regretted not having a chance to finish college. Yet I have thought this was seriously to his advantage. So often, it seems, people get their college degrees and then are content to let mental faculties atrophy from disuse. He, on the contrary, perhaps because of being denied the credentials of an education, retained his appetite for knowledge and became an avid reader. He had wonderful eyes (azure blue; I inherited the colour but less optical quality) and boundless curiosity, so he read everything within reach: books, magazines, and of course, many newspapers. Everything in print seemed to be grist for him – and when he found something that struck him as interesting, important or in some way useful, he would cut the item out of the magazine or paper with a small penknife he carried. Then, to be sure he wouldn't lose it, quite often he would pin it (with a straight pin; he carried a supply) on his lapel or, when that area was filled, almost anywhere else on the front of his jacket. One of my earlier vivid recollections is of him sitting in a chair surrounded by newspapers, penknife in hand and neatly (always neatly, like a surgeon) excising something pertinent.

He kept on doing this all his life. Eunice says that one of her own enduring images of him – one of those impressions that somehow are selected and stored in the mind from among the many – was when he was well along in years, probably in his seventies. He was visiting us at Hyannis Port and was sitting in his favourite perch there, a chair at the far end of our big, bright, comfortable living-room, with a sea view and the sunlight streaming in behind him. 'There were masses of newspapers all over the floor around him, and he was clipping. He wouldn't get through a page or two without pulling out something. And he'd say, "Now look at this! Look what the women are doing" – anyway, always he'd be finding something interesting.'

And what he read, he remembered. He had a stupendous memory for facts and figures, points of law, historical facts, quotations, anecdotes, and of course anything to do with Boston – all of great advantage to him in his political speech-making and in debating with an opponent. He had a famous ability to talk about anything, rapidly, persuasively, cogently and with swarms of facts seemingly produced from the thin blue. Someone put this verse in a Boston paper:

> Honey Fitz can talk you blind
> On any subject you can find.
> Fish and fishing, motor-boats,
> Railroads, street-cars, getting votes,
> Proper ways to open clams,
> How to cure existing shams,
> State Street, Goo-Goos, aeroplanes,
> Malefactors, thieving gains,
> Local transportation rates,
> How to run the nearby States;
> On all these things, and many more,
> Honey Fitz is crammed with lore.

I expect that here again his character left some imprints on mine. I mentioned earlier my scrapbooks – looseleaf Commonplace Books filled with useful facts and notable ideas and quotations, the gleanings of many years of clipping items from newspapers and magazines and transcribing favourite passages from plays and books. Also for years I have carried a small spiral-back notebook in my purse, which I use for jotting down similar treasures that I encounter on the hop; and I'm sure I would feel rather lost and deprived without it.

The life of a Customs clerk could not contain my father's energies for long or ever satisfy his ambitious nature, so after three years of it he resigned and started an insurance business with an office in the North End. He was already mixed up in so many civic, fraternal, social and athletic affairs that he was widely known there, and with his natural gifts of salesmanship he soon was prosperous enough to marry the girl he had been in love with for years, Mary Josephine Hannon, daughter of Irish immigrants who had settled in the little town of Acton north-west of Boston. They married in 1889, and I was born the next year. Proverbially, a man wants his first child to be a son. But with nine boys in his family, and no female relatives in this country and none that he knew of in Ireland, my father was overjoyed to have a girl. He seems to have regarded me as a miracle, an impression from which he never really recovered.

By the time I arrived he was already active in ward politics. Soon he was elected to Boston's Common Council. And then to the State Senate. And then – a meteoric rise – to the US House of Representatives. He was one of the youngest men in Congress, the only Democrat from the whole of New England, and the only Catholic. He was re-elected twice, so his tenure in Congress lasted six years, from 1895 to 1901.

Meanwhile our family was increasing. I had a little sister, Agnes; then a little brother, Thomas; and with three small children and the promise of more to follow, my father decided to vacate our small flat and move us to a place in the country with space and a yard and fresh air. It was a big, old, rambling, architecturally hybrid but wonderfully comfortable house in West Concord, just a few miles from Acton, where my mother's parents, my Hannon grandparents, lived on a hill, with lovely woods behind, and it was there that I spent the rest of my childhood.

They were wonderful years, full of the traditional pleasures and satisfactions of life in a small New England town. Years of serenity, order, neighbourly human relationships, family affection: trips with horse-and-buggy to my grandparents' house, climbing apple trees and gathering wildflowers in the woods behind the house. I knew and remembered from year to year where the lady's slippers were hidden, and where to look for the Solomon's seal and all my other favourite spring flowers as they appeared, each in its time. There was the hand-cranked ice-cream freezer, and tantalizing visions of getting to lick the ladle – which never could be soon, because making ice-cream was a big job, hard work, and it was only for Sundays and birthdays and other special occasions; warm milk fresh from the cows at a neighbour's farm. My memories seem to dwell on food. Fresh peas and salmon were Fourth of July for us and everyone else in the area (no one outside of New England, it seems, has ever heard of the idea), and peas in season were a Sunday staple. We did our share of shelling. Baked beans and brown bread: every household had a special, perfect recipe and in all cases the smells were delicious every Saturday night, because that was the night for baked beans and brown bread. My father loved them. And, on Friday nights, lobsters brought in from Boston. I remember how happy he looked sitting at the table with his family and devouring lobsters, sucking the claws and pulling them apart with great gusto.

Except when Congress was in recess he could be there with us only for weekends. And these visits were feats of endurance. By the time he had left his Congressional office in Washington to board the train to New York, and caught a train from there to Boston, and another from Boston to Concord, and ridden in a carriage from Concord to West Concord where we lived, at least fourteen hours had passed. Then, to get back to Washington for the Monday morning session of the House, it was all to do over in reverse.

He never complained or even commented on this outlandish commuting arrangement, so far as I can recall. On the contrary, it seemed to stimulate him. He loved excitement and every train connection was a gamble. As soon as I was old enough to handle the reins I was usually the one to go along with him to Concord station and drive the carriage back home. He never wanted to leave until the last minute, and he would calculate it by having all us children look for smoke puffing up from the train as it approached – still a couple of miles away – through the woods to Concord. Then, depending on the report and what must have been some intricate mental arithmetic, he would regulate the speed of the horse. Now and then, not often, he cut his chances too fine or ran into delays and lost his bet with himself and missed the train. But that didn't seem to faze him. He accepted most things as they came – or went. He would shrug his shoulders and tell me he'd use time getting a shave and reading the papers and a book or two he always had with him and wouldn't be missing a thing, no time really lost at all.

Losing time, wasting time, doing nothing – these were matters that really bothered him, so he always made sure there was something to do, something he could feel it was useful to do. And I think I have always been the same way.

I think there is truth in the idea that 'opposites attract', because it was certainly true in the case of my parents. Father was an extrovert; mother was innately rather shy and reserved. He would talk with anybody about anything. When she spoke, it was usually directly and to the point. Small talk and other social lubricants bored her and she was not adept at them. He adored being with people – of all kinds, complexions, religions, attitudes, conditions and ages, so long as they were alive and responsive. She was happiest with close friends and members of her family, yet she also needed time to be alone, in peaceful solitude for reflection and prayer. He loved being 'on stage' and feeling the vibrations emanating from an audience. She could enjoy the show and the glamour but, as it were, as a spectator in the audience; when she was obliged to be on stage herself, as from time to time she was, she was likely to respond with a nervous uncomfortableness that she controlled somewhat stiffly and formally. When he was happy everyone knew it. When she was happy there were few symptoms but smiles and serenity, yet when she was unhappy (she must have been sometimes; who hasn't been?) she rarely showed it. She was unselfishly devoted to her husband and her family and to our welfare as she saw it.

Mother was an immaculate housekeeper with a strong sense of the value of money and a sharp eye for any waste or any short-changing. And a good thing: for my ebullient father's inclination was to cut a figure, bestow benefits, set a fine table and think of the money a little later. He had known poverty and knew the meaning of nickels and dimes. But his nature and the nature of political life made him more spontaneous than frugal. Mother minded the budget.

When I try to identify traits in myself that my mother may have had a special influence in forming, I would guess this is one of them. I grew up with the idea that one should be careful with money, that none should be spent without good and sufficient reason and there should be something – tangible or intangible – to justify each expense. I have never changed in this belief, not even after money was no problem for us. Thriftiness is a famous Yankee virtue and I suppose I would have acquired it, to some extent, just from living in the Boston-Concord region, but my mother's example was probably decisive. This was a principle I tried to instil in raising my own children.

I also was influenced by her conviction that children need firm discipline. She, perforce, was the disciplinarian in our house because my father was not there most of the time. She brought us up quite strictly by today's standards. She made it clear we were to behave ourselves, study our school work and our religious lessons, be punctual, neat and mannerly. If we didn't obey the rules, we were spanked.

A most precious gift that came in large measure from my mother was deep faith in the Church and its teachings and practices. My father was a devout and dutiful Catholic who took Holy Communion regularly and observed the holy days and obligations of the church calendar. But he was so deeply involved in the affairs of the world that he took religion for granted without thinking much about it. Going to Mass was simply natural and normal and gave him the opportunity (I say this with love and without sacrilege) of communicating not only with God but with many of his friends and political constituents.

To my mother, however, the Church was a pervading and abiding presence, and she instilled these feelings in us. She drilled us in our Catechism and other religious lessons, and talked to us about the fasts and feasts and special seasons of the Church. May was the month of the Blessed Virgin. There was a little shrine to her in our house, with her statue, and all month we kept it decorated with fresh flowers and offered a prayer there each night. Every night during Lent my mother would gather us in one of the rooms of the house, turn out the lights – the better to concentrate – and lead us in reciting the Rosary.

I'm sure my knees ached and that sometimes I wondered why I should be doing all the kneeling and studying and memorizing and contemplating and praying. But I became understanding and grateful, and in my own time I tried to pass on to my own children this precious gift of faith.

Yet along with these qualities of dutifulness and piety and austerity of temperament my mother also knew how to enjoy life. She went on vacation trips with my father, leaving us children (two more, John F. Jr. and my sister Eunice were born in these Concord years) in the care of a nursemaid and housekeeper. One year they went to one of the spas that were so much in fashion in that era, and came home with a matched pair of beautiful black horses, Black Hawk and Maud. My mother loved riding and excelled at it. One of my most vivid memories is of her riding side-saddle at a gallop on one of these black horses, its mane and tail flying and her own long, thick, lustrous black hair – fallen loose from the hairpins – streaming behind her. She was magnificent and, it seemed to me, perfectly beautiful.

She had dark Irish looks, with a fine complexion, and a small, lithe, trim figure which she never lost. From the time she married to the end of her life (at the age of ninety-one) her weight seldom varied much from 115 pounds. She was fine-boned and finely proportioned, standing only about 5 ft 3 ins, but seeming taller because of the dignity of her bearing. Even in her last years her black hair was only flecked with grey. She liked clothes and dressed with instinctive taste.

My father was enchanted with her and very proud of her. When both were old, and someone asked him to look back and name the happiest day of his life, he said: 'When I got the girl I wanted, Mary Josephine Hannon. We've lived together now for forty-five years. The first time I met her, I knew.'

We lived in Concord when I was between the ages of seven and thirteen. There were many good times and many warm memories.

I remember the sweet and peaceful Sunday afternoons when, after morning Mass and a bountiful country-style noontime dinner, we got into a carriage or two and – still in our Sunday best – clattered away in the countryside for an airing. Naturally, there was an ultimate destination, a purpose: most often my grandparents' house, sometimes a farm where we children could admire the animals and chickens and my father could do a little political pulse-taking with the farmer, and tell him a few remarkable facts about the origin and proper care of guinea-fowl or something. Or sometimes it would be swimming in a nearby freshwater pond.

How I remember the lessons! There was a makeshift raft at the water's edge: that was my father's headquarters for the session. He had put together a contraption consisting of an old-fashioned cork circular lifesaver into which we were tied, the lines leading to a strong fishing line, in turn attached to a strong bamboo fishing rod, which my father grasped in his hands as he stood on the raft. Then I, or one of us, was in the water . . . Shouts of instruction: 'Kick your feet,' and 'Move your hands and arms' . . . and shouts of encouragement . . . and, whenever I or the contraption went out of kilter, a swift yank from the pole to the line to the ropes and the lifesaver and me, putting everything temporarily right. That is how I learned to swim. And although I never got much beyond the dog-paddle and breast-stroke, swimming has been one of the abiding pleasures of my life; and to this very time, when the weather is half-way decent, I swim every day.

Those Sunday outings became even pleasanter when my father bought a two-horse carriage that was half-moon shaped, like a truncated bay window or part of a theatre-box on wheels, a congenial design big enough to hold us all – parents, children and grandparents – side by side but in view of one another. As we jounced along, behind our spirited Black Hawk and Maud, we chattered back and forth and sang our favourite songs.

By the time I was twelve or so I had my own rig – a gentle horse and small carriage – of which, of course, I was quite proud. I used it for all kinds of errands and explorations, but I remember best the summer days when school was out and time was heavy and I used to drive back and forth to the Concord library for books. I loved to read, another enthusiasm I got mainly from my father. Yet I was far more interested in fiction than fact, especially 'romantic fiction'. Most of the authors, titles and plots have long since faded from memory, but I'm sure that in the spirit of the age they were, without exception, moral, inspirational and sentimental. A usual theme, as I do recall, was that love (aided by virtue and hard work and pluck) somehow conquered all. I attribute to this my later girlhood conviction that I must, absolutely, marry only for love. The books I remember best were those by Louisa May Alcott. She had lived and written in Concord and was one of the famous literary names of the region, along with Emerson and numerous others who brought about the literary 'Flowering of New England'. The library had her complete works, and I'm sure I read them all. *An Old-Fashioned Girl*, *Little Men* and others, but her most popular book was also my own favourite: *Little Women*.

Every summer, then and later, our family spent two or three weeks at the seaside at Old Orchard Beach, Maine. It was a pleasant place for both old and young, but especially attractive to my parents because so many of their friends also went there. Not surprisingly, practically all of them were Irish Catholics from Boston and my father's Congressional district, and many of the men were involved in politics. They all knew one another. They came with their families, and visited back and forth and picnicked together while the children played. It was nothing at all like a conclave: the attractions were as simple as they seemed, salt water and sunshine and congenial company, and families came and went without discussing any topic more serious than the weather. Yet mixed with the salt air there was often the whiff of politics. One of the men who came there fairly regularly, with his family, was a greatly respected businessman and political leader from East Boston, Patrick Joseph ('P. J.') Kennedy. Needless to say, he and my father knew each other well.

So it was at Old Orchard Beach that my future husband and I first saw each other. Neither of us had the faintest recollection of that 'historic' encounter until, many years later, someone turned up a yellowed clipping from a Boston newspaper: a group photograph of the Fitzgeralds and Kennedys and a dozen or so other families lined up for the camera on part of the beach, with a caption identifying everyone. And there was Joe, a rather spindly-looking nine-or-ten-year-old; and there was I, not so much to look at either, but apparently taller though two years younger. I have managed (through one of the many helpful friends who have taken an interest in this book) to get a copy of the photograph.

3

Boston politics of this era were not unlike those in Ireland before the Anglo-Norman conquest. The Irish had their local chieftains, who often warred against one another for fancied glory and advantages for themselves and their followers. They made unstable alliances that could find one year's ally another year's foe, and vice versa. Yet they produced especially strong leaders, super-chieftains who reigned as kings over large regions, allying and defecting and forming new constellations as the winds blew. Occasionally one would be successful enough to claim the status of 'high king' but never without challenges, direct or brewing, against his authority. The famous folk hero Brian Boru, through extraordinary prowess in battle and diplomacy and statecraft, managed to unite most of the island and is revered as 'the one real king Ireland ever had' – but his reign lasted only twelve years.

I won't go into further analogies. I have said I was not involved in or even much aware of the 'practical politics' of the time. My only role was as a supporting character in a political tableau designed by my father, who was a sort of political Shakespeare: author and actor and stage-manager in one.

The Democratic party was predominant in Boston, but it was less a party than a label for a multitude of neighbourhood and district interests and leaders, often in contention, with alliances of convenience quickly formed and broken, with rare intervals of relative stability and equivocal discipline under some especially strong leader or a pragmatic working coalition of several of the most important leaders. Around 1900 there were four men who used to meet regularly, usually in a private room of the fine old Quincy House Hotel, and iron out differences and make plans over luncheon and coffee. They were nicknamed 'The Strategy Board'. One of them was my father. Another was my future father-in-law, Patrick Joseph 'P. J.' Kennedy.

My father's position as Congressman for a district that took in all of Boston was obviously reason enough for him to be included as one of 'The Big Four' on the Strategy Board. But why Patrick Joseph

Kennedy? I must now digress briefly to bring this part of the story up to date.

As I have said, his father Patrick migrated from Ireland during the Great Famine and settled in the region of Boston harbour now known as East Boston. There he made his living as a cooper; married Bridget Murphy and had a family of four; and there he died nearly penniless at the early age of thirty-five – the same age that death took my grandfather, Thomas Fitzgerald. His widow opened a little stationery and notions shop and managed to eke out a living. Her children helped as they grew old enough. Patrick Joseph, the youngest, worked in the store, ran errands, found innumerable odd jobs around the waterfront and, when he was big and strong enough, became a stevedore. Because of the family's grinding financial need he had to drop out before finishing grade school; but he, like my father, was a great reader, with a special interest in American history.

After several years of scrimping he saved enough money to buy a neighbourhood saloon. He prospered, and put his profits back into his business, which expanded until he had partnerships in other saloons as well as a retail, wholesale and importing trade. He went into the coal business too, and into banking. His was a second-generation-immigrant American success story.

In Ireland as in England the neighbourhood pub was 'the poor man's club' and the tradition also existed in Boston. As bar-tender, host and proprietor P. J. Kennedy found himself in the middle of East End news, gossip, celebrations, hopes and fears, troubles and tragedies. He was a good listener, knew how to keep confidences, and had a compassionate spirit. He helped people with loans, gifts and advice. Often he passed the word on to somebody that so-and-so needed this-or-that and P. J. Kennedy would appreciate it, asking nothing in return but good-will. Everyone knew that he was an honourable man, and everyone respected him. He was 5 ft 10 ins, with a brawny physique, blue eyes, a rain-washed, rosy complexion, reddish hair and a handlebar moustache that swooped gracefully, adding to his air of composure and dignity. Predictably, he became a political force in East Boston. And before long, he was the most influential figure of that whole region of the city.

He served a term in the Massachusetts House of Representatives and another in the state Senate, and was a delegate to three national Democratic conventions. But elective office, with all its demands for public appearances and speeches, was not his style. He preferred to work quietly behind the scenes, which ideally suited him to the work of the Strategy Board.

He and my father had been friends, or at least close acquaintances, for a long time. Temperamentally they were opposites, and I suppose they must have grated on each other's nerves at times. But they had many things in common too: their immigrant background, the early deaths of their fathers, poverty, the personal determination, foresight, and hard work that raised them to their positions, and of course, a sophisticated understanding of politics. I'm sure they understood each other and each in his way liked and admired the other.

I am reminded now of the analogy with which I began this chapter. And of a comment my son Jack once made about political relatives as he encountered them in his own career and described with his succinct wit. He said: 'In politics you don't have friends. You have allies.' He cited a book by Frank Sullivan, one of the best political reporters early in this century, called *The Great Game of Politics*, a title that conveys a lot about the necessity of teamwork, of allies – and the possibility of upsets, and finally, the desirability of handshakes after the 'game'.

My father had first run for Congress and won in 1894 against the opposition of the Strategy Board, of which he was not yet a member, though P. J. Kennedy was. (A fabled independent chieftain, Martin Lomasney, was his strong ally: 'My political godfather,' my father said.) A few years later, when my father came on to the Board, the past was smoothed and he and P. J. Kennedy became allies.

But in 1900, as my father was ending his third term in Congress and expecting renomination and re-election, there were seismic movements, shifts, realignments. I had no idea at the time what it was all about. In any case, P. J. Kennedy and the other Board members (and a new Mayor with whom my father disagreed) blocked his renomination. He might have won against them in the primary as he had the first time, but a look at the odds persuaded him not to try.

His Congressional career ended in 1901.

My father then bought a moribund little weekly newspaper called *The Republic*, which he managed to pick up for only $500. He thought he could turn it into a money-maker, which was urgent because he no longer had his Congressional salary. But he also knew the power of the press in politics, and in *The Republic* he saw a potentially valuable instrument for advancing his political career. He was both resilient and audacious, and his goal was to become Mayor of Boston.

He had no experience in newspaper publishing, but he had many friends in Boston papers to give him advice, and he learned quickly. He knew what was interesting and how to present it in an appealing way. He was also shrewd.

As he said later: 'I knew the success of a newspaper depended on its advertising revenue, and that advertisers looked to women, who spent most of the money in the big stores that did most of the advertising. I accordingly made the paper more readable to women . . .' Although women did not yet have the vote, John F. Fitzgerald was aware of their power even then. I think he influenced some of the campaign strategies Jack adopted when he entered public life.

With his ideas and energy and salesmanship, my father soon made a success of *The Republic*. After a few years he was said to be clearing as much as $25,000 a year with it, five times his Congressional salary. True or not, I do know that by 1904 he could afford a fine, spacious fifteen-room house in the Boston suburb of Dorchester.

Dorchester was outside the Boston city limits, and my father was preparing to run for Mayor of Boston. Yet his legal address, his 'voting residence' had continued and still continued to be in the old neighbour-hood, Ward Six, the North End. He was always in touch with the voters there, as well as with the solid dependable lieutenants who were the foundation of his strength. He was the 'boss' of Ward Six and, if not yet the 'boss', at least the leading political chieftain of the whole North End.

He was a very sentimental man. When he talked about the North End, it was 'the dear old North End'. When he ran into some former neighbour or acquaintance who had gone to another part of the city or region, he was inevitably moved to reminisce about 'the dear old North End'. Here is a sample of his manner and style, as he once described a visit to the old neighbourhood:

'As I came up old Hanover Street this morning – up the dear old North End – every man and child had a smile for me. It seemed as if the very paving stones rose up and greeted me. I met old Johnny Doolan on the corner. "God bless ye, little Johnny Fitz," he said to me, "you deserve to win." '

Someone, probably a newspaper reporter who heard the phrase often, contracted it to the generic term 'Dearos' for all who lived in the North End or had ever lived there and had any association at all with my father. The name caught on, and it became one of those trade-marks that can be useful in politics. He was the king of the Dearos, who became part of the language of Boston politics.

Despite my father's love for the dear old North End and his Dearos, he preferred his own family to have the fresh air and open spaces of small town and suburban Dorchester. Indeed, Concord had been some twenty-five miles from the nearest border of his Congressional district, which caused some of his critics to call him a 'carpet-bagger'.

We lived in Dorchester very comfortably and happily for a good many years. Another baby, my youngest brother Frederick, was born there: the last of us six. I went to the Dorchester High School, and soon made many friends while managing to do well in my studies. I was in the college preparatory curriculum and had my eye set on Wellesley College, where in fact I was accepted in my junior year. I resumed the dancing and piano lessons I had begun in Concord, both of which I liked and am everlastingly grateful to my parents for giving me. I was also rather interested in boys, and they seemed interested in me. But our relationships were predictably strained and giggly.

My mother went on serenely and conscientiously with her domestic and motherly duties. My father, despite the proximity of Boston and Dorchester, was no more and perhaps even less visible in the household than he had been in Concord. He was busy with *The Republic* and actively preparing his campaign for the mayoralty. He attended meetings, banquets, church parties, parish reunions, clubs, societies and sodalities. There were hundreds of speeches to make, thousands of hands to shake, jokes, songs, warm glances and cheery smiles, patient listening, good advice and favours to grant. It was a rare night he was home to have dinner with us.

I was certainly not happy about that, at the time. I'm sure none of us were, especially my mother. Yet I have come to realize this is a price which members of a 'political family' have to pay. I watched my own sons, and their wives and children, go through the same strains and disappointments.

But there was a compensatory side to my father's infrequent presence at home. Modern candidates seem to have to live with political matters all the time. I noticed with my sons that key supporters and assistants were practically part of the family; that there were reporters and photographers often around the house; that strategy meetings and staff consultations frequently took place in the living-room. In short, public and private life had become inextricably mixed.

In my father's time a politician's home was still his castle. The planning, consultation, horse-trading, persuading and razzle-dazzle took place in political clubhouses, hotels, and campaign offices. Home was a place for peaceful rest and quiet away from the fray. This is what my father wanted. My mother did much to give him a healing balm to his spirit and refreshment for his energies.

We children had only a hazy idea of what was happening when, in 1905, he announced his formal candidacy for Mayor of Boston and began his campaign. Of course there were some posed pictures taken of us and our school-mates looked at us with a new curiosity. We also saw pictures of my father and articles about him in the papers and we were excited. Yet the sounds of the battle seldom reached us.

As I learned later, from reading and from hearing my father and some other old combatants reminisce about it, it was one of the most hard-fought, noisy, complex political mêlées ever seen in Boston, which says a good deal.

Again the Strategy Board opposed him in the primary. Further, his former mentor, the independent chieftain Martin Lomasney, whom my father had been counting on for support when he decided to run for Mayor, switched to a temporary alliance with the Board members and declared to the press that if elected my father would be the worst Mayor in Boston's history. The outgoing Mayor, close ally of Lomasney, also denounced my father. An awesome combination.

But my father adroitly turned events to his advantage by making the main issue of the campaign 'Down with the bosses! The people, not the bosses, must rule! I want a Bigger, Better, Busier Boston!' He had his picture and his slogans all over town on billboards. He toured the city in a gleaming red horseless carriage, followed by a caravan of supporters and reporters – the first time such an automobile caravan had been used in a Boston election. His Dearos were everywhere, cheering and working hard for him. He averaged ten speeches an evening. On primary election eve, with his red horseless carriage to speed him from meeting to meeting, rally to rally – a technological breakthrough – he managed to visit all twenty-five wards of the city and deliver thirty speeches, emphasizing that: 'I am making my contest single-handed against the machine, the bosses and the corporations.'

And so, through foresight and long and careful planning, through indefatigable attention to the needs of others and establishment of personal relationships, through energy, ingenuity and boldness (and, I should add, some timely defections from the 'machine' by several ward leaders and rising younger politicians), my father won the nomination.

That night, after a proper celebration at his Ward Six headquarters, he visited other wards to thank his supporters and begin the job of fence-making needed to unify the party for the general election. At East End headquarters the place was full of rather sombre-looking election workers. My father moved around the room, shaking hands, and as P. J. Kennedy remarked with the unblemished admiration of one pro for another pro's fine performance: 'He knows them all. I don't know half of them, even though they are in my district.'

My father made his way to P. J. and said:

'Now that the fight is over, let's get together.'

They shook hands on it and that was that. They were allies once again.

His opponent in the general election was Louis Frothingham, a distinguished member of an old Yankee family. It was quite a campaign. Martin Lomasney – a fine friend but a fierce foe (an enigma nicknamed 'The Mahatma') – bolted the Party and swung his support to the Republican.

Nevertheless, my father won.

On election night there was such excitement, with such crowds of celebrants, that my father could not even get inside the Quincy House to attend his own victory party. His shouted remonstrances – 'I've just been elected Mayor and they're all waiting for me. I'm John F. Fitzgerald' – were to no avail, such was the crush of his admirers outside the entrance. Suddenly some of those nearest him saw a solution, seized him and boosted him up to an iron awning above the doorway: there, ten feet in the air, he made his victory speech to thunderous rounds of cheers.

4

And so in January, 1906, not far from his birthplace in the dear old North End, my father was inaugurated Mayor of Boston. His one regretful thought, he said, was that his parents were not alive to see the day. 'It would have been a great delight to them . . . I am the first son of foreign parents to become Mayor of Boston, thus my parents were the first persons of immigrant stock to have a son a Mayor.'

As for us at home, back in Dorchester, his new status made little difference in our lives. Later on it would, but not then; we were all still so young.

Although he was very busy, he still made all the important family decisions and a good many less important ones. Among the latter, I particularly remember one. There were Saturday afternoon dances at our high school. They were 'mixers', with the boys and girls allowed to invite friends from others schools in Boston and the region. It was all quite decorous, but I was never allowed to go. My father was a great innovator in public life, but when it came to raising his daughters no one could have been more conservative. When you put the 'Yankee ethic' and 'Irish Catholic ethic' together, the results were formidable. Which was sad. After all, you're only young once and young people should be able to get the most from those special years which last such a short time. But my father was adamant. He believed I was too young to be going to public dances and that was the end of it. I never thought of remonstrating with my father.

In those days, at least in Dorchester, high school consisted of three years with a fourth, post-graduate, year for those who were going on to college. I took the fourth year, and so left high school at the age of sixteen. But although I would have been seventeen the next fall my father decided that I was still too young for Wellesley and insisted I take an extra year at the Convent of the Sacred Heart in downtown Boston. I was disappointed but managed to like the school and did well enough there. I also took piano lessons again but in a more serious way, with enrolment and regular attendance at the New England Conservatory of Music and an hour and a half of practice a day.

It was still a time when some skill in music, playing or singing, was considered a social adornment and almost *de rigueur* for any proper young lady, so I was encouraged in my musical studies by my parents. But I also truly enjoyed them. I had a good ear, and still have. In those years, as I tried to look ahead and imagine what I would be doing until that future time – unknowable, unpredictable, beyond the horizon but surely there, someplace – when I married for love and devoted myself to a husband and family, I thought very seriously of becoming a music teacher. That didn't happen. But my ability to play the piano turned out to be a wonderful asset, then and for a great many years to come, in ways I couldn't have guessed.

Also, as events turned out, I never did go to Wellesley – and that is something I have regretted, for I'm sure it would have been an interesting and rewarding experience. However, I had one instead that probably was of equal value.

The Mayoralty term in Boston at that time was two years, so in 1908 my father came up for re-election. Once again, there were new outbreaks of factionalism. This time the Strategy Board – with P. J. Kennedy still a member and a strong ally of my father – worked hard for him. But there were others who didn't. A decisive factor was a third party sponsored by the Good Government Association ('Goo-Goos', as they were nicknamed) which cut deeply into the regular party vote. My father was defeated by a plurality of a little more than 2,000 votes and a Republican took office.

Although I'm sure the defeat was a sore blow to my father, there were few signs of it in our household. Election night, when someone asked him about his future, he replied: 'We held a conference a little while ago and began our planning for the next election.'

Meanwhile, he apparently decided to enjoy a respite from the political arena. He and my mother spent a winter vacation in Palm Beach, where they had been going for the past few years. Then, in that summer of 1908, they took my sister Agnes and me along on a trip to Europe.

There were crowds of Dearos and others, friends and relatives and well-wishers of all sorts, to see us off when we sailed in July from Boston harbour. It is worth remarking that the only one from the Strategy Board was P. J. Kennedy.

Anyway, with all flags flying and music playing and handkerchiefs being waved between dabbing of tears, and many smiles and shouts and embraces, and flares and smoke of flash-powder for photographs –

in quite a few of which my father managed gracefully to insert himself – and boat-whistles and orchids (boutonnières for the men) and bon voyage baskets and packages and confetti and balloons and all those marvellous trappings and ceremonials that used to make a departure on an ocean voyage on a big liner such an exciting and glamorous experience, we were off to Europe.

In my school studies I had learned at least a little about the countries and peoples of Europe and the British Isles, some of it superficial, I suppose, and some clogged with dry facts and statistics; yet I became entranced with the idea of seeing these places. On many a Saturday afternoon I had sat enthralled in Boston's Symphony Hall listening to Burton Holmes – whose illustrated travelogues were among the famous and popular entertainments of the era – and envying his experiences, wishing I could visit some of those places. These were the beginnings, I expect, of a lifetime wanderlust and global curiosity that to this point have taken me to every continent but Antarctica and to scores of countries. In July of 1908, with an excitement one can imagine, I was setting out on the fulfilment of a girlhood dream.

We went to Ireland, England, Belgium, France, Switzerland, Germany and Holland, all by the end of the summer, about two months, which in those times was a rather hectic schedule. But I loved it, as I'm sure Agnes did too, though both of us had a little trouble keeping up with our energetic father, who liked only about five hours of sleep a night and could go twenty-four or thirty-six hours without signs of fatigue.

I remember that as we walked through Phoenix Park in Dublin, laced with paths and full of flowers, my father pointed out the place where a member of the underground Irish republican army had assassinated the British Chief Secretary for Ireland, Lord Frederick Charles Cavendish, on May 6, 1882. Among many things I could not have known was that someday I would have a daughter, Kathleen, who would marry Cavendish's grand-nephew, Billy Hartington.

We went on to England and visited Stratford-on-Avon. Mind you, my father had read Shakespeare and revered him and sprinkled his speeches with quotations. Nevertheless, he took twenty minutes to gallop our rented horse and carriage from the railway station to the village of Stratford. Thirty minutes to get us through Shakespeare's house and garden and the village and tell us more than we knew about them. Then another twenty minutes to force the horse back to the station again in time to connect with our train to Scotland. As I said, he didn't like to waste time.

I remember that in Germany he was impressed with the neatness and discipline, the warmth and companionability and sentiment, the reverence in religious matters, the respect for secular learning, and above all the vitality and forceful energy of the people. He said to us that the area they were in, about as big then as our own state of Texas, could not contain them and they would burst out sooner or later and there would be a war. It occurred six years later practically to the month.

I remember also that wherever we went he was comparing the countries to the US and the cities to Boston, almost always to the advantage of our native country and city; and went back with ideas that might be useful to both. But the problems of city government, and the solutions and attempted solutions that he saw, were especially fascinating to him. The slogan 'A Bigger, Better, Busier Boston' was to him less a political catch-phrase than a summary of a grand design. The ambition of an immigrant son who wanted to repay thrice-fold his city and his country.

Toward the end of that summer, it was decided that Agnes and I would stay on for a year of school. In those times, it was considered a great advantage for a young person to have gone to school 'abroad' and I find myself still in agreement with this. The place my parents chose was a convent boarding-school called Blumenthal (a German word translatable as 'Valley of Flowers') in Holland, near the German border and Aachen or, as the French call it, Aix-la-Chapelle, the ancient capital of Charlemagne.

I would have preferred going to school in France, because I had been studying French (preceded by years of Latin) and I knew the best way to improve my skills would be to live there. However, as the result of a dispute between church and state, the teaching convents in France had been closed. Since Bismarck, the teaching orders of nuns had been banned in Germany. Yet the government of Holland was tolerant, and Blumenthal was haven for a number of French nuns and even more from Germany. It was a little Franco-German-and-much-mixed Roman Catholic enclave in the peaceful Dutch landscape. Girls enrolled from many countries, with classes conducted in both French and German, and with some Dutch on the side.

So I was able to polish my French after all, as well as my German, to which I had already devoted three years of study in Boston. A great arrangement. I became proficient in both languages and they have been assets all the rest of my life.

(I say 'proficient' but of course it is difficult for anyone who wasn't 'born in a language' to acquire perfect pronunciation and unconscious grammatical accuracy. I have been plugging away at my French and German ever since.)

Because a convent education was impossible in France and Germany and many Catholic families in both countries wanted one for their daughters, Blumenthal's students were predominantly German or French and mainly from the aristocracy or at least the well-to-do. No distinctions were made, no talk allowed about titles. But a number of the girls were from some of the oldest and noblest houses of Europe, including such other nations as England and its then dominion, Ireland, as well as a share of well-connected gentlefolk here and there. Agnes and I, Miriam and Margaret Finnegan from Cambridge and Worcester, Massachusetts, and two or three others were at that time the American delegation.

We all seemed to get along together quite well, managing to communicate across language barriers in our fractured French or German or English or Dutch. I seemed to have a degree of natural facility (or determined interest) in languages, so one of the things I remember from that time is sitting in a group and translating back and forth, in and out, English and French and German, for girls who had not yet acquired the 'ear', to help keep some of those schoolgirl conversations going, and classroom duties accomplished.

Actually, though the atmosphere was religious as in all convent schools, Blumenthal's curriculum was unusually concerned with the practical things of this world. It was assumed that the girls, when they married, would be devoting their lives to *Kinder, Kirche und Küche* – children, church and cooking – and needed to prepare for all the duties implied in that expression. It was further assumed that as wives of *Offizieren* they would have servants to do all the actual work; but in order to instruct and supervise the servants and to run an efficient household they should be proficient in what has been called 'domestic science'. So at Blumenthal we were all coached in cooking, sewing, and the other arts of housewifery.

Another forte of the school was music, with excellent choral and instrumental instruction, so I was able to continue my music lessons to great benefit. Further, wonderful music, wonderfully well played, was practically as much part of the surrounding scene as church spires. In Boston I had been allowed to go to the Friday afternoon concert rehearsals of the Boston Symphony and, for 50c admission, sit on the stairways at Symphony Hall. Although they were called 'rehearsals' I cannot remember a time when the conductor stopped the orchestra to correct a badly rendered passage. Whereas at a similar afternoon rehearsal in Aachen with Richard Strauss conducting, I remember

Strauss four or five times halting everything in mid-flight and putting instrumentalists or sections or the whole orchestra through the music again, demanding nothing less than perfection.

Because so many of the nuns and girls at Blumenthal were German and the border was so near that we could drive to small towns such as Vaals, or to the city of Aachen, to buy our toiletries and little gifts to send home, I had a chance to observe 'the German character' and learn to appreciate its virtues. There are too many to inventory but let's say, for instance, the industry and ambition and ready acceptance of hard tasks; the respect for learning and the way children paid attention to their studies, especially foreign languages (I wish more American children would do the same); the respect children had for the authority of their parents, the deep sense of spiritual responsibility parents felt for their children, as demonstrated in such a lovely, open way – I saw this often – such as the sign of the cross they made on a child's forehead when they met after separation.

I have been to Germany seldom since then. I have been to France often, have lived there for months at a time, and French is the foreign language I know best and enjoy most. I know the horrors of Nazi times and destructive policies undertaken by several German regimes in the name of the people. The German people are nevertheless, in my opinion, fine, decent and richly endowed, and all too often have been betrayed by leaders whom they have trusted too much.

At the beginning of this book I mentioned that many family letters had been saved through the years and had turned up when I sent out a general alert for help in writing this book. To my amazement, they included scores of letters I had written home to my parents from Blumenthal and some places we visited (under scrupulous care of a chaperone from the convent) during holidays. I will not put them here verbatim. Most of the contents are, of course, just as inconsequential as those of practically all schoolgirl letters: lovingly written and lovingly read at home at the time, but of faint, if any, interest to posterity.

However, looking at them sixty-odd years later, I think that excerpts from them can be useful in conveying some of the flavour of that scene and those times, and the warmth and closeness of our family relationships. They reveal something about my own outlook on life and my own character at eighteen, when I was leaving girlhood and becoming a young lady. To ensure that they do not clog the story, I am going to put them in a compartment of their own.

But before the letters I should tell you a little bit about my sister Agnes. She was very pretty. When I was seven and she was five, and our father a Congressman, he took us to Washington, and to the White House to meet President McKinley. The President was an imposing man but warm and friendly. He liked my father and my father was very fond of him, despite their difference in political parties. He handed me a carnation from a vase on his desk, and then one to Agnes, and said to her: 'This is for the prettiest little girl I have ever seen in the White House.' I thought it was a wonderful thing for him to do and through the years I told the story often, until by the time Jack was a teen-ager I guess he had heard it often enough. He looked at me, his face a perfect mask of innocence, and asked, 'Why didn't he say it to you, Mother?'

I had to agree that Agnes was the beauty of the family.

As for temperaments and tastes, we were as complementary as in colouring. I was the one with lots of ideas. I would be the one to say, let's have a party. She would think that was a marvellous inspiration, and would plan the menu and arrange the table. I would say, let's take a trip to so-and-such; again marvellous, and she would pack our bags. I liked one kind of beau. She liked another kind. So there was never really any reason to argue.

The letters were addressed mostly to 'Dear Mother' but were meant for both parents. I might make a remark directed specifically at one or the other, which caused them no confusion but might cause some for the present reader without this word of explanation.

Here, then, are the collected and much abbreviated letters in rough sequence and by the month:

September

Well, here we both are safely packed away at last in Blumenthal. We have a dear little room just above Miriam's and after we put our rugs in, and the pictures on the walls I am sure it will look real homelike. The nuns are simply lovely to us, and do all in their power to make everything as agreeable as possible. We have our milk or our cocoa – in fact everything we can wish for in the line of eatables.[1] The girls talk German nearly all the time. Then all the recommendations are given in French, and we have French stories and French conversations while we are walking in the garden. Give my best love to everyone who asks for me. With many, many kisses and hugs and my dearest love to all, believe me ever, Your daughter, Rose.

Well, our first week of school is over. I am glad, because I think the first week is always the longest. We had an hour's instruction this

[1] We were also offered beer every day.

week in politeness. We do not take gymnastics, because I thought it would take up our time too much and Agnes did not seem to favour the idea *at all*. My music lessons have begun. I am to play twice for the celebration in November. The singing teacher said I had a good voice, and told me the hoarseness in my throat would soon disappear. The bell has rung. Goodbye. Much love and kisses to all and my dearest for you and Papa. Rose.

Another new pupil arrived, a girl of about twenty, who comes here to study German in order to prepare for entrance examinations to Dublin University. [This was Mary Magiore, the future Mary Colum, wife of Padraic Colum.] She has to take examinations in Irish, too. Oh yes! She is very much interested in politics, so I think I shall be able to learn a great deal about Ireland from her. I should like it very much if you would send me a *Sacred Heart Review*, a *Republic* and a *Transcript* about once a month. Please send wrapped inside them the songs 'Are You Sincere', 'Take Me Out To the Ball Game' and one or two more of the very latest. Our very dearest love and kisses to you and dear Papa. Rose.

Your pictures are standing on our writing tables, so whenever we raise our eyes from our books, there you are. I have a splendid one of Pa with Vice-President Fairbanks and all the nuns are very much interested in it. Our black uniforms are all made and really are not *very* repulsive-looking after all. This morning we had a fitting for the white ones, which we wear on feast days. Wait till you see them. Our hair we wear straight back from our forehead and braided down with two ribbons. We had it shampooed a week ago and you should have seen the rubbing and scrubbing it got. This operation is performed every three weeks. This afternoon we are going to make a pilgrimage (on foot, of course) to some shrine about an hour's distance from here. By the way there is a German countess staying here now for a few days. She is only about nineteen but wears her hair up, and looks about 23. Miriam says they all look much older than they really are. Agnes is quite happy, I think. She and I both hope everyone at home is perfectly happy. Very dearest love to you and Father and the rest. Rose.

We had a very exciting time here entertaining the sisters, who had their feast day, with five or six short plays. You should have seen Agnes. As she cannot speak German, she took the part of a bell, and chimed. I played the part of a child who did not want to go to church. I told the girls that it was mean to 'give me away' like that. It is time for lunch now. I know Father will be glad to hear that I usually succeed in being on time here. Dearest love. Rose.

October

School has started in dead earnest. We have not wasted a second. I am rather glad, for when I have a great deal to do the time goes more quickly, and I feel as though a year ought not to be very long in passing, and then I can go home, and never have to go away again. We try to talk together at night when we are getting ready for bed. We do not have much opportunity during meals for we have conversation only during breakfast-time for a few minutes. During dinner there is German reading, and during supper French reading, and we are silent. I am used to this regulation now, but at first it was very hard. The bell has rung. I enjoy *The Republic* more and more every day. So glad Pa is not bothering with politics. Love to all and my dearest and best to you and Pa. Rose.

November

The Americans entertained at Recreation by singing 'Yankee Doodle Boy' and 'School Days' and quite a few others. My singing lessons are going along well. The teacher said that the hoarseness in my throat would disappear after a short while. Everything is marked out for a certain period of time and we have hardly any free periods. Do tell me soon who is President. I did not realize Election came off so soon. Dearest and best love and kisses. Rose.

We just received the loveliest box of candy from home, and we have been having a regular little party to celebrate Agnes's birthday eating it and talking about what we would be doing a year from today, etc. The little pin was very pretty, too, but unfortunately we wear no jewellery whatever. You should just see how *demure* we are in our plain black dresses with our little black aprons on. I should like to see a *Ladies Home Journal*. Any number will do. Vera wrote me that Taft was elected. Dearest love. Rose.

'Well, another week has gone by. As I am an 'angel' [a neophyte in the sodality] I arise at six o'clock (fifteen minutes earlier than the others) and go to meditation nearly every morning. So you see my piety is increasing. If I am extremely angelic, I may become an aspirant for the Children of Mary; later I may become a Child of Mary. That is the highest honour a child of the Sacred Heart can receive. So I shall have to be a model of perfection for the next few months. My French and German are coming along fairly well, I think. It is such a funny combination here. The French girls wish to

Founding Fathers

1 *Above* John Francis Fitzgerald and Mary Josephine Hannon Fitzgerald

Below Patrick J. ('P.J.') Kennedy and Mary Hickey Kennedy

2 *Above left* Agnes, John F. Jr and me
Joe with his sister Loretta, 1892

Joe and I first met at a family picnic. I am second from the left
standing beside my father, who sits on the post. Joe is in the second
row centre, to the left of his aunt in white dress

Early Years

3 *Above* My father, the Mayor of Boston, presented my High School diploma to me

Aboard Sir Thomas Lipton's yacht. Agnes sits below him and I am on his left

Below In 1909 I graduated from Blumenthal. I am in the last row, fourth from the right

Young Marrieds

4 *Above* Me in 1927 and Joe in the early years of our marriage

Below Joe and I skating, Poland Springs, Maine, 1915, and at Palm Beach, 1925

speak German or English; the Germans want to talk English or
French, and the girls from English-speaking countries want to speak
French or German. My dearest love and kisses for you and dear
Pa. Rose.

Dearest Father,
I have something very important and exciting to tell you so I hope
my words will be persuasive and you will say 'Yes.' Christmas is
coming and there is to be a fifteen-day vacation, from December 23
till January 8. We love Blumenthal very dearly, but we do not at all
relish the idea of spending our vacation here, when all the others are
home, having a happy time with their families. We can take a two-
week round trip from Aachen to Hanover, to Berlin, to Dresden, to
Leipzig, to Cologne and back to Aachen, with room and board and
incidentals, for about $140. This amount seems very large, but I hate
to get away and not have enough. The cities we want to visit will
prove interesting. They contain famous picture galleries and churches.
An opportunity would also be afforded us to go to the theatre, and
see some of Goethe's and Schiller's plays. We would get a chaperone,
so we would be perfectly safe. The Mothers here at school approve of
our plan and will write ahead and engage room and board in convents. We could see the Celtic Art Collection too, about which the
Republic spoke. We do not want to spend the holidays here. It would
make us too lonesome. I do hope Mother will approve. If I could
only talk to her I am sure she would. We will think of you when you
cut the *Turkey* tomorrow. Dearest love and kisses to you and Mama.
Rose (If you send money send it to me in cheque for bank at Aix-la-
Chapelle.)

Dearest Mother,   *December*
I was delighted to hear that your whist party was such a great
success. Of course I knew it would be. I am glad, for your sake, that
it is over, for it is apt to cause you a little trouble and care. What did
you think of the letter I wrote Father? By this time, he will have
received one also from Mother Esterhazy. I had her write Father,
because I thought you would be better satisfied about the chaperone.
Now do let us go. While we are in Europe it is worthwhile to travel,
for we can see new places and things, and perhaps we shall never have
a chance to see them again. My dearest to you and Papa. Rose.

Your letter just arrived. To think of anyone saying that we really
ought to stay here at least two years! It is very nice for girls who are
used to boarding-school life, but I prefer to be home in America.

Everything points to the approach of Xmas now. Miriam heard from Rome today and has the names of some dandy *pensiones*, and the mother of one of the nuns knows of a convent where we can stay in Berlin. So you see all we are waiting for is a word from you and then we can trot off. Send us a cablegram and just say 'Yes'. We would understand what you mean. Your affectionate daughter. Rose.

Father's letter arrived and how we jumped and talked and laughed when we received it. It was just lovely of you both to give us the permission to go. We both were so happy and vowed you and Pa were the best and the dearest father and mother in the world. We shall both think of you at the Midnight Mass, and pray for you. We have a great deal of opportunity to pray here. Happy New Year. Your loving and devoted daughter. Rose.

January

The Reverend Mother and Mothers General stayed up to welcome us back again. We have been kept busy talking about our trip ever since. We seemed to have seen everything. New Year's Night in Berlin we heard *Tannhäuser* and it was truly wonderfully beautiful. We had to wear *decolleté* gowns and you should have seen us. We took the yokes out of our light dresses, and threw veils over our heads and there we were. The Kaiserin and Crown Princess as well as other members of the royal family had a loge directly below us . . .

This evening the Retreat begins. Three days of complete silence will be quite an experience for us all. Of course the Retreat is a great blessing. There is hardly any news except the Kaiser's birthday. At dinner each nation stood up and wished the Kaiser a happy feast. The French did not like it very well; they were the last ones to wish the Kaiser well and they would not stand up during the singing of the national hymn . . .

I was so rushed about the Retreat that I forgot to tell you and Father about what we sent him for his birthday. We received permission from the Mother General to make fudge. It really tasted very good when it left here. It may have been hard when it reached Pa, but he knew we thought of him anyway.

Now we are preparing more or less for Lent. There is going to be a retreat for the women who work in the factories, about 700 of them. Don't you think this is perfectly splendid for the poor working girls? Reverend Mother is so good. If we are very good this week, she has promised to take us over and show us where all of them will eat and sleep. Of course we shall not come into contact with them at all, for they will all be in a building entirely separated from ours – where the poor children usually go to school. We shall think of you all on Washington's birthday, when we wear our stars & stripes . . .

March

We were so sorry that the candy arrived so late. Easter will be here soon. We plan to remain at Blumenthal until June, then go to Paris for a month or two at the Sacred Heart convent there, get in a little Français and buy our clothes at leisure. We really shall need two suits apiece and one or two light dresses for the boat going home. We cannot get anything satisfactory in Aix-la-Chapelle. I prefer to wait and get something à la mode in gay Paris. These plans will completely fall to the ground if you are thinking of having us stay here another year, so tell us quick if you are thinking about it at all, so we will not go on planning and then be terribly disappointed. I do hope Pa will not run for Mayor. He has been so happy and carefree since he left City Hall.

April

We went to Aachen for shopping, and Agnes and I bought two captivating little black hats, just the kind you and Pa like, plain and small but oh! so coy! I hear they are wearing huge ones at home, but I prefer something small and serviceable. After our shopping we had afternoon tea and cakes. Here abroad people, even men, have afternoon tea and cakes . . .

Father's and your letter arrived. It would be too much of a sacrifice for you and for us to remain away another year. If I did not *love* you all so *madly*, I might consider another year or two. But I often think, how could I ever forgive myself if anything should ever happen to you or Papa while we are over here. Mother seemed to say that Pa would run for Mayor. How I hope he will not use all his strength and tire himself out, bothered with politics. It is so much better to have him in good health and free from worry . . .

I must go directly and practise the piano. You see I am the orchestra for the play which we are going to give, so I shall be kept quite busy. Jeanne d'Arc is what is going to be presented, and a French girl is to play the part of the heroine! It lasts about two hours and promises to be quite grand . . .

[This was Schiller's version of the 'romantic tragedy' of Joan of Arc, *Die Jungfrau von Orleans*.]

May

We had quite a celebration here after the news came of the birth of Holland's little princess. We sang the Dutch national song, and made speeches at dinner, telling how glad the representatives of the different nations here were that the Queen had a little successor.

[That 'little princess' was Juliana, who succeeded her mother as Queen in 1948. She herself is the mother of four daughters and several times a grandmother. Recently, at a dinner party, I found myself with a Dutch noblewoman and told her I had been in Holland and helped celebrate the birth of her Queen. She looked at me with astonishment as if thinking, How can you – or anybody – be that old?]

We are wild to see you and dear papa again, besides Eunice and the boys. We are wondering if you all look the same. Miriam's father wrote her that his hair was turning grey, but of course our father is too young to meet with any such catastrophe.

I received my medal for the Child of Mary today. As I told you before, this is the highest honour and blessing a Sacred Heart girl can get and one which we all strive for. We are supposed to be a model and a help in the school, and someone to be depended upon, etc.

The Finnegans are going to Liège for clothes and I thought we might go with them and buy a new suit. We have not a thing to wear . . .

June

This is the Feast of the Sacred Heart and I could tell you a great deal about it and a great many other feast days which we have been having lately. First I must finish the important things. I had a fitting of my white dress yesterday. It looks too pretty for words, and I am so pleased with it. I got slippers for my dress and they match beautifully. I am going to be St Peter in a French play at Graduation so I got black suede slippers, too.

[In mid-June we had a letter from our father saying he had decided to run for Mayor again. And that if we wanted to we could come home, at least for the summer. But, in that case, he would come to escort us on the journey.]

We just received Father's letter and it seems best to us to come home and home we shall be. It seems like some lovely dream. I would not have Father risk the mayoralty fight for the world just to see us. It is not for his sake alone, but for the sake of the whole party – the men who work and sacrifice so much in order to help him. They might not think it was the honourable thing to do, to rush off in the middle of the campaign almost. Write to the Captain and tell him to take care of us. We know how to behave ourselves anyway I think. We shall need no extras in wardrobe – something stunning to land in, that's all . . .

July

   I am telling the nuns that you are so well acquainted with the captain on the boat that it is perfectly natural for us to return alone. I suppose we shall offer the same explanation to people at home. I do not dare to think about home much because my imagination runs away with me . . .

My father cabled that he was coming over on the next boat. He met us with tears and open arms.

Together we did sightseeing in Holland and in Belgium, and went on to Paris too. Agnes and I did a little shopping for 'something à la mode in gay Paris'. I remember, especially, that we bought two large velvet hats and two white ostrich plumes to put in them. That was our idea at that age of 'something stunning to land in'. Also, if we wore them they would qualify as used clothing and we wouldn't have to pay duty on them.

On the way back we stopped off in England for a few days and were at Cowes at the time of one of the great boating regattas. My father had earlier become a warm friend of Sir Thomas Lipton, the famous merchant and yachtsman who used to bring his ocean racers (the sequence of boats numbered but all named *Shamrock* in honour of his mainly Irish ancestry) to our waters to race for the America's Cup. We had entertained him in Boston. He was always full of compliments for us, and of invitations to visit him. We had already been aboard his big sea-going residential yacht *Erin* several times, so she was a familiar enough sight. And so, as my father related the story:

Rose sighted Lipton's *Erin* in the distance and we went down to a wharf, hoping to find a motor-boat that could take us out to the *Erin*. There was no boat there, but we noticed the King's launch and thought one of the members of the royal family was aboard. The launch came up to the wharf where we were, and the skipper looked around and was about to start away when the officer in charge came up to where I was and asked if he could be of any service, seeing that I was anxiously looking about. I told him I was a friend of Sir Thomas and was looking for a boat to carry us to the *Erin*. The officer graciously said the King's launch was at my service.

As we approached the *Erin*, Sir Thomas saw us through his glass, and figuring it was some members of the royal party, possibly the King or Queen, he had all his crew brought forward on the deck to receive these eminent guests. Among his guests were some Americans, and they were all anxiously asking Sir Thomas as to the etiquette to be followed immediately upon the approach of the King or Queen. Sir Thomas was busily explaining when the boat arrived and as I popped my head over the rail he nearly fell on the deck, so great was his surprise. 'My heavens,' he said, 'it's my friend, John Fitzgerald of Boston, with Rose and Agnes.'

In his own memoirs, Sir Thomas told the story from his viewpoint on deck, and added a few touches:

'You could have knocked us all sideways with a feather,' he wrote, 'so great was our astonishment and bewilderment.

' "My word, Fitz," I exclaimed, "but you have arrived in great style."

' "What do you mean?" he asked blandly: "I took the best boat I could see available to bring me over to you." Then he went on to say that being in London, he had decided to run down for the day and give me a call. Arriving at the seafront of Cowes he and his family had strolled along to "that building over there", pointing to the sacred steps of the Royal Yacht Squadron, and he "hired the only launch he could see idle at the moment!" '

Apparently, there was a small crisis when the King and Queen arrived to find their launch gone and 'nowhere to be seen' while they were 'waiting impatiently on the jetty'. But there was a happy ending. Sir Thomas explained everything. King Edward VII was not irritated but amused.

In August, we were back at Boston and Dorchester. Our mother greeted us with tears in her eyes. She had been terribly lonely. It was decided we would not go back to Europe for another year's study. Instead, Agnes went to the Sacred Heart convent at Providence, Rhode Island, a rather short distance from Boston, and I went to the Sacred Heart convent at Manhattanville, New York, farther away.

Meanwhile, my father won the nomination for Mayor. As I think my letters from Blumenthal indicate, he had not even been sure he wanted to run again; but once in the race he was sure to run hard. J. J. Storrow was as worthy a rival as he would ever meet, a patrician of old proper Bostonian stock, Harvard crew captain and graduate and Overseer, successful in business and enormously wealthy, a patriotic political independent, leader and benefactor of good causes from the Boy Scouts to the beautification of the banks of the Charles River. He and my father had always got along well together. But then came this political encounter, head on, so to speak, and things became noisome and acrimonious and bitter – mostly for the Democrats, because all but one of the Boston papers had lined up on Storrow's side. I would awaken practically every morning to find my father accused in headlines of being guilty of nearly every sin short of murder. Storrow's managers also ran a series of large advertisements, each headed in screaming type FITZGERALDISM followed by some fervid accusations against my father and 'the Fitzgerald ring'. 'Never,' according to a leading historian of the Boston political scene, J. H. Cutler, 'was character assassination more brutally practised in a Boston campaign.'

As I mentioned earlier, I had been too young to pay much attention to my father's earlier campaigns. This, in fact, was the first political campaign of any sort of which I was fully aware – the first one that I clearly remember. When the mud began flying, my instinctive reactions were shock and outrage; I seethed. But my father seemed to take it more or less for granted. Some of the accusations and personal slurs undoubtedly angered him, but outwardly, at least so far as I could see, he was unperturbed. I remember bringing the morning papers in to him at 9 a.m., when he would be waking up from a hard day's and evening's campaigning. He would sit up in bed and go through them with great interest, and now and then would reach for his penknife and excise an item he wanted to make use of or to rebut, but with no more visible emotion than my mother might display when, for instance, cutting out a recipe or an advertisement for a bargain at Filene's department store. Sometimes, after catching up on the latest news of his alleged infamies, he would drop off peacefully for an extra catnap before rising and returning to the battle.

And so, taking my cue from his example, I calmed down and began to accept the idea that gossip and slander and denunciation and even vilification are part of the price one pays for being in public life. As Jim Farley once commented, 'You have to have the hide of a rhinoceros to stay in politics.' It is a lesson that is hard and unpleasant but necessary to learn; for unless one does learn it and knows what to expect and is prepared to cope with it emotionally, life in a 'political family' such as ours could become miserable.

This was on my mind when my sons married. They had all had a taste of it, one way or another, from a fairly early age, and could take the penalties more or less in stride. But neither Ethel nor Jackie nor Joan had been brought up in a political atmosphere. Jackie had some knowledge of political life because of having worked on one of the Washington newspapers, but even so that is another side of the matter: writing about someone is different from finding oneself written about. So each time, in turn, Ethel then Jackie then Joan, I made sure to warn them in advance of what they were in for: that they might be hearing and reading all sorts of scandalous gossip and accusations about members of our family, about their husbands and for that matter about themselves and eventually even about their children; and they should understand this and be prepared from the beginning, otherwise they might be very unhappy. They took the burden with the blessing and all three have managed well.

Poor Jackie, married to a beloved young President of the United States; an entrancing First Lady and entrancing in her own right; cruelly widowed; later married to one of the richest men in the world, though to worldwide surprise. Rumours and stories and *exposés* swarm around her wherever she goes. She and I were talking about this not long ago, because she was feeling the pressures. I wanted to give her the best advice I could, but what it came down to in essence was what I had told her before and had been telling myself for many decades:

'You're bound to have publicity of that sort, the world being as it is, so why pay attention to it? Don't waste the time. We're a strong family unit and we can face it in confidence and go on with our lives. Not only for ourselves but for the sake of the children; we must do whatever is important for them. There are people in this world who have to gossip, it seems. There are people who chronically want to believe the worst. Yet most people are kind, decent and good-hearted. So you can always hope for the best in humanity and expect it.'

I was at Manhattanville while Father's campaign roared along through the final weeks – perhaps mercifully for my feelings, since the mud-slinging increased. I understand that up to within a few days of the election the Storrow forces were sure of victory, and that most of the signs, such as public opinion polls, pointed that way. But my father put on one of those whirlwind finishes in which he was a specialist. There was the biggest turn-out of voters in the city's history, about 95,000, and when the count was over my father had upset the predictions and squeezed through by a plurality of 1402 votes.

In thanking his supporters, he said: 'No man could ask for a greater victory. My family appreciated the triumph especially, because there

had been so much injustice in the attacks made on me – so much mis-
representation and vilification. For the sake of my boys and girls I
wanted to win the election as a vindication.'

My school year at Manhattanville passed peacefully and productively. I
was able to get home on school holidays and for weekends a few times.
Old friends were able to visit me; there were excursions and diversions;
the months went by quickly. In June of 1910 I received my graduation
certificate, listened to the advice of the saintly nuns and then departed,
at last, for Boston. I was no longer a schoolgirl. In fact I was on the
verge of leaving girlhood, for I was to be twenty years old the next
month, and the following winter I would be making my debut, the rite
of passage that would make me a full participant in adult life and the
perils and excitements of the world.

5

'There is a time to laugh and a time to dance,' and those next few years were such times. I was 'the Mayor's Daughter' again but now old enough to enjoy the attentions and participate in the pleasures that came my way. Further, with a change in the city charter the mayoralty term had become four years instead of two. My father could relax a bit, which relaxed us all. I myself was, as they said in a term of that day, 'in the bloom of youth and beauty'. My spirits were further uplifted by the fact that Joe Kennedy and I were in love and knew we wanted to marry.

Yet it was not all fun and frolic. Aimless frivolity has never appealed to me. What does anyone get out of it? A life of partying and socializing would have bored me to death. I took afternoon courses at Boston University in French, German, and Art. I kept up with my music and studied the history of piano at the New England Conservatory. I joined a 'little theatre group' and appeared in a play and some musicals. I conducted catechism classes and taught Sunday School. I sewed for the poor and did settlement work. I went to educational lectures. I was the youngest member of the Public Library Investigating Committee, a principal function of which was to recommend books and make reading lists for Boston children. (Needless to say, I staunchly supported Louisa May Alcott's works.) I was a member of the French and German friendship and cultural associations, the Alliance Française and Deutsche Gesellschaft and attended and contributed to their meetings. And much else.

I even founded a club composed of young women who had been to school abroad and were interested in studying and discussing worldwide current history and meaningful current events. Thanks to my father, we were able to get all sorts of visiting dignitaries to address us. One of the first was the Rev. Bernard Vaughan, SJ, himself one of the most distinguished of English clerics and brother of Cardinal Vaughan of London. He was also a man of keen wit. Knowing that Boston was full of clubs of all kinds and degrees, proliferating in all directions, I asked him for a suggestion as to what to call ourselves, and he said: 'Why not "The Ace of Clubs"? Meaning the first and the foremost and the most important of all clubs.' The motion was seconded and carried with enthusiasm. Rather soon, inevitably I suppose, even among serious-minded young women, the club sprouted some social activities, notably an annual charity ball (for years, as president, I led the Grand March), and became quite fashionable, with a long waiting list. One result of this was that some reporters and quite a few readers made mental slips and miscalled it by such names as the Ace of Spades or Ace of Hearts club, and as I recall there were some who thought of it as a gambling club. But it was the Ace of Clubs and it had a truly serious purpose.

My debut was not lavish, at least by the standards of those times. It was just a beautiful reception and tea at our home in Dorchester. Though it was the dead of winter, my parents had turned the house into a bower of roses for me. There were other flowers too as accents, and ferns and palms and garlands, but roses were the motif of the day. I wore a white satin dress with a short train; the bodice and skirt were embroidered in white, with just a touch of yellow silk ribbon showing through the embroidery along the hemline. Long white kid gloves; no jewels or ornaments except a bit of white ribbon in my hair; a corsage of violets and lilies of the valley. With my mother in black chantilly lace, and my father in cutaway and winged collar, I received the guests in the drawing-room. I was so excited by the occasion that I felt no fatigue standing three or four hours and shaking hands and chatting with more than 450 people, among them the new Governor, two Congressmen, and numerous other dignitaries including the entire Boston City Council, who had accepted my father's invitation and closed down for the day. In fact my debut – thanks to my father's boundless enthusiasm for the event – was treated as a municipal celebration, with yards of photographs and write-ups in the newspapers. There were messages from far and wide, including one from Sir Thomas Lipton – that kindred spirit of my father – who cabled: 'I extend my heartiest congratulations to you on the occasion of your coming-out. I suppose that in a short time I will be sending congratulations for another occasion of great joy. Before that occurs I hope that you pick out a man who is the equal of your father.'

In my heart, I had already done that. Joe was there. So were a couple of would-be rivals and a number of other young men and girls, all good friends. After the older people had left and a dozen or two had settled down to an evening of their own, we went upstairs to a room festooned with ropes of roses, where we had a sitdown dinner and sang and joked and laughed and danced. No champagne, no alcohol in any form, for none of us used it so far as I knew, and certainly on that evening none of us needed anything for a good time but our own high spirits.

Actually there were two societies in Boston. That was because the population itself, despite a continual influx from Italy, Russia, Germany and other countries, consisted mainly of two predominant groups. One of them was almost entirely Protestant and was mainly of English descent, though with admixtures of Scotch, Scotch-Irish and even some Irish plus a soupçon of French and others; in any case all descended from colonial or early American settlers, blended into the general breed called Yankee or Old American or (in a term coined later) 'proper Bostonians'. Their main citadel and symbol was the region known as Back Bay where wealthy and distinguished families such as the Cabots and Lodges lived serenely amid ancestral portraits and mahogany sideboards and silver tea services in spacious houses in large grounds. With the advantages of inherited wealth and status and close-knit inter-family ties, they controlled the banks, insurance companies, the big law firms, the big shipping and mercantile enterprises and almost all the usual routes to success, and thus were a self-perpetuating aristocracy. They had many admirable qualities. But they were a closed society.

The other predominant group consisted of Irish Catholics, descendants of those impoverished hordes who had fled from the Great Famines of the 1840s to 1860s. Through hard effort and much ingenuity, often by way of politics but in every other way open to them, large numbers of these second- and third-generation offspring had achieved prosperity and many had achieved a cultural level fully equal to that of the Back Bay Brahmins.

Between the two groups feelings were, at best, suspicious, and in general amounted to a state of chronic mutual antagonism.

The reasons are too much a part of familiar history to need any exposition, but I will mention just a few factors. One of them, anachronistic but none the less powerful, stemmed from the ancient unhappy relationship between England and Ireland. Despite having broken away from England, most of the old Yankee families had strong cultural roots there and shared many of the ancestral biases, such as anti-Catholicism and a diffuse image of the Irish people as being inferior and troublesome; whereas the Boston Irish, of course, had their ancestral image of the English as a callous cold-hearted breed of apostates, exploiters and oppressors. The old biases might have died away in the new land, but instead were reinforced by the circumstances of the mid-nineteenth-century migrations. Children of the immigrants heard at their parents' knee the dreadful stories of mass suffering and death while the English absentee landlords, the English government including Queen Victoria, and presumably the English people in general, had remained unconcerned except for a few tokens of sympathy and a good deal of fretful worry that their usual sources of income and tax revenues in Ireland were shrinking.

On the Yankee side, precisely because the immigrants were so poor and distressed and came in such sudden great numbers, there were natural fears of being inundated, swamped and overwhelmed by a tide of unfriendly, uneducated, uncouth aliens with customs and religious belief at odds with their own. In their alarm and disdain they gave the Irish nicknames such as bog-trotters, clodhoppers, Micks, Harps and – because so much of the pick-and-shovel labour of digging ditches and canals, levelling hills and filling-in swamps and oozy tidal flats was done by Irishmen – 'blacklegs' and 'muckers'. They worked long hours at backbreaking work for any subsistence wage they could get, and many businessmen exploited them for every penny to be gained from their sweat. There were others who could not abide them even to exploit them. In the Help Wanted columns of the classified ads, or even in large lettering on cards in shop windows, those feelings were put in such cold blunt terms as 'No Irish Need Apply'.

All this overt hostility had fairly well died down by the early part of the twentieth century. On both sides, nevertheless, mistrust and resentment remained. The two co-existed, having as little as possible to do with each other. In fact it was so difficult to find a common meeting-ground that my father and James Jackson Storrow and other men of good-will got together and founded a club, the City Club, to give prominent leaders of both elements a chance to meet in a neutral and socially relaxed atmosphere.

I'm sure both sides were to blame. Both being too myopic, too preoccupied with old grudges, too little able to realize that there were new circumstances that appropriately needed fresh and different responses; too little, by far, of the quality of mercy and the capacity to forgive and forget and go on. I remember, for instance, that when my father appointed an old-line Yankee Protestant, Charles Cole, as Boston's Fire Commissioner, there were Irish Catholics who grumbled to me, 'Why didn't he appoint one of his own kind?' And later on after Joe and I married and had our first child and I asked my obstetrician, of Irish Catholic descent, to select the best paediatrician he knew to take medical care of our baby and he chose a doctor of Scotch-Irish descent and Presbyterian faith – oh! what a commotion there was then among some of my friends and my o.b's other patients Why was this, they wanted to know! Why an Orangeman, even if he was supposed to be one of the best paediatricians in Boston?

And what a scandal when this same doctor called to attend a sick little boy, the Cardinal's own nephew, on St Patrick's Day – wearing an orange tie!

With such 'cultural lags' still widespread then in Boston, I suppose it was inevitable and even in some atavistic way 'natural' that there should be two societies. And so there were; even to such a degree that separate 'Society Columns' were published in the newspapers, one about them, one about us.

In later years people who know me and my personal background have asked me what my reactions were. Well, the fact is, at the time I really just took it for granted. I was aware that there was an incongruity but I don't think it occurred to me to be surprised. I had known since young girlhood about the social division, had grown up with it, and accepted it as one of those elementary facts of life not worth puzzling about. I knew that was Boston: that's the way it was. I would not be mixing with the Back Bay set. None of them would be mixing in ours. No regrets, and certainly no feelings of inferiority on my part. I knew some of those girls well enough to know that in education, talent, appearance, social grace and practically every other quality that might count in a human equation I was every bit their equal, if not their better.

The two social sets did more or less the same things in the same ways, at the same times, often at the same public places, dressing and behaving and enjoying themselves in ways so nearly the same that to an observer from London or Paris or Berlin or outer space there would have been no discernible differences. They had their Junior League, we had our Cecilian Club, equally dedicated in principle to unselfish good works; and although we might have thought of ourselves as 'holier than they', mature judgment inclines me to doubt it. They had their Benefits and Bazaars and Charity Balls under various labels, and we had ours under different ones. There were some advantages to the arrangement. They all knew one another, and so did we, so in each environment there were minimal needs for explanations and defences and the best of chances for spontaneous conversations about common interests. Catholic young men were extreme rarities at their parties, just as Protestant young men were at ours. For example, although our Abbotsford Club gave three subscription dances a year, and for several years I was at all of them, I can't recall meeting a Protestant at any of them. The principle was wrong, of course, but the practical effects were to help prevent romances leading to 'mixed marriages', with the eventual unhappiness, often really searing consequences, that awaited such a marriage in the world as it was. As for the separate Society Columns, there was an advantage to that contrivance, too, in fact quite a convenience. We always knew exactly where to look for the news of our friends. The Church was very strict in those days about mixed marriages, and even non-Catholic schools.

I think I have made it clear already that my father was a 'natural performer'. The political arena was his stage. And like any skilled performer he achieved rapport with his audience, and played to it not only in his manner of delivery, which ranged from the hortatory-pontifical-inspirational to the merriest laugh, but also in the content of his script, which ranged from the most serious issues of statesmanship to song-and-dance.

Indeed, he did a great deal of singing instead of speechifying. A favourite song of those times, 'Sweet Adeline', became one of his political trademarks. Since I played the piano well and often accompanied him on his rounds during those years, I was a participating partner in some of his musical productions.

'Sweet Adeline' is as inseparable from his legend as Al Smith's 'The Sidewalks of New York' or Franklin D. Roosevelt's 'Happy Days Are Here Again'; probably more so. I have played it a few thousand times.

Although he sang it innumerable times 'in answer to popular request', he needed little encouragement and frequently none. He often entered a meeting hall or stadium warbling the unmistakable message that Fitz had arrived and wished everyone well. He was invariably greeted by responsive voices with emphasis on the last two lines:

> *You're the flower of my heart,*
> *Sweet Adeline.*

He sang it at the summer White House for President Taft. On a trip to Central America he sang it so often, with such feeling, to such applause that years after, when President Franklin D. Roosevelt was on a good-will tour of Latin America, he was met in one country by a band playing 'Sweet Adeline', which was believed to be the USA's national anthem – an incident that F.D.R. related later to my father with the greatest delight.

The song became so closely identified with him that I must mention that he knew others – at least one of which I can document from my scrapbook of those years. News clippings describe a visit to Boston by a large group of students from Germany, and described how my father entertained them with a banquet and 'informal musicale' at the Hotel Somerset. The German students burst into song at a certain point (one reporter used the word, 'inevitable') and my father, after words of appreciation, responded in kind. 'The Mayor did not let the chance of singing what he termed "the municipal hymn", "Sweet Adeline", go by and insisted that the visitors should join in the chorus.' But also, as the news story goes on to say, he sang 'Love Me and the World is Mine'. It's true. I was there and had a share of the spotlight myself: 'Miss Rose Fitzgerald . . . made a short speech in German, in which she welcomed the visitors to these shores.'

Since my father spoke no foreign languages, he asked me to speak to dignitaries from abroad who came to Boston and needed some form of official greeting or hospitality from the Mayor, or wished to talk with him. My mother also certainly did her part and did it well, and my father delighted in showing her off. I remember that at one reception a reporter who recognized me asked me to point out Agnes for him. Then he said: 'And the very slim one in blue – which of the daughters is she?'

'Her name?' I laughed. 'Why, don't you know her? Her name is Mother!'

For reasons both of time and temperament Mother had a limited capacity for the official social whirl. She still had young children at home who needed her. Moreover, as she declared to one interviewer, 'I want my home to be a place of inspiration and encouragement to all my family. I am a home woman in every way, and my one ambition is to make the home the most happy and attractive place for my husband and our children.'

Frankly, I don't think any woman, however gregarious and heedless of other duties, could have kept up with my father on a regular basis. His strength and energy were just overwhelming. On his fiftieth birthday in 1913 he announced to the press, 'I feel no older than I did twenty-five years ago,' and illustrated his point by running a hundred-yard dash at seven a.m., a quarter-mile at nine, wrestling at noon, and boxing at one. His schedule was a whirligig of dedications, corner-stones, receptions, banquets, picnics, parades, orations, rallies, greet-ings, grand marches and ceremonials – from attending important wakes and funerals to crowning beauty queens – besides other things that popped into his head spontaneously. When she was out with him, my mother never knew what to expect next. Once, when they were the guests of honour at a dressy party at the Dorchester Club he brought her home on a fire engine, sirens howling through the night.

Obviously, my mother could use help and was happy I could give it. We reached a perfect arrangement.

I was his companion, hostess and assistant on a good many of the trips he took. He loved to travel, and as Mayor he could always find a good official reason for a jaunt of some sort, and at least a plausible reason to take me. I was with him in Chicago for an international meeting of municipal executives. And in Baltimore for the 1912 Democratic Convention where Woodrow Wilson was nominated. On some of the trips, Agnes was along. One winter my father led the Boston Chamber of Commerce to Panama to ponder the possible effects on Boston of the recently opened Panama Canal. I was along as hostess-companion-helper. Another time, for the same purposes, he took a Chamber of Commerce delegation to Europe to examine the big ocean port cities such as Hamburg and Brussels and the highly developed systems of inland waterways that carry such a large traffic of goods to and from those ports. Agnes and I accompanied him, and with our fluent German and French and a smattering of Dutch, and our basic knowledge of Europe, we performed valuable services for the group while also having a fine time in our own ways with our own interests, which had less to do with rivers and harbours *per se*, and more with them as places to sail around on, preferably with some young beaux.

During most of the trip we were joined by Hugh Nawn, an attractive young man a year or so older than I. He was the son of near neighbours and close friends of my parents in Dorchester. His father, Harry, was one of the leading contractors of the region, successful and in fact quite wealthy, and a man of charm and other attractive qualities. He was a great pal of my father's. In fact, on many a night when my father came back to Dorchester after a hard day and evening's campaigning he would head first for the Nawn house, and – I have heard – Harry would pour some milk or cocoa and whip up some peanut butter sandwiches, of which my father was excessively fond, and the two would sit in the kitchen trading jokes and discussing the affairs of the day and nation and world. Hugh Nawn, after graduating from Harvard, had joined his father's firm with clearly foreordained prospects of someday owning it. Thus he had the soundest of prudent business reasons, having just come to the end of a European tour on his own, for joining our Chamber of Commerce inspection of rivers and harbours for good ideas for a busier Boston.

He and I had been good friends for a long time, and we were quite fond of each other. He was the proverbial 'boy next door'. In the later years we were at many parties and dances together. Sometimes he was my escort. We had lots of fun, we were congenial, and it would be easy to imagine that our relationship could blossom into romance and marriage. Perhaps Hugh had hopes that it would. There were signs that so did our parents, especially my father and his crony, Harry Nawn.

Anyway, Hugh joined our group at Ostend and was along for the rest of the time, and that was great good luck for Agnes and me. One of the beautifully happy memories of my young life was a night we sailed from Vienna down the Danube and Hugh and I danced on an open deck in the moonlight to the strains of 'The Blue Danube' waltz.

6

I want to tell you about Joe Kennedy, the boy I fell in love with, the man I married, the father of my children, and the architect of our lives.

We saw each other again about eight summers after our first meeting at Old Orchard Beach, Maine. During the few days we were together, we became friends, then affectionate friends, and later began to think of ourselves as sweethearts. At least I did.

Joe Kennedy was tall, thin, wiry, freckled and had blue eyes and red hair. Not dark red, orange red or gold red, as some Irish have, but sandy-blond with a lot of red lights in it. His face was open and expressive, yet with youthful dignity, conveying qualities of self-reliance, self-respect and self-discipline. He neither drank nor smoked; nor did I. Nice girls just didn't. He was a serious young man, but he had a quick wit and a responsive sense of humour. He smiled and laughed easily and had a big, spontaneous and infectious grin that made everybody in sight want to smile, too. Even then, he had an aura of command, an attitude of being competent to take charge of any situation. At Boston Latin School, from which my father had graduated, he was captain of the baseball team, player-manager of the football team, captain of the tennis team, a star on the basketball team, colonel of the all-Boston prize-winning school regiment, and president of his class.

The following autumn he invited me to the first dance of the season at Boston Latin. My father refused to let me go. He disapproved of a girl of sixteen going around to dances in strange places and meeting people who might cause trouble. This didn't seem logical to me since it was his school and he was proud of it. He knew Joe and the Kennedys; and besides it was an afternoon dance, so I would be home before dark. I also knew my way around Boston on the street-cars and took them often. But my father made the rules. In politics he was known sometimes as 'the Little Napoleon' – and he could be Napoleonic in matters of home and family as well. Argument would have got me no place.

So Joe asked somebody else, after first telling her she was his second choice. I thought that was very honest of him, and I admired him for it.

The next spring, when I was finishing my post-graduate year at Dorchester High, there was a big graduation dance there. I was still sixteen but soon to be seventeen; the school was nearby; the time was afternoon. It was a sentimental occasion, so after some pondering my father let me attend. Obviously, I invited Joe Kennedy.

Formal 'dates' were very rare events among my age-group in those days. Regular dating was taboo and 'going steady' was completely out of the question. This was a serious problem for Joe and me, and one we had to work out, as best we could, through 'innocent' stratagems.

For instance, could anyone object if by coincidence we happened to be at the same place at the same time? Joe was captain-manager of the Latin School tennis team. When I went for a weekend visit with an aunt of mine in Concord, he arranged a match between Concord High School and his team, at Concord. We spent quite a few hours together that day.

We also met at informal get-togethers with friends at somebody's house, usually in the afternoons and always, of course, with a responsible adult on the premises. We would push back the parlour furniture, lift the breakable bric-à-brac out of the way, make lemonade or punch and cookies and fudge, and someone would play the piano. We gathered around and we sang and we danced. Joe and I had many mutual friends. If I were invited, he would just drop in.

We also met at lectures, the library, and walked part of the way home together. (That was the beginning of a good habit. For many decades Joe and I took long walks together, not for dutiful exercise but for pleasure. I still take a walk, by myself, almost every day.)

It took teamwork and conspiracy, because we needed reliable allies.

Some were girl-friends of mine in Dorchester and the area, girls from nice families living in nice houses, their parents known to my parents. They gave more 'drop-in' parties – well planned ahead – than they would have otherwise. Another ally was my father's chauffeur. He was a very good man. He was devoted to my father. But he was also a sentimentalist, and was fond of me, and liked Joe, and knew young love when he saw it. He helped to smooth the way. Sometimes, when he picked me up in the car he would ask what route I would prefer, and I might give him a roundabout one. And there to the surprise of neither of us would be the recognizable figure of Joe Kennedy waiting for a trolley, or lurking on a bench, or strolling along. This would suddenly remind me that there was something I wanted to speak to that young man about, so would the driver take the car to the end of the block and wait a few minutes? The minutes might stretch to half an hour. Then Joe would walk me to the car, open the door, greet his benefactor, and

I was sped home, dutiful as usual. There was always a faint smile on the chauffeur's face. He never gave me away.

During that last year at Dorchester High and the following year, when I was commuting to Sacred Heart in Boston, Joe and I managed to see each other rather often. Less often than we would have liked, but more often than my father was aware of, and enough in any case to reaffirm in our hearts how deeply we cared for each other.

But then I went to Blumenthal, an ocean away. I could only write and wait. When I came home again, it was only for about six weeks. At Manhattanville, we exchanged more letters and made a few visits back and forth. When I returned to Boston to stay, I became involved in public functions and far-flung travels with my father.

Scarcely had the roses from my debut faded when my father announced that in honour of my new status in the world he would take me on a winter vacation to Palm Beach. I was thrilled by the prospect of southern sunshine instead of a Boston February of snow and slush, of exciting new scenes, new friends; to say nothing of summer frocks and evening dresses. Palm Beach was even then known as a centre of style and fashion. But then I discovered that the trip conflicted with the date of the Junior Prom at Harvard. Joe had invited me, and to make it easier for me to get my parents' permission he had even arranged for one of his college room-mates to invite a girl who was one of my best friends.

It was an awkward choice to make, but a clear one. I thanked my father gratefully but told him I had already accepted an earlier invitation, to the Prom. My father replied that he would hear of no such thing and I would be going to Florida.

I didn't argue with my father since, as I have said, I wouldn't have dreamed of doing so; but I was visibly upset, downcast, teary, and melancholy. My father began to show signs of weakening. But then my mother, with all the firm common sense of her character, told me to stop being foolish, for I might never again have a chance to go to Palm Beach.

So I snuffled a bit and submitted and boarded the train for a trip of some 1200 miles, each of which I heartily regretted. I kept hoping for a major disaster in Boston. Nothing that would kill or injure people, of course; just something like a two-foot snowfall or a fire that would burn down a few acres of the port and warehouse area, enough that the Mayor of Boston would feel duty-bound to go back home and I could feel free to go to the Harvard Junior Prom. But nothing happened.

In 1911, Florida was still sparsely populated, with only about 800,000 people in the whole state compared with the many millions now. There were few cities of any size, and Palm Beach itself was hardly more than a village, with a population of less than a thousand. Today aeroplanes make the trip in a few hours, but early in the century it meant two days and one night on the train from New York to Palm Beach, plus more hours in carriages or taxis and on the ferryboat that connected the mainland with Palm Beach island. Getting there was a tiring adventure. But having arrived, one could see why people made the trip. For behold, there indeed were the palms and the beaches, and balmy breezes and white clouds in limitless skies, and beautiful blue-green water just the right temperature for swimming. A couple of splendid hotels with every convenience, and a dozen fine private homes in large grounds along the sea. In short, an aquamarine gem in a perfect setting.

We had a wonderful visit, full of fun and razzle-dazzle and high spirits, with lots of sun and sea and blue skies. If it hadn't been for missing the Prom I think I would have enjoyed it immensely.

A few months afterwards, my father and Agnes and I and our Chamber of Commerce cohorts sailed off on the *Franconia* (my father serenading dockside friends, and an honour escort of Hurrah Johnny Cadets in small boats, with you-know-what song) to look at the European port and river systems.

And so it went. Europe, Central America, Palm Beach, Kansas City, St Louis, Chicago, Baltimore and here and there, meeting many people including a certain number of attractive, eligible young bachelors along the way. Did my dear Pa have a plan?

Did he object to Joe? He did not. How could he? There was nothing to object to. The only fault that anyone could find with him was that he had to take an extra year at Boston Latin to make up some languages; furthermore, when a few acid-tongued acquaintances remarked that with those low grades he must be 'dumb in school' my well-founded reply was, 'I don't see how he has time to study at all, he's so busy with all those sports and leadership activities and winning all those high honours and awards.' Furthermore he ended up with an academic record good enough to be admitted to Harvard: one of the few Boston Irish boys of that era to go there.

He played football (his senior room-mate and best friend, Bob Fisher, was captain and All-American) and baseball, his favourite sport. My father and I saw him the day he won his 'H', when he made the winning play against Yale. He was widely popular and respected. He was elected to Hasty Pudding Institute of 1770 and to one of the best fraternities, Delta Upsilon. He was involved in all sorts of things but still did well in his major studies, history and economics, and graduated with a creditable average. During his senior year he made money as coach of the freshman baseball team. I doubt this escaped my father's notice, for much as he valued academic achievement, he placed a high premium on popularity and respect, athletic skills, physical fitness, energy, ambition, and a practical capacity to make money. All of these were obviously part of Joe's equipment and credentials.

It has been said that my father objected to Joe Kennedy because of his political feuds with P. J. Kennedy. Yet I never then nor later heard either say an uncomplimentary thing about the other. They were never meant to be close personal companions – and they never were – because of their different temperaments. But they could be friends and from all outward signs they were. Their paths crossed amicably on many occasions, including holiday resorts such as Old Orchard Beach. There is a photograph of them taken at Asheville, North Carolina. They are on horseback and ready to take off on a fox hunt, of all things.

In those days a debut meant that a girl had reached marriageable age and was to be looked at by various young men and in turn she was to be surveying the field of eligible suitors. She wasn't supposed to make up her mind for a while, perhaps a year or more. If a couple became engaged directly after the debut, or worse, already had a 'secret understanding', it was considered foolishly romantic, if not pitiable. People were likely to say: 'Think of all the fun they missed before they settled down.' The accepted opinion was that when ardour had cooled and nostalgia had set in, they would suffer marital discontent. Or worse.

Also, my father had extravagant notions of my beauty, grace, wit and charm. As I entered young womanhood these delusions deepened. I suppose no father really thinks any man is good enough for his daughter. But my father was a hopeless case. Therefore, believing that I could take my pick of any beau, and happy that through his own hard won success he could give me the opportunity to meet a large cross-section of suitable admirers on several continents, he didn't want me to make the rash, short-sighted and ungrateful mistake of pledging my heart prematurely to any young man, nice and fine as that young man might be.

My father never said any of this to me explicitly. There were no scenes and no lectures. Actually, his temptation to issue Napoleonic orders (if elected, you will go to Palm Beach) gave way to sweet reason. He pointed out that I was fortunate enough to have unusual advantages and opportunities. Therefore I shouldn't say yes to the first man who fell in love with and who wanted to marry me. I should take my time and I should look around. This theme was often repeated and endorsed by my mother.

So there I was, wobbly and often tearful in private, as I tried to find an equilibrium of my own. I adored Joe. I also adored my parents, and knew how much I owed them. I didn't want to be ungrateful, and certainly didn't want to offend or deceive them. Thus it was with pangs of conscience that I began to see Joe more often than I was supposed to.

As the years went along I found myself a willing accomplice and imaginative co-conspirator in stratagems we devised to be together.

Some of them were really rather funny.

Our finest hour in clandestine meetings, as Joe and I later agreed, came on a walk one day when we thought we saw a newspaper reporter. We were just then passing a church, so we quickly went inside and sat in a rear pew, rather breathlessly, not paying close attention to our surroundings for the moment. Then we looked at the literature in the pew racks and discovered we were in a Christian Science church. As Roman Catholics we were not supposed to be there. But we immediately decided to accept that venal sin and answer for it later. Anyone else who came in and thought we looked like Rose Fitzgerald and Joe Kennedy – scions of well-known Catholic families – would have to assume this an interesting example of coincidental resemblance, since we could not possibly be who we really were. After we were married, Joe and I drove past that church many times, and in fact Joe would go out of our way to do so. We would grin at each other, thinking how wicked we had been. Joe would say that as soon as he could afford it, he would give a contribution to the church in honour of us and for its blessings received in a time of need. And when he was able to, he made an anonymous gift, for he wanted no personal notice or thanks.

Another conspiracy concerned the important dances of the year. At the beginning of the season Joe would say to me: 'Now remember, you are invited to the Cecilian Club dance, the Newman Club dance at Harvard, the Ace of Clubs dance and any other dances I can't think of now – remember that I invited you to all of them.' I agreed cheerfully, while knowing, as he did also, that most of the time he would be my escort only in theory. For my mother, as the Mayor's wife and leader of Catholic society, was a chaperone or 'matron' at many of the dances, and when this occurred, I was expected to go with her and come home with her instead of being escorted by a boy.

Yet all was not lost because there were 'dance orders' in those days. I understand the practice still exists in a less formal way in some places. What it came down to was that no matter who invited whom to a dance, once the couple arrived there each person was a free agent.

Customarily they had the first and last dances together, and one or two in between, but otherwise any boy was free to ask any girl 'for the honour of a dance'. If she accepted he wrote his name or initials next to the appropriate number on the girl's programme or 'dance order', a card or little booklet she carried, usually on a ribbon at her waist or around her wrist. The most popular girls had their cards filled within minutes at the beginning of the evening. The least popular had dances to spare and became wall-flowers. The system had its cruelties, both for girls who didn't get asked and for boys who asked and got turned down. But the general effect was to add excitement and variety and let people circulate, instead of couples being stuck with each other all evening. For most people it was really quite a good idea. But not for Joe and me. We didn't need excitement and we didn't want to circulate and we did want to be stuck with each other all evening. What to do?

Joe's solution was bold and elegantly simple. Forgery. Well, not forgery literally because he didn't sign the names of real people on my card, but instead names and initials that he made up out of thin air. He had half a dozen or so that he liked best and used often, mixing them up and scrawling in different handwriting. His favourite one, though, and mine too, was Sam Shaw or just S.S. for short.

Since I was not supposed to be dancing with Joe all the time and since my mother was usually there, sitting near the dance floor, one may wonder how our deception worked. Shrewdly, Joe would leave a couple of dances open for Hugh Nawn or other beaux. At those times I contrived to dance in good view of where my mother was, and perhaps wave to her or even stop to chat with her for a minute or two. As the boy who had invited me, my official escort of the evening, Joe was entitled in her eyes to the first, last and a few other dances. The others, we sat out, vanishing amid the potted palms or into the arcades and verandahs of the hotel or country club, and in fine weather on to the terraces and paths. Some of my sweetest memories are of music floating in the night air and the distant sounds of gaiety and laughter, while I took walks hand in hand with 'Sam Shaw'.

After Joe graduated from Harvard in 1912 there was less need for subterfuge, and finally there was none. Part of the reason, I suppose, was that my father, with his capacious sense of realism in political and public matters, finally became realistic about our romance, faced the facts, and adapted himself to them. Another reason was simply that Joe had a Harvard diploma, a symbol of respectability and capability; and for a boy or young man, college graduation was a rite-of-passage, rather like a girl's debut, both signifying that the person was ready for adult relationships and responsibilities. Furthermore, there were soon signs that Joe had special talents in certain activities where the prizes were tangible, practical and, to my father's pragmatic parental eye, quite comforting.

Joe was as fascinated by the world of finance and business, with its infinite variety and possibilities, as my father was with the world of politics. Soon after graduation he took the examinations to become a state bank examiner. They were difficult and conducted in a rigidly honest fashion; he passed and received his appointment, and during the next year and a half visited banks all over eastern Massachusetts. The job was still another factor limiting our time together; but also it was highly educational for him – he learned far more about finance than he had in all his Harvard economics courses.

I mentioned earlier that the financial institutions of Boston were controlled by proper Bostonians. They sat on their fortunes like broody hens on fertile eggs, and intrusions into their henhouses were met with resentful cluckings. I remember my father telling of an encounter he had with one old-line Boston banker. 'You have plenty of Irish depositors,' he commented. 'Why don't you have some Irishmen on your board of directors?' The banker replied, 'Well, a couple of our tellers are Irish.' 'Yes,' said my father, the indignation still in his voice long afterwards, 'and I suppose the charwomen are too.'

As a result of this oligarchical control over finance and credit, P. J. Kennedy, together with a few other of the more prosperous Irish businessmen, had founded an independent bank in East Boston called the Columbia Trust Company. After nearly two decades it was still a rather small bank, but it had grown large enough that one of the big Boston banks wanted to absorb it, and offered the stockholders a good price. Most of them – holding a majority of the stock – wanted to accept. P. J. Kennedy did not. He wanted to preserve the bank as an independent neighbourhood institution under local control. He hadn't money enough of his own to buy out the others and block the deal. So he called on his son Joe – who by then had grown wise in the ways of banking, and knew allies to seek and moves to make – to lead the fight against the take-over.

It was quite a battle. It caught the imagination of financial reporters on the Boston papers, and there were practically blow-by-blow accounts as a young David defended his people against the financial Goliath. When the tumult and shouting had stopped, Joe was the victor. Columbia Trust was saved intact and secure. And Joe Kennedy was its president. He was then twenty-five years old: the youngest bank president in the United States, probably the youngest one in the world.

The Boston financial writers were enchanted, not only with him as a financial prodigy but as an appealingly fresh face and colourful character in a scene that for so many years had been coloured in tones of grey. Within the financial community, and in the general community of Boston Irish, he was no longer just P. J. Kennedy's son but suddenly well-known in his own right.

My father now had to agree that if any young man were worthy of my hand in marriage, Joe Kennedy would be as good a choice for me as anybody.

The Columbia Trust battle occurred during the latter part of 1913. We waited nearly a year more before we married. This may seem strange to some people. There was Joe with a fine job and fine prospects; both families had money enough to spare to give us a good start in our married life, so why wait? The answer lay in an attitude of the times: before a couple married they should be sure they could stand on their own, without financial gifts or subsidies. The man should have a secure job with a certain income. The woman should be able and willing to live on that income. Until that came about, they waited. To us, it was a matter of personal pride, dignity, self-respect.

In those days we unquestioningly believed that life was meant to have certain basic forms and structures. We felt that, 'To everything there is a season, and a time for every purpose.' There was courtship, there was the discovery of love, there was engagement, there was marriage, there was parenthood; each in its season and marked by traditions and rituals which, believe me, were sources of strength to young people then and I hope will continue – in some way – to be so for others for a very long time to come.

Having said this, I now find myself slightly embarrassed because in that procession of events, each of which should be engraved in memory, there are two in my case that I can't quite remember. Try as I will, they are absolutely gone. One is the time Joe asked me to marry him. The other is the time he gave me my engagement ring.

I feel fairly easy about the first, because I don't think he ever *did* ask me, not just straight out. That's not the way it was. It was less a matter of 'Will you marry me?' than of 'When we get married . . .'

As a matter of fact, while on the topic of proposals, the only direct one I ever had was from Sir Thomas Lipton and was neither meant nor taken seriously. Sir Thomas was a perennial bachelor, and one of the most eligible bachelors in the world. Consequently there was much speculation about the lady he sooner or later would choose, and good-humoured joshing by his friends about his hesitation. One evening when he was in Boston, and at a private dinner party my father gave for him and some friends at one of the hotels, this banter started again and it was demanded he speak out at last and declare his intentions.

He looked over at me, and said:

'If you want to know who Lady Lipton is going to be, she is right here in this room. Come along, Rose, we'd better let them in on our secret. Stand up, Rose!'

'I won't accept you, Sir Thomas,' I replied with what I hope was not too much of a blush. 'I think you are altogether too fickle!'

'Well,' he said, when the laughter subsided, 'now I know how it feels to be jilted!'

From that bit of by-play the rumour spread that Sir Thomas wanted to marry me (or in other versions, my sister Agnes) and in time, as so often has happened, this began to be transmuted into 'fact' and turned up as such in articles and books. The truth is that of course I loved Sir Thomas, as I would a grandfather, and that he loved me too, as he would a granddaughter, for we were just about that far apart in age.

Joe gave me the engagement ring, I'm certain, during late winter or early spring of 1914. Also, I remember his telling me he had bought it through a Harvard college friend, Arthur Goldsmith, who had graduated and gone into the family jewellery business in New York. Further, I am practically certain that he gave it to me one evening in my home. Beyond that, everything is hazy: no dialogue, no details, not even the general scene. I can hardly believe it myself. But there we are. Perhaps I was too excited by the event and perhaps also a bit stunned by what I saw: for when I opened the ring box I found a two-carat stone, pure white, flawless, superb.

The summer of 1914 was of course a time of high drama and crisis in Europe. The assassination of the Austrian Archduke in June was followed by political and diplomatic storms, the mobilizations of armies; and the outbreak of war in August between the Allies and the Central Powers. Warfare between Germany and France, the countries I loved best and admired most after my own United States, was deeply distressing to me. Joe was saddened too; for only the summer before he had gone to Europe for the first time, with a group of Harvard friends. They travelled in Germany and France, and he had come home with fine memories of both countries and peoples.

Nevertheless, we were young and in love and the Atlantic lay between us and that tragedy. President Wilson declared America's neutrality. We could assume that the war would be settled by somebody, and somehow fairly soon, since all the nations had intelligent leaders and intelligent men could not fail to look for and find some reasonable compromise before events became too serious. We assumed that it would all be done with, peace restored, before it could possibly affect our own life together in any direct way.

Thus that summer of 1914 passed for us in much the same ways that earlier summers had passed. We went to the Boston 'Pops' concerts and loved the music and ate ice-cream. Usually on Friday nights some friend was having a small party; a dozen or two of us would gather around the parlour piano and sing old favourites and new hits, and some of us danced. On weekend afternoons, at one of the clubs or good hotels, there was likely to be a tea-dance with an orchestra. Between numbers we chattered with one another and drank tea or lemonade or one of the new popular soft drinks such as Moxie.

We always had good times at these little soirées, partly because I loved dancing and Joe was such an extremely good dancer. He always knew all the current steps: the waltz, of course, was the perennial favourite, but others such as the two-step, the Turkey Trot, the tango (both those considered rather wicked) and the latest rage then, a dance called 'the Boston'. It had come along very recently, during his senior year at Harvard, and he hadn't had a chance to master it until he discovered that one of the young novitiates into the Hasty Pudding Club was greatly adept at it. There was 'hazing' for new members, certain duties the upper-classmen assigned to them, and Joe plucked this boy out and gave him the full-time special duty of teaching him 'the Boston'. The boy worked hard, and Joe learned well.

It goes without saying that we talked a good deal about ourselves, our plans for our wedding and honeymoon, where we should live, what kind of furniture we should have – all that. And I'm sure we exchanged special hopes and dreams about our future together.

Joe and I were married that October of 1914 in a service attended only by our families and close friends – neither of us wanted a public fiesta – in the private chapel of Cardinal O'Connell, who officiated. Agnes was my maid of honour. Joseph Donovan, an old friend of Joe's from boyhood through Harvard, was best man.

We had a beautiful honeymoon trip of two weeks at the Greenbriar in White Sulphur Springs, West Virginia. Then we returned to Boston, to the home we had selected and had already furnished so it would be waiting for us.

7

Most of our young married friends lived in rented apartments, and as a place to start our life together an apartment would have been perfectly fine, for me. But not for Joe. From the very beginning, 'home' was the centre of his world and the only place that really, finally, counted in his plans, no matter where those plans took him from time to time. Moreover, despite all his capacities for persuasion and leadership – tête-à-tête across a table, or as a team captain, or as administrator of vast enterprises in business and government, as he would be in years to come – he had a strong need for privacy, for independence, for being able to choose the people he wanted to be with in close association. In later years when he became a leading figure in Wall Street he was known as a 'lone wolf'. These traits of temperament were manifested in the first big decision he made for us. Home could not be an apartment but had to be a house. I gladly seconded the motion.

We looked around, that summer before we were married, and found one we both liked and decided would suit our needs. It was a nice old wooden-frame house with clapboard siding; seven rooms plus two small ones in the converted attic, all on a small lot with a few bushes and trees. It would have blended perfectly into most of the Main Streets of America. It was in the Boston suburb of Brookline, yet only about twenty-five minutes from the centre of the city, by trolley, the usual means of transport in those days. There was a sense of openness in the neighbourhood, with a vacant lot on one side of us and another across the street, and fine big shade trees lining the sidewalks. It is built up now and to my eye seems rather congested and drab. But our house, our first home, is still there at 83 Beals Street.

It is now a public museum, part of the National Trust, and is visited by many thousands of people a year. The house has been restored with most of the original furniture, some of which Joe and I had saved through the years and some we had lent or given away, but which could be traced and collected. It is good, solid, serviceable, conservative furniture in the taste of the times, which favoured the English and Anglo-American designs of the seventeenth and eighteenth centuries, the muted colour scheme set off by reproductions of the great master-pieces I had seen and especially admired during my travels in Europe. We have done our best to put it all back together the way it was, including the beloved Ivers and Pond grand piano that was a wedding present from two of my uncles, and the set of teacups and saucers blazoned with shamrocks that Sir Thomas Lipton gave us as a souvenir of his next (as always, unsuccessful) effort to win the America's Cup.

Tastes change. Nowadays I use a lot of bright colours in our houses at Palm Beach and Hyannis Port; but at the time, the Beals Street house seemed to us just right, beautiful and comfortable, a dream realized, even if seeing it now it reminds me a little of a museum. I had no way of knowing that eventually women from all over the country, and for that matter most of the world, would be forming their opinions of my taste while looking into my parlour, dining-room and kitchen, and the second-floor bedroom that was Joe's and mine and the adjoining two bedrooms that became nursery and dormitory for our children. The centre of attention in the nursery is the small bassinet that in succession held all nine of our children.

I think our worldly ambitions as a young married couple were about the same as those of other young couples then and now. With a home of our own and furniture of our own, the next goal was to have a car of our own.

Only a few of our friends had cars, so it wasn't as if we felt deprived. Most of us took the trolley-cars or, if we were in Boston, either the trolleys or the subways.

One of the great thrills of my life was the day my husband drove home in our very own brand new, gleaming black Model T Ford. No Rolls has ever seemed so beautiful to me. Naturally Joe was proud and excited about this surprise he had brought into our lives and was eager to take me out for a drive. And so, immediately after supper, in the summer twilight, off we went heading towards a neighbourhood shopping centre called Coolidge Corner. That very afternoon I had walked there to buy a few things and on the way had noticed workmen digging a ditch preparatory to laying some water pipe. They had left two or three kerosene oil lanterns to mark the excavation. But these produced only dim light in the dusk. Joe was occupied with the challenging job of steering our new vehicle. I was so excited that it slipped my mind entirely to mention the excavation, and by the time I saw the lanterns and shouted a warning it was too late, and into the ditch we went.

There was a terrible lurch and bounce; noises of metal grinding on pavement, motor racing, rocks and dirt flying, yells from Joe and from me; total confusion. But Joe went to full throttle, gripped the steering-wheel while I gripped the side of the car with one hand and his coat-tail with the other, and with another great bounce seconds later we were up and out and upright on the other side.

Neither of us was hurt except for a few black-and-blue bruises. And our beautiful car was relatively undamaged. They made tougher springs in those days. Joe had no loss of nerve. I expect he saw I was a little pale and decided for my sake to turn around and get us back home to Beals Street.

Except that Joe and I had a house and a car a little sooner than most of our friends, and a few other blessings that came our way, there was little to set us apart from our peers. There is a time for everything. And one of the lessons of my life is that people have a better time at any interval of their lives if they stay with their friends who have similar backgrounds, interests and resources and are contemporaries in age, and thus have experiences together. I continued as president of the Ace of Clubs (as I did for many years more). Joe's time was his own, as it had been and always would be: school and college had once taken much of it, and now it was business that did so. We shared as we had before, except more so. I loved music, especially the classical composers, and since Joe had not been exposed to serious music in his earlier years, I suppose I had something to do with introducing him to this great pleasure. Yet the natural taste was there, and one of the joys of his life remained the collection of classical records we accumulated. Years later, it was primarily Joe who enabled Arturo Toscanini to leave Fascist Italy and live in the US.

He also introduced me to pleasures I might otherwise have missed. While he was at Harvard he had become a great admirer of Professor Copeland of the English Department. 'Copey', as he was known with affection by many generations of students, was famous not only for scholarship but for showmanship: his 'readings' from the classics were literary feasts in which he enabled his audiences to savour all the drama of plot and nuance of character. Joe and I were especially entranced by his readings from Dickens.

Joe loved football. He had roomed in his senior year at Harvard with Bob Fisher, the team captain and All-American, who by this time had become the Harvard coach. The combination of interest, school loyalty and his great friendship with Bob was enough, of course, to make Joe want to turn out for every Harvard game he could possibly get to and he wanted me to come with him. At Harvard Stadium on Saturday afternoons, in the middle of huge excited crowds, the pennants and pom-poms and banners and bands and noise, sharing as best I could in Joe's enthusiasm, hoping the best for the team and for our dear friend Bob, was something special and thrilling, and I had a great time.

The great new experience we shared, a most fundamental one that to some degree affected our thinking about everything else in life, was parenthood. Since most of our circle had married at more or less the same time we were having our children at about the same time. I don't recall that there was any great amount of conversation about them, or comparing of notes about bottles and safety-pins. Certainly not on my part, at least: for me, there were always a multitude of things more interesting to think about and talk about than whether one brand of talcum powder might or might not be slightly better than another for diaper rash. Yet we were all interested in each other and hence in each other's families; in fact, taking us as a group, we had some resemblance to an 'extended family'; and without boring one another with senti-mental details, we felt profound new meanings and grand new dimen-sions in our lives, and we were aware that God had given us incalculable blessings and responsibilities.

Joe, Jack, Rosemary and Kathleen were born during the years we lived at Beals Street.

They arrived in a space of less than five years, counting from Joe Jr's birth to Kathleen's. The nursery was becoming cramped and on the verge of overflowing, since I was soon pregnant again.

True, there were the two small rooms on the third floor but they were occupied by live-in help. We had started out with a maid of all work who cooked and served and cleaned and laundered and kept house, with an afternoon a week and every other Sunday off, all for $5.00 a week, the usual wage and conditions in those days. When the babies began coming we added another helper, a hospital-trained nurse-maid: as I recall she was paid $6.00 a week, the going rate. With the fifth child on the way I couldn't do with less help and probably would need more, at least for a while, and obviously I needed more space. This was equally clear to Joe. So we began looking for another house. As always, my primary concern was that it be near good schools, good transport, and a good shopping area. It also must be in a quiet, un-congested area with plenty of fresh air and play space for the children. We found what we needed in our same neighbourhood: a bigger and better house for our busier family, only about a five-minute walk from Beals Street, at 131 Naples Road. Consequently, early in 1921, Joe sold the Beals Street house and bought the one at Naples Road, where Eunice, Pat and Bobby were born.

When Patricia, our sixth, was born, Joe had to be in New York on complex and time-consuming financial operations involving Wall Street and the Hertz-Yellow Cab interests and couldn't get back home to Boston until about two weeks later. When he did, the five older ones all wanted to greet him at the station and were driven down in the limousine to wait for his train. So when he came on to the platform (he loved to tell this story) and looked around, there they were, the five of them ranging from ten to two, all hanging their heads out of the car windows and waving and yelling and laughing: 'Daddy! Daddy! Daddy! We've got another baby! We've got another baby . . .' And as the other arriving passengers saw and heard all this and saw Joe walking towards his children with his arms outstretched and a big grin on his face, their faces were a study in mixed emotions. Joe related: 'They were smiling, they were mellow, but with a touch of perplexity and maybe sympathy, as if they might be thinking to themselves, "What that fellow there certainly *doesn't* need right now is *another baby*." '

Joe always gave me a special present of some kind to celebrate the birth of each child. After our eighth, Jean, arrived he turned up at my bedside with three diamond bracelets, which he had taken on approval so I could have my choice. A girlhood friend of mine had dropped in to visit. I put all three bracelets on at once, the better to compare them – and to say the least it was a glittering sight. My friend's eyes opened wide, she seemed to have a little trouble breathing, and she turned to Joe and gasped, 'What can you possibly think of to give her next if she has the ninth baby?' Joe glared at me. 'I'll give her a black eye,' he said gruffly, and broke down with laughter.

We did have the ninth, of course, and Joe gave me something more enjoyable than a black eye. I can't remember quite what it was (a trip to Europe?) He loved giving me things and any pretext or none would do. In any case, Teddy himself has been treasure enough. He is the only son I have now, and is my joy and support and solace.

And as I think any mother who cares deeply about her children and their individual welfare and development will know – as any good father will know, too – much as I welcomed and counted on help from maids and nursemaids, I was extremely busy.

And though sometimes distracted or excited or tired – feelings familiar to parents of young, active children – I was also happy, optimistic and proud. I had made up my mind to raise my children as perfectly as possible. What greater aspiration is there for a mother than the hope of raising a great son or daughter?

8

People who have admired my children often ask me about 'early influences', with an implication that I must have found and applied some private formula to make them turn out so well. This is flattering and I do wish I could claim original discoveries in the field of child-rearing, but I must confess there would be nothing to support it. When they were old enough to understand the rules of right and wrong, to learn responsibility, and to have their interests broadened and channelled from those of babyhood to childhood and thence to youth, my methods with them did depart somewhat from the norm, but practically always in the direction of the old-fashioned rather than the newfangled. As for the earliest influences, those of birth and infancy, they could hardly have been more old-fashioned since I followed the customs of my time, which also had been those of my mother, and my forbears.

Women had their babies at home, wherever and whatever 'home' happened to be. And so did I, except for the last two. Women nursed their babies during early infancy. And so did I with most of them, though by the time the last two arrived the paediatric fashion was fast changing to bottle-feeding almost from birth. (I am amused at such reversals of scientific fashion among great and famous experts: breast-feeding is now once more highly recommended, and there is even a noticeable trend towards giving birth at home.)

When Joe Jr was born on July 28, 1915, 'home' temporarily was a cottage we had taken for the summer at Hull, a pretty town near Boston on a sandy hook of land that curves far out into Massachusetts Bay. I don't know how my husband afforded the rent and didn't ask, but I expect that he rented the house because he thought the fresh sea air would be good for me and for our firstborn. He was fully as excited and reverent about this incipient miracle as I was.

Once my obstetrician, Dr Good (whose fee for pre- and post-natal care and delivery was about $125) had confirmed pregnancy, the next important step was to engage a trained nurse for the expected time. Since babies show their individualism from the beginning by arriving on their own schedule and nobody else's, during the last week or fortnight she stayed at her own home on call around the clock, until I telephoned her that I was feeling contractions or other signs that the baby was coming, and she hurried over. From then on she lived in the house, available at any time of the day or night to care for me and for the baby, until I was up and feeling fit and the baby was making the usual healthy gains, generally a period of a few weeks. For these responsibilities she had a salary of $25 a week. Meanwhile, at the same early signs of labour, Dr Good was notified, and soon he arrived with an assistant, whose main job was to administer the anaesthetic, which was ether. (His fee was $25.) Meanwhile, too, my bed would have been moved next to the sunniest window, if this was daytime, or if at night-time to the best sources of light, because I did want Dr Good and all concerned to be able to see exactly what was happening and what they were doing. Meanwhile, the housemaid and nursemaid would be busy with all sorts of paraphernalia and supplies – fresh sheets, towels, ice-bags or anything the doctor ordered, especially pots and kettles of hot water.

The rest was up to me. I put my faith in God, accepted directions and encouragements from Dr Good and the others, and tried to sublimate my discomfort in expectation of the happiness I would have when I beheld my child.

For any normal woman in normal circumstances there is bound to be a special excitement and joy when she holds her first baby in her arms. It was so with me when the first tiny, amazing creature in swaddling clothes, Joseph Patrick Kennedy, Jr, was presented to me. But with each one it was a new thrill and joy, and I have cherished all of them equally.

It may seem unusual, but I did not want my husband on hand for the birth of the babies

I knew he worked hard for us, went on working hard even when he wasn't feeling well or sometimes when he was in severe pain. Yet there was nothing that he could do to help me in bearing a child, just as there was nothing I could do directly in helping him bear the burdens of business. None the less, indirectly I could help. If he weren't required to be away on business, I told him to go away, to take a vacation and get some rest. He was all the happier and exultant and loving and joyful when he came home to me and our new baby.

This was another aspect of the 'synergistic' quality of our marriage. We were individuals with highly responsible roles in a partnership that yielded rewards which we shared.

I remember once, for instance, when he was in California and telephoned me within a matter of minutes after I arrived home from a car accident that had put a good-sized gash in my forehead. I was feeling shaky: in fact when the call came I was lying on my bed pulling myself together. But I spoke naturally, gave him news of the children and told him what a fine day it was: a perfect day for golf. Then I went to the hospital and had my forehead stitched.

Characteristically, the family chauffeur whom Joe counted on to take care of us decided that news of the accident and my injury would be on the radio and Joe would quickly learn of it. He felt it was his duty to telephone Joe first. When he got the call, Joe called in a state of great anxiety. I then had to convince him it was just a minor accident. No one was hurt seriously, including me. He was not to worry.

Thus, nothing was gained from his knowing about my accident and something was lost: time and energy that both of us – he out there, I back East – could have put to good use and really couldn't spare, because both of us were very busy.

Joe was delighted and enchanted with his children from the time each child was born. He spent as much time as he could with them. Yet those times soon became scattered and unpredictable. Early in 1917 – with only Joe Jr born and Jack still on the way – he turned Columbia Trust over to his father to run and became assistant general manager of Bethlehem Steel's huge Fore River shipyard at Quincy, Mass. With America's entry into World War I, he was under such pressures that, except for Sundays, he came home just long enough to sleep. The shipyard broke all production records. And Joe developed an ulcer.

It was during those times that he became acquainted with Franklin D. Roosevelt, who was then Assistant Secretary of the Navy.

After the war, Joe went into the brokerage business, and later into the private banking business, which enabled him to spend much more time at home. But, as always with Joe, one idea easily sparked another; he was quick to see opportunities and to seize them before others did. Before long he was in all sorts of enterprises that kept him busy, travelling more and more. For instance, he formed a syndicate to buy control of a chain of New England movie theatres. This led him into movie distribution as well as exhibition, and thence into movie production, which in turn led to studio ownership and operation. This required a lot of time in New York, at that time the financial centre of the movie industry, and in Hollywood, the production centre. He worked away from home for days, weeks or even months at a time. He telephoned me nearly every day; and each Sunday at noon he called and spoke with the children. I had them all lined up and waiting, in the order of their ages, so that even the smallest could hear his voice. To them he never seemed far away. His influence was felt in our house even when he was away. When he was home he was deeply involved with our children. Yet for quite a few years I was responsible for most of the child-rearing.

Eunice and I were talking recently, trying to come to a definition of the roles Joe and I had in their lives. She states things clearly and directly, a quality I admire, and she puts it this way. 'You were in charge of us and raised and trained us while we were children. And then, when we began turning into young people, Dad took charge the rest of the way.' I think perhaps this was so.

'As the twig is bent, so the tree inclines' – an elementary home truth that apparently psychologists of most schools now accept. I now realize that I had a considerable part in forming the characters of our children. Naturally, I had very good material to work with. Yet I knew what I wanted from them. I didn't always succeed in all my aims, but it was never from lack of effort. I looked on child-rearing not only as a work of love and duty but as a profession that was fully as interesting and challenging as any honourable profession in the world and one that demanded the best that I could bring to it.

I was more fortunate than most women in having the domestic help and money that I required. On the other hand, with nine young children the needs were extraordinary and demanded not only personal effort but a lot of planning, organizing and supervising. I learned to become an executive.

I did little diaper-changing, but I had to be sure there were plenty of good-quality diapers on hand, and that they were changed as needed and properly washed and stowed for use. One of my continuing memories is of two decades of rows of diapers hanging up to dry on the backyard clothes lines. In the winter they often froze stiff and then had to be thawed and further dried before being put away. I learned that the best method was to put them on the steam radiators – and I remember all those radiators sizzling away, draped in white.

There was also the daily supply of bottles and nipples to be cleaned and sterilized. I didn't do much of it myself, but I had to be sure it was done properly, and on a schedule that wouldn't interfere with another vital schedule. If the nursemaid were in the kitchen boiling bottles and nipples and preparing formula and puréeing vegetables (there were no canned baby foods then) when the cook needed the stove and some of the same utensils to prepare supper, there could be a kitchen crisis, sharp words and bruised feelings and, from a management point of view, a precipitous drop in morale and efficiency.

In passing, I would like to pay tribute to whoever invented zippers.

In my antediluvian times all we had were snap-fasteners, hooks-and-eyes and buttons. Primarily buttons, buttons, and more buttons. In warm weather with light clothing the button problem was only moderate. But in winter, whenever the young children were outside they were dressed in long leggings, and I can't begin to calculate the hours the help and I spent buttoning and unbuttoning them. Also, no matter how strong the thread or how well sewn, it was forever pulling loose or wearing thin or breaking. With daily inspection and some luck we spotted loose buttons while they were still dangling. With less luck they were lost and had to be replaced from the button box, with its collection of spares of miscellaneous sizes and colours, from which I could usually find something to fit if not quite match.

I liked sewing, so this was a job I often did myself. There was a little room on the second floor at Beals Street that I fixed up as a combination sewing-room and office: a desk on one side for correspondence and record-keeping, my sewing gear on another side. I spent many hours there seaming, sewing, mending and darning. In those days children wore long stockings; in winter they often managed to wear holes in them, particularly in the knees, which were always tearing.

Having deplored old-fashioned inconveniences, I want to praise an old-fashioned convenience, the front porch. Nearly all houses had a front porch in those days: it was almost as much taken for granted in home architecture as walls and windows. In my experienced opinion the front porch is one of the greatest arrangements ever imagined for the benefit of mother and child.

Young children need fresh air, exercise and activities that stimulate their interest, some of which I could supply by taking them for a daily walk. Most mornings, while the domestic chores were getting under way, I would put the current toddler in a kiddycar and, with one or two older ones on either side, set off to the shopping centre. I didn't buy much – perhaps a box of talcum powder, or some other household item that needed replenishing – but it was an interesting adventure for the children and good for me. Sometimes we went into the Five-and-Ten, and that was especially exciting for them. Almost always, on the way home, we stopped in at our parish church. Part of the reason was that I wanted them to understand from an early age that church isn't just something for Sundays and special times on the calendar but should be part of daily life.

So the walks were fine and full of fun but they weren't enough, and the front porch thus became a blessing. With a folding gate to block the entrance, the children could play there in fresh air and in full safety and, moreover, with the full panorama of neighbourhood life to entertain them. Cars passing by: people walking along (many of them acquaintances who waved); the letter-carrier, the milkman with his wire basket loaded full as he came to our house and empty as he left; the policeman passing by on his patrol; the grocery-boy, tradesmen, visitors and friends of all degrees and kinds – everybody with a smile and cheerful greeting for the children.

Imagine Naples Road, with its big front porch, in 1925. Joe Jr and Jack by then were nine and a half and soon to be eight and playing (in their buttoned leggings) someplace in our yard or nearby where I tried to keep track of them while keeping an eye on activities on the front porch. There, probably – or perhaps outside with the boys – would be Rosemary, by then about six-and-a-half; and Kathleen at the age of five, and Eunice at three and a half, and in the baby carriage would be three- or four-months-old Bobby.

With that many children – the seven of them counting Joe Jr and Jack, who would be in and out – we discovered it was a good idea to divide the porch into sections with folding gates: two, three or four of them as the situation at the time indicated. That way they could be with each other and entertain one another for hours at a time with a minimal risk that they would push one another down or stick one another with something sharp or perhaps pile heavy objects inside or on top of the baby carriage.

What a blessing is the old-fashioned front porch! Not only for mothers and children but for all humankind, since it is also lovely for chatting with neighbours and to sit on in the summertime. In my travels I have been pleased to see that they still exist, but almost always on older houses, very rarely on the modern ones. What's the matter with our architects? They talk about 'functionalism' but they ignore a most functional part of a house. I hope, one day, it will be rehabilitated.

With all our children and all the statistics that needed to be remembered each week, month, year and for years ahead, I found my head beginning to spin. One day, therefore, while passing a stationery store in our shopping area, I stopped in and bought a supply of file cards and index tabs and set to work cataloguing names, dates and events in a systematic way. I continued to do this for many years.

As each new baby came along, he or she was indexed and the card contained all the primary vital statistics such as date and place of birth, church of Baptism, names of godparents and any other pertinent data. In due course I added the date and place of Confirmation and First Communion. Meanwhile there were entire cards on anything of importance concerning health and physical welfare. The child was weighed each Saturday night and if there was loss of weight two weeks in a row I took measures: perhaps a richer diet and less exercise until the scale went up. Vaccinations, Schick tests and results, eye examinations, dental examinations. Everything went on to the cards, including dates and notations of childhood diseases and after-effects, the names of the doctors in case of relapse or complications or the need of more information later on. Thus, I maintained a healthy summary on small cards, literally at the reach of a fingertip.

When Joe became Ambassador to the Court of St James's and we all went over there the English press treated my card file as a phenomenon of the magnitude of Henry Ford's assembly line. My dutifully kept box of file cards thus became a symbol of 'American efficiency'. Actually, it had just been a matter of 'Kennedy desperation'.

But I must say that it is really impossible to know what it meant to me and to Joe, when I wrote those brief notations. I think any mother will understand what I mean.

Each card evokes a biography.

Joe Jr was a healthy infant and child, big and strong for his age, and there are few notations about him in the early years.

Jack was a healthy infant too, but then, as noted on his card: 'Has had whooping cough, measles – chicken pox,' childhood diseases that were expectable in those days but that of course caused worries about him.

Then: 'Had scarlet fever – February 20 – 1920.' It was a terrible time for us. Rosemary was only a few days old; and with that very contagious disease in that small house on Beals Street there were fears that Joe Jr would get it, and that the new baby might also and so might I. And yet there was no place in Brookline where Jack could be taken – the hospital wouldn't admit patients with contagious diseases – and our family wasn't eligible for use of the Boston hospitals because we didn't live in the city. Finally, through my father's influence, Jack was admitted to the Boston City Hospital, which had a special ward and facilities for these diseases. By the time he got there Jack was a very, very sick little boy. Joe was in church praying for him, and in his prayers he promised that if Jack were spared, he would give half of all his money to charity. When Jack did recover, Joe fulfilled his pledge by giving a cheque to the St Appollonia Guild, which had a programme of taking needy children to dentists and doctors for good care but lacked money for a bus for the purpose. Joe's contribution was, I expect, just about the right amount. His cheque was for $3,700 – which was exactly half his 'fortune' at that time.

9

'To exist is the fleet joy of becoming,
to be a channel for life as it flashes by
in its gaiety and courage,
cool water glittering in the sunlight –
in a world of . . . anxiety . . .'

Markings – DAG HAMMARSKJÖLD

File cards show the milestones in the lives of our children when they were young; but, of course, life isn't a matter of milestones but of moments. They tick away like the heartbeat of time itself, and as we begin to think of the last tick-tock we can look back and count the years and remember that it was so-and-so year when such-and-such happened, but how do we cherish the moments, minutes, hours that hold 'the fleet joy of becoming'? A child's smile, or tears, a first tooth, a funny little expression or remark, a good or naughty deed as he discovers the world for himself and grows into it in his own ways, developing his own personality. Impressions, feelings, sights and sounds and smells – of a snowfall or a sea breeze – bits of life soon gone and, unfortunately, relegated to the recesses of one's memory as life goes on happening. Becoming.

I take some comfort in some lines Jackie brought to my attention by the writer-director Garson Kanin:

'The past, recalled, is a flowing cornucopia . . . We do not remember chronologically, but in disordered flashes. We are not, after all, programmed memory machines. People are less efficient and less orderly – but consider the compensations: freedom to associate; to roam and rummage in the attic of our yesterdays; to let one thing lead to another.'

Our home at Hyannis Port is a big, old-fashioned rambling house with a big rambling attic that has served us well for four decades as storage space for the memorabilia that became too bulky to keep around the house, but too precious to give away or throw out. I'm sure all families know the problem.

My daughter Patricia said recently: 'That's a memory of mine, and of all of us, growing up, that Mother was in the attic, putting things away. And now that we're grown up she's *still* up there, taking things out.'

True, it is time for the collection to be dismantled and the parts sent to the places they best belong: to family members and friends, to Jack's Presidential archives, and to the files I have been building to help me with these memoirs.

For example, I found that I kept a diary during 1923.

I had started diaries before, during childhood and girlhood, but they have not survived. Obviously, I was just as bad as my own children have been in beginning diaries with good intentions that soon, after a few beautiful entries, begin to trail off into white space. My nephew Joey Gargan, who spent many summers with us, recalls: 'One of my memories of Aunt Rose is her saying we ought to keep diaries, because they would be so interesting for us later. But we didn't quite get around to it. And now, all these years later, of course I'm sorry. I wish we had taken her advice.' I wish that I had taken my own advice; for the fact is that I did not keep a full diary until the time of Joe's Ambassadorship.

Yet let us now be thankful for small blessings, among them the 1923 diary. I must have begun it in the spirit of a New Year's Resolution since it starts on January 1 and continues in almost unbroken sequence all the way through January 21, with the entry: 'Stormy day. Could not go to church. Children in all day.' Thereafter, the entries tend to become fugitive, with sturdy intervals lasting until into December. Thus it does cover most of a typical year in Brookline.

My diary summons all sorts of memories. Disordered memories. Bits of time I remember.

January 1, 1923: Came up to Poland Springs December 27 with Joe Jr and Jack and Mary Moore. Eddie and Joe Sr came later. Two horribly snowy days and boys had to stay in the house. Very gay crowd. College boys and girls. Went to Mass . . . then coasted at Auburn on Sunday. Stormy on Monday. Joe Sr and Eddie went home in afternoon . . .

In those times 'winter sports' as we know them now – the ski-lifts and long manicured ski trails, the artificial snow, the sheltered hot-water pools, the chalets, hotels, motels: the whole huge business didn't exist. But there was Poland Springs, a well-known spa that stayed open in the winter. We had been going there for some years, beginning about 1916, and enjoyed ourselves thoroughly. Sleighs met us at the railroad station and we were bundled into racoon coats, with blankets over our legs, and taken to the hotel with bells jingling and steel runners crunching in the snow. We revelled in the adventures of skiing the gentle slopes and coasting on the snow and skating on the ice rink. Our skates had to be screwed on to the soles of our shoes with a key and secured with leather straps bound around our shoes and ankles, an irksome job that gave uncertain results. The skates were likely to come loose and fall off, and we were likely to trip on the straps and slip and slide and fall down. But that is how Joe Jr, Jack and some other children learned to skate – the numb fingers, lost skate keys, bumps, and fun.

The Mary Moore and Eddie mentioned in this first diary entry were Mr and Mrs Edward Moore.

Eddie Moore was a devoted friend to my father and had worked for him as secretary and confidential assistant during the years of the Mayoralty. He knew our family well. When my father left office he joined Joe in the same role but, in a sense, even more so. For, as I have said, Joe had a rugged individualist's need for privacy; there were very few men he liked, trusted and could relax with entirely. Among these Eddie Moore became his closest friend, someone he trusted implicitly in every way and in all circumstances. His wife, Mary, became an equally great friend, confidante and unfailing support to me.

They were older than Joe and I and we felt the full affection and confidence and unquestioning mutual acceptance that might be felt for a beloved aunt and uncle.

They had no children; so they turned to ours, in love and duty, bringing their parental emotions to them, and rejoicing with us in every childhood triumph and sharing in every sorrow. The children adored them. When our ninth child, and fourth son, was born, we named him Edward Moore Kennedy.

January 2: Joe Jr and I went home on afternoon train leaving Jack and Mary, as I think Jack needs a few days longer. Train 1/2 hour late. Jack said he had to put his hand over Mrs Moore's mouth last night, because she was humming (she really was snoring).

January 5: Ace of Clubs dance – wore blue and silver Hickson dress.

I was still president of the Ace of Clubs, as I continued to be until we moved away from Boston, so I was still responsible for the general arrangements including those for our annual gala ball. That accounts for the first part of the notation. As for the second, the 'Hickson dress', that really was quite special.

I'd been brought up to dress well. My mother had a fine sense of style: nothing frilly or fancy, always an emphasis on quality and cut and fit and simple, classic lines, little or no ornamentation, everything just right to set off her special beauty. My father had the same sense of what was right. My friend Mary O'Connell Ryan remembers, somehow, a special prudence of mine about hats:

'Rose liked millinery. And she would take a hat home – whatever she would buy – and she would study it and think about it some more; and then, if she decided she didn't like it, as happened fairly often, she would take it back and exchange it. She was always a careful shopper. And always cautious, never extravagant about money.'

I had been buying most of my clothes off-the-rack in Boston and Brookline shops and having them fitted. Others I made myself or had run up by local seamstresses working with patterns and my own ideas. But never had I splurged on the total luxury of *couture*: a dress made by a famous designer – as Hickson was – one of its kind, fabric chosen with only me in mind, design inspired by his artist's vision of what I should look like. It was wildly expensive: something like $200, as I remember. But also it was a fiery success, much complimented at the Ace of Clubs ball and much admired by Joe. And I liked it so well I kept it for years and had my photograph taken in it. That, of course, was before colour photography so the blue and silver can't be seen; but I hope you can see even in black-and-white that it was a beautiful dress.

Joe always wanted me to dress well. It pleased him, in fact it delighted him, to have me turn up in something quite special, even though it might be quite expensive. I submitted happily to his whim.

January 10: Children's nursemaid came back tonight. Rose home from school on account of grippe epidemic, though she is feeling okay.

Rose here is Rosemary, our third child and first daughter, who by this time was about four and a half; the school mentioned is, of course, a kindergarten.

She was born a retarded child. No one knows why – there are only hypotheses. Eunice, though several years younger, even in childhood was particularly good and attentive and helpful with her, encouraging her to do her best; and later on, because of this loving and unremitting interest in her older sister, she became a lay expert in the field of mental retardation and is director of the foundation[1] our family has created to study the root causes of this misfortune that afflicts so many children – so many more, we now realize, than anyone knew in the dark era when retardation was considered somehow a disgrace to a family. Eunice says: 'Probably it happened – we think – because the doctor was delayed someplace and was late getting to the delivery; and the nurse, not

[1] The Joseph P. Kennedy Jr Foundation

knowing what to do, didn't let the baby arrive; and that went on for nearly two hours. But we're not sure, nobody knows.'

She was a pretty baby girl, and it was only slowly, as she grew to be a toddler and beyond, that I began to realize she might be handicapped. The signs were hard to accept. I saw that she did not learn as quickly as the others; yet, of course, children are different, and not all in the same family are equally endowed. I saw that her physical coordination was poor. She had trouble steering her sled. When learning to write she did it backwards, right to left. Yet these also might be things that time and training would correct. I worried about her, puzzled over her and finally in mounting dismay took her for examination by neurologists: one the chairman of the department at Harvard, the other a scholar-priest in Washington. They told me she had a low IQ. When I asked, 'What can I do to help her?' there didn't seem to be a satisfactory answer.

January 11: Eunice went back to Saranac . . .

This was not my daughter Eunice but my younger sister, for whom she was named. She had fallen ill with tuberculosis, and Saranac was a leading centre for treatment.

January 13: Went to Harvard–Princeton hockey game, then to Brunswick with Mary and Joe O'Connell. Big gay crowd there.

Joe O'Connell was one of my Joe's oldest, closest friends . . . God-father to our firstborn, Joe Jr . . . Brother of Mary O'Connell (Ryan) who was one of my own closest friends, and who has been quoted here in earlier pages . . . the two of them respectively nephew and niece of Cardinal O'Connell, who had married Joe and me in his private chapel, with his niece Mary as his hostess afterwards, pouring coffee for us at His Eminence's residence. Quite a complicated relationship, to be sure. But we always had a fine, happy time with Joe O'Connell. And we did this time, too.

January 16: Joe Sr left on 5 o'clock for Palm Beach with Eddie Moore and a couple of other friends who joined them in New York.

This was synergism in action. He wanted to get down to Florida with three reliable pals to make a golf foursome, and he needed the rest and sunshine and could arrange his business affairs to be away at that time. I couldn't be away, for obvious reasons – children with bad colds and worse, at the worst time of the year for more colds and complications – so I sent him off with loving blessings. Partly, of course, or shall I say largely, because it was already well understood between us that soon I would have a trip of my own, accompanied by someone I wanted as a companion, to some place I wanted to see. And that, of course, is exactly what happened, with his loving blessings to me.

The trouble with a bad cold is that it isn't serious. Although one may feel at death's door one can't get much sympathy from others, especially half a century after the fact. Obviously, in 1923 our family was prone to this plague – and a common cold in a large family is very common.

February 14: Eunice walking alone and talking a lot. Best little talker of all. Also tries to take a bow and say, 'Little Partner dance with me,' etc . . .

She was only one and a half then, but I think these jottings foretold something about the girl she became. Wonderfully well coordinated and with quick reflexes, one of the best athletes in our active family. A 'talker' with a special way of expressing herself in a pithy and witty manner that made her one of the livelier participants in our family conversations. But she was also a good listener, and marvellously generous in her interest in others, especially her brothers and sisters, but including waifs, strays, and anybody who needed her. And so through vigour, candour, wit and comprehending sympathy she endeared herself to all of us. A special girl, no one like her.

What could be more interesting for a woman than to watch one's very own child grow and develop, or more rewarding than to guide the child, with understanding, imagination, patience, perseverance, to bring out the best that Nature has given? As I found out from raising our nine, all of whom have shared some qualities and traits yet also have been so different from one another, each child is a continual surprise. Each baby is truly 'born to be different'. None should be compared with another, for each has God-given potentialities which depend for full realization on influences in his or her environment. In the early years, this depends primarily on the mother. I mean the guidance, the imagination and the 'emotional climate' a mother can provide.

February 20: Kathleen cut her cake . . . (And a notation two days later) Kathleen goes out now in her little sleigh.

She was three years old, a beautiful and enchanting child, finely made and with the soft Irish colouring. Everyone made much of her, as we did, obviously, but I don't think we could have spoiled her if we had tried. Her disposition was sunny, bright, gay and full of fun, and with a special sweetness, and a wisdom that seemed to be born in her.

February 23: Joe Jr went inside altar rail today at early Mass at St Aidan's to practise being altar boy, but has not been one yet. Has Cassock all ready.

He was seven and a half, a very young age to be an altar boy. But he was responsive and responsible, energetic and full of initiative. A manly, straightforward, visibly intelligent little boy, quick to smile and laugh and yet with a certain forcefulness of character that marked him as a natural leader. That was a quality we all recognized in him early. Kathleen once wrote that 'somehow we all looked up to Joe and everything he did.' And my father, his Grandpa Fitzgerald said, 'No sweeter personality ever lived . . . He loved life. He liked to meet people. His sincerity was apparent when he shook your hand.'
Yet he also got into his share of mischief.

February 25: Joe Jr and Jack have a new song about the Bed Bugs and the Cooties. Also a club where they initiate new members by sticking pins into them.
I believe this needs no comment from me.

February 28: Their Aunt Agnes sent boys alligators from South. They named them after their best friends Jerry and Charlie. Charlie has a dog whose name is Brandy, because his father is a bootlegger.

March 30: Jack did not care much about wishing for happy death, but thought he would like to wish for two dogs.
Joe Jr went to Stations of the Cross all dirty.

April 1: Easter. All went to Winthrop, except Jack who had little cold. Eddie and Mary Moore over to dinner. Went to concert at night. Very cold day. Rose stuck her tongue out at Winthrop.

Winthrop is a town near Boston where the elder Kennedys lived. Patrick J. was sixty-five by then and in semi-retirement: still a political power but in the role of elder statesman. He took great pride and satisfaction in Joe's accomplishments, of course, and for his own part Joe was a very affectionate and dutiful son. So, in the months of good weather, we often used to pack the children in the car and drive up to spend Sunday with them. Alternating, more or less, with Sunday visits to my parents. There were large families on both sides so usually, besides ourselves and our brood, there would be assorted relatives around – from great-aunts and uncles to infant cousins – and the scene was warm, congenial and sentimental.

Our Growing Family

Rosemary, Jack,
Joe Jr and me in 1919

Our 1927 Christmas
card

Bobby, Jack, Eunice,
Jean, Pat, Kathleen,
Joe Jr and Rosemary
on the beach at Hyannis
with our dog Buddy

Ambassador Kennedy

6 *Above* Justice Reed swore Joe in as Ambassador to the Court of St James's, as President Roosevelt witnessed the occasion

Below Kathleen, Bobby, Ted, Pat and Jean are with me as we depart for England

7 *Above* The coronation of Pope Pius XII. Kathleen, Pat, Bobby, Jack, Teddy, Eunice, Jean and Rosemary are with Joe and me

Below With King George VI and Queen Elizabeth

8 At the Embassy, 1939

April 3: Jack said, 'Gee, *you're* a great mother to go away and leave your children all alone.'

He was then nearly six. As I have indicated, he was a rather frail little boy. Not small for his age but with a tendency to be thin, so I was perpetually concerned that he got enough of the right things to eat. At family meals, if there happened to be an extra portion of food, or perhaps some rich gravy left in the bottom of the pan, I would usually tell the cook to give it to Jack because he needed it. He had a rather narrow face and his ears stuck out a little bit and his hair wouldn't stay put, and all that added, I suppose, to an elfin quality in his appearance. But he was a very active, very lively elf, full of energy when he wasn't ill, and full of charm and imagination. And surprises – for he thought his own thoughts, did things his own way, and somehow just didn't fit any pattern. Now and then, fairly often in fact, that distressed me, since I thought I knew what was best. But at the same time that I was taken aback, I was enchanted and amused. He was a funny little boy, and he said things in such an original, vivid way that I felt they were worth recording, as these diary entries show.

As for the one just noted above, it was brought on by the fact that I was about to leave with my sister Agnes on a trip to the West Coast. Having an insatiable curiosity about the world, I managed, in those times and later ones, to get away every year or two to a place I hadn't seen before. In this country I hadn't been to the Far West. Joe arranged his business plans so he could be in Boston, or within easy reach, while I was away; and so, with Mary Moore always ready to lend a hand in any emergency, I could travel without undue worries about the children.

I must say that Jack's comment made me feel a little hard-hearted. And the next day, April 4, when I said goodbye to the children on the porch, I felt miserable. They looked so forlorn, and when I kissed them goodbye I had tears in my eyes. After I was down the street a way I suddenly realized there was something I had forgotten and I came back – to find them all playing quite contentedly on the porch and apparently not missing me much at all. I resumed my journey with an easy conscience.

That little scene illustrates something too about the benefits of a large family. They take care of, and are good company for, one another, and in those respects it seems to me the bigger a family is the better for everyone. That is a theme I will have reason to illustrate in a number of ways in other parts of this book.

Agnes and I were gone for about six weeks, during which I made almost daily diary notes. Reading them now I must admit there is not much in my jottings that could fascinate others.

While we were in the Los Angeles area we visited Hollywood, as most tourists did, for by that time the movies had become a national habit and Hollywood was established in the public mind as a glamorous and fabulous place. That same year, Cecil B. DeMille released *The Ten Commandments*, one of the first of the super-epics, advertised as having cost the then staggering sum of more than a million dollars and 'with a cast of thousands'. The star system was then coming into its glory too, and many a girl, I'm sure, sat in front of her mirror wondering if she might possibly resemble Mary Pickford or one of the reigning movie queens.

Besides the movies, California seems to have impressed me most for its oranges, to judge by my notes: 'Countless orange groves, with wonderful fragrance . . . Stopped at Sunkist factory . . . Pasadena – Orange Grove drive . . . mountains country and orange groves, most attractive.' But we did all the sights up and down the Coast, from Catalina to the Redwood country, with side trips to Yosemite and elsewhere.

Back in Brookline, I was met with joy and learned that there had been an epidemic of measles in the house. Joe hadn't told me because he didn't want to worry me and perhaps to cause me to cancel part of my trip. Mary Moore was there, we had a good doctor, good household help, and he managed. They all recovered without after-effects.

June 7–8, 1923: Moved to beach, cool but pleasant. Joe Jr and Jack at McElwain's with pony.

The 'beach' for us was not yet Hyannis Port – that came a few years later, and meanwhile we tried several places along the extraordinarily long, convoluted coastline of Massachusetts. For a while we were at Hull, where, as I mentioned, Joe Jr was born, and my father had bought a big and rather elegant old Victorian house where he and my mother and the younger children summered. By this time we had taken a place a few miles farther south of Boston, on the way (as it turned out for us) to Cape Cod, at Cohasset. In any case the whole Boston-Cape Cod region is fairly compact, with good roads even in those days, so we were within reasonable driving distance of both my parents' summer home and Joe's parents' farther down at the village of Sagamore. Hence there was a lot of visiting back and forth.

June 13: Down to Sagamore with Kennedys . . .

June 15: Joe up all night on business. Boys now down here for rest of the summer.

June 19: My sister Eunice going back, cannot sleep here . . .

'Going back' must have meant back to Saranac to the TB sanatorium. She had responded well enough to treatment to be released for a while, but she had relapses.

She was a beautiful young girl with very lively ways, much of the spunk and spirit and wit of my father, which made it seem all the more cruel that she should be stricken by this wasting disease.

June 21: Celebrated my birthday by trip to Cape. Men golfed at Wianno, we went to Hyannis. Joe gave me blue and gold vanity case from Cartier's.

My birthday was a month away, on July 22, but Joe had to be gone then on business so we celebrated early. Not for the first or the last time, and I expect it has happened to quite a few millions of other couples, especially in these days when so many men have to travel away from home so much.

October 26: Boys went to store and saw, 'No dogs allowed in this Restaurant', and they put in front of it 'Hot'.

October 28: Boys stole false moustaches from shop.

November 21: Boys were down cellar collecting milk bottles to sell when I found them.

December 5: Jack said, 'Daddy has a Sweet Tooth, hasn't he? I wonder which one it is?' His teacher is coming over to tell on him. He says, 'You know I am getting on all right and if you study too much, you're liable to go crazy.'

It was at about this time – with a few other episodes such as finding one of the boys, Joe Jr, I believe, on the roof of a neighbour's garage and Jack in one or another state of quixotic disgrace – that I decided to take the boys out of the local public school and enroll them in a nearby private school, Dexter, where there would be after-school supervised play. Their father and I had both gone to public school, and we appreciated the advantages of public education and believed in the ideal, facts I point out to make clear I was driven to my decision.

My 1923 diary entries end in early December, I imagine because our family was already deeply involved in preparations for Christmas, always the greatest event in our house.

We always had a Christmas tree selected with care by Joe or some of us together but as bushy and as big as our living-room would allow. That would be pretty small at Beals Street, bigger at Naples Road. But, whatever the size and place, decorating it was a family event with everyone involved, from parents and often grandparents, to toddlers. Everyone having an opinion about which ornament should hang where. There was a lot of chatter, a lot of fun.

Meanwhile someone, usually Mary or Eddie Moore, after many whisperings and long preparations, would have taken each of the children to the Five-and-Ten at Coolidge's Corner, where they would choose presents for one another and for us and others in the house. From the age of five they had an allowance, beginning as I remember at ten cents a week, an amount that was supposed to cover not only their lollipop expenses but leave something for birthday and Christmas shopping. Each had a little bank. Some of them were more frugal than others and had their reward at the Five-and-Ten when they could afford something that took their eye for someone they loved. A storybook with large colourful pictures – what could Jack like better than that? Or a bubble pipe for another one, or a little wind-up toy or, for the baby of the moment, a rattle or teething ring or set of jingle-bells. For their father perhaps a fancy pencil holder, for me perhaps a gay red and green cloth pen wiper.

Then the wrapping, getting the edges stuck down with seals full of elves and holly wreaths and smiling Santas and flying reindeer, and trying to fix ribbons and festive fancy bows, and hiding everything away in the most unlikely places because everything had to be secret until Christmas Day.

It was an excitement prolonged and heightened because we waited until after our mid-day Christmas dinner, while we still sat around the table, to open the wrappings and see what Santa had brought and what each had given to the others, each child opening his or hers in turn according to age, with exclamations of wonder and delight.

10

I have always felt that the more experiences a child has and the more things he sees and hears the more interested in life he is likely to be, and the more interesting his own life is likely to be.

On the whole I think my conviction that my children should have many 'learning experiences' and should use their minds to the fullest capacity, discovering the world for themselves through personal encounters with the world outside, worked out well and perhaps had something to do with their vivacity. But I am frank to admit that there were some miscalculations.

I remember, for instance, the time I decided it would be interesting to take the children out to pick blueberries. In those days wild blueberries grew in profusion on most parts of the Cape; and the wild blueberries have a much fuller flavour than the big plump cultivated kind. So the governess and I loaded five children in the station-wagon and set off over sandy rough roads with everyone bouncing and jouncing and laughing, until we were about ten miles into the wilds and saw a big sunny patch of bushes with ripening berries, with the Cape's multi-coloured wild flowers sprinkled among them like Impressionist dabs and accents.

Each child was given a little tin pail, the accepted receptacle for berry-picking. Soon they were all busy trying to find the bushes heaviest with berries, calling back and forth, vying to see who could cover the bottom of a pail first. They were having a marvellous and memorable time.

Suddenly Eunice came running up with a piercing shriek. A bumble-bee had stung her on the arm. We had no ointment with us to allay the pain. As the others stood around watching her they all began imagining they felt bumble-bees alighting on their arms and legs, even if it were only a mosquito.

When Eunice's suffering and their apprehensions lessened and they all went back to berry-picking, Eunice was still sniffling a little, but being brave.

Minutes later Jack ran up to me yelling and waving his arms. He had been sitting on the ground, presumably to get at the lower berries on a bush, and had sat on an ant hill. Ants were swarming all over him. We took off his clothes and shook them. The ants departed.

Then, with a small harvest and my deflated educational ideas, I re-packed our little darlings into the station-wagon and we drove off towards home, stopping on the way to buy three quarts of blueberries at a neighbourhood store.

I never mentioned picking blueberries again.

Some outings were more successful. We liked family picnics, usually at one of the excellent Cape beaches. The menu tended to become standardized. We filled a big Thermos jug with creamed chicken and bought a big container of ice-cream at a drugstore on the way, along with a package of crispy cones. We always brought lollipops. And all sorts of fresh fruit. And, as the crowning glory and favourite of all, a chocolate cake.

Jack, at age six and observant, noted his father had a 'sweet tooth', but I recall that we all did. Another extremely popular dessert was a luscious concoction called Boston Cream Pie, a light fluffy cake with custard cream in the middle and a firm, semi-hard chocolate frosting on top. These pies were easier to transport than the cakes, since they survived jostling and never ended in a chocolate mess. We always took them on our longer trips. After we moved to Bronxville and had to travel to the Cape and back, a trip that also involved a couple of large automobiles and a long train ride, a Pullman drawing-room or two and some aisle space became our temporary home-on-the-road. Rather than go to the dining-car it was much more fun for the children if we packed a picnic lunch and spread it out on fold-down tables. The climactic display, the cutting and serving of the Boston Cream Pies, always anticipated and cheered, helped make our sooty, cindery, often hot and humid trips not only endurable but also memorable. We often served this same confection at home. The children associated it with good times together, unto the next generation.

Most of the grandchildren are at Hyannis Port at least for a while each summer. They come and go, in and out of our old house, as informally and freely as their parents did. There are so many now I couldn't keep track of them if I tried. But once or twice a week I have a few over for lunch, in groups of the same age so we can discuss things suitable to their age and experiences – as I did with their parents. Naturally, as I see them sitting there in the dining-room, often in the same chairs where long ago their parents sat, I want them to get a little sense of family history, our family life – where they are, where they came from, what it was like, what good times there were. I give them the old reliable menus, the things their parents liked best. Not long ago I had a TL[1] from Jack's little boy, John Jr, who was down to the Cape with his mother and sister, Caroline. Somebody asked him if he liked coming to lunch with me and he said: 'Yeah, she has really good food! She has very good creamed chicken and Boston Cream Pie.'

Except for picnics, where informality is half the fun, our family meals were subject to definite rules of procedure. First, everybody should come to the table on time, neither sooner nor later, no nibbling and no loitering. There were practical reasons for this, one being that in a family of our size, and with increasing numbers of friends and relations and drop-ins, meals really had to be timed with some precision to avoid near-chaos, resulting in disgruntled cooks and exhausted kitchen help packing their bags and leaving us to fend for ourselves from the icebox. Second, mealtimes were the only times we had a chance to sit down together and find out what each of us had been doing. Moreover Joe and I believed strongly that time is a precious commodity. There's only so much of it, never enough to do all the things that need doing. Thus promptness was a self-evident virtue. *Res ipsa loquitur* – the thing speaks for itself.

Our reasoning was so obviously sound that it should have worked to produce the logical result: promptness from all. Alas, this did not turn out to be the case. Again, one of the interesting things about having a large family is the gradual discovery of the various responses the same influences can elicit. Most of our children were reasonably prompt. But among them Jack was generally at the bottom of the class.

We frequently went to a beach club a few miles from Hyannis Port – a station-wagonload of children, ten or a dozen counting visiting cousins and friends. The rule was to reassemble at the car at twelve forty-five so we could be home for one o'clock lunch. Jack invariably was nowhere in sight. So, in an effort to teach him a lesson, I would drive off without him. He always managed to 'hook a ride', as he said, with somebody else and would show up cheerfully at the luncheon table ten or fifteen minutes after the rest of us had sat down. By then the first course was gone and we were partly through the second. I had made it quite clear that tardiness meant starting in the middle of the meal – no asking for a first course. Just pot-luck. Jack knew better than to ask for an exception, so he frequently had a meagre lunch.

Afterwards, on the sly, he would slip into the kitchen and charm the help into filling him up. I knew what he was doing. And he knew that I

[1] TL: 'Trade Last' a term for compliment or praise

knew. But I let him get away with it, despite my theoretically inflexible rule, because he was so skinny I felt he needed the nourishment more than the discipline.

If Jack was tardy I think Bobby was prompt. Or at least the most spectacularly prompt. While each child knew what was expected of him or her, Bobby really worked at doing what he was supposed to.

Perhaps this had something to do with his position among his brothers and sisters. He was the seventh child, which is supposed to be lucky. On the other hand, by then even the most enthusiastic parents may feel less excitement about 'another baby'. We were all happy he was a boy baby, after four girls, because it was wonderful for the girls. And for us. I suppose it is every boy's dream to grow big and strong. As a boy Bobby was not big, but he was very strong. Our next child was our sweet and beautiful daughter Jean. And by the time Teddy arrived in 1932, Bobby was already more than seven years old. So there he was, with two older brothers and one very much younger one, none of whom was much use to him as boyhood pals, playmates.

I don't think I worried much about this situation, but I remember my mother did. 'He's stuck by himself in a bunch of girls,' she would say, 'he'll be a sissy.'

Manifestly just the opposite happened. He never did become tall but he became strong, muscular, fast, – a fine athlete, in fact, a rather famous varsity football player – a full back at Harvard. I think this was the result of raw will-power. He not only accepted challenges but in later years invited them, almost as if he felt it necessary to overcome obstacles. When he was grown up and in politics, reporters wrote about his toughness and said he was ruthless. I think this is mistaken. He was determined, dedicated, loving and compassionate. He was a beautiful, considerate person. He always had the capacity, and the desire, to make hard decisions. Those who loved him saw this in him, and understood. As I did, as we did.

And, as the family knows, Bobby was prompt. Sometimes even to the point of rashness.

Our daughter Pat remembers an episode soon after we moved to Bronxville, New York, into a big house there with a lot of rooms and corridors and alcoves, and still weren't quite used to where things were. That was 1929, so Bobby was not quite five years old; but he was already working hard at being dutiful. Pat says:

There was a big living-room, and that's where Bobby was when the call came for supper. We had been brought up to be prompt, *very* prompt – one had to be on time – about such things. And not just by

Mother. Dad was extremely punctual, and he said he didn't like to be kept waiting so why should he keep others waiting. He really impressed the idea on us. So Bobby was in the living-room, and between it and the dining-room there was a passageway under sort of a grand staircase and in that was a big heavy sheet of glass. I suppose it slid back into a groove in the wall, to join the rooms, but it was closed then. When the call came Bobby took off and ran right into it and smashed it. And the pieces cut his head and he fell down and there was blood all over the place, a horrendous scene. It turned out to be not nearly as serious as it looked, no effects on Bobby after he'd had some stitches taken – and none on me. I'm always still on time. I guess it's just habit.

Pat collected personal reminiscences from many people about Bobby after his assassination and made a book, *That Shining Hour* – privately printed for our family and friends – from which several excerpts are adapted here for this book. One is from James Noonan, a good friend of Bobby's at Hyannis Port for many years.

He recalled an episode that matches the one above, at least for eagerness. It was during the summer of 1948 – when Bobby was twenty-two – and Bobby stopped by one day and invited him out to crew for him in his fine sailboat, of the class known as a Wianno Senior, although knowing 'only too well my knowledge of sailing and sailboats was limited. As we cruised, he mentioned that most of his family was at the Cape and that his father had arrived the previous evening. As was the custom, when Mr Kennedy was at home [especially then!] luncheon was served at an appointed time and all members were expected to be prompt. Time slipped by quickly. Bobby realized it was later than he thought. He came-about and headed for the 'Compound'. As we approached the shore, to my complete amazement, Bobby stood up and dove into the water. He yelled back that mooring the boat was up to me. *He* was expected to be on time for lunch. In desperation I tried to hail any passing boat. Finally, a power-boat came alongside and helped me to a safe mooring. That evening I could hardly wait to tell Bobby of my ordeal. But it was obvious his moments of concern had long passed – *he* had made lunch on time. To him my story was comedy. His reaction was – 'Terrific, but we've got to do something about your sailing!'
We certainly wanted him to be prompt. But not *that* prompt.

I don't want to give an impression that our lives somehow revolved around meals and mealtimes, but the fact was these were about the only times for Joe and me to talk with them and – more important, we both felt – to encourage them to have their own ideas and learn to speak up for them. I also had a bulletin board someplace the children were sure to see it, which meant a place on their way to meals, and I would clip items from the papers and magazines and pin them up there. The girls and boys who were at the age of reading and reasoning were supposed to read or at least scan these enough to say something about the topics of the day – opinions, comments, questions, or confessions of sheer confusion or bewilderment or disbelief, at least something about current events during the mealtime conversations. Surprisingly, these were spontaneous conversations. They were fun. Yet they were certainly not meant to be pointless chatter, and I led them and popped in questions or made comments according to the flow of talk.

A few examples:

A Florida item could cue me to ask how the state got its name. What does the word mean, what language is it from? Think of Spanish names of towns there. Sarasota, Tampa – no, not Miami, that's Indian. Where else in the country are there a lot of Spanish names. Yes, California, where their cousins, the Lawford children, live. What about San Francisco? – what does that mean, who was it named after? You know about that from Church? Think of some other saints' names out there. San Diego, San Gabriel, Santa Barbara. And what about Los Angeles? Do you know how to spell it? L-o-s, meaning 'the'. And A-n-g-e-l-e-s – what do you suppose that means? And why is our part of the country called New England? Think of English names *in* New England. New Hampshire, New London, New Bedford, Acton.

And they would become very interested in this educational game. At first, some of them wouldn't know many answers. Yet they would the next time the subjects came up.

Easter is coming. Why was the priest wearing those special pink vestments last Sunday? Why do we have Lent? Does Easter come the same time every year? What's the term the Church gives to something that changes like that? It's a 'moveable feast'. How is the date calculated? It's the first Sunday after the first full moon after the vernal equinox. What does 'equinox' mean? What does 'vernal' mean? The days are getting longer now – why is that? When is the longest day of the year? The shortest? When are daylight and dark exactly even? Why is that?

Or, Thanksgiving is coming, so I would put a clipping on the bulletin board to get us going on a conversation about it. The Pilgrims lived right in our Boston – Cape Cod region, I would remind them, so we ought to be especially interested in them. What do you think they would be doing at this time of year? What would *you* be doing if you had to raise or catch all your own food? What would it be? Clams and seafood, yes, of course, those were always important, but what about birds? Why do we have turkey on Thanksgiving? And vegetables – what was the great vegetable the Pilgrims got from the Indians and that no one in England or Europe had until seeds were brought over from America? Maize. We call it corn. What did they do for meat? What wild animals do you suppose lived around here then? Which ones do you see now? And what about fruits and berries? Why are cranberries part of our Thanksgiving dinner? You've seen them growing around here. What else have you seen that the Pilgrims would be able to find? Grapes, beach plums, blueberries, blackberries. And why do you suppose we put chestnuts in the turkey dressing? Who had that idea? And how did the Pilgrims get their clothing? Don't you suppose the women and girls had to be awfully good at sewing? And, do you know that if you're really good at something you get great satisfaction from it? You have to like football to become good at it, but then, *because* you're good at it, you like it more and more. The Pilgrim women and girls learned to be so good at sewing that they took pride and pleasure in it, and they passed on their knowledge to their daughters and grand- and great-granddaughters, who did 'fancy work' sewing like that big 'sampler' we have framed on our living-room wall at Hyannis Port. So, you see, if you're good at your work it is a pleasure. Something that might at first seem very boring can turn out to be very exciting. The main difference is how you feel about it. The Pilgrims had to work terribly hard, against great obstacles, but they won out because they were dedicated to their ideals. And though they were often in danger they weren't afraid. And those are some of the reasons we honour them.

With our large family there couldn't be family conversations that would interest all the children at the same time. Or older ones would give quick answers and the younger ones would never have a chance. After all, there were seventeen years between the eldest and the youngest; which meant, for example, that by the time Teddy was six and learning to read Joe Jr was twenty-three and a Harvard graduate, and more. As the years went along we decided to have two tables and servings. The small table, for the little ones, would be in the nursery or perhaps a breakfast-room or alcove; away from the main table. I would sit with them, usually at supper. The conversation would be adjusted to fit. If for instance it was the Christmas season, we might talk about Christmas trees. Did they like them? Yes, of course, the fatter and bushier the better. What do you suppose a tree needs to grow that way? Sunlight and space and fresh air and good nourishment. Why do you suppose we have Christmas trees, and who first thought of the idea? Because they are 'evergreen', green all year around, and they remind us of Jesus and His birthday, because He never changes and is always part of our lives, every day, all year. The idea began in Germany. I would tell them a little about my Blumenthal; maybe sing a few lines from the German Christmas tree song, *O Tannenbaum*, in German and tell them what the words meant.

And I would tell them that when they saw a big Christmas tree outdoors in a public square or park or village green, all decorated with lights and ornaments for everyone who passed by to enjoy, *that* idea had begun with their grandfather Fitzgerald. He felt sorry for people who couldn't afford a Christmas tree. Perhaps they didn't have a home, or had to be away from home. So their grandpa had a big tree put up in the middle of Boston Common, a Christmas tree for everyone. And the idea spread, until thousands and thousands of cities and towns and villages all over the country have public Christmas trees every year.

Thus at 'the little table' as at 'the big table' everyone had the chance to learn and converse at their own level of understanding. Nevertheless, I had to ensure that an older or more mentally agile or more assertive child didn't monopolize a conversation or try to put down the others by interrupting the others in an intimidating way. For the silent, it could lead to shyness, diffidence, a sense of inferiority and self-doubt. The main point of our conversations was to encourage precisely the opposite qualities.

If a child is encouraged to have ideas and speak up for them, with no fear of ridicule, in an atmosphere of mutual respect for others and their ideas, not only are wits sharpened but his confidence grows. So, with practice, does a child's ability to communicate. In my Commonplace Book I have written a notation, 'The destiny of the world is shaped by those persons who get their ideas across – for better or for worse.'

Later, when I have heard them stand up and speak before large audiences – thousands of inquisitive, often sceptical people – and speak well and directly and reasonably, and perhaps have to defend their statements against vigorous challenges from an opponent, as in Jack's televised debates with Nixon in the Presidential campaign, I liked to think that those spirited discussions when they were young contributed to their effectiveness.

If children are to develop into effective people, the process has to begin when they are small. They can't suddenly as teen-agers, for instance, bloom into remarkable conversationalists or speakers or suddenly acquire the mental quickness, emotional poise and the breadth of knowledge that is needed. It doesn't happen at fourteen or fifteen or sixteen without preparation and effort that begin, at the latest, at age four, five, or six. We've heard a lot from psychologists in the past forty or fifty years about the importance of early childhood influences. In my years as a mother of young children we didn't read the books. The books hadn't been written, or at least weren't in circulation. Dr Freud was only a name to us, and as for Dr Spock I am nearly old enough to be *his* mother. Obviously I don't hold with the *tabula rasa* theory that a little child's mind is a 'blank slate' on which anything can be written. I hope I have made that unmistakably clear. But I think that helpful things can be written there, with effects that last a lifetime. This is one of the great responsibilities and joys of a mother.

It isn't easy. Mothers get tired, or feel uneven or become inundated in obligations and demands. Also, children can be uncooperative. Or worse: shirk, interrupt, show off, rebel. Break into arguments among themselves. Punch one another over the table and kick one another under the table. So it isn't now nor was it then as simple as I may have made it sound. But almost always there are ways to overcome the problems, and the results are worth the efforts.

I don't want to leave the impression that these mealtime talks were mental drill sessions, because they weren't. There was nothing cut and dried at all. It was spontaneous, natural; there would be mistakes, wild guesses; no one was graded or rated – it was a game. People told jokes, made wisecracks, hurled friendly insults, and hooted and 'hollered' at silly mistakes. They joshed and kidded and made faces and fooled around (within limits) and talked about things that popped into their minds. Things that had happened at school, news or friends, opinions, likes and dislikes, a certain amount of chatter and gossip. The stuff of life, well spiced. I enjoyed listening to them talk. I could be sharp with them, I could be quite sharp, but I could laugh with them too, and there was no lack of laughter or fun.

There was another game that I got from my father and used to spring on them to help them with their arithmetic. I still do it with my grandchildren. My father called it 'Examples' and my grandchildren have for some reason decided to call it 'Snakes'. This is the way it goes (for Example). I would say:

'Five times three, add one, divide by four, times eight, take away two, divide by three, divide by two. What's the answer?'

I had had so much training from my father in these gymnastics that I could do them as fast as I could say them. Finally, one after another, the children began writing down Examples I had given, or that they created for themselves, and bring them to me. It was good practice for them: they really learned arithmetic. So this game worked very well.

(The children don't know this – or won't until they read this page in my book – but when Teddy was just old enough to know arithmetic, I had gone through two of these Examples with him and shown him how they worked and what the answers were. The first answer was 4, and the second was 2. I would reel off the numbers to the others, and while they were still groping, Teddy could sprint up and say that's 4 or that's 2. They all thought he was amazingly smart at maths. He supplied an incentive: they wanted to catch up with the little brother. So that worked very well too.)

These multi-flavoured encounters and activities were not limited to mealtimes. They happened in much the same general way wherever we happened to be: on those train trips I mentioned, for instance, or at home during evenings in the living-room or just in the course of a drive in the countryside. On a trip, the children might form two teams and compete to see who could spot the most animals on either side of the road. (And identify them, and thus learn a little more about animals.) Or there would be guessing games and charades – we always loved those, and Jack usually was the best at them.

If we were passing through a pretty little New England town where so much American history took place, and I happened to know the historical significance of, for example, Salem (witchcraft), or Sandwich (glass), or Cape Cod (canal), I would bring that up, tell them some interesting facts, quiz them a little and try to lead them on to think about what they had just seen. I did this for many years and do it still – whenever I get the chance – with my grandchildren.

My daughter-in-law Ethel was asked about her recollections of the first time she met me, her first visit to Hyannis Port. She was Jean's room-mate at Manhattanville, a great friend, and that's how she met Bobby and started going with him. They came to Boston – they and a few other friends of theirs – and I went up from the Cape with a car and driver to collect them and their baggage.

Ethel says:

> It was a big chauffeur-driven limousine but there were a bunch of us, so the car was crowded. Very, very crowded. And it was raining. That gives the general picture: a pile of kids and luggage driving for two hours in a closed car on a rainy day. Mrs Kennedy spent practically the whole ride giving us a history lesson – and she was great. It was October 31, Hallowe'en, so there were Jack-O'-Lanterns on

people's porches and in windows, and that's what started her off. She said, 'Now why do you suppose people have Jack-O'-Lanterns, how did that custom ever begin?' That led back to All Hallows Eve and witchcraft and all that, and then to the Church and Saints' Days, and then up into American history and Pilgrims and pumpkins and super-stitions and autumn harvest and protect-the-crops and pumpkin pies and apple cider and . . . anyway, I thought she was fascinating, she knew so much, and twitted us a little if we didn't know perhaps as much as we should've, and she got us all involved and probably all of us did learn something and pretty soon the trip was over and we were at Hyannis Port.

And I remember arriving at the Cape and going to Jean's room and thinking how everything was so well thought out for the happi-ness of children and guests. There were fresh flowers. There were interesting books on the bedside table. It was all so comfortable and pleasant and beautifully done – all those niceties that can make life so pleasant. She had thought of them all. Nothing showy, just very nice.

Obviously, I didn't do too much damage to the romance because they were married (he was the first in the family to marry) while Bobby was still in law school. I had misgivings about that. But I have always been glad he married Ethel. She was a wonderful wife to him, and was and is a wonderful mother to their children. Some years after their marriage they bought a house next door to our house at Hyannis Port, and Ethel still comes there every summer and most of the children are there too for at least part of the time; which is a joy for me.

Everyone knows that reading is the most important instrument of knowledge, so naturally a parent is gratified if a child reads early and enjoys books and worries if the opposite happens. I was the most concerned that my own children learn to read well, enjoy it and have the right books. When they were pre-schoolers I read them bedtime stories. A bit later on, when they were sick and needed to stay quiet in bed but also needed some entertainment, I read to them, often hours at a time. And I was careful about the books, selecting them from the PTA, New York Women's Exchange, and library lists for their educa-tion and inspirational values – not only entertainment, but books with useful ideas and artistic design and illustrations. They were never chosen hit-or-miss.

We also always had a governess who had been a schoolteacher so we were assured she always spoke grammatically correctly to the children, was well acquainted with literature, had advice about what to read, and was aware of current events.

A good time for the children to read was after lunch. An orthopaedic doctor also told me that an after-luncheon rest period is good for growing children.

Jack and Bobby, as youngsters, were very different in their reactions to my well-laid plans. Bobby just didn't care about reading. If I gave him books he was likely to skim them and put them aside. I said, 'Well, why don't you go to the Library and pick out some books for yourself,' and with enough bamboozlement from me he would; but even then he wouldn't spend much time with them. Yet in later years he became an assiduous reader. And in the fields of law, political science, history, sociology, for example, he became almost omnivorous, simply stuffing himself with knowledge and feeding his mind on the great ideas of past and present.

He became a wonderfully well-educated man. Why? He had travelled and seen and learned things for himself, with his own eyes, in his own way, and had developed the essential intellectual curiosity; and he had fallen in love with Ethel; and he had been swept up in ideals of service and excellence that his father and I had communicated to our family; and indeed I could think of a score of possible reasons, but they add up mainly, I suppose, to the fact that he matured, 'found himself' and his own goals and from then on spent his life running hard to achieve them. And among other things that meant catching up on a lot of reading he hadn't felt like doing when he was younger.

On the other hand, Jack was a 'natural reader'. The fact that he was so often sick in bed or convalescing in the house and needed entertainment only encouraged what I think was already a strong natural bent. He gobbled books – not necessarily the ones I had so thoughtfully chosen for him from the PTA and library-approved lists. When he was little his greatest favourite was a book called *Billy Whiskers*, the fictional adventures of a billygoat, of all things. It seemed to me very, very poorly illustrated, with the pictures in brash flamboyant colours. I wouldn't have allowed it in the house except that my mother had given it to him. Jack adored it. As I recall, Billy married and he and Mrs Whiskers had twins – twin 'kids' – and the goat family had many adventures in a series of books, all of which Jack found vastly interesting and I felt were a waste of time. However, one day he came to me to ask, 'Mother, where are the Sandwich Islands?' I confessed I didn't know but said I'd find out, as I did, and then showed him in the atlas. 'Those are the Sandwich Islands but the name is changed and now we call them the Hawaiian Islands. Why are you interested – are you studying about them at school?' He said No, but Billy Whiskers had stopped at the Sandwich Islands on his way across the Pacific. So it is really difficult to predict what may awaken a child's interest and imagination in constructive ways. Billy Whiskers after all was teaching him some geography and history; and, in this case, teaching some to me, too.

Another favourite, when he was a small child, was the series of little stories about animals – fictionalized and with a continuing cast of characters with such names as Reddy Fox – mixed up in an endless series of simple, but I guess exciting, adventures. They were written by Thornton Burgess and appeared for many years in the newspapers. Jack never forgot the pleasures he had from them when he was a little boy; and many years later, when he was President, he had Mr Burgess, who by then was quite elderly, as his guest at Hyannis Port. As I recall, they had lunch together and relived some favourite episodes about Reddy Fox and other memorable characters.

As he grew older his tastes broadened and began to include a number of the books I thought he should read. He liked stories of adventure and chivalry, such as Sir Walter Scott's Waverley Novels and biographies of famous or interesting people and, in general, subjects having to do with history, so long as they had flair, action and colour. He had a strong romantic and idealistic streak. In fact he was inclined to be somewhat of a dreamer. I often had a feeling his mind was only half-occupied with the subject at hand, such as doing his arithmetic homework, or picking his clothes up off the floor, and the rest of his thoughts were far away weaving daydreams. I was deeply touched but not surprised to learn long years later (after his assassination) that he and Jackie had taken Camelot as a small, personal, private symbol of their sweet and glorious life together. I remembered him in his boyhood reading and re-reading his copy of *King Arthur and The Round Table.*

Many people have asked me about the books he read when he was a boy. With the help of various friends and family members I have been able to put together a list of most of the books for children and young people that we owned as part of our own library. I expect all the nine children read some of them, and some read most of them, but my strong guess is that Jack read almost every one of them. Here is the list, in the order in which I have written it down in my notes.

Arabian Nights
Billy Whiskers series
Kidnapped by Robert Louis Stevenson
Treasure Island by Robert Louis Stevenson
A Child's Garden of Verses by Robert Louis Stevenson

King Arthur and The Round Table by A. M. Hadfield
Lays of Ancient Rome by Thomas Babington Macaulay
Sinbad the Sailor
The Jungle Book by Rudyard Kipling
Kim by Rudyard Kipling
Bambi by Felix Saltern
Uncle Tom's Cabin by Harriet Beecher Stowe
Peter Pan by J. M. Barrie
Far Camel of Baghdad
Black Beauty by Anna Sewell
Story of A Bad Boy by Thomas B. Aldrich
Wing and Wing by James Fenimore Cooper
Biography of a Grizzly by Ernest T. Seton
At The Back of The North Wind by George MacDonald
The Pope's Mule by Alphonse Daudet
Pilgrim's Progress by John Bunyan
Wonder Tales From East and West;
   Introduction by Maud Wilder Goodwin
Young Folks' Book of American Explorers
   by Thomas Wentworth Higginson

There were others, I'm sure, and books borrowed from friends and libraries, and story and history books and others that were part of school instruction, but these are enough to give the general flavour. Some of them are still there at the Beals Street house, others are in his Presidential archives at Harvard, and others have been passed on as I'm sure a great many parents do, if the books happen to survive, to the various grandchildren. I know that Caroline and John Jr have several of Jack's favourites.

With reading aptitudes and skills and enjoyment there would come, I fondly supposed, both facility in using words properly and effectively and mastery of the essential mechanics of written expression: grammar, penmanship, spelling. After all, any good craftsman respects and relies on his tools, the farmer or fisherman or carpenter or writer, as I pointed out to them. So if they wanted to write such things as they would want to read they must master the tools.

To my distress, most of them seemed to be afflicted with deafness about the proper uses of 'who' and 'whom', 'I' and 'me', 'shall' and 'will', 'may' and 'can'. They split infinitives with abandon, and put in commas or left them out as the spirit (an evil spirit) moved them, and they ended sentences with prepositions. Eventually, with continual reminders and repeated explanations of the really very simple rules governing these matters, they did absorb proper usage, and in later years some of them went on to become extraordinarily good writers. Bobby's mature writings, for instance, were admired for their fluency, force and precision of meaning. Some of Jack's writings have been compared with Lincoln's, and there are scholars who have ranked him as one of the masters of modern prose.

His spelling, however, which had been terrible, never progressed beyond the point of being unreliable. And his handwriting, which had been a mess, never evolved into more than a semi-legible scrawl. At least there was progress. His writing requires some deciphering, so here, for convenience, is my transcription, line for line, of a letter he wrote to his father. It is undated, but I think he must have been about ten years old:

A PLEA FOR A RAISE

by Jack Kennedy
Dedicated to my father Mr J. P. Kennedy

Chapter I
My recent allowance
is 40c. This I used for areoplanes
and other playthings of childhood but now I am a scout
and I put away my childish
· things. Before I would spend
20c of my c.40 allowance
and in five minutes I
would have empty pockets
and nothing to gain and
20c to lose. When I became
a scout I have to buy
canteens, haversacks, blankets
searchliagts ponchos things
that will last for years
and I can always use it
while I cant, use a
chocolate marshmellow
sunday with vanilla ice
cream and so I put in
my plea for a raise of
thirty cents for me to buy

out things and pay my
own way more around.

Finis

John Fitzgerald Francis Kennedy

I should add a couple of notes about this letter. I don't know why he included 'Francis' in his signature. Perhaps it was to invoke the blessing and help of that gentle saint.

His father, after brief deliberation and consultation with me – since I was the one who handed out the allowance money to them once a week – granted the raise. So Jack didn't have to write a 'Chapter II'.

Clearly, we did keep a close rein on their finances. And that, too, was part of their education. We wanted them to know the value of money, the foolishness of squandering it and the painful consequences of heedless extravagance – as painful, let us say, as not knowing at age five where your next gumdrop is coming from. As I mentioned earlier, that was the age at which they began receiving weekly allowances of ten cents. Usually their first thought was of the candy store. At Hyannis Port, two short blocks from our house, there was a tiny 'variety store' with indeed a rather amazing variety of goods including a rich, colourful, tantalizing assortment of penny candies. There would be a temptation to spend the whole dime at a swoop – but that would not leave the penny or two that ought to go in the bank for Christmas shopping. Then, whatever the amount bought, came the following temptation to gobble it all up in the first few days, leaving nothing but sorrow and regrets for the rest of the week until next allowance-day.

This was fully as important for the girls, I felt, as it was for the boys; for, after all, when girls grow up and marry it is ordinarily they who actually spend most of the family income on food, clothing and other necessities. They have to know how to budget, keep track of the dollars, how not to waste. I have always felt sorry for a couple when the wife is heedless about money, piling up bills, forcing the husband into debt or to work harder and harder to provide the means. It must be very disappointing and discouraging if he finds he has to follow her around pointing out unnecessary expenses. Constant argument about money leads to all kinds of other quarrels and difficulties; and, as I have often read, this is the most common root of marital discord and thus of a great many broken marriages.

We followed the same principle in our Christmas, birthday, and other special-occasion gifts to them. When they were little they had their share of the things children like: the dolls and go-carts, the train sets and cap pistols, the Parcheesi games and wind-up cars and stuffed animal toys and the rest that most parents want to give and manage to afford. But we made it a point that these were not particularly expensive, just the normal toys, and that they came only a few at a time. None of those elaborate criss-crossing toy railway systems full of switches and semaphores that fill a big table, and no menageries of stuffed toy animals that fill a closet or a couch. Galsworthy said, 'Variety of choices leads to confusion of the mind,' which I think is likely to be true in adulthood as well as childhood. People need some simple certainties in their lives, more solutions and fewer problems.

As a general guideline in all such matters – allowances, gifts, perquisites and privileges, clothes, and in due course clubs, boats, cars, and travels and other things involving a degree of mature responsibility – we wanted the children to have whatever was needed for them to fit in normally, naturally, easily with their environment. As the environment changed, so did the needs. It is a long distance in more ways than one from Beals Street, Brookline, to Ocean Boulevard, Palm Beach.

Within the family, we just didn't talk about money. It wasn't a forbidden subject, but simply didn't meet the criterion that if you want to talk, have something interesting to others to talk about. If you need or deeply want something special, then discuss this privately with your father or me; if it's something you just happen to want, something extra and unusual, then find a way to earn the money for it yourself. We wanted them to learn the value of work, of efforts and rewards, and to respect it for its own sake – the idea of 'the dignity of work'.

Bobby had a paper route. That pleased us, of course. The 'paper boy' is practically an American symbol of boyhood spunk and ambition. Then, after a while, I found he had talked the chauffeur into driving him. There he was, riding around all over Hyannis Port – making his deliveries from a Rolls-Royce. Needless to say, I put a stop to this at once. Shortly afterwards something interfered, perhaps he came down with summer 'flu, and Bobby was out of the newspaper delivery business.

When some of the children went into politics and public life, with the implication that they had been spoiled rich brats and their father, spreading around his money and influence, more or less bought and paid for their success, I want to say this was rubbish. When the children were growing up, at the 'impressionable age', they neither had nor expected any privileges whatever. They lived at the level of their 'peer groups'. Being intelligent and observant, they realized at some point in their maturation that although we lived on a lower scale than some families we lived on a higher one than others, and they realized that was because their father was successful at his work. They knew as they grew older what this work was. They did know, for a period of years, that some of his work had something to do with the movies, because there was visible evidence.

When he came home from his trips to Hollywood he brought souvenirs or mementoes. One time, I remember, he came back with Tom Mix cowboy outfits for Joe Jr and Jack. Anyone old enough to remember Tom Mix can understand what a sensation those caused with the boys and among their friends.

Gloria Swanson was our house guest for a couple of days in Bronxville and brought along her small daughter, who was about the age of our Patricia, who was about ten. The two got along well together, and Pat took her down to show her the Bronxville public school and meet her classmates and perhaps show off a little, as she did by introducing her – 'her mother's Gloria Swanson.' Nobody believed her. They all just grinned, thinking it was a joke. After all, Gloria Swanson was, to them, practically a supernatural being, so she wouldn't be in Bronxville and wouldn't have a daughter and Pat was just doing some silly spoofing. I can't recall the exact details but I do remember how completely indignant Pat was when she and Gloria's little girl came home and told us.

We needed a convenient place to screen films, and so at Hyannis Port, in what used to be part of the basement, we installed a little theatre, which still exists much as it was. I do mean little: fixed chairs – the old-time kind with iron legs and fold-up-down wooden seats – for an audience of about two dozen, with space on the steps and sidelines for sitting or reclining by others, maximum uncomfortable capacity for a hit show on a wet night for as many as forty; or, with standees jammed in shoulder to shoulder for a super-hit, maybe even fifty. It had a little stage for the children's theatrical productions, but primarily it was a movie theatre. Because of Joe's position in the industry he was able to borrow practically any film from practically any studio, which of course was useful to him as an exhibitor and producer but which also gave us an inexhaustible supply of home entertainment. Naturally, anything shown for our young audience was recommended or checked by someone in advance as being suitable for family viewing. If there was a slip-up and the plot became lurid, the projector was switched off and they were sent out. But that seldom happened. Consequently,

our summers at Hyannis Port took on something of the character
of a modern movie festival, with a different film shown three or
four evenings a week. Everyone in the house, including the staff,
was invited, and almost always the children would have some of
their friends over too, so there was always a large, appreciative
audience.

Well now, obviously not everybody in the world has two very nice
houses, a couple of boats, a tennis court, a swimming pool, and a
Rolls-Royce or two in the family. The children realized their father
made a lot of money for us to afford all this, and it was a clear presump-
tion – from the way we encouraged them to save – that he must have
quite a lot in the bank besides. But they had no real idea that their
father was 'a rich man' and that we were 'a rich family' until Joe
entered politics and public life.

That began in 1932, when he became one of Franklin D. Roosevelt's
strongest supporters and chief advisers in the campaign for the Democratic nomination and the Presidency. Thus he was suddenly in the
national limelight and the press took an interest in him.

He was already something of a celebrity within the movie industry
and in the stock market, but the stories about him usually appeared in
trade journals or on the financial pages and dealt with specific deals or
operations in which he happened to be involved. Now the political
reporters got to work on him and raked up all sorts of information
from all quarters and put it into news and feature stories – especially, of
course, in the Boston papers. Usually there was mention of his wealth:
he was 'multi-millionaire movie mogul and stock market operator
Joseph P. Kennedy'.

Thus the time came when we felt we had to tell the children. Their
father had made millions. He was an extremely rich man. And because
of this, eventually each of them was likely to come into a lot of money.

With this information, however, came large continuing doses of
cautionary advice and moral principle. With money, we emphasized,
there comes responsibility. Money isn't for spending but for using – for
necessities and, up to a point, for comforts and pleasures, but beyond
that point only for things that are truly important and worthwhile. A
worthy goal in life for yourselves; a worthy cause; a worthy enterprise
for the benefit of others, such as public service, schools, libraries,
hospitals, civic and recreational facilities and, of course, the many
needs and good deeds of the Church. Money doesn't make this family –
doesn't make you – the least bit better than anybody else, just luckier.
Remember it wasn't you who earned it. Your father did that. And when
some of it comes to you, remember it comes with his hope and faith,

his expectations and confidence, that you will use it wisely. Money is never to be flaunted. There is nothing more vulgar than a display of wealth. Some of the greatest people in history have lived lives of the greatest simplicity. Remember it isn't the clothes you wear, the car you drive, or the diamond rings or stickpins – it's the you, the you inside, that counts. Money doesn't give you any licence to relax. It gives you an opportunity to use all your abilities free from financial worries, to go forward, and to use your superior advantages and talents to help others – at school, in the neighbourhood, and later in working for social gains in the community and in government. I'm glad to say that my grandchildren have inherited this sense of responsibility.

As I think anyone would say who knew the children then or in later years, or even knew anything much about them at second- or third-hand, the message soaked in. They have had a decent respect for money and what it can do, for themselves and others, and at the same time a dislike of waste and contempt for ostentation, and an almost aggressive disdain for 'appearances'. Sometimes I have thought they might even be overdoing it a bit, as when I have seen them – girls as well as boys – habitually running around our house and environs in old, half-wrecked blue jeans, soiled tennis shoes or sneakers, and with shirt-tails out under ravelled sweaters, and sometimes no shoes.

Once again, in that spectrum of attitudes, undoubtedly Jack held the championship. The others offered challenges, but he was beyond reach. For example, once Jack was travelling around someplace and had no money with him. He had simply forgotten to bring any. It hadn't occurred to him. Several of his old friends – friends during his grown-up years – have remarked about this. They would be having lunch together, let's say, and when the time came to pay the check, Jack would fumble around and then say with an apologetic smile that he hadn't any money along to pay his share, so would the other person take care of it and he'd square accounts later.

His attitudes about dress and appearance were apt to be equally off-hand. We have a snapshot of him at the time he graduated from Harvard, with a suitably serious expression in his black academic gown but with his feet in a pair of worn brown-and-white saddle shoes.

Yet I think that his disregard for money, appearances and posses-sions was not simply a strong reaction, or over-reaction, to the parental advice and teachings I have described but was part of his natural character, and reflected an engaging absent-mindedness.

For example, while I didn't mind him and the others dressing like roughnecks for play I did want them all to look brushed and neat at school, church and in public. I bought them good clothes, and very often dressed them alike: there would be identical sailor suits, say, for Joe Jr and Jack, and identical middie blouses and skirts for Rosemary, Kathleen, Eunice and Patricia, in descending sizes. On school days I was always with them at breakfast, partly to be sure they were properly groomed and dressed. On Sundays before Church I would be at the foot of the stairs to inspect them as they came down, making sure they had their prayer books and rosaries and handing each of the girls a fresh pair of white gloves.

Joe Jr and Jack usually had similar outfits. It would happen from time to time that Jack would absent-mindedly help himself to Joe Jr's clothes, even though they were too big for him.

Joe Jr's temperament was different from Jack's in a great many ways, one of which was a better defined sense of neatness and order. Another was a strong sense of ownership and of responsibility for the appearance of his personal possessions. A third was that Joe Jr had a quick temper. The consequences were predictable. There were times when I had to pry them apart.

Being boys and brothers and less than two years apart in age had its advantages and its disadvantages. Generally, they were good pals and playmates and shared all sorts of experiences and adventures, including getting into mischief together. But I suppose it was inevitable that they were also rivals. With their different temperaments, this brought flare-ups, including personal combat.

I remember, for instance, one time when they were very young and sitting across from each other at their little table in the dining-room at Beals Street, with Joe and me at the big table, and suddenly there was an awful outcry which brought us to our feet. Once we sorted things out we discovered that what had happened was this: it was dessert time, we had one of those favourite cakes with the rich gooey chocolate icing, and Joe Jr had taken off the top icing of his piece and put it aside to save for last. When Joe Jr wasn't looking, Jack reached over and took it and gobbled it down. Joe Jr gave him a whack, and Jack let out a big yell, and hit back. I don't recall exactly what Joe and I did, probably spoke sternly to both and sent them off to bed.

Did Justice triumph? The punishment is supposed to fit the crime. Was it worse for Jack to have stolen his brother's chocolate icing or for Joe Jr to have given his brother an angry punch? And if assault and battery are more serious than petty theft, should Joe Jr actually have been punished more severely than Jack, even though Jack had provoked him? I'm sure that throughout history mothers have faced similar conundrums and have agonized over the right answer.

In any event, during the earlier years of their boyhood there were fights, few of which I saw but some of which I have been told were real battles. Joe Jr was older, bigger, stronger and better coordinated – but Jack, frail though he was, could fight like fury when he had to. Thankfully, they probably fought no more than other brothers so close in age do, and in fact possibly less.

I once bought them a pair of identical bathing suits, black with white stripes. Joe Jr's was of course quite a lot larger than Jack's. They were about eight and six years old and Joe Jr was a good four inches taller as well as broader and heftier. We wanted a snapshot of them in these stylish outfits and in the commotion of getting their regular clothes off and into the suits there was a mix-up, and Jack ended in the one meant for Joe, and Joe in Jack's. Probably I had bought the suits a couple of sizes bigger than needed so they could last several seasons: that would account for the fact that Joe Jr felt comfortable in the wrong suit and didn't notice until a minute or two after the snapshot – when he turned away from the camera and saw Jack in a suit ludicrously too large – that somehow his brother had done it again. And gave a yell of outrage. The same mix-up recurred and Joe Jr's ire rose. One day at Hyannis Port, Joe Jr came out of the house and saw Jack trotting over the lawn down to our beach – in the big bathing suit.

I was out at the time, so I didn't witness the scene, but I discovered that Joe Jr exploded and took off after his brother. Jack looked back over his shoulder momentarily and then sensibly took flight down to the beach looking for either protection or refuge. A hundred yards or so away, a bit beyond where our beachfront joins that of the old Taggart place, there is a breakwater: a structure of huge boulders and stone blocks that curves out for an eighth of a mile or so into Nantucket Sound, a nineteenth-century engineering marvel that afforded safe harbour to coastwise and ocean-going ships and thus gave Hyannis Port its function and its name as a port. A little more history was added to it that day when a future President of the United States climbed up on it and headed out over those great blocks and boulders towards the open sea, leaping the waterworn barnacled crevasses with a strength born of terror, with his elder brother leaping along behind shouting promises of awful punishments for his sins.

Joe Jr was gaining on him when, thank goodness, Eddie Moore arrived on the scene. He realized instantly that Jack had done something wrong and Joe Jr was chasing him for it, but this time the situation could be dangerous. He shouted: 'Stop that. You two get yourselves back here. Right now!' They did, but it chilled me to think what could have happened if Eddie hadn't turned up at the right time. I dare say Jack thought about it, too.

The friendly enmity between those two veered this way and that during their childhood and early youth. As the years went on their affection and understanding for each other deepened; and in maturity, as young men, they had a very deep bond – tacit but evident – of love, loyalty and confidence.

After Joe Jr's death, Jack made a collection of essays about him by people who had known him well. They were privately printed for family and friends in a book titled *As We Remember Joe*. Jack began the foreword saying: 'My only hesitancy in collecting these essays was that I doubted that Joe, if he had had a voice in it, would have approved. But I have disagreed with him before, so here they go.' Jack himself wrote the first essay in the book. He headed it simply, 'My Brother Joe', and wrote, in part:

> Joe did many things well, but I have always felt that he achieved his greatest success as the oldest brother. Very early in life he acquired a sense of responsibility towards his brothers and sisters, and I do not think that he ever forgot it. Towards me who was nearly his own age, this responsibility consisted in setting a standard that was uniformly high. I suppose I knew Joe as well as anyone and yet, I sometimes wonder whether I ever really knew him. He had always a slight detachment from things around him – a wall of reserve which few people ever succeeded in penetrating. I do not mean by this that Joe was ponderous and heavy in his attitude. Far from it – I do not know anyone with whom I would rather have spent an evening or played golf or, in fact, done anything. He had a keen wit and saw the humorous side of people and situations quicker than anyone I have ever known. He made friends with admirable ease, and wherever he went, his popularity was assured.
>
> He would spend long hours throwing a football with Bobby, swimming with Teddy, and teaching the younger girls how to sail. He was always close to Kick [our family nickname for Kathleen] and was particularly close to her during some difficult times. I think that if the Kennedy children amount to anything now or ever amount to anything, it will be due more to Joe's behaviour and his constant example than to any other factor. He made the task of bringing up a large family immeasurably easier for my father and mother, for what they taught him, he passed on to us, and their teachings were not diluted through him, but rather strengthened.

Jack was being modest about his own contributions. He did his share of pitching footballs and teaching sailing and swimming, and others were projections of his own interests and personality. His love of reading, his fascination with history and great events, and his rather romantic approach to life impressed his brothers and sisters. The open, friendly, disarming and wholly charming way he had about him helped form that unique quality he had when he was President that has been called 'a Special Grace'.

Eunice says:

> I'm sure it's normal for girls to look up to older brothers with some admiration and sense of dazzlement, but in our case it was fairly extreme. To us they were marvellous creatures, practically God-like, and we yearned to please them and be acceptable. Not that any of us would necessarily show it in any overt way, and nothing sugary, which would have turned them off and wasn't our style anyway. But we had this great feeling about them – as they did about us– as we all did about one another – and part of it was that they were such fun to be with. They treated us in a loving but off-hand way, occasionally sternly bawling us out, but most of the time considerately and humorously, and affectionately.

Just as Joe Jr and Jack passed along certain attitudes and values to the older girls, so did they to the younger ones, and so on down the line.

In later years people remarked about the unity of the family, the close bonds of loyalty and faith among them and their spontaneous understanding of each other. There was talk of 'the Kennedy clan', a term I dislike. The idea of 'clannishness' has, for me, connotations of narrowness, exclusivity and suspicious rejection of other people and indifference to their interests. This is diametrically opposed to the ideals of our family, and those which they brought with them into public life. I can see one merit in the expression, however: in a clan there is a pervading body of common beliefs, customs, modes of acceptable behaviour, community of interest and purpose, so that members know what to do without having to ask or explain themselves to one another. And in truth this fairly describes our family.

For parents who have or expect to have a sizeable family, my strong advice would be to work hardest on the eldest, for in the direction they go the others are likely to follow. Children are naturally imitative, and although at first they tend to imitate their parents' examples, as the years pass they tend just to imitate those set by older children, especially those in the family. And the elder ones, in my experience and also in my observations of other families, enjoy the responsibility of setting an example, of correcting mis-steps, of deserving the confidence of the parents and the respect of the younger ones.

Indeed, if they are properly encouraged to take an interest they will begin taking over functions that in a small family might be thought of as parental – and do so not only willingly but in many instances more effectively than the parents themselves could. If one of the girls, say, at age seventeen was using too much lipstick and I spoke to one of her older brothers and had him express his disapproval to her, she was sure to listen. Or, again, if she was going out with a beau of the wrong sort, some remarks from a big brother would be a hundred times more effective than a speech from us.

This also applied to the boys. Bobby wanted to be like his two big brothers and strove with all his might and main to be. And the three of them profoundly influenced Teddy.

I haven't said much about Teddy so far in these pages, for the reason that until quite late in the period I have been describing he hadn't been born. He arrived on February 22, 1932. With my own July 22 (1890) birthdate, I was exactly thirty-nine and a half at the time.

After Bobby, our seventh, was born in 1925 some of my best friends began indicating delicately but unmistakably that he should be the last one. When Jean, our eighth, arrived three years later, the broad hints turned to admonitions. And if I was with acquaintances and they learned I had eight children, they tended to regard this as a phenomenon and wanted to discuss it with me.

Finally I evolved a stratagem. If a conversation turned towards family and children I would quickly ask if the person had children and, if so, what ages they were. Usually I would be able to say I had children of just about those same ages, and at those ages – say of 5, or 10, or 15 – children are fascinating. I'd change the subject.

Mary Sanford is an old and close friend of mine who was also a friend of Joe's – she was Mary Duncan, of the movies, before she married 'Laddie' Sanford, the great polo player and racing stable owner – and who for many years had lived down the road from us at Palm Beach. She was saying some things about me, bringing back some memories for this book, not long ago, and said:

> She used to go to the polo games with me. Laddie was playing a lot of polo, and Joe Kennedy wasn't so famous then, and this must have been at least forty years ago when she had all those children, you know. And I would take a delight in introducing her to someone and then mentioning she has eight children, or whatever she had at the

time, because she always looked like a young girl. She's always had a beautiful figure. I never happened to see her when she was large with child: I suppose she must have put on weight then. Anyway she would say, 'Mary, please don't talk about how many children I have.' And I said, 'Why not? I think it's so fabulous because you look like such a young girl and you have all these children.' She said, 'Thank you but . . . it makes me . . . well, just don't do it, don't bring that up.'

Then I learned I was to have another baby.

So I made a firm resolution that this was not going to be any disadvantage to me or to the baby. None, none whatsoever. The baby, boy or girl, would always know it was a welcome and cherished member of our family, always feel loved and would grow up knowing the profound meaning of love: family love, Christian love, the love that 'passeth all understanding' in joy and confident service and happy relationships with others.

When Teddy was born I went out of my way to make sure that these resolutions – for me and for him – were kept in every way I could do so.

There were many factors that counted in the formation of his special character and personality. During Teddy's later boyhood and his youth he was more exposed to his father's direct and frequent hearth-and-home influence than his older brothers had been. This was a great source of inspiration and strength. I suppose the fact that he was the little brother of them all got him more attention – and affectionate indulgence – than the older ones would have been inclined to give one another. I expect if the next elder had been a brother there would have been rivalry. Girls, however, tend to be protectively fond of little brothers. Pat had a special empathy with Bobby. Jean has always had a special relationship with Teddy. They were a pair; they trotted around together; she sometimes admonished him and sometimes scrapped with him but mainly was his valiant friend and big sister, as she still is, though he is now nearly twice as big as she is. They shared a lot, including a quirky sense of humour. When they were teen-agers we sent them on a trip to Europe together – taking care of each other – but with a scolding note saying they had been spending too much money and should be more careful. From London we had a cablegram, which I'm sure they worked out together: 'After reading your letter I decided to travel tourist and I put Jean in my duffel bag. Lucky no one weighed the duffel bag. (Signed) Teddy.' Which reminds me of another we had from Teddy from the Riviera: 'Having barrels of fun. Send more money for more barrels.'

Teddy always was big and strong for his years. Who knows where this came from? There were athletes on both sides of the family. From some place in his ancestry, no doubt on both sides, Teddy got the right genes to give him all the physical attributes a boy needs to excel at sports and the spirit to go with them.

His father was of course delighted. His older brothers were of course delighted too, as well as amazed, amused, and challenging. This was fine, provided the little brother could respond and live up to the challenges. Teddy could and did, or at least he always tried his best. Sometimes at the risk of injury.

I remember an incident on the Riviera at Eden Roc, a beautiful hotel with grounds that end abruptly on a thirty- or forty-foot cliff with the Mediterranean below. The water below is deep, so it is a great place for high-diving provided one knows how to do it. And I remember Teddy up there on the cliff and Joe Jr yelling up to him to jump in. And he did. To my consternation and concern he kept doing it, egged on with great applause. I didn't interfere because the big brothers wouldn't be putting him up to it unless it were safe. And he seemed to be having a great time. I think he had confidence in Joe Jr's confidence in him. And that is something I did not want to disturb by being a solicitous mother.

I knew each of them would have to work things out for himself and each would need all the pluck and experience that circumstances could provide. There are, therefore, risks that a parent must take, nervous though some may make one feel.

It is a difficult line to draw. In Teddy's case I especially remember a time during Jack's Presidential primary campaign in Wisconsin during the winter of 1959–60. There was lots of snow at a ski resort there, a ski-jumping meet was in progress. Teddy, who knew how to ski but had never been on a ski-jump before, was challenged by somebody to try the jump. He went down an Olympic-size jump and flew through the air and managed to land upright without breaking his neck. I read about it in the papers next day; I was appalled. I thought it was a crazy idea, as I told him when I spoke to him on the telephone. Yet, privately, I really admired his spirit and courage and his loyalty to Jack, the fact that he would do such a thing for his brother to show the mettle of the family and pick up some votes. Yet I wished he could have found a less dramatic way to do it.

Eunice was recently talking about the differences among the boys. She said:

Teddy had a different physical constitution from Jack. He's always had enormous physical energy. He could do all the sports and do them well. Jack was, in a sense, envious of that. Or 'envious' would not be the right word – more like 'admiring', and because Jack was so much older and Teddy wanted his admiration it made him more, say, extroverted and more interested in doing all those things Jack wished he could do but couldn't because he had an injured back. In a sense Jack did the best on all the intellectual things and sort of monopolized them, and so the younger boys looked for something a little bit different. Probably all of them were more or less equally bright. What makes the difference in the way one goes, or the other, I don't know. Mother treated us all the same. I never felt there was any favouritism in terms of my mother at all.

Teddy's brothers and sisters took care to build his character. Here is the best piece of direct evidence imaginable, which I am taking verbatim from Jack's book of essays about Joe Jr. The first lines, those in italics, are Jack's introduction to the essay by Teddy (age 12) which then follows.

One day last Fall, Eunice and I were discussing this book when Teddy interrupted and said that he wanted to write about Joe, too. Eunice started to explain how Teddy should write and tell 'how wonderful and strong and calm' Joe was, when Teddy burst in with, 'But he wasn't calm; he threw me in the ocean.' So I told him to go ahead and write about that, and here it is with capitals and periods falling where they may, just as Teddy wrote it.

I recall the day the year before we went to England. It was in the summer and I asked Joe if I could race with him. He agreed to this so we started down to the pier, about five minutes before the race.

We had our sails up just as the gun went for the start. This was the first race I had ever been in. We were going along very nicely when he suddenly told me to pull in the jib. I had know Idea what he was talking about. He repeated the command again a little louder tone, meanwhile we were slowly getting further and further away from the other boats. Joe suddenly leaped up and grabbed the jib. I was a little scared, but suddenly he seized me by the pant and through me into the cold water.

I was scared to death practully. I then heard a spash and I felt his hand grab my shirt and then he lifted me into the boat. We continued the race and came in second. On the way home from the pier, he told me to be quiet about what happened in that afternoon. One falt Joe had was he got very easily mad in a race as you have witnessed. But he always menat well and was a very good sailor and swimmer.

Teddy had a wonderful sense of humour. In our family solemnity would have been intolerable. We were serious about serious things but we liked laughing at things that weren't, including, sometimes, some of our own foibles as we perceived them through others. Humour is a necessary part of wisdom; it gives perspective; it frees the spirit. Here is a verbatim letter from Teddy to his father.

Dear Daddy,
I have been to the Worlds Fair today with jimmy Murphy. I went into the swimming pool with my clothes on but the pool was empty. Write to me soon.

Love from
Teddy

Speaking of Teddy's boyhood leads me to his first cousin, Joey Gargan, my sister Agnes's son. During most of the summers of boyhood and youth they were together at Hyannis Port and became great pals and inseparable companions, sharing all sorts of adventures together. We were so glad to have Joey with us, as he was a wonderful pal of Ted's. Ted had no brother near his own age. Bobby was seven years older and was advanced in sailing, tennis, and football. So Joey found a warm welcome with us.

Agnes had married Joseph F. Gargan, originally of a Lowell, Massachusetts family. He had graduated from Notre Dame, had been a Captain in the Marine Corps and had returned for a law degree, and was by 1929 a lawyer practising in New York City. By Agnes's choice their wedding was a private ceremony, as mine and Joe's had been. I was her only attendant. It was a fine, happy marriage soon blessed with three children: Joseph Jr – 'Joey', Ann, and Mary Jo. They were still very young when Agnes died suddenly in 1936.

I felt a deep, personal loss. I was also very concerned about her children, knowing how the thought of leaving them would have grieved her.

Faith is always necessary, but especially at such times. For Faith sustains, and without it Hope is dead.

There were many letters of condolence, all of them appreciated beyond measure, but perhaps they can be represented by one that came from the president of my alma mater, the College of the Sacred Heart at Manhattanville. Rev. Mother Donnalley wrote:

. . . May God comfort you . . . I know how much your faith sustains you at this moment. How do those bear sorrow who have not that hope? I remember dear Agnes as such a charming, lovable, beautiful character. God is rewarding her now with unlimited joy for all she did for Him during her full life and she will watch over and protect from Heaven those poor little children who cannot have her visible care.

Yet I have always believed, and have tried to live my life in the belief, that Faith without Works is dead.

Joey Gargan, who is now a man in his early forties, father of his own large, loving family, says:

My first real memory of Aunt Rose was when my mother died and she came to our house, and naturally she was very upset because this was her sister and they were very close. But also she was there to see about us children, and that we were taken care of and what we were going to do now, or what my father was going to do about the problem of having to raise three children without a mother. I was only six. My first question to Aunt Rose was, 'Oh, are we going to have a step-mother now?' Apparently I was very much afraid of the idea of having a step-mother and quite concerned. And she said to me, 'No, no, Joey, everything's going to be all right.'

One of the benefits of being in a large family is that in tragedy there are always many people who care deeply and can be counted on to rally to do whatever must be done. Both Agnes and Joe Gargan came from good-sized families. My husband and I took the three children into our home. After many consultations with their father and among the relatives, it was decided, partly because Joe had become a high official of the Roosevelt Administration and a trouble-shooter for the President, making our family plans unpredictable, that they should live in Lowell with their father's brother and his wife. But of course the rest of us continued to have them in our thoughts and to do everything possible for them. In the years following, as Joey and Ann and Mary Jo grew older, they began to spend summers and some of their school vacations with us. This lasted many years, and in a real sense they became members of our own family.

Although I have said a good deal about education, I am far from finished with the topic. For I feel it has meant not only the formal categories of knowledge – history, literature, grammar and the rest – but also education in the simple social graces. On the subject of good manners, the children were taught to speak politely to the servants, not to yell at them. For instance, they were to ask the chauffeur when it was feasible to take them into the village, not to demand that he drop everything and take them. I also stressed that punctuality was important, and that first impressions are highly so.

I was just as rigorous with Joey Gargan in such matters as I was with his pal Teddy – and with all the others – and a few decades later he has recalled:

> Aunt Rose wasn't severe with us but she certainly, almost constantly, supervised us. Appearance and Conduct. Don't wear white socks with dress suit. Wear dark shoes with blue or grey suit, not brown shoes. Suit sleeves short enough so shirt cuff hangs below suit sleeve one inch. Don't say 'Hi' to people when addressing them but particularly don't use it when greeting Cardinal Cushing, James Forrestal, Arthur Krock or the like.
>
> We got the natural instructions at the dinner table about good table manners in eating, and right forks and so forth and deportment, such as proper seating and 'ladies first'. That reminds me of a classic scene with Aunt Rose and Jack.
>
> They had a wonderful relationship, but at the same time they were often in a way at cross purposes so far as household disciplines were concerned because he didn't fit into them too well. Aunt Rose, for instance, would always be seated at the far end of the table, that is the end farthest away from the entrance to the dining-room. And of course the idea was, when a meal was over, the ladies and particularly Aunt Rose were to leave the dining-room first. That was good manners, just basic, Aunt Rose would lead the way. But very often Jack would forget. He would have been having an interesting conversation, or his mind was on something else, or someway he would absent-mindedly and unintentionally forget the order of departure. That happened so often that when a meal was over Aunt Rose would start for the door. And then, quite clearly, it could be a race between her and Jack as to who was going to make it. And she would frequently mention this to Jack and he would say, 'Oh, yes, Mother, I'm sorry' – and they would both kind of chuckle – but it would only be a couple of days later when it would happen again. The rest of us all knew what was likely so we would all sort of stand by our chairs or move towards the door slowly – to give her a chance to get out first.'

I remember those episodes quite well. Joey is telling the truth. One thing he hasn't mentioned is that during those Hyannis Port summers I chased him around a lot making *him* behave. He goes on to say:

> She was always very much aware of where we were going and what

our activities were, whether going to a movie on a rainy day down at Hyannis (by the way we rode our bikes down and back, about three miles each way, and we were given just the price of admission, no extras) or going out in a boat – particularly the boat or anything to do with the water. If we were going sailing she wanted to know where we planned to be, what time we were coming back: and we were always to watch the flag on the flagpole in front of the house. If she wanted us to come in for some reason she'd take the flag down and that was her signal. Sometimes she'd ask Wilbert, the gardener-caretaker, to handle this but if he wasn't in sight she'd just do it herself. Ropes and pulleys didn't faze her. In sailing, she was especially concerned to know if we were taking any other children with us and, if so, who they were and did their parents know – so that the parents wouldn't miss them and start wondering and worrying about them. She was very much conscious, always very aware and considerate, about the feelings of other parents, and she was in touch with them about all the activities of our group of friends. When we were older and dating and going to dances and driving cars, she had to know the names and addresses of our dates – just so she could be in touch with the parents in case of any problems that could involve not getting the girls home on time. The club dances ended at twelve midnight in those days. We were supposed to take our dates directly home and then be back at the house ourselves at a definite time, depending on where the girls lived, but that would never make it longer than about 12.30. And if we missed by more than ten minutes or so, we'd hear about it from her the next morning. That went on until we were well up into our late teens. And it really went on – with the rules relaxed and less monitoring – all the way through until we were out of college.

I have always been a rather light sleeper, so I would hear them – as they grew old enough to drive and be out at night – when they came into the driveway and put the cars away in the parking space in back of the house. If they were later than they should have been they drove in very slowly, with the least possible noise, turning the head-lights off, and careful not to slam the car doors or the back door of the house. They would take their shoes off and sneak upstairs in the dark to their rooms. But I knew what was happening. I asked Pat to keep vigil one night, but she fell asleep herself.

My niece Mary Jo Clasby says:

The rules were a little different for the girls than for the boys. If I stayed out an extra fifteen minutes I could expect to see Aunt Rose looking for me. And that is the absolute truth. She had a little blue car – and she'd come looking. We'd always have told her where we planned to be, and there wasn't much of anyplace to go anyway. We could be at the golf club or down by the post office and variety store. But if we weren't home on time she'd come out and find us and say, 'Dear, it's time to come home,' and home we'd go. And everyone recognized her headlights on the little blue car and knew she was coming. She was, for us, even then a very strong personality. I think she knew us all very well – she had had an awful lot of experience raising children.

But I can't ever remember her putting anybody down. That was one of my biggest memories of her about raising children. She probably would remind you of what you had done wrong. If I was late or something, and she had gone out after me, or gone out after one of us, there'd be a note on that person's pillow: 'The next time be sure to be in on time.' She made herself clear and that was it: she didn't upbraid you, you were never chewed-out. And over a period of time, this method really worked, it got to you.

After I had stayed awhile there at Hyannis Port with her and Uncle Joe I became very close to her, because I liked her very much. And loved her, really. And I think that when you feel that way about somebody, you don't – even if you're quite young – want to hurt them by doing things they would consider wrong. And this was especially so with Aunt Rose. There's something about her. She believes in people. You just didn't want to do anything to disturb her or make her upset. If she said, 'This is the way I think you should do it,' you probably would find yourself thinking, well, I would kind of like to do it that way. And usually it did turn out her way was the best in the end.

Later, I sent Mary Jo to the convent of the Sacred Heart, where I had been a pupil, and she graduated from Manhattanville, as had my daughters. Joey was sent to Notre Dame, where his father had studied. Later, my husband arranged for all the nieces and nephews to follow the same pattern. I can say with pride and pleasure that all the members of the family responded willingly and with deep appreciation.

I do think that a parent who has a child's love and confidence has the most effective of all instruments, in the long run, for shaping character and good behaviour. But there are times when even they are not enough: particularly when children are very young and their physica

1

safety depends on learning certain lessons soon and clearly. For instance, if I found a child playing with my sharp scissors I would take them away, explain how dangerous they could be and then, to make this immediately clear, stick the points against a finger or arm just enough for him to feel some pain and to understand. Or again, if I found him too near a hot stove I would hold one of his fingers close enough to the flame or the oven door for him to feel the heat uncomfortably, and thus realize what it could mean for him if he weren't careful.

People have asked me if I ever spanked Jack when he was a boy. I suppose it is part of the mystique surrounding the Presidency that anyone who occupies the office is endowed with qualities that are extraordinary and must have passed through childhood in a glow of virtue. I can verify that this was not the case with Jack, nor was it with Bobby or Teddy or any of the others, and whenever they needed it they got a good old-fashioned spanking. I believe this is one of the most effective means of instruction.

I should add that if a spanking is necessary it ought to be a parent – not a baby-sitter or nursemaid – who gives it. Since Joe was away from the house so much of the time, that duty fell to me. And I saw it as a duty, never to be done in anger or a fit of irritability. I also believe that physical punishment should not be the first choice of instruction but the last. Nevertheless, there are times and situations in which some solid whacks on the backside may be the only thing a very young child understands.

I kept a ruler in my desk and used it for measuring out punishments. After a few times of being whacked on the hand or the breeches, the mere mention of the ruler would have a healthy effect on a child's behaviour. Since justice should be both sure and swift, as I said, fairly often I didn't even wait to get to the desk but took the nearest thing at hand, which was likely to be a wooden coat-hanger. With our big family there had to be a lot of clothes and therefore of closets and therefore of hangers – they were always within reach. A hanger didn't hurt any more – probably less – than a ruler, but it is a rather unusual implement for this purpose, and as adults the children have liked to rag me about how 'cruel' I was to 'beat' them with coat-hangers. (They weren't beaten, they were spanked – just hard enough to receive the message.) The coat-hangers have become a part of our family lore. When Eunice was having her fifth child some few years ago I went down to help with her older children and the household while she was in the hospital, and I found that my reputation had preceded me. Her boys had taken all the coat-hangers in the house and put them down the laundry chute. It may have been a joke, but I've never been too sure.

In any case, when they were beyond the spanking stage, and especially when they were grown up and married and faced with their own problems of child-raising, they accepted the idea of corporal punishment with perfect equanimity. Teddy says:

One of my memories of when we lived in Bronxville was walking home one day from kindergarten, which I wasn't supposed to do, and getting spanked by Mother. There was always someone to pick me up in a car and bring me home, and Mother's point was that the person wouldn't know where I was and she wouldn't either – and something might have happened to me – and I had caused needless worry to others. So she spanked: I think it was a ruler or hairbrush or maybe a coat-hanger. Whack! And she was right.

I think that if discipline is immediate and direct and responsive in proportion to the size of the mistake, then physical punishment can be good. If the mistake is dwelt on and there's a sense of accusation around – that's no good. When I was nine I went to boarding-school at Fessenden. The school had sent off a notice to all the fathers of the entering boys for permission to paddle their sons, and my father was the first one to send it back, approved. In four years there I was paddled thirteen times. (That may not be good campaign material for a US Senator but there it is, thirteen.) Sometimes we'd even be paddled just before going out to do our best for the old school in an athletic event. But I never resented it, because if I broke a school rule I knew I was supposed to be corrected and it was a matter of preference. The boys whose parents hadn't given permission would have to stay over during Thanksgiving, get days cut off their Christmas vacations, or couldn't come to the school's 'Saturday Nights' or had to spend hours writing repentant inspirational slogans on blackboards.

The disciplinarian did most of the whacking but I didn't hold that against him at all, and after I was out of there I used to go back to see him and visit with him. I considered him a good and trustworthy friend: he was that kind of man. And of course this is a tremendously important factor, the personality, the character, of the individual on both sides of the equation. With some kids an experience of corporal punishment would be absolutely horrendous. Could bruise very badly, psychologically. Anyway, as for Mother, I never felt I was getting more nor less than justice from her, although it was a justice tempered by mercy and compassion and love. You knew those qualities were there. Even when – after the exercise of her motherly duty – your behind was sore.

I do remember that some of the boys, knowing they had been naughty and would be punished, would, if there was time, stuff a pillow-case into their pants to lessen the anguish. Those were vintage years for the Sunday 'funny papers' including The Katzenjammer Kids, who were always in mischief and being spanked and trying to pad their breeches in advance; perhaps that's where our small sinners got the idea. I was seldom deceived. But sometimes I'd let them get away with it.

I believe that while a child is still very young the parents should let him know he is not to 'have his own way' and is not to say 'No'. He should have this explained – and soon should understand – that his parents love him very much and are advising him on everything for his own good. And he is not to contradict them.

This idea worked so well that I can remember only one instance in which a child said 'No' to me directly, even though I realized, sensibly, that some of them were probably saying 'No' to themselves and didn't always do as they were told. The exception was our eighth, Jean, who one day in Florida announced that *No!* she was not going to the Bath and Tennis Club for a swimming lesson. After I recovered from the shock I said to her, 'Every little Kennedy goes to Bath and Tennis and takes a swimming lesson so you just run along like your brothers and sisters!' Perhaps she sensed something in my tone of voice. Anyway, she went.

Jean disapproved of my telling anybody about her rebellion, because, as she said, it made her seem like the black sheep of the family. Yet she is now amused by it, perhaps because it gave her a unique place in our family history or because rebels are popular.

Eunice says:

We were really organized. It was an extraordinary thing the way she had us all . . . I guess the word is disciplined. And scheduled. We went to dancing lessons once a week, which bored us, but we did turn out to be good dancers. The same with sports. She wanted us to do swimming and tennis and golf and those things properly, so schedules of lessons were laid on, which sometimes were a drag, but we did develop the skills and they've been important assets. In fact if Jack hadn't been such a good swimmer he probably couldn't have come through alive – let alone do all that rescuing of crew members –

after his PT boat was sunk in the Pacific. A lot of Mother's things have paid off both in general and in special ways. For instance that so-called 'flashing Kennedy smile' that got to be part of the trademark after we grew up and some of us entered public life. You don't flash unless your teeth are good. And Mother really organized and scheduled that, first of all by monitoring our intake of sweets. She kept a box of assorted candies in her bedroom and after dinner each of us was allowed to pick out a favourite piece. One piece, and that was it, and this got to be such a custom or habit that we would hardly have dreamed of asking for a second. Then the tooth-brushing. After every meal. Dentists have always recommended it but we actually did it because Mother made it a rule and was there to enforce it. I remember it, for instance, as part of the morning drill. She'd always come down, in her robe, for breakfast with us, to make sure we had the right food and ate it and then brushed our teeth. There was a down-stairs bathroom and we'd file in and out one by one. Then stand inspection for any spots on our clothes and general neatness. These things get to be a habit – if you're brought up that way you think it's natural. And then also we had our teeth straightened. All of us: we all had braces. We could have gone to some local dentist in Bronx-ville, I suppose, but Mother is a perfectionist, so every three weeks five or six of us had to hop in the car and be driven about an hour down to New York to a super-dentist. We'd wait our turn, and go to the chair, and be driven back home with all our braces tightened. I remember doing this for five years. With the age-spread in our family there must have been close to twenty years of continuous tooth-straightening among us, with Mother keeping tabs on it all the way. A rather staggering statistic.

Eunice's mention of habits, good and bad, reminds me of some we tried to discourage; the use of tobacco and alcohol. Joe never smoked. As a schoolboy and college athlete – and as a fit, trim, enormously vigorous sportsman until the vascular accident that led to his death late in life – he knew that smoking is bad for wind and health; and as an ambitious young businessman he thought it was a stupid way to spend money he needed for better purposes; and, besides, his whole nature rejected any idea that he could become dependent in the least on any-thing but his own physical and mental resources. He had a drink or two now and then, but only on social occasions, and never before an important meeting. He wanted his mind completely clear.

As for me, I never thought of smoking. When I was a girl and young wife any woman who smoked a cigarette was typed as a scarlet woman.

Drinking? In my young married set we knew that some of the men took a nip, but any over-indulgence or visible inebriation was considered an insult to us and we would cut that young man dead and try never to be seen in his company again. My father, by the way, though he might have a drink with friends in private, never drank anything in public; for he believed it would contribute to the caricature of 'drunken Irish politicians – a glass of whisky in one hand, a pipe in the other'. The Boston Brahmin image of the Irish he resented deeply and wanted to dispel. Times and outlooks change. 'Thé Dansants' gave way to 'cocktail parties' and sometime in the early 1930s, in Florida, I tried my first cocktail, an 'Orange Blossom'. I found the sensation pleasant. It made me feel quite hospitable. However, I found the only alcoholic beverages to which I am not allergic are products of the grape, and among those the only one that really agrees with me is champagne, in small quantities. So through the first half of my life I was teetotal and for the rest of it I have been abstemious.

Joe and I both realized that as the children passed through their teens they undoubtedly would be exposed to provocations and temptations. We had always believed in rewards for good behaviour as well as penalties for bad; in encouragement, praise, recognition, prizes, such as the silver cups and trophies they accumulated. I therefore had a flash of inspiration when I read that the Rockefeller children, not many years older than our own, had been given a thousand dollars each for not smoking or drinking until they were twenty-one.

I am not, in fact, certain as to the amount. Governor Nelson Rockefeller told me he remembered it as three thousand. However, sitting next to his elder brother, John D. III, at the opening of the John F. Kennedy Center in Washington, I asked him about that figure. He said, 'Well, I think it was only one thousand. Perhaps when Nelson and the other younger ones came along my father raised the amount. But I think I got one thousand.' In any event, Joe and I agreed upon a thousand dollars for not smoking, another thousand for not drinking, to each child if he or she on his or her honour made it all the way to age twenty-one. This was not a bribe for good behaviour because they already realized they would come into considerable money when they reached that age, since Joe had arranged trust funds for them. Rather it was an interesting and enticing trophy. From age twenty-one onward they were presumed to be adults in command of their own futures.

I think it worked as well as we could have expected and perhaps even a little better. Joe Jr went through his twenty-one years without faltering and got his prize. One or two of the girls did begin to smoke because, they said, it helped them cut down on sweets and they were afraid of losing their figures. I didn't approve but I could sympathize. In general the no-smoking prize was more successful than the no-drinking reward because of circumstances. All the children were abroad at one time or another during their late teens; and, of course, beer and wine are considered staples of life in most parts of Great Britain and Europe and are served as part of a meal. So when Teddy was in the Army and was stationed in Germany and France – he had two years, age nineteen and twenty – his father told him he could drink beer and wine during that time, without penalty. However, when he was twenty-one Teddy wouldn't take the money because, he said, it wouldn't be fair since he hadn't stayed the whole course and he felt this was a matter of principle.

Actually, the overwhelmingly favourite beverage in our house always was and still is – milk. Sometimes with some cocoa or other flavouring but essentially just milk. Mary Jo Clasby says:

> After coming back from a dance or a party we drank milk or cocoa or whatever was there but not beer. A couple of boys in our age group did drink beer and one is now the headmaster of a country day school: we kid him about how bad he was. I didn't drink at all. The boys in the family told me I shouldn't. It was never anything for them until they were old enough, around twenty or twenty-one. But the one who impressed it on me the most was Pat. She was a beautiful girl and just had everything, so far as I was concerned. I was seventeen or eighteen and starting in college and she told me not to drink because, she said, you'll have a much better time if you don't – and Pat was my idol.

Ethel has a memory in a later time – this would be December of 1960, just before Jack's Inauguration, and a lot of us were at Palm Beach, and in and out were as large a variety as one could imagine, from Cabinet appointees to seamstresses. A very busy and exciting but slightly dishevelled period when days ran into nights. She says:

> I remember going into the kitchen and there were several of us there, talking about whatever we were talking about, past-present-future, with glasses in our hands. And Oleg Cassini joined in and he couldn't *believe* we were all standing around drinking *milk*.

Joe was absolutely devoted to his children. He loved them and he let them know it, realize it, absorb the understanding of his love from their earliest childhood and in the most outgoing demonstrative ways. In business and politics many people found him 'hard-headed' and 'tough':

but they should have seen him at home, warm and gentle with the little ones. He would sweep them into his arms and hug them, and grin at them and talk to them, and perhaps carry them around. Also, as each one became old enough to talk – had enough vocabulary and under-standing for a simple conversation, which would be roughly at about age two and a half or three – he would want that child in bed with him for a little while each morning. And the two of them would be there propped up on the pillows, with perhaps the child's head cuddling on his shoulder, and he would talk or read a story or they would have conversations. These were on any topic whatsoever that the child wanted to talk about. He would be responsive, understanding, amused or mock-horrified, always affectionate but if necessary corrective with advice or plain declarations of Yes or No and Good or Bad. Even when they were that young he treated them, in a sense, as equals, respecting each one as a unique and wonderfully interesting individual and trying to bring out whatever that individuality was. Except to adjust his vocabulary to theirs, he never 'talked down' to them, never patronized them from the lofty holier-and-wiser attitude that I have seen some parents take. He said what was on his mind and in his heart. There was a marvellous combination of sternness and warmth, severity and great good humour, the greatest of expectations along with a knowledge of human frailties and a very deep sense of justice. I think children understand parental qualities and attitudes: they just soak them in. Ours grew up with feelings of awe and reverence and respect and friendship and camaraderie and love and duty toward their father.

Physical punishment was not his style at all. (It wasn't mine either once they were old enough to be reached by the power of reason.) He may have and probably did give some of them a paddy-whack at one time or another but I can't remember a single time that he ever spanked any of them. Instead he enforced his ideas by the sheer strength of his personality – an almost physical emanation of energy and power and mental quickness and forthrightness. He did not, in the phrase, 'suffer fools gladly' and if there was foolishness going on the culprits knew it and usually all it took was a look. He had bright blue eyes with a remarkable range of expression. They could change, in a moment, from sunny affection and merriment to a look that – as a young house-guest who was there to see it happen a few times described in a later time – 'was ice-cold steel blue, piercing right into and through you and stripped you to the soul; and you felt naked, shrivelled.' That may be a little elaborate. It was known in the family as 'Daddy's Look'.

Mary Jo recalls:

I can't remember him raising his voice. Or even thinking of doing anything. But he had a way of putting his glasses down and *looking* at you over the glasses. I never found out what was beyond that but I really never felt that I wanted to find out. It was just one of those things. The fear of God was there and why tamper with it.

Her brother Joey says:

He didn't have to say anything to you. All he'd have to do was look down the table rather sternly over the top of his glasses and that was enough to indicate it had better not happen again; and it very rarely did. At the same time he was very kindly and, I always felt, extremely understanding. If you did get into trouble – with a car or a boat, say, even foolishly – he would make it clear he was upset about it, and the person should have had better sense, it was unnecessary. Once he'd made it clear that he was unhappy and hoped it would never happen again, the subject was not mentioned again. It was a past incident, you had learned an important lesson and life went on from there.

Once, when I was old enough to drive, he called me in Boston and asked me to bring his new Cadillac down to the Cape. On the way, a truck came out of a side road and hit the left front fender. The car went off the road and into the trees and one of them crumpled the right front fender, so now there were smashed fenders on both sides of his new Cadillac. The car was still driveable, so I took it on to Hyannis Port and into the parking area back of the house. Bobby and the chauffeur, Dave, both saw it and of course were horrified and suggested I take it to a garage for repairs before Uncle Joe saw it. I decided to be brave. So, with my face the colour of cement, I went in and told him what happened. He said, 'Let's see the car' – which was a mess. Instead of tearing me apart he said, 'Joey, you're lucky to be alive,' and that I should take it back to Boston on Monday to get it fixed and meanwhile, just then, I ought to get into the touch football game that had begun out front on the lawn. There was often a little good-natured ragging going on in the household. And if somebody was in trouble with Uncle Joe all the others were delighted it was that person, not them, who was in a hot spot, and they might even bait Uncle Joe a bit and encourage the situation – just to see the fireworks. That evening at dinner Jack, who was a Congressman then, began this operation by remarking very innocently, 'Dad, I hear Joey had a little accident with the new car.' At that, Uncle Joe put his glasses down a little, peered at Jack with that special 'look' and said: 'Joey and I have discussed the car, and I don't want to hear it mentioned again.' And it never was. In fact a week later he asked me to drive Aunt Rose to the airport. It was his way of telling me and showing others that he still had confidence in me.

When any one of them got into trouble (I didn't say 'if' but 'when') his first approach was to demand all the facts. He would say: 'Tell me the truth. Come clean. Tell me everything about it, the whole truth. Then I'll do everything I can to help. But if you don't give me the truth, I'm licked.' Painful as truth-telling might be in some situations, they all understood what he meant and, I think, almost always brought forth the truth as they saw it. (Sometimes giving themselves the benefit of the doubt, I dare say.) Then, if on the basis of the facts he decided they had been in the wrong, he would tell them so, straight out, logically, emphatically, and carefully explain why they had been wrong and how they could and should guard against getting into that sort of difficulty again. If he thought they needed a stronger speech he would give it and if there was some really serious lapse he would give them blue-blazes. But then, as Mary and Joey have indicated, when it was over – it was over completely. He had made himself entirely clear. He assumed they understood and realized, and had made their own vows to themselves, that they were not to engage in any such nonsense again. Teddy remarks:

> When I got into that mess at Harvard in my freshman year at eighteen and was suspended, and called to tell him, his initial reaction was very calm. What exactly was the situation I'm involved in? What impact could this have on my life and relationships? And then about eighteen to twenty-four hours later, after he had got a 'feel' for what it meant, he was absolutely wild and went up through the roof. For about five hours. From then on he was calm. It was just 'How do we help you?' And he never brought the thing up again.

Many years later in 1964, after Ted had his nearly-fatal aeroplane accident and while he was in the hospital recuperating, he collected essays from family members and friends about his father, and these were published in a privately printed book that he titled *The Fruitful Bough* after a passage in Genesis (49: 22–24), 'Joseph is a fruitful bough, even a fruitful bough by a well, whose branches run over the wall . . . his bow abode in strength, and the arms of his hands were made strong by the hands of the mighty God.' Here are excerpts from the essay that Teddy himself contributed to that book:

> My first consciousness of how important Dad was to me began

when I was allowed to crawl into bed with him in the morning and listen to him read Donald Duck.

From our earliest days, I think all the Kennedy children were made to feel that our father's principal interest in life was his family. As the youngest, it appeared to me that the family was his only interest.

I have always felt the greatest gift Dad gave to each of us was his unqualified support. His purpose was to encourage and to sift the relevant from the irrelevant. His criticisms were always positive and constructive and made sense. His guidance was for our own good and the family's. Perhaps we might not agree with his conclusions, but the final decision was sounder because of discussions with him.

Even when he was away from home, he made sure to get reports on our conduct. At a very early age each of us realized the need to speak to Dad frankly and forthrightly. 'Applesauce' was not for him, and he wanted no 'monkey business' at school or at home.

When Dad was away from home, he kept up with everything going on in the family. The children who were away at school reported to him regularly by letter and phone. No matter how busy he was, he seemed to have a moment to listen and to encourage us.

Dad wanted us to be natural, and able to smile no matter how tough things were. He wouldn't let any of his children feel sorry for himself. 'I don't want any sour-pusses around here,' he would say. Yet he was quick to scold a child who tried to smile too readily, or to charm his way through life. 'Remember,' he would say, 'a smile and a dime can only get you a ride on a street-car. You are going to need a lot more than that to get somewhere in life.'

Clarity, frankness and honesty were basic parts of his character. He was never afraid to state his case. Typical expressions were, 'He doesn't have the brains of a donkey,' or 'enough brains to find his way out of a telephone booth'. One whose personal honesty or ethics might be in question was described as one who 'would take a red hot stove'.

Although we loved him as a father, we also admired him as a man, who was eminently successful, extraordinarily knowledgeable, and thoroughly enjoyable. His handshake was strong and firm, and he looked you straight in the eye. His broad smile and whole-hearted laugh were infectious. His welcome was warm and genuine – a special one for each of us.

He was generous to a fault, but woe unto him who made the mistake of taking advantage of it. Dad was a taskmaster, too. He was also quick to admonish us for errors. He tolerated a mistake once, but never a second time. Because he was interested, because he did care, because he wanted to help, he brought out the best in each of us. We were ashamed to do less than our best because of our respect and feelings for him.

Ted's last remark brings up a question that has often been asked of me: 'What has made the Kennedy children strive so hard for individual excellence?' The answer is a combination of elements.

Superior achievement – or making the most of one's capabilities – is to a very considerable degree a matter of habit. This was the reason why Joe used to say to the children, 'We don't want any losers around here. In this family we want winners.' They were encouraged to be winners, leaders, and victors in whatever they set their hand to, and to develop the habit. 'Don't come in second or third – that doesn't count – but win.' If they lost in a sport – or lagged in school or other activity – the reasons were analysed. If these turned out to involve some negligence or lack of effort or 'monkey shines', that was dealt with in very clear terms. Eunice has recalled:

> Mother and Dad put us through rigorous training in athletics. Dad wanted his children to win the sailing and swimming races (I remember racing fourteen times a week when I was 12 years old!)

Joe's attitude has been much written about, particularly after the boys went into public life with such conspicuous success. Journalists and others pondered what had caused the so-called 'Kennedy phenomenon'. The main point of the whole exercise was not 'winning' *per se*. It was rather that we wanted them to do their absolute best. Always give their maximum effort. 'From each according to his abilities and to each according to his needs' might be one way of saying this. Another could be, 'God wants a different thing from each of us . . . which only we can do and for which we were created.' Joe and I knew they were not perfect. We knew they were each different, yet we wanted each to develop his or her individual abilities and to do the very best that was in them to do. In *The Fruitful Bough*, Ted has explained this very well:

> His standards were the highest for each of his sons, but they were different standards for each one – standards which recognized our individual strengths and weaknesses. Often, he compared us to each other, but only in a way which raised each of our expectations for what we hoped to accomplish. Comparisons between children are delicate to handle, but Dad could put each of us on our mettle, without creating resentment between us.

And Bobby, in his essay in that book, said:

> He has called on the best that was in us. There was no such thing as half-trying. Whether it was running a race or catching a football, competing in a school – we were to try. And we were to try harder than anyone else. We might not be the best, and none of us were, but we were to make the effort to be the best. 'After you have done the best you can,' he used to say, 'the hell with it.'
>
> Most importantly, he has been there when things went badly. Our opponents became his opponents, our problems his problems . . . and he was there to help. In bad times it has been he, more than anyone else, who has seen the bright side. 'Call up Dad, he will be cheerful,' my older brother used to say. The greater the disaster, the brighter he was, the more support he gave.
>
> And so it has been this interesting combination – his demand that all his children strive for excellence – strive for it, perhaps not achieve it, but continuously strive for it; and – what made this demand tolerable and in fact enjoyable – the interest and support we felt we always had from him.

I think the most important lines in these paragraphs of Bobby's are: 'After you have done the best you can, the hell with it.' I was saying the same thing to them, more sedately. The important thing was to *try*; then, if it didn't work, too bad about that but no regrets, go on to the next time or the next project; and *try* again. For surely there is no way to excellence, achievement, leadership without full effort, and I'm certain that is true in every field.

The other most pertinent remarks are about his father's invariable support in times of troubles and the infectiously optimistic reassurance he could always manage. How many times I have heard him declare: 'That may be one of the *best* things that ever happened to you!' And sometimes it really was. Meanwhile, it helped.

Another of Joe's statements that everyone in the family heard often enough was: 'We don't want any crying in this house.'

It too was picked up by some of the writers and misunderstood or misused in a way to make him seem hard-hearted or as if he were trying to convert the children into Spartans and Stoics. What he really meant was that there was to be *no self-pity*, and no burdening of others with your personal misfortunes by making a commotion about them. He knew that for almost everyone life is likely to hold many knocks and bruises, and that people had better get used to that idea at an early age.

I have a favourite passage from Dag Hammarskjöld's *Markings*: 'Keep alive the incentive to push on further, that pain in the soul which drives us beyond ourselves.'

And another that I jotted in my Commonplace Book, regrettably without noting the author: 'A healthy attitude can change a burden into a blessing, a trial into a triumph.'

One especially appropriate example was the way Jack happened to write his book *Profiles In Courage*.

Ever since the war and his injuries during the PT 109 ordeal he had a serious problem with his back. He was seldom if ever really free of pain, although he bore it with such few outward signs that nobody but his doctors, the family and a few close associates realized his condition. Meanwhile he had plenty of reason to think about courage. Finally during 1954 the problem became so bad that he had to be on crutches; and rather than face going through life as a cripple he agreed to a spinal operation. Not only was it a failure but an infection set in. He nearly died: he received the last rites of the Church. But he did pull through, and after the danger was past he was flown – on a stretcher – to our Palm Beach house for recuperation in the warm climate. In a few months he was 'healthy' enough for the doctors to try the operation again. If he wanted it. He did. So it was back to the hospital in New York, where the second operation was successful (relatively speaking, for he was always afterwards in discomfort, which he ignored) and then back again to Palm Beach for more months of recuperation. It was there, during those times, that he did most of his work on *Profiles In Courage*. He had, as I said, been fascinated since boyhood by history and biography. In his own life, and from life in our family, he knew the meaning of courage. The theme of the book was a natural one for him. He worked on it most of the time during the long period of trial and risk and suffering – in his hospital bed, with a writing-board propped in front of him, in bed at the Palm Beach house, other places – but my vivid memory is of him sitting in a wheelchair and later a comfortable camp-chair out by the sea wall.

There is a little promontory, about the size of a big bay window and shaped like one, that protrudes from the wall, with beach and ocean on three sides. On calm sunny days this was an office and studio for him. Literally an office because all the most important mail and messages and items of Senate business were sent down to him from Washington. Literally a studio because Jackie got him interested in painting, as a good relaxation, and sometimes he would be out there with easel and palette trying his hand at seascapes and beach scenes or, for practice, copying a painting he had taken off a wall some place in our house. (Rarely with a by-your-leave to me. Not that we have any valuable paintings, but still . . . ! And he would say, 'Oh, yes, Mother, sorry,' and then I'd find another one gone.) And literally an office-studio-library – or whatever the best term is for the working habitat of a writer – because so many times I remember looking out from the house across our sturdy green lawn and past the tall white royal palms towards the tropical sea, the aquamarine white-capped ocean and blue sky and passing clouds and ships in the distance, and there was Jack in his sea-wall alcove with his writing-board and a thick writing-pad clamped to it, and a folding table or two piled with books and note-books and file folders – paperweights or perhaps some rocks from the beach to hold things down against the sea breezes – and his head would be forward and he would be writing away on that book. From full heart, mind and spirit.

It turned out to be a very fine book. One he could take satisfaction in for several reasons: first because it expressed ideas and ideals he believed in and believed were very important in the life of this nation; and not last nor least because he realized he had expressed them well – and as I said, before he happened to go into politics, his ambitions had revolved around writing, journalism, teaching.

Furthermore, its excellence was recognized and rewarded. It received a Pulitzer Prize. It was admired by historians and influential figures in government and journalism and other 'opinion makers' of the so-called Intellectual Establishment – whose good opinion in political life in this country usually has been and hopefully always will be of great importance. After publication of the book, Jack was no longer just an interesting, attractive but relatively inexperienced and comparatively unknown junior Senator from Massachusetts, but was someone dis-cussed and weighed and measured nationally. He was chosen to give Adlai Stevenson's nomination speech at the next Democratic Conven-tion, in 1956 – and he himself came within a hair's breadth of becoming nominated for the Vice-Presidency. From the force of that momentum he went on to the Presidential nomination and election in 1960. Quite obviously there were many complex elements – oh, indeed, a very great many, greatly complex, involving a great deal of very hard work by a great many people – that led to those victories. What I am saying is that an early and important and possibly even crucial one was Jack's own response to his own misfortune and sufferings back in 1954-55: a positive, affirmative, constructive response that – to an extent that I'm sure he never even faintly imagined at the time – did 'change a burden into a blessing, a trial into a triumph'.

I think the spirit of endurance and affirmation can be overdone sometimes, and in particular I am thinking of an incident about Bobby as related by Kenneth O'Donnell, sometime classmate and ever afterwards close friend of Bobby's, and later a campaign assistant to Jack and his Appointments Secretary in the White House. Since this has to do with football, I should mention that, as a senior, he was Harvard's football captain. In Pat's book about Bobby, *That Shining Hour*, Kenny O'Donnell recalled that when Bobby came back to Harvard in the fall of 1946, after serving as an enlisted man in the Navy:

> By this time, the GI Bill allowed even the poorest of boys to seek an education in our best universities and Harvard was overflowing with the finest collection of athletes . . . with transfers from all over the United States – most of the boys had played some one or two years at Notre Dame, Wisconsin, etc. Because of Bobby's size, the coach exhibited very little interest in him, and consigned him to sixth or seventh squad. By the middle of fall he had been promoted to the Varsity. By the end of the season, Robert Kennedy was a member of the Varsity Club, admired and respected. In 1947 he started the opener against Western Maryland. We defeated Western Maryland 47 to 0, and Bobby caught his first and only touchdown pass of his collegiate career. A week later we were scrimmaging and he and I were playing side by side, missing block after block. The coach was raging at me, and I was raging at number 86. After nearly half an hour, Bob collapsed on the field. He had been playing with a broken leg all that time . . .

That, needless for me to say, was over and beyond the courage and fortitude that Joe and I wanted to instil. Even so, it had an ultimate and unexpected reward for Bobby, for as Kenny goes on to say, even though that 'ended his football career, he did play briefly in the Yale game to earn his letter', which is the Harvard player's dream, and which I suppose was the coach's way of recognizing and rewarding Bobby's extreme bravery and dedication.

In training them for excellence, Joe and I always worked towards the same goals, although not necessarily in quite the same ways. Nor even the same times. Eunice remembers:

> It was not one of those things where the father commutes and goes away in the morning and comes home at night. He was away a lot. When he was there, it was his personality that dominated. Our

mother was articulate about everything but more so when he wasn't there – when he was home she let him sort of take over. By the time I got to know my father really well it was later, because he was around so much more when I was eighteen or nineteen. By that time we older ones were all trained. He made it possible for us to do things but I think the terrific drive – for me – came much more from my mother. That more so for the girls than for the boys, because he took charge more of the boys, but she was the one who was there. And she could be quite stern. She knew there were certain ways to behave. It wasn't a great emotional thing with her, as it is with some mothers, she was more a teacher and an inspirer. She was interested in whatever you were doing, reading or taking skating lessons. I remember she would take us ice-skating in Bronxville, and you just wouldn't go skating off into the blue yonder: she'd say use your right leg or use your left leg better; again it was this terrific drive, she wanted everyone to do their best. There was quite a little pressure around. If you weren't doing very well there weren't any excuses for it. She'd say, you just get along there, don't be stupid about it, or something like that. Never, Oh, you poor thing, you may not feel well today. She wouldn't excuse you. Oh, you can't do Latin well and that's too bad so drop Latin and take another subject – no, you go in there and you learn Latin, and she made sure you did. She would do homework with me, and if I couldn't do it right she'd get cross and say you just learn this and you sit there and learn that verb.

And she was always very energetic and expected us to be. Today, children stay in and watch television or listen to radio or records, but we were packed up and out we'd go, no matter what the weather was. On the porch, or sled-riding or ice-skating, or playing tennis – she played tennis with all of us. I suppose if we were really sick we stayed in, but so far as I can remember the first time in my life I ever stayed indoors was when I was in my thirties and had a baby and had to stay in. And I walked around in the hospital and thought, How odd, some people stay in and read all day . . .

This may make her sound like she was sort of an ogress, but actually none of us felt that way in the least. We always understood she wasn't doing any of these things for her sake but for our sakes. You felt that she felt you had more in you than you thought. She always assumed you did. She was a great believer in opening up many opportunities for us. Some of the things were difficult, but she'd say, well, you ought to try them. Such as taking trips on our own while we were young. And encouraging my father to let us go. At first he might say an idea we had for some trip was no good, but

she'd talk him into it. I can remember that very well when I was
sixteen and my sister Rosemary and I wanted to go to Switzerland.
Dad's first reaction was no, it was too risky. We went, and there were
no problems. Mother believed we could do it and believed young
people ought to be exposed to lots of experiences.

In any case, something seems to have had a lasting effect on Eunice
because I have known few people in the world to match her for initiative and energy and drive. I was looking over her schedule during
the 1972 election when she was out helping Sarge[1] in his campaign
for the Vice-Presidency. On one typical day she flew from New York
City to Utica, NY, met and talked with county Democratic leaders,
addressed an assembly at a local high school, took part in a rally at the
State Office Building with Democratic officials and candidates, attended
and spoke at a big fund-raising luncheon, spent an hour at a Day
Centre for Senior Citizens, was interviewed on a radio show, took part
in a television panel show, flew back to New York and was there in
time for dinner and an evening of other activities. In three months,
either on her own or with Sarge, she travelled thousands of miles,
attended several hundred meetings, rallies, political breakfasts,
luncheons and dinners, gave innumerable talks or 'remarks', gave
dozens of interviews on radio and television, visited scores of schools
and centres and other institutions, and was introduced to and shook
hands with thousands of people. Meanwhile she was also attending to
various important projects and duties that are part of her normal life,
and also, and by no means incidentally, attending to the health and
welfare of Sarge and their five energetic children and to the operations
of a large house and staff in Maryland. She thinks I have a lot of energy,
but she amazes me.

Jack once remarked of me that I was 'the glue that held the family
together'. I'm not so sure I like the metaphor, but the sentiment is all
right. Bobby once wrote that I 'was the stabilizing influence, performing all the functions that a mother can for children'. Pat has said she
remembers a lot of 'care and interest' and that I was 'very solicitous
and kept up with whether one was doing well or not'; adding that, as
for my praising her, 'Well, she must have, though that's not one of my
strong memories.' Eunice, writing in a sentimental mood, remarked
on 'Mother's compassion, and ever present, ever constant love and

[1] Robert Sargent Shriver

example of goodness and faith'. Teddy, in an interview about me, spoke of 'gentleness and understanding, and support and encouragement that made the high family standards liveable and perhaps reachable'.

I am indulging in these quotations, making a little mosaic of them, because together they may help illuminate a question that naturally could come to people's minds after what has been said about our aim to bring out the best in each of our children. It is true, as Eunice put it, that in this sense 'There was quite a little pressure around.' But Rosemary was a retarded child.

People who have read the preceding pages may well wonder how she fitted into the scenes that have been described, and about her personal relationships with her brothers and sisters, and the ways in which Joe and I adapted our aims to her needs.

I'm sure it will be understood this is not an easy matter for me to write about, but I will do my best, while also drawing on the memories of others in the family circle.

After Joe Jr and Jack it was of course a special joy for Joe and me when our third child was a girl, a daughter for us and little sister for them. She was a very pretty baby and she was sweet and peaceable and cried less than the first two had, which at the time I supposed was part of her being a girl. I delighted in her. And because the nursemaid was so busy with the two boys, still very young and needing a lot of attention, I took care of her most of the time myself. Physically she was very healthy, and there were no signs I recognized that anything might be wrong. She crawled, stood, took her first steps, said her first words late, she had problems managing a baby spoon and porringer – and yet, as everyone knows, babies always have their own individual rates of growth and of acquiring skills, so I was patient, concerned, beginning to be a little apprehensive, but not worried, partly, I suppose, because of wishful thinking. Then it became apparent that Rosemary was born a retarded child. No one knows why – there are only hypotheses. Eunice, though several years younger, even in childhood, was particularly good and attentive and helpful with her, encouraging her to do her best; and later on, because of this loving and unremitting interest in her older sister, she became a lay-expert in the field of mental retardation and is director of the foundation our family has created to study the root causes of this misfortune that afflicts so many children – so many more, we now realize, than anyone knew in the dark era when retardation was considered somehow a disgrace to a family. Eunice says: 'Probably it happened – we think – because the doctor was delayed some place and was late getting to the delivery; and the nurse, not knowing what to do, didn't let the baby arrive; and that went on for nearly two hours. But we're not sure, nobody knows.'

She was a pretty baby girl, and it was only slowly, as she grew to be a toddler and beyond, that I began to realize she might be handicapped. She was slow in everything, and some things she seemed unable to learn how to do, or do well or with consistency. When she was old enough for childish sports I noticed, for instance, that she couldn't steer her sled. When she was old enough to learn a little reading and writing the letters and words were extremely difficult for her; and instead of writing from left to right on a page she wrote in the opposite direction. She went to kindergarten and first grade at the usual ages for those, but her lack of coordination was apparent and as time went on I realized she could not keep up with the work. In the Brookline school system intelligence tests were given to all the children very early. I was informed that Rosemary's IQ was low, but that was about all the concrete information I received, and it didn't help much. This was in the early 1920s, the tests were still quite new and unrefined, and neither those who created them nor those who used them could say, really, how accurate they were or what the scores meant except in a general way. Joe and I looked for experts in mental deficiency, at Harvard as well as in hospitals, and I talked with some of them. They were not very helpful. They could venture certain theories to account for her condition – 'genetic accident', 'uterine accident', 'birth accident', and so forth – but when I would ask, 'What can I do to help her?' there didn't seem to be much of an answer. I was frustrated and heart-broken.

If science had no answer, it was up to us to find our own as best we could. Love her, accept her, encourage her, help her along in every way we could.

There were a few private schools in those days that offered living facilities and care and training for children with neurological defects, and it was suggested we put Rosemary in one of those. Much as I had begun to realize how very difficult it might be to keep her at home, everything about me – and my feelings for her – rebelled against that idea, and I rejected it except as a last resort. In the inevitable atmosphere of such a place, living in a population of neurologically maimed children, gaited to their pace, she would soon understand and feel deeply her difference from her brothers and sisters, and that might remove the incentive for her even to try her best to learn. I decided that care, understanding and encouragement, and enough special attention and tutoring and coaching, would be the way to bring out the best in her and develop her capacities to their fullest, whatever they turned out to be. Eunice has written:

> My mother had carried the main responsibility for Rosemary – taking her to doctors, educators and psychologists. My father supported her, but he was much more emotional and was easily upset by Rosemary's lack of progress, her inabilities to use opportunities for self-development.
>
> His belief in family loyalty, however, was again an influence. When psychologists recommended that Rosemary be placed in an institution he said, 'What can they do in an institution that we can't do better for her at home – here with her family?' So my sister stayed at home. He believed that Rosemary should have every opportunity that the rest of us had, even though she could not make the most of such opportunities.

This did, of course, involve a good deal of time. The less progress Rosemary seemed to make, the more time I would spend trying to bring her along – time that had to be subtracted from that spent with the other children. Kathleen, the next down the family line, was such a beautiful, lively, outgoing child and girl that I became convinced she never felt at all neglected. I was less sure about Jack. He was the next eldest, and as I have said he was rather sickly and therefore needed attention: perhaps more of it than in my worry and distraction about Rosemary I gave him. In the later years I sometimes wondered if he had felt neglected by me. Not long ago I asked Jackie if he had ever mentioned this to her. She assured me he hadn't, nor had indicated it in any way. But the thought still bothers me a bit that he may have felt neglected when he was a little boy, and only realized later on why I spent so much time with Rosemary.

Joe and I, knowing we wanted her to be brought up and treated in the most normal way possible, steeled ourselves as best we could and did not indicate either within the family (except as necessary, and then casually and indirectly) or outside that there was anything extraordinary about her. I think there were only very few outside the family circle to whom she seemed noticeably 'different' from the others in our family, or other children. Mary O'Connell Ryan, one of the dearest and closest friends during the Brookline years, and a dear friend still, who has been quoted here earlier, recalls:

> I had small children of my own and loved to sew and design clothes for them, so I opened a children's shop and Rose was one of my first customers and was a steady one until the family moved from

Brookline down to New York. She would bring her children in – four or five of them then – all beautiful children, and Rose didn't treat any of them differently from the others. She kept all of them on the mark. Oh, yes, always right on the mark! But she never showed the slightest difference with her affection and attention. I remember Rosemary as a little shy, but nothing was made of it at all. There is a mutual friend of ours, Miriam Finnegan – she was with Rose as a schoolmate at the Blumenthal convent in Holland, and later one of our charter members when Rose founded our 'Ace of Clubs' – and of course she saw Rose and her family from time to time, and she noticed that Rosemary seemed a rather shy little girl. Miriam, I remember, mentioned this to me and said: 'I think there's so much made of Kathleen' – that's 'Kick' as they called her later, and there was a lot made of her, for good reasons, she was so vibrant and alive and everything – 'that Rosemary is a little conscious of that and feels a little bit in the background.'

So that's the way it was, nothing to indicate that Rosemary had any special problem, because I'm sure lots of little girls could feel inhibited by an especially beautiful baby sister. And on Rose's part, nothing, nothing at all. Nothing was ever said even to very close friends. No one outside that family – except, I suppose, some doctors – knew or suspected that Rosemary's condition was that unusual. I didn't know anything about it for all those years, not until 1960, when Joe gave an interview explaining she had been a retarded child. That was when Jack was running for the Presidency and I suppose there were rumours around and the family decided to quell them by putting the cards face-up on the table.

I felt that if she could acquire enough of the basic skills in reading, writing and arithmetic, a little history and geography, and sports and dancing, at least well enough to participate and enjoy them, she would manage to be happy. If she was attractive and well groomed and well mannered she would be able to have a reasonably satisfying life. With special attention, which we arranged at the schools she attended, and private tutoring at home and many special lessons, and great effort on her part, she did achieve reasonable performances in all these matters. Yet success bred its own problems from time to time. Since we treated her in every possible way as if she were normal she couldn't understand why, for instance, she couldn't take a row-boat out alone in the harbour the way other children did. In fact, she couldn't manage the oars. She resented having someone always go with her to the station when she took the train to her school. Because, she said, other girls went to the station alone. Sometimes she would run away from the person accompanying her.

The other children in the family must have realized that she was rather different from them and from children of her age group, but Joe and I tried hard to minimize this. They were merely told that Rosemary was 'a little slow' and that they should help her and encourage her. When she did something well, tell her so. If she made a joke, laugh with her, don't give her a quick retort. If she has on a pretty new hair-ribbon or blouse say something about that; but don't talk about her lack of tennis skills. If there is some activity going on, let her participate, invite her to be involved. All of them were very understanding and cooperative. Eunice was particularly good with Rosemary. Eunice is three years younger, but she became very close to Rosemary and gave her companionship and all sorts of encouragement. She recalls:

> Rosemary was never hidden away or anything, she was pushed right on with the rest of us. Even though she was slow she was always given every opportunity that everybody was given. As I said, we took a trip all over Switzerland together; I was sixteen, so she was nineteen. There was no tension in the family about her, and she didn't cause scenes. There was never any bursting into tears or running to her room. She laughed and she was always rather jolly. We all had the feeling she was just a little slow, so jolly Rosemary along. But my mother spent a lot of time with her, a lot of effort and concern. If you were going down the hall on the way to swimming she'd call out to ask, Will you take Rosemary? And she would say to me, Will you play tennis with Rosemary? She wasn't very good, Rosemary, but I played tennis with her. Or she would say, Will you take her sailing, racing? I was quite good at racing in those days and I could handle a boat all right by myself, so I'd take Rosemary. Then I'd tell my mother she had done well on the boat, and Mother was pleased – it meant a lot to her. But the situation never depressed her. Then also the boys were always very good with her. Like Jack would take her to a dance at the club, and would dance with her and kid with her and would make sure a few of his close pals cut in, so she felt popular. He'd bring her home at midnight. Then he'd go back to the dance.

I'm sure that the children who were old enough to sense the need (Teddy, so many years younger, says he thought of her as 'just a very sweet much older big sister'), and those such as Agnes and the Moores and others who were in the inner family circle and thus knew or sensed the problem, always did things to help her along without mentioning or even thinking much about them at the time. It was a conspiracy of kindness.

About this time I changed my handwriting. I was brought up to write 'a fine Spencerian hand' with all the letters of a word gracefully flowing and connected one to another. It was called The Palmer Method. Yet, because of Rosemary's neurological problems in recognizing written letters of the alphabet and being able to reproduce them with a pen or pencil, or to read them, she was taught to use the printed forms: thus the words in a book would look like those words as she would write them and so they would be easier for her to read. When she was old enough to receive postcards or little notes from me when I was away, I took up this same method so she could read my messages and so that she wouldn't think my way of writing was different from hers. It became a habit with me and my writing has ever since been more printed than written. Of course, much later on, this form of 'cursive' handwriting came into fashion and millions of people use it today.

Rosemary was an affectionate, warmly responsive and loving child. She was so willing to try to do her best, so appreciative of attention and compliments and so hopeful of deserving them. I have been looking through letters from and to and about her, and perhaps a few passages from these may tell a good deal:

October 1934, from the Sacred Heart Convent at Providence, R.I., where she spent that school year of '34–'35, when she was sixteen, and where Joe had visited her.

> Dear Daddy
> I had a lovely time on Saturday.
> Thank you ever so much
> for coming down to see me.
> Sunday I also had good
> time.
> I would do anything
> to make you so happy.
> I hate to disapoint
> you in anyway . . .

That same year, in a letter to Joe and me. Examination time; and she wrote,

> Pray very hard that I will get some-
> place, I tried as hard as I could.

A letter to us in the winter of 1936, when she was seventeen:

> . . . Thursday, I went to Girl Scouts.
> I am taking Nature up. Sunday, Joe
> and Jack, and I, Grandma, Grandpa,
> went to Aunt Agnus for lunch, then
> Jack took Grampa, Grandma, and I to
> St Joseph Cermtory. Also Grandma
> took me to the movies. Jack is taken
> me to the next dance. He is going to
> take me in his new car . . . I gave Jack
> 1 $ he diddn't ask for it either. 2 cents
> I paid for his papper . . . thanks loads
> for calling me up. I miss you so
> much. I try to keep my spirit up all
> the time. Lots of love kisses your
> darling daughter

She adored her father, and he was wonderful with her: joking with her, congratulating her warmly for achievements, chiding her forthrightly – as with all the others – for unseemly behaviour or carelessness about her personal appearance. She tended to become overweight, for instance, so Joe gave her a kind but firm talking-to about watching her diet and getting exercise – for these were things that lay within her own competence to do for herself. After war broke out in September 1939, Joe, while of course staying at his Ambassadorial post in London, sent the family home, except for Rosemary. We had her in a small school deep in the Hertfordshire countryside, safely remote from any military target, and she had made such exceptional progress we decided to leave her there for another term. Joe was especially attentive to her during that time, supervising everything from her studies to her pocket money and dental care, and writing to her often and visiting the school. Which accounts for the following correspondence (she was twenty-one):

Joe to Miss Gibbs, a headmistress and also Rosemary's special tutor-companion:

I was more than pleased to see Rosemary Sunday. She was looking very well and seemed to be in excellent humour. I do feel that she is getting altogether too fat and I told her so in no uncertain words. So I wish, if you could, you would try to build up the idea that she should lose weight. I told her that her mother would be very disappointed and also that I could not have her picture taken for

America if she remains as stout as she is. Both these arguments seemed to make some impression. It really makes me very happy to see the great improvement she has shown and I can never thank you and Mother Isabel enough . . .

Miss Gibbs to Joe:

You *must* have made a big impression on Sunday – because when she was showing a new lot of snapshots today she remarked, 'Yes, my figure does look fat, doesn't it?' Thereupon she said, 'What do you suggest I can do about it?' So we can proceed peacefully, and we will.

Rosemary to her father:

Many, many thanks for coming to see me. You were darling. I hope you liked everything here . . . Mother says I am such a comfort to you never to leave you. Well Daddy, I feel honour because you chose me to stay. And the other suppose are wild . . . PS, I am so fond of you. And love you very much. Sorry, to think that I am fat you think.

She came to the US the next spring, 1940, and in her first letter to her father included the proud news that:

The Saks men wanted to hear about my trip. And he things I am the best looking of the Kennedys.

Her following letter was to tell him she had a job as a Junior Counsellor at a summer camp for girls, and was teaching Arts and Crafts to the younger girls. 'Another girl, Alice Hill, has the bigger girls. So the two of us run it. They were looking for somebody else to teach it. And they have me now. Mother went to talk to the Sullovans girls about it and Judge Sullovans' daughters run it. But isn't it interesting abt me being a Junior Counsellar the first year.'

Joe wrote to her:

I couldn't have been more surprised to hear you had gone up to camp as a junior counsellor. It looks to me like all the rest of the Kennedys are still going to school, including the boys, while my eldest daughter is out working. Good for you!

We go occasionally to Windsor [where we had a country house] when it is a nice weekend, but I am living regularly at the Embassy. There are so many things to be done in the office all the time. I certainly miss those weekends with Eddie, Mary and you and we haven't had any good laughs since you left.

Incidentally, I have gained four or five pounds myself and am starting on a diet right now. I guess while you were here I was so busy trying to keep you thin, I didn't have a chance to eat and have been making up for lost time.

Give my love to all and keep right on working and setting a good example for your brothers and sisters.

Joe always made it possible for me to have a nursemaid or governess to help caring for the children. There were several during the years, wonderful young women who really became part of the family and were trusted by us and loved by the children. None was more efficient or delightful than Elizabeth Dunn (later Mrs Anderson) who came to us at Hyannis Port in the summer of 1936. I asked her for some recollections for this book:

One of the first things I remember on arriving at your home was the regular noontime swims with you and Mr Kennedy and all the children down at Taggart's pier. The children all looked forward to being with you and displaying their swimming and diving ability and how they improved. It was great fun when you and Mr Kennedy would form a big circle with the other children and then Teddy, Jean and Bobby would swim first to the one nearest them and gradually work up to the one farthest away. Of course the first summer Ted could only do the dog-paddle from you to Mr Kennedy, or from me to one of the older children who was closest, but you always made him and Jean as much a part of the group and games and fun as the others. They had no fear of the water and when it was time for you and the older ones to have your swim, he and Jean would put their arms around my neck and one of the older ones and we'd swim back to the pier steps where they were very content to dog-paddle and watch the rest of you play ball or have water fights.

They all had the same colour bathing hats so you could identify them in the water.

The children all ate together with the whole family and any guest who might be present, which enabled them to meet many dignitaries and benefit from grown-up discussions of world affairs. This aroused their curiosities and interests and made them more conscious of what was going on around them than the average youngster. It also awakened their interest in history.

After lunch they were all required to have a rest and be quiet for a while – when they couldn't sleep, they were allowed to read quietly.

You used to read to them a great deal, and they looked forward to you telling them stories of when you were in school, growing up, and going on different trips with your father when he was in politics, and particularly loved hearing you tell of Sir Thomas Lipton and his boat.

I also remember that you used to encourage them to play with their puzzles and you would work on them, with them, often at the Cape.

In the evening after dinner at the Cape, the children looked forward to your playing the piano for them and they loved singing some of the old songs, as well as the new ones you'd teach them. It was fun time for them and they had much fun with the musical games.

They all wore navy coat sweaters with nametags inside to identify them. Each spring the girls all had navy dress coats, navy shoes and purses and white gloves. They weren't too clothes conscious – just always wanted to look well – and didn't borrow one another's clothes too much, mostly sweaters.

During school time, it was a bit of a ritual after breakfast to check children's nails and spots on uniforms and sweaters.

Faith in God and His wisdom and mercy and goodness and in the teachings of the Church had been instilled in me from my earliest years. One of my nephews became a priest. A niece, Ann Gargan, youngest of Agnes's children, was training to be a nun when illness forced her to leave that vocation. So religion was 'in the family'.

I didn't think of myself as being particularly 'religious'. One of the strange stories that was printed about me much later was that at Blumenthal convent I used to spend an hour at a time at Confession. Another was that after I was home again I moved to the attic to 'mortify' my flesh and spirit. This is nonsense. You already know from the Blumenthal letters I was a lively young lady who chafed more than a bit under convent restrictions and found some of the ceremonials rather tiresome. I'm sure I never had a 'holier than thou' attitude because it would never have occurred to me that I was any 'holier' than anybody I knew. I was just an ordinary, staunch, believing Irish Roman Catholic.

This also meant that my Faith and my Church had great importance for me; that I realized their values; and that when I had children of my own I wanted to pass those beliefs and values on to them as they had been passed to me.

Rosemary's misfortune did not incline me in the least towards doubt; but rather, if anything, strengthened my belief, and sheltered my spirit

The London Embassy

9 *Above* Kathleen, Rosemary and I were presented at Court

Below Joe with Jack and Joe Jr

The London Embassy

10 Joe with (*above*) George Bernard
Shaw; Lord Halifax
Left Mrs Churchill

ack and Bobby on the balcony of
ne Embassy

Teddy waiting to photograph us as
we leave Buckingham Palace

Wartime England

12 *Above* Joe watching air drills near Windsor Castle with Princess Helena (daughter of Queen Victoria) and Prime Minister Neville Chamberlain

Kathleen in American Red Cross uniform auctioning a sheep in aid of the Red Cross

Below Joe talking to rescue workers during the London Blitz in despair. I asked myself endlessly why this had to happen to her. I felt it was so unfair for her to have so many handicaps and the others to be so blessed. The more I thought, the more clear it became to me that God in his infinite wisdom did have a reason, though it was hidden from me, and that in time, in some way, it would be unfolded to me. 'God wants something different from each of us.'

Religion was never oppressive nor even conspicuous in our household, but it was always there, part of our lives, and the Church's teachings and customs were observed. We went to Mass on Sundays, Holy Days, First Fridays. We said Grace before meals. I would choose a different child each time to say the Grace. At Sunday dinner after the Mass, we generally had a little discussion of what the sermon had been about, what the Gospel message meant, so the children would pay attention during Mass. If it was a Holy Day or a favourite Saint's Day, we discussed its meaning and asked what the Saint's life could teach us. At Easter, of course, we asked the meaning of the Resurrection and Life Everlasting. Why did Jesus accept crucifixion and suffer and die for us? What was He doing for us, and by His example telling all of us? Faith, I would tell them, is a great gift from God and is a living gift, to sustain us in our lives on earth, to guide us in our activities, to be a source of solace and comfort, so we should do everything we can to strengthen its roots, to nourish it, and to help it grow and flourish, and try never to lose it. Many of the institutions of the Church are meant to help us in this way, and of course do. Catechism: I would hear them recite their lessons every week before Sunday School. I also encouraged the idea – in youth and adulthood – of making a yearly Retreat, spending a weekend or fortnight away from the world in a quiet, wholly religious environment of devotion, instruction and contemplation.

When they were little they accepted their religious training with few questions; the normal, innocent, curious questions. As they grew older, towards and into adulthood, they responded and questioned or accepted in their individual ways.

Dave Powers, a close friend and political associate of our family for many years, Boston Irish Catholic born and bred, has a story about Teddy:

This is at Hyannis Port and Mr Kennedy and I and young Ted – he's a big, strong, very healthy boy or youth of maybe sixteen, anyway old enough to be driving – are having breakfast together that morning and Ted is telling his father about the weekend he's got planned for sailing and racing. They're sailing up to Edgartown from the Port, and he's talking about the crew and how they're going to race. Just then his mother – who had just returned from Mass and Holy Communion – walked into the room and when the discussion had slowed a bit she said, 'Ted, I made arrangements for you to attend Retreat up at Lawrence.'

And I looked at him, thinking what I might have said to my own mother in a situation like that. He said, 'Yes, Mother, I'll be ready to go.'

And then she went upstairs to change. His father, realizing how Ted must have felt after all those plans and all that, said, 'Ted, you can drive my new car up to the Retreat.' Ted thanked him, and a minute or two later he left the room.

His father was gazing at him as he went. And then Joseph P. Kennedy turned to me and said, 'Dave,' he said – and those blue eyes were a little misty – 'Dave, you know, he's a good boy.'

I wanted all the children to have at least a few years in good Catholic schools, where along with excellent secular education they would receive thorough instruction in the doctrines of their religion and intelligent answers to any doubts or perplexities. A child thus educated, I maintained, would have more poise, more peace of mind, more confidence about settling the problems of everyday living, and a better concept of his duties towards his God, his neighbour, and himself. This was one of the very few instances in which Joe and I were in disagreement. He said that a child learned faith and morals at home, and that with a religious atmosphere, instruction and reassurance, that's all that was needed. And he said that for the boys in particular, when they grew up, they would be dealing with people of all faiths or none, and he wanted them to meet all men on their merits without consciousness of religious factors which were matters of personal belief. As a consequence, all the girls did have some years at convent school, but the boys were educated almost entirely at secular schools: Joe Jr, in fact, entirely; Jack, part of a year at a Catholic prep school; Bobby had a year or two at Portsmouth Priory, and Teddy had a term there when he was very young.

Yet, in retrospect, it's clear I needn't have worried. The boys as well as the girls seemed to have deep religious convictions, though as usual each manifested them in his or her own individual way. Eunice says:

I don't remember any of my grandparents or aunts or uncles being intellectually or emotionally super-devout. Mother was, always was within my memory, and where it came from I don't know. Of course I was fifth in the family, so by the time I was old enough to understand anything a lot had already happened and obviously I wouldn't know. I do have clear impressions later, and I remember we were doing all the First Fridays and all that and Joe Jr was quite serious about it. He was in the St Paul Catholic Club at Harvard and later on, when he was training for naval aviation at Jacksonville, he was head of the Catholic club there. Bobby was really quite religious. He was at Communion on Sundays all the time. He was very strong on this.

Pat says:

I remember Bobby wanting to be an altar boy, that would be at St Joseph's Church when we lived in Bronxville. I suppose they all were altar boys, but he was next youngest to me and for some years there he was the little brother, so I was conscious of this ambition and how much he worked at it. My room was between his and Mother's. I used to go into his room to hear his Latin. Then Mother would come in, or he'd go into her room, so he could show her how much he'd learned. He worked hard at it.

We always had a rosary on our beds; and then, of course, she'd hear our bedtime prayers and do our Catechism with us every week for Sunday School. But I don't recall any abnormal pressure at all.

I felt that each should have at least one summer at a 'summer camp' away from the seashore, so they would know about camping and life in the fields and forests. I must add in all candour that by the time Pat and Bobby, the sixth and seventh, came along the idea had begun to seem even better to me, since it meant I would have one or two fewer children to struggle with during the summer. However, this turned out to be one of my least successful ventures in child-rearing. Most of the older ones went, as I recall, for short times but didn't really care for the experience at all and said loudly and clearly they would rather have been at home with the family at Hyannis Port. With Pat and Bobby my plan led nearly to disaster. The summer when he was twelve and she was barely fourteen, both went to camp and both became dangerously ill: she with acute appendicitis and emergency operation. She was joined at the same hospital a day or two later by Bobby, another emergency case, with pneumonia. Neither knew the other was there. Pat says:

They told me at the hospital that there was a little boy down the hall who really liked Cokes and comics and things but they didn't say who it was – they thought I'd be so upset. I think we traded a few comic books and sent a few oral messages back and forth, but it was days before we realized we were doing this with each other.

It was in this ordeal – and needless to say, Joe and I were terribly upset and worried – that we had the great good fortune to meet and know Luella Hennessey. She was a special nurse at the hospital and was put in charge of Pat's case; and, knowing her brother was down the hall, she was in and out to see him too. It was she who delivered the messages and comic books and I think she also broke the news to them about each other. In any case both children became extremely fond of her, with the result that she became an integral part of our family life. I now have twenty-eight grandchildren and she has been on hand to take care of twenty-seven of them from birth. (As it happens, the exception was Pat's own firstborn, Christopher Lawford: he came a few days early, and I was visiting the Lawfords at that time, so I took charge and took care of him.) Luella wrote in Pat's book about Bobby:

I suspect that Bobby and Pat connived to have me to go Hyannis Port with them; and then later to England with the family at the time their father was Ambassador to Great Britain. Thus, it may very well be that these two young people conspired to alter the course of my life . . .

Even at twelve, Bobby was 'people-minded'. People interested him, and the problems and troubles of people concerned him deeply. Not only were his eyes quick to see, but his heart and mind were prompt to follow thought.

At the Brompton Oratory [our church and parish house in London] Bobby noticed that each priest had to supply fuel for the fireplace in his room. He also observed that when his priest-friend was short of funds, he was also short of fuel! He spoke to his father about this predicament, and Mr Kennedy arranged for a year's supply of wood to be sent in. This deep love for people made me think that perhaps Bobby would be the Kennedy who would one day enter a seminary and follow the religious life. But it was not to be so; his was a lay apostolate.

And what about Jack, who was destined to be the first Catholic President of the United States? Eunice goes on to say:

He tended to be casual about religious rituals and observances as in a lot of other things. I personally felt so strongly about them that when I was at college at Manhattanville I used to call him up, and he must have thought I was crazy – here I was, nineteen years of age, and calling and asking him why he wasn't going to church on First Fridays. But he went to Sunday Mass. I lived with him a long time while he was a Congressman in Washington, and he always hustled off to Mass. People who were with him on his campaigns and travels say he always did, wherever he was. With his inquiring mind I think he was always a little less convinced about some things than the rest of us. But that didn't make him less truly religious. He prayed. Lem Billings, his room-mate through prep school, has said: 'Never can I remember Jack not saying his prayers on his knees every night before going to bed.' And this lasted right on through. One night when Dad was visiting at the White House, it was late and he started into Jack's bedroom to mention something he had just thought of. Then he stopped short and left without being noticed – because there was the President kneeling by his bed, saying his prayers.

So the training Mother put us through, and her own unquestioning strong belief, made an impression that lasted. She was successful in instilling firm faith in all her children.

I always felt the children should have as much continuity as possible in their educations. At best, changing schools is unsettling; moreover, since curricula and text-books are not standardized from one school and locality to another, as they are, for example, in the Soviet Union, a transferring student may find himself at a serious academic dis-advantage. It was for that reason I stayed on in Brookline with the children a couple of years after Joe's first big venture in the movie business obliged him to spend his work-weeks in New York City. Only when he was certain this business was solidly successful and would be taking most of his time in the foreseeable future did I consent to move from our Boston suburb to a New York suburb, with the proviso that it be a place with excellent schools, preferably within walking distance of home. Walking to and from school is healthful exercise; it is fun in good weather and teaches perseverance and acceptance of discomforts when the weather is bad. It teaches punctuality and respon-sibility by making the child accountable for lagging and tardiness; and in the coming and going he becomes acquainted easily with all the children of different ages living in his neighbourhood. Eddie Moore was put in charge of the problem and produced a good temporary solution in a large and handsomely furnished house, formerly the home of Chief Justice Charles Evans Hughes, in Riverdale, on the Hudson, a small, quiet, pleasant community that lies just north of the city and has an excellent Country Day school for boys and girls. We lived there two years. Meanwhile Eddie kept on looking and found a rather ideal spot and situation for us a few miles farther north. This was Bronxville, a very attractive village of only a few thousand people whose average per capita income, however, was among the highest in the country, so they supported an outstandingly good public school system. There was also a private school for girls, and a private kindergarten. Yet the village was only a mile square, which put the schools and churches and everything else within walking distance.

We bought a big house set in six acres of grounds: a property well scaled to the needs of our increasingly large and energetic family. Joe Jr and Jack continued at Riverdale, riding the school's bus that made the rounds of the area; they had adjusted to the school and were doing well and we didn't want to uproot them so soon again, especially since they were old enough (fourteen and twelve) and obstreperous enough for us to foresee we would be sending them off to boarding-school. All the others, including Jean and Teddy when they came along, had a portion of their schooling in the Bronxville public schools, which remained our home and main base of operations for nearly thirteen years.

We debated whether the children should stay at home and go to day school until ready for college, or at some point in their teens go off to boarding-school. If the latter, which school? At what age?

Joe and I had agreed that the responsibility for education of the boys was primarily his, and that of the girls primarily mine. My conclusions were easier to reach.

I sent Kathleen off to Sacred Heart at Noroton when she was thirteen. She was quite pretty and was getting altogether too popular with boys, which she enjoyed. She was on the telephone with them for hours at a time and was being distracted from her schoolwork and other duties by boys taking her to the Saturday afternoon movies and so forth. My answer to the situation was to send her away to school.

Eunice never liked this story because, she said, it made her seem like a wallflower by comparison. Otherwise we would have sent her away too at thirteen, instead of letting her stay on in Bronxville several years more.

As usual, things did not always work out according to my ideas and plans. In writing this book, I have learned many things I may have suspected but never fully understood till now. Recently Pat was talking about life in Bronxville and her school days:

That was my first home, at least the first I have any real memories of, because we moved there when I was five and stayed until I was seventeen or eighteen. We had very, very happy times there. Particularly on weekends when Jack and Joe would come down from their schools for weekends, usually with some friends along. We had a big lawn. The boys would be playing football or kickball or something, and they would always let us join in. There would be five or six big boys and a small mob of younger children because each of us probably would have a friend or two over too. Joe and Jack were terrific with us and of course we thought they were marvellous. To us they were heroes, young gods. Part of Mother's general idea of having the older children bringing the younger ones along, in the best possible way. Then all of us, and the school friends, would be together, with Mother and Daddy, for a big Sunday lunch, which was a very happy time. A very happy house.

We always had dogs – I remember especially a wirehaired terrier named Skippy. We'd skate on the ponds and go sledding and tobogganing, because there were a lot of hills and open spaces. I liked that town. Even the tradespeople were especially nice. There was a drugstore, Bellis's, on a corner just up from the public school, and it had a great soda fountain, so that's where the kids congregated at noontime and after. It also had great gum and Life Savers, and the trick was to get in there and steal the gum and Life Savers without being caught. The owner knew what was happening and kept a sharp eye on all of us. But I guess he charged up a few gum and mint losses to normal cost of doing business in a place like that full of kids. Anyway, he never turned any of us in to our parents, which was kind of him, because they would have been very upset, my Mother especially. I liked the school, the people, my friends, the whole scene. So when the family came back from England in 1939 I was returning to a place I was happy to be.

But then a question about schools. I was fifteen and a half and would be going into my last two years of high school. Kick and Eunice had both been to Sacred Heart at Noroton and Mother felt it was time for me to go too, and graduate from there. But from being away in England – some different subjects there and taught in different ways from those at home – she thought I might possibly have to repeat a year back here, stay back a year to catch up before going into junior year. And if that happened I would stay home during that time and go to day school. But the only way to know would be for me to go up to Noroton and take the exams.

So I went there and they asked me the date of the Battle of Hastings, and I said it was 1740.

They asked me about the Declaration of Independence and I said it was 1812.

They asked me to recite the Apostles' Creed and I recited the Our Father – something like that.

I came home and they called Mother up and said, 'This child really has to stay back.'

Mother then put me in a convent school at Maplehurst, which is about a fifteen-minute ride from Bronxville. Of course, within a matter of about two weeks they put me up to junior year there. But by then Mother decided it was too late to send me off to Sacred Heart at Noroton, because everything would have started and I'd be behind, so she settled for the other, which is also a very good school.

So that's how I could stay home. In fact, I never went to boarding-school until college.

I never told her what I had done.

Pat was so bright that I suspected there might be something unusual – possibly even a little fishy – to account for her poor performance on that exam. Now the truth is out.

While the children were young I always felt I could manage the boys in their little escapades and their schooling and everyday problems, but as they became teen-agers I was increasingly uncertain; and it was at this point that I was especially grateful for my husband's experience, sympathy and judgment.

Joe was a perfect father in dealing with our teen-age sons, not only because he had their love and respect but also because he took every bit of time needed, in any or all circumstances, to think about them and their needs and what was best for each of them. In the matter of schools, he decided for various well-considered reasons they should have their college preparatory years at boarding-school, and that the school should suit the boy. A big one such as Andover or Exeter would be right for a boy with a certain temperament, ability and interests; a smaller one with a different atmosphere might be much better for a boy with a different personality and interests. Joe did a lot of investigating, thinking and discussing. For a time his chief adviser was Mr Pennypacker, who had been headmaster of Boston Latin, whom he knew well, and who became Dean of Admissions at Harvard. I wanted a school nearby so that the boys could visit us on weekends. But these plans never materialized.

It was decided to send Joe Jr to Choate School, in Connecticut, and after finishing grade school at Riverdale he was enrolled there.

It was a fortunate choice. The school suited him, and clearly he suited the school. His grades were excellent. He entered enthusiastically into school activities and demonstrated qualities of leadership that brought high praise from his masters and, of course, made Joe and me very proud of him.

As Joe noted later, in the introduction to his book *As We Remember Joe*:

> At Choate he played end on the undefeated football team of his senior year, was Vice-President of the St Andrews Society, editor of the Year Book, and won the Harvard football trophy, 'awarded to that member of the Choate football squad who best combines scholarship and sportsmanship'.

He wanted to go to Harvard and was accepted there, which of course deeply pleased his father, a loyal alumnus. However, Joe and I wanted the children to have a year of study abroad. The question was, should this come after college or before? The decision for Joe Jr was before. Which country, which school? There were many consultations. Finally we had a long talk with Felix Frankfurter, the Harvard Law professor and later Supreme Court Justice, who at that time was on an exchange professorship at Cambridge University. Joe then decided to send our eldest son to the London School of Economics to study under Professor Harold Laski.

Professor Laski was one of the best-known theoreticians and leaders of British Socialism, and interpreters and scholars of Marxism in its various forms.

I must say I was rather taken aback by this choice. I asked Joe why he chose the London School of Economics rather than send Joe Jr to Oxford or Cambridge to study under some of the renowned professors at those great and famous places. After all, Joe was by that time – 1933 – quite a well-known capitalist. His answers, which puzzled me then, make perfect sense now. The US and most of the western world were in the grip of Depression, and there were many revolutionary currents and ideas – Marxist and semi-Marxist – in the political atmosphere. Roosevelt had taken office and the New Deal had barely begun. It was still unformulated and no one could be sure whether the new Administration would succeed in restoring stability and a sense of confidence in the free-enterprise system. Therefore, he wanted our son to understand the challenges he might be facing as put forth by a brilliant challenger, Professor Laski. He already had the same plan in mind for Jack. For after all, he said, 'These boys are going to have a little money when they get older, and they should know what the "have-nots" are thinking and planning.' As he said later in an interview, speaking of Professor Laski: 'I disagreed with everything he wrote . . . But I never taught the boys to disapprove of someone just because I didn't like him. They heard enough from me, and I decided they should be exposed to someone of intelligence and vitality on the other side.'

It is interesting to know what Professor Laski thought about this youth of barely nineteen, who arrived in the autumn of 1933 to attend his extremely sophisticated classes in economics.

When Jack was doing his book about Joe he asked the Professor for any comments or memories he might have about his brother. I am going to quote from those pages, beginning with Jack's own lines of introduction to them:

> When Professor Laski was asked to write about Joe, he wrote back, 'Joe is one of the most vivid memories among all the students I have had, so that I am glad, indeed, to do what you ask.' The year that Joe spent with Professor Laski was a decisive year for him, and under Professor Laski's encouragement, a career in Public Service became Joe's dominant ambition.

Professor Laski wrote:

> A large part of every teacher's life is in the students for whom he feels a special affection; and when they die, something in him, I think, dies too. Joe came to work with me at the London School of Economics and Political Science in 1933–4, for the year before he entered Harvard. He was adorably young and still more adorably unsophisticated. He went to some seven or eight lectures each week and did a weekly essay for me; and he accompanied my wife and me when I went to lecture at the University of Moscow in the summer of 1934.
>
> Three things, above all, stand out in my recollection of young Joe in that year. Above all, his astonishing vitality. He was interested in everything and only disturbed by the limitations of twenty-four hours which Nature has put on the day. And, second, there was his astonishing capacity for enthusiasm. What he liked, he liked with all his heart. He had nothing of the cynic's pose which sometimes affects the undergraduate. He gave all of himself to what he did with immense energy and eagerness. The third thing was his profound interest in politics. He had set his heart on a political career; he has often sat in my study and submitted with that smile that was pure

magic to relentless teasing about his determination to be nothing less than President of the United States.

At the stage when Joe worked with me, of course, his mind was only just beginning to discover the enchantment of thought. But his essays were written with great care, and he took criticism with a disarming friendliness. He never stopped asking questions. I had him join a seminar of mine which was intended for third-year students; and I can see now the quick shift of his attention as the argument moved from one undergraduate to another . . . He was very popular with the other students. He was so simple and so frank and so forthright. They loved to tease him about his American ways, and I think he enjoyed being teased if only because the process enabled him to affirm, with that special kind of laughter that has intense conviction behind, his love for America . . .

He never posed. He was always anxious to know. He repaid one's efforts with a fidelity of heart that was deeply moving . . . I am glad I knew Joe . . .

The combination of famous professor and young pre-college student, of London and Boston, of Jewish descent and Irish descent, of erudite scholarship and eager curiosity, of deeply compassionate interest in the welfare of humanity on both parts and mutual desire to do something to better it, was one that I think few men but my husband, in his situation and at that time in history, would have ventured – and then stepped back to see the consequences. And then, if necessary, to take his own stand with his son, defend his own beliefs in his own way. I have always felt that this was intellectual honesty and courage of the highest order.

It has been said that when Joe Jr came back from his studies with Professor Laski and that summer with the Laskis in Russia, he and his father had heated arguments about the comparative merits of capitalism and communism, that emotions became high, and that at least one time Joe Jr 'bolted from the table' and another time Joe Sr 'stalked away'. Well, all I can say is that I was there and nothing of that sort happened.

I do remember a couple of incidents within that context. Joe Jr did come home well immersed in the idea and ideals of socialism, and he did declare himself in favour, for instance, of all people sharing equally in the world's wealth. I suggested that in that case he should give up his boat and just fish off the pier or play baseball or do other things that most people do for recreation. Joe Jr objected to that vigorously: for, he said, one person giving up one boat would not make enough difference in the social objective of sharing the wealth. Joe often said, 'If I were their age I probably would believe what they believe, but I am of a different background and must voice my beliefs.'

Another time, after one of these Sr and Jr debates, I remember Jack – then around sixteen or seventeen – commenting to me, 'Joe seems to understand the situation a little better than Dad.' I mentioned this later to their father and he said:

'I don't care what the boys think about my ideas. I can always look out for myself. The important thing is that they should stick together.' That thought dominated him and them all their lives. Bob and Ted had the same philosophy. Very important.

As Jack went on to record in his book about Joe:

> The following year he entered Harvard, and his success was immediate. He played football and Rugby for four years, was a member of the Freshman Union Committee, Chairman of the Smoker Committee, on the Student Council for three years, and was Chairman his senior year. He managed the financial end of his class Year Book, was elected Chairman of his Class Day Committee, was a member of the Pi Eta, Hasty Pudding, and St Paul Catholic Clubs, and in 1938 graduated cum laude . . .
>
> Though a glance at Joe's record shows that he had great success, things did not come particularly easy for him. I think his accomplishments were due chiefly to the amazing intensity with which he applied himself to the job on hand. I do not think I can ever remember him sit back in a chair and relax. Even when still, there was always a sense of motion forcibly restrained. And yet, this continuous motion did not have its roots in restlessness or nervousness but rather came from his intense enthusiasm for everything he did and his exceptional stamina . . .

Thus, for Joe Jr, this combination – Choate, the London School of Economics and Political Science, and Harvard – evidently came close to being ideal.

In 1945, when Jack was writing these words about his brother, it was before he entered politics or had any clear idea of what he wanted to do with his life, or whether he would ever amount to much. Yet I expect that in the back of his mind he may have been thinking how different his own academic career had been in so many ways, with the same opportunities and at most of the same institutions.

Many people have asked me about Jack's teen-age years. Did he like school, did he do well, what were his favourite subjects, what didn't he like, did he have any 'adolescent problems', and so forth.

The best way to tell that story is to let it tell itself through a series of letters, with such comments and explanatory notes as may be needed from me to supply the missing links.

Jack went through his fourth, fifth and sixth grades at Riverdale Country Day School and did reasonably well; I think it levelled out to around a B-average. Meanwhile Joe Jr had gone to Choate and was doing so well there we decided it would be a good place for Jack too, so we put in his application in the spring of 1929, in advance, as one must do at such places, for enrolment in the fall of 1931. We were advised that he should first have a year away, at some other boarding-school, so he could mature and become accustomed to boarding-school life. As I have said, I wanted each of them to have at least a while in a Catholic school, so it was decided he would go to the Canterbury School in Connecticut.

It was not one of his better years. As I look back over his letters home – I discover that his spelling remained peculiarly his own ('I learnt how to play baggamon today . . .'); that his right eye was bothering him ('I see things blury even at a distance of ten feet'); that he had a sledding accident ('The hill is all ruts and all icey for 1/2 mi. You go from 35 mi. to 40 mi.'); and that 'my Latin could stand improving'; and, PS, that 'We have Scott's "Lady of the Lake" in English.' Then, during Easter vacation of 1931, with his chronic bad luck in matters of health, he was stricken with appendicitis and had to have an operation. By the time he recovered, the school year at Canterbury was nearly ended, so there was no point in his going back. Instead we engaged a tutor to work with him at home, in the hope that with concentrated study he could pass the entrance examinations for Choate that summer and thus still join his elder brother there that fall.

I see that on July 3 I wrote to Choate's headmaster, George St John, from Hyannis Port:

Jack and I were delighted to hear that he passed the English and Mathematics. His tutor and he were extremely doubtful about the Latin – so he was not too disappointed. I am arranging for him to work down here every day with an experienced teacher, and I hope and I will make sure that by the end of September he will know his first year Latin. As a matter of fact he hates routine work but loves History and English, subjects which fire his imagination.

Again let me thank you for your interest and patience with Jack. He has a very attractive personality – we think – but he is quite different from Joe, for whom we feel you have done so much.

Sincerely yours,
Rose Kennedy

After intensive drill during the rest of the summer he took the Latin exam again. He passed. And that fall entered Choate, for which we all were thankful.

As usual and for a long string of reasons – from scarlet fever when he was two to the appendicitis when he was thirteen – I was concerned about his health, and I see from correspondence that I was in touch fairly often with the school about that, usually with Mrs St John: who, as wife of the headmaster, stood *in loco parentis* for the mothers of all those boys and, I expect, heard from quite a few of them. I see that Jack was soon afflicted by a bad cold, or virus of some sort, that gave him some badly swollen glands, and I wrote to her with some of his medical history. He'd had the same trouble before. My next letter was:

Dear Mrs St John,
I understand from Jack's letter that he is much better, and he also said something about eating in the Tuck Shop in order to get 'built up'. I was a bit worried at that suggestion because the 'Tuck Shop' usually means sweets to me, and Jack has no discretion; in fact, he has never eaten enough vegetables to satisfy me.

I do not want to bother you but will someone please investigate this matter a little? . . . I do want him to go along the right track.

How is his weight? My records show 114 1/2 – 115 in January – after supper.

Sincerely yours,
Rose F. Kennedy

And in due course, as the years went along, messages from me such as:

I received your letter regarding the condition of Jack's feet. It is probable that his fallen arches are the cause of the trouble. He has inherited that weakness in his feet and he has persisted in wearing cheap rubber-soled shoes during the last two or three years.

I shall be interested to hear whether or not he finds relief when his shoes are built up. Please write to me . . . Let me thank you for your interest and attention.

And:

Dear Mrs St John,
  I should like very much to hear about Jack's knee . . .

And so it went. At least once he was hospitalized with a football injury. For despite his proneness to illness and injury he went right ahead with activities in several sports including football, in which he made the Choate varsity team. One of his team-mates spoke of him later as 'a tiger on defence'. And the coach has said:

> The most burning thing I can remember about Jack was that he was a fighter. You take Joe, he was a real athlete. But Jack made up for what he lacked in ability with his fight.

So I was often anxious about his physical health in those years; and so was his father. Yet by that time, I suppose, both of us were accustomed to the idea that every now and then he would be laid up by some disease or accident. What concerned us as much, or more, was his lack of diligence in his studies; or, let us say, lack of 'fight' in trying to do well in those subjects that didn't happen to interest him. Like practically all the old-established eastern prep schools in those days, Choate had a highly 'structured' set of rules, traditions and expectations into which a boy was supposed to fit; and if he didn't, there was little or no 'permissiveness'. Joe Jr had no trouble at all operating within this system; it suited his temperament. But Jack couldn't or wouldn't conform. He did pretty much what he wanted, rather than what the school wanted of him.

After his first year there, with a poor set of marks, it was decided he should stay on for the summer session to improve his standing. Mr Steele, the director of the summer school, wrote to my husband:

> You may count on us in every way to do everything in our power to stabilize Jack this summer and make him appreciate not only the necessity but the advantage of consistent and well-balanced effort . . .

But Mr Steele was doomed to disappointment. The more pressure that was put on Jack, the more he seemed to find ways to frustrate and annoy those in charge. Once, as I remember particularly, I sent him a crate of oranges from Florida, and he amused himself by pegging some of them out his window at friends who were passing by below. It was a silly thing to do, but one of the masters caught him at it. He received another demerit. Once he collected all the pillows from all the rooms in his dorm and put them in some boy's room, filling up the whole room top to bottom, so that when the boy came back from a class and opened his door there was just a solid mass of pillows. At the end of his second year, his house master, Mr Maher, filed a despondent report with Mr St John.

I'd like to take the responsibility for Jack's constant lack of neatness about his room and person, since he lived with me for two years. But in the matter of neatness, despite a genuine effort on Jack's part, I must confess to failure.

Occasionally we did manage to effect a house cleaning, but it necessitated my 'dumping' everything in the room into a pile in the middle of the floor. Jack's room has throughout the year been subject to instant and unannounced inspection – it was the only way to maintain a semblance of neatness, for Jack's room was a club for his friends.

I regard the matter of neatness or lack of it on Jack's part as quite symbolic – aside from the value it has in itself – for he is casual and disorderly in almost all of his organization projects. Jack studies at the last minute, keeps appointments late, has little sense of material value, and can seldom locate his possessions . . .

Hoping against hope, or perhaps grasping at straws, Mr Maher did go on to say in conclusion:

Jack has had a thoroughly genuine try at being neat according to his own standards and he has been almost religiously on time throughout the [last] Quarter. I believe Jack . . . has and is trying to be a more socially-minded person.

The outstanding talent Jack had demonstrated in school to that point – as Mr Maher indicated – was a talent for making friends and enjoying friendships. He had, it began to seem to me, innumerable friends, for during vacations and special weekends when he came home he invariably had at least one, usually two, three, four or more school-friends with him. We never knew who to expect or how many. It became a joke in the family, a little shorthand expression that evoked a lot, 'Jack's surprises'. After a while, though, it was no surprise to see LeMoyne ('Lem') Billings, who became Jack's best friend and finally his room-mate. They had great rapport; and they sparked each other to various pieces of nonsense, including one at the expense of the long-suffering house master, Mr Maher, who certainly deserved a better life than he had with those two around.

It was shortly after Jack returned to school from his summer vacation [Lem relates] and we were dragging his trunk down the stairs to store it in the cellar. We were making a good deal of noise. Our house master, Mr Maher, came out of his room. He reminded us this was during study period and the noise was a distraction for people who were trying to work. He ordered us to take the trunk back up and bring it down to storage the next morning instead. So Jack and I got up at 6 a.m. We dragged the trunk out and down the stairs, bumping all the way down. Mr Maher came tearing out of his room, in his bathrobe, wild-eyed, and demanded to know what we thought we were doing. 'But Mr Maher,' Jack said innocently, 'you *told* us to take it down in the *morning.*'

Besides talking things over with Jack at home and writing to him his father was having correspondence with Mr St John. It seems to me the headmaster showed a great deal of forbearance and understanding. In Jack's junior year he wrote:

The fact of the matter is that I cannot feel seriously uneasy or worried about Jack. The longer I live and work with him and the more I talk with him, the more confidence I have in him. I would be willing to bet anything that within two years you will be as proud of Jack as you now are of Joe.

Jack has a clever, individualist mind. It is a harder mind to put in harness than Joe's – harder for Jack himself to put in harness . . . A more conventional mind and a more plodding and mature point of view would help him a lot more right now; but we have to allow, my dear Mr Kennedy, with boys like Jack, for a period of adjustment. All that natural cleverness Jack has to learn how to use in his life and work, even to cover it up at times, how to subordinate it and all the rest. I never yet saw a clever, witty boy who at some stage in his early development was not considered fresh . . . the final product is often more interesting and effective than the boy with a more conventional mind who has been to us parents and teachers much less trouble.

. . . By and by, when Jack is in college, and especially when he can choose his own subjects, his academic output will correspond more nearly with his high IQ.

Considering how much Joe wanted for our sons and how much he wanted them to respond to their opportunities, his response to Jack's pecadilloes was, I should think, a model of reasonableness.

Now, Jack [he wrote in one of his letters], I don't want to give the impression that I am a nagger, for goodness knows that is the worst thing a parent can be. After long experience in sizing up people, I definitely know you have the goods, and you can go a long way. Now aren't you foolish not to get all there is out of what God has given you?

After all, I would be lacking even as a friend if I did not urge you to take advantage of the qualities you have. It is very difficult to make up fundamentals that you have neglected when you were very young, and that is why I am urging you to do the best you can. I am not expecting too much, and I will not be disappointed if you don't turn out to be a real genius, but I think you can be a really worthwhile citizen with good judgment and understanding.

By the end of the first quarter of his senior year, Jack evidently was beginning to see the light clearly, for he wrote to his father:

Dear Dad: I thought I would write you right away as LeMoyne and I have been talking about how poorly we have done this quarter, and we have definitely decided to stop any fooling around. I really do realize how important it is that I get a good job done this year if I want to go to England. [To study under Professor Laski, as Joe Jr had done.] I really feel, now that I think it over, that I have been bluffing myself about how much real work I have been doing . . .

I really feel that we will get something done this quarter as LeMoyne seems to feel the same way as I do.

Love, Jack

Nevertheless, it was about the same time, or a bit later, that these two antic characters formed a little enterprise to pull the headmaster's leg that nearly pulled the roof down on their heads.

Mr St John often addressed the student body assembled for convocations or at chapel. His remarks were designed to inspire, guide, if necessary chastise, and in general to expound the ideals of the school and the kind of responsible citizenship he expected from the students. Any boy who did not uphold those ideals, behaved irresponsibly, disrespected the aims and disciplines of the school, did not belong to Choate, and he had a descriptive term that summed up all such unworthy qualities. The term was 'mucker'. 'Muckers' were everything that was not wanted at Choate.

Lem Billings, at my request, wrote me a letter recently explaining – close to forty years later – just how it happened that he and Jack organized a 'Muckers' Club':

In those times part of the daily schedule at Choate was compulsory evening chapel, starting about twenty minutes after supper. And in

those times Seniors were the only students allowed to have combination radio-phonographs – and Jack and I had a very good one.
As it happened, our room was directly above the dining hall, and with
the stairway close by it was very convenient for us to get down and
back for meals – and also, of course, very convenient for other boys
to get from the dining hall up to our room, and with those twenty
minutes to kill they were coming up by the dozens to listen to the
radio-phonograph. The congestion became so bad that sometimes
Jack and I couldn't get into our own room. So we decided to form a
club – and only club members could be in the room during that
period.

We chose thirteen of our best friends as members. All of them were
top athletes of the school; but there were none representing student
government.

There was nothing wrong so far: the unfortunate thing was the
name we chose. Mr St John used the word 'mucker' as the epitome
of the worst element. Therefore, in our juvenile way we found it
amusing to call our group the Muckers Club. We even had little
gold charms designed in the shape of shovels and engraved 'Choate
Muckers Club'. I don't know what ever happened to Jack's, but a
couple of Christmasses ago I gave mine to Caroline.

Naturally, I suppose, rumours began to spread. The worst things
Jack and I ever did at Choate were to keep a messy room and be late
for classes. Some of our members, I expect, did break the school code
of conduct by going into town and smoking, drinking and so forth.
Anyway, the rumours centred on our room because that's where the
club met nightly. The school gossip reached Mr St John, and when
he heard the name of the club – he saw red. He was furious.

Jack and I were the prime targets of the wrath.

He called my mother – my father had died two years before – and
she had to come all the way from Pittsburgh to have a session with
him and me about my part in the Muckers Club. She decided it was
much ado about very little.

He called Mr Kennedy in Washington and asked him to come up
to Choate to discuss Jack's part. Mr Kennedy was Chairman of the
Securities and Exchange Commission and there were many important matters to occupy his full time and attention in Washington.
But he came up anyway.

Many years later Mr St John was asked to recall this episode and
meeting for a book about Jack, *John Fitzgerald Kennedy* . . . *As We
Remember Him*, and he said:

He was the chief mover in the group . . . They weren't wicked kids, but they were a nuisance. At one time, it came to the point where I was saying to myself, 'Well, I have two things to do, one to run the school, another to run Jack Kennedy and his friends.' And they weren't bad, you know, but they had to be looked after. In other words, they just weren't maturing. So I wrote to Mr Kennedy and I said, 'I think you and Jack and I ought to have a three-cornered talk, Mr Kennedy. Could you come up here . . .' We held nothing back. I was angry . . . Psychologically I was enormously interested. I couldn't see how two boys from the same family could be so different. But Mr Kennedy and Jack and I sat together, in my study, and I rehearsed the chapter and verse of things that had happened . . .

Well, we reduced Jack's conceit, if it was conceit, and childishness to considerable sorrow. And we said just what we thought, held nothing back, and Mr Kennedy was supporting the school completely. I've always been very grateful to him.

There are lots of boys who go through a period like that, and the greatest kindness is some severity. Jack's father didn't hold back. In fact, he spoke very, very strongly, and also with Irish wit. You know, in dealing with Jack, you needed a little wit as well as a little seriousness. Jack didn't like to be too serious; he had a delightful sense of humour, always. His smile was, I think, as a young boy, when he first came to school – well, in any school he would have got away with some things just on his smile. He was a very likeable person, very lovable.

The final outcome of 'The Muckers' escapade was that both boys graduated with their class at Choate in 1935, in no disgrace. Jack, in fact, though his cumulative grades placed him slightly below the middle of his class, was voted 'most likely to succeed'.

Lem went on to Princeton, did well there and afterwards has made a distinguished career for himself. He remained Jack's lifelong close friend, confidant, sharer in old memories and new experiences: as he has continued to be to this day for all our family, a wonderful friend to all of us, in all weathers, in all times. Lem is always there whenever he feels help may be needed. He has really been part of 'our family' since that first time he showed up at our house as one of 'Jack's surprises'.

As for Jack, I think that this silly episode of 'The Muckers' may well have been a turning-point in his life. I'm sure he didn't like that confrontation with the headmaster and his father, that 'three-cornered talk'. Something certainly soaked in, and deeply. There would be no way to measure the influence of this embarrassing necessity to talk things out – and to have a good talking-to, in open forum, from his father. Probably it was also, or even more, as Mr St John has indicated, a matter of 'passing through a phase' and thus of getting a little experience leading to adult maturity and perspective. At any rate, his life took on a new momentum from then on.

II

As Joe's wife and hostess, and with his expanding activities in so many fields of business and government, I found there was seldom a dull moment. I was involved, for example, in the golden age of films because I was Joe's wife, and he very soon became one of the leaders of the movie industry. Others such as Louis B. Mayer, Jessie Lasky, the Schenk brothers and Adolph Zukor were shrewd entrepreneurs and showmen. So was Joe – but he had the advantage of knowing the world of stocks and bonds and corporations. When he went to Hollywood there were predictions that this Boston Irishman soon would be sadder and poorer. Instead, in less than three years after entering film production he headed or controlled three studios, and had merged them with Radio Corporation of America to form a major new studio – RKO – contending with Paramount, Metro-Goldwyn-Mayer, Fox, Warners, and Universal, and other large studios of the period. Consequently I knew a number of the stars, some of whom visited us at Bronxville or Hyannis Port.

One who thrilled our children especially was Fred Thompson, a handsome and highly intelligent Princeton Ph.D., who with his horse Silver King (highly trained and, for a horse, very intelligent) was one of the popular heroes of the Westerns. Joe paid Fred $15,000 a week. When not carrying Fred around through gulches and gullies, Silver King enjoyed a life of ease in his mahogany-floored $25,000 stable.

There was so much money to be made in the movie business in those days the stars began to feel that, even with their huge salaries, they were not being paid a share commensurate with the profits generated for the studios. Douglas Fairbanks, Mary Pickford, Harold Lloyd, Charlie Chaplin and others therefore decided not to renew their studio contracts but form their own companies to produce their own pictures, taking the possible financial risks involved but also reaping the potential great gains. Gloria Swanson wanted to do this too. While she could earn $20,000 a week on contract at Paramount, it

followed that if she could have the right business advice and management, she might earn even more in independent productions.

Obviously the best adviser-manager-financier in Hollywood was Joe
Kennedy. I knew few of the details of his business ventures, whether
buying and selling an office building, or stocks and bonds, or movie
properties, but I do know that Gloria wanted his advice and he did
help to set her up as an 'independent', under the label of Gloria Productions Inc., and became the managing director of this additional
enterprise.

Gloria was grateful. She told me she was in a financial morass. Mary
Pickford had her mother to advise her. Harold Lloyd had his brother,
everyone seemed to have a fully trustworthy adviser, but she had none
and really needed someone like Joe. She was married to the Marquis
Henri de la Falaise de la Coudraye. But although 'Hank' (as his Hollywood friends called him) was a very attractive, charming, witty and
delightful man, a perfect consort for Gloria, he knew little about
business, finance, or the complexities of film production.

Among the films Joe made for Gloria Productions, I have special
personal memories of *The Trespasser* (1928). Joe felt it had potentialities
for becoming a great box-office hit, and to that end he decided on a
campaign of international publicity, with successive premières in Paris,
London, New York and Los Angeles, building to a tremendous climax
when the film was released to the general public.

Joe and I and his sister, Margaret Burke (née Kennedy), therefore,
sailed in June 1928 for France, and were joined by Gloria in Paris.

There was a lot of excitement, of fun, and crisis.

Much of the excitement revolved around clothes. Gloria and I both
needed some things to wear. Gloria had to have something not only
becoming but spectacular, something that would draw gasps and ohs
and ahs and would photograph well. Since there would be four
different premières she needed four different outfits. And she was not
easy to dress, because she was small. Tall women have many more
options in dress than short ones; and while I am short, less than 5 ft
3 ins, Gloria was smaller.

There was, even to begin with, a set-back that probably only women
could understand fully. Gloria had a chinchilla coat. This at a time
when there were only about half a dozen such coats of that delicate,
beautiful and rare fur in the world, so of course hers was not only
becoming but worth a small fortune. She planned to wear it to two of
the openings. Imagine, then, her chagrin when her maid unpacked the
trunk in which it had been shipped and found it had fallen apart.
Gloria made the best of a bad situation by having a satin wrap made,

trimmed with chinchilla, and it was very attractive, but not what she had in mind for herself.

The leading couturier of Paris in those times was Lucien Lelong. We went to his salon. I had been there when I was a schoolgirl travelling with Agnes and our father, and later travelling with Joe, but this was my first full exposure to the *haute couture* at the height of its dazzling elegance. I sat fascinated as the beautiful mannequins slinked and slithered the length of the ornate salon showing M. Lelong's creations. And of course being with Gloria magnified the experience, for the vendeuses and management hovered around her, attentive to her every whim; and both the girls and the customers kept stealing glances at her. She was the great celebrity. I, by comparison, was a nobody, just the wife of the producer. But it was fun being with her and sharing in the excitement she generated.

My own special interest in clothes developed during this period: not just from this episode but from the general circumstances of which it was an especially vivid part.

During Joe's years in the movie industry he was surrounded daily by some of the most beautiful women in the world, dressed in beautiful clothes. Obviously I couldn't compete in natural beauty, but I could make the most of what I had by keeping my figure trim, my complexion good, my grooming perfect and by always wearing clothes that were interesting and becoming. And so, with Joe's endorsement, I began spending more time and more money on clothes. Eventually I began landing on some lists of 'Best Dressed Women'. Eunice wrote recently:

> We'd go shopping together in New York, and I'd pick out something and she'd be terrific: I always liked to go with her because she always had better ideas than I had. She'd suggest a dress or two for me, and it was always very nice, the right dress. But if I found another one a bit prettier, I'd find she had already picked that one for herself and she'd have it off in a corner.
>
> Or in Paris we'd see some beautiful dress and I would refuse to buy it because it cost so much; but then she'd buy it and give it to me. She has always been very generous, in addition to her other wonderful qualities. She's fantastic with her children but she's got her own thing too.

Pat has a comment:

> I remember in Bronxville when she'd go out at night with Daddy . . .
> I remember her coming to kiss me good-night, and she was always

so beautiful. My room was dark and this vision just sort of appeared, smelling absolutely marvellous with her perfume.

I was fascinated by the perfume, we all were, and as we girls grew older we'd ask her what it was. But she wouldn't tell us. She didn't want even her own daughters to have it. We'd sneak in and try to find it, but we never could. Finally when she was seventy-five she told us. Now we all wear it; it's our favourite perfume.

Even Ethel took it over.

But when we all started to smell alike, Mother changed hers to something else.

Eunice continues:

She has a wonderful sense of colour. I was with her lately and we were looking at some dress materials. I picked one out, and she picked one afterwards and said, 'I would get this one if I were you,' and I looked at it and it was definitely better. She can always do that. She'll do it with me and with my sisters. She has a fashion sense that none of us have ever had. We had the same resources she had, not as much money but it was enough, in other words we could afford, but we just never . . .

I suppose it goes back to the fact that she really likes clothes and likes design – and she likes to look very, very well whenever she goes out. She goes to Mass every morning. I was there at Palm Beach and at church too, and saw her, and afterwards – putting her on a bit – said, 'A joy to see you at Mass.' But I had been sitting back in my slacks which were too tight and she was up in front with a French dress on.

We went up to Deauville for a few days, back to Paris for our fittings, and everything was going well, with that mounting nervous euphoria that happens before an 'opening night'.

At this point, unexpectedly, Gloria told Hank (the Marquis de la Falaise) and Joe, and all of us, that she was suing for divorce immediately and Hank could not escort her or be seen with her at the opening night in Paris – just a few evenings away – or any of the other openings.

Joe was flabbergasted. Hank retreated to other quarters in the hotel. Gloria's attitude was one of cold, regal rage. Joe's sister, Margaret, and I were, to say the least, concerned and perplexed. There were two or three close, trusted members of Joe's staff who were there to see that everything went gloriously well, and these seasoned veterans of show-business and publicity and studio diplomacy were also in a state of high commotion.

When emotions had cooled enough, we began to take stock. Joe had a lot of money in the movie, and of course so did Gloria – since he was not, after all, subsidizing her but acting as her financier and charging the usual rates of interest for monies he advanced – and he wanted at least to make a profit. So we sat around for long hours discussing the problem. Would it be better 'box-office' if Gloria were involved in a sensational divorce (as this one was bound to be) or would it cause a boycott of the movie? Some of the sessions at the Ritz reminded me of what it must be like to negotiate a complex international treaty among friendly and unfriendly Powers. After hearing all the accusations and arguments and suggestions, Joe finally brought everything back into focus by declaring that he had put money and time and effort into this picture, and so had other people, and these were *not* going to be lost just because of a disagreement between a husband and wife. He proposed that Hank and Gloria *act* out the relationship they had before the trouble began. Until the premières were finished they should appear in public as a devoted, happy and glamorous couple.

And that's what happened. Gloria, of course, was a wonderful actress, and Hank showed that he was quite an actor himself. At the Paris opening they walked hand in hand, all smiles. The movie was a grand success and Gloria's performance was greeted with great demonstrations. Lavish bouquets, congratulatory telegrams, parties and banquets that went on in the temples of *haute cuisine*, with speeches and gallantly phrased toasts to The Star.

There was a similar scene in London, and then again in New York. Except that in New York the crowds were more boisterous – perhaps because of the advance publicity from Paris and London – and Gloria, riding with Joe and me in our car, was afraid that someone might break the windows and she would cut her face. That had once happened to a friend of hers. I realized her face was more valuable than mine, but I got rather nervous myself.

After Paris-London-New York I decided to get back to our children in Bronxville. And I did.

Not long after the Los Angeles opening, when *The Trespasser* was well along to being the great hit that it became, Gloria and Hank were divorced and he married Constance Bennett. He was divorced from her and married a wealthy Latin American girl. I saw him from time to time in the later years, at Capri, Eden Roc, Paris, or New York; the same smiling, urbane Marquis Henri whom we had all enjoyed so much.

Gloria's next vehicle after *The Trespasser* under the flag of Gloria

Productions was *Queen Kelly*, which achieved enduring fame in Hollywood as one of the great disasters of all time. Briefly, this is the story:

Following a rash of scandals among Hollywood celebrities and a trend towards salacious movie scenes that caused denunciations of Hollywood as a capital of wickedness, the leaders of the industry had formed the Motion Picture Producers and Distributors of America Inc. and hired Will Hays, the former Postmaster-General and a greatly respected figure in public life, to take charge of the moral contents of films. The 'Hays Office' established a strict and precise 'Code'. It reviewed all films, and if there were scenes that violated the Code they had to come out. Otherwise the film would not be handled by any reputable distributor or exhibitor. Joe was a firm supporter of the Hays Office and moreover became a close personal friend of Will Hays.

The second element of the *Queen Kelly* fiasco was that Joe and Gloria engaged Erich von Stroheim as the director. Von Stroheim was considered one of the great directorial geniuses of films and was one of the very few who could demand complete 'artistic control', including 'improving' the script as he went along. This time he altered the story in ways Joe would not have dreamed of. From von Stroheim's fertile mind came a graphic scene of a convent girl being seduced. And another of a young priest giving the Blessed Sacrament and Last Rites to the madam of a house of ill-repute who was dying.

Gloria, naturally, had begun to worry a good deal about all this, and one day she called Joe who was then back East to tell him: 'There's a madman in charge here. The scenes he's shooting will never get past Will Hays.'

At this point, however, Joe was in an emotionally heart-rending situation. His father was very ill and according to the doctors might die any day. Joe felt he couldn't leave. A round trip to the coast meant at least a week just in travel time. So he stayed on and supervised the production as best he could by telephone, with Gloria becoming more upset and von Stroheim more stubborn; while his father faded and rallied again and again as the days and weeks went by. Finally Joe decided to take a chance and go to California.

While he was away, his father died. Joe couldn't even get back in time for the funeral; a matter that to him, with his very deep family love and loyalty, I know was a source of painful regrets for the rest of his life.

While he was on the Coast, he saw the twenty thousand feet of film that von Stroheim had shot, realized that the personal vision of the story by the Great Director wouldn't pass the Hays Office and, even if it did, could not be presented under his own aegis as a 'Joseph P.

Kennedy Production'. So he dismissed von Stroheim and engaged another fine director, Edmund Goulding, who saw no way to salvage it except by re-shooting a large part. Costs were already around $700,000, the price of a great 'epic' in those days. After trying various remedies, while costs rose to $800,000, Joe decided the only rational thing was to cut the prospective losses and scrap the whole venture. That is precisely what happened. Thus ended the sad saga of *Queen Kelly*. Almost.

Many years later, when both Gloria and Erich von Stroheim had retired from the movies, they came back to star, with William Holden, in a remarkable film called *Sunset Boulevard*. Gloria played the part of a former great star. Von Stroheim played the part of her former great director, who was now her butler. During one episode, when the former star was entertaining by showing films of herself in some of her great roles, with the projection machine being run by her former director, there was a sequence from *Queen Kelly*. Time heals enough that by then it could be taken as an 'inside joke'.

Gloria and Joe made one other picture together, called *What a Widow*, which was a hit and quite profitable. I believe he had an advisory role in Gloria Productions for a while longer, though not as executive head and producer. During 1929–30 he liquidated all his movie interests except for his chain of theatres and a few minor properties.

I didn't see Gloria again until a long time afterwards, just a few years ago, when I was lunching at the Ritz in Paris and recognized her at another table with a woman who turned out – when I was leaving and stopped by to say hello – to be her daughter: that former little girl whom nobody at the Bronxville school could believe was 'Gloria Swanson's daughter' and who now was expecting a child of her own. We chatted together a couple of minutes in a very friendly way, recalling old times. I gave the daughter a Kennedy half-dollar as a keepsake for the baby. I haven't seen Gloria since.

From 1929 on, for the next couple of years, Joe was at home with us in Bronxville. That is to say, generally he commuted to his office in New York City during the week, as did most of the men of that suburb, and ordinarily was home at nights and during weekends. This was a golden interval for me and for the children. He and I were able to play a good deal of golf together, and also able to resume those long, conversational walks that had been so much part of our life in Boston and Dorchester and Brookline. Pat says:

I remember every Sunday afternoon, after lunch, Mother and Daddy

would go down the long driveway there together and 'way up
Pondfield Road around that whole area there, which has a lot of
hills and by-ways. Sometimes a couple of us would start out trailing
behind them, but they walked so fast, or so long, we'd get tired and
go back home. We weren't included, they weren't talking with us,
they were talking to each other. And they walked: those Sunday
afternoon walks, they were *their* walks. It indicates something about
their relationship. They were interested in each other, they enjoyed
each other, they wanted to talk with each other.

While Joe had been active in the movies he had also continued to be
substantially involved in the stock market. Part of his genius was an
amazing sense of timing: his ability to analyse a situation in the most
clear-headed way, refusing to be swept along in tides of opinion, and
to reach the right, hard-headed, rational answer at just the right time.
There was no better example of this than in that boom-and-bust year
of 1929.

While the stock market was soaring, and the newspapers were full
of statements from famous political and business figures about 'limitless prosperity' in a 'new era', Joe took a long hard look at the scene
and decided this was a bubble that was bound to burst. He began
taking his money out of the market. By the time of the famous crash
of 1929 (as again I know from reading; he didn't tell me) nearly all of
his major assets were in cool hard cash in safe banks. Thus not only
had he saved his wealth from the disaster but was in a position to 'sell
short'. Consequently, he made money as the market went down.

Years later, when Jean was of an age to be going out with young men,
one of her escorts remarked to her that during the market débâcle of
1929–31 her father had been a famous 'Bear'.

Jean wasn't too clear about the meaning of the term but the image
struck her as hilarious, and when she came home she said to her
brothers and sisters: 'Did you know that Daddy used to be a Big Bear
on Wall Street?' They were enchanted by the idea, and when Joe
appeared that next morning they all gathered round and joined in the
refrain, 'Daddy is a Bear, Daddy is a Bear!' Joe was momentarily
perplexed but then caught on and laughed and began giving them all
bear hugs.

So Joe's 'bearishness' became another part of the family lore, something to tickle the fancy and elaborate on in poems and playlets and
valentines and birthday cards and joking pseudo-*sotto-voce* asides in
family conversations. One of those really 'inside' jokes that gets better

with the years because it evokes so many scenes of silliness and kidding and laughter and banter from the past; hard to explain; one would have had to live there.

While Joe took normal satisfaction in the way his judgment was confirmed, he was at the same time becoming increasingly worried about the state of the nation. The market collapse did not 'cause' the subsequent general economic disaster, but it did cause widespread loss of confidence among businessmen and the secondary effects spread as bankruptcies and unemployment and mortgage foreclosures rose and the 'recession' became a 'depression', which gave way to the Great Depression. As hardships increased with no end in sight, people began losing faith in the whole structure of the American system of government and economics. There were powerful voices raised for radical changes – Norman Thomas, the Socialist; Father Charles E. Coughlin, the 'radio priest', with his message of 'social justice' and audience of millions every Sunday; and others to the left of them who were fomenting revolutionary change.

Joe had never been directly concerned with politics, and was not particularly interested in the political processes except as, from time to time, they directly affected his own interests. But, with the same analytical intelligence that had enabled him to see through the pronouncements of a 'new era of prosperity', he now saw that the country was heading towards a potential explosion that could wreck not just the monetary system but, more important, the very principles on which American Democracy had been founded.

Joe admired and liked President Hoover; and continued to in later years. They worked closely together on the 'Hoover Commission' to improve the efficiency of government. But, regretfully, Joe decided Hoover was not temperamentally suited to the role demanded by this extreme emergency. The times required bold decisions, made by a man who, through force of personality as well as reason, could command the confidence of the country, restore a sense of optimism, unite disparate elements in a common effort for the good of the nation.

Who could this man be? Where was he? I remember Joe turning this over in his mind, discussing it at dinner at our house, or in New York, with experienced political figures including my father (who at first thought Al Smith was the man who . . .), as well as with influential leaders in business and journalism such as Bernard Baruch and Herbert Bayard Swope.

As I have mentioned earlier, Joe was manager of the Bethlehem Steel Company's shipyards at Fall River, Massachusetts, during the First World War, while Franklin D. Roosevelt was Assistant Secretary of the Navy with responsibilities for shipbuilding. Both were giving their energies to their jobs, which resulted in arguments and mis- understandings but also in a good deal of mutual respect. Joe had had very little contact with FDR for at least a decade, though each had enjoyed remarkable success. Roosevelt had become Governor of New York State, a key state in any national election. His name, therefore, came up in any conversation about the Democratic nomination and the national election of 1932. I think it was Henry Morgenthau who brought them together again, for close conversation and mutual reappraisal and exchanges of ideas. Joe and Morgenthau went to Albany for a talk with Governor Roosevelt. Joe returned with his mind made up that Roosevelt was the man who could save the country.

Once Joe had decided on his goal – in this case the nomination and election of Franklin D. Roosevelt in 1932 – he worked ceaselessly to achieve it. I won't go into details of that campaign. But I do know that Joe was one of the earliest, most ardent and most effective of FDR's supporters. By then he had contacts throughout the financial com- munity from New York and Boston to Los Angeles and San Francisco, and he knew how to talk with financiers in ways they would under- stand and respect. Indeed, he knew people in influential places all over the country, and if he didn't know them personally he knew people who could pave the way for talks with them. Thus, for instance, he had talks and correspondence with Father Coughlin, the apostle of 'social justice', and convinced him that Roosevelt was the man for the times and to speak out for him. In lining up delegations to the Demo- cratic Convention (in those days it took two-thirds of the votes to choose a candidate) his work was one of the decisive factors, and possibly the decisive one, in getting the nomination for Roosevelt.

During his years in the movie industry Joe was on close terms with William Randolph Hearst, the powerful publisher. In 1930 Joe began to persuade him to back the Roosevelt candidacy. Hearst decided to wait, however, and let the field of candidates develop before making a choice. Meanwhile, to prepare a strong position for convention-time, he supported John Nance Garner of Texas, the then Speaker of the House, who consequently came to the convention with the votes of the Texas and California delegations, both of which were under Hearst's control. After the first three ballots it was evident that a stalemate had developed between the forces of Roosevelt and those of Al Smith, and that unless it were broken the convention would either settle for a 'favourite son' or a minor 'dark horse' candidate. Many people were trying to reach Hearst by telephone in California before the balloting resumed, but Joe's call was one of the few accepted. Arthur Krock, the

great political reporter-commentator of the *New York Times* and a
warm friend and admirer of Joe's, was with him in his hotel room
when the call went through, so he heard Joe's end of the conversation.
As Krock recalled in his *Memoirs*: ' "If you don't take Roosevelt,"
Kennedy warned Hearst, "you'll get Newton D. Baker," perhaps the
nominee least acceptable to the press lord at San Simeon.' And as
Krock declared, it was Joe's 'successful interview by telephone with
William Randolph Hearst, Sr, that clinched Roosevelt's victory on the
fourth ballot'.

Mr Hearst had plenty of advice of various sorts from other men, I
dare say, and in my later reading about the era I would come across
names of those credited with influencing his decision and asked Joe.
The best evidence he had, he told me, was indirect. A symbolic act
that nevertheless had a very clear meaning: when Hearst made his
financial contribution to the Democratic Campaign, it was Joe through
whom he channelled it. 'I'm the one who got the Hearst cheque and
gave it directly to Roosevelt,' Joe explained, 'and in politics that meant
I was the one who had "delivered Hearst" at the convention. WR
meant it that way and FDR understood it.'

Joe was very closely involved throughout the course of the campaign, though not in a publicly conspicuous way. He always preferred
to 'work behind the scenes'. This was probably one of the reasons he
declined FDR's invitation to serve on the campaign's executive committee. Another was that it would involve working closely with Louis
McHenry Howe, a strange, wizened, brilliant, vindictive little man who
had spent most of his life as Roosevelt's personal assistant and political
secretary, was utterly devoted to him and was jealously resentful of
anyone he perceived, in his rather warped way, as a rival to his role of
chief confidant and lieutenant. Joe had long since been aware of Howe's
suspicions and animosity, and had no stomach for them. He did,
however, accept an invitation to go along on the train in which the
candidate – with scores of 'close' advisers, speech writers, secretaries,
arrangers and organizers, and members of the press – toured the
country during the last six weeks or so of the campaign. Usually, when
the train stopped long enough at some town or city, he would go off
on his own to seek out the local financial and business leaders, explain
to them why Roosevelt was the man to save the nation and perhaps
get some pledges from them for much-needed campaign funds.
During that time also, travelling and living with that distinguished
aggregation, he made many friends who not only were pleasant but
also useful in the years ahead.

Joe was elated when the election returns showed that Roosevelt had swept the nation. This was a result he had worked hard towards, with dedication and great effect, for the better part of three years. He naturally expected to be a part of the new Administration, in a role commensurate with his efforts and abilities. To him this meant appointment as Secretary of the Treasury. He felt he could do that job as well as anybody in the country. He wanted the post and let people know that he did. Instead, to general surprise, Roosevelt appointed William H. Woodin, another and even earlier supporter, a competent businessman (president of American Car and Foundry Co.) but rather colourless and certainly more pliable and submissive to White House wishes than Joe would have been.

Joe was keenly disappointed. He was again disappointed, or more, when Mr Woodin retired because of health two years later and President Roosevelt again passed him by and appointed Henry Morgenthau – an uncritically devoted friend and Dutchess County neighbour – to the Treasury. Meanwhile he and the President had a friendly, though more or less remote, relationship. There were exchanges of greetings and good wishes and invitations to drop in, we at the White House whenever we were in Washington, the President and Mrs Roosevelt if their travels happened to be nearby our houses, which by mid-1933 included the house we bought at Palm Beach.

There and at Hyannis Port and Bronxville and New York we entertained various of Joe's old close companions, such as Professor Raymond Moley, the founding member and recruiter of the famous 'Brains Trust', and authoritative interpreters and critics such as Arthur Krock. Thus Joe was kept very well informed as to what was happening inside the New Deal.

The outstanding personal experience for me during that interval was when Joe and I, and Jimmy and Betsy Roosevelt, went to Europe together in 1933. Jimmy, the oldest of the Roosevelt boys, was of course his father's stalwart support and closest attendant during the campaigning, and thus circumstances had brought Joe and Jimmy together and they became fond of each other and established great *rapport*. He and Betsy, and Betsy's sister, Mary Cushing (they were daughters of the famous brain surgeon Harvey Cushing), had been visiting us at Palm Beach, and we all had such a good time together that when Joe had to go abroad on business it was decided we'd all go and make it a party.

Joe's reason for the business trip was yet another example of his sense of timing. Foreseeing that the Prohibition Amendment would soon be repealed, he felt that anyone franchised to distribute the good British and Scottish brands of liquor was bound to do very well. Thus he decided to go straight to the sources of supply and negotiate agreements with the heads and owners of the big distilleries. James Roosevelt accompanied us. They were mainly family firms; the families were mainly of old lineage with titles and castles and lodges and mansions galore, and they entertained us as if we were, at the very least, visiting nobility of high station.

Joe, knowing we would be entertained at the houses of some of these people and it might be embarrassing if I came up with a question such as how does Scotch whisky differ from Spanish sherry, gave me a cram course in elementary terminology and genealogy on the boat going over. It was, if I may use the term, like a daily catechism. Joe said if I got in difficulty it would be a good idea to discuss our children.

The trip turned out to be a great business success for Joe. He secured the US franchises for the distribution of the products of Haig and Haig Ltd and John Dewar and Sons Ltd – which as I had learned were among the most highly esteemed manufacturers of Scotch whisky – and also those of another well-known firm, the Gordon's Dry Gin Company Ltd. I mention this because I want to make a point. In later times there was a story that Joe had used his official position as US Ambassador to Britain to get these contracts. In fact, he got them as a private citizen, an independent and quick-witted businessman, years before it had even seriously occurred to him that he might become Ambassador. I don't know the origin of such stories. Anyone who wanted access to the facts could have found them in the records very easily.

Soon afterwards Joe returned to New York because of some emergencies there. The rest of us went on with our itinerary to Rome. I had never been there before. And, as any tourist with an eye for beauty and a sense of history would be, I was fairly overwhelmed by its grandeur, past and present. We had an audience with the Pope, then Pius XI; and this was a tremendous event for me. It was my first visit to Rome and an opportunity to see St Peter's, the Vatican, the Papal Chambers, the Guards, the Chamberlains, the Attendants, the Pope, and I think I must have been deeply impressed because about all I really remember are my feelings of beauty and majesty and awe and reverence.

In the summer of 1934, more than halfway through President Roosevelt's first term, Joe finally found a job in the New Deal that challenged and excited him.

During the electoral campaign he had contributed many ideas for

reforms that could help restore health and vigour to the country. Few
were as specific and complete as those for reforming the rules (or lack
of rules) by which financial institutions operated, particularly 'holding
companies' and the commodity and stock exchanges. Joe handed these
suggestions to Ray Moley, the original and foremost Brains Truster.
They became the basis of one of Roosevelt's most powerful speeches
and, subsequently, a solid starting-point for New Deal legislation
culminating in a new arm of government, the Securities and Exchange
Commission. Who should be the chairman, the guiding spirit? Moley
wanted Joe because, as he wrote the President, '. . . of executive ability,
knowledge of habits and customs of business to be regulated, and
ability to moderate different points of view on the Commission.' There
were objections, however, from others who considered him too much
an 'insider' and adept 'professional' in the markets' operations to
enforce the new rules firmly and impartially. Joe naturally took this as
an affront to his pride and a slur on his honour. There was to be a
decisive meeting in Washington. I well remember that as Joe left our
house that morning he said to me, 'I'll probably be back tonight
because I'm not going to be on the Commission unless I get the
chairmanship.'

There was a full confrontation that evening at the White House with
the President, Joe, Ray Moley and Bernard Baruch. Joe had been
heavily attacked by the Scripps-Howard chain that very day, with a
declaration from Roy Howard that there would be more to come if
Joe were named Chairman. (I'm indebted to Ray Moley's memoirs for
the following account.)

The President nevertheless said he wanted Joe as Chairman.

Joe said: 'Mr President, I don't think you should do this. It will
bring down injurious criticism.'

Ray Moley said: 'Joe, I know darned well you want this job. But if
anything in your career in business could injure the President, this is
the time to spill it. Let's forget the general criticism that you've made
money in Wall Street.'

Moley goes on: 'Kennedy reacted precisely as I thought he would.
With a burst of profanity he defied anyone to question his devotion to
the public interest or to point to a single shady act in his whole life.
The President did not need to worry about that, he said. What was
more, he would give his critics – and here again the profanity flowed
freely – an administration of the SEC that would be a credit to the
country, the President, himself, and his family – clear down to the
ninth child.'

I think Ray may have been exaggerating the 'profanity', around the house he never used anything but the mildest cuss-words, but I do know Joe didn't come back that night, because he had been appointed to the Chairmanship of the Securities and Exchange Commission.

Once again we had a decision to make about our family. Should we move to Washington? That would mean changing schools again for the younger children, uprooting the life we had established by then in Bronxville. We decided not to move. For one thing, Joe would be spending some time in New York City, since it was the financial capital of the country and the securities and most commodities exchanges there dominated other exchanges elsewhere. For another, Joe hoped and believed he could have the whole SEC apparatus set up and running well within a year's time; then he planned to give his resignation. Actually it took sixty-six days longer, at which point he resigned, leaving behind a great record of accomplishment within the Administration and one of the still enduring monuments of the New Deal.

That September of 1935, Joe and I, accompanied by Jack and Kathleen, sailed for Britain and Europe. Jack had graduated in reasonably good standing from Choate, and the time had come for him to take his year with Professor Laski in London. Kathleen was fifteen and old enough to get something out of a year of schooling abroad, which I wanted her to have in a French convent so she could absorb French culture and language. And Joe needed some rest and relaxation, and he and I wanted time together free of pressure after the long high-voltage demands of his SEC job. So there was a combination of worthwhile purposes.

I seem to have a reputation in some quarters as a planner and organizer. But as the poet Burns observed so wisely, 'The best laid schemes . . . gang aft agley.' Joe and I travelled in Britain and France and did have a lot of marvellous times. On the other hand, as an *ex officio* but still intensely loyal member of the Roosevelt New Deal team, he undertook (at the President's request) a private survey of the European political and financial scene, talking at length with such figures as Sir Montagu Norman, head of the Bank of England ('The smartest banker I ever met,' he commented to me), and formed extremely pessimistic judgments about the chances for economic stability and chances for peace. All of which he reported to the President, and which I'm sure was useful to Mr Roosevelt, but not good for Joe's ulcers.

Further, the convent school where I had placed Kathleen turned out to be so severe in its rules and customs, and so remote from the general life of the country, that she felt oppressed and forlorn. So I had to change that plan and put her in another, more sophisticated convent school in the Parisian suburb of Neuilly, where she stayed a year and did have a pleasant and rewarding experience.

The thing that really went wrong was that Jack developed hepatitis, or jaundice, and had to drop out of the London School of Economics after only a month. By that time Joe and I were returning from our Continental travels, so we took Jack home on the boat with us.

He felt well enough by the time we were home again in November to think he could manage all right at an American university. The place he wanted was Princeton, because his Choate room-mate, Lem Billings, and several other good friends were there. Joe, of course, as a Harvard man, was not happy about that. But, once he and Jack had a full discussion and each had made his points, he let Jack have his choice without argument.

Jack was accepted at Princeton, even though classes had started a few weeks earlier. He was always bright enough to catch up whenever he really needed and wanted to, and he did well and liked the school. I remember his being in a bit of a quandary at the time of the Princeton-Harvard football game. There he was, a freshman of only a few weeks standing. His father was a former Harvard athlete who always rooted hard for all Harvard teams. His brother Joe Jr was in the Harvard football team. Jack said: 'I'm not sure who I want to win the game.'

However, that December, after he had spent only two months at Princeton, his hepatitis flared up again and put him out of commission once more. I think it was around that time that someone in the family – probably Bobby, who would have been ten or eleven – made a *bon mot* that the other children took up and made a family joke. He said, 'If a mosquito bit Jack Kennedy, the mosquito would die.' Jack took that sort of joshing in very good spirit. Even when he was laid out flat in bed from some new accident or disease, with his face thin and his freckles standing out against the pallor of his skin, he could always smile or grin about his own bad luck, as if he had been victimized once again by some absurd nonsensical joke that he should have been on guard against. He never, never mentioned his ailments until he had to, and even then he didn't accept them. He went along for many years thinking to himself – or at least trying to make others think – that he was a strong, robust, quite healthy person who just happened to be sick a good deal of the time.

Writers have sometimes portrayed Joe as a relentlessly demanding, Spartan father. This was not true. He worried about Jack. He was tender with him – very tender in his own masculine, 'bearish', fatherly way, as I think can be shown quite well in a letter he wrote soon after Jack had enrolled at Princeton:

Dear Jack,

I had a nice talk with Doctor Raycourt . . . and we have decided to go along on the proposition as outlined by Dr Murphy and see how you get along until Thanksgiving. Then, if no real improvement has been made, you and I will discuss whether or not it is best for you to lay off a year and try and put yourself in condition.

After all, the only consideration I have in the whole matter is your happiness, and I don't want you to lose a year of your college life (which ordinarily brings great pleasure to a boy) by wrestling with a bad physical condition and a jam in your studies. A year is important, but it isn't so important if it's going to leave a mark for the rest of your life. So let's give it a try until Thanksgiving and see if you are showing any improvement, then you and I will discuss what's best to do.

You know I really think you are a pretty good guy and my only interest is in doing what is best for you.

Love, Dad

Jack left Princeton a few weeks after Thanksgiving. I might add that many years later, among Princeton contemporaries who didn't know him and most of whom were not even aware he existed, the story went that he left because he 'flunked out'. We sent him out West to recuperate. Most of the rest of that school year of 1935–6 he spent in Arizona, since the sunny and dry climate there was said to be good for health and especially good for asthma, because he had that also. Joe Sr had it too, and several others among our children had it, and some of our grandchildren do also, so apparently it is congenital. The form it takes with us evidently has some connection with allergies.

Nineteen-thirty-six was a busy year for Joe.

At the request of David Sarnoff, the head of Radio Corporation of America, he reorganized the entire financial structure of RCA.

Then, at the request of the board of directors of Paramount Pictures, an ailing giant of the movie industry, he reorganized the company from top to bottom, both the financial and the studio operations. That took him back to Hollywood for a while, and Jack was able to spend time with him there.

Then, at the request of his friend William Randolph Hearst, he studied the financially troubled Hearst publishing empire, and produced a reorganization plan that resulted in drastic changes there.

Nineteen-thirty-six was a Presidential campaign year, with Roosevelt running for re-election to a second term against Governor Alfred M. Landon of Kansas. In the course of his first four years the President had alienated many of the most important persons and special groups in the country, and the resentment against him among business and financial leaders was especially wide and deep. Joe, though often at odds with these men, was obviously still highly respected and accepted by them. He knew that Roosevelt needed him, and responded by writing a book titled *I'm for Roosevelt*, in which he showed that the New Deal was not the enemy of business but, in fact, by its reforms, had saved capitalism and the free-enterprise system in America. He then went on to take a very active part in the Presidential campaign, all through the late summer and fall, right up to election day. He was happy when the returns came in, showing the greatest landslide in US political history, knowing that his words and deeds had contributed to the tremendous victory.

Despite all the things he was doing – an incredible list as I contemplate it now – we managed to have more time together than we had had, except in rare intervals, for many years. There was time for opening nights of Broadway shows, usually preceded by dinner at the Colony. Joe had many friends and acquaintances in showbusiness; and we would always encounter a number of them in the restaurants and theatre lobbies, and everybody was called 'darling'. It was, 'Oh, darling, so marvellous to see you!' and 'Oh, darling, when did you get back East?' I got used to that. There was one situation, however, in which I didn't. Joe wanted to give me a new mink coat, and it seemed unusual to me when the furrier who designed it and was doing the fittings kept addressing me as 'dearie'. (That wouldn't have happened in Boston.)

Another vivid memory came directly after the election. Cardinal Eugenio Pacelli, who was then the Vatican's Secretary of State – and later became Pope, as Pius XII – was visiting this country and before returning to Rome wanted to consult with President Roosevelt. Bishop (later Cardinal) Spellman, who was a close friend of Cardinal Pacelli's, and Joe worked out an arrangement for him to do so, informally, at Hyde Park, since the US did not recognize the Vatican as an independent state and had no diplomatic relations with it.

The President invited Joe, as one of the nation's leading Catholic laymen, and me to join Cardinal Pacelli's entourage in New York and ride up to Hyde Park in the private railway car. On the car we were presented to His Eminence. I was struck by his appearance. He was a tall, rather thin man of rather dark and sallow complexion and dark eyes behind rimmed spectacles set on a Roman nose. He was not a handsome man: yet his eyes shone with great intensity and compassion, and in his bearing and movement there was an unearthly dedication. I truly felt I was in the presence of a mortal who was very close to God.

At Hyde Park there were cars waiting to take us the additional few miles to the President's home. This was early November, and it was one of those flawless autumn days, crisp and bright and fair, with the sky blue and most of the colourful foliage still on the trees. Suddenly, about halfway there, there were hundreds of children – from local and nearby parochial schools – lining the road, all rosy-cheeked and excited and waving their little US and Papal flags. The Cardinal could have waved and smiled and passed by; but instead the thoughtful, inspired, humane and godly man stopped our caravan, left his car and – with the red robes of his Cardinalate moving with the shift of the autumn breezes – passed among the children, smiling and patting heads and with his right hand making the Sign of the Cross or raised in a gesture of Benediction. So I shall never forget the future Pope, striding in his robes among those children on a rural roadside near the Hudson River in apple- and pine-tree country in New York State. Then he walked along the road for a great distance while the children waved small flags. It was such a happy and spontaneous gesture.

There were quite a few people at the Roosevelt house at Hyde Park, and I was in the background. I remember FDR's mother, Sara Delano Roosevelt, who was quite an imposing person, a handsome and impressive *grande dame*. Her appearance and attitude clearly demonstrated that she was in charge of the household.

What I remember with total clarity is that on the way back to New York City the Cardinal left his special railway car and came to take tea with us at our house in Bronxville. It was a most unusual gesture on his part. The visual memory that stays most clearly in my mind is of His Eminence sitting on a sofa in our living-room, and of Teddy – then four years old – being much interested, and liking him very much, and finally going over to sit on his lap. Whereupon, of course, Teddy got a good close look at the pectoral cross the Cardinal wore on a long chain and was fascinated, and took it and gazed and turned it over and around and gazed some more. The Cardinal accepted all that with smiles and complete understanding; he had a wonderful way with little children, and he loved them, I believe, as Jesus did. I have regretted that we didn't happen to have a camera in the house at the time to record the scene. But I have kept that sofa ever since, through many moves and changes, and it is now to this day – along with so many other artifacts of our lives – in our house at Hyannis Port.

The third particular memory I have of that extraordinary year, 1936, was of a trip to the Soviet Union. This came in the late winter of the year, and Joe had finished his analysis of RCA's financial problems but was already deep into the far greater ones of Paramount; which meant he would be busy in New York and on the Coast. Kathleen's school in France allowed an Easter vacation of several weeks, and inasmuch as I wanted to see her and thought we could have a good time together some place during her holidays, I sailed from New York early in April. But then what? Both our imaginations had been considerably fired by Joe Jr's impressions of the Soviet Union and the sometimes warm discussions these had occasioned at home. So Kick and I agreed it would be a grand idea to go and see for ourselves.

In those days, to most people, the Soviet Union seemed as remote and mysterious as the other side of the moon, and when I made the arrangements in Paris for the two of us, mother and young daughter, to travel there on our own, everybody seemed to think I was slightly out of my mind. However, I knew that once we were in Moscow we could stay at the Embassy, and that Ambassador William Bullitt would take charge of us and arrange for us to see everything that was open to foreigners.

Actually, the most exciting part of the whole adventure was simply getting there, for the European commercial airlines went only as far as Latvia, where we were to change to a Soviet plane. While we were waiting for it at the airport I saw a small old-fashioned plane being trundled across the field. It had a pair of ropes looped around the back, evidently to hold the fuselage and wings together. Imagine my consternation when, a few minutes later, I saw our luggage being carried out and put aboard.

It was our aeroplane, all right, and in fact it was all ours, for there were only four seats, including two for the pilot and co-pilot. Anyway, we got in, Kick and I in back, the pilot and co-pilot in front, and strapped ourselves firmly to the seats, and as I recited Hail Marys silently to myself and thought of my other children at home, perhaps so soon to be motherless, the plane went yawing down the runway and with a convulsive shudder lifted off, and we were airborne.

More or less, that is, for we seldom were more than a few hundred feet off the ground. I don't know if there was anything but a compass in the way of navigation equipment, but if so the pilot apparently wasn't using it – perhaps he was too proud, or wanted to show off his skill – because he flew by visual landmarks, now and again tipping a wing so he could peer down. I can't imagine what he saw that could help him, because to me it looked like nothing but endless expanses of dark, dense, impenetrable forest, which for variety was sometimes obscured by fog or low-hovering clouds, in which case he would dive down to tree-top level for a closer look. The landscape kept looming up at us. The pilot would then pull out the choke, pull back on the rudder or whatever it is, and we would rise sharply – leaving our stomachs, Kick's and mine, back on the latest cloud-number.

Actually the pilot was very friendly and solicitous. Often, after one of these near-misses, he would take his eyes off the terrain altogether while the co-pilot took over and turn to us and give us a smile and a little wave, indicating that despite the extreme turbulence everything was just fine and we should have complete confidence. I'm sure he must have been a very good pilot. After some hours we landed safely. Neither Kick nor I had become airsick. Probably because our normal reflexes were paralysed.

Anyway, Ambassador Bill Bullitt was a perfect host. We saw everything there was to see, so to speak, both in Moscow and in Leningrad, the old Czarist St Petersburg. We went to the ballet and the museums (which included many of the grand palaces and glorious churches built by the old regime and taken over by the new), and schools and hospitals; and Lenin's tomb on Red Square, of course, and the famous Moscow subway where every station is a work of art in marble and mosaic.

We saw the former private apartments of Nicholas and Alexandra, the deposed and slain Czar and Czarina. While reflecting on that human tragedy I also noticed in their bedroom – where a great many of their personal things remained, just as they had left them – that they had had twin brass beds, with icons on tables next to them. I understand that some of the artifacts we saw are now in museums.

I remember too that in the living-room of the royal apartment, down at one end of the room, there was a secret door in the wall that would open and close leaving no sign of itself, and this led to a hidden staircase that in turn led to the outside of the palace. And this, in case of betrayal or attempted *coup d'état* or assassination, none of which were in the least uncommon in Imperial Russia. In turn, this reminded me of something Sir Thomas Lipton had told me one day about a cruise Nicholas and Alexandra had taken with him on one of his *Shamrocks*. Alexandra evidently was having a happy and reposeful time, and she said to Sir Tom – as he related – that this was one of the few days of her life since she married Nicholas that she felt safe from assassins. Otherwise, she said, home in Russia she was haunted by the idea that any day someone might try to kill her and her husband and their children.

Bill Bullitt told us on our arrival that, for example, if we made any telephone calls from the Embassy we should be discreet about anything we said because the switchboard operator – a pleasant, efficient woman who was fluent in English, and I suppose French and German also, besides her native Russian – was a spy and would be reporting everything we said that might be of interest to the authorities. He told us we would be under surveillance all the time, and this turned out to be true except that there was nothing 'secret' about it; any time Kick and I left the Embassy to drive somewhere, there was a little car parked down the street with two plainclothesmen in it and they would trail along – to see where we went and what we did. On our visits to the factories and schools I, of course, was curious about many things and was asking questions. But soon one of the Embassy people told me I mustn't do much of that, because if our guide-translator interpreted the answers or made comments in ways that didn't quite fit the official doctrines, other guides who might be present and overhear would report these lapses and our guide would be in trouble.

Bill said there was no escaping the police-spy apparatus so we might as well get used to it, and told us a story about himself. It was about a visit to the Black Sea, the Russian southern resort area. Bill was a strong athlete, a confident swimmer, so he swam far out in the water and was floating there on his back and looking at the azure sky and thinking peaceful thoughts such as that finally, for a while, he was free of the police 'shadows' who always trailed him. Suddenly he was aware of gurglings and splashings from another swimmer, and he turned to see a familiar face, that of one of his customary NKVD followers, who had surfaced about a hundred feet away and was nonchalantly pretending to be looking the other way as if he were out there just because he liked long-distance swimming.

The idea of being followed was unpleasant. At the same time I realized this couldn't have been happening to more than a small fraction of the Russian people themselves. After all, if the regime was trying to build up the economy and 'build Socialism' it couldn't employ half the population to spy on the other half. For anyone suspected of disagreeing with government policies it must have been terribly difficult, nerve-racking and dangerous. I'm sure I thanked God every day for the protections we Americans have under our Constitution. Yet I could understand why the broad masses of the people would accept the Communist system. Not just because they had to and not only because of the incessant propaganda that was dinned into them, but also because the masses really were better off in a good many ways than they had been under the Czarist system, which was the only alternative most of them had known.

I remember, for instance, talking privately with one of our guides, a very nice and attractive young woman, who told me about her life. She had been educated by the State, she said, and now had a good well-paid job which she enjoyed. Her husband was finishing higher education, in college, at State expense. They had a young child who was being educated, and being taken care of during the hours she worked, by a State school and child centre, and who in turn would be assured of opportunities for advancement and ultimately of a job – since all able-bodied people worked and there was no such thing as involuntary 'unemployment'. She said that none of these advantages could possibly have come to her or her husband – their families lacking money or influence – under the old regime; so naturally they liked the new one – and why shouldn't they?

I remember, too, a day when another of these attractive young guides was showing us around one of the big libraries and said proudly: 'We can read any book in the whole library that we want to.' I was touched by her naïveté because, of course, in the US we all are so accustomed to our public libraries and to perfectly open access to books; and besides, books critical of Communism or contrary to its doctrines had been purged from the Soviet libraries. Still, that left a large part of the world's literature, including many of the familiar American classics: the works of Thoreau, Emerson, Bronson, Hawthorne and others dear to my childhood (I forgot to ask about Louisa May Alcott, but I expect she was there; I hope so), and Poe and Whitman and Mark Twain and Dreiser, and of course Jack London (a favourite in Russia) and numerous others. So in this case, too, I saw that ordinary citizens had much greater opportunities to educate themselves and better themselves, and that they appreciated this and had good reason to.

So although there were many things I saw that dismayed and repelled me – one which I need only mention, without elaboration, being the official doctrine of atheism – I did see why the Soviet system could be acceptable to the people of the USSR; moreover that many of its aims, if not many of the methods, were worthy of respect and discussion and study in some of our western societies. I did, at least, understand a lot better what Joe Jr had been talking about; which was bound to be of some satisfaction to a mother with a very bright eldest son, on whom many hopes rested.

Eunice has always been one of the most faithful correspondents in the family. I had a letter from her which, though dated merely 'Mon. 18' I am certain was 1936. I must have received it in Paris or London on my way home, so it was late spring or earliest summer. It gives a flavour of the family news at that time:

Dearest Mother,
We all received your letter and were very glad to hear from you. We are awful glad your coming home. Bob has sold 4 rabits at 75c each and so is doing very well. Dad called up yesterday and said Jack was staying in Cal. with him and he also said he would be home the end of the week or the 1st of next week. Eddie is taking me to the horse races next Sat. at Long Island. Jack wrote and said he is having a wonderful time out West. Smokey [Jack's then current dog, a shepherd dog of some sort] is out there with him now. School is just the same and I am certainly anxious to get to the Cape. It is very warm and it has been above 85 during the week. Well thats all.

All my love
Eunice

And here is another, dated 'about Jan. 20th', which I must have received in Florida, having stayed down there a while after the children had to go back north to school after the Christmas holidays.

Dear Mother,
I suppose you are having a wonderful time. My exams started today and get over in two weeks. Bob went to Boston today and was very excited as he is planning to see Joe, Jack [Joe was at Harvard; Jack hadn't yet gone West], Grandpa and Grandma and he wont have to go to school tomorrow. Yesterday the lights went out about four thirty over most of New York and it was terrible . . . It snowed the other day but the rain washed it all away. How do you like this writing paper. Mrs Moore gave it to me. Please excuse this letter but Teddy is running around my room shouting like a maniac, as he put a huge piece of gum in his hair and Kicko [the resident nursemaid] is trying to get it out but has not succeeded and Pat is practising so I cant think straight. Well I hope you come home soon as we all miss you *loads*.

Love from us all
Lots and Lots of Love
Eunice

PS   Have a nice time.

Active as Joe was in 1936, busy accomplishing things that many talented businessmen would have considered the climax of a lifetime career, he rather soon began feeling uncomfortable at being out of the thick of things in Washington. While he was merely reshaping great corporations, FDR and other friends and former colleagues were reshaping the life and institutions of the nation. It was becoming increasingly difficult for him to stand on the sidelines.

Consequently, the following year, 1937, he accepted FDR's request that he head a new federal agency, the US Maritime Commission, which was supposed to bring sense and order and profitability into the chaotic, fast-declining US merchant marine. The long skein of circumstances, beginning back in 1916 when FDR was Assistant Secretary of the Navy and Joe was manager of the Fall River shipyards, made Joe the President's first and logical choice, and Joe took the job, releasing the same house he had near Washington during his SEC chairmanship. I visited now and then, as I had before; he managed to take every weekend back in Bronxville, but the heavy demands of his new job and his determination to keep a reasonable semblance of home and family life put a heavy strain on him, vigorous as he was. First the SEC, now the MC, both important, no doubt, but the New Deal was teeming with 'alphabetical agencies', all of which presumably had some important reason for existing. I felt that Joe deserved something better, something really special, in the government, and I told him so. We discussed the situation at home and with close friends in the Administration and with a few trusted and knowledgeable friends in the press, such as Arthur Krock.

What Joe had always wanted, as I mentioned, was to be Secretary of the Treasury, but there was really no chance left for that after FDR appointed Henry Morgenthau. The President wouldn't have removed Morgenthau even if he had been otherwise inclined to, because Mrs Morgenthau and Eleanor were such great friends, and dispensing with Henry could have resulted in friction not only in the Dutchess County neighbourhood but in the Roosevelt home; and FDR had enough problems without adding that. The other Cabinet-level jobs were of little or no real interest to Joe. A high-level Ambassadorship would, of course, be another and attractive possibility. But Joe spoke no foreign language and had no 'ear' or natural facility in languages; thus the suitable possibilities really were reduced to only one post, that of being Ambassador to Great Britain. That was occupied by Robert Worth Bingham, a most competent and respected man. However, it was rumoured, and rather soon confirmed, that Ambassador Bingham was seriously ill and would have to resign.

I began to question Joe when he came home for weekends. 'What has the President said?' I would ask. 'What have you done about it? Why should you, with all your brains, spend all this time away from me and our children doing odd jobs for the President unless there's an important reward? Why don't you demand specifically what you want?'

Joe finally said to me, 'Well, I can't just walk into the office of the President of the United States and say, "I want to be Ambassador to England."'

Through other means behind the scenes, however, eventually it was understood that if he did his usual excellent job at the Maritime Commission the next step beyond would be the Ambassadorship. He was confident enough of this to confide the approaching event, in fall of 1937, not only to me but to Joe Jr and Jack so that they could make their plans too. Arthur Krock broke the news on an unofficial 'well-informed sources' basis in December, and early in 1938 it was confirmed by the President's official appointment of Joe as his Ambassador to the Court of St James's.

12

Our family seems to have an affinity for involvement in major episodes and events at precisely the time they happen. If the President had made Joe Secretary of the Treasury, the job he so very much had wanted, he would have missed the more exciting – and some would say, more important – challenges of building and running the Securities and Exchange Commission. Or again, if the Ambassadorship had come in 1932 or soon after, it could have been rather forgettable except to us, to recherché historians, and to archivists at the State Department. Coming instead in 1938, it landed us in the centre of those dramatic, still almost unreal events that led to World War II.

The political and diplomatic history of that time has been written about from all sorts of national and personal viewpoints. I can add only some footnotes – interesting ones, I hope – from the viewpoint of the American Ambassador's wife, official hostess and companion and mother of his numerous children, who were transported from a more or less 'normal' American environment to the complicated world of diplomatic London.

I was sure this would be an important experience for them, and indeed it was. In fact, in retrospect, it probably put Jack on the first rung of the ladder to the Presidency. However, there was also the immediate, practical matter of schools for them.

Finally it was decided that Bobby, then thirteen, and Teddy, six, would live with us at the Embassy Residence but go to day school in London. Eunice and Pat and Jean would go to a Sacred Heart board-ing-school near London similar to the one at home. Rosemary, because of her condition, would go to a special school. Kathleen, who had graduated by then from convent school and had been going to Parsons in New York to learn design and decorating, would drop out for a while and live with us at the Residence, helping me a bit with my duties as hostess and also having her debut in London. Joe Jr, who was in the last semester of his senior year at Harvard, would stay on to graduate and then come over to gain embassy experience as a very

junior secretary to his father, and to travel on the Continent as his
father's unofficial but bright observer of the troubled scene.

As for Jack, who when last seen in these pages had hepatitis and
asthma and had dropped out of Princeton for the academic year of
1935–6, he would also stay on at Harvard to the end of the semester.
Meanwhile he had recovered enough health to go to college again and
this time had chosen Harvard instead, to his father's hardly concealed
pride and joy, and entered there in the fall of '36 for the academic year
of 1936–7.

He had done well. Promptness was still not among his greatest
virtues. This accounts for the opening paragraph below. Never mind
about that. The letter from his father in February 1937 from Palm
Beach is evidence of larger change:

Dear Jack,

I was not particularly upset about your not getting back on time
as I feel you are doing such a good job up there, but some little thing
like that might put you off on the wrong foot and then again it may
give people the idea that you were expecting privileges that other
people could not enjoy. However, I am glad you are back and I
think you and Joe did a swell job on your marks.

I am impressed with the almost complete turn-around you have
made in yourself in the last year. You know I always felt you had
great possibilities and I think now you are starting to avail yourself
of them. You are making a great hit with the older people and they
are very much impressed with your discussions and looking on you
with a great deal of respect. For your own satisfaction this is really
worthwhile.

I talked with your Mother on the phone last night, she is coming
down this week. Said she had a grand time in Boston and she was
more than pleased with you and Joe. Rosemary had a marvellous
time also and really does not require many gestures like this to make
her life worthwhile.

The weather after you left was bad for almost the whole week, in
fact it was raining for three days, so you were most fortunate . . .
My golf is completely gone, I can't beat anybody . . . Good luck to
you on the swimming and as to football, remember to be as good as
the spirit is. You ought to weigh somewhere about 170.

Love, Dad

Jack had run for class president that first year and been swamped.
The next school year, 1937–8, he ran for student council, and lost. I
think that this was his last venture into student politics. He continued

during those years to show rather more interest in social activities and sports than in grades. He went out for swimming, football and golf.

He was a strong contender for the varsity swimming team, in the backstroke, but as the crucial meet with Yale approached he came down with a hard case of influenza and had to be in the infirmary. He made a secret pact with his room-mate, Torbert Macdonald, who remembers:

> Guts is the word. He had plenty of guts . . . he had the flu, but he was set on making his letter. So every day I'd sneak into the infirmary with some food for him. [Lots of steaks and thick malted milks, to keep his weight from dropping.] As soon as he'd eaten, we'd slip out the back door, and I'd drive him to the indoor athletic building, where he'd doggedly practise his backstroke. Then I'd drive him back to the hospital.

Alas, in spite of all that valiant foolhardy effort he was eliminated in the trials for the meet. (To Richard Tragaskis, who later on became a well-known journalist, author and broadcaster.) As for football, he tried out for the varsity although he weighed only 149 pounds, which again showed a lot of courage but not much sense on his part. He dropped back (I'm sure with much regret but with good grace) to the 'junior varsity' and was doing a good job there until one day in practice he was hit by a hard block or tackle and landed at the wrong angle and ruptured a spinal disc. This injury ended his football days and marked the beginning of troubles with his back that were to haunt him the rest of his life.

As his father's letter shows, he had begun in a significant way during his first Harvard year to 'avail' himself of his 'great possibilities' and his elders were already becoming 'very much impressed' with him. Between his first and second years at Harvard, the summer of 1937, he and his pal from Choate and Princeton, Lem Billings, travelled around Europe together, and as Lem has recalled:

> I went over with very little money because my father wasn't alive. This is another side of Jack's character: he was perfectly happy to live at places for forty cents a night, and we ate frightful food . . . but he did do it, and that was the only way I could go with him. We had a terrific time. [The two toured France, Germany, Holland, Italy, Spain, and parts of England.] London was last . . . and Jack broke out in the most terrible rash, and his face blew up, and we didn't know anybody and had an awful time getting a doctor . . . Food poisoning of some kind . . . [Probably it was an allergic reaction.] This was just before the war, and Jack decided to report

to his father what he was finding out – he was constantly asking questions . . .

When he came back to Harvard in the fall he decided to major in government. He still had no particular idea of going into politics himself, or participating directly in government. His ambition inclined towards journalism; but studies in political science and government would be very useful background for him in that profession. In any case his new curiosity and interests were reflected in improved marks and also helped prepare him to be an intelligent observer, and for a while a participant in the events of his father's Ambassadorship.

Joe preceded us to London. My travel plans and preparations were interrupted by an inconvenient attack of appendicitis. There was nothing to do but have the thing out, so without informing anyone but Joe, the Moores and the help – why worry the children? – I did so. When I was ready to leave the hospital someone tipped off the press and my exit was made in a commotion of photographs and interviews.

Eunice wrote from Sacred Heart at Noroton:

Dear Mother,
    Of all the surprising things that occurred in the Kennedy family within the past few months the greatest shock came when I heard that you had your appendix out . . . we are praying for you up here so I am sure you will be up and even running around dear old England in no time . . .

Actually it didn't take long. I was able to sail by early March, bringing Kick, Pat, Bobby, Jean and Teddy with me. It was an exciting and slightly hectic sailing, because so many friends of all ages were there to wish us bon voyage and a marvellous time in England, to say nothing of a great many members of the press. Among these was our old friend Mary Pickford, pretending to be a reporter because she was about to play the role of one in a movie and wanted to get a little practice in an authentic scene.

Our first port on the other side of the ocean was Cobh, Eire, and this brought back some memories and reveries to me. I had been there with my father in 1908 when I was eighteen – Kick's age – and it was Queenstown, Ireland, and I remembered the sight of young men and women on the quays saying emotional farewells to relatives and friends before sailing off to America, more than likely to Boston. In similar scenes and far worse circumstances my ancestors and Joe's had departed. Now our family returned, momentarily, in circumstances that could hardly be more dramatically different. There were many thoughts in my mind that day.

As I approached London, the Embassy, and the Court of St James's as the wife of the American Ambassador, to take up responsibilities as my husband's hostess and partner, I realized I would be under special scrutiny and that if I made mistakes in my role, or if I even inadvertently gave my opinion about some delicate matter to the wrong person at the wrong time, there could be damaging consequences.

I freely admit to feeling a bit nervous and apprehensive. Any woman who didn't have similar such feelings, in that situation, would have to have had supreme self-confidence. Curiously, my nervousness gave way to expectations. The adventure ahead was surely to be one of the more interesting experiences of our lives.

The British press seemed fascinated by the idea of a large and lively Boston Irish family descending on the London diplomatic scene. There had already been a good deal of advance publicity about us, and once there we became practically public property. I almost began to feel that we had been adopted, as a family, by the whole British people. Wherever we went, we were greeted with smiles and waves and bright looks – a spontaneous outpouring of human warmth. I shall never forget it.

This was all very stimulating, but the pressing need was to attend to the business of settling in. The Embassy residence stood six stories high and was part of a long row of similar, connecting houses fronting on a street called Prince's Gate, in one of the pleasantest parts of London, almost opposite the beautiful park called Kensington Gardens. In back, it shared a large enclosed expanse of lawn and garden with the other houses of the block. It had been given to the US Government by J. P. Morgan. It sounded like a nice location.

Although I supposed it would be furnished in silk and damask and precious objects, I had inquired of the State Department, through Joe's office, if there was anything I should bring or have sent over. With our large family, I was also curious about the sleeping arrangements.

A letter soon arrived from 'Department of State: Division of Foreign Service Administration', initialled BK, from which I will quote:

'There are no bed linens and no dining-room linens of any description; no towels of any kind; no bath mats.

'The only dining-room silver consists of 4 solid silver sauce-boats. A list of the Lenox and other china is attached.

'There is a sewing-room which does not seem to be equipped with a Government sewing-machine.'

(This meant acquiring a complete assortment of linens and towels on the massive scale needed for our family and for the luncheon, dinner and overnight guests we were sure to have; plus a complete silver flatware and hollow-ware (less four sauce-boats) service for at least two dozen, considering the official entertaining we would be expected to do. And the essential sewing-machine.)

As I read further, I found some good news: 'A careful comparison of the attached lists with the inventory cards indicates that the Embassy residence is quite completely furnished with high grade furniture.' However, BK continued, 'Of course I have no way of ascertaining the present condition of the various pieces . . .'

More good news: 'Curtains and drapes appear to be adequate for the whole building, as well as rugs and lamps.

'There are mattresses and springs for all beds.

'In 1931 the Department paid $506.52 for 68 blankets.

'There are eight baths and three servants' baths.

'There are eight bedrooms, 2 single and 6 double. All appear to be well furnished. For the servants there are 13 bedrooms, 19 beds.'

How on earth was I going to fit our family into the Residence, which had sufficed nicely for Ambassador Andrew Mellon and, I suppose, for all the previous Ambassadors to the Court of St James's. We were eleven people and there were only eight bedrooms.

Double everybody up, one may suggest. Yet this would have caused complications, besides which only six of the rooms were big enough for double occupancy. And the beds for three bedrooms were in storage. I solved this problem in a practical way. We certainly didn't need 19 live-in servants in 13 bedrooms which occupied the entire two top stories of the Residence, so we poached on that territory and had rooms enough for ourselves and for our guests, as necessary. Actually, with three of the girls at boarding-school, Jack at Harvard about half of our time there, our travels, and Joe Jr's trips to the Continent, it all worked out.

Andrew Mellon had of course been one of the great art collectors of this century, and during his tenure at the Residence the walls were hung with masterpieces. Upon endowing the National Gallery in Washington, however, he had transferred all his art treasures there, leaving the walls of the Residence practically bare. In the interval no one had seemed to have ideas about what to do with the bare walls. Fortunately, Joe and I knew another fabulous art collector, William Randolph Hearst. He owned a castle in Wales, with many fine paintings, and he arranged for a number of them to be sent up on loan to the Residence.

The staff that lived in, or came daily to the Residence – butler, chef, secretaries, maids and others – was almost wholly British and wonderfully well trained and proficient. I also was able to call on, in case of need, the services of the Embassy staff. I sometimes have been asked how I could know quite what to do in such a delicate but important matter as the order of precedence in seating people at a large formal dinner at the Residence.

The answer is that I didn't know, but there was always someone on the staff whose job it was to know, and to whom I could turn for advice and guidance, and in fact confidently entrust nearly all the arrangements. Almost invariably everything came out just right.

There were three American staff-members, though, who had come along with us and, within the family, had far higher ratings than any of the others could possibly have achieved. One was Luella Hennessey, the trained nurse who had been in charge of Pat at the time of her appendectomy and had become a great friend of Bobby's when he had been in hospital with pneumonia – and who by this time was the person we looked to first when any one of us needed skilled and loving nursing care. She was, by turns, nurse, nursemaid, companion and friend to the younger children.

Another was Elizabeth Dunn, our governess. The third indispensable American was our cook, Margaret Ambrose, who kept the family supplied with creamed chicken, strawberry shortcake, and Boston Cream Pie.

Another item of interest:

Our six-storey Residence had a 'lift', or 'elevator'. It was a large fancy cage that went up and down smoothly and majestically on a system of hydraulics involving a couple of enormous weighted steel pillars that alternately pushed or gave way: a most impressive and fascinating machine. In no time at all after our arrival, Bobby and Teddy discovered it and how to make it run and decided it was the greatest thrill in the world to get inside the carriage and work the controls and go gliding up and down, up and down. The butler discovered them at the game and tried to coax them out but, poor man, he wasn't used to small American boys, and it was I who ordered them to disembark and never again to treat this useful machine as a toy.

Those first months passed in a whirl of introductions and social and official events. This was compounded by the fact we had arrived at the beginning of the London 'Season', when gentry arrive from far and near for a round of balls, parties and Court functions. This is also the season for English girls to make their debuts. Kick, being eighteen, had reached the customary age for coming out and it was logical she should do so in London. There were many preparations to make. For instance, I had to be introduced to the mothers of all the other debutantes. Unless they had met me personally, etiquette would have forbidden Kick to be invited to the parties they gave for their daughters. There were many other formalities to thread my way through. A pleasant but exhausting one was to call on the wives of all the other ambassadors to introduce myself. It was interesting seeing the other embassy residences, and meeting these women and getting a sense of who-was-who in the diplomatic colony, but the list was long, and it took me months to work my way through it.

The first protocol visit, which was quite exciting, came only two days after my arrival while I was still unpacking and getting my bearings.

Ambassadorial wives – accompanied by their husbands – were always 'received' by the Queen, a gracious form of welcoming them to the country. So, on March 18, Joe and I arrived at Buckingham Palace, and precisely to the minute of our appointed time were ushered into a beautiful and very comfortable sitting-room, where Queen Elizabeth came forward to greet us.

She had such a happy, natural smile and friendly manner that I felt at ease with her at once. She indicated I should sit beside her on a small sofa near the fireplace (in which a cheerful, warming and most welcome fire was flaming) and that Joe sit in a big, comfortable-looking chair opposite us. She and Joe had already met, so they chatted a bit about Anglo-American relations, but she soon wanted to hear all about our children, their ages and school plans, their feelings about coming to England, and so forth.

Again I found it a great conversational convenience that ours were spread over such a range of ages, because the two royal children, Princess Elizabeth (the present Queen) and Princess Margaret Rose, were about the ages of our two youngest, Teddy and Jean. Her Majesty and I could compare notes and agree that these were extremely interesting ages in child development.

Soon afterwards Joe and I received a Royal Invitation to spend the weekend of April 9–11 at Windsor Castle. The other guests were Prime Minister and Mrs Neville Chamberlain, Lord and Lady Halifax (he was the new Foreign Minister), Lord and Lady Elphinstone (she was the Queen's sister) and, I suppose as an 'extra man', Major the Hon. Sir Richard Molyneux.

We came up from London in an Embassy car to Windsor, and through a large and beautiful park to arrive at the castle at 7 p.m.

There we were met by the Master of the Household, Brigadier-General Sir Hill Child, who conducted us to our rooms. They were in one of the towers, with a lovely view of the park, and were upholstered in red damask and white linen paper; there were accessories in gold and white. In my bedroom was a huge bed, also upholstered in red damask and set high, so that one had to use a step-stool to enter it. There were numerous servants in evidence, in full livery; soon one of them brought us sherry. Another, who as well as livery wore a peruke, was especially appointed to attend us and lead the way whenever we left our suite.

After a few minutes of contemplating the scene, Joe turned to me and said, 'Rose, this is a helluva long way from East Boston.'

That weekend at Windsor was one of the most fabulous, fascinating experiences of my life. I took many diary notes. These are excerpts which I hope will be interesting to others:

At 8.20 the footman came to escort us to the Green Reception Room. At 8.30 the King and Queen came in and greeted everybody by shaking hands. All the ladies curtsied. Dinner was announced and the King and Queen walked ahead . . . they sat opposite each other at the middle of the table, I at the King's right and Mrs Chamberlain on his left. The Ambassador sat on the Queen's right and the Prime Minister on her left. Lord Elphinstone was on my right and was extremely agreeable. I talked a good deal to the King about my children.

On the wall behind the Queen was a portrait of Queen Victoria with the Ribbon of the Order of the Garter. Conversation led to this and to the story that Queen Victoria had declared the ribbon was not painted the correct hue and had one sent to the artist so he could do retouching. He somehow thought he was being decorated with the Order, and when after correspondence and dispute he learned this was not the case, he refused the royal wish – so the colour was never made right.

Table decorations consisted of high flowers, which made it difficult for the King and Queen to see each other and caused some good-natured teasing when he could not communicate to her that she should rise, the signal to leave the table.

After dinner, the Queen stood in front of the fireplace in one of the drawing-rooms. Each of the men bowed to her, then went into an adjoining room to talk with the King, the ladies remaining with the Queen. She talked with me first for about fifteen minutes, then Lady Halifax brought up each of the other ladies in turn. Joe told me that the same procedure took place with the men, in regard to the King. Meanwhile a Scottish piper walked through the rooms, piping away. The Queen is of Scottish descent. We are of Irish descent. The pipes are equally Scottish and Irish; so this was a congenial touch. I found it very difficult to accustom myself to saying 'Ma'am' when addressing the Queen and she told me not to bother; putting me at my ease. She has a very pleasing voice, a beautiful English complexion, great dignity and charm; is simple in manner, stands very erect and holds herself well and is every inch a Queen. We talked, among other things, about the difficulty of sleeping in London, and the Queen was very much amused that I put wax in my ears.

After a while the King and the men came back, and after mixed conversation the King and Queen showed us some of the treasures of the castle, in a room off the drawing-rooms. There were jewellery and trinkets worn by Mary Queen of Scots and the original blue garter from which the Order of the Garter has its name.

At 11.00 the Queen said goodnight and shook hands again with all. In bed, but before sleep, we heard the sounds of the Changing of the Guard, and the clock striking in the tower.

The next day, April 10, was Palm Sunday. My diary notes continue:

We had breakfast in our sitting-room. Then went to Mass in the town of Windsor, where the priest met us at the church door. On return we saw the Changing of the Guard – very impressive – then walked in the park that surrounds the Castle and ran into Princess Elizabeth hiding behind the shrubs. She had on a pink coat and was hatless and she smiled at us. Walked around the golf course and had a lovely view of the Castle.

At luncheon the Queen wore a bluish-green dress, no hat and an aquamarine bracelet. The Princesses were in rose dresses with checked blouses, red shoes with silver-coloured buckles, white socks, and necklaces of coral and pearl. Princess Margaret had a ribbon in her hair. She sat next to her mother, and Princess Elizabeth sat next to Joe. I sat on the right of the Prime Minister and had Viscount Gage on my left. I told the Prime Minister he was very much like my husband, with his business background and both of them so fond of music and walking. (Joe later told me I could compare him with anyone I wanted to, but to keep such opinions private.) I found I was not suitably dressed, as all the ladies were in afternoon dresses and I had remained in my tweeds.

After lunch there was a band concert. Then it was arranged for us all to take a walk, very informally, with the King and Queen and the two little Princesses. Everybody changed into comfortable shoes and tweeds. We walked to Frogmore, one of several mansions that monarchs have built in Windsor Park as domiciles for visiting family members and guests. It is very stiff Victorian, with yellow damask curtains, though the entrance hall is rather sweet in white delicate chintz. The King told us that his parents – with their large family – had used it as a schoolhouse and he had studied there. We also saw many of the natural and cultivated beauties of the park, such as the mulberry bushes. Margaret Rose was very much interested in a Californian pine tree of great height and said it made you giddy to look up to the top and she thought that was funny.

We left at mid-morning the next day and were back at the Embassy Residence in time to have guests of our own to lunch there.

For various Reasons of State, British and American and others, we were to find ourselves associating with the King and Queen fairly often in the many months ahead. And, indeed, with many other royalties and members of the highest nobility, both foreign and domestic. Within two weeks of my arrival, as I see by my diary (March 29), we were 'received' by the Dowager Queen Mary at Marlborough House. My notes of the day read:

Were there promptly. Ushered into a sitting-room where we met Dowager Countess Airlie and another lady-in-waiting. The ladies-in-waiting are always Peeresses, usually serve two weeks at a time and may go home nights except at Windsor . . . Met Her Majesty in a small sitting-room. She was dressed in grey wool crepe with silk dots scattered. She wore a small diamond and coral pin. She sat very straight, was meticulously groomed. As usual, discussion was of children.

In May we gave a coming-out party for Kathleen: actually a joint debut for her and Rosemary, who was also of an appropriate age. As I have said, we always wanted Rosemary to participate as fully as possible in the activities of the family and of her general age group. On such an occasion as this – a big, somewhat confusing scene with much music and dancing and lots of people she didn't know – we naturally had a few apprehensions. But she looked quite pretty, she was happy and everything went well. Rosemary went to some parties, but as she was rather shy we always had one of the men from the Embassy escort her to see that she had dancing partners and wasn't left too long with one partner. I say this because parents who have retarded children may be discouraged because they think their child could not undertake a social occasion. We made special provision to see that Rosemary was included.

Also, that same month, Kick, Rosemary and I were Presented at Court, one of those British royal ceremonies that has since disappeared but at the time was glamorous beyond belief. Being presented was at one and the same time one of the most utterly simple and intensely complicated events imaginable.

The simplicity consisted of the act itself. One went to Buckingham Palace, sat a while in a reception room, and on cue from a functionary of the Court entered the Grand Ballroom, at one end of which, on a dais, sat the King and Queen and two or three other members of the Royal Family. One walked out in front of them, curtsied to each, then walked to the side of the room and stood there, or perhaps sat on an available gilt chair. Others would have been doing this before you, others would do it after, there would be several hundreds of girls and matrons at any given session of Court, of which there were four that year, ours being the first – and literally that's all there was to it: a couple of brief curtsies to the enthroned monarchs.

Not only were the selected debutantes presented, but also the wives and daughters of the diplomats, and of visiting dignitaries from far parts of the British Empire, and anyone else who had the means to get to London, afford it, and could somehow wangle an invitation, a process that in most cases involved the various embassies.

The pressure on the US Ambassador from socially ambitious American women to arrange presentations for them had been intense for many years. Joe decided to put a stop to that, and he did so forth-rightly by announcing that the only Americans presented in his ambassadorship would be wives and daughters of men attached to the US diplomatic mission or of American families who for other reasons were actually residing in England. That caused some heartaches at home, but Joe had secured approval in advance from Washington – where Senators and State Department officials and others were glad to be rid of the pressures – and officials of the Court told Joe, too, privately, that they thought it was a very good idea because the competition for presentation was getting to be too fierce. After all, even the facilities of Buckingham Palace are limited.

It was decided that about ten of us who were associated with the Embassy – we three, the wife of the military attaché, the wife and daughter of the naval attaché, several others – would go to the first evening of the first of the four Court presentations. As there would be matrons and girls from other embassies, as well as many members of the British 'ruling classes', we wanted to do our best to represent our embassy and country properly; and this was especially incumbent on me and the girls.

An important matter was proper gowns. Our British friends, and ladies of the Embassy who had been presented in earlier years, said they should be by a British designer since he would understand the exact needs, including the dimensions of the train. I went to Molyneux, the foremost British designer of the time (who also had a salon in Paris), for my dress of white lace beautifully embroidered in tiny silver and gold beads. For Rosemary we selected a white net trimmed in silver. Kathleen's dress was from Paris, selected at Lelong during a long weekend, and was also of white net and trimmed with silver croquettes. (I was amused afterwards to see in the British press that my gown and Rosemary's were described in detail and credited to the great British designer Molyneux; whereas Kathleen's very lovely one was, I suppose by inference, also ascribed to Molyneux.) The girls and I had decided in advance that we should be in white, or else a very light pastel shade of ivory, because this would look best with feather plumes that we called Prince of Wales feathers which every woman presented wore in her hair.

I as a matron would wear a tiara in my hair. I didn't own one. It had simply never occurred to me before coming to England that I would ever need one. My new and sympathetic friend Lady Bessborough lent me hers and it proved to be almost exactly right, most flattering and magnificent. (It fitted very well and had many brilliant diamonds, including a gorgeous marquise diamond in the front. With a few temporary adjustments and arrangements, it was perfect. I was so grateful to her for the thought. I remember that my children – Bobby and Teddy as well as the girls – were extremely impressed.)

We at the Embassy who were to be presented had many discussions about all the paraphernalia. And we also had rehearsals. To save time and strain the matrons and girls would be presented together in pairs. It was important that there be carefully calculated equal space among us three, not only for harmonious design, like a ballet, but to ensure that we would not become entangled in or tread on one another's trains. Further, precision was a crucial matter. We were all to curtsey, and this must be within a split-second of the same time: for it would not have done to have one of us bobbing up while others of us were bobbing down. After all, the eyes of the Court and the Diplomatic Corps would be upon us; we must do it right. So we practised. We had had years of curtseying at the convent, like all Sacred Heart girls.

The great night arrived.

I had already been to the hairdresser that afternoon and my hair was done in a way to receive Lady Bessborough's tiara. I had an early supper on a tray in my bedroom. I was carefully inserted in my lovely embroidered gown by a covey of enchanted, murmuring maids. The man from Molyneux came over to check details and to pin and secure our three head feathers at the proper angle, as I had no idea about how this should be done. A hairdresser was there to place the tiara on my carefully constructed coiffure. The maids helped me draw extra-long white thin kid gloves almost all the way to my shoulders. My jewels were added.

I viewed the complete picture in a long mirror and was perfectly amazed at myself. I had never dreamed of looking this way and being part of such magnificence. I felt a little like Cinderella.

I went into my husband's room to show him my elegance. He wasn't quite finished dressing, but he turned and looked at me, and his blue eyes lit up, and he grinned in the most loving way and said – as he *would* say – 'You're a real knockout,' which was the highest compliment I could ever want.

The girls meanwhile had been having their own special attentions and in a few minutes, fully as excited or more so than I, came running in to see us and be seen. More exclamations all around. Then downstairs to be viewed by the younger children who were duly impressed, then to stop in the hall for the staff to see us, then followed by a session with photographers; and then in large cars off to Buckingham Palace. As we neared it we saw people who had gathered hoping to catch a glimpse of glamorous ladies in their Court gowns and gentlemen in their regalia. They waved to us; we waved to them.

The rest was a gigantic theatrical. The Palace illuminated; the Guards resplendent; the Beefeaters in costume with maces lining the Grand Stairway; passing through anteroom after anteroom attended by footmen in full livery; at last the ballroom and a sight of the royal dais, and being ushered to our place among the Diplomatic Corps – our place determined by length of tenure (everything governed minutely by protocol) which put us after the Chinese Ambassador but before the German Ambassador – and looking around at the grandeur of the room with its vaulted and frescoed ceilings and its walls of murals and gilded pilasters and elaborate details, and looking around also at the others there, the men immaculate and in their decorations, and the women striking and regal in their beautiful gowns and jewels . . . the Duchess of Buccleuch in the famous emeralds of her family; the glittering diamond tiara of the Duchess of Devonshire; the glowing ruby necklace and earrings of Madame Patiño, the dark-eyed vital wife of the

Bolivian Ambassador. I won't ever forget the beautiful embroidered dress worn by the wife of the Chinese Ambassador.

It is a strange aspect of human nature – that almost all of us tend to expect the best and discount the possibilities of the worst, even though experience shows us that the worst can and often does happen. Human beings seem to have been designed (by a Divine Plan, I think) to be optimistic. Otherwise why would anyone have children, strive to do the best for them, plan for their future, while realizing that every hour and day is problematical, and that for all of us, as individuals or families or communities or even nations, there may be in fact no future at all on this earth?

I am led to these thoughts because, while all the pomp and circumstance and romantic story-book traditions that I have described were continuing without a ripple to blemish them, events were in fact building towards the general disaster (and for us, very personal disasters) of the Second World War.

May 4, 1938: Lunch at Prime Minister Neville Chamberlain's home at 10 Downing Street. Prime Minister has several characteristics like Joe. Both had a business background, both love to walk with their wives for recreation, both have music for relaxation. He talked easily but does not smile as often or with as much gaiety as Joe. Joe has told me not to compare the two of them, when I am talking with people.

As a matter of fact, however, they did have much in common and they soon established a close, confident, personal relationship. They were friends; they understood each other easily; and especially they shared a deep desire to avert war and to use every practical means to that end.

May 17: Gave dinner in honour of Foreign Minister Lord and Lady Halifax. Had shad roe sent over from America which arrived frozen and in very good condition and tasted delicious. Surprised how many people were familiar with it and enjoyed it.

After dinner we had a moving picture, *Test Pilot*, with Myrna Loy and Clark Gable. Colonel Charles Lindbergh, who sat next to me, said the aeronautical display was very authentic. He came with his wife and mother-in-law, Mrs Dwight Morrow. This is the second time I have met him – first being at Cliveden, home of Nancy Astor. He acts very shy, smiles in a boyish sort of way and seems to retire to a corner where he stays most of the time. Anne is all poetry and light, simple, natural and lovable with an enchanting smile.

Mrs Morrow is an alert, keen, pleasant woman who pleased me enormously by saying that even though she is a Republican she is glad to see Joe here.

May 19: Photographers from *Vogue* and also two women interviewers. They inquired again about the card catalogue, about which I had told the numerous reporters who came last week. I mean the file where I keep the list of the children's illnesses, dentist visits, eye-examinations, etc. This idea has created a furore in the press.

May 25: Dinner for Mr and Mrs Henry Luce. A box arrived later with a gift from them, reading:

'We wanted to send you flowers when we left London. But you seemed to have so many that we decided to send these frozen ones instead. The clip, they tell me here, are the flowers of the Empire – the Rose for you – and England – the thistle and the Clover for luck – and the shamrock for Joe of course. Again thank you for all your sweetness to us. Love.

Clare and Harry.'

June 1: Went to Epsom Downs to see the Derby with about fifty of Lord Derby's guests. Took a train down. Joe and I rode with Lord Derby, who is the jolliest, the most interesting, the most cordial of the Englishmen I have yet met; grey moustache, stocky in build, has a ruddy complexion and a ready smile.

I knew that this race had originated with his family, had become one of the most famous such events in the world and was the progenitor of many others, such as our own Kentucky Derby. So I asked him about the history of the race and the next day I received a very long letter from him, written in his own hand, telling me all about the Derby. I was honoured and flattered, and most of all, impressed by such personal thoughtfulness.

Of course, he was part of the Victorian-Edwardian era of good manners and graceful living, in which personal correspondence was regarded as important and almost as an art form. I have often wished our society had retained more of that feeling: so much correspondence nowadays comes off a typewriter and lacks the personal qualities of handwriting; and, of course, there is such a great deal of telephoning now, instead of writing, and the words spoken are lost forever.

June 14: Left Embassy about 11.15 to arrive at Ascot about 12.45.

Met Sir John Monk who told us to be on hand after the first race to dine with King and Queen. We walked up the curved stairway with its white rails and a bronze balustrade, and on arriving in Royal Box met the King, Queen, Dukes of Gloucester and Kent, and Duchesses, and Princess Royal, and former Queen Ena of Spain. All the ladies wore long dresses of lace except the Duchess of Kent, who wore a short white crepe. It was the most perfect day, warm, bright sunshine . . . an atmosphere of contentment, of joy, of interest and satisfaction . . . When we went to lunch, I was escorted by the Duke of Kent and on my other side was the Maharajah of Rijipla, who had on a sort of black homespun coat with five buttons of diamonds and rubies and a turban of a mixture of green with yellow stripes swathed around his head . . . Joe took in the Duchess of Gloucester. Marvellous view of race-track, straight down and completely made of grass. In the US it is always dirt; also it is straight, while in the US it is almost circular.

June 16: Gold Cup day at Ascot. Said to be the day when women wear their finest, most luxurious dresses, hats, etc. Beautiful day. In early afternoon came the procession of the carriages containing the King and Queen and all their royal guests from Windsor. It starts at the beginning of the long green race-course which seems miles off in the distance, and we see a faint moving colourful something advancing. Promptly at 2.10 the first carriage, containing the King and Queen, arrives followed by the others, and all proceed down the course and then around in back of the grandstand, where all alight and proceed up the stairs to the Royal Box. There are vast throngs to see them and to view the carriages, which carry two footmen in back and two in front, dressed in navy blue coats with scarlet trimmings. The carriages are open barouches.

When Joe first saw the royal procession, he commented, 'Well, if that's not just like Hollywood!'

I wore black organdie dress and black hat, more unusual than lavenders and pinks and other pastel shades of the crowd. It came from Patou.

June 22: Lady Abingdon's to lunch. She shops at Patou's for her clothes and is rather smart-looking . . .

After luncheon returned home to greet Mother and Father, just arrived from America on the *Manhattan.*

My father was then seventy-five, my mother seventy-three, and both were hale and hearty and active and really had no trouble at all about

As We Remember Joe

13 *Above* Joe Jr receives his commission from his father, May 1942, and Joe Jr in flying kit

Below The dedication of the Joseph P. Kennedy Jr Hospital for Rehabilitation of Handicapped Children in Brighton, Mass. To Joe's right is Cardinal Cushing (then Archbishop Cushing)

A Bouquet of Weddings

14 *Opposite* Kathleen and Billy, with the
    Duchess of Devonshire and Joe Jr
    Pat and Peter
    Jean and Steve
    Eunice and Sarge
    (*inset*) The Father of the Brides

15 *This page* Bobby and Ethel
    Teddy and Joan
    Jack and Jackie

16 I christen the
   Esso Richmond

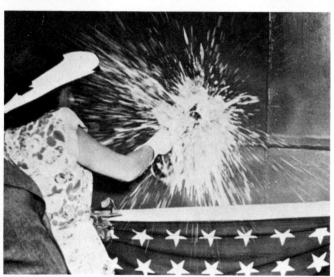

Jean christens the
Joseph P. Kennedy, Jr

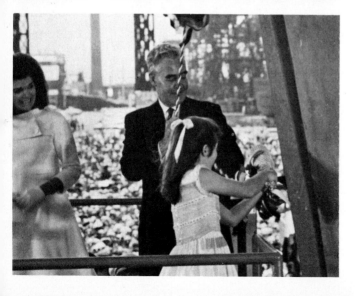

Caroline launches the
John F. Kennedy

making the trip. Naturally I wanted them to come over and see us in our rather amazing setting, and to participate in the life we were leading.

Earlier that year in February, on my father's seventy-fifth birthday, there had been a testimonial dinner for him by the Boston Chamber of Commerce, with seven hundred and fifty guests and with Charles Francis Adams – the most patrician of all Back Bay Bostonians, descendant of two US Presidents, former Secretary of the Navy, a man of immense and diverse talent – as the featured speaker. I am going to quote the gist of his speech:

> It is a pleasure to testify to the good Irish qualities that are in you, John. And I am glad to thank you personally for what you have done for us and the city of Boston.
>
> At times in your past, you, John F., have found it politically expedient to say things about my class that have sometimes hurt. You have even called us degenerate sons of splendid ancestors. Quite possibly that is true. But it takes a man of supreme gifts to tell us a thing like that without arousing rancour. Yet it was said so pleasantly, with such good humour, that no one could take offence or long be angry with a man of the charm – the Irish charm – of John F. Fitzgerald. In everything you have done and in every way you could, you have tried to develop Boston and to improve our community. Even today you are sweating your heart out to bring this port back to what it was, to make it what it should be.

My father replied in his special way, saying among other things:

> I told Charley recently that I might go abroad pretty soon to meet the King and Queen . . . and asked him for tips. You see, Charley Adams's great-grandfather and his grandfather were Ambassadors to Great Britain in times of great stress, too. Before I go, I'm going to get some pointers from him.

They stayed at the Embassy Residence with us for several weeks: 'us', at that period, meaning mainly me and the younger children because Joe had returned to the US briefly, for consultations with the President, and to be present at Joe Jr's graduation from Harvard (*cum laude* and Chairman of his Class Day Committee), and to bring both Joe Jr and Jack back with him. They arrived, appropriately, on July 4.

I showed my parents around London and made sure they had a good time. There weren't many weeks together because they also wanted to tour England and Scotland and Ireland once they were on that side of the water. Further, there were not as many festivities as I would have wanted for them, because the morning after their arrival the news came that Queen Elizabeth's mother, the Countess of Strathmore, had died, which of course put the Court in mourning and cancelled all the royal receptions and social engagements for a while. I see from my diary notes that on June 27 we went out to Cliveden, the huge and beautiful estate of Lord and Lady Astor. Although the Astors didn't happen to be there at the time, we could wander as we liked in the magnificent house and around the endless grounds.

Another day Mother and I went off to Wimbledon for the tennis matches. (Helen Wills Moody, Helen Jacobs, Sarah Palfrey Fabyan, Alice Marble; and Donald Budge and other immortals – if one cares about tennis.) The Dowager Queen Mary was there, and in passing up the aisle between matches saw me, stopped to speak and so was introduced to Mother. Queen Mary at once recalled that my parents were to be visiting me and that she wanted Mother to feel most welcome in England, a heart-warming example of how well trained the Royal Family has been to remember such things, which are so important in public life, as I used to remind my sons. She then also invited us to have tea with her group of dignitaries and accompanying royalties; an invitation it would have been unseemly and inappropriate to refuse.

There were several other memorable occasions, but I think the one that gave the greatest thrill to my father was when we went to tea at the Prime Minister's residence. My diary notes say:

> Mrs Chamberlain very charming. Seems to have time for all of her guests, has a quiet leisurely manner and a very calm unruffled expression. Told Father her family was Irish. In fact Fitzgerald was their name, which quite pleased him.

Naturally my father, during that visit with us, could not help but indulge his sense of humour and his sense of politics. One day he went down to a secretary's office, helped himself to a lot of engraved Ambassadorial invitation cards – which had the blank spaces to be filled in, in handwriting, as to the occasion and the hour people were to arrive – and mailed them off to great numbers of his old pals in Boston, inviting them to the Embassy at tea-time five days hence. Now, of course, as he knew perfectly well, by the time they received the invitations it would be impossible for them to get to London, even if in some delirium they had wanted to cross the ocean for a tea-party.

When Joe heard about this he was considerably annoyed. But my father, the former Congressman and Mayor, was not in the least disturbed. He thought it was a nice gesture, one that had made many people happy, and that he had been quite clever to have thought of it.

Anyway, Father and Mother both had a very good time. And we could enjoy it together, three generations, because they didn't leave until the later part of July and by then Joe Jr and Jack were there, the girls had come down from boarding-school, and Bobby and Jean and Teddy were on hand, so it was a full assemblage. I was happy to know my parents had lived that long, beyond the three-score-and-ten, and had remained unimpaired in their capacity to enjoy life, that their resources were strong and their wits keen, and that they could have the pleasure of being there with us at that time; because I know it was a great joy for them.

I spent most of the next two months near Cannes, on the Riviera. the younger children with me and older ones floating in and out and Joe dropping over from London when he could get away from his duties.

July 27: At Eden Roc for bathing. Saw Elsa Maxwell at lunch so I introduced her to children, who later saw her walking with Marlene Dietrich and they requested her autograph.

Am trying to inspire Pat and Eunice to be interested in collecting autographs. Begged three of Anthony Eden the night of our July 4th dinner. Marlene is gracious, animated, pleasant to meet, seems to be taking a holiday with her hair thrown to the winds and no worry about make-up.

August 3: Joe and Kathleen flew down from London which is easily best way to come and not any more expensive than by train as latter entails extra meal and sleeper. Joe did not come before this as he had to wait until Parliament had risen. Kathleen had been house-guest of the Duchess of Devonshire a few days at the end of July.

August 4: All lunched at Eden Roc Casino, which is quite good, with a special plat du jour. Laughed at waiter yesterday who did not charge for Teddy, saying the little fellow did not eat much, though he had a full course.

August 5: Joe has told Jack that though the milk has a peculiar, to us, sour taste, it is really the flavour that milk has which is not pasteurized. He says he drank that sort of milk in Wales for three or four days – at Mr Hearst's castle. Jack is more resigned.

August 7: All went to church. Priest told Eunice that he was most appreciative of all the francs we give him as usually there are only the smallest coins in the collection. Says Mass very quickly. Mass and Benediction are finished in twenty-three minutes.

August 13: Almost go mad listening to discussion of diets, as Jack is fattening, Joe Jr is slimming, Pat is on or off, and Rosemary (who has gained about eight pounds) and Kathleen and Eunice are all trying to lose.

August 17: Joe planning to send Joe Jr to Paris as it looks as though there would be a crisis in the government at any minute and if he is on the spot it would be a wonderful opportunity for him to see history made. Also he can see how the Embassy there is run by Bill Bullitt and pick up ideas that may be useful to us in London Embassy.

August 28–September 13: Joe Sr flew to Paris. I took train up by night . . . luncheon next day at 2 Avenue d'Jéna which Bill Bullitt [Ambassador to France] gave in honour of Senator Barkley [majority leader of Senate] and Mrs Barkley and some other Americans. See Joe Jr every day . . . Joe's birthday [Sept. 6] and phoned him in London; party for him at Embassy . . . Paris rather chilly and I will be glad to go back to Cannes again and to the sunshine tomorrow . . . Shops here filled with Americans as usual. No one seems to enjoy it all and both agreed that it is difficult to weigh actual advantages and experiences of his stay in Europe. This year will be an accumulation of meeting and seeing men who are shaping the world's destiny.

Arrived at Cannes from Paris. Rainy day . . . Margaret preserved dozens of yellow peaches which have the most delicious flavour in the world and grow here in great profusion . . . Ted has a bad cold, and it is so damp we have kept him in bed all day . . . Teddy adores pedal-boats which he can run when he does not swim . . . Went to church in a modern good-sized church. Few men present, but more than at Valbonne. No Communion, and though I wanted to go I was afraid the Priest would shout at me as he did at Eunice the first Sunday, so I desisted . . . Beautiful day. Ted is so much better that I have decided to send him to London by air in the morning, with Jean and Miss Hennessey. The other children, Rose, Eunice, Pat, Bob, with Miss Dunn, started on a week's tour of Scotland . . .

When Joe phoned at night, he said things were terribly agitated in London and perhaps I should have to leave in the morning.

September 14: No seat on the plane so I am going by sleeper to Paris tonight. I think I should be in London as Joe has Teddy on his mind and, also, there are these crises in world politics. Everyone fearing war. The French all took part in the last war and are almost frantic at the spectre of another one.

As I wrote that, I had in my mind a heartbreaking conversation a couple of weeks earlier with a Frenchwoman I had met. She said: 'My grandfather was killed in the War in 1870 against the Germans. My husband and brother were killed in the War in 1914, and my cousin was blinded. And now they are asking me to send my son to war in 1938. I cannot, I will not.' I was terribly sad. Moved. Little knowing then what tragedies were ahead for me.

September 15: Arrived in Paris about 9.30. Was told that Chamberlain was on his way by air to Berchtesgaden to talk to Hitler.

Several comment on fact that Joe has been on hand constantly and has aided by his presence. Feel that he has given great moral support. First air flight of Prime Minister who is almost seventy years old. Position much more acute and more urgent than PM had realized. Hitler determined to march in and risk a world war if Sudetenland Germans do not get the right of self-determination.

September 18: Church at Brompton Oratory, then golf. Children brought back ties, etc. from Scotland with the Ireland Kennedy colours in the plaids, also some Belleek china for me which I love.

The telephone rings constantly and insistently for Joe. Sometimes from London and sometimes from USA.

Telephoned to Father and Mother. They were fine and it is their 49th anniversary.

September 22: Prime Minister went back to Germany, to Godesberg on Rhine which is a more convenient place than remote Berchtesgaden . . . Profound shock to Prime Minister when he was told the original proposals were not acceptable and were to be replaced . . . Memorandum and map received which was an ultimatum rather than a memorandum, which the Prime Minister felt would profoundly shock public opinion. Hitler to occupy Czechoslovakia October first. Hence, the urgency of making all plans.

Bobby and Teddy return to Gibbs School, a day school.

September 23: Scotland, Gleneagles Hotel. No particular scenery as days are usually rainy and wet in the morning. Have ordered a high pair of rubbers, the like of which I have not worn for years, in order to play golf in the heavy turf . . . Went to dinner at Mrs Buchanan's . . . They were quite shocked when one of my compatriots asked for pheasant yesterday, as they expect all the world to know that one does not start shooting pheasants until October.

Shoots:

Grouse shooting	August 12
Partridge shooting	September 1
Pheasant shooting	October 1

September 24: Foggy and drizzly. Prime Minister back in London with memorandum which was transmitted to Czech government.

President Roosevelt sent two messages to Hitler, also messages around the world to try to get all the people to exert moral support against aggression.

September 25: Czechs say demands absolutely unacceptable . . . Chamberlain seems hopeful. Mike Scanlon phoned from London, said trenches were being dug in Hyde Park and sandbags were being put up around the Air Ministry building.

September 26: . . . Cannot seem to find quiet walks here in the woods or surrounding country like we have at home. There also do not seem to be any specially attractive places to sit out of doors . . .

French Ministers informed us if Czechs were attacked, France would support them. Speech of Prime Minister on radio. His voice filled with sadness, with loathing of war, with discouragement as to result of his efforts but still urging people to keep calm, to co-operate quietly and with confidence and not to give up the last shred of hope.

September 27: Today, individual, brooding silence was general, as were unsmiling, unemotional faces. Everyone unutterably shocked and depressed, feeling from the Prime Minister's talk that his hopes for peace are shattered and that war is inevitable.

Went to launching of the *Queen Elizabeth*. Queen came without King as the times are so uncertain. She was dressed in grey with a smart small hat and looked much thinner than in the spring. Little Princess Margaret Rose saw me in the group, smiled, told her sister Princess Elizabeth, who immediately told the Queen, who looked over and bowed.

September 28: Joe phoned this morning. Said I should come back tonight, as we must make some sort of plans for the children because war is imminent. Everyone here depressed and sober . . .

Took golf lesson. Then played first four holes and last three on Queen's course which was wonderful. Beautiful large greens . . .

Lunched in rather a subdued atmosphere as few people are at hotel, though the races are on at Perth. Took ride to Perth and visited Frazer's tweed shop, said to be the last word for tweeds. While there, the proprietor told us that the four great powers were to go to Munich to discuss peaceful ways of settling the controversy.

Everyone immediately felt a vast relief and unspeakable emotion. From the depths of despair we were moved to a new hope . . . I decided to stay on at least over the weekend.

September 29: Joe called. Said everything was packed, though nobody wants to go except Teddy, because he thinks if he has his tonsils out back home he can have all the Coca-Cola and ice-cream he wants.

Talked to Kathleen who went to the horse races at Perth yesterday which is a big drawing card here now. Called at Lord Forteviot's Castle yesterday and saw her for a moment as she was just returning from a cocktail party after the races . . .

Everyone expects Prime Minister's visit to be crowned with success though preparations for war are still being carried out. Trenches are being dug and gas-masks fitted . . .

September 30: Everyone feels relieved and happy. Chamberlain arrived home last night and he was given a wonderful reception by the people and received a tremendous ovation when he appeared with the King and Queen.

We all feel that a new psychology for settling issues between countries has been inaugurated and that henceforth war may be out of the question.

Chamberlain's words, from Shakespeare's *Henry IV*: 'Out of this nettle, danger, we pluck this flower, safety.'

The result of the Munich settlement, he said, would be 'Peace in our time.'

In the end it was an illusion; but one that everyone clung to until the Nazis broke their pledge six months later and took over the rest of Czechoslovakia. As Jack wrote in his book *Why England Slept*:

The situation came to a head in March when Hitler invaded Prague. It now became evident to all that the hope of a permanent peace for Europe was doomed. The invasion of Prague meant the end of the Chamberlain policy of appeasement; and it meant, in addition, the desertion of the traditional policy of refusal to make commitments in Eastern Europe. The Government realized that something would have to be done to build back British prestige, to bring to the world a realization that from this time on appeasement was officially dead, and that England now was really determined to resist German attempts at Expansion.

The outcome, as we know, was that England officially guaranteed the borders of Poland – the next likely target of German aggression – and that in September 1939, when the Nazi armies did invade that country, England declared war.

Jack was an observer and even to some degree a participant in those events that finally led to war. After the summer and early fall of 1938 and the scenes I have described, he went back to Harvard for his junior year. However, his father, realizing that momentous history was being made in London, Paris and the other capitals, and that it would be infinitely more instructive for Jack if he were on the scene, suggested he defer his second semester and rejoin us. He could help in the London Embassy and, by arrangement with Bill Bullitt, in the Paris Embassy, and also do some travelling in other parts of Europe.

So he came over in February 1939 and was there the rest of the time, seeing it happen with his own eyes. So was Joe Jr. The boys helped their father and not least by the reports they sent to him on their impressions – from very broad cross-sections of society – during their work and their travels.

Here are other notes – from my diary, from letters – that convey the terror of our lives during the period that remained for us in England.

Teddy had his tonsils out on October 3 [1938] in a London hospital, and everything went well, but he was disappointed in his hopes for endless Coca-Colas and ice-cream.

Kathleen and I investigated a couple of colleges for her in London, with the idea that while helping me at the Residence and having her social life she could also be continuing her education with part-time courses. The trouble was that so very few English girls went to college then and few arrangements were made for them. That was especially true of the girls of the 'upper classes' and aristocracy – the debutante set – who in the fall and winter stayed in the country, at the ancestral places, and went shooting and riding and would give and go to house parties. (I'm sure this has changed, but that's the way it was then.)

Joe gave the principal speech at the Navy League on Trafalgar Day, an annual event of great symbolic importance, since it celebrated Lord Nelson's decisive victory. He cleared the speech with Washington and had very few suggested changes from that end. The gist of the speech was that:

> It is true that the democratic and dictator countries have important and fundamental divergences of outlook, which in certain areas go deeper than politics. But there is simply no sense, common or otherwise, in letting these differences grow into unrelenting antagonisms. After all, we have to live together in the same world, whether we like it or not.

This was in fact President Roosevelt's own attitude at the time. After Munich he had sent a personal message of congratulation to Prime Minister Chamberlain, which Joe personally delivered and read to him.

During November and December the fine high hopes of peace had already begun to deteriorate, though there was still a lot of optimism both among officials and the public. Joe, with his 'feel' for a situation, was becoming pessimistic, and in December he returned to the US for consultations. He told the President that in his opinion a general European war might very easily break out in the spring of 1939. He testified before Congressional committees that America should hurry on with a rearmament programme, both to preserve itself as 'an island of freedom' if worse came to worst, and meanwhile to help supply arms to the democracies for their defence. He knew that couldn't be very much very soon, first because the Neutrality Act would have to be revised; second because, as the very recent Chairman of the Maritime Commission, he knew – and told the British Government – how inadequate the USN merchant marine was to carry great tonnages of materials across the ocean on more than a slow schedule.

While he was in the US, Joe spoke out on the international situation:

Excerpt from Winchester speech, July 12, 1938:
> In those parts of the world where the idea still exists that the national good is the sum total of the welfare of all its individual inhabitants, we are now being called upon to stretch our already hard-pressed resources to cover the care of refugees cast out of their native land because they belong to certain races or profess certain religions or think the thoughts of free men. Let us do what we can to take care of this immediate emergency.
> It is hard for us to realize that intolerance such as is abroad in so much of the world may conceivably threaten us and the bases of our national lives. We must always be on the alert to defend the thesis

that no permanent national happiness can ever be achieved, in the kind of society to which we are accustomed and which we wish to preserve, by one segment of our populations at the expense of another.

Excerpt from Manchester speech, November 29, 1938:

I am inclined to believe that we place too much emphasis upon the political side of international relations, and not enough emphasis on the economic side. Most of our current difficulties, I believe, are an outgrowth of the disturbed economic conditions with which we have been burdened for the past twenty years. It seems to me, therefore, that a solution, if one is to be found at all, probably will be found in the realm of economics.

The world is today wallowing around in a sea of discord. It is going to take some exceedingly skilful piloting to keep us off the rocks.

During recent years there have arisen two conflicting viewpoints with respect to foreign trade. Some nations have preached the doctrine of autarchy, or national self-sufficiency; others, while yielding here and there, have endeavoured to preserve the fundamentals, at least, of a liberal trade policy. The course taken by Great Britain and the United States undoubtedly will influence, to a considerable extent, the course to be taken by other countries.

It appears that the totalitarian countries, together with areas now controlled by them or likely to fall under their sway, account for about a third of all international trade. Great Britain, France, the United States and other countries account for the rest. It will be seen, therefore, that while the totalitarian regimes have made considerable headway with the regimentation of foreign trade, two-thirds of the international business of the world is still transacted on a reasonably free basis. That fact should encourage us to hope that the type of commercial policy which we consider desirable will yet prevail. Meanwhile, it is up to us to show the world that our system is better. We must do everything within our power to make the democratic system of trade work, and to make it so attractive that those nations now committed to a different system will join us in a great movement to restore to international commerce the flexibility which it once enjoyed.

We of the United States want trade. We want to enjoy the plenitude made possible by differences in climate, soil and human aptitudes. We want others to enjoy those products in which we excel. We know that an exchange of goods between countries, as between individuals, means better products, lower prices, and a higher standard of living. Therefore we shun the doctrine of self-sufficiency and seek to trade with other nations.

Great Britain and the United States have a great opportunity for economic collaboration. If we succeed, other nations undoubtedly will follow our lead. If we fail, there is no telling what will happen to the trade of the world. Perhaps we shall have a world made up of self-contained economic units, each attempting to produce the needs of its own people and all suffering from their inability or unwillingness to take advantage of the specialities of other nations. That is the road to hardship; that is the road to internal unrest; that is the road, finally, to increased tension between nations.

No one will contend that the liberalization of trade is a panacea for the ills of the world. Nevertheless, it can be said that a greater exchange of commodities between nations would contribute to the solution of most of the problems with which we are confronted.

Interviewed on arrival in New York by several newspapers, December 16, 1938.

NY Journal American, December 16, 1938:

Mr Kennedy brought back to his native shores a host of definite views on the troubled situation overseas, the most definite of which was an urgent plea that the United States 'keep out of it'. 'That's the chief thing I'm campaigning for now,' he said. 'I come home more pro-peace than ever. I strongly favour our policy of rearmament, particularly in strengthening our air force and navy.

'But so far as the US of America is concerned, I feel more strongly than ever, in the light of what I learned in recent weeks, that this nation should stay out – absolutely out – of whatever happens in Europe.'

Before leaving for his White House chat, the Ambassador warned that there was not too much hope that peace will be preserved in Europe. 'I truly think that nothing has been accomplished in the way of appeasement,' he said. 'But we must keep trying for peace or we shall have only two alternatives and both are very bad – economic chaos or war.'

New York Wall Street Journal, December 16, 1938:

On the subject of the Munich pact, Mr Kennedy pointed out, 'There are two alternatives, one of which is economic chaos and the other war. If there is any way of doing better than either of those, there is every justification for trying.'

A reporter recalled that President Roosevelt had said with regard to the European situation, 'Whatever comes, stay out of it.'

NY Times, Washington, Associated Press Interview of December 16, 1938:
    Mr Kennedy brought a pessimistic view of political developments to the White House. He indicated that recent events had changed his mind about the prospects of peace. 'Last summer I predicted there would be no war in Europe. Well, I am going out of the prophet business on December 31,' he said grimly. He did not discuss in detail what he told the President. Mr Kennedy was particularly outspoken in his condemnation of Jewish persecution in Germany which he has called 'the most terrible thing I have ever heard of'.

The fogs and grey skies and chill of the English winter were beginning to bother me. Further, as I see from a letter I wrote to my mother, I was thinking: 'Joe will not stay here for a very long time and I may as well see all the places around here.' (He didn't like staying in any job a long time, and he wasn't planning on this one for more than about a year to a year and a half.)

I talked to Joe three or four times about living in England after he left the Ambassadorship. He had really enjoyed his sojourn there, and he agreed he would like to stay, on the condition that he could get to Palm Beach for a few weeks each winter. Therefore, not long after Joe Sr and Jack were re-ensconced at the Residence, I left on a southern tour that took me to the Riviera, to Genoa and Naples, Athens, and the Greek Islands, Turkey, Palestine, Egypt. Then back to Italy – because Pope Pius XI had died, and I received word that President Roosevelt wanted Joe (and thus, informally, me also, and our family) to represent him at the coronation ceremonies for the new Pope. This was the first time an American President had sent an official representative to such an occasion. And the new Pope Pius XII was our gracious friend Cardinal Eugenio Pacelli.

There were a lot of logistics involved, with our family spread in several locations, but we did, with the exception of Joe Jr, assemble by the date of the Coronation, March 12. The Spanish Civil War was at a climactic stage then and Joe Jr was in Madrid. Because communications from Spain to the rest of the world were so fragmentary and chaotic, he didn't receive his father's message that he was to come to Rome. Perhaps he couldn't have got there in time anyway.

Joe Sr and Jack came down on the same train with the Duke of Norfolk, the leading Peer of the Realm, and a Catholic, whom the King had sent as his representative. Joe and I had time, before the

ceremonies, to move around Rome a bit and pay some official respects
to other dignitaries who had come in from all over the world. It was a
special joy for us to talk with Cardinal O'Connell of Boston, who had
known both of us since we were in our teens, and who had married us.
He had been deeply interested in us and our family all these years.
He was now about eighty and becoming feeble, yet he retained his
poise, kindness and wisdom.

The next morning His Holiness received us in private audience.
First he and Joe were alone a while, talking I dare say about the state
of the world and the prospects for war or peace. Then I came in from
a reception room and we reminisced a bit about his visit to Hyde Park
and Bronxville. Then came the children, with Elizabeth Dunn and
Luella Hennessey, and Mary and Eddie Moore. The Pope seemed
pleased to see everyone, especially Teddy, whom he remembered fondly
as the little boy on his lap who had been so curious about the crucifix.

I noted in my diary:

Miss Hennessey must have had twenty dozen rosaries to be blessed.
In fact, we had to carry a small suitcase to hold hers and the rosaries
of all the children.

And two days later, March 16, I have another note which, to me,
means too much to try to express.

Teddy received his First Communion from Pope Pius XII.

April 4: Lunch at 10 Downing Street, Prime Minister and Mrs
Chamberlain plus their married daughter. Joe and PM did all the
talking. Prime Minister looks very worn down compared with last
spring but does not look his seventy years as he has plenty of hair.
Is not over-optimistic as he cannot tell what Hitler has in view. I
asked him if Hitler died would he be more confident about peace,
and he said he would.

I said I wondered at lack of knowledge of British Government
about preparations in Germany. He said there . . . reports. They must
be analysed . . .

April 7: Everyone away for holiday extending over Monday. Played
golf with Joe and when we finished, about one o'clock, he had a
tense look as he had just received word the Italians had marched in
Albania and it might mean war. He came home, went to Foreign
Office. Chamberlain is in Scotland for a much-needed rest . . . Feel
so sorry for the Prime Minister as Mrs Chamberlain said he was so

looking forward to the long holiday. Now a plane is waiting to bring him back . . .

April 23: At Cliveden. Nancy Astor has the most amazing energy of anyone I have ever seen. She went to Christian Science Church, had huge lunch with about twenty-eight to thirty, went off to play eighteen holes of golf . . . I like her because I think she is inherently good, works hard to help out others, strives to do the right thing, is passionately devoted to her family (her own children, her nieces, etc.). I have heard someone say she dominated her own children too much so it's difficult for them to be around her. She is great fun any place, talks about everything, anything, intelligently and with gusto and with an inexhaustible sense of humour. Also imitates inimitably, such as Lady Asquith for us, and when she puts in a pair of false teeth she changes her whole facial expression and is marvellous.

May 1: Debutantes' Party at Lady Hood's
This was Eunice's first debutante party. The custom is for the mothers to go to the debutantes' party and spend most of the evening and come home with the girls. Of course, this is not done in America. As Kathleen has been out, it is considered perfectly proper for her to chaperone Eunice, although I will go occasionally when I can. All the mothers say it is rather difficult to sit night after night and watch the young things dance until two or three o'clock in the morning, but most of them do it at the beginning of the season. Occasionally one mother chaperones several girls. Towards the end of the season, they send the car with the chauffeur and it is supposed to be all right for the girl to come home in her own car, but she must never invite a young man to accompany her and the worst possible offence is to go on to a night-club afterwards. Of course, they always say there is very little drinking here compared with American debutante parties.

Eunice seems to be enjoying herself and, of course, Kathleen's having had the experience last year makes it much easier for her.

May 4: Very busy all day preparing for the dinner for the King and Queen. The flowers arrived from Paris about 1.30. As we found we could get more unusual flowers there and much less expensive, Offie had them flown over by plane. Everyone was rather nervous until they arrived because it always takes quite a long time to arrange them, and get the right colours for the right rooms. The flowers for the table were particularly lovely. They were like baby orchids, some white and some orchid colour. They were called moth-orchids, or fillanopsis. I did not want the press to get the idea that I was decorating the table with orchids, which would sound too nouveau riche, or too extreme, so I called them 'fillanopsis' to the press. As we had old-fashioned strawberry shortcake, the strawberries also came from Paris by plane, as we thought they would be better. Everyone seemed very calm and confident but I know everyone in the house was terribly excited, including myself and the Ambassador.

During the day men from Scotland Yard came up to interview our butler to find out who the men were who were helping out in the evening. The butler, who has been in London for a long time, had chosen men who had all served at Buckingham Palace, so Scotland Yard was reassured and there were no detectives present. I suppose they are especially careful at this time because of the Irish terrorists in the IRA.

The six youngest children were seated at a small table at the end of the room. The conversation was naturally quite informal. I told the King about the shad roe which we had sent for from America for a big dinner last year and which had not arrived on time as the boat was twelve days late. Therefore at the last moment I had to substitute filet of sole. As the menus had already been printed for shad roe, we had to leave them. And one English lady was quite astonished to find that shad roe tasted so like her own filet of sole and so I had to explain the difficulty.

We also talked about the King's coming visit to America. The menu was purely American, and the Virginia ham had come from America, as had the shad roe.

At the end of the dinner the Queen and I left the table, I giving a slight curtsey as I left the King; and as the ladies left the room, they each curtsied towards the King. We then went to the French Room. The Queen and I went upstairs to my bedroom for a minute for a little powder. I showed her my reflector mirror, something she had never seen before. She asked me if I got up in the morning to see the children off, and I said I used to in what I called the good old days, but that now I was usually up late at nights and rested in the morning. To my astonishment and humiliation, she said she usually got up, half-dressed, to see her children, and then went back to bed again.

When we joined the ladies for coffee, she chatted with two or three of them, and I brought up two or three of the American ladies with whom she chatted about seven or eight minutes. We followed the regular procedure of the hostess, bringing up different ladies to speak to her for a few minutes each. Lady Halifax, who was lady-in-waiting, had already told me in advance with whom she would chat. After about twenty-five minutes, we were joined by the gentlemen, and we went into the pine room which had been arranged for the cameramen and had two pictures taken, one serious and one laughing.

The Queen had on a beautiful pink satin gown with paillettes, a crinoline style which she wears, the same length all around. I had on a turquoise satin dress, also with paillettes which, when I was near the Queen, seemed to become entangled in her paillettes. Consequently, in the picture mine were rather pulled to one side.

Then we went into the back room for the film. We had two of Walt Disney's, and *Goodbye, Mr Chips* which was long, as it had not been cut – to use moving picture parlance – but excellent and marvellously acted. I think it was an American picture made over here. It was quite sad, and after it was finished, it was very plain to see that the Queen had had a little weep, as had most of the people.

After that we stepped into the hall where we had something to drink. Again they chatted with a few of their friends and then went downstairs. They shook hands with almost everybody as they left. I said goodbye in the hall and the Ambassador went to the car with them. After a minute's interval, the other guests said goodnight and the party was over.

May 5 and 6: It was so nice to receive letters from several people who wrote saying they had enjoyed the party and that they thought everything had gone off so well . . .

Early in May, the King and Queen left England for a good-will tour of Canada and the US, and inasmuch as Joe and I had talked with them and their staff a number of times about their US itinerary, and Joe of course had many consultations about the visit with our State Department and others back in Washington, it seemed useful and almost necessary that I should be there at the same time they were.

I sailed on May 25 and I returned on June 22. Here are some entries concerning that visit:

Great argument on whether it is befitting for the President to serve hot dogs at a picnic to the King and Queen . . .

That was at Hyde Park. The President did serve them, as a 'typical American delicacy', and their Majesties were delighted, and it all caused a great sensation in the press and, I dare say, helped build a reservoir of goodwill in this country towards Imperial Britain.

And now, just a few more social notes. Because very soon there would be no more at all.

June 22: Met Joe and went with him to Waterloo Station to meet the King and Queen who arrived at 4.50. All the members of the Cabinet were there and it was the first time I ever saw Joe look small; he was standing talking with Lord Halifax (six feet five inches) . . . The King and Queen drove off in their coach with the famous grey horses with a rider in front. The Queen and the Princesses wore dresses of light shades so that they could be readily identified by the people and the photographer, even at a distance. They received a wonderful ovation all along the route . . .

That night was Eunice's debut party. She wore a peach-coloured dress from Paquin . . .

About half past two they all started doing the 'Big Apple' and everybody got very gay. I was quite surprised and even a little shocked. However, I was assured by some of the chaperones that the party was a huge success . . . The Duke of Marlborough had asked if he might come, although the fathers don't usually come to the debut parties. He was one of the leaders of the 'Big Apple'.

June 27: Four of the children, Joe, Jack, Eunice and Kathleen, went to a reception at the Prime Minister's at 10 Downing. They were shown through the house and went into the room where the Cabinet meets.

This reminds me of when Jack first came over to London, and I was showing him a few of the sights and we drove past the Prime Minister's residence. I pointed it out to him, and he was so excited. 'Is that really *Number Ten Downing?*' he asked. He was awestruck.

July 3: The papers are full of war; many articles about evacuation schemes and lists of supplies which should be stored at home. The Duchess of Marlborough and Lady Astor are getting their houses ready and the people on their staffs organized so they can turn their houses into hospitals or homes for children in the event of war.

July 4: We had the Fourth of July party and received in the dining-room . . . The entire group was very nice-looking and quite representative, I thought, of an American gathering. There were quite a number of people from Boston.

That evening, at a large official dinner, I sat next to Duke of Kent, who accidentally told me he had seen Kennedys at every table at 400 Club, which is supposed to be rather gay and not a place for Kathleen.

Joe reprimanded Kick for being there. (A few nights later, the Duke apologized to Kick to telling on her.)

July 12: We went to the Court . . . Joe stood next to the German Ambassador (protocol, as before) who remarked that it was much easier now than in the days of the previous King, George V, who used to insist on the Diplomatic Corps going to four or five Courts. He said Queen Mary is much less shy now and much less difficult than when King George was alive. She now has time to go to things which she enjoys.

The German Ambassador considers the whole Court procedure a waste of time.

July 13: We gave a small luncheon for the Prime Minister. Mr Lamont, a banker from New York; Justice and Mrs Felix Frankfurter; and Mr and Mrs Joe Patterson, New York newspaper people, were present. It was a small luncheon so that Mr Chamberlain might get over his point of view to the men.

All the Americans feel that they may be seeing some of their English friends here for the last time as everyone feels that war is more or less imminent. Although many people think that since it has been delayed so long there is still a chance, or a way may be found, to put it off.

August 1: Now there seems to be a bit more confidence, though no one really knows. But everyone in these countries is possessed of an ardent hope that war may still be avoided.

August 12: Jack and Torb McDonald leave for Germany. They would like to go to Prague, but we are told no one is allowed to go there.

August 16: Reports keep coming that war is imminent and August 29 seems to be the date as the harvest in Germany will have been reaped and all the reserves have been called.

And that is the last entry in my diary. There was too much to think about, too many plans to make. The war didn't break out on August 29. The estimate was off by three days. On September 1, the Nazi armies invaded Poland. Two days after that, September 3, the British Government fulfilled its pledge and declared war against Germany.

Joe Jr and Jack and Kick and I were there in Parliament to hear Mr Chamberlain's heartbroken, heartbreaking speech (the text of which the Prime Minister had shown to Joe a few hours earlier) with its tragic lines: 'Everything that I have worked for, everything that I have hoped for, everything that I have believed in during my public life has crashed in ruins.'

While we were on our way home from the House of Commons the air-raid sirens began to howl and we ran for refuge into the nearest shelter we could find – which was not a bomb shelter but just happened to be the basement at Molyneux. I thought later, what an ironic way for a woman to begin her war experiences. At the time I was simply scared for us all. No bombs were dropped on London that day, but it was a vivid experience and a premonition of what soon would be happening in deadly earnest.

It was time to get my children back home.

That wasn't particularly easy. Space on the American and other neutral ships was jammed; and the seas suddenly were dangerous for ships of any combatant nation. On the fourth day of the war the British ship *Athenia*, heading for Canada with 1400 passengers including 300 US citizens, was torpedoed and sunk. The survivors were landed in Scotland and brought to Glasgow. Joe sent Jack up there to interview the Americans – most of whom had survived – and to file a report to the Embassy as to the circumstances of the sinking, and also to do for them whatever it was possible to do, within the powers and resources of the Embassy, to help them with food, clothing, shelter, funds and other transport. Joe trusted him to do a proper, thorough and understanding job, young as he was, at twenty-one. He did it well.

All but two of us were back in the US by the end of that month. As I have explained earlier, we decided to let Rosemary stay on a while because she was doing so well at her special school, which was deep in the countryside and almost surely safe from any bomb damage. The other missing member was Joe, who was duty-bound to stay at his post, and did so for more than another full year; save for trips home for rest and consultations and to help President Roosevelt in his bid for a third term.

Jack resumed his undergraduate studies at Harvard and by taking extra courses was able to graduate the next year, in the class of 1940. He decided to do his senior thesis on the reasons why the British Government, under Stanley Baldwin and then Neville Chamberlain, had not armed the nation sufficiently to meet the growing power of Hitler's Germany – thus making the Munich Pact necessary. The title he chose was 'Appeasement at Munich'. Naturally, he and his father had a lot of correspondence about the subject-matter. The thesis was rated *magna cum laude*, which enabled Jack to graduate – despite his fragmented collegiate career – *cum laude*.

13

When the war broke out, the use of the transatlantic telephone between the US and England was limited to high priority messages. At first Joe was told that he couldn't call us at all. Finally, he was allowed ten minutes every Sunday. Inasmuch as there were ten of us – the nine children and I – arranging for each of us to have his or her budgeted minute or minute and a half required precise organization. Everything had to go like clockwork. I stayed in the living-room, by the telephone, with two of the older children to act as escorts for the younger ones, who were waiting in the nearest room. When a child had finished his time he was hustled out while another child was being hustled in. Thus each got to hear Joe's voice, and he got to hear theirs.

Obviously there was no time for any real exchange of news and views; and so all of us fell back on that old-fashioned method of communication, letter-writing.

A great many of the letters survived. In reading them after all these years, it seems to me they form a remarkably complete and vivid family narrative of our life during that time. It was a crazy time in the world – outrageous and frightening at first, then exasperating as the war fizzled into what was called the 'Phoney War'. Then, terribly and suddenly, the Nazis swept through Denmark and Norway, the Low Countries and France; and began the full-scale Battle of Britain with massive day and night bombings of London.

From the great number of letters exchanged I have selected excerpts from a few dozen; not because they are 'important' but because they seem interesting. Some of the dates are missing, but the letters are in approximate chronological order. I have added notes as needed.

Eunice to Father
September 17, 1939
On Board *SS Washington*

It is really amazing the number of people they managed to get on board. People are sleeping in the lounge, swimming pool, gymnasium, in fact everywhere thinkable, but it is all great fun. Nobody has their bags and Kick and I wear the same costume for breakfast, lunch and supper, but then, so does everyone else . . .

Bob is rushing around trying to get Tilden, Budge and Montgomery's autograph, but today two people asked him for his, so at present he is feeling very important.

Hope to see you soon, Dad, and don't work too hard. Everyone we have met on the boat, even the young people, think you have done and are doing a marvellous job . . .

Kick to Father
September 26
Bronxville, NY

Well, we have been home a week. I can't believe it even though everything is just the same. That's the amazing thing when one's been away, one expects things to have changed and they haven't . . .

I have been to the World Fair twice . . . I went to the polo game on Sunday with Peter Grace who was playing on Tommy Hitchcock's side and he played very well. I went to the theatre with him last night. He's just the same . . .

I couldn't get into Sarah Lawrence so I am going to Finch's in New York. It is a Junior College and one can get a diploma, which is something.

Everyone is just the same. Eunice is working hard and comes home every night. Jack is taking out Frances Ann this weekend so we can all hardly wait.

['Frances Ann' was Frances Ann Cannon, an attractive girl in whom Jack seemed to be quite interested at that time, and evidently she was interested in him too. At least Kick seemed to be implying that some 'announcement' was in the offing.]

Eunice to Father
September 29
Postcard from Richmond, Virginia

We have had a marvellous day and everyone is talking about how well Mother did. She made two marvellous speeches . . .

People, particularly women's groups, were interested in my experiences and impressions as wife-hostess-consort of the American Ambassador at that time in history; so I was invited to speak at a number of places. I prepared a few talks on non-political subjects, and usually they did seem to go over well with the audiences. Richmond had and has a large population of English descent, so I expect people there were more receptive than could have been the case in some other places at that time, and thus I was encouraged to accept other invitations. Perhaps, indeed, I was made a bit giddy and incautious by success. I remember later on speaking to a group of predominantly Irish Catholic women in Boston and saying something like, 'Now, of course, you're all familiar with Windsor Castle . . .' I heard a woman in the front row turn to a friend next to her and whisper loudly, 'What does she *mean* – we're all *familiar* with *Windsor Castle!*' And I didn't blame her a bit. She was right, I had been wrong, and I carefully didn't make any more such remarks.

Pat to Father
Early in October
Bronxville

We are all thinking of you on your anniversary. [October 7, 1914.] Mother is up visiting Bobby at school this weekend. I haven't been to the Fair yet but I am going . . . How are you and Rosie? Don't work too hard. Teddy is going to Lawrence Park West and loves it there. Jean goes into the convent every morning with me. She likes it very much. [Teddy's school was a few minutes from Bronxville; Pat's and Jean's was Maplehurst, of which we heard here before] . . . Noroton next and our great ambition is to beat them . . . Miss Hennessey went away for the week and Teddy is getting away with anything, but Miss Dunn is coming today so he will be under control . . .

Father to Pat
November 3
From London

You are doing yourself proud on letters. I certainly think that you are having a much gayer time there than you possibly could have had over here . . . I still go out to the country every night [at Windsor Park, near London] and between you and me it is pretty lonesome. I live alone except for the weekends when Rosie and the Moores . . . come out. Work hard, dear, have fun and think of me. Love.

To our joy Joe returned in December for consultations with President Roosevelt and US officials and others most concerned with the war, and later was able to join us at the Palm Beach house for Christmas. Rosemary did not come with him. Transport was difficult and tiring at best: the best being a four-engine Pan-American flying-boat that came from England by way of Portugal, the Azores and other way stations on this side. It would have been an unpleasant trip for her, possibly a complicated one for Joe. Also, as I have said earlier, she was making encouraging progress at her special school in England, so all in all it seemed wise that she stay there and miss this one Christmas with us.

From the time Joe bought the Palm Beach house in 1933 we had been spending the Christmas-New Year's holiday time there. Most of us travelled from Bronxville in a Pullman car and we filled several drawing-rooms. Meanwhile, two or three automobiles would have started south, occupied by household help and vast amounts of personal luggage, and tied and bowed Christmas presents.

The logistics were formidable. There were eleven of us, and there was a present from each to each of the others and (11 × 11) that accounted for 121 presents. In addition there were presents from grandparents, aunts and uncles and cousins and friends such as Mary and Eddie Moore, and from other close associates and assistants, and also presents to the young from Santa Claus. We had lots of ornaments: many that the children had made in times past, many we had collected on our travels, bought and had saved through the years. With the small mountains of gifts under the tree, it was a cheerful Christmas scene.

And then we went out into the warm sunshine to swim or play tennis or touch football, or golf, or just to walk under the palm trees, or up and down the beach with the waves and eddies swishing in.

Joe wished he didn't have to leave the family and go back to London. But the President wanted him to, and so he returned to London early in 1940.

Thus the family correspondence continues.

Teddy to Father
Mr Santa Claus
J.P. Kennedy
January 1940
From Bronxville

Dear Santa Claus,
    Thank you very much for the toys you gave me. You can give some more any time you want too. I liked the watch best. Thank you again. Lot of love. Happy New Year.

Bobby to Father
January 1940 (but later; school holidays don't coincide; too bad)
From Palm Beach

Joe has a pretty good sunburn but the newest bulletin is he thinks he is going to peel. He has been giving all his speeches around here. [Joe Jr was about to run as a delegate to the Democratic National Convention of 1940.] They are pretty good. Last week Jack told us all about himself now Joe is telling us about himself.

Grandma and Grandpa are still down here and are fine. I am sorry but I have run of ink . . .

I have been playing quite a bit of tennis and swimming a great deal but I only went fishing once when I caught 2 or 3 small fish. I have to be back at school on the 8th.

Teddy flew back yesterday. He is as fat as ever and rising steadily in weight.

My report was much better, Miss Dunn said, but I'll have to do better in my marks I think.

This is about all the news. I will write you again soon. Give my love to Mr and Mrs Moore and Rose.

The Kennedys in America send their love to the Kennedys in jolly old England.

PS   I am offering up my Mass for you and Mother a lot.

Jack to Father
February
From Harvard

. . . Mother looks very well and is getting quite academic as she is taking some college courses.

. . . I am taking as my thesis for honours England's Foreign Policy since 1931 and will discuss the class influence in England. Will get in touch with Jim Seymour [one of Joe's close personal assistants at the Embassy] if I want him to send me stuff. Am taking a course under Prof. Friedrich which is very interesting. I am still incognito but expect to go up and shake his palm and start discussing what a big impression he made on you when these papers start getting marked.

Everyone is getting much more confident about our staying out of the war – but of course that is probably because there is such a lull over there . . .

Am getting along fine here – have been doing quite a bit of work as my courses are really interesting this year. That year is really standing me in good stead as I am quite a seer around here.

Joe Jr to Father
April 5
From Palm Beach

The Easter vacation is just about over and soon back to the law School for the last two months of the grind . . .

Grandpa left today and looked very well but says that he doesn't feel very well. He had been feeling pretty well up until a couple of days ago when he took a look at the stock market and saw that one of his stocks had dropped four points and from then on his stomach started to go badly . . .

Everyone has been very well and we have had plenty of sun. Teddy is fatter than ever and looks as healthy as it is possible to look. Jack finished his thesis and Arthur Krock thought it was excellent . . .

Primary election will be on the 30th of April . . . There was some criticism of me not being on the voting list but that was straightened out OK and the protester finally got his only consolation in stating that it was sending a child on a man's job.
[Joe Jr was twenty-four at that time. The 'third term' question was still very much up in the air – President Roosevelt was not saying yes or no. Jim Farley was against a third term for anybody, even his close friend Roosevelt, and announced his own candidacy; and Joe Jr was running as a Farley delegate.]

It looks like Dewey will get the Republican nomination OK and it is still a mystery as far as the Democratic one goes. At the present time it doesn't seem that anyone could be elected except Roosevelt. The Republicans are rather afraid that Hull would be nominated for that would take a lot of the wind out of their sails. Farley has come out and said that his name will be presented at Chicago regardless of what happens. That's about all the news . . .

Jack to Father
Mid-April
From Harvard

Just got back from the South. It was great down there – the weather was about the best I've ever seen. An awful lot of people were down – three girls to every man – so I did better than usual. The girls [sisters] having a bit of a battle at first but finished up the week in a blaze of glory.

Mother was in great shape and seems to be feeling fine. Bobby has increased in strength to such a degree that I seriously believe he will be bouncing me around plenty in two more years. He really is unusually strong and that school seems to have done him an awful lot of good as he has improved immensely as everyone has noticed – in every way. He looks 100 per cent better too. [That 'school' was Milton Academy.]

I am sending my thesis . . . Arthur Krock read it and feels that I should get it published. He thinks that a good name for it might be *Why England Slept* as sort of a contrast to Churchill's *While England Slept*. Krock felt it should be brought out in the spring – May or June – but it would depend on:

1st   When you resigned, and

2nd   If you thought it was worth it –

3rd   If you stayed on thru the summer whether it could be published while you are in office. You can judge after you have seen it . . . I thought I could work on rewriting it and making it somewhat more complete and maybe more interesting for the average reader – as it stands now, it is not anywhere polished enough although the ideas are OK . . .

Whatever I do, however, will depend on what you think is the best thing . . .

Harvard's baseball team looks none too good but Torb has been batting 400 for the 1st 8 games . . . Planning to put the boats in the water shortly . . . That's about all the news. Please let me know what you think about the thesis as soon as you can – Am sending it to an agent Krock gave me – and see what he thinks – the chief questions are:

1. Whether it is worth publishing if polished up.

2. If it can be published while you're still in office.

Best to all,
Love, Jack

The professors at Harvard thought so highly of the thesis, in fact, that they suggested Jack expand it somewhat and interest a book publisher in it. The book came out that summer, with a foreword by Henry R. Luce, under the title of *Why England Slept*. It got excellent reviews and sold extremely well.

Before the finished book could arrive in England, Joe had written to Jack that he had already heard good reports and:

I am very anxious to read the final copy. I am sure if it reaches the problem as they now visualize it in England, the book will have quite a sale and at least will get a very good standing. Chamberlain, Halifax, Montagu Norman, and Harold Laski have all asked me about it. So, whether you make a cent out of it or not, it will do you an amazing amount of good, particularly if it gets a good standing. You would be surprised how a book that really makes the grade with high class people stands you in good stead for years to come. I remember that in the report you are asked to make after twenty-five years to the Committee at Harvard, one of the questions is 'What books have you written?' and there is no doubt you will have done yourself a great deal of good.

As usual, Joe was right. In addition to making a handsome amount of money for Jack (most of which he gave to repair bomb damage in England) it gave him an invaluable credential, as a young man wise beyond his years, when he later entered public life.

Eunice to Father
Early May
From Manhattanville

I made the tennis team. Last week we had our first match and we won. However, when I arrived at the court I had on white shorts, very respectable, and the same type we wear each day for gym, but the nuns wouldn't allow me to play in them, so I was forced to wear a girl's skirt and shorts who must have had a size 64 waist. Both proceeded to fall off in the middle of the match. Such is life!!

I also bought a big lizard at the circus which jumped out of the box, and what a commotion! You would have thought I had let a lion out of his cage. Everyone started to shriek, one lady shrieked out 'my heart, my heart,' and I was running like mad trying to catch him which I finally did. If looks or words could kill I would be 90 feet under. Anyhow I gave him back and got my money back. Now the nun is staring at me with fire in her eyes so I shall sign off. Please ask Rosie and the Moores to say a prayer for my exams and do say one Dad or else!!

Joe Jr to Father
May 4
Harvard

The only great excitement over here was the election and Grandpa thought I did quite well, so I guess the Kennedy name is a pretty good vote-getter. I came in second by about 100 votes . . . [This gave him a place on the delegation.] It kind of looks like Roosevelt is going to run . . .

People over here still feel the same way [about the war]. However every once in a while now you hear people talking about the need to go over now and not wait till it is too late.

Grandpa is still making speeches and going strong. His latest remark is that Curley tried to sell the Boston Common but he stopped it . . .

Kick to Father
May 21
Bronxville

At the moment it looks as if the Germans will be in England before you receive this letter. In fact from the reports here they are just about taking over Claridge's now. I still keep telling everyone 'the British lose the battles but they win the wars'. I have received some rather gloomy letters from Jane and Billy. Billy's letter was written from the Maginot line. Daddy, I must know exactly what has happened to them all. Is Billy all right?

['Billy' was young Lord Hartington, eldest son and heir of the Duke of Devonshire. He had been one of Kick's most attentive beaux while we were in London; and she liked him a great deal.]

Jack just returned to Harvard after being home a week. He really is the funniest boy alive. He had the Irish maid in fits the whole time. Every time he'd talk to her he'd put on a tremendous Irish brogue. He still misses Cannon quite a bit.

[Frances Ann Cannon married John Hersey, who became both an excellent journalist and novelist. A few years later on, when Jack had been through his harrowing war experiences in the Pacific and was back in Boston in a hospital recuperating, John Hersey, then a war correspondent for *Time-Life*, and having heard something about Jack's story from mutual friends, came to interview him. From their conversation, and details supplied by members of the crew, Hersey wrote a memorable article in *The New Yorker* titled 'Survival'. That is how the saga of PT 109 came to public attention. The world is indeed small.]

The house in Bronxville looks beautiful at the moment. All the trees and flowers are out . . . Mother came back from White Sulphur yesterday and looks very well.

Teddy is very upset over the pictures of him in his birthday suit.
Much love to Ed and Mrs Moore and Rosie.

Jean to Father
May 29
Bronxville

How are you? . . . The nuns are all praying very hard for you.

We are all very excited that Rosie is coming home. The house has been turned upside down with spring cleaning.

Teddy now has to go on a diet. Miss Dunn has to get extra large size suits for him. We are all working very hard for the tests. I go to Mass every morning to pray that I pass them.

Oceans of Love and Kisses

Joe Jr to Father
June 12
From Harvard

Well it's over except the shouting. I am confident I got through all right, however I would like to get some decent marks, as I really put in the time . . .

It seems rather petty to talk about examinations when the whole world seems to be going to the devil. The country has gone through the most amazing change of public opinion. [This was after the Nazis had destroyed the French armies and two days before they entered Paris; the Pétain government capitulated on June 22.] All the professors around here are crazy with fright that America will not arm quick enough . . . There is a feeling around that we are going to get in before very long. No one has a reason for their feeling but they just have an idea that it is inevitable.

I am going to investigate the possibility of joining the reserves of the Navy or air force, so that if anything happens I won't be a private. I think that compulsory military service is coming . . .

I go to the Convention on the 15th of July . . .

Jean to Father
June 20
Hyannis Port

We are all down at Hyannis Port now. Today Mother, Rose, Eunice and Bob are all down at Harvard for Jack's graduation. Joe went on a trip on a boat so Teddy and I are the only ones in the house now . . . Teddy is learning to sail by himself now, he is going in some of the races with the skipper. Pat is not down yet because she had to take a Latin exam but she is coming down today. The water is very good. We go in twice a day . . .

Teddy to Father
June 20–21?
Hyannis Port

We are down in cop-card. Mother has gone to jacks graduoin. joe is
here. The weather is very bad. Would you get me the kings autograh
for me. I will send you an other letter soon . . .

Eunice to Father
June
Hyannis Port

Here at the Cape at last and is it a grand feeling. The boats seem to
be in fine shape so here's hoping we take a few prizes this year. As
yet there are only a very few people here and as for the Hyannis Port
races it looks like the *Tenovus* will race the *One More* and nobody else
but you can't tell.
[We had a boat called *Tenovus* because there were the ten of us. Then
Teddy was born. We needed another boat anyway, with a crowd our
size, so we bought one and christened it the *One More*.]
    I have been out in New York, Penn, and Cleveland, Ohio, visiting
and playing in tennis tournaments. I had a marvellous time, although
I didn't win any of the tournaments but I am going to work on my
tennis this summer. I received plenty of attention and I don't think
it was because of my delightful personality (however I never know).
I had my picture in the paper a couple of times and if I won a round
it would be in big black type and if I lost they put it in tiny small
letters in the corner of the last page . . .
    The chief topic of conversation during the trip was your brains
and what a wonderful job you were doing. Also how young-looking
Mother was. You can imagine how upset Mother was when I told
her this. She almost jumped over the table in her excitement.
    Jack's graduation was really wonderful and we are sending you
his picture in a cap and gown.
    Everyone is screaming for me to come as we are all going out
with one another per us . . .

Jean to Father
June 24
Hyannis Port

The weather has been very bad these last few days. Today we went
swimming and it was the coldest water I have ever been in . . . Rose
wanted to go to the movies so I went with her. She is going to
camp soon . . . Pat fell in the water a second time so she has been

spending most of her vacation falling in the water . . . Mother went up to New Hampshire to see about Rose's camp.

When Eunice went up to Cleveland she brought a newspaper article back with her that said she would give Hedy Lamarr a run for her money because she was so *beautiful*. I think she is going to send it to you . . .

Joe Jr to Father
July 22
From Oshkosh, Wisconsin

I am up here visiting Tom Schriber after the Convention and I thought I would give you some of my reactions.

Even before the Mass. delegation left Boston there were arguments as to whom they would support, Farley or Roosevelt . . . We had a caucus the first night and it was the stormiest session that I have ever seen. They called each other liars and thieves . . . On the other hand there were those who felt that they had pledged themselves and they were bound by this pledge. [The delegation was pledged to Farley] . . . I had seen Krock previously, and he thought that I should stick with Farley . . . Of course someone demanded a poll of the delegation so I gave my vote orally. A lot of people came up to me afterwards and said that they thought I had done the right thing, and now I am more than ever convinced that it was the right thing . . .

[It was a complicated scene, but in Joe Jr's mind and conscience the issues were clear enough. He didn't like the idea of a 'third term' for anyone. And, having run as a Farley delegate, he considered it morally dishonest to vote for anyone else unless and until Farley withdrew, which Farley did not. A lot of pressure was put on him by Roosevelt's managers; and pressure too on his father, by transatlantic telephone, to which Joe – even though he himself supported the third term – characteristically replied that the decision was up to Joe Jr: 'I wouldn't think of telling him what to do.' Joe Jr stayed steadfast with Farley all the way through.]

There is a note worth adding here, a letter that Joseph M. Patterson, president of the *New York Daily News*, wrote on that same date to Joe Sr in London:

Dear Joe,

I was at the Democratic Convention in Chicago and wish to tell you what an excellent impression your son, Joe Jr, made on the delegates and spectators. When the Massachusetts Delegation was being polled, he was kind of on the spot, as everybody knew, but he got up and said firmly, 'I was pledged to Farley and I vote for Farley.' He seemed to gain the respect of everybody there. I am sure he can have a political future if he wants one.

With best wishes,
Sincerely yours,
JMP

Joe's response to Patterson's letter was, I think, very interesting, and I am going to quote from it at some length because it not only shows his pride in his eldest son's behaviour but also gives his view of the war situation and of what America's policy should be – matters that have been often misunderstood or misrepresented:

One is always surprised – although I suppose one shouldn't be – when a busy man with lots on his mind has time to do as kind a thing as this: first of all to note the fact that Joe Jr was even alive and second, that any action he took at the Convention was worthy of your notice, and, third and most important, that you took time to write me about it.

I judge that great pressure was brought to bear on him, because Johnnie Burns called me from Chicago . . . Of course I told Johnnie that Joe Jr would have to make his own decision and that I thought it would be manifestly unfair for me to mix in it one way or another. I thought that if he intended to go into public life, he might as well find out now if calling the play as he saw it was going to cause him difficulty. I wrote him a letter when it was all over and praised his stand. Jim Farley, from the thick of the campaign in Chicago, sent me a wire commending Joe for showing plenty of guts, so I was very happy . . .

I remember well the last time I saw you before I left America. The immediate cause of a dispute that day between Bullitt and me was whether the United States should continue to loan money to other countries. I said I thought it was like pouring money into a sieve. I still think so. In fact, I think everything they are giving to South America will go the same way. If, however, our rich country can afford to give this money away – in the interests of foreign policy – why that is one thing. I just don't think it makes sense . . . Now that doesn't mean that we shouldn't arm and that we shouldn't prepare, but, while we are doing that, we ought to have a well-formulated policy as to what our economic future is to be . . .

The situation on this Island is as I have felt it was for some time.

If Germany can knock off the British Air Force and gain supremacy in the air, then I don't believe that all the plans made for the protection of England will amount to a tinker's damn. I believe that the Germans will invade the Island whenever they please, provided they attain air supremacy . . . If they haven't air strength enough . . . then this Island will continue as long as it is possible to get ships into the country and their resources in the United States permit them to purchase supplies . . .

As I see it, we are going to be faced more and more with the argument that England is our line of defence and that will serve as a reason for every action we want to take, even up to the declaration of war . . . To me, whatever our country wants to do of its own free will is fine, but if we ever enter this war we will be signing a blank cheque, not only for our resources but for our manpower and our social and political life.

Don't misunderstand me. There is nobody in the world who would rather see the Germans beaten than I would, but it strikes me that my job here is to keep as realistic as I can and to call the picture as I see it, which I am doing every day in my dispatches to Washington.

It is rather dismal here with my entire family in the United States and I hate to have Mrs Kennedy burdened with the whole responsibility, but . . . I felt I couldn't leave here until I had seen the bombing through. After that, we will see.

And two footnotes now about that Chicago Democratic Convention of 1940. Because they help illuminate what the term 'politics' has meant in our family. A cable from Jim Farley to Joe Sr in London:

I WILL EVER BE GRATEFUL TO YOUR SON JOE FOR HIS MANLY AND COURAGEOUS STAND AT LAST NIGHT'S CONVENTION.

And Joe Sr's cabled reply:

. . . AS YOU CAN IMAGINE I HAD HEARD ABOUT THE STRUGGLE TO GET HIM TO CHANGE HIS VOTE AND WAS DELIGHTED HE TOOK THE STAND HE DID. AFTER ALL IF HE IS GOING INTO POLITICS HE MIGHT JUST AS WELL LEARN NOW THAT THE ONLY THING TO DO IS TO STAND BY YOUR CONVICTIONS. AM MOST HAPPY TO SAY HE NEEDED NO PROMPTING IN THIS RESPECT. MY BEST WISHES . . .

Jean to Father
July 29
Hyannis Port

Everybody went to the Edgartown Regatta except Teddy and I. They all said it was piles of fun. Jack raced in the senior with some boys. He came in second going over and won coming back . . .

Jack's book has come out, he went to New York or some place yesterday.

Mother went up to Maine and she is going to go to camp for a week and get a rest.

Teddy has gone out to race today. He is first in his series. He is learning to swim much better and . . . thinks he can do swan dives and everything . . .

Grandpa and Grandma came down here yesterday afternoon . . .

Everybody is very well and Teddy thinks he will go on a diet. He has been thinking that since he came down here although he has got a bit thinner.

We all hope you will come home soon, Daddy.

Well, that's about all the news just now.

Oceans of Love and Kisses . . .

Father to Jean
August 2
London

Your last letter, which arrived yesterday, was a nice newsy one and I was glad to hear about what's going on. I wish you would get hold of that Teddy and tell him to send me some news. All he says is, 'I am racing. Get me the King's autograph. I will write soon.'

I am glad that you are sailing and doing so well. I think if you really got interested in it, with your good little head, you could make your sisters hustle. Also do keep after tennis because being proficient in sports helps you to get a lot more fun out of being with people . . .

I have moved back into the Embassy for five days a week, because there are so many things going on that I can't afford to take a chance on staying out at Windsor, but I have only opened my own bedroom and study, so the house looks pretty lonesome . . . We are getting along very nicely, but I miss you all terribly. However, we had lots of fun when the going was good and one can't walk out on a job just because one wants to. Obligations must be fulfilled. Anyway I am hoping to have a few swims with you before you go back to school – if I am very, very lucky.

Love to all and hugs and kisses to you.

Father to Eunice
August 2
London

I have had a lot of laughs at your observations re the members of the family.

I have also been getting plenty of requests from Mother re your golf clubs. Where in the name of heaven did you leave them? Or, at what golf course did you use them, or to whose house did you ever take them on weekend parties? There is no sign of them at the Embassy and we are sure we took everything away from the Wall Hall. So, if you can give me any clue at all, I will get busy.

I certainly was plenty homesick when I saw the picture in *Life* of you all sailing at Cape Cod . . . I still haven't given up hope that I may get the month of September there, or at least part of it, but that depends on Hitler . . .

Keep up your tennis and start playing golf. I am still going to make a champion out of you.

Jean to Father
August 5
Hyannis Port

Thanks loads for your nice long letter. It was awfully sweet of you to write all of us. It must have been an awful job.

Mother arrived home last night from a camp in Maine which she stayed at for a week. She looks wonderful now.

Jack's book seems to be a great success. All his friends wanted theirs autographed by him.

Pat is on a diet and she has lost eight pounds and she really looks awfully well.

Teddy says he is going to write to you more often and he is going to write you longer letters. He is getting bigger and broader every day . . .

Teddy has won one cup. I think I have won one but I have been protested so I won't know yet. We had a long-distance race a couple of days ago. It was loads of fun. We brought our bathing suits and our lunch. We raced over and back and was it windy. Teddy steered going over and won by 3 mins and 8 sec. I steered coming back and won by 11 mins and 5 secs. We get a cup for that. Eunice and Bobby are doing quite well.

I go to the Red Cross and make bandages every Monday and Thursdays . . . It is really awfully nice . . .

Kick is knitting a scarf for Billy and I am going to start knitting one for one of the soldiers . . .

Eunice got a lovely painting from an elderly gentleman who came down one day with Condé Nast and he went crazy over Eunice. It is too bad nobody goes crazy over me.

Don't forget to come home soon.

Joe to me
August 13
London

I have a chance to get this off again on the North Atlantic plane so am rushing it along. I went to see about your china and they haven't been able to give me much satisfaction yet. I have to get a sample of the plate and a sample of the colour. They say they are still trying . . .

I am also busy on the chintzes and I won't buy anything unless it meets all your requirements. Frankly, however, I am not at all taken with the one you sent me. I don't think it is sufficiently light and airy for that place . . .

As to the situation here, there is little if any change. People are getting more confident that the home defence in the air is getting stronger. I am not prepared yet to make this judgment. If Hitler has the strength in the air he pretends he has, sooner or later it is bound to tell, and it is for that I am waiting. I hate to think I am going to be here indefinitely considering that the work is not as important as I should like to be doing. However, as I have said, I shall have to wait to see what is going to happen in the next few weeks.

I read Jack's book through and I think it is a swell job. There is no question but that regardless of whether he makes any money out of it or not, he will have built himself a foundation for his reputation that will be of lasting value to him. Tell him I am taking the book today to Laski and I am going to have Laski give me some suggestions as to what people here might be helpful to get letters from for Jack, and I am also looking up who would be likely to do the best job publishing it.

I am still taking very good care of myself and I am having surprisingly little trouble with my stomach considering the strain we are under . . .

By the time the next letter is due we will know a great deal more about Germany's possibilities in the air. Until then, best love to you all.

Father to Eunice
September 11
London

I received your stories on Sunday and I sat myself right down on the porch and read them all. [Eunice had sent her father four essays.] You know, I think they are really wonderful . . . I knew you had a good sense of humour but I didn't know you could handle the descriptive part so well . . .

There has been plenty of bombing going on . . . and they are still dropping them all 'round 14 Princes Gate. Last night they dropped one in the pool of Buckingham Palace . . . The prospect of bombing every night is driving them frantic. I don't know where it is all going to end but everything I see confirms what I always thought, that it ought never to have started. The unfortunate part of this war is that poor women and children are getting by far the worst of it. The soldiers aren't suffering in any such degree . . .

I can't tell you what my state of mind would have been if any of you had been over here . . . I think I should have gone mad . . . The Germans are pursuing, I think, their usual methodical manner. I am not one of those who believe they are looking for maternity homes and hospitals to bomb. They are bombing their military objectives; and when you do that at night from fifteen or twenty thousand feet up in the air, you are bound to hit other things . . .

Well, old darling, keep praying for civilization because heaven knows it needs it . . .

Father to Jean
September 11
London

You have been one of my best little correspondents and I got another sweet letter from you yesterday. I certainly wish you could get that fat little brother of yours to write a little more frequently and tell me what he is doing. He was very good on the record [We sent a phonograph record, entitled *Voices*, for Joe's birthday. Each child recorded a birthday greeting.], but I think he should have a little more practise writing letters, because it looks to me as though the Kennedys are going to be good writers and I should hate to think that the Dude is not holding his end up, so will you see what you can do with him.

The house at Windsor that I live in is such a bright colour that the Air Ministry came in the other day and said it was such a perfect landmark for the German aeroplanes that it will have to be camouflaged, so they are trying to fix it up before the new moon. From this you can see all the problems that one has over here during the terrible war that this is.

[As a matter of fact, bombs were dropped nearby. One of his staff aides, walking around the grounds, found a piece of bomb casing that bore the initials JPK. Probably a coincidence that Joe's initials were on it; nevertheless, they were.]

Father to Teddy
September 11
London

I certainly don't get all of those letters you keep telling me you write . . . your sisters do very well and you and Bobby are the worst correspondents I have in the family. It is very good practice for you to write, so I hope you will plan to send me a regular letter for so long as I am here. Incidentally, I certainly was thrilled to hear all your voices . . . [The recording.] You are a great little cheer leader, and that Hip! Hip! Hooray! couldn't have been better . . .

I was terribly sorry not to be with you in swimming at Cape Cod this summer, but I am sure you will know I wanted to be, but couldn't leave here while I had work to do . . .

I thought you might be interested to know, and you might tell this to all your brothers and sisters, that the other night when I was going to the concert and afterwards to have dinner with Duff Cooper, the Cabinet Minister of Information, I dashed home to 14 Prince's Gate, put on my dinner jacket and left to go to the concert. When I got to Queen's Hall I found out the concert was cancelled, and then I went back to my office, and after sitting there three-quarters of an hour I noticed by the merest chance that I had forgotten to shave for a couple of days, and I was going out to a dinner party without having shaved. So you can see how busy I am. I am sure everybody will laugh at this.

I don't know whether you would have much excitement during these raids. I am sure, of course, you wouldn't be scared, but if you heard all those guns firing every night and the bombs bursting you might get a little fidgety . . .

It is really terrible to think about, and all those poor women and children and homeless people down in the East End of London all seeing their places destroyed.

I hope when you grow up you will dedicate your life to trying to

work out plans to make people happy instead of making them
miserable, as war does . . .

Joe came back the next month, at his own insistence, for discussions
with President Roosevelt about the war situation, American policy
and – a matter that had been angering him – the State Department's
penchant for working through special emissaries and otherwise
operating behind his back without keeping him informed on develop-
ments he needed to know about. The first evening after his arrival,
he and I had dinner at the White House with the President and his
personal secretary, 'Missy' LeHand, and Senator and Mrs James
Byrnes. Joe made his points in his most forthright way – which was
very forthright. The President not only agreed with him about the
State Department operations but went on to give the persons involved
a verbal blistering. In fact, in describing his remarks I see that in my
notes I have used the term 'harangue'.

The Presidential election of 1940 was less than two weeks away
and looked as if it would be a very close one; the 'third term' issue was
hotly debated, and the Republicans had an energetic and attractive
candidate in Wendell Wilkie. The President asked Joe that evening for
his support and a public announcement. Joe agreed, and a few evenings
later he went on a national radio hook-up of 114 stations (paying the
expenses from his own pocket, as his personal financial contribution
to the Democratic Party) and examined the issues and endorsed
Roosevelt for re-election. His main point of emphasis was that he
believed FDR could and would keep us out of the war. He closed by
saying:

> My wife and I have given nine hostages to fortune. Our children
> and your children are more important than anything else in the
> world. The kind of America that they and their children will inherit
> is of grave concern to us all. In the light of these considerations, I
> believe that Franklin D. Roosevelt should be re-elected President of
> the United States.

At the request of Betsy Cushing Roosevelt, I too went on the radio
and said I was sure the President would not lead us into war.

There were nagging doubts in our minds as to just how far, 'short
of war', FDR's policies could lead the country in safety. Yet Joe could
in all sincerity agree with FDR, at that point in history. Give England
all the aid possible, while also rearming this country to make it im-
pregnable against attack in case England fell and we were next on
Hitler's list. Meanwhile, we should not fight unless attacked.

Peace was a continual theme in Roosevelt's campaign speeches. An evening or two after Joe's speech, FDR was in Boston – incidentally, welcomed there at the station by dignitaries including my father, with Jack in tow – and before a great crowd at the Boston Garden gave one of his most eloquent speeches which included these memorable lines:

> And while I am talking to you mothers and fathers, I give you one more assurance. I have said this before, but I shall say it again and again and again: Your boys are not going to be sent into any foreign wars.

I must confess that I was as susceptible as most people to Roosevelt's charm and blandishments. He was undoubtedly a genius in his personal relationships. He knew that one of the easiest ways to get around me, and therefore to influence Joe a little in his favour, was to tell me complimentary things about my father. I knew what he was doing (and later one of the Roosevelt boys told Jack it was true, and Jack told me). Nevertheless, even while I knew I was being charmed, the charm was difficult to resist. He even beguiled my father, who was a beguiler himself. For instance, Father, with young Jack, met the Presidential train in Boston. Roosevelt gave my father his special, jovial attention and said: 'Everywhere I went on my South American trip they were asking after you. They all remember your singing "Sweet Adeline" when you were down there.'

The day after President Roosevelt's re-election, Joe sent in his resignation. The President wanted him to stay on, and in fact persuaded him to keep the title until a successor could be selected. Thus his resignation was not formally accepted until February 1941.

He never re-entered Government service again except as a consultant and adviser and, many years later, a member of the 'Hoover Commission', under his old friend, the former President, to reorganize the Executive Branch of the Government.

Yet he was never any less concerned with national and international affairs than he had been during the decade when he was helping to shape them.

14

For most of the year following his resignation, Joe organized sentiment against US intervention in the war and the policies that could lead to it. He testified before committees of Congress, wrote articles, gave interviews, made speeches and talked with influential friends. Yet direct involvement became steadily more likely.

With the imminence of war, and the feeling that it might be the last good time for a long time, I took a trip to South America. I had never been farther south than Panama. With Joe now back in the US and able to cope with the children, I could travel with my mind at ease. I invited Eunice to come along for companionship. As soon as she finished her spring term at Manhattanville we cruised through Caribbean islands and thence south to Rio de Janeiro. From there we travelled by air.

We were joined briefly by Jack. He was still having a hard time deciding on a career. He had thought of law school. Then, perhaps because Joe Jr was to be a lawyer, he thought of becoming a businessman. He had great love and admiration for his father, who had made such a great success in business. Jack evidently figured that if the life of a businessman and financier was interesting enough for his father it should be interesting for him. Consequently in the fall of 1940 he had enrolled in courses in economics and finance and business administration at Stanford University. But he had no real appetite for it, so he left after the first semester. Then, impelled by the same urge to travel in the world and sharing my curiosity about South America, he had taken off by air about a fortnight after Eunice and I sailed, and met us in Rio.

After a time together he went on his own way alone, seeing whatever interested him, forming impressions of countries and their peoples. I dare say that his trip found echoes twenty years later when he was President and created the Alliance for Progress.

Eunice and I had quite a fascinating time. We learned a lot, we had fun and we also had a few thrills and chills, including flying over, and between, the towering snowy Andes in a plane bouncing wildly in the treacherous air currents. The windows frosted over completely and many people inhaled oxygen from overhanging tubes. I didn't need oxygen. I used my breath to clear a little space in the frost so I could look at the mountains.

Here are a few diary jottings beginning early in the trip:

May 14: Barbados. On our arrival at shore, we were delighted with the atmosphere of the town. The people are happy and gentle. Visited the Cathedral which is as old as Plymouth, and found some graves in the church as old as any in Massachusetts, written in old English . . .

Hired a car and visited the Convent of Ursulines, where Sisters were teaching children, little coloured and white children sitting together . . . Was struck by the cleanliness of all the children.

May 21. Rio de Janeiro. Jack and Eunice and I invited by Ambassador Jefferson Caffery to dinner at the United States Embassy. The first dinner in an Embassy I have attended since I left London. Seemed reminiscent of many of my own in London. There was the guest of honour, Señor Aranha, the foreign minister of the nation. There was the Papal Nuncio. There was an Austrian Archduchess and her Polish husband. A few visiting Americans like us, and the regular quota of two or three American attachés from the Embassy who are always at hand to fill in or drop out of an official dinner, so that an official hostess need never worry at the last moment about a guest's sudden absence . . . The china and glass at the US Embassies are the same the world over. White Lenox china with the gold crest; glassware is plain crystal with the Coat of Arms etched on. Menu cards, 4 ins by $6\frac{1}{4}$ ins, are ivory white with gold Coat of Arms at top and the courses are printed or handwritten in French. Although for the dinner we had for the King and Queen before they travelled to the US we wrote them in English, because all the food was American-style and how could we say 'Georgia picked peaches' or 'Old-Fashioned Strawberry Shortcake' in French and have it mean anything . . .

On my arrival I was presented to the Papal Nuncio in his cardinal red robes, and I chatted with him in French until dinner was announced. I sat next to Señor Aranha, whose family has been five generations in politics. We discussed the attitude of the Brazilian government in the present world crisis, and he seems to feel it would be strongly influenced by which side won the victory abroad. For that reason he seemed to think America would be compelled to enter the war so that England would not be defeated.

It seems to me that the idea of a family serving in the government generation after generation, and as is the case with so many English families as well, is one we might do well to think about and encourage in our own country . . .

Eunice and I travelled on to Argentina, across the Andes to Chile, thence to Peru, Ecuador, on then to Panama and to Cuba. We arrived in Hyannis Port about June 20, full of stories of our adventures and just in time to get almost the full benefit of a Cape Cod summer.

At our house the summers had some rather special qualities. For help in recalling them fully I wrote to Charles Spaulding, a friend of Joe Jr's and Jack's. He replied with a letter describing the summer of 1940, just after Jack's book was published, but the scene was essentially the same in earlier summers and again in 1941.

Dear Mrs Kennedy,

Perhaps the best way for me to answer your letter is to recall the first time I met your family.

George Means brought me to your house on the Cape at the end of a day in the summer of 1940. The two of us walked up on the porch. There was an uproar of voices, laughter and insults pouring from every room – Billings's notes quite clear in the orchestration. Somebody yelled above the din that we should stay for supper.

We walked into the house and I remember being startled to see so many young people – children then – who looked so alike when they grinned and somehow managed to keep the atmosphere in the house at fever pitch even while involved in something as lack-lustre as getting ready for supper.

George went into Jack's room which was downstairs. There was a large inventory of *Why England Slept* stacked on the floor. 'They're going like hot cakes,' the author explained as we were introduced. I noticed a letter of praise from a very famous man in Europe lying on the floor, half under a bathing suit, and was about to pick it up when the former Mayor of Boston entered. He carried a clipping from a Boston paper that made a flattering reference to himself, the justice of which he was at some pains to make clear to his grandson.

Dinner followed shortly with the whole family and four guests present. A supermarket must have been cleaned out to supply the vegetables and the berries that were consumed at that sitting. The talk was about the Federal Reserve System and the argument lasted through the meal with the head of the house leading the company through a strenuous exercise on the subject.

Afterwards, there was a movie. When George and I left much later, the place was having difficulty calming down. Those who had gone to bed early were pounding shoes on the floor demanding a quiet that was coming with a grudging reluctance. A lot had gone into that day and it was dying hard, leaving behind a diary of activity that included a sailing race, an aggregate of twenty-three sets of tennis, a debate on the forces involved in the Spanish Revolution, some stories by the emperor about plungers of the 'twenties, a paper contributed by the girls listing the qualities that should be present in the ideal husband, the daily game of touch football, and finally, a local war that broke out after the movie over the issue – would Ingrid Bergman go to fat.

On the way home with George, I went over the evening in my mind and wondered about what had made it so good. There was the excitement of the unusual achievement of the house coupled at the same time with a complete lack of pretence. There was the constant spur of competition which brought out an intense appreciation of excellence. There was the feeling shared by everybody that anything was possible and the only recognized problem was that there would never be enough time. And this combined to produce the most heightened group of people, much less one family. I thought to myself – that's the best I've seen.

All of this was many years ago. I have been close to the act off and on since. It's still the best I've seen. It never loses its fascination or inspiration for me. When one has stumbled and come back and been exposed again to your vivid point of view, one finds the energy to try again. When one has succeeded a little and returned, he quickly sees how small his achievement has been and gets the impulse to start at once on something else much more demanding. All in all, it amounts to a considerable influence, I think the strongest I have known.

This is as close as I can come in a few words to describing what I have found of value in your house.

Chuck Spaulding

There are a few footnotes worth adding to this wonderful letter of Chuck's. One is on the subject of radios and phonographs. I don't know how many we had in our house, but certainly there were six or eight or so, including 'portables'. Several were operating morning, noon and night around the house and grounds. During most of the daylight hours one could fairly well count on music coming from the directions of the tennis court, the beach and the front porch – each according to the taste of the person running the machinery.

And then there were the telephones. There were several lines coming into the house, with instruments in nearly all the bedrooms and strategically placed in other areas. The telephones rang morning to night.

I mustn't neglect the barking of the dogs.

I have read someplace that I have an idiosyncratic dislike of dogs. Actually I grew up with dogs, in Concord and Dorchester. I think we always had a dog in the house. So I knew what a dog could mean to a child. When my children were old enough we began to acquire a series of dogs. There were so many through the years, including mutts from the pound as well as purebreds, that I can't begin to sort out their identities and eras. But we had a 'house dog' until Jack was fourteen or so and began developing asthmatic troubles. He was apparently allergic to dog hair. It was sad for him because he loved animals, but it meant no house dogs so long as he was at home. However, it did not mean an absence of dogs: it merely meant that there would be 'yard dogs', which rather often would be allowed inside.

Pat says:

One of Jack's dogs was a Dobermann Pinscher called Moe. Jack was in Arizona for his health and living in a rather remote place and bought the dog both for company and as a watchdog. Then he moved on someplace where he couldn't take the dog, so he shipped him home. It was supposed to be for Mother's birthday, or something like that. The dog arrived one day on the front porch in a big, slatted, open crate with a big sign on it: MY NAME IS MOE AND I DON'T BITE. Everybody gathered around, and Teddy opened the door of the crate and the dog jumped out and bit him.

We immediately sent a telegram to Jack: THIS DOG THAT DOESN'T BITE JUST JUMPED OUT OF HIS CAGE AND BIT ME. (signed) TEDDY.

Mother took the dog out for walks, and Moe became very attached to her. Only to Mother – a real one-woman dog. And Mother rather enjoyed him. For the rest of us it got to be terrifying. There were a couple of us old enough to go down to Hyannis to the movies at night. Daddy always made us put the car away in the garage when we got here. But after a few nights we couldn't do that, because to get from the garage to the house with Moe around was absolutely terrifying. Finally it got so we couldn't do anything, because he was so attached to Mother. He was biting everybody in sight. Except Mother. He adored her. But not the rest of us – if you kept all your limbs, or fingers or toes, you were lucky. He lasted about five weeks and then Moe had to go. Mother I'm sure found a good home for him with someone who needed an insanely dedicated watchdog.

My own feeling was that the dog was an exceptional judge of character. However, since it had become a matter of keeping Moe or my children, I chose the children.

Summarizing the sounds of our summers: the thunks of tennis balls, the shouts of touch-football players, the cars 'revving up' and back-firing, departing and arriving, the cries of welcome and farewell, the yapping and barking of dogs, the cacophony of the radios and phonographs, the piano being tortured by someone learning to play, the merry chases down the hallways and stairs, the ringing of the telephones and the maid's knock on my door to ask, 'Mrs Kennedy, what should I . . .' I resolved to get away for an hour or two of peace and quiet each day, though near enough in case something happened I should know about.

I bought a little prefabricated one-room house and had it erected down at one corner of the beach. It was about the size of a tool shed – or of my little sewing-room at our house on Beals Street – but big enough for a desk where I could take care of personal correspondence, an easy chair where I could sit and read, a cot on which I could nap, and space enough so that I could change clothes there if I felt like walking down to the water for a swim. Other 'Hermitages' have been grander, but this was perfect for me.

Imagine my horror when a summer or two later we had a hurricane and I watched it bob in the waves and then disappear towards the open sea. I was so sad that I had it replaced the following summer, at a little higher and safe elevation from the shore. The children referred to it as 'Mother's Little White House'. I used it contentedly for several years. But then came another and even bigger hurricane and Little White House II also went off to sea without trace. By then the Hyannis Port scene was quieter and Joe and I had begun to spend part of each summer abroad. I didn't erect White House number III. But I remember numbers I and II with deep nostalgia.

The summer of 1941 was the last one our family would ever have together.

Ordinarily Joe Jr would have been returning to Harvard that fall for his last year of law school, but however much he regretted the prospect, he felt sure the US would be drawn into the war. He felt he should prepare himself for a role in active service. Accordingly he volunteered for training as a Navy flyer; and in July, shortly before his twenty-sixth birthday, he reported for his primary training at the Squantum Naval Air Station near Boston. It was close enough so that he could come home for several weekends during the rest of that summer. Afterwards he went for advanced training at the big Naval Air Station at Jacksonville, Florida. In the book, *As We Remember Joe*, Jack wrote:

> As a cadet at Jacksonville he was President of the Cadet Club, President of the Holy Name Society, and at the last, upon graduation, was awarded the Cutler Wings, given to that cadet as elected by his fellows who is best fitted for his duties as a United States Naval Officer.
>
> After being awarded his wings in May 1942 by his father at a graduation ceremony, he flew Caribbean patrols, and it was not until September 1943 that he finally realized his ambition and was sent to England with the first Naval squadron to fly B-24s with the British Coastal Command . . .

Jack had come to the same conclusion as Joe Jr at practically the same time. After returning from his South American travels early that summer (soon after his twenty-fourth birthday) he volunteered for the officers' candidate school of the Army. However, because of the spinal injury he had suffered in Harvard football, he failed the physical exam. He tried the Navy, and was rejected for the same reason. Instead of being downcast he refused, as usual, to admit there was anything wrong with him, so during the rest of that summer he did all sorts of calisthenics and corrective exercises to strengthen his back. In September he applied again to the Navy and this time he was accepted. He went through the Navy's officer training course and early that winter received his commission. At first he had a desk job in Washington, helping prepare a digest of relevant news and 'Intelligence' for the Navy's Chief of Staff, a duty he found dull. After Pearl Harbor he quickly applied for sea duty. Nothing happened for some time. Then he was assigned to instruct recruits at a training base in South Carolina. His pal Lem Billings saw him 'in action' there and told about it later – in *John Fitzgerald Kennedy . . . As We Remember Him* – in such a funny way that with Lem's permission I am including it here:

> He was stationed for a while in Charleston, South Carolina. My

brother got married down South, and so I was there, and I went over after my brother's wedding just to see what was going on. He made, as far as I know, his first public speech. And I was there. He had to give a talk on incendiary bombs. He knew very little about the subject and did very, very well. I was impressed, because I had never heard him speak before. When we were at Choate, we both avoided public speaking – you could do that if you went into Dramatic Club. Neither of us was a good actor, but we avoided public speaking by doing that. After the speech was over, he was so pleased with himself that he said to the crowd, 'Now, are there any questions?' The first question was, 'Well, you have told us about these two kinds of bombs; tell me, if one lands, how do you tell which is which?' Jack said, 'I'm glad you asked that question, because a specialist is going to be down here in two weeks and this is the kind of thing he wants to talk about.'

He spent most of his first year and a half in the Navy in similar duties, which didn't appeal to him at all. He did manage to get home to Hyannis Port on leave during the summer of 1942. In the late fall of that year he was transferred to PT boats. He trained for about six months, and early in 1943 was sent off to the South Pacific, where by March that year he became skipper of PT 109.

Thus Jack, although he had been accepted into the Navy a couple of months after Joe Jr, was in a 'combat zone' of the war, subject to all dangers of enemy action, six months or so before Joe Jr arrived in England. As most spirited young men do in a national patriotic war, as this one became for all of us after Pearl Harbor, both had wanted to get away from routine military matters and into direct combat as soon as possible. In their long brotherly, friendly rivalry, I expect this was the first time Jack had won such an 'advantage' by such a clear margin. And I dare say it cheered Jack and must have rankled Joe Jr.

One may wonder what I thought about all this. I hated it. I suppose there are mothers someplace in the world who can send their sons off to war, to kill or as likely to be killed, with pride and pleasure that they could supply warriors to defend whatever the needs of the tribe or nation might be. I thought, 'Why should my sons be killing the sons of the girls I knew at Blumenthal?' War has always seemed to me 'the ultimate insanity'. Violence, and war as the maximum demonstration of man's capacity for inhumanity to man, was against my religious beliefs, my sense of morality, and my common sense. The future confirmed my beliefs in ways that in that period I could barely have imagined.

Yet, like nearly all mothers everywhere, I was caught in events and forces and circumstances utterly beyond my control. There was nothing I could do but put on a cheerful face, to hope, and to pray.

The summer of 1941 was also the last one that Rosemary could be with us.

She had been making good progress for some time past, and Joe and I had every reason to be optimistic about her future. Not that she could be brought all the way up to the level of normality; this was an unrealistic hope. Yet there are many millions of people in the world with IQ's below 100 who have satisfactory lives and do work that is satisfying to themselves and helpful to others. This was our ambition for Rosemary, and it seemed close to being achieved.

Yet in the year or so following her return from England disquieting symptoms began to develop. Not only was there noticeable retrogression in the various mental skills she had worked so hard to attain, but her customary affectionate good nature gave way increasingly to a state of tension and irritability. She was upset easily and unpredictably; some of these upsets became tantrums, or rages, during which she broke things or hit out at people. Since she was quite strong, her blows were hard. Also, there were convulsive episodes. Manifestly there were other factors at work besides retardation. A neurological disturbance or disease of some sort seemingly had overtaken her and it was becoming progressively worse. Joe and I brought the most eminent medical specialists into consultation, and the advice, finally, was that Rosemary should undergo a certain form of neuro-surgery. The operation eliminated the violent or convulsive seizures, but it also had the effect of leaving Rosemary permanently incapacitated. She lost much of what had been gained during the years by her own gallant efforts and our loving efforts for her. It was soon quite evident that she had lost all possibility of ever again being able to function in a viable way in the world at large. She would thenceforth need custodial care. We searched for the proper place and found it in a convent in Wisconsin where the nuns were understanding of her condition and gave her all the care and compassion and cheerful loving-kindness that her misfortune and her sweet nature deserved. She has been there for more than three decades. She has remained physically healthy and generally happy. I visit her every few months. Eunice goes about every six weeks. The other family members see her at least a few times a year. So she sees one or another of us every few weeks. She functions on a somewhat childlike level but is able to be out for pleasant excursions in her motor-car and to do a little personal shopping for her needs – always with an attendant

– and to enjoy life to the limit of her capacities. She has grown quite used to being where she is and would be confused and disturbed at being anywhere else. She is always happy to see us and knows that she is a much-loved member of our family.

Rosemary's was the first of the tragedies that were to befall us. I have never before this moment explained anything about it to anyone except those in the family and the few outside it who needed to know. In writing as I have, I have felt grief and pain hardly lessened despite the years. Yet there have been so many strange stories (that Rosemary was incognito at Jack's Inauguration) that I have felt obliged to relate the story as it really was. As I said at the very beginning of this book, a principal reason for writing it was to set the record straight. I am eighty-three years old now – in my eighty-fourth year – and it is now time for candour.

That summer of 1941 was also the last of the long times we had with Kathleen. She was twenty-one by then and, having finished her second year at the Finch school in New York that spring, spent much of the summer with us at Hyannis Port. She wasn't sure what to do next but liked the idea of journalism. So, that fall, encouraged and aided by her father, who was a friend of the owners, the McCormicks and Pattersons, she got a job reporting for the *Washington Times-Herald*. As her father pointed out, that would keep her in the thick of things in the most important capital in the world at one of the most important times in history.

Lest the fact that Joe helped her get the job be taken amiss, I should add that once she was in it she worked as hard as anyone – probably harder – because she wanted to prove herself. She won everyone's respect as an excellent reporter and writer, and she tried her best to avoid any attention or privilege that could come her way due to her father's fame and fortune. In fact, she strove so hard to blend into the staff and be just another cub reporter whose name was Kathleen Kennedy that one amusing incident is worth telling here.

Joe gave each of the girls a fur coat on her twenty-first birthday, mink or her choice of some fine fur and in any style she felt was most becoming. Kick's, as I recall, was a long, lustrous mutation mink in a shade that would set off her glowing, lightly pink Irish complexion. Naturally she didn't wear it to the *Times-Herald* office. Except early one evening she did. She was supposed to attend a diplomatic reception, which obliged her to dress up in her best. She wore an expensive dinner dress and her elegant mink coat. Then she suddenly realized there was something she had to do at the office, so on her way to the party she had her taxi wait while she hurried up to attend to it. In the interval, she encountered a couple of her older female colleagues, who looked at her as though they couldn't believe their eyes and didn't want to. Later the grapevine had it that they feared their sweet innocent little Kathleen had gone wrong, succumbed to the temptations of wealth, become a loose woman. She obviously couldn't afford such raiment on her wages as a cub reporter!

From her childhood Kick had been, in effect, our eldest daughter because of Rosemary's disability. She was small, quick, radiant, witty, and exceptionally bright. She was an enchanting child, girl and young woman. She adored her two big brothers, and they in turn were delighted by her. When she was a teen-ager, and with Joe Jr only five years and Jack only three years older than she, these three reached such near-parity that they shared friends and experiences. During the Embassy years, for instance, while Joe Jr and Jack were becoming popular swains in London, Kick was becoming a rather spectacularly successful debutante and post-deb in the same set. They knew the same people, often went to the same places, heard the new songs and learned the new dance steps and listened to the latest jokes and youthful gossip, and talked about it together.

Consequently, when Joe Jr and Jack went off into the armed services expecting shortly to be sent into theatres of war, I think Kick felt rather left out. She too wanted to become directly involved in the war, and to make her own contribution that would be constructive. Early in 1943 she left her newspaper job to join the Red Cross Training programme. She wanted to serve in a theatre of war, and hoped that this would be England.

She had developed a great fondness for that country and its people during our years there. She had many English friends and she wanted to share their wartime ordeals. There was a young man who meant far more to her than I realized at the time. This was William John Robert ('Billy') Hartington.

She got her wish. She was on her way to England by late June 1943, which was only a few months after Jack had arrived in the South Pacific and taken command of PT 109, and was actually close to three months before Joe Jr arrived in England with his squadron to begin working with the British Coastal Command.

Her letters to us – and to Jack out in the South Pacific – form a very interesting narrative. I am going to quote from them at some length, with my notes and comments as needed.

To the Family
June 27, 1943
On Board the *Queen Mary*

After talking with you I went back to the hotel and got myself together. At 7.00 promptly on one of the hottest days of the year, dressed in winter uniforms, raincoats, gas-masks, wearing tin helmets, carrying 35-pound musette bags, not to mention the canteen and First Aid Kit strapped to the waist – we boarded the *Queen Mary*. There are eight of us in a cabin and when I say on top of one another I do mean on top of one another! Nearly 18,000 troops are packed in all over the ship. They are sleeping in the hallway, decks, etc. It really is the most pathetic sight in the world . . .

There are about 160 Army nurses and they are certainly a lot of tough babies. There are also about 300 Officers of every nationality. Most of the Red Cross girls don't pay attention to them as it certainly isn't any compliment to be sought after when the ratio is so uneven . . . The girls are quite nice but you certainly get sick of a lot of giggling females and they still like to sit up until about 1.30 a.m. every night . . .

We have had Mass every afternoon at 3.30 – a wartime measure, and guess where we have it – in the Synagogue. I have been serving Mass as the soldiers don't seem to show up . . .

I really am becoming quite excited at the thought of seeing England again and I am quite prepared for the changes. This arrival certainly is going to be different from our last one. This life on an Army transport has been an eye-opener. It seems so unreal and far removed from anything I've ever known that I can't believe I'm a part of it. Sometimes it almost feels like a dream.

I still haven't any idea about my assignment, but hope like anything it will be London for a while . . .

No one really knows I'm coming. What a shock they'll get when I get on the other end of the phone.

About a half-hour after each sharp swerve we are informed that this good ship has just missed a sub. There's another one. It was probably about nine miles to starboard.

Tell Eunice I shall keep her constantly informed of all happenings as maybe she could join me after graduation. Or, Dad, do you think you could go through another session with the Red Cross? . . .

Love to all and eat a lot of ice-cream for me on Sunday.

To Jack
July 3
Hampstead, England

At the moment I am sunning myself in the Gores' garden. Still recovering from a rather hectic trip over . . .

London seems quite unchanged. Food is very good. Blitzed areas are not obvious . . .

Sissy and David Gore have two wee ones now. Talked to Tony [Tony Rosslyn. A good friend of Kick's] on the phone. Am going to get down and see them tomorrow. Lady Astor wrote me a note of welcome but she's at Plymouth at the moment. There are a great many in the country on manœuvres, etc. . . .

The Gores were Mr and Mrs David Ormsby-Gore, an attractive young couple. David was just a year younger than Jack, and Sylvia ('Sissy') was, I suppose, about Kick's age; they had married some six months after our family had to come back, so they had done well to produce two 'wee ones'. David and Sissy, Jack and Joe Jr and Kick had been great friends together during our family's time at the Embassy. So Kick's comment was just a newsy note about old friends. David and Sissy, David particularly, would later have a conspicuous role in Anglo-American relations and in the life of our family.

To 'Dearest Little Kennedys'
July 14
London

I haven't heard a word from any of you but expect all letters take a long time these days . . . The job is going very well. Slowly but surely I am catching on as to what exactly I am up to. I simply can't get over how nice everyone is. I must say that I expected old friends to be kind but they have exceeded all expectations. Anytime anyone ever says anything against the British in front of me they'll hear about it. Yesterday Lord Beaverbrook rang me up and asked me down for the weekend but of course weekends are impossible for me, which is very sad. However, I am going to dine with him next week even though he said, 'This admirer is the combined age of all your other admirers.'

. . . Billy and I went out together for the first time in London last Saturday. It really is funny to see people put their heads together the minute we arrive any place. There's heavy betting on when we are going to announce it. Some people have got the idea that I'm going to give in. Little do they know. Some of those old Devonshire and Cecil ancestors would certainly jump out of their graves if anything happened to some of their ancient traditions. It just amused me to see how worried they all are . . .

There were very great difficulties in the way to a prospective marriage between Kick and Billy, and I think I must make them clear.

Kick had, of course, been brought up in the Catholic Church, had been convent-educated from early to late teens, an important and very impressionable time in any girl's life. Not only had she been thoroughly indoctrinated in her religious beliefs but she had that 'gift of faith' to which I have referred and to which I shall return. She also knew how much the Church meant to me, to most of her close relatives and, historically, to her ancestors. It had, in fact, as I think historians of almost any persuasion would agree, been the cohesive force that had – far more important than language, custom, any circumstance – enabled the Irish people to survive and in some ways prevail during the course of many centuries of domination by the English.

Billy's ancestors for many generations had been occupants of highest offices – lords-lieutenants or governors-general or numerous other titles – in the English government of Ireland and almost invariably had done their best to suppress 'home rule' or any sentiments for independence among or on behalf of the Irish. Indeed, on both sides of the family, the Cavendishes (Earls, Marquesses, and Dukes of Devonshire) and the Cecils (Earls and Marquesses of Salisbury), they had been among the most conservative and, in the Irish view, most oppressive of the members of the ruling class. I think it would be fair to say that both the Cavendishes and the Cecils deeply mistrusted the Irish people and in turn were regarded as arch-enemies by Irish patriots, who to a greater or lesser degree had been in a state of rebellion ever since the Norman-English conquest of Ireland quite a few centuries before. Billy's grandfather, Marquess of Hartington and 8th Duke of Devonshire, had been Secretary of State for Ireland – that is to say, the British ruler or Viceroy – in the 1870s, a post he hadn't wanted and from which he emerged with such bias that he later broke with his party, the Liberals, and defied his Prime Minister, Gladstone, in order to form his own party to oppose Irish 'Home Rule'. Meanwhile his younger brother, Lord Frederick Cavendish, was appointed to the same post as Secretary of State for Ireland. But he had barely been in office when a gunman of the Irish independent movement shot and killed him in Phoenix Park, Dublin, in 1882.

On the basis of what I have just related, there was little in the family backgrounds to encourage a romance between Billy Hartington – who by this time bore the title of Earl of Burlington, and was heir to the title as 11th Duke of Devonshire – and Kick, whose ancestral circumstances, only four generations removed, had been so entirely different.

This was one reason for Kick's remark in her letter about 'Some of those old Devonshire and Cecil ancestors . . .' But there was far more to the matter. The Cavendish and Cecil families had always been among the strongest pillars of the Church of England. Moreover, Billy's father, the tenth Duke, was a keen Freemason. And Freemasonry had been under condemnation by the Catholic Church for more than two centuries. Kick had said in her letter she wouldn't 'give in': wouldn't leave her church to join Billy's. It would have been equally unthinkable for Billy to leave the Church of England and become a Roman Catholic.

It was an apparently impossible dilemma in terms of 'announcement' and marriage. And Kick was realistic to have written, therefore: 'It just amuses me to see how worried they all are.'

To Jack
July 29
London

I have just returned from a day and a half spent in the country with Billy at Eastbourne. It's right on the South Coast, has been blitzed quite badly but the family continues to go there during the summer months. For 24 hours I forgot all about the war. It's the most lovely spot . . . Billy is just the same, a bit older, a bit more ducal, but we get on as well as ever. It is queer as he is so unlike anyone I have ever known at home or anyplace really. Of course I know he would never give in about the religion and he knows I never would. It's all rather difficult as he is very, very fond of me and as long as I am about he'll never marry. However much he loved me I can easily understand his position. It's really too bad because I'm sure I would be a most efficient Duchess of Devonshire in the post-war world, and as I'd have a castle in Ireland, one in Scotland, one in Yorkshire and one in Sussex, I could keep my old nautical brothers in their old age. But that's the way it goes. Everyone in London is buzzing with rumours and no matter what happens we've given them something to talk about. I can't really understand why I like Englishmen so much as they treat one in quite an off-hand manner and aren't really as nice to their women as Americans, but I suppose it's just that sort of treatment that women really like. That's your technique, isn't it? . . .

Well, take care, Johnny. By the time you get this so much will have happened. The end looks nearer now than ever. Write to me . . . God bless you . . . Much love.

'Well, take care, Johnny. By the time you get this so much will have happened . . . God bless you . . .' Kathleen's letter was prophetic. Four days later, PT 109 was cut in two by a Japanese destroyer. I did not know anything about his ordeal until after it was all over and he was safe. A message had come from the Navy Department that he was 'missing in action' but it had been delivered to Joe and he didn't show it to me. Joe did not want to torment me with uncertainty or give me bad news until it was absolutely necessary. Several days later, when Joe had gone riding at eight a.m. as was his custom, I turned on the radio and heard the announcement that Lieutenant (JG) John F. Kennedy, earlier reported missing, had been found. I waited for more news about him, but there was none. I called Joe, who was twenty minutes' distance away. He came home immediately and confirmed the details, and he told me that he had known and that he had been trying to spare me until the facts were established.

To the Family
August 24
London

Of course the news about Jack is the most exciting thing I've ever heard. There wasn't a very big piece in the English newspapers but quite enough for me to gather that he did really big stuff. Rang up Baby Carcano to tell her and she hasn't stopped ringing me since, she was so worried. I rang up Mr Raymond Daniell at the New York *Times* and he told me where I could read all about it in last week's *Times* . . .

I am having lunch tomorrow with a Father Darcy, the famous English Jesuit . . .

They are keeping us very busy here at the Club and one does receive enormous satisfaction from doing lots of little things. The boys really crowd in here every night and most of them have got over the fear that I am some extraordinary being because I happened to have a father who really was (extraordinary, of course!) . . .

As no one liked my hair, I have changed it back . . . All the news for the moment. Please send things somehow . . . Much love to all.

To Jack
September 10
London

Goodness, I was pleased to get your letter. Ever since reading the news in all the newspapers over here I have been worried to death about you. All sorts of people have rung up about it and sent congratulations. I read the clippings from the *NY Times* but long to hear the whole story.

When the shouting and the tumult dies I don't know where we Red Cross girls will be. Very tired – of that I'm sure. It's a great joy, a great job, but sometimes you don't know whether you are going to shoot yourself or that GI over there in the corner. However, there never was a job that was all milk and honey, was there?

. . . God bless you, much love.

To the Family
October 5
London

. . . We had our big day last Saturday. [This was a carnival party at the Red Cross club.] Lord and Lady Astor dropped in and she had a remark for everyone, starting with me, 'You don't work in a Red Cross club, you work in a lunatic asylum.' To a big tough top sergeant she'd make a remark, 'You don't need to be entertained. I should give you a lecture on temperance.' She kept looking for a boy from Richmond or any place in Virginia. Lord Astor just looked amazed and I really don't blame him as the place looked like a mad-house. She was very sweet to come and as she said to me afterwards, 'I just wanted them to know that there are lots of people concerning themselves about you over here.'

. . . Talked with brother Joe last night. [Joe Jr had arrived at a Coastal Command base in southern England.] He sounded very well but didn't have any idea when he could get up here. I'd go down there to see him on my leave but he says it would be silly as there's nothing to do and it probably wouldn't be a very good rest . . .

To the Family
November 17
London

Haven't had a minute to write but there's lots to tell. The party went off very well, at least I think it did. We couldn't possibly have jammed another soul into the house [they had borrowed Violet Cripps's house for the party] and they all stayed until the bitter end at 1.00 . . . People swarmed in, it was the first party London had had for the young for two years. There were about a dozen girls who hadn't been to a party since the beginning of the war. Every-body brought some drink so we were never short on that end

. . . Joe Jr arrived with his entire squadron who were feeling no pain.

Before dinner I was putting on my dress at Marie Bruce's when Irving Berlin rang her up . . . She told him I was giving a party and to come along. Then I spoke to him and told him he must come . . . People don't pay much attention to celebrities over here and when he walked in he might have been Joe Snooks for all the glances he got. I planted him at a table with the Duchess of Devonshire, hoping she'd strike up a lively conversation. Marie Bruce hadn't arrived and Joe had just gone to fetch her and I was praying she would arrive very soon. Sheila Milbanks suddenly appeared and as she had known Berlin on his honeymoon I knew he'd be well taken care of in her hands.

I asked him to render us a few pieces and he finally agreed and got up saying he had known the family for years and he would do anything for any of us. (Please thank him again, Daddy, when he gets back home.) He played his new piece, 'My British Buddy', and then a lot of his old ones. We all sang with him so it made everything go very well. The climax came when someone requested 'Over There', which he said he didn't write but he'd finish up his performance with . . .

We wanted the band to stay on but they refused past 1.00. It was probably just as well . . . We had an incident before it was all over. Lord Edward Fitzmaurice, a young Guardsman of 21, had rather too much to drink and set a match to Elizabeth Cavendish's new evening dress. She is Billy's younger sister and it was the first party she had ever been to so we were all afraid it could have scared her away from other parties. She stayed on and told her mother, 'Before I was set on fire the boys didn't pay much attention to me, but afterwards I was very popular.' An American boy put the flames out. I was very relieved that it hadn't been the other way around. Angie Laycock said that she said to her brave husband, General Laycock, 'Why didn't you do something about putting those flames out?' He replied, 'I thought it was a fireworks display.'

I really think every one had a good time and I have received lots of letters saying 'Why aren't more parties like that given?' . . .

Monday Joe and I did some shopping . . . Last night he and I dined with the Biddles, then went out to join some of his pals. We all went on to the 400 club. Joe seems to be having a good time but no special girl-friend. Goodness, it makes a difference having him over. He is in wonderful spirits . . .

To 'Mother and Daddy'
November 26
London

First, if possible, could you get my typewriter over to me somehow. I am in awful need of it . . . I suppose Eunice or Pat have carried it off to school by this time. I am always borrowing somebody's, which I hate.

Joe finished up his leave a bit tired. But I suppose that is the way with everyone. One feels one must pack all the fun possible in the shortest space of time . . . On Monday evening Sissy and David Ormsby-Gore and another couple came for dinner. We were praying that Lady Astor wouldn't ring up and find the house full, her food being eaten while she was taking a rest in Cornwall. Michael kept saying, 'Give us the good food and let the politicians have the other old stuff next weekend.' . . .

Got a letter from Joe yesterday. He was down with a cold like everyone else. People just don't get the right food here and they catch all sorts of diseases . . . I shall go down to see him before Christmas . . .

Margaret Biddle's son has lost the sight of one eye, and one leg. Isn't it awful? Much love to all . . .

The romance between Kick and Billy continued and deepened greatly during this period and in the months ahead. So did their dilemma, one in which not only they but naturally the parents on both sides were painfully involved.

There were many transatlantic cables and telephone calls, and much correspondence. There was, I expect, enough material for a large novel. But the point of it all was simply – if that is the term – to find a way through innumerable complications to make possible a marriage that had everything sentimental in its favour. The two young people were much in love. Joe and I and the Duke and Duchess were friends. We were very fond of Billy. They were equally fond of Kick. This would have been 'a marriage made in Heaven' except for the special and ironic circumstances of religious loyalties.

During the winter and spring of 1944, all of us – Joe and I, the Duke and Duchess, and of course Kick and Billy – tried to find some way by which, through some stretch of the rules, the marriage could be sanctioned or at least tolerated by both the Roman Catholic and Anglican churches.

One of our closest friends among the Catholic clergy in America was Francis Spellman, once Bishop in the Boston archdiocese of

Cardinal O'Connell and by then himself a Cardinal and Archbishop of the New York archdiocese. We enlisted him as our adviser and also as our friend at court, so to speak, with Pope Pius XII, the former Cardinal Pacelli. Since it was wartime and all letters, cables and telephone calls were read or listened to and subject to censorship, we worked out a rough kind of code with Kick as we talked or corresponded back and forth. His Eminence Cardinal Archbishop Spellman became 'Archie Spell'. So it was Archie Spell suggests this, or is doing that, or wants to know about the latest difficulty on the other side.

But finally it couldn't be worked out. The only way for Kick to marry Billy within the Sacraments of the Catholic Church – and even this would be a civil ceremony – would be for Billy to agree that their children would be raised as Catholics; and of course he could not agree to that either.

They decided to be married in a civil ceremony on May 6, 1944, at the Chelsea Registry Office. It was a very brief ceremony. The Duke and Duchess and a few other close kin were there for Billy, and Joe Jr represented our family.

In *As We Remember Joe*, Kathleen wrote:

Never did anyone have such a pillar of strength as I had in Joe in those difficult days before my marriage. From the beginning, he gave me wise, helpful advice. When he felt that I had made up my mind, he stood by me always. He constantly reassured me and gave me renewed confidence in my decision. Moral courage he had in abundance and once he felt that a step was right for me, he never faltered, although he might be held largely responsible for my decision. He could not have been more helpful and in every way he was the perfect brother doing, according to his own light, the best for his sister with the hope that in the end it would be the best for the family.

Another pillar for her was my dear friend Marie Bruce, who has been mentioned here several times. Many years afterwards, while I was gathering my materials for this book, I asked Marie to send me her own direct account, thinking it might be of interest to others.

Here is the information you asked for. Kick's dress was very pale pink crepe, dull surface, made quite plain. Little half-hat was made of two pale pink ostrich feathers and one pale blue with a veil over it (pink). She carried my gold mesh bag with sapphires and diamonds, which I gave her for 'something old and something new', and a new posy of pink camellias I made for her; Duke had sent a basket of them from Chatsworth that morning . . . Best fitter in London, Miss Jarvis, sat up all night to make the dress. There was no time for fittings, so she copied one of Kick's American dresses. We did not have enough coupons for material, so milkman gave us his. She looked enchanting.

Charles Rutland [Duke of Rutland] was the best man. Only others at marriage in the Registry were Devonshires, Anne, Elizabeth [Billy's sisters], Lady Salisbury [from the Cecil side of the family], Lady Astor, young Joe and me.

Eddy and Moucher [the Duke and Duchess of Devonshire] gave her a diamond bracelet . . . I gave her and Billy an Augustus John drawing. I said it was from you and Joe. Anne Tree [Billy's sister who later married a son of Ronald Tree] has it now. I gave five pounds to the head waiter at Claridge's and had a chocolate cake made for us without ticket! [Ration was one egg per week.] Reception was held at Lord Hambledon's house in Eaton Square. Carlton House Terrace [Devonshire's house] was already bombed and they lived in Mayfair Hotel.

Kick went away in cherry-coloured coat and pink and white print dress with a white hat made of white gardenias. For her trousseau, I gave her all my Porthault underclothes. They were more feminine.

Honeymoon was spent at Compton Place, Devonshire's house at Eastbourne. They had about a week . . .

It was three weeks. In any case far too short. Billy had to return to his regiment. He was an officer in the Coldstream Guards and they were in training for the Allied invasion of Europe that came a month later.

Meanwhile Jack, because of his injuries in the PT 109 episode, had been in a Naval hospital in the South Pacific and then finally had been brought back for treatment at the Chelsea Naval hospital and the New England Baptist Hospital in Boston. He continued his recuperation, which was slow, during the first seven months of 1944, partly in hospitals and partly with us at Palm Beach and Hyannis Port. It was obvious he couldn't be on active duty soon.

Meanwhile Bobby had become old enough to volunteer for the Navy, and had entered the Navy's officers' candidate school. Jack wrote him:

The folks sent me a clipping of you taking the oath. The sight of you up there was really moving, particularly as a close examination showed that you had my checked London coat on. I'd like to know what the hell I'm doing out here while you go stroking around in my drape coat, but I suppose that's what we are out here for – so that our sisters and younger brothers will be made safe and secure – frankly, I don't see it quite that way. At least, if you're going to be safe and secure, that's fine with me, but not in my coat, brother, not in my coat.

In his introductory essay to *As We Remember Joe* – published in 1945, before the war was over, thus under restrictions of military security – Jack summed up briefly Joe Jr's war service from the time he arrived with his squadron in England in September 1943.

> This squadron, flying in the bitter winter over the Bay of Biscay, suffered heavy casualties, and by the time Joe had completed his designated number of missions in May [the month of Kick's wedding] he had lost his former co-pilot and a number of close friends.
>
> Joe refused his proffered leave and persuaded his crew to remain on for D-day. They flew frequently during June and July, and at the end of July they were given another opportunity to go home. He felt it unfair to ask his crew to stay on longer, and they returned to the United States. He remained. For he had heard of a new and special assignment for which volunteers had been requested which would require another month of the most dangerous type of flying.
>
> This work that Joe did and which led to his death is still a Naval secret . . . It may be felt, perhaps, that Joe should not have pushed his luck so far and should have accepted his leave and come home. But two facts must be borne in mind. First, at the time of his death he had completed probably more combat missions in heavy bombers than any other pilot of his rank in the Navy and therefore was pre-eminently qualified, and secondly, as he told a friend early in August, he considered the odds at least fifty-fifty, and Joe never asked for any better odds than that.

It was not until several years after the war that we were able to know the circumstances of that 'mission'. Several accounts have been written. Probably the most accurate was that in 1948, the 'Tenth Anniversary Report, Harvard College Class of 1938', by a friend of Joe Jr's who, in the course of a long eulogy, said:

> Joe, regarded as an experienced Patrol Plane Commander, and a fellow-officer, an expert in radio control projects, were to take a 'drone' Liberator bomber loaded with 21,170 pounds of high explosives into the air and to stay with it until two 'mother' planes

had achieved complete radio control over the 'drone'. They were
then to bail out over England; the 'drone', under the control of the
'mother' planes, was to proceed on the mission which was to cul-
minate in a crash-dive on the target, a V-2 rocket launching-site in
Normandy. The aeroplane . . . was in flight with routine checking of
the radio controls proceeding satisfactorily, when at 6.20 p.m. on
August 12, 1944, two explosions blasted the 'drone' resulting in the
death of its two pilots. No final conclusion as to the cause of the
explosions has ever been reached.

Joe was posthumously awarded the Navy Cross . . . and also the
Air Medal . . . In 1946 a destroyer, the USS *Joseph P. Kennedy, Jr,*
destroyer No. 850, was launched at the Fore River Ship Yards as
the Navy's final tribute to a gallant officer and his heroic devotion
to duty . . .

He left a lasting mark on the hearts of an extraordinarily large
number of people, and his success and popularity indicated the
promise of great achievements. That his progress should have been
cut short is tragic, but in the words of Professor Laski he has entered
'that supreme immortality which belongs to all who proudly give
their lives in the service of freedom'.

Surviving Joe are his parents, Mr and Mrs Joseph P. Kennedy, Sr,
of Palm Beach, Florida, and Hyannis Port, Massachusetts, and eight
brothers and sisters . . .

I remember that it was Sunday afternoon and we all had lunched outside, picnic style, on our big porch at Hyannis Port. It was about two
in the afternoon, and Joe Sr had gone upstairs for a nap. The younger
children were in the living-room chatting quietly so as not to disturb
their father; I sat reading the Saturday paper. There was a knock at
the front door. When I opened the door two priests introduced themselves and said they would like to speak with Mr Kennedy.

This was not unusual: priests and nuns fairly often came to call,
wanting to talk with Joe about some charity or other matter of the
church in which he might help. So I invited them to come into the
living-room and join us comfortably until Joe finished his nap. One of
the priests said no, that the reason for calling was urgent. That there
was a message both Joe and I must hear. Our son was missing in action
and presumed lost.

I ran upstairs and awakened Joe. I stood for a few moments with
my mind half-paralysed. I tried to speak but stumbled over the words.
Then I managed to blurt out that priests were here with that message.
He leaped from the bed and hurried downstairs, I following him. We

sat with the priests in a smaller room off the living-room, and from what they told us we realized there could be no hope and that our son was dead.

Joe went out on the porch and told the children. They were stunned. He said they must be brave: that's what their brother would want from them. He urged them to go ahead with their plans to race that day, and most of them obediently did so. But Jack could not do it. Instead, for a long time he walked on the beach in front of our house.

There were no tears from Joe and me, not then. We sat a while, holding each other close, and wept inwardly, silently.

Then Joe said: 'We've got to carry on. We must take care of the living. There is a lot of work to be done.'

Kick asked for leave when she heard the news and hurried back home to be with us. Meanwhile the Allied invasion of France had begun in June and Billy and his regiment, in the tradition of the Guards, were among the earliest units ashore, and had fought through France and into Belgium.

In mid-September, while Kick was still with us, the news came that Billy had been killed in Belgium. He died on September 12, a month to the day after Joe Jr died. We could scarcely believe it. It seemed too cruel that another tragedy had so soon befallen us. Kick then heard directly from the Cavendishes. It was true.

She left us then to be with them in their sorrow, and to continue with her duties in the Red Cross. We did not see her again until the war in Europe was over.

VE-Day was May 8, 1945, only months after the death of these two fine young men, each of them so beloved, each of whom had so much to give to the world.

Our friend Arthur Krock's *Memoirs* contain a paragraph that I quote without comment:

The death of Joe Jr was the first break in this circle of nine children, nearly all extraordinary in some way: handsome, intelligent, with a father and mother to whom they were devoted and who were devoted to them. It was one of the most severe shocks to the father that I've ever seen registered on a human being . . .

He is, I'm sure, religious: at least we used to go to Sunday Mass together whenever and wherever I was visiting him. But his wife attended Mass . . . nearly every morning. At any rate, she bore up better than he did in the sense that he was truly stricken, whereas

J.F.K.

17 *Left* Jack at his Harvard graduation. Note the brown and white saddle shoes

Below Jack demonstrating how he towed a shipmate to safety

Captain Frederic L. Conklin awards Navy and Marine Corps medal to Lieutenant John F. Kennedy, 1944

he Making of a President

ft My father, John Francis
tzgerald, aged 83, and my
n, John Fitzgerald Kennedy,
ter Jack's election as a
ongressman. The desk
own is the original one
ed by my father in
ongress
ght Jack and Jackie
low Eunice, Pat, Jack and I
fore a 'Kennedy Tea'

The night of the
nomination in
Los Angeles

With love
Rose Kennedy

The Making of a President

20 *Above* Jack's nomination, Los Angeles, 1960

Below The morning after Election Day in Hyannis Port. Seated,
l. to r.: Eunice, me, Joe, Jackie, Ted. Standing: Ethel, Stephen Smith,
Jean, Jack, Bobby, Pat, Sargent Shriver, Joan, Peter Lawford

the philosophy of her religion clearly helped her. Joe Kennedy was so deeply distressed and hurt by the death of his boy, his eldest son, that when a number of us got together and wrote chapters in a little book called *As We Remember Joe*, each contributing some personal reminiscence, Kennedy looked at it, opened the cover, closed the cover, and, I am told, has never been able to read a line in that book.

Joe took his own advice that we should carry on, take care of the living, do a lot of work.

One of the best ways to assuage grief, as we first learned fully at this time – and which would help us survive future tragedies – is to find a way to turn some part of the loss to a positive, affirmative use for the benefit of other people. I do believe that God blesses us for that and the burden is lightened.

In Teddy's volume of essays about his father, *The Fruitful Bough*, Eunice wrote:

. . . All my father's qualities were particularly alive to me when I watched him in the work of the Kennedy Foundation. Again, it was his great devotion to his children that brought him into this work. After my brother Joe's death in 1944, my father – still in grief – decided he wanted to build a memorial to his son. He had never believed much in building buildings. He wanted to invest in men. He asked us all at the table one day what could be done to best perpetuate Joe's memory.

We gave him ideas: a gymnasium at Joe's school, an orphanage [Joe had spent much time in college working with underprivileged children]. We all thought that since Joe, as our older brother, had taught us so many activities, his memorial should try to do something for young children.

Dad then asked Sargent [Sargent Shriver was then a close and highly trusted staff assistant to Joe; he was just a few months younger than Joe Jr, and already we felt he was a member of our family – as in fact he became when he and Eunice were married later on.] . . . to get judgments from around the country on what programmes for children were most neglected by private foundations and the federal government. Sarge reported that foundation and federal efforts in the field of mental retardation were practically non-existent.

My father decided immediately to enter this field. He was particularly enthusiastic because my sister Rosemary was retarded, and he felt a great sympathy for parents who had suffered as much as he and my mother had over my sister . . .

It was not surprising then that Dad wanted all his children to work together on the Foundation for retarded children. He believed that together we were almost unconquerable. Every major city in America needed a school for the retarded. Since each of his children [this of course came later] lived in major cities – Pat in Los Angeles, Jean in New York, me in Chicago, the boys in Massachusetts – Dad established schools over a fifteen-year period in each of these cities, and encouraged each of us to take part in the school's development.

Each of us served on the boards. Pat initiated the largest benefit for retarded children ever held in Los Angeles. My sister Jean and sister-in-law Ethel ran benefits in New York and in Washington to raise money for these homes. My mother supported all these benefits by attending them and giving wonderful talks.

I described to Dad that mental retardation had no national status, that almost no legislation had been passed on the subject, that the needs were enormous. He listened and then said, 'Go to Jack (who was then President of the United States). This movement needs the federal government behind it. The President can give it the prestige and momentum we can't give it if we work for 100 years and had 100 times as much money to put into the field.' He knew, too, from his own experience, that what we were doing was very, very small.

Jack recognized the problem and the possibilities and the need immediately. 'That seems like a good thing for the country,' he said.

We had the meeting, and the President's Panel on Mental Retardation – the first of its kind in history – was launched. The result was the first federal legislation ever specifically directed at mental retardation.

It has been said that time heals all wounds. I don't agree. The wounds remain. Time – and the mind, protecting its sanity – covers them with some scar tissue and the pain lessens but it is never gone.

How can one endure in the face of tragedy? people have asked me. And surely I have often had reason to ask myself.

Joe was right in his words: '. . . carry on . . . take care of the living . . . there is a lot of work to be done.' And right, most right, in his instinctive and immediate recognition that even in the fates that overtook Joe Jr and Rosemary there could be a way, in the largest sense for humanity and to some degree for us personally, in which those tragedies could count for good and peace of mind, and peace of spirit.

15

When Jack was discharged from the Navy in the spring of 1945, he worked for the Hearst papers as a special correspondent, covering the British election, the Potsdam Conference and the founding of the United Nations at San Francisco. He liked the work and he did well. In fact, Arthur Krock – who was certainly one of the best-informed journalists in the world – said in his *Memoirs* that Jack had been '. . . the only source of my expectation that Churchill would be turned out of office. This he strongly indicated in his dispatches, and more definitely in a private letter.'

Many people think that his decision to enter politics was made for him by his father; that Joe practically forced him into it. That would have been completely out of character on both sides. Anyone reading Joe's letters to Jack and the others can see that giving orders to his children would have been contrary to the relationship he had with them. And Jack, quite as obviously, would not have submitted to such a parental command even if it had been given. (I can imagine his smiling agreeably and saying 'Yes, Dad,' as he used to smile agreeably and say 'Yes, Mother' when I told him to put on a sweater – and then go off without it.)

It is true that the role he chose probably would have been different, and would have come later, had it not been for Joe Jr's death. Joe Jr would have made a career in elective public office. That was his ambition and, I think, his destiny. Everyone thought so. And he had practically every asset for that role. As Jack wrote, 'His success was so assured and inevitable that his death seems to have cut into the natural order of things.'

Kick, in her essay about Joe Jr, finished with this paragraph:

Without Joe there will be always a gap in the Kennedy family circle, but we are far, far luckier than most because there are so many of us. And I know Joe would always feel that Jack could easily take over the responsibility of being the oldest. I know the one thing Joe would never want is that we should feel sad and gloomy about life without him. Instead he'd laugh with that wonderful twinkle shining out of his Irish eyes and say, 'Gee, can't you all learn to get along without me?'

The period when Jack was confronting the fact that his older brother was gone – and it took a while for all of us to emerge from a feeling of unreality, a bad dream – was a 'hinge time' in events in Jack's life, in the life of our family and eventually in the political life of the country.

James Michael Curley, who had succeeded my father both as Congressman and as Mayor of Boston, and who was subsequently in and out of those two offices, and the Governorship, during three decades, had run for Mayor again in 1945 and had been elected. This left his Congressional seat vacant; and, since Mr Curley seemed to have no strong preferences about a successor, the way was cleared for a wide-open race and a chance for the best man to win the Democratic nomination, tantamount to election.

Further, this Congressional District, although its boundaries had been redrawn, was essentially the same region my father had represented when *he* went to Congress. It included the North End of Boston as well as the East End.

The combination of time, place and circumstance made the idea of Jack's running for Congress attractive and reasonable, inexperienced in electoral politics though he was. I can say for certain they appealed enormously to my father, who at that time was a hale and healthy eighty-three. The idea that his grandson might be going to Washington to fill the same position that he had held, filled my father with delight. Thank Heaven he lived to see it happen.

But if he were directly associated with this campaign Jack would have been seen by many people as an heir to the old ways, which were of course inappropriate for his time. Moreover, my father, in his love and pride for Jack and thinking of him as torchbearer of the Fitzgerald name and fame and achievements, would have thought of Jack as an incarnation of himself and have tried to mould him to his own pattern. And that, frankly, would have been a disaster. They loved each other dearly but seldom were two people less alike.

Although Father wasn't asked to take the stump for his grandson in the campaign – as he would have dearly loved to do – that didn't prevent him from telling his innumerable friends about this marvellous young man. It didn't inhibit his appearances at campaign headquarters or stem his flow of stories about bygone campaigns. Nor did it deprive

Jack of his advice. By then my parents had moved from the big house in Dorchester to an apartment suite at the Bellevue Hotel in Boston, a favourite place for political gatherings of all sorts and thus a place where my father felt very much at home. It was also where Jack had his headquarters, on the same corridor. Joe and I had an apartment not far away. Other family members were also in town. So there were gatherings in Boston and also from time to time during that busy campaign summer at Hyannis Port. 'Grampa' had plenty of opportunities to spin his tales of the past and to tell Jack what to do and how to do it. Some of the other descendants and relatives had begun to find my father's stories slightly tedious – but not Jack. He always listened with interest and respect, and with affection for 'Grampa' shining in his eyes.

As John Henry Cutler relates in his biography of my father:

> On primary day he [Jack] went to the polls with his Fitzgerald grandparents, then went to see a movie, *A Night in Casablanca*. When the votes were counted, Honey Fitz hopped on to a table and danced a jig as he led the singing of 'Sweet Adeline' . . . After the victory celebration, Billy Sullivan, a former assistant attorney general, patted Honey Fitz on the back.
>
> 'Congratulations, John F.,' he said. 'Some day – who knows? – young Jack here may be Governor of the Commonwealth.'
>
> 'Governor?' Honey Fitz smiled. 'Some day that young man will be President of the United States.'

Jack was in a complex situation, containing many elements that he had somehow to put together in an effective political way. While he would listen to advice receptively and cheerfully enough, he made his own decisions which usually incorporated the best of many different suggestions. His mind was open and inquisitive and he weighed the elements of a problem in order to see it in the round.

At twenty-nine, Jack knew a lot about political science, government, diplomacy, national and international affairs. He had learned a good deal through his father's involvement in them, and as an author and journalist in these fields. He also knew something of 'practical politics' from having read, observed and listened to his 'Grampa' Fitzgerald. Jack always considered 'Grampa' fabulous. He never tired of listening to him; and he soaked it all in.

So he was by no means a naïve youth. (He always, to the end, looked younger than his years, but during this time especially so because of his war injuries and – as I had forgotten to mention – a case of malaria which cost him much loss of weight; at this point he looked like a nineteen-year-old who needed a lot of feeding-up.) He understood that in this congressional district the names Fitzgerald and Kennedy were enough to get him off to a good start. In other parts of the district, notably Charlestown, where Irish ethnocentricity prevailed, the two names were held in some reverence.

One of Jack's assets was the fact that people laughed at the charge he was a 'carpet-bagger'. Some of his rivals brought it up, on the grounds that he hadn't lived in the district since he was eleven and never had voted there and wasn't directly acquainted with the people and their problems and desires. This was absolutely true. Yet there is no Massachusetts law stating that a candidate has to live in the district he represents. But there is a law requiring that he be a registered member of his party twenty days before declaring his candidacy in that party's primary. Jack didn't know about this, and no one else thought of it until a few days before the deadline. Jack hustled down to City Hall and quietly joined the Democratic Party.

While Jack knew about politics, he knew very little about the actual mechanics of organizing and operating a campaign.

For that matter, neither did my husband. Joe was wise in the fields of national and international political affairs, but his interest dwindled as the political unit grew smaller. Events at the level of district, city, town and ward left him progressively more bored. Particularly in Boston. It was a milieu he had left behind him long ago without the faintest regret. Yet he realized how important the organizational matters, personalities, strategies, itineraries, handshaking and speech making were going to be for Jack in this campaign. Therefore, as his own close adviser, and as Jack's teacher and coach, he sought out his own favourite hard-bitten, long-experienced political realist, Cousin Joe Kane.

Cousin Joe was quite a rough diamond, with abrasive style of thought and speech. My husband wasn't at all sure how he and Jack would get along, but they hit it off quite well. Jack was surprised, entertained and informed. Having got into the race he was determined, of course, to win it, and Cousin Joe could tell him about the winds and tides, the ropes and sails, the shoals and channels in this particular form of navigation. He also had some good overall ideas such as a slogan for the campaign: 'The New Generation Offers a Leader.' There were some echoes of that in Jack's Inaugural Address.

Obviously, to my father and to Cousin Joe Kane and to other relatives and close family friends, Jack looked like a promising neophyte and got the benefit of any doubts. It is worth asking how he looked to others who had no personal connection with us.

Some interesting answers have been supplied – from direct experience – by Dave Powers, who met Jack at the very beginning of this campaign, had no intention at all of joining it but did so, and stayed with Jack afterwards as a close associate to the end of the road in 1963:

I was just out of the Air Force myself – a sergeant, mostly in China – and starting to look around and catch up on what was happening. Meantime I was on the 52-20 – that was $20 a week for unemployed veterans up to 52 weeks – and living with my widowed sister and her eight children on the top floor of a three-decker tenement house in Charlestown.

That day I'd been talking with John Cotter. He lived two streets away from me. A great, great guy. I'm having a beer with him and he's telling me about the fight. Curley is Mayor, that leaves the seat in Congress open and there's going to be a battle royal for it. Mike Neville of Cambridge is running, and he's the number one 'tough guy' because he used to be mayor of Cambridge, is very strong there, and Cambridge has thirty per cent of the votes in the district. Cotter tells me he's going to run, too.

Now mind you, Cotter has two things that give him great strength. He was administrative assistant in Washington to Curley and before that to Congressman Joseph P. Higgins, which meant that all the requests and important matters back home in the district were channelled through him. He had helped do a lot of favours. And also, when Higgins left to take a judgeship, he had run for the spot himself and almost got it. So everybody in the district knew him, and he knew the district like the back of his hand. Cotter tells me he's running and he asks, 'Will you be with me?' And I agreed.

At that point I don't know that Jack Kennedy is even thinking of being in there. Then I got this call from Bill Sutton. I told him I was already with Cotter. And a few nights later – it was January 21, 1946 – somebody knocked at the front door.

In Charlestown in winter we shut off the front of the house and heat the kitchen. We don't have central heat, it's a stove here or there. People who know you come up the back way. Nobody comes up the front stairs – the front of the house is shut off. So, when somebody knocked at the *front door* – and I was baby-sitting for my sister that night – I went out there. And I saw this tall, thin, handsome guy. He introduces himself and says he's Jack Kennedy and could he talk with me a few minutes? I invited him in. We started talking and he

said he was running for Congress. I said, 'Gee, John Cotter's running for that seat. I'm going to be with him. We grew up together
and we stick together.'

So now he spends the next half-hour picking my brains. He was
sort of shy. But – I thought of the description of it later – he was
'aggressively shy'. He said, well, what would you do if you were
like me a candidate running here for Congress?

Here's a millionaire's son from Harvard trying to come into an
area that is longshoremen, waitresses, truck-drivers and so forth. I
said, 'To start with, I'd get somebody on the waterfront for sure,
somebody tied up with the labour unions and all that.' And he's
writing this stuff down, and I'm thinking to myself, 'It won't do
him any good. A millionaire's son from Harvard, for Christ sake,
they're going to laugh at him down there.'

And he asked more questions. As he did the rest of his life. He
wanted to know everything about everybody and everything. If you
sold papers he wanted to know how many you sold and how much
you charged. He was interested in bootblacks, how many shoes they
shined. He was incredible, this guy.

As he was going out the door he said, 'Dave, will you do me a
favour? I'm speaking to a group of Gold Star Mothers at the
American Legion Hall next Tuesday. I don't know anyone in
Charlestown. Will you come over with me?'

Well, you'd do that: you'd do that for *anybody*. But can you imagine
that – imagine feeling sorry for a millionaire's son? And I said all
right, all right, I will.

That Tuesday I met him at the Bellevue and he said, 'Shall we
grab a cab?' I didn't know him that well – then – but thank God I
said let's take the elevated. Because if we'd taken the cab I would
have paid for it.

I said earlier Jack had an absent-minded way about money. Never
about the taxpayers' money but about carrying some of his own; so
he was often in difficulties about luncheon checks, taxi-fares and the
like. In fact, I remember a time some years after this. I was in New
York and going in a taxi to the Plaza Hotel, and in the course of
conversation the driver learned I was Jack's mother. 'I'm glad you're
in the cab,' he said, 'your son rode with me a month ago and it turned
out he didn't have any money with him. He said he'd make it good the
next time he saw me. I haven't seen him since. He owes me $2.45.'
Of course, I promptly paid Jack's overdue taxi-fare.

Dave Powers continues:

We're on the El riding over and here he is looking around. We're coming from North Station to Charlestown and out the windows we're seeing Old North Church and East Boston and Old Ironsides and stuff like that – it's a long ride – and he's looking down at the longshoremen loading ships, and all that, and I said to him, 'This is almost a panoramic view of your district.' And solemn as hell he went, 'You know, this is the kind of district I would like to represent.'

So we go over there and he's talking to these Charlestown Gold Star mothers – we had an awful lot of boys die in the war, there was a National Guard unit and they were at Guadalcanal and places out there – and there were several hundred in the hall. And it seems to me he's making the world's worst speech. He's talking about the need for peace and the sacrifices of war, but he's certainly no orator. And I am getting nervous as hell. I'm the only other man there, they're all women. At the end he looked out at all those wonderful ladies, and in a kind of awkward but direct way he said, sort of blurting it out from deep inside, 'I think I know how you feel because my mother is a Gold Star mother too.'

I could hear them – where I was sitting on the fringe – saying, 'He reminds me of my own' – the John, Joe, Peter they had lost. When he finished his little ten-minute talk he was surrounded by these wonderful Charlestown ladies. In all my years in politics I've never seen such a reaction.

So now we come out of there. He's solemn as hell. I said, Why don't we walk back over? It's still afternoon. We're walking, and he's looking – in fact, we stopped in at Faneuil Hall and Paul Revere's house in the North End.

Along the way he said, 'How do you think I did?' And I said, 'You were great!'

And he went on, 'Then you'll be with me?' And he put out his hand, and in the excitement of the ordeal I shook his hand and said, 'I will.'

I walked back over the bridge thinking, 'What will I ever tell Cotter?' Luckily, the fight developed between Kennedy and Mike Neville, not Kennedy and Cotter. In the meantime I was getting a good deal of static from a lot of friends in Charlestown. Jack knew about it, and he'd cheer me up with one of his Classical jokes: 'Just think, Dave,' he'd say, 'some day you can say you were with me from the beginning.

We few, we happy few, we band of brothers;
For he today that sheds his blood with me
Shall be my brother; be he ne'er so vile
This day shall gentle his condition;
And gentlemen in England now a-bed
Shall think themselves accurs'd they were not here,
And hold their manhoods cheap whiles any speaks
That fought with us upon Saint Crispin's day.'

(*Henry V*, Act IV, Scene III, lines 60–7)

With Joe Kane, Bill Sutton and other adepts such as Dave Powers involved, Jack's campaign had plenty of 'professionalism'. But also and at the same time it had a great supply of 'amateur enthusiasm'. It was a marvellous combination, a very effective one that continued throughout Jack's political career. Later, when Bobby and Teddy began running for office, it was a characteristic of their campaigns too.

Friends began turning up from all over the area, and for that matter from all over the map. One of the first, naturally, would be Lem Billings. Lem has recalled:

> When I heard from Jack what he was doing I came over to Boston, mostly from curiosity but also thinking I might give him a little friendly encouragement in this amazing development. I never thought he'd go into politics. Neither had he. I figured he must be about as surprised as I was.
>
> He was living at the Bellevue Hotel, in two rooms there, bedroom and living-room, and it was just beyond belief, because anybody could walk in. The rooms were filled with these old pals who had been connected with his grandfather, and they were always there, smoking cigars. He never turned anybody away; he wanted every vote he could get and every bit of help he could get. Slowly, young people began to be attracted. He needed some help over in Cambridge, where he had a headquarters, so I thought I'd run it for a week or two until he got somebody, and I ended up staying with him for the entire campaign.

Torbert Macdonald, his room-mate at Harvard, was back there (after war service in another PT boat squadron) working on his law degree. He did a lot of work for Jack in the Cambridge office and also in the one at nearby Somerville, where the head of the local head-quarters was Timothy 'Ted' Reardon, a Harvard classmate and room-mate of Joe Jr's and also a very good friend of Jack's. Paul 'Red' Fay, a PT boat pal, even came out from his home on the West Coast and pitched in to help. There were many others – friends from the Navy, friends from school days, and friends of no particular label; in any case, scores of them, drifting in and out for longer or shorter periods and all pleased to do what they could for Jack. They were more or less his age and their presence gave the campaign a look that matched the slogan, 'The New Generation Offers a Leader.'

And then, too, of course we of his family wanted to be helpful. By that campaign year of 1946 even Teddy, at age fourteen, was old enough to make himself useful doing office chores, running errands, bringing in coffee and sandwiches. Eunice, who was twenty-five, handled the telephone calls and was general office manager at the Bellevue headquarters. Bobby, who would be twenty-one that November, had withdrawn from officers' training after Joe Jr's death and finished his military service as a seaman on the destroyer *Joseph P. Kennedy Jr*. After his discharge that summer he came into the campaign full-time and took over the East Cambridge section. Pat, who was twenty-two, and Jean, who was eighteen, did the innumerable office chores that are involved in a well-organized campaign, made suggestions, kept tabs, pepped up rallies and pushed a few thousand doorbells to tell the bemused householders they were Jack Kennedy's sisters and he would be a wonderful Congressman, and to leave literature describing the reasons why.

Needless to say, Joe was intensely interested in the campaign and was active in it day by day, though he carefully stayed behind the scenes. Because of his pre-Pearl Harbor position as a non-interventionist, which opponents twisted to label him an 'isolationist' (which he was not), he had become a controversial public figure and he didn't want any of this to rub off on Jack's candidacy. Moreover, as Dave Powers indicated, there were always those who could be easily inflamed against Jack as a 'millionaire's son' and a 'spoiled rich kid'. Therefore, and wisely, Joe was as invisible as he could be, while knowing exactly what was going on, and why, and where and how, and with hardheaded analytical judgments and prescriptions to offer when needed. He was deeply involved, working hard behind the scenes.[1]

One of his favourite practical aphorisms which he had picked up from his friend Will Hays was 'Things don't just happen, they are made to happen.'

As for my own role in that campaign, I really had none in the sense of any plan that I thought of or was thought of for me. While Dave

[1] In Jack's Senatorial campaign, for example, he made the decision to use television rather than billboards to promote Jack's candidacy.

Powers has some stories to tell, I'm not sure I swallow all of them whole, because Dave is a raconteur and like all practitioners in the art he has a tendency to add flourishes for effect. On the other hand, he is famous for having a remarkable memory:

She was important to Jack politically in 1946 because she made herself available for appearances any place, and because with the double-barrelled name Fitzgerald and Kennedy she was better known than any in that Eleventh Congressional district. She had gone around with her father so much when he was in office or campaigning, and we were forever meeting people in Charlestown and East Boston and the North End and South and West who were Honey Fitz fans and they remembered her as the girl who had accompanied him; they were tied to Rose Fitzgerald Kennedy, they related to her.

You have to grow up in politics to really know it. She wasn't 'in' politics – she wasn't running or seeking – but she was looking and listening. I remember one rally that she spoke to and she was appalled that there wasn't somebody there taking the names of everyone who showed up – because that's what her father used to do. She was forever writing notes to us about things like that. In 1946 she had a greater understanding of precinct politics than anyone in our organization. And when you say 'precinct politics', you only understand it by doing it or maybe absorbing it, in her case, by osmosis. She not only loved meeting people, but she cared about the people she met. This is the key.

She didn't do a lot of speaking. We used her just at special times where it could count most, like with the Veterans of Foreign Wars. Remember, this is 1946, a great year for veterans. Each time, she was the Star of the Show. She must have been about 56 then, but she looked more like 35. I recall when she was speaking to a VFW audience at Brighton – that's ward 22, part of the district – and of course they all know she's a Gold Star Mother and that Jack almost got killed in the war. But she doesn't mention anything about how Joe Jr died or how Jack's PT got cut in two. She talked about raising the family, with the index cards and all, and about living in England, and told some interesting little stories about the Embassy. And that's one way I knew she was a real 'pro'. People want to hear about something different, and that's what she gave them, and when she finished she got a standing ovation. Then she introduced her son, the candidate for the nomination in the eleventh Congressional district.

And Jack is slightly overwhelmed. Because he couldn't talk as well as his mother, then. I came up front with him as she was finish-ing and he stood there, before he went on stage, listening to her – and he is sort of overwhelmed that his mother could talk that well to an audience. As she was coming off the stage and he was going on, he stopped her and said, 'Mother, they really love you.'

He didn't say anything like 'Thank you, Mother.' The Kennedys are funny about saying things like that to each other, because there's so much loyalty there they assume – they know it – each one is going to *try* to help the others. They don't want thanks for trying, they want to be told if they've done it well. It would have been corny as hell for him to say, 'Thank you for making that speech.' He was saying more like, 'Mother, you did a great job. I admire you for such a great job.' A Kennedy would rather get applause from another Kennedy than from ten thousand other people.

Actually it was just a little, rather rambling talk I had put together – and for that matter I wasn't much of a speaker. I began with small groups and audiences I knew were going to be friendly, and later spoke to larger, more diverse and more sophisticated audiences. Gradually, I gained the confidence which comes with practice and experience. So by that time, in that friendly setting, I was pretty much at ease and I spoke pretty well. Jack, as we know, developed into one of the finest public speakers of his generation. But at that time he truly embodied the old bromide, 'Unaccustomed as I am to public speaking . . .' He needed experience and also advice, which needless to say came from many directions, including some from me.

He spoke too fast, as I had also at first. When I was a child in school, if the teacher wanted a story read quickly in the class – if the bell was about to ring – I was the one always chosen because I could do it so fast. I suppose I passed this on to my children. But staccato delivery is a handicap in a campaign. So I would often remind Jack of Churchill and Roosevelt – both of whom he had heard speak in person – and of their measured and effective pace.

Years later, when he was campaigning for the Presidency, I would sometimes hear people say he spoke a bit too fast. And I would see him on television with a hand thrust into a jacket pocket. But by then those characteristics, along with the little repertory of gestures he developed – such as that short punch into the air with his forefinger to emphasize a point – had all blended into a personal style that was pleasing and effective. He was receptive to advice, but he used it in his own way. *If* he decided to use it.

During this campaign I was reminded anew of certain boyhood

characteristics. His loose sense of time: he was the one who often wasn't there when the rest of us were ready to drive home from the beach. His competitiveness: humorous and in some ways modest though he was, once he was in any race he was in heart and soul to win it. His quirk about hats: he wouldn't wear one unless I reminded him, then would pick up any hat in sight and stick it on without a care whether it fitted or how it looked. Later, he almost never wore a hat except when official rules – or perhaps a driving rain – made it necessary. He was out of my control by then.

But when he began running for Congress – hatless in January of a New England winter – it became Joe Kane's turn to worry. He explained that *all* politicians in the Boston region wore hats; that without a hat Jack looked like a college boy and nobody would take him seriously as a Congressional candidate; that with a hat he could come closer to fitting the expected 'image' and could gain many votes. Jack listened pleasantly and remained bareheaded. Losing all the battles, Joe Kane was determined still to win the war. He kept on mentioning the hat problem to Jack and enlisted allies who also mentioned it.

Competitiveness, tardiness, hatlessness – all are intertwined in this next skein of memories Dave Powers has contributed:

Jack was the hardest-working candidate I ever saw. Nothing was ever too much if he figured it could help the cause. If he heard some other candidate had been to some benefit or church affair or something like that earlier and made an impression, he'd say to me, 'Dave,' he'd say – and this, let's say, is in the evening after already going that day for twelve, fourteen hours' campaigning – 'Dave, how about it, shall we go over and show them the real candidate?' And tired as you yourself might be feeling by then, you'd say sure, let's go, even if it's half an hour away through traffic, because he was trying so hard, giving it everything he had, and with a guy like that – inside you're groaning for bed and sleep – you feel that you've got to do your best for him. And every place he goes, he makes votes. People warm up to him. Some days I'd go wake him up at the Bellevue around six-thirty in the morning, which would give time for us to get over to the shipyard or a factory to hit the incoming shift and for him to shake a few hundred or a thousand hands. We'd have some breakfast and then start ringing doorbells in the three-decker neighbourhoods, house to house, floor to floor, down the block. The mothers took one look, heard him say his name and mission and a few more words – and they loved him.

We'd stop at some joint for lunch: this was always the same menu for him, a hamburger and a frappé, a frappé being a milkshake with ice-cream in it. In the afternoon, more calls, maybe stopping in poolhalls, grocery stores, taverns, anyplace the voters were; or maybe a special meeting someplace, a club, whatever.

Back to the Bellevue for him to take a hot bath and rest his back and change clothes. And then go right through the evening. Lodge halls, VFW, Knights of Columbus, Knights of Pythias, name it, but the most usual thing was a string of what we called 'house parties'.

I would arrange – somebody would arrange – for various women or young ladies in nearby neighbourhoods to invite some friends over to their homes for refreshments and to meet John F. Kennedy. Who shook hands all round, had a Coke and mingled around in a relaxed sociable way, then on cue made a few remarks about why he wanted to be elected to Congress and hoped for their votes; and thanked them and good evening – and on to the next place, maybe five or six in one evening.

Now, with a guy like that – with that desire, and making votes everywhere he stops in – you tend to make a very full schedule. But here's something else. Jack has a funny sense of time and distance. He'd get interested in these people and he'd forget about time, and it was hard to disengage him and drag him away. And anyway he has the feeling that every place else is only fifteen minutes away. Christ! I've been with him in his apartment in the middle of Boston and he's soaking in his tub at a quarter of eight, and we're due in Worcester at eight, and he'd say, 'Dave, how far is it to Worcester?' And I'd say, 'Well, if we're driving, we're late already.' It would go like that. We'd run late.

Now, I remember there was one of these big veterans' rallies someplace in the district and his mother was there, at our request, to say a few words and to introduce him as the candidate. We were running late. We got there late.

Afterwards, Jack and his mother were chatting, with several of us who were in the campaign also in the conversation. Well, Joe Kane had that day evidently been pursuing his programme to get Jack to wear a hat, because it's on Jack's mind. And he says, 'Mother, they're all telling me I should wear a hat, because it will make me look older.'

And she looked him right in the eye and said, 'I think it's more important to be on time.'

That's the same way she'd get her message across at a dinner or luncheon with family and friends. There would be a flow of discussion about something and she might not be saying much, but then she'd come in with just a word or two or a sentence that made them all blink and think.

I saw this have an instantaneous effect that evening. Jack did a quick mental doubletake and then he turned around to the fellows who were handling his schedule and said, 'How the hell do you happen to be scheduling me to be in Somerville at 8.00 and Charlestown at 8.30 and Brighton at 9.00? It's impossible.' So, through her remark, it brought them awake too, and the scheduling got looser, at least for a while. He kept on the fourteen-hour day. He never asked for anything but time, more time than it turned out he ever had. You know, he was so casual and easy and so interested and yet he was so hard-working. All he needed was if there had been a thirty-six-hour day.

I'm sure there's no such thing as a 'women's vote'. Women make up their minds individually and on the basis of numerous factors just as men do. Obviously, however, there are appeals that weigh more heavily with one sex than the other. For instance, men were much more likely to be interested in and impressed by Jack's war record. He didn't want to exploit it; in fact it embarrassed him that it should be any factor in the campaign. Once when somebody brought it up and asked him how he happened to be 'a war hero', he replied, 'It was involuntary. They sank my boat.' Nevertheless the story was well known and it was a plus for him among men voters.

Eunice and I and some of the other women in the campaign were wondering what could be done that might have a similar, special appeal for women. He had a natural appeal that was built-in, as it were. It has been said that the older women wanted to mother him and the younger ones wanted to marry him, a thought I find more than reasonable. However, for his youthful and manly charm to be effective, they had to meet him. Someone – I'm pretty sure it was Eunice, although she's not sure – suggested I give a reception and tea in his honour, and invite a lot of women and introduce them to the candidate.

It occurred to us that we already had a good model in the annual Fourth of July reception we held at the Embassy in London. This was an open house. Everyone was welcome. There were refreshments, people strolled about and mingled after meeting the ambassador and perhaps members of his family.

Where should we try out our idea first? Well, as Dave Powers has mentioned, Cambridge was the biggest ward and its favourite son, Mike Neville, was Jack's strongest rival. We rented one of the big public rooms at the Hotel Commander, and engraved invitations were sent to every registered voter in Cambridge.

That evening our receiving line consisted of me, as hostess, Eunice as my co-hostess, and Jack between us. Jack was feeling dubious about the whole thing. Some of the seasoned politicos in the campaign had been more than dubious – openly and discouragingly sceptical. Jack, Eunice and I waited expectantly to see what would happen.

What happened was that 1500 people came to the reception. At times the line stretched all the way through the hotel lobby, through the entranceway and outside and far down the block. For all of them there were handshakes, smiles and some words from each of us. There were a few men there, but most were women, all of whom seemed to have done their hair for the event. Jack was marvellous with them.

After the primary was over, Mike Neville's campaign manager was ruminating the results and was quoted as saying, 'That reception was the clincher.' I don't know about that. I hope it helped. Neville was supposed to take Cambridge by a landslide vote that would negate for Jack's predictable strength in the North End and East End and other friendly territory. But it turned out to be a very close race there with Neville just managing to win Cambridge.

As for the outcome of the district primary – in which, as I hadn't mentioned, besides Jack Kennedy and Mike Neville and John Cotter, there were seven others, a grand mêlée of ten candidates – Jack won decisively with 42 per cent of the vote, about twice as many as Neville and well beyond three times more than Cotter.

Jack won the general election that fall, defeating the Republican candidate by better than three to one, entering Congress at the age of twenty-nine, a year older than my father had been when first elected to the same Eleventh District seat.

It was a convincing victory, and subsequently Jack's performance as a Congressman was difficult for anyone to fault. When he ran for re-election two years later, 1948, no one in either party bothered to make him run in the primary and he continued in office by acclamation, so to speak. In 1950 he had five opponents in the Democratic primary, but he was renominated with five times the combined total of their votes, and then beat the Republican nominee by five times.

Presumably he could have gone on in the same way, in this same 'safe seat', for the next thirty or forty years, rising by seniority through committee chairmanships and cloakroom camaraderie to become an extremely influential old man, perhaps Speaker of the House. The prospect of spending his life that way bored Jack intensely.

By the time his third term in the House would be over, Senator Henry Cabot Lodge, Jr, would be coming up for re-election again. It was difficult to imagine that Jack could win against him. He was tall, handsome, charming and intelligent. He was a hard worker in government and an excellent campaigner. Although his ancestry and background were Back Bay, he was one of the foremost liberals of the Republican Party in the state and nation. 'An enlightened Republican.'

Lodge's ethnic appeal included the French-Canadians, many of whom had settled in the state, for he was fluent in French, and thus could speak to that segment of voters in their own language. He had a beautiful sister-in-law who could accompany him to important meetings in Italian neighbourhoods and introduce him, gracefully, in that language; for she had been born in Italy, a daughter of the noble family of Braggiotti. He had an excellent war record; a name known and respected everywhere; the prestige of his years in the Senate and party leadership in several of the important Senatorial committees.

Furthermore – a factor of very great importance – he was mainly responsible for persuading General Eisenhower to run for the Presidency that year, a feat that endowed him with a share of the General's enormous popularity and prestige.

Thus, if ever there was such a thing as an 'unbeatable' candidate, it seemed to be Senator Henry Cabot Lodge, Jr.

However, my husband believed Jack could win and encouraged him to make the race. I must say that at first I was taken aback by the idea. If anybody had asked me, I would have advised strongly against it. But in our thirty-eight years of marriage, I had seen his judgment vindicated so consistently that I didn't question it. If Joe said it was so, for me it was so. Jack took his time, weighing all the pros and cons carefully, sounding out opinions from people all over the state, then as usual made his own decision. He would run.

He was unopposed in the Democratic primary. No one else had any desire to take on the invincible Lodge, who also, of course, had no contenders in his own party for the nomination.

Kennedy v. Lodge developed into one of the most famous battles in modern US political history, and much has been written about it in many other books – easily available to anyone who wants a play-by-play account.

Suffice it that in all essential features the pattern was the one developed in 1946 in Jack's first election, except, of course, that by this time everyone was older and more experienced, and the scale of the effort was very much larger because this was not a district but a state. Joe and I took an apartment located conveniently in central Boston at

81 Beacon Street. From there Joe kept a supervisory eye on everything and did many things to smooth the way for Jack. He was aided by a secretary, by his lifelong friend and assistant Arthur Houghton, and by his much younger and equally trusted assistant Sargent Shriver.

Bobby, by then twenty-six and recently graduated from the University of Virginia law school, had an interesting job in the US Department of Justice and was eager to get on with his own career. He and Ethel had barely settled in Washington, and he had no intention of taking part in the campaign. Nevertheless, when problems developed and he was needed, and was asked by his father and by Jack, he put aside his personal concerns and – not happily but willingly – came in as campaign manager. Some of the old politicians who had joined the troops were disgruntled by this, considering Bobby a politically innocent boy sent to do a man's job. But Bobby already knew a good many of the ropes from the 1946 campaign. Further, he had as his 'director of organization' Lawrence O'Brien, a man Jack's age and a veteran even then of fourteen years' experience in local, district, state and national politics. What Bobby didn't know about organizing a detailed campaign, Larry O'Brien did. And Bobby also brought in a number of his friends, notably the talented, tough-minded, loyal and tireless Kenneth O'Donnell, who, with Larry, spent the next decade working in close rapport with Jack and Bobby in politics and government.

By this time some of the young relatives were old enough to have a part in Jack's exciting adventure. My niece Mary Jo recalls:

I was between my sophomore and junior years in college and it was one of the greatest summers I ever had, because we had such a good time. I worked mostly in the Boston headquarters. Bobby was there, Kenny O'Donnell was there, Chuck Roach and my brother Joey and a lot of others. Ted wasn't there that year because he was in the army, in Europe. Uncle Joe would call the switchboard every morning. Freddy Fitzgerald was on the switchboard [my nephew, son of my brother Fred] which was unusual too, because he was only about fourteen or fifteen. Everyone told Uncle Joe he was a nut to have all these young people down in the headquarters. Finally they did get a girl to run the switchboard but she was quite young too.

Jack was out campaigning all over the state but most of the time he'd manage to get back to headquarters at night, get the latest word, and cheer us on.

A bunch of us lived in the same rooming-house on Marble Street. Bobby and Joey, and Jean McGarnigal who was a secretary, and

Pat came and stayed and then later she and Eunice got an apartment. The woman who ran the rooming-house couldn't figure out what was going on, because there were all these young men and girls coming in and out. But she looked happy. We always paid the rent on time. There were about eight of us there.

We used to open the office early in the morning and work through until evening, sometimes later. There wouldn't be any cocktails afterwards. Some of the men might have had a drink elsewhere, but nobody drank to my knowledge. Instead, we used to go over to the Ritz – and we would be covered with mimeograph ink and really not looking the 'Ritzy type' – and we'd all have a profiterole, a cream puff filled with ice-cream with a lot of chocolate sauce over it. So that's what we'd do instead of having a drink: everyone would go to the Ritz and have a profiterole.

Kenny and Bobby would go out at night and make speeches. Eunice and Pat and Jean would be out making talks and showing sound films of a terrific interview Jack had given on the TV programme *Meet the Press*. All of us were doing something ten to fifteen hours a day. Usually everyone would be back and in bed by twelve. Then we were up again before eight. We just had a wonderful summer.

Jack campaigned harder than anyone else. He had been travelling around the state for several years, taking long weekends from the House, to meet people, make friends, seek allies and, most important, to let voters see him and feel a personal relationship with him.

Soon his back was again causing severe and prolonged pain. Kenny O'Donnell has written about this:

He travelled with crutches, which he concealed in his car when he arrived at the hall where the audience was waiting. Dave would notice him gritting his teeth when he walked with a determined effort from the car to the door where the chairman or the committee members were waiting to greet him, but then when he came into the room where the crowd was gathered, he was erect and smiling, looking as fit and healthy as the light-heavyweight champion of the world.

Then after he finished his speech, and answered questions from the floor, and shook hands with everybody, we would help him into the car and he would lean back on the seat and close his eyes in pain. Dave says, 'When we got back to the hotel, out would come the crutches from the floor of the back seat and he would use them to get upstairs, where I would fill the bathtub with hot water, and he would soak himself in the tub for an hour before going to bed.'

The size of our family – and our 'extended family' counting our numerous relatives – again turned out to be advantageous, since each of us had had varied experiences and had individual skills that could be put to use. We always checked to see which of us could do the best for Jack in a given situation – then that person did it. For instance, among the many ethnic groups that have come into Massachusetts on the tides of immigration over the years, there is a sizeable portion of Lebanese; and of course, like others, they have their clubs and associations. As it happened, Eunice had been to Lebanon, and furthermore had bought a beautiful shawl there. When there was a Lebanese meeting Eunice would put on her shawl and go, and tell the people how much she had enjoyed visiting their country and why they should vote for Jack. I had been in Portugal and had pleasant memories of that country, so I was the logical one to speak in New Bedford, which has a large population of Portuguese descent. And so it went.

I had a few extra strings to my own bow. For one thing, I spoke French. I certainly never dreamed when I was a girl at the Blumenthal convent, studying French, and then working on it through the years, that someday I would be using it to help elect a son of mine US Senator. My French was not nearly as good as Senator Lodge's, but it was pretty good. I was interested and informed about French and French-Canadian history and culture. For some reason the Democrats had not done much to solicit the French-Canadian vote in the past. So the situation was made to order for me.

I bought French-language newspapers, followed the news and opinions and various activities that were of special interest to these voters, and attended their fraternal and church meetings to say a few words about my experiences travelling in France. I said that Jack had worked and travelled there and greatly admired the French, so that he would be a good man both for Massachusetts and for the French heritage.

Dave Powers, talking about this not long ago, said:

I remember we were having a great deal of difficulty in the French sections of Lowell. Father Morriset was very influential. In fact, later on he ran for Congress. Father Morriset endorsed Henry Cabot Lodge, Jr. Jack figured there was no one better to send up there than his mother. So Rose Kennedy went through the French-speaking sections of Lowell, talking French to them at meetings, and all. And, do you know, she pulled out the city of Lowell for us.

Remembering the surprising success of the reception and tea we had given in Cambridge in 1946, we decided to try the idea again. I would be the hostess, though always assisted by two or three of the girls so that it would be a family affair – the general purpose of the invitation would be 'Come and meet the candidate and members of his family.' At some point I would take the platform, say a few words of welcome and introduce Jack, who would make a short, informal speech stressing the points of his campaign and, above all, giving the guests a chance to look him over and feel the warmth of his personality.

Polly Fitzgerald, the wife of my father's youngest brother Edward, was in charge of the arrangements. I asked her to send me a few of her memories for this book:

When Frank Morrissey [Jack's aide] called and asked me to see Jack about setting up some teas I learned that you were to be the attraction that would lure women to these events. Once they were there they would of course meet Jack, be impressed, and go on to work and vote for him . . .

I remember saying to Jack that I didn't know anything about politics and he said, 'You don't have to. Just go about arranging the teas the way you would for any civic or charitable activity.' But Jack himself talked with me about all the little details when we were planning the format.

We went out and found many, many women who 'knew nothing about politics' but who would like to serve on a committee to arrange a tea for the wife of the former Ambassador to Great Britain. They were thrilled to be identified with you and your family. They even lent their silver services and lace tableclothes. They didn't cook proper meals for weeks and neglected their housework in their efforts on the committee for your teas.

The first one was on May 18 in Worcester. Several thousand women turned out for it. Once we saw how it went there, we followed the same pattern everywhere. You were the one through whom we got the women to meet Jack. Those 33 tea parties in '52 ought to go down in history!

And in fact they have. When it was all over and Jack had won, Lodge said: 'It was those damn teas that beat me.'

Later, Jack became irritated when they were given so much credit, and someone said that he had 'floated into the Senate on an ocean of tea'.

General Eisenhower took the Presidency that year by a large majority, and he swept Massachusetts by a margin of 208,800 votes. Yet Lodge, who was so closely identified with Eisenhower and had his most vigorous endorsement (in fact, Eisenhower came to Boston for the wind-up speech of his campaign, specifically to help Lodge), went down by 70,737 votes. At those 33 'Kennedy teas' we had about 70,000 guests, nearly all of them women. The close matching of the figures is, I dare say, coincidence. But I also think that the tea-parties helped.

I have been asked if Jack was an emotional person. I suppose the reason for the question is that he always seemed so self-possessed, unruffled, equable, with a certain air of 'detachment' as though he were in the scene and living it fully and yet observing the scene with himself in it. I think by and large this was true. He had an even temperament, perhaps due to the continual bad luck he had with his health. Some people could have given in to self-pity, but Jack inured himself against pain and misfortune and lived life to the fullest. He chose to be optimistic. When he was going on a trip or had just won a race he would be excited and happy. When he was bedridden or had just lost a race he was not visibly depressed, just rather subdued. One of the few times I remember seeing him really nervous was election night of '52.

His headquarters – which oddly enough were across the street from Lodge's headquarters – were near our apartment on Beacon Street, so he spent time in both places. At his headquarters, according to O'Donnell and Powers, although 'the vote was so close that as late as midnight on election night the television and radio commentators were naming Lodge as the winner . . . Kennedy was so calmly sure of himself . . . that he remarked to his Harvard friend Torbert Macdonald, "I wonder what kind of job Eisenhower will give Lodge." ' Back with us at the Beacon Street apartment, as the returns came in, changing every few minutes with Lodge ahead or Jack ahead, he kept pacing around from one room to another. I remember especially he kept taking his jacket off and then soon putting it on again, sometimes pulling it off in such a way that the sleeves were inside out, then putting it on that way, and doing the same motion again, so that part of the time the sleeves were rightside in and part wrongside out. Torb Macdonald was with him, and my husband told him to keep calm. Jack calmed down.

I remember that in the morning, soon past eight, Jack and Torb came back to the apartment. Lodge had just conceded. Teddy was still

doing his military service overseas, and the first words I heard Jack
say were, 'Let's send a cable to Ted.' Then he went to see his father,
who advised him to have a Turkish bath and then go to bed.

Four years later, in 1956, Jack was called on to make the nomination
speech for Adlai Stevenson in Stevenson's second try against President
Eisenhower. The speech was so good, and his platform manner and
personality were so attractive to the delegates and to the public
watching on television, that there was a spontaneous movement to
put him on the ticket for the Vice-Presidency.

The reaction was a surprise to everybody concerned, and not least
for Jack himself. Once he realized what was happening and that he
actually had a fair chance for the nomination, his competitive nature
took hold and he decided to go for it. Bobby, Teddy, Kenny O'Donnell
and other loyal lieutenants went into action and worked furiously in
the little time available, in about twenty-four hours.

Among the most surprised were my husband and I. We were spending most of that summer in a house we had leased on the Riviera. We
had heard Jack's speech on short-wave radio and thought it extremely
good, and Joe had kept up more or less (less because of the wide
difference in time-zones between the Riviera and Chicago) with the
news of the convention. That Jack could be a candidate for the Vice-
Presidential nomination was, so far as we knew, only a rumour.
According to Kenny O'Donnell and Dave Powers:

> Kennedy waited to get an idea of just how much support he could
> count on before declaring himself, particularly in the Protestant
> Southern states. He was still waiting, leaning in the direction of
> running but not yet quite decided, when a delegate from Louisiana
> came to him and pleaded that he had to run. The Louisiana delegation
> had voted against their governor in favour of supporting Kennedy.
> 'We went out on a limb for you, and you can't leave us hanging
> there,' the Louisiana man argued. 'You've *got* to run.' That gave
> Jack the push that he needed. He turned to Bobby and said, 'Call
> Dad and tell him I'm going for it.'
> Bobby placed a telephone call to the Ambassador's home on the
> French Riviera, by no means an enviable assignment. Jack dis-
> appeared . . . when the call came through, the Ambassador's blue
> language flashed all over the room. The connection was broken
> before he was finished . . . Bobby quickly hung up the telephone and
> made no effort to get his father back on the line. 'Whew!' Bobby
> said. 'Is he mad!'

Joe's remarks were not very 'blue' but they were certainly emphatic. He felt sure that President Eisenhower would be re-elected over Stevenson, and that Jack – in second place on a losing ticket – would suffer damage to his political future, since they might blame Stevenson's defeat on the fact that Jack was a Catholic. Jack was being very short-sighted, he said. He did say it vigorously.

But Jack, having made up his mind, went right ahead anyway. There was a tremendous battle for delegates between Jack and Senator Estes Kefauver. (Kefauver had made a strong race for the Presidential nomination; many people admired him for his pluck, and Stevenson had already agreed, privately, that Kefauver ought to have the nomination for the Vice-Presidency.) At the peak, Jack was within an eyelash, only $33\frac{1}{2}$ delegate votes, of winning and surely would have except for manœuvres by several senior members of the party leadership. Kefauver won. Jack went to the convention hall, from his command post at the Stockyards Inn, and made a graceful acknowledgment and endorsement and introduced a resolution that the nomination be made unanimous. It was so moved, and passed.

Soon afterwards, back at the Stockyards Inn, he called his father to tell him the sequence and the outcome. I remember my husband saying: '*That's one of the best things that could ever happen to you!*'

Again, he was right. For Jack, not being on that losing ticket, didn't suffer from the fore-ordained defeat.

The historian James MacGregor Burns, writing about Jack's role at the '56 Convention, said:

He appeared as calm in defeat as in the prospect of victory. At the convention hall, he pushed his way to the rostrum: 'Ladies and gentlemen of this convention. I want to take this opportunity to express my appreciation to Democrats from all parts of the country. . . .' Despite his grin, Kennedy looked wilted and disappointed. Yet as things turned out, this was his greatest moment – the moment when he passed through a kind of political sound barrier to register on the nation's memory. The dramatic race had glued millions to their television sets. Kennedy's near-victory and sudden loss – the impression of a clean-cut boy who had done his best and who was accepting defeat with a smile – all this struck at people's hearts in living-rooms across the nation. In this moment of triumphant defeat, his campaign for the Presidency was born.

A year after the '56 Convention Jack had arrived at a personal perspective that enabled him to say:

Joe was the star of our family. He did everything better than the rest of us. If he had lived, he would have gone into politics, and he would have been elected to the House and to the Senate, as I was. And, like me, he would have gone for the Vice-Presidential nomination at the 1956 convention, but unlike me, he wouldn't have been beaten. Joe would have won the nomination. And then he and Stevenson would have been beaten by Eisenhower, and today Joe's political career would have been in shambles . . .

In 1958 Jack was up for re-election to the Senate. He won, this time, by almost a million votes, the biggest majority that any candidate in any campaign in the history of Massachusetts had ever received.

On that momentum he just kept on running for the Presidency, which was two years away.

With my wildest hopes and dreams for him, I could hardly believe that, in a matter of only fourteen years, he would move from a rather shy, slightly embarrassed, sometimes awkward young candidate for Congress in 1946 to a still youthful-looking but mature and wise President of the United States.

16

Meanwhile, from that first campaign of Jack's to the one for the Presidency, we were concerned with a great deal else besides politics. In fact, except during election years, politics was rather far down the list of topics that occupied my thoughts. In the Kennedy family, as in all others, life and death went on happening. It is surprising to look back (I expect this happens to anyone who has lived a long time) and to feel that so much happened so quickly.

After the end of the war in Europe, when it was possible to travel freely again across the Atlantic, Kathleen would come to visit us, for a few weeks or more at a time, at Hyannis Port and Palm Beach. And of course was always a blessing to us.

Her letters give some sense of her love for Billy and of her affection for the English people. In fact, she used to say that when she was here she spent most of her time explaining the British to the Americans and, when she was there, explaining America to the British.

After recovering, outwardly, from the shock of Billy's death in the war, she went on to make a good life for herself in England. The Duke and Duchess took her with utmost affection into their family circle. She bought a little house in London. She found pleasure in the subdued but still pleasant London Seasons and in country weekends. She worked to do her part to bind up the wounds and dreadful damages of the war. She travelled in the British Isles and on the Continent. England became her home.

In 1948 she had taken a spring holiday on the Riviera and was flying in a private plane with a few friends to Paris, where her father was waiting to meet her. On the way – a route threading the edges of the French Alps – the weather turned bad, navigation equipment was not adequate, and the plane crashed into a mountainside, killing all on board. Joe was notified and hurried to the scene. He watched as the body of his daughter was brought down the mountainside.

We lost our beloved Kathleen on May 13, 1948.

The Duke and Duchess wrote to us. A beautiful and heartfelt letter. I cannot bear to quote from it. They said how much they had loved Kathleen, and how grateful they had been to her because of the happiness she had brought to their son Billy. The Duchess suggested the epitaph on her gravestone: *Joy she gave, and joy she has.* Kathleen was buried at Chatsworth, Billy in Belgium, where he fell leading his troops during the war.

My father remained hale and lively, full of wit and cheer and enthusiasm, well on into his eighty-eighth year. His formula for keeping young so far beyond three-score-and-ten included ingredients that I dare say would be endorsed by scientific specialists in gerontology, such as: get plenty of exercise, keep active, keep interested in the world, spend a lot of time with younger people, especially grandchildren. In his later years he and my mother had a house at Hyannis Port, on Lighthouse Lane, about a ten-minute walk from our place. We saw them in those summer times even more than we usually had.

While my father was growing old, Teddy was a boy growing up; and since my father was in semi-retirement (the year of Teddy's birth he was sixty-nine) Teddy probably saw more of him than any of the other children had. He has some vivid memories:

My first recollections of Grampa were at the Cape. He'd sit on that marvellous wall right outside the sun-porch, sit for hours facing the south-west in the afternoon sun and sunset, enjoying the sea and salt air and sun. Or now and then he'd walk down to the sand and sit in all the seaweed and cover himself with it, because he thought the iron and the bromides from the seaweed could come into his skin.

Another early recollection was the newspapers. I used to go down to the store and pick them up for him. He wouldn't just get the morning and afternoon papers, he'd have placed an order for every edition. And his pockets would be bubbling with notes and papers and clippings. They were all over his room; sticking out of his pants' pockets; pinned to his suits, coats. He was interested in everything. And of course he knew so many people. He would see an item that somebody's son or daughter or grandchild was married, or some-body's son was on the police force or had done very well at school or in sports. And he would write a little note to these people. And he collected information. He would take some of the clippings back to the Bellevue Hotel, where he kept files. But with a lot of the others he wouldn't need to do that because he had such a terrific memory.

When I was going to boarding-school at Fessenden, I'd go into downtown Boston to the Bellevue Hotel and have Sunday lunch with him. In his and Grandma's apartment there he'd go around dressed very comfortably and informally. But by the time we went out, he was spruce, immaculate, a splendid sight. Downstairs on the way to lunch he'd take me through the kitchen and introduce me to any of the cooks or dish-washers I hadn't already met. Then the same, in the dining-room, on our way to his table. He knew everybody because almost the same people came every Sunday, sat at the same place and ordered the same lunch; it was a sort of ritual.

On a number of occasions Bob was there. He was in the Navy at the time, based nearby, and he'd join us.

Afterwards, Grampa might take us for a walk through the Boston Commons and point out where the British soldiers had been camping when they left to fight at Concord. Or we'd go down to the Old North Church and he would give us the story of Paul Revere's Ride again. Or down to the old well on Spring Street. Or maybe over to the *Constitution*. Or out to Franklin Park. Each Sunday he had something different. Once in a while we'd start out and Grampa would run into a few old friends and they'd get wrapped up in conversation and telling stories and we'd never get there.

He was a marvellous story-teller. I heard my first off-colour story from Grampa. But he was laughing so hard while he was telling it that I don't think he ever got to the punch line. He enjoyed his own stories. He would start out telling a story, and start laughing and then pretty soon be laughing so hard he cried. It was very infectious. I can't remember any of them, but that's probably because they weren't such great stories – it was the way he told them.

I do remember his talking on about his 'Bigger, Better, Busier Boston' – and saying what was the matter with people that they didn't bring it about sooner. He'd say, 'My own daughter doesn't even have fish chowder. This is the trouble with the fishing industry, people just don't eat enough fish. They only eat it on Friday and they ought to eat it every day.' He'd go into Hayes-Bickford's and want pumpkin pie and they wouldn't be selling it that day. He'd say, 'Now you know up in Acton pumpkins are selling at three cents a pound. Why don't you buy pumpkins?' Also he'd try to get restaurants to serve squash. It was one of the things that was grown in some quantity in regions around Boston. He'd ask if they knew what a bargain squash was these days at the market. He was tremendously interested in the whole life and vibrancy of the city and everything that had to do with it.

People seem to wonder how it happened that we as a family, and especially perhaps in this generation – my brothers and sisters and I – became so much involved in public life. Obviously there were several influences: but Grampa surely had a part in it. He knew people's problems and motivations and needs, and what he talked about could easily be transformed into a current setting. And those little historical tours: I think that when you're a boy, you're going to be interested in the *Constitution* as a boat and as a fighting ship. But history, obviously, brings life into these monuments and characters and events. It's a reasonably easy transition to move from the issues of those times into the issues of these times.

My father's health began failing. I don't know the cause, if there was any precise cause: 'circulatory troubles' mainly.

He passed away on October 2, 1950.

Joe had an office and a staff of perhaps a score of people in New York, and he had other trusted agents in other places where he happened to have large holdings or current operations (for instance, after Sarge and Eunice married they lived in Chicago, because Sarge was assistant manager of The Merchandise Mart). He also had a skilled full-time secretary and, nearby or quickly available, two or three trustworthy assistants who had worked with him through the years and who understood – without the need for detailed instructions – what he wanted done. Consequently there was plenty of time for golf, swimming, walking (we again could have our long walks together), travelling, reading, talking, being with close friends, being with our children and then, in due course, with our grandchildren – enjoying the things that can make life so pleasant. What made it possible for him to conduct all sorts of intricate business while sitting in the solarium at Palm Beach with a beach-towel around his middle and a straw hat when needed, or at Hyannis Port in equivalent ease and informality, was that fabulous invention, the telephone. I'm sure that if Joe had ever had to choose among all the marvels of modern technology the one thing to preserve from some holocaust, he would have discarded automobiles, airplanes, radio and TV and all the rest, including electric lights, in favour of the telephone.

This predilection went back a long way. When we were courting he used to call me every evening. After we were married whenever he was away, he would call me almost every day or evening. Eventually it became a family habit and quite a wonderful one in a way, because of course it is marvellous to have a direct conversation instead of having to wait for the mails to get back and forth. Most letters leave questions unanswered or unasked anyway. Still, there are grounds for regret, for once a call is finished it's gone for keeps, whereas letters last. When Jackie became part of our family, the way the Kennedys used long-distance appalled her. She said she had been brought up to think that a long-distance call was only for an urgent or special occasion.

As I have mentioned, Joe's various new ventures obliged me to keep adding to my vocabulary and knowledge, not to become expert, but enough at least to keep up a conversation in case I found myself at a dinner with people who were experts. In these later years I found this happening again several times, but the example that stays in my mind with vividness is that of horse-racing.

Joe came home one night and told me he had just bought a large share in the Hialeah race-track in Miami. It was the portion of the track ownership that had belonged to Colonel E. R. Bradley. I was used to surprises, but this was a rather extreme case.

Col. Bradley had been one of the early entrepreneurs in the Palm Beach and south-east Florida coast area, and among other contributions to the landscape and entertainments had built a big restaurant and casino. It was quite a beautiful place. Dinners, with superb food, were about $5.00, and the service was swift and courteous. So everyone turned up at Bradley's sooner or later, for luncheon or dinner, and afterwards went into the casino and usually lost some money, enabling Col. Bradley to recoup the losses on his delicious meals and pocket a profit besides. Everyone seemed to accept this as a fair arrangement for fine food in beautiful surroundings among friends and acquaintances. Bradley's, in fact, was a Palm Beach institution. Col. Bradley himself felt so deeply about the place, regarding it as the fulfilment of his highest ideals, that he specified in his will that it not be sold as part of his estate but simply torn down. (And that is exactly what happened.)

Joe and I used to go to Bradley's fairly often. Joe was not a gambler, except in the sense of taking closely calculated risks with the possibility of significant rewards. At Bradley's we would play roulette but seldom bet on a number, almost always on the red or black; and Joe would rely on 'the law of probability', waiting for either red or black to come up in a long series or five or six in a row, and when that happened place a bet on the opposite colour; and if we lost, then double the bet, and keep on doing that to the allowable limit. Usually we came out a little ahead. Of course, we always kept the bets small. And it was fun.

During the years Col. Bradley and Joe became good friends, partly, perhaps, because Joe, like himself, was a self-made man of Irish descent. Shortly before he died, he asked Joe to buy his interest in Hialeah, which he had helped to found and develop into a beautiful place (especially famous for its ponds with flocks of flamingoes) because, as he told Joe, he wanted it to go to an Irishman. I can't think of a more whimsical reason for buying substantial ownership of a race-track, but I guess Joe was touched by the gesture. Besides, he thought it might be a good investment, which it turned out to be. Meanwhile, he thought it could be an interesting sidelight to our Florida life, since the track is only about an hour and a half away from our house. Many people we knew went there.

We had a big box with one of the best views of the track and infield. There was a fine restaurant. Friends and interesting visitors were all over the place. As the major stockholder, Joe of course had every facility at his disposal; the service to him and us and our guests couldn't have been better. I used to go down a couple of times a week for lunch and spend the afternoon.

I was obliged again to learn a new world and new vocabulary, including the names of the leading racing stables and their owners, since they were likely to be mingling with us or visiting our box. I learned the names and locations of other leading tracks around the country, and something about their owners, for the same reason. And, of course, I had to master the form sheet and to understand the tote board and how to place bets intelligently on the basis of past performance, track condition, and all the rest of the highly fallible information available to the better. I can't say that I became an expert handicapper, but my record wasn't so bad. And since I seldom ventured from the $2.00 window, my losses, if any, during an afternoon were bearable. Meanwhile I had fun.

There was always something to do. In fact, there was a great deal to do, including the incessant dinner-parties, cocktail-parties, balls and galas of various sorts that dotted the winter season. Joe loathed big noisy cocktail-parties, couldn't have cared less for the big splashy and glittery charity balls (he would gladly send a cheque for the charity; but did he have to *go*?), and as for dinner-parties, he would say: 'The food is better at our house and the conversation is a lot better. All they want to do is to fight about Roosevelt and ask whether the stock market or real estate is going up or down, or what do I think about the fifth race on Saturday at Hialeah . . .' It has been said that Joe was a highly gregarious person who loved dining out, talking with many selected peers and enjoying all the social perquisites of his success. Nothing could be more untrue. His idea of a good time was to rise early, read the papers, take a swim, have a light lunch, have a nap, play golf with me or a few close friends, have dinner at home with me and with members of our family and perhaps just two or three really good friends; then read, listen to some music, look at TV or screen a recent movie (he had equipment that was easily set up on our big patio at the Palm Beach house, and it was very pleasant seeing movies there in the tropical air under the moonlit or starry sky) and turn in early, around ten or eleven and no later than twelve. Meanwhile, of course, he would have dictated a lot of letters and had a dozen or two telephone conversations with people all over the country. But his heart and his real interests were always at home: he was actually – a strange term for a man of his tremendous vitality and interests – a homebody. Others have noted, but I can affirm (and who better than I?) that his over-riding and guiding concern was for me and our family.

The children were with us during the Christmas holidays which stretched to various dates in January (why don't the schools learn to coordinate their vacation schedules?), and then again during the Easter holidays.

In any case, after they had gone back to school from their Easter vacations, and provided the weather was becoming mild by then in the north, Joe and I would go up to New York and stay for several weeks in a small apartment we owned facing Central Park.

Hyannis Port was our principal residence, our base of operations, as it were, for seven or eight months of the year from 1941 onward through all the years I have been describing. For all of us it became Home. The children had their Christmas and Easter holidays in Florida, but they had their summer vacations and all the spring and fall weekends they could manage at Hyannis Port.

It was a complicated household, especially during the late 1940s because by then the three Gargan children, Joey and Mary Jo and the youngest, Ann, were teen-agers and were spending the summers with us. So the age and circumstance of the inhabitants ranged from Jack, a US Congressman in his early thirties, to Ann, a girl in early adolescence. None of our older children was there all the time, because by then, like Jack, they had other things to do, but all were there for at least part of the summer and they tried to make their visits coincide or overlap. Moreover, they were likely to invite a friend or two along for a week-end or a week or so. It was a busy house and I was sometimes hard put to keep it passably well organized.

Evelyn Jones, who began working for us as a maid during that period, has recalled:

Mrs Kennedy always had so much on her mind. She was always going around with these notes. At the time I was first working there, they were wearing those twin sweater sets and she would have so many things to think of that she'd have all her sweaters pinned with notes. One day she ran out of space and tried to pin some on me. I wouldn't let her: it made me feel like a human bulletin board; but I sympathized with the problem.

I don't remember trying to enlist Evelyn as a message centre, but I wouldn't be surprised.

Except for a few elementary rules and regulations such as being at meals on time, it was a very informal household. Joe and I wanted it that way. We wanted people to feel relaxed. Yet sometimes the relaxation got to be a bit extreme. For instance, there was a general tendency, especially among the boys, to leave towels and sweaters and sweatshirts and tennis racquets and tennis shoes strewn about the house. I remember that several times I came into the house and found tennis shoes parked any place from underneath the table in the entrance hallway to the top of the baby grand piano. I considered that to be extremely inappropriate, and I said so so vehemently that one day they ganged up on me in the following way. This is a Lem Billings story and I can't guarantee it in all details, but it goes like this:

One of them, just to bait me, deliberately left a pair of very dirty white tennis sneakers on the dining-room table. I saw them and left a note sticking out from the top of one sneaker: 'Bobby, are these yours?'

Bobby came along, saw the note, and left another one with: 'Dear Mother, no, they're not mine. Jack's.'

Jack came along, saw both notes, and left another: 'Dear Mother, that's wrong. They belong to Teddy.'

Teddy came along, saw and read the three notes, and left one of his own: 'Dear Mother, that's a lie, they belong to Eunice . . .' And so forth, through several others. I never did find out whose dirty sneakers those were on the dining-room table. But in the dining-room that evening I noticed a lot of silly grins around the table; to which I paid no heed. (Lem Billings, by the way, was one of the worst at leaving things around. Was it Lem . . . ?)

As for the strewn towels, that reminds me that after showering the boys often used to go around any place in the house with one of our big bath towels knotted at the top around their waists, sarong-style. I made no objection; but to say the least it lent an informal touch.

When the cook was off, we'd gather in the kitchen and usually each of the girls, sometimes the boys too, would try cooking a dish of something, and then everybody would try it out. And comment on it. Some of them would be sitting on the table, or on chairs, or on the floor while the tasting went on. And then we would all sit around the kitchen table when everything was done, and there would be compliments – or razzing – about the food, and we would talk and gossip. They all enjoyed the experience and they also learned something: for instance, don't take an egg out of a cold refrigerator and expect it to be properly soft-boiled, even in rapidly boiling water, in just three minutes, because it won't be. I don't recall that any of them developed any specialities. Except perhaps for Eunice, who was apt to be involved in telephoning or something when the dishes were to be washed or some other onerous kitchen task to be done. At least she was accused of that.

During the late 1940s I still had a sizeable population of teen-agers on my hands at Hyannis Port, and of course I felt obliged to keep track of them and, hopefully, to instruct them in good manners. My niece Mary Jo, whose age put her near the middle of this age-group, has special memories of the time:

> There were Friday night dances at the golf club and Aunt Rose would drive over in her little blue car and look in on us, very unobtrusively, to see how we were doing. The next day some of us probably would get some coaching from her about dancing. I had my heels going in some funny way and she'd give me a demonstration of how I looked, and how to correct it. The boys would be pumping their dates' arms and she'd show them how not to do that. Bobby was a terrible dancer for a while. He not only pumped, he hopped. My brother Joey was probably even worse. He danced like a longshoreman. Aunt Rose tried to show him and then gave up and made him go to dancing classes. Teddy was a good dancer. He had a lot of rhythm, like Grampa Fitzgerald, who was a marvellous dancer.
>
> On Saturday nights there could be a dance at the other club at Wianno beach, which was a few miles away, and practically all of us would go over there. Aunt Rose would dance with Uncle Joe if he was there and alternate with Bobby and Ted and my brother Joey to see how they were coming along.
>
> Uncle Joe was in on most of what was going on because he really cared so much about his children (and about nieces and nephews), and as he used to say, 'You'd better believe it.' Another of his expressions about his children, was 'All my ducks are swans.' And

he really felt that way: his family was his life, Aunt Rose and the children.

For a man who valued domestic peace and quiet, Joe always showed remarkable forbearance. When the stream of traffic – friends and relations, Jack's continuing 'surprises', those of others – grew even heavier than usual, I do remember him saying, more plaintively than complainingly, 'This isn't a hotel. You don't have to have every room filled all the time.' Actually, not only were all of them filled practically all the time during the summers, but there often had to be double and triple occupancy. It was not at all unusual to have another 'surprise' arrive in the driveway at eleven o'clock or so at night, and then we'd have to do some rearranging. If it was an extra boy, and there were no vacant beds or cots left in any of the boys' rooms, we might have to start moving girls into other girls' rooms; or of course vice versa if the arrival was a girl; or if perhaps a boy and a girl arriving together, it could become quite a checker game. We were, I expect, in the forefront of what now would be called 'communal living'.

Somehow we always managed to fit everybody in. Even if some of them might awaken next day with muscles a bit stiff or a crick in the neck from sleeping on the floor on a spare mattress or inflatable raft, they all seemed to have a very good time. I expect that in part at least this was because of the informality and openness of the household.

There were rules (largely implied) of manners and consideration which are part of civilized living. I assumed that people realized this was a large, involved, hospitable but still personal household which took some thought and energy on my part to operate: otherwise, it was understood that everyone was to be him or herself and have a fine time.

Mary Jo: Aunt Rose kind of ran the whole show, I would say, in that she planned everything about how the house would be run, planned the meals, the schedules, coped with the help, directed and supervised that whole big enterprise and yet it was really practically unbeknownst to us. At the time I never had the idea that anything was a big bother.

It would have been somewhere around that time, with Teddy at about the age of eighteen – he was a freshman at Harvard – that Richard Clasby first came into our lives. Not many years later he married Mary Jo. I am told that he was one of the very few athletes in Harvard's history to have won nine varsity letters, which he did in football, hockey and baseball.

Dick Clasby says:

What really drew my attention first was that I was out for football,
freshman football, and I kept getting hit and hit very hard. In
athletics your greatest respect is for someone who really belts you,
and even if you don't like the bruises you sort of have to like the
guy because he's good and he's playing hard, and that's the game.
Well, this turned out to be Ted Kennedy. We happened to be walking the same way to and from football practice, and everything just
seemed to fall into place and we became friends.

Now, it's important to understand something about my personal
circumstances. My dad was a cop, a good honest one but a cop, and
my mother had to work most of her life to help make ends meet,
so there was no money, and to me a rich kid – I knew very few of
them – was a spoiled sissy and was a kid I fought. Automatically,
the first thing you do is fight them. The first one I ever liked or
trusted was Ted, and it was sort of incredible to me but we became
close friends.

It was sometime late that spring I first went to Hyannis Port and
began to know the rest of the family. As I remember, Ted just said
how about taking a ride down to the Cape and get on the beach.
So we did that, except that was only part of it, a small fraction.

When you arrived, there probably would already be a touch
football game going on out on the front lawn, and before you even
got your bag in the house you were playing football, and you might
still be in the suit you'd gone to church in that morning.

I looked at the game, the girls playing it along with the boys, and
it didn't look like anything I would take seriously. You got tagged,
so what? But they get you so involved, it's like Harvard versus Yale.
Everybody is participating one hundred per cent. If there's a little
boy in the game and they throw the ball to him – and they do – and
he doesn't try his best to catch it, that is considered bad. And if
you're a big guy and another big guy has the ball and you are chasing
him, you run as fast as you can, you do everything within your
power to stop that ball. I think some of the guests were left slightly
battered and bruised. There would be people from Washington,
Senators, high officials, and if you met them inside the house they
would be dignified. But outside, they'd be running around in a pair
of shorts and striving. It was like, 'I don't know what you can do
for the country, but can you catch the ball, that's what's important
right now.'

The game they played wasn't the normal game. They could throw the ball all over the field. Ordinarily in football you can't throw a forward pass except from behind the line of scrimmage, but they could throw it from any place and then the person who caught it could forward pass again. So it became part football, part basketball. There was no blocking. You would change goals after each touchdown, and also you would change them because of the wind conditions because the yard is so close to the ocean. There were no kick-offs, you threw it to the other team. I don't know where the rules came from. I had never heard of them before but I just took them for granted and tried to learn this wild game.

It was an extremely competitive situation. But it was a competition that was hard for me to understand, because when you have young people in competition it often leads to hard feelings in the person or side that loses. Even now, when I play with my children I sort of try to make the game come out tied. That wasn't their way, they were out to win. But then when the game was finished there wasn't anything from the winning side that would even hint at gloating and 'ha ha, you lost'. There was a great comradeship. They'd say, great game, Bobby, or Ted, or whoever it was. So you didn't feel like you had lost although five minutes before you thought – this is before I knew them that well – if you lost you were going to be ribbed about it all weekend. During the game they did a lot of that sort of thing to each other. But as soon as it was over, it was over, and it had all been just for fun. And probably there'd be another match tomorrow at 2.30 with players changing around to different sides.

But they loved kidding and playing these rather fantastic jokes on each other. Again on football – and this would be a few years later on – we went down to Washington and there was going to be a 'grudge' championship game between Bobby's team and Teddy's team. Well, there were guys I didn't know, but they were friends of Bobby's or Teddy's and it was 'Dick Clasby, I'd like you to meet Joe Somebody' and it was natural they both would have rounded up some of their best football-playing friends for 'The Big Game'. You wouldn't necessarily recognize their names or faces. It soon developed that they were *very* good football players. And that about three or four of Teddy's friends were members of the Baltimore Colts. But it also turned out that Bobby had had the same idea and that three or four of his friends played for the Washington Redskins. It didn't take long for this double deception to come out into the open, and of course there was a riot on the field and on the sidelines among the rooters and everybody had a hilarious time. In the end

Teddy's fake-out team lost to Bobby's fake-out team, but I don't think anyone was really keeping much track of the score.

Jack couldn't get into the rough action entirely because of his bad back – people did remember to be a little careful with him on account of that, but he participated. Pat has a story about that:

Jack was President-elect. He was forming his Cabinet and was having some of his meetings at Hyannis Port. The rest of us were out on the lawn playing football. A rainstorm came along – one of those sudden terrific storms – but we kept on playing anyway. From where Jack was, inside the house, he could look out and see us and it got to be too much for him to resist. During a break in his meetings he came outside, in this driving rain, and ran out for a pass. It was high, so he had to jump to catch it, and he came down hard on his heels. Bobby couldn't believe what he had seen and he yelled a typical compliment to the President-elect: 'Lots of guts, no sense!'

Dick Clasby continues:

When you were with Jack there at Hyannis Port, if you weren't outside involved in something you would soon find yourself involved in something that was going on inside, such as various intellectual games which Jack organized and led. There would be, for instance, 'Categories'. One category might be Shakespearean characters, and when you had to produce a Shakespearean character beginning with 'M' you would have to think of Macbeth or Macduff or one of those or else lose the point and pass the question.

I'm sure that Jack would have been attracted to such games in any case, as nearly all our children were, but one thing that fixed his and their interest, I believe, was the experience in England of taking 'country weekends' in the English countryside at some of the great houses. Those were the late 1930s, the pre-television age, and although country life was bountiful in the daylight hours there were, at dinner and after dark, some hours when people were dependent on their own mental resources for entertainment. As a result, conversation was a highly developed art. Another result was the invention of amusing, intellectually stimulating and challenging 'parlour games'. I remember Kathleen talking about Anthony Eden and what a marvel he was at them. He was a weekend guest at a place she had in Ireland, and the group was playing a game involving historical names – persons, places, battles, and so forth – and he knew everything and always won.

Jack was great at keeping conversation going and bringing every-one into it, making it lively and humorous but interesting and worth-while; and I expect the experiences in England helped him bring out that talent, and those English country-house games suited him exactly because of his great background in history and literature and the endlessly curious nature of his mind. In turn and in due course, when Bobby was old enough, Jack's interest in these games stimulated Bobby's interest and he too became an inveterate inventor and organizer of parlour games. Ethel and I were talking about all this not long ago:

ETHEL: I remember that often after dinner you'd play the piano – always if there was a birthday – and everybody would gather around and sing with great gusto. Not in tune. You'd do old songs and newer and current ones; popular songs. People don't seem to do that much any more. And we'd play games afterwards. Charades, and Murder, and Sardines, and Twenty Questions, and Ambassadors.

RK: How did Ambassadors go?

ETHEL: Two people leave the room, and they decide who they are. They could decide to be people who weren't even of the same historical time: for instance, one could be Julius Caesar and the other could be Mrs Roosevelt. So they come back into the room and carry on a dialogue, and the others try to guess who they are, and they do that by contributing to the conversation with remarks or questions which have to make sense to the historical personage – you know, something you really might say if you were having a chat with Julius Caesar or Mrs Roosevelt. If you've guessed right, you don't announce it but the personage accepts you into the conversation and is friendly towards you. But otherwise he or she just ignores you, which is a terrible put-down. The one who first gets accepted into the conversation by both personages wins the game. It's a marvellous game, just straight fun.

RK: Jack must have been good at it.

ETHEL: Yes, he was very good. Another one he liked was Indirect Questions. It's like Twenty Questions but it's more fun. The same as in Ambassadors you decide who you are, let's say you're Charle-magne, and we try to guess, but the way we do it is through indirect questions. We'd say to you, 'Are you a seventh-century Irish poet?' and you have to think of one and answer with, for instance, 'No, I'm not Claimon,' and if you couldn't you'd say, 'I pass,' and then the one who asked would be entitled to a direct question, such as 'Are you living?' or 'Are you an American?' or 'Are you an astronaut?' and get a direct Yes or No answer. It would go on that way and finally get winnowed down to where somebody'd guess 'Are you Charlemagne?' and be the winner.

RK: Which ones did Bobby like best?

ETHEL: He liked those, and Categories and Charades and Sardines.

RK: You were good at those games. I remember you and I had a discussion about Paul Revere's Ride and I was quoting the poem that goes 'T'was the nineteenth of April in 'seventy-five . . .' and you said it was the eighteenth of April. I said, 'Ethel, dear, one of my brothers was born on the nineteenth of April and it's been a big celebration half my life, so you're wrong.' And you said, 'Do you mind if I get the book?' And you got it, and of course it was the eighteenth of April.

About this time, Joe and I began to wonder when we were going to have grandchildren.

It was Bobby who blazed the trail. Ethel was Jean's room-mate and best friend at Manhattanville; and that's how Bobby and Ethel met. Their romance flowered, they married in 1950 and their first child, Joseph Patrick Kennedy, was born in 1952 during Jack's run for the Senate against Lodge.

Eunice and Sarge married in 1953, Pat and Peter in 1954, Jean and Steve in 1956, Ted and Jean in 1958. Once the idea took hold it became a veritable processional down the aisle, and with our children, our nieces and nephews, and the children and nieces and nephews of our friends, Joe and I would count on a wedding every few months during that decade.

Jack was the oldest to marry. By the time he was approaching his mid-thirties his father and I had really begun to wonder if he was going to remain a bachelor for years more and then perhaps marry late in life. We weren't worried – that would be much too strong a term – but we knew that for us marriage had brought such great satisfactions, that a good marriage is one of the happiest conditions of human life, and of course we wanted this for him. And so, while not worrying, we were in a sense waiting and wondering.

The first I ever heard of Jackie was sometime during the winter of 1951. She – and her younger sister Lee, as I recall – were vacationing at their family home at Hobe Sound up the coast from Palm Beach. Jackie worked in Washington on one of the newspapers and knew several of our children, since by that time Jack, Eunice and Bobby all were working in Washington, and she was invited to spend a few days at our Palm Beach house while some of them were there. I wasn't there myself at the time; I was detained on other matters and arrived a little later that year. Soon afterwards, however, I received a thank-you letter. It was signed, Jackie. I thought it was from a boy, and how extraordinary for a boy to write such a charming letter. I wondered, who is Jackie? It turned out Jackie was a girl and I began hearing all sorts of good things about her from members of the family, and that Jack was taking her out often and liked her a great deal.

Then one day, glancing through the society pages of one of the papers, I read she was engaged to Cass Canfield, Jr. I thought to myself, 'What a pity, everybody says she's such a nice girl and she's a Catholic, and the right age, and she's been well educated and she would have been a good helpmate for Jack. And now he's lost her.' I didn't know she had a sister. The item turned out not to be about Jackie but about Lee; so my fears were allayed.

I didn't meet her until the next year, in the summer of 1952, at Hyannis Port. I liked her at once. Jackie, of course, has her own special memories of coming there for the first time, and meeting her potential mother-in-law, and what the general ambience of our household was like:

The first time I met her was about a year, a little more than a year, before I married Jack, when I came that summer for a weekend. I remember she was terribly sweet to me: for instance, I had a sort of special dress to wear to dinner – I was more dressed up than his sisters were, and so Jack teased me about it, in an affectionate way, but he said something like, 'Where do you think you're going?' She said, 'Oh, don't be mean to her, dear. She looks lovely.'

She did everything to put one at one's ease. She was so friendly ... everything. So that was really nice. Because I expect I was nervous. It was the first time I'd seen all of Jack's family together. I'd met him in Washington when he was in Congress, and he used to come to Bobby's and Ethel's house, so I knew him with Bobby and Ethel well, and I knew Eunice, but I'd never seen the whole group together. Obviously, if you really liked the elder brother and were rather shy you might have been a little nervous. So that's it: she went out of her way to put me at ease, and I liked her enormously. I had already met Jack's father when I'd gone for a weekend at the Palm Beach house. He was the same – so welcoming and kind. I adored him.

It was a marvellous weekend. How can I explain those people? They were like carbonated water and other families might be flat.

They'd be talking about so many things with so much enthusiasm. Or they'd be playing games. At dinner or in the living-room, anywhere, everybody would be talking about something: they had so much interest in life – it was so stimulating. And so gay and so generous and so open and accepting to outsiders. I thought they were wonderful.

I must now explain that when the children married, Joe and I – and of course their spouses too – faced the problem of what we should be called: 'Mother and Father, Mom and Dad', any variation on those? The problem, a delicate one, must be familiar to many people. My feeling, in which Joe concurred, was that both we and they would be slightly uncomfortable if the husbands and wives of our children addressed us as parents. We weren't their parents: to my ear it sounded artificial. But then what? When they began to have children, who would be calling us 'Grandpa and Grandma', it seemed both simple and seemly if we were known that way by our in-laws as well as our grandchildren. And that became the general principle. When someone refers to 'Grandma' or 'Grandpa' in the next pages the references – unless otherwise noted – are to me or to Joe. However, two additional notes on this note. When Jackie came into the family it didn't seem appropriate to her to call me 'Grandma' and she has always used the expression 'Belle Mère', a French colloquialism for a mother-in-law one really likes. And needless to say, I have always liked that. I wish there were some equivalent expression in English. 'Grandma' has its perils. Before a recent party, I was fresh from the beauty parlour, had put on a new Paris gown, and when the ensemble was complete, my maid exclaimed, 'Oh, madam, you don't look a day over fifty!' Sarge, in his late fifties, with his portion of grey hair, was at the party and when I entered he greeted me from across the room in loud, clear tones: 'Hello, Grandma!' I was immediately deglamourized and very conscious of my eighty years.

Jackie and Jack became engaged early in the summer of 1953, and the announcement set off various festivities including an engagement party given by friends of ours, the Harringtons, in a big house they had there in Hyannis Port at the edge of the golf course. The party involved – for the younger element – a 'scavenger hunt' which became rather famous, or perhaps the better term would be notorious, in our family.

Ethel and I were talking about this:

RK: There was something about taking the policeman's hat.

ETHEL: Yes. That was the night Pat 'borrowed' a bus. One of the things we were supposed to hunt for was 'the longest object' and so Pat found the bus. I guess the driver had disappeared into the station for a minute or two. And the next thing he knew . . .

RK: Where was the bus?

ETHEL: In Hyannis. And she drove it right to the Harringtons' and parked it in the driveway.

RK: A big bus like that?

ETHEL: Yes. I can't remember who, but one of them appropriated a policeman's hat. By the time they got home there were three squad cars of policemen talking to Grandpa.

My nephew Joey has some illuminating memories about the scavenger hunt:

Bobby and I and Pat were part of a team. You had to get different things like 'A monster from the sea', and I remember we went in and got one of Uncle Joe's frozen salmon from a refrigerator. Another one of the things on the list was 'A menu from a famous restaurant'. There was a place called 'Charlie's' so we drove there and I went in to get the menu. But also on the list was 'A show of courage', and at Charlie's in those days they had a police officer on duty. Somehow I decided that as 'A show of courage' I should take the policeman's hat. I grabbed it, ran out the door, leaped into Bobby's car – Pat grabbed the bus – and down the street we go. We went around picking up more items.

When we got back to the house at Hyannis Port that evening, there looking for us were some of the maddest-looking policemen I've ever seen.

Uncle Joe came up from the movie room as this confrontation was taking place. The policemen were quite upset, naturally, but Uncle Joe was fit to be tied. Bobby and I got the royal dickens. We heard him very clearly in no uncertain terms.

The next morning Uncle Joe was sitting in the sun-room and I went in and said, 'I'm sorry about last night, we just got carried away,' and he said, 'Well, Joey, don't worry about it, but I certainly expect it's *not* going to happen again' – and he kind of smiled. And I said, 'No, I'm sure that won't happen again.'

There were many preparations for Jack and Jackie's wedding to be made, and Jackie goes on to say something about that:

We got engaged in June and the wedding was going to be in

September at Newport, so I remember one day my mother invited Jack's mother over to Newport for lunch and to discuss the plans. Jack was there for the weekend. And the situation amused me so much. Because here was Jack, he was 36 at the time and he was grown up and he was a Senator. And his mother was coming to have lunch with my mother and we were going to the beach and he and I would have a swim first. The two mothers were dressed up – Bailey's Beach was dressy then – and I remember she had on a beautiful light blue silk dress and a big hat. Jack had on some undershirt and a pair of bedroom slippers, and I expect she was rather mortified at the sight her son presented. I had on something not quite as casual but knockabout. I remember that on the way over, the two ladies were in the front of the car and we were sitting in the back seat sort of like two bad children.

Anyway, it was, I'm sure, one of his least favourite days – the two mothers sitting there in their hats and pearls and white gloves chattering away about the wedding. So we went swimming. I came out of the water earlier; it was time to go for lunch, but Jack dawdled. And I remember she stood on the walk and called to her son in the water, 'Jack! . . . Ja-a-ck!' – and it was just like the little ones who won't come out and pretend not to hear their mothers calling. 'Ja-a-ck!' but he wouldn't come out of the water. I can't remember whether she started down or I went down to get him, but he started coming up saying, 'Yes, Mother.'

It was a grand wedding, with all the traditional ceremonials and a large group of attendants. Numbers of Jack's schoolboy, college and Navy 'surprises' such as Lem Billings, Torb Macdonald and Red Fay, and newer ones such as Charles Bartlett, were on hand in cutaways and striped trousers, as were Teddy and Joey, as was Sarge, who by then was a brother-in-law (he and Eunice had married in May that year). Bobby was 'best man'. Jackie was perfectly beautiful in ivory silk taffeta and rosepoint. Her matron of honour was her sister Lee and she too had a numerous entourage, including Ethel and Jean. Archbishop (later Cardinal) Cushing presided at the ceremony and also read a special blessing on the marriage sent by the Pope. There were 800 in the church, including all sorts of notables and dignitaries, and more than 1200 at the reception. I read in one newspaper account that: 'So great was the traffic that cars were backed up nearly half a mile and it took almost two hours for the guests to pass through the reception line to greet the couple.' I dare say Jackie must have got a little tired smiling and shaking hands, but I can't think of a more appropriate introduction to her new life as the wife and helpmate of a political figure.

I have read Jack and Jackie had some problems in their marriage. Really, now, wouldn't *that* be a surprise to everyone in this world? Wouldn't that simply astonish all married couples? Good marriages may be made in heaven, as it is said, but they are worked out no place else but on this earth, between two human beings who are, after all, individuals with their own personalities. If there weren't some problems I should think it ought to be a source of universal amazement, on the order of a miracle. I would like to add that so far as I knew, they had one of the most loving, understanding and devoted relationships that I can imagine.

He loved her and was proud of her and appreciated her. And it would be hard to imagine a better wife for him. She brought so many things that helped round out and fulfil his character. She developed his interests in art, music and poetry – especially poetry, in which he had had only a mild interest before. He learned to delight in it because she had such pleasure from it. In fact, she wrote a poem about him. It is dated October 1953, a month after their marriage.

So far as I know this has never been seen except by those of us in the family and by a few good friends and associates. It is a treasure in several ways and I include it here, in its entirety.

Meanwhile in Massachusetts Jack Kennedy dreamed

Walking the shore by the Cape Cod Sea
Of all the things he was going to be.

He breathed in the tang of the New England fall
And back in his mind he pictured it all,
The burnished New England countryside
Names that a patriot says with pride
Concord and Lexington, Bunker Hill
Plymouth and Falmouth and Marstons Mill
Winthrop and Salem, Lowell, Revere
Quincy and Cambridge, Louisberg Square.
This was his heritage – this his share
Of dreams that a young man harks in the air.
The past reached out and tracked him now
He would heed that touch; he didn't know how.
Part he must serve, a part he must lead
Both were his calling, both were his need.

Part he was of New England stock
As stubborn, close guarded as Plymouth Rock
He thought with his feet most firm on the ground
But his heart and his dreams were not earthbound
He would call New England his place and his creed
But part he was of an alien breed
Of a breed that had laughed on Irish hills
And heard the voices in Irish rills.

The lilt of that green land danced in his blood
Tara, Killarney, a magical flood
That surged in the depth of his too proud heart
And spiked the punch of New England so tart
Men would call him thoughtful, sincere
They would not see through to the Last Cavalier.

He turned on the beach and looked toward his house.

On a green grass lawn his white house stands
And the wind blows the sea grass low on the sands
There his brothers and sisters have laughed and played
And thrown themselves to rest in the shade.
The lights glowed inside, soon supper would ring
And he would go home where his father was King.
But now he was here with the wind and the sea
And all the things he was going to be.

> He would build empires
> And he would have sons
> Others would fall
> Where the current runs

> He would find love
> He would never find peace
> For he must go seeking
> The Golden Fleece

All of the things he was going to be
All of the things in the wind and the sea.

Jacqueline Kennedy
October 1953

Jackie is a rather quiet and shy person and soft-spoken – at least in comparison with most of our brood – and there may have been doubts about her among one or another of Jack's brothers or sisters or cousins at first, but that marvellous poem, which they read, immediately resolved them. Here indeed was an admirable new member, someone who could contribute a new dimension, who had insights and sensitivities challenging to them, and a fascinating person to know.

I should add that she gained full respect also by being 'in there' in athletics. She was a most accomplished horsewoman, and she was quite good at swimming, golf and tennis. She had not played much football. Well, neither had I, so I will turn this over to Dick Clasby:

> I was there and playing with or against Jackie many times. She is a most misunderstood person by the public. People think of her as being elegant, but she was just as much at home in a sweat shirt and a pair of blue jeans. She would be running the beach or the golf course every day at Hyannis Port, and as far as the girls go, Jackie would be right in the middle. On football, I was there in fact at the time she broke her leg. She was running for a pass, she cut quickly – or someone bumped in or something like that – and she did break it or badly sprain it. It stopped the game for a little while. That was more or less the end of her career. She wasn't as fast afterwards.

I admired the fortitude and courage she showed when Jack had to have his back operations. The first one, when he almost died, was in October of 1954: and there she was, still a young bride, deeply in love with her husband and faced with being widowed. She showed 'grace under pressure'. When he was brought down – still on a stretcher – to Palm Beach to recuperate we had a nurse with him the first few weeks, but then the doctor said she wouldn't be needed any more provided there was someone else to change the dressings. Jackie took that on: the doctor taught her how to do it. The incision was very large, it was still draining, and the dressings had to be changed several times a day. She did this skilfully and gently and calmly, and made no comment about it to anyone.

From the very beginning, Jackie and I always got along quite well. When there is friction between a mother-in-law and a daughter-in-law I expect that two main reasons would usually turn out to be that the mother-in-law feels possessive and protective about her son, as if she can't quite accept the fact he's not a little boy any more but a grown-up man with a life to lead; and also that the mother-in-law simply doesn't have enough else to do to occupy her thoughts. Our situation was quite different. Joe and I always encouraged our children to be individuals and to take responsibilities; we loved them and they always knew it, but there was no clinging on our part. I also had so many things to do, so many interests outside the family as well as inside, that I couldn't have found the time to make a nuisance of myself to my daughters- or sons-in-law even if I had been so disposed.

Jackie was remembering:

We spent every Christmas and Easter vacation with them, until the White House. We spent the first four summers with them at Hyannis Port – we didn't have our own house there until Caroline was born. During Jack's convalescence from the operations we spent the whole time with them in Florida, and I had every meal with them. So for long periods I really lived with them.

And I think it's so sick when you hear those mother-in-law jokes on the radio or any of the media. They used to make me sad even before I had a mother-in-law. They really used to make me almost angry when I heard them; because I'd think, are people really like that? And then this woman, my mother-in-law, she just bent over backwards *not* to interfere. If she gave a suggestion, it was in the sweetest way. She sort of set you – set Jack and me – up as an entity.

I think it's doubly extraordinary coming from that strong family where all the ties were so centrifugal.

And so: everything. I loved her very much. And I do now. She was just the most extraordinary mother-in-law, Belle Mère.

As the children married and the tribe increased, we began to have a housing crisis. It never was really solved – still isn't – at the Palm Beach house, because there was only so much space and it seemed foolish to build on or to buy another nearby house or two just so that everybody could be there at the same time for Christmas and Easter and another weekend or two totalling only a few weeks of a year.

Evelyn Jones, who worked for us a lot during that period, has some vivid memories of the logistical situation:

There were always people waiting to get into rooms – there were always more people than rooms. Once Teddy was in a room, it was next to Mrs Kennedy's, and somebody else was arriving. I think it was Mrs Jack and the baby, Caroline. There was no other place to put them but that room – we knew that Teddy was leaving sometime that afternoon or evening, but he hadn't said when. In the help we used to say, 'It's a military secret around here when something's going to happen.' So Teddy came back from wherever he'd been in the afternoon and all of his things were out in the hall. Somebody had to leave that room! He came downstairs and was mumbling to Jean, 'Who put my things out in the hall?' Well, after all . . . And then another time, one day when Mr and Mrs Jack were here – he was President – and they were leaving, Mrs Shriver had been renting a house nearby and she couldn't wait. She had all their bags out and put them in the front hall downstairs, even before they were really out of the room. But all that was quite frequent.

Our house at Hyannis Port had only about the same number of bedrooms but there the problem soon began to solve itself, for the children could take a much longer cumulative time – the summer vacations, and weekends all the way through from after Easter to Thanksgiving – and this made it sensible for them to buy their own houses, especially as their families increased. Bobby and Ethel rented a place the first two or three years; then a house next door to ours came on the market, and they bought it. And that was the beginning of what came to be known as 'the Kennedy Compound' – though that is a misnomer if I ever heard one. A few years after Bobby and Ethel bought their house, another came on the market: it is diagonally opposite ours and directly back to back with Bobby's and Ethel's, and thus the three back yards adjoin, separated by some shrubs and outbuildings. This one became Jack and Jackie's house. It was a spacious and congenial arrangement – everyone in any of the three houses being able to walk back and forth through the back yards – but according to my dictionary a Compound is 'a group of residences enclosed by a barrier'.

Actually, that group of three is bounded on the street-sides by a tall, split-picket, closely nailed fence – enough to give us a bare modicum of privacy from people driving past, which I think anybody would want. The other two sides are open: the beach, and also the lane coming into the properties. Up from those, at the beginning of the lane, Jean and Steve in due course bought a house, a charming one, one of the oldest in Hyannis Port. But there are other houses around them, around us, so if there is a 'compound' Jean and Steve are out of it. So are Eunice and Sarge, who have a house ten minutes' walk from these, below the golf course, facing the ocean. And so are Teddy and Joan, who have a house another ten minutes or so away, with an even better ocean-view, near the top of a high hill known as Squaw Island.

In any case, by 1960 there were houses galore, with plenty of space for Pat and Peter and their children whenever they came to visit, and for friends and everyone's 'surprises', and we were all close enough to see one another as easily and often as we wanted to, which was often.

Joe and I by then were seventy-two and seventy. Both of us were healthy, very active, enjoying life fully. We had suffered grievous losses but we rejoiced in our children who remained, and in our grandchildren. And we had the excitement, the drama, the pride, the great thrill that our eldest surviving son was running for the Presidency of the United States.

17

'Public life is the crown of a career and to a young man it is
the worthiest ambition . . . Politics is still the greatest and
most honourable adventure.'

John Buchan, Lord Tweedsmuir, 1940

'Some men give up their designs when they have almost
reached the goal. Others, on the contrary, obtain a victory
by exerting, at the last moment, more vigorous efforts than
before.'

POLYBIUS, *ca* 150 BC

There were plenty of reasons why it would be impossible for Jack to
get the Democratic nomination, and even if he got it why he would
be unable to win the election.

First, he was too young. In 1960 he would be forty-three, and no one
so young had ever been elected President.

Second, he had no experience in the Executive branch of government, either state or national, whereas the presumed Republican
nominee, Richard Nixon, had two terms in the Vice-Presidency and
had been closely involved in many of the major undertakings of the
Eisenhower administration.

Third, he had little or no support among the Party's established
national leaders: former President Truman, Mrs Roosevelt, Sam
Rayburn, and Lyndon Johnson.

Most important, he was a Catholic. A good many of the more
influential state and city leaders were Catholics themselves. But they
knew how important anti-Catholic bias had been in defeating Al Smith
for the nomination in 1924, and in his loss to Herbert Hoover in the
election of 1928. True, there was now a new generation and religious
tolerance had grown. But how much, how far, and how effectively,
was debatable. There were strong doubts, and in some cases strong
convictions, among Catholic as well as Protestant and Jewish leaders

that Jack's Catholicism would prove to be too severe a handicap. All political leaders dislike backing losers.

Nevertheless, after thinking the matter over and talking with his father, among others, Jack decided to run.

From the moment of the decision, everybody went to work. It wasn't until after Jack made his formal declaration of candidacy – January 2, 1960 – and the state primaries began that I had any direct role in the campaign. But there had been a great deal of preparation that went before, and naturally one couldn't be the mother of the candidate and the wife of Joseph P. Kennedy without knowing something about some of those preliminaries.

It was understood that when Jack ran, Bobby would be his campaign manager. And so, after Adlai Stevenson's nomination in 1956 and when that campaign got under way, arrangements were made for Bobby to travel along in Stevenson's entourage of helpers and advisers and press during the rest of that summer and fall. (For people who haven't been involved in a big campaign, I'm sure it would be rather amazing to see the sheer 'logistics' of getting the candidate and his staff and all concerned from point to point, fed and sheltered, besides arranging for all the conferences with local leaders, for speeches, for radio and television appearances, and for shaking hands up and down Main Street.) Joe wanted Bobby in on all this so he could observe how a national campaign is run, understand the problems, and benefit from any lessons that could be learned. Jack was very much in favour of this. For much of the summer and fall of 1956 Bobby travelled with the Stevenson campaigners. It was a rich experience and Bobby learned a great deal, including some mistakes to avoid, all of which was put to good use later.

Bobby's assignment was characteristic of Joe's way of training our children for public life. It was also another way in which he and I reinforced each other, because I knew the purpose and encouraged it in my own ways. Bobby had been a rather shy and retiring little boy, hemmed in as he was by sisters, and his ego needed boosting and he needed to feel he was interesting to other people. So his father sent him off to Russia. This was meant to be part of his political education, of course, and a valuable addition to his general knowledge and sophistication about the world, but also so that he would have some interesting observations to deliver to Rotary, Kiwanis, Knights of Columbus, Chambers of Commerce, Elks, Masons and other civic and fraternal groups, for their benefit and his. Theirs, because they always need speakers. His, because he would gain poise and confidence in facing an audience and practice in public speaking.

I remember that Bobby was loath to go and really rather depressed about the whole idea. He came back with a lot of colour slides and reams of notes for his lectures. According to a family friend who attended some of these: 'Bobby wanted to do well, he tried, but at first the results were dismal. Sometimes almost embarrassing. But he began to improve. He got better.' And that was the point. He improved with practice, and finally became eloquent.

Joe believed that experience was the best teacher and he was always alert to ways in which the children could be trained for public life. If he made a donation for a hospital, school or charity it was not he who was photographed and applauded and made the presentation speech, but one of the children. When he gave a new gymnasium to Manhattanville in memory of Kathleen and it was ready for dedication, it was Teddy who represented the family, went through the ceremonies, shook the hands and made the speech, though at the time he was barely in his twenties.

Teddy was wearing a dark suit, which was proper for the occasion, but had tan shoes. His father was as quick to notice as I was, and he said, 'We must tell him about that.'

I don't know why Jack, Bobby and Teddy were so hard to educate about such simple rules of dress – *black* shoes with any shade of grey or black or dark blue. Among many reasons for my admiration of Jackie, Ethel and Joan is that they did manage to get their husbands to pay attention to clothes, even to the extent that they finally became known as being quite well dressed. It was something the wives could do, while I seemed doomed to frustration.

Jack was making speeches throughout the country during the late 1950's, and Dave Powers usually accompanied him, doing all sorts of things, from telling jokes and giving political advice, to carrying and unpacking his baggage to save strain on Jack's bad back, and Dave remembers:

> She was great for notes. I might be going somewhere with the Candidate and I'd have his bag and I'd be opening it to unpack and get his things put away. And if we had left from Florida or Hyannis Port or someplace his mother was, there inside could be a note to me: like, make sure he doesn't have holes in his socks. You know, when you're in politics and you're on a stage, sitting up there and the audience looking you over and you begin to feel a sock slipping down, you have to go for that sock and pull it up. Well, evidently

one time when this happened and she was there she noticed a hole in one sock – not a big one, but big enough to notice, so that was the message: 'Make sure the socks Jack wears do not have holes in them.'

I felt that if he were going to take the time to travel and prepare a good speech, why have people distracted by a hole in his sock? I have always felt that appropriate dress and grooming are part of good manners, and that good manners are important – as I freely reminded the children from time to time.

Ethel and Bobby began saving my notes and letters to them on that topic; and not long ago, while Ethel was going through various papers at her house that might help with this book, she came across a round-robin letter from me that she considers a good example of the genre. I defer to her judgment and am putting it in. The date, June 19, 1958, would place it fairly in the hole-in-the-sock episode, at the time Jack was getting up full steam in his pre-primary campaign.

Dear Children,

This letter which I am sending to all of you may be of some help to you in the future.

When there is a clergyman present at luncheon or at dinner, the hostess asks him to say grace and no one is seated until after he has done so. The same thing applies at the end of a meal . . .

When travelling abroad, bring calling cards with you. Send them around to the embassy by courier or leave them yourself with the corner turned down and possibly the address of the hotel. You then will probably get a phone call for luncheon or tea. A lady is supposed to leave a card on every lady of the embassy. A man leaves them on every man, as well as on the ladies. For instance, last year when I was in London, I went to the embassy and left two cards: one for Mrs Whitney and one for her daughter Sara Roosevelt. If your father had been with me, he would have left three. However, you know your father (Grandpa).

Also, when you have gone to a luncheon or dinner at the home of an important person, it is well to write a note of thanks immediately. For instance, when the Cardinal gave a luncheon for Grace Kelly, she wrote a note of thanks that very afternoon and it made a tremendous impression.

I am just giving you these few hints. Perhaps, if you follow them, you will be more of a success socially.

Much love,
Grandma

Ethel has unearthed and given to me another note from those times, and although it doesn't deal with proper manners as such, it does have to do with respect for the value of one's personal possessions – which for most people in the world have always been hard-won. It is dated November 17, 1959, and so fits in here:

Dear Ethel,

Bobby took me to the top floor of your house the other evening and I noticed a Jaeger-Le-Coultre clock in one of the maids' rooms. Since these sell for $50 or $60 in Switzerland – probably $90 here – I would think that you would like to keep it for travelling. It is very easy to get a good electric clock for $4.95 and this would be most suitable . . .

The Jaeger clock is sometimes difficult to set because it has just the one knob; but if you like, I will show you how to operate it . . . when you come for Thanksgiving.

We are already stuffing the turkey and cooking the cranberries.

Much love to all,

G. Ma

And another item from Ethel's collection that probably belongs here simply because of my belief that attention to details, even the minor gestures that are part of human communication, are important in all human relationships. Sometimes it may be inconvenient to give them one's attention, as I dare say it was for Bobby when he received my note dated March 7, 1960, addressed to him at Kennedy Campaign Headquarters, Wisconsin Avenue, Milwaukee:

Dear Bobby,

Will you autograph a copy of your book for the Duke of Windsor and then send it to me here in Palm Beach. I will then see that the Duke receives it.

I believe that the inscription should read: To HRH the Duke of Windsor.   Much love,

G. Ma

I'm sure that Bobby did sign and send the book as soon as he could, although probably not that day or week, because Wisconsin was a terribly important primary and Bobby had a lot on his mind.

I remember so well in that time, especially the winter of 1959–60, Joe's activities behind the scenes on behalf of Jack's candidacy. He would be in the solarium – the 'bull-pen' as it came to be called by the children –

at the Palm Beach house, with a hat, a towel, a cool drink and a telephone, contacting influential leaders all over the country. He worked especially hard on Governor David Lawrence of Pennsylvania who, a Catholic himself, was unable to believe that a Catholic could be elected President and therefore why sacrifice the Democratic Party by giving Jack the nomination. Joe wrote many letters also. And often he would go to Hialeah (and often I would be with him) because some influential political leader or editor or someone able to exert leverage at the Convention would be there that day and Joe would want to talk with him.

I remember also that Jack and his father were in almost daily communication. There would be long conversations. And if Jack had some really bad news to report I would hear his father saying – as usual – 'You know, that may be one of the greatest things that could happen to you . . .' After putting down the telephone he might sit a minute or two looking dejected, or start pacing the floor muttering denunciations of someone. Then, quite likely, he would sit down and start making some more telephone calls.

My active participation in the campaign began in the Wisconsin primary on March 15, a date I would not be able to give with precision, except for another letter that Ethel saved. It was dated March 14, from Palm Beach, and was from me to Bobby's and Ethel's eldest daughter Kathleen (namesake of our beloved Kathleen, 'Kick'), a little girl of only about eight or nine. She was and always has been a delight to me. I am including the letter because I think it helps show that, for us, politics had become a normal part of life:

Dear Kathleen,

I was very glad to hear from you. I wish you were not so far away because I would love to have you come over here often for luncheon or dinner. It would be nicer still if I could read you a story every night.

I have not forgotten about our date for the ballet. The next time I see you I will tell you the story about the Nutcracker Suite, for that is the name of the ballet we will see, either this year or next year.

The weather has been quite cool down here, but we go in swimming just the same. And then we all yell because it's so cold. But after a while we get used to it and then we like it.

I am on my way to Wisconsin to make speeches for Jack. I hope you will be able to take a trip with me some day, but right now, it is very important that you work and study hard in school. When Jack

T.R.

was a little boy, he studied very hard and so he knew all about Paul Revere and George Washington. And when he was older, he studied a lot of European history. I hope that you too will work hard in school.

Grandpa has gone to a ball game, but I know that he would want me to send you his love.

I had some oranges shipped to you last week. I think you and your brothers and sisters will enjoy them. Tell them I send them all a kiss and hope to see them soon. And much love to you, dearest Kathleen.

Affectionately,
Grandma

I spent eight days in Wisconsin. My schedule began around 8.30 a.m. – with a talk to a breakfast club, or a radio or TV appearance, and ended in mid-to-late evening, time enough for seven or eight hours' sleep. There were comments about my stamina, but actually that's all the rest a mature person is likely to need. Of course, as one grows older one needs less sleep, and at the time I was seventy.

The general design of Jack's campaign, as in most of the primaries and then later in the general election, was mainly an extension and elaboration and refinement of the ideas that had been effective in 1946, '52, '58. It was marked by great effort and attention to details on the part of everyone: friends, supporters, allies, recruits and draftees, volunteers, cousins and cousins-in-law in our extended family, and above all the immediate family included. The 'Kennedy teas' and the 'house parties' (coffee or tea or some light refreshment at someone's house, with the neighbours in), with Polly Fitzgerald coming on again, as she had before and always would, tirelessly and gallantly, to make so many necessary arrangements. There are too many people to thank. I can't put all their names in here and I hope they will understand. Everything was handled so efficiently that I was never exhausted in spite of what might seem to be a rather hectic schedule – a schedule that was made for me, without my advice but with my consent, by Bobby and his campaign associates, who decided where and how and when I could help most effectively.

I remember I did have one bright idea that was vetoed. Although it had been many years since I learned German at Blumenthal, I had kept up at least a fair proficiency in it through the years. I knew that Wisconsin has a large population of German descent and I thought this was a situation made to order for me. I could address some German social and community organizations, *Turnverein* and so forth, and perhaps introduce some German expressions into my radio and television interviews, thus capitalizing on my German as I had on my French in the 1952 Senate campaign. But apparently memories of the war were still too strong and the German language was out of fashion even in Milwaukee, so my idea was turned down. I accepted this with disappointment (all those years of study!) but with good grace.

The point was, what could we do for Jack? This was true for all of us. Even at peril. I have already mentioned Teddy's ski-jump as an example. But here is his own version of the event:

It was rather like Jack saying, when someone asked him about being a war hero, 'It was unintentional. They sank my boat.' I went to a ski-jump event near Madison because there was a big crowd there, eight or ten thousand people, and the idea was that somebody would introduce me on the public address system and I would say a few words about the election and vote-for-my-brother and then go around and shake hands. Someone in charge said I should go to the platform at the top of the jump and be introduced from there. So up I went and there were several people waiting and one fellow with an official's badge introduced me and ended by adding, 'Maybe if we give him some encouragement, he'll jump.' The crowd applauded.

I had on ski clothes, more or less, so I would blend into the scene of the day. I could ski pretty well. I should've by that time because my parents, Mother in particular, started me out when I was six or seven, and Dad was in the embassy and Mother took us over to Switzerland for the Christmas and New Year's holidays. And I remember seeing my brother Joe go down that dangerous one-man bob-sled run, and skiing with him and Jack – they were trying to teach me – and I twisted my knee, and they took me down to the hospital and I was laid up for a while. But I had done a lot of skiing later and I was pretty good at the usual things, though I hadn't jumped. I had 'pre-jumped' several times – you go down a short slope and fly out as far as you can get, which could be anywhere from nothing to thirty feet, learning to control the skis and poles and body angle. I knew the principles.

This was an Olympic-size ski-jump, and naturally I had never been on one before, but I thought I'd try. So down I went. In the circumstances, it seemed I should. Somebody was kind enough to offer to lend me a pair of skis. I didn't show the grace of an eagle but I managed to keep everything going in the right direction and landed upright about seventy-five feet or so away and skied on down the slope and was very happy still to be alive. There was applause. Maybe there were some extra votes for Jack . . .

I certainly never went around looking for things like that. But I did find myself involved in a similar situation later on during the general election. They put me in charge of the campaign in the Mountain States, so one day I was at a big rodeo in Montana. I was there with the same idea, to be introduced and say something about my brother and shake some hands. But they said no political figures were going to be introduced. They said, 'If you want to ride, you'll be introduced like everybody else.' Which would be like, 'Ted Kennedy, now comin' out of chute 4.'

I knew how to ride a horse. I never had been on a bronco. But if that's the way it had to be . . . so I got on the bronco and we went out the chute and I think I may have lasted six seconds – it seemed like an eternity – before I was thrown. No real damage, no broken bones. People seemed to think I had done all right for an amateur. They like to test you in that part of the country. Possibly I had conveyed something about our family – about Jack – that resulted in a few more votes.

Jack called me shortly after that to say that he had just talked with the State Chairman in Wyoming, who told him I was coming to Rock Springs the next Saturday night. They were arranging to have a sharpshooter shoot a cigarette out of my mouth at 20 yards. Jack said, casually, that he didn't think I had to go through with that if I didn't want to, but . . .

Teddy was always stalwart and optimistic from the time he was a little child. I think none of us was surprised by his ski-jumping and bronco-riding. (Jack had been kidding Ted about the Wyoming sharpshooter.) If anyone among us was surprised about any of us, I suppose it would have been about Jackie. This was her first experience of hard campaigning. She had been out with Jack a few times in the 1958 Senatorial campaign but there had been no question about his winning, only about winning a landslide victory that would help establish him for 1960. We knew she had plenty of spunk and courage, but we also knew she was a rather shy person who found a lot of public attention uncomfortable. She was not a natural-born campaigner.

But there she was travelling with Jack in motorcades, standing in receiving lines, shaking hands along Main Street, and even taking off on her own now and then into supermarkets to announce herself as the wife of John F. Kennedy, Presidential candidate, and urging the shoppers to give him their votes. All of us were newly impressed. She was a wonder.

There were numerous candidates for the Democratic nomination that year. Among them were Senator Lyndon Johnson, Senator Stuart Symington, and former Governor and twice nominee Adlai Stevenson, who was being encouraged by many admirers such as Mrs Roosevelt to seek the Presidency again and who found that prospect pleasing. The only candidate, however, who was willing to contest the primaries with Jack in 'neutral' states (those uncommitted to a 'favourite son' or other leader) was Senator Hubert Humphrey of Minnesota. Thus he was Jack's opponent in Wisconsin.

He seemed to have all the advantages. The two states are neighbours; both with a predominantly rural, farming character and economic interests; both noted for their Progressive, Farmer-Labour, Populist, Socialist sentiments. Senator Humphrey was almost as well known and admired in Wisconsin as in his own constituency of Minnesota, and deservedly so. He is a fine, sincere, intelligent and effective public servant. Jack liked and admired him and this was reciprocated by Senator Humphrey. Actually there weren't any essential points of disagreement between them except one: who was going to be the Democratic nominee? Jack ran as an Easterner, the son of a well-known 'capitalist', and with little or no record to offer as a champion of the special interests and concerns of the Midwest farm-belt.

Consequently, when Jack won against such odds it seemed to me that it should have been a cause for celebration and satisfaction. Yet somehow the loser seemed to be in the position of being the winner, or at least the presumed winner in the next primary. Political chess of this sort has always baffled me. I quote Kenny O'Donnell, Bobby's friend and assistant and later Jack's assistant at the White House, who was there all the time:

Kennedy won in Wisconsin with more popular votes than any candidate in the history of the state's primary, carrying six of the ten Congressional districts and getting two-thirds of the delegate votes. That seemed good enough to me, but it was not good enough to satisfy the experts, because Kennedy failed to carry the three so-called Protestant districts in the western part of the state and lost to Humphrey in the Second District, around Madison, where we had expected to win. In the hotel room at Milwaukee Eunice Kennedy was puzzled to see her brother glancing at the impressive popular vote figures with a glum expression on his face. 'What does it all mean, Johnny?' she said to him.

'It means that we've got to go to West Virginia in the morning and do it all over again,' Jack said. 'And then we've got to go on to Maryland and Indiana and Oregon, and win all of them.'

As older readers may remember, West Virginia attained fame in national politics in 1924 when its delegates at the Democratic Convention steadily, through dozens of ballots, voted for Oscar W. Underwood in order to prevent the nomination of Governor Alfred E. Smith of New York, primarily because Smith was a Catholic. The population of West Virginia was still almost wholly Protestant and still suspicious of 'Catholic influences' in US government and thought that a Catholic President might 'take orders from the Pope'. To all of us, and probably most of all to Jack, this would be about as sensible to say that American members of the Episcopalian church would 'take orders' from the Archbishop of Canterbury about secular matters. But illogical as it was, 'the Catholic issue' had to be faced, against almost the worst odds imaginable, and with Catholic political leaders such as Governor Lawrence of Pennsylvania waiting to take their cue from the outcome and filled with pessimism about his chances in West Virginia.

A public opinion poll had been taken in the state a few months earlier and showed Jack winning against Hubert Humphrey – if they ever ran against each other there – by 70 per cent to 30 per cent. But a similar poll taken after the primary campaign was actually under way reversed the figures, showing 70 per cent for Humphrey. Kenny O'Donnell has described the welcome that he, Bobby and Larry O'Brien received when they arrived from Wisconsin and went to a meeting of West Virginia campaign workers:

'Well,' Bobby said to them pleasantly, 'what are our problems?'

A man stood up and shouted, 'There's only one problem. He's a Catholic. That's our Goddamned problem!'

The room broke into an uproar with everybody yelling at us that nobody in the state would vote for a Catholic in a contested Presidential primary . . . all over West Virginia they were getting abuse and ridicule from their own friends and neighbours because they were supporting a Catholic. I began to gather that apparently Kennedy's Catholicism was not well known to most West Virginians until the recent reports of his religious problems in the Wisconsin primary were given widespread coverage by local newspapers and television news shows. Overnight our whole situation in West Virginia had changed, and all of the careful and hopeful planning . . . was on the brink of going down the drain. I looked at Bobby. He seemed to be in a state of shock. His face was as pale as ashes.

When we left the meeting, Bobby went to a telephone booth and called Jack in Washington . . . Jack was taken aback by Bobby's discouragement. 'It can't be that bad,' he said, and reminded Bobby of the pre-campaign poll. Bobby said, 'The people who voted for you in that poll have just found out that you're a Catholic.'

In 1952 I had been made a Papal Countess by Pope Pius XII. In the terms of the scroll or patent-of-nobility delivered to me by Cardinal Spellman, this was in recognition of an 'exemplary life and . . . many charities'. Understandably, I considered this a tremendous honour, especially as it was the only one conferred by Pius XII during his long reign. I had used the title very seldom, only at special events and ceremonies of the Church; and only in Italy or France or other predominately Catholic countries. But in West Virginia, with 'Popery' suddenly the big issue, the media surely would bring this up in interviews and feature articles if I came into the state to campaign. I would have been, to say the least, 'counter-productive'.

So I wasn't invited. I don't recall any discussion of the fact that I might be a problem. Bobby just said something like, 'Mother, after you worked so hard in Wisconsin, go on back to Palm Beach and get some rest for a few days. Then we're booking you into Indiana, and Nebraska, and Maryland, and maybe some other places . . . we'll work it out and Polly will have the list.'

I was entirely used to this procedure. I never knew – and it never bothered me – who chose the places for me. They were places where the committee thought I could attract a group and be effective with it.

Although I wasn't involved in the West Virginia campaign, I do have one vivid memory of it. Franklin D. Roosevelt, Jr was visiting us at Palm Beach earlier that year. We all had dinner and then went out to the patio, in the tropical moonlight, and the talk went on. Of course it turned to politics, and then to West Virginia and the questions as to whether Jack should contest the primary there and, if so, whether FDR Jr would go into the state to campaign for him.

This scene, the conversation and situation, stays in my memory for two reasons because I felt that young Franklin had so many qualities and assets that almost no elective office seemed beyond his reach. He had a marvellous personality. He had the smile, the voice, the facility and vocabulary, the stature and bearing and stalwart good looks, the 'charisma'; and above all, in terms of practical politics, he had the magic that was associated with his name. I remember that when Joe and I retired that evening we agreed we were thankful that FDR Jr was not a candidate in the primaries or election against our son, because we thought that Jack or anyone in the world would have had an extremely hard time winning any election against him.

I quote Kenny O'Donnell:

Kennedy's most valuable campaigner in West Virginia was Franklin D. Roosevelt Jr, whose famous name is held in reverence in the coal-mining state. Roosevelt's father pushed NRA legislation that gave coal-miners the right to organize and to get decent living wages . . . Recruiting Franklin Roosevelt for duty in West Virginia was Ambassador Kennedy's idea. The Ambassador [this, of course, had become an honorary title; just as anyone who has been a Governor or Senator or General is usually addressed by that title thereafter] also saw to it that letters to voters in West Virginia, praising Senator Kennedy and signed by Roosevelt, were shipped to Hyde Park, New York, to be postmarked and mailed from there. . . . Roosevelt spoke for Kennedy all over the state and was mobbed by admirers wherever he went. Appealing to the militant patriotism of the West Virginians, he heavily emphasized the Senator's war record, sometimes making it seem as if his own destroyer and PT 109 had fought in the same battles . . . [and] one of his often-used and most effective lines: Holding up two fingers tightly pressed together, he said, 'My daddy and Jack Kennedy's daddy were just like that!'

Jack decided that the only way to deal with the religious issue was to face it head on, bring it up himself in his speeches, invite questions from everyone about any and every aspect of it. To the great credit of the people of West Virginia they listened, understood and responded to the man and the real issues. They voted for Jack by such a majority that Senator Humphrey withdrew from the race in the remaining primaries.

It was said later Jack had, in effect, won the Democratic Party's nomination by the victory in West Virginia, but that was far from being so. He could have *lost* the Party's nomination there. But what the win meant, mainly, was that the religious issue could be surmounted and thus Jack's candidacy was still alive and well and it was possible to glimpse an ultimate success – provided everybody went on working as hard as possible to achieve it.

The White House Years

21 At the Inaugural Ball, 1961. My dress, by Molyneux, is the one I wore
for my presentation at Court twenty years earlier

The White House Years

22 *Above* Jack chatting with President Khrushchev, Vienna 1961

Below With Mrs Khrushchev, Jackie and me

I receive with Jack at the White House reception for Haile Selassie

23: *Above* Jackie and I chat with Mme de Gaulle upon Jackie's arrival at Orly Airport for the State visit in 1961

Below Jack and Jackie greeting Casals after his White House concert

The White House

24 *Left* One hour after this photograph was taken J suffered the stroke that him paralysed, Decemb 1961

Below Jack with Caroli John in the White Hous

I kept some diary notes during that time. Here are a few, dated June 23, 24 and 25:

Jack and Jackie, Jean and the children down at Hyannis this weekend for the summer. Went for dinner Friday and Saturday nights at Jackie's house, but Jack looked tired and went to bed early. Saturday he played golf in the morning with Jean and later when I went over they all were playing croquet. Caroline was out there too, and the dog Charlie, racing back and forth chasing Jack's ball. Whereupon, Jack harangued the dog at the top of his lungs.

. . . Jack on the phone and particularly incensed because Governor Meyner of New Jersey will not come out for him. After dinner, we call up Dad. As usual, he was reassuring, said it was 'in the bag', and that everyone got nervous about these things near the end.

As Jack's mother, I am confident that Jack will win because his father says so, and through the years I have seen his predictions and judgments vindicated almost without exception. And so, I believe it. He also says, and has said all along, that if Jack gets the nomination he can beat Nixon.

We are all furious at Governor Brown of California and Governor Lawrence of Pennsylvania because they will not come out for Jack now. Their support would clinch the nomination for him. Joe has worked on Lawrence all winter but he still can't believe a Catholic can be elected. He has been one of the most exasperating and tantalizing forces . . .

This was only about two and a half weeks before the Convention opened at Los Angeles, and Jack had been campaigning actively as a declared candidate for nearly six months, and as an undeclared one for almost four years.

The Convention itself is rather blurred in my memory, perhaps because I was excited. We all were in or near Los Angeles except for Jackie, who by then was in mid-pregnancy and Jack didn't want her exposed to the tumult of Los Angeles so she stayed home. Jack had two places, a hotel suite and a small apartment which was far from the Convention scene where he could relax. Joe and I and other of our family members stayed at Marion Davies's house. Joe said he would much rather remain there on the evening of the balloting, away from the crowds and the photographers. The rest of us were at the Convention hall. Pat was a member of the California delegation. Teddy was a floor manager. Bobby was at his command post. I went to

Convention hall and sat in one of the boxes with Eunice, my niece Ann Gargan, and a few of the older grandchildren.

After Jack won the nomination on the first ballot and came to the hall, Eunice and Pat and I were called to the platform to stand with him as everyone cheered and waved. It was a very proud moment in my life.

Afterwards I was on the road during a good deal of that summer and fall, and when it was all over Jack gave me a map of the United States which he had marked to show the places I had gone to take part in some function of special importance and signed it, 'For Mother – With Thanks.' The map shows that I was in 14 states and made 46 appearances significant enough for something to be put on the record. Actually I was in a number of other places as well, coming or going or stopping over for a rest. Somewhat to my own surprise, I found myself turning into a regular 'politician'. I didn't miss a chance to ask anyone directly to vote for Jack. I talked with taxi-drivers, elevator operators, waiters and waitresses, porters and bellmen, manicurists and anyone with whom I might have a brief chance to strike up a conversation.

Taxi-drivers are, of course, proverbially great conversationalists, and on the way from the airport to my hotel the dialogue would begin with my remark: 'Well, how's business? Probably it will be better when a Democrat gets in.' Some of them would sort of size me up in the rear-view mirror and I often thought they felt I was too well dressed to be a Democrat and was a Republican *agent provocateur*. Others would respond readily but often objected to Jack because he was too young for the job. 'He's young in years,' I would say, 'but not in experience, and isn't that what's most important?' Or I would hear, 'We always have a war with the Democrats in office.' I would reply that John Kennedy had had tragic deaths in his own family in the last war. He had seen good friends killed or maimed, and had himself been severely wounded. Surely this had given him a horror of war. Often, the problem of his Catholicism would arise. I remember hearing variations on the theme, 'I don't want the Pope running things over here.' I would answer that the Pope lives in Italy but certainly doesn't run things there, even though it's a Catholic country; and that France is mainly Catholic and De Gaulle was a Catholic but the Pope certainly did not give any orders to De Gaulle; and that Catholics in the US Congress never voted as a bloc; and therefore the whole 'Catholic issue' was nonsense. If, by the end of the trip, he hadn't figured out that I was related to Jack I would tell him who I was; in which case, usually, his face would light up, he would say he was glad to meet me and he was certainly going to vote for Jack. The same thing generally happened with waitresses, baggage porters and others: they might have a rather vacant, detached look at first, but almost always they would end up assuring me that Jack would get their votes. I remember sitting next to another woman on the airplane. We got into a conversation which I drew around to my favourite subject, and by the time we landed she asked me to send her a large supply of campaign buttons.

Teddy was asked recently about what I might have added to the campaign:

> Mother is superb in talking with a group. She puts out; she turns on right away; she works at it and knows what the audience's interests and sentiments are likely to be. She has a feel for these things and also she has done her homework and is very much aware, plugged-in, and she has been thinking.
>
> But where she comes through best is in a person-to-person relationship. She's interested in people as individuals, genuinely very interested in them as individual human beings, and I think this is a very important part of her success, not only in campaigning but in all the aspects of her life. People feel the interest she has in them: she is able to communicate that to them.
>
> Time and again people say about Jack that even when he was President he had this very personal interest in anyone he was with. He was listening, responding, communicating, fully. And this came from her.

Here are some other diary notes of the late summer and fall of 1960, the first one at Hyannis Port soon after the nomination.

> Jack is home today. We all went to his house last night. Ethel, Joan, Jackie and I. He eats ravenously of lobster and corn on the cob. According to Dr Jordon of the Lahey Clinic, corn and lobsters are the worst things for a tummy like I have and Jack has. The roses are so beautiful now at the Cape. The fogs and the climate here seem exactly right for them. In the paper this morning there was an article about the superb Kennedy organization. The efficiency – the results – all this because it is a family team at the centre, with Jack, his brothers, his sisters and brothers-in-law, and the overall strategy of their father, who I doubt will ever get credit for the constant, unremitting labour he has devoted to making his son President.

October 7, 1960; Jacksonville, Florida: It was our anniversary today but

I almost forgot it this morning when I telephoned Joe . . . as I am campaigning now. Had planned to take a plane but ran into an electric storm just before Jacksonville so decided to stay here all night. I went to headquarters this morning and photos were taken. As they were last night on arrival, although I had not expected them and I was in flat shoes and a tweed coat. With my hair windblown, after having been matted down half the day by perspiration from the television lights and from the humidity which seems to pervade the South at this time of the year.

I have been thinking all day of Jack and his debate with Nixon and praying, praying, praying. It must be such a strain with all the world watching, waiting, and then reacting, and discussing, criticizing.

The immediate reactions, I suppose, depend upon the community. Like Hot Springs [I was there during the first debate], where most people said the debate was even because Hot Springs has a strongly Republican audience who did not discuss it in an analytical way.

But so many women in the reception lines in the days since then seem to regard Jack almost like a new Lincoln. 'Thank you for giving us someone like your son.' Or, 'I am praying for your son every night,' or 'I heard his speech and I just know that he is going to save this country,' or 'I am a Presbyterian (or Methodist, or Baptist) and I'm for your son.' Others might say with a giggle, 'I love your son,' or 'I touched him. He is so good-looking.'

October 8: I watched Jack last night on the debate, praying through every sentence. As I had prayed during the day. He looked more assured than Nixon and looked better physically. Jack seemed to have all the initiative and once or twice rose to inspiring heights of oratory . . . Jack really looks, sounds and acts like young Lincoln . . .

October 9: The policeman came into the hairdresser's and said comment was that Jack had won the debate, or rather people had liked him better.

People think that Jack speaks too fast. I agree and have already told him, because the audience has to become accustomed to his Boston accent as well as to the inflections and the modulations of his voice. The newspapers have also commented on this.

It has often been said that the series of debates tipped the election in Jack's favour and were really the crucial factor of the campaign. If so, it was an odd turn-about. For Mr Nixon had been the star of his college debating team, a lawyer trained in presenting evidence and making

rebuttals, a Naval Intelligence officer trained in gathering and presenting information, a Vice-President seasoned in national campaigns. As
Lem Billings pointed out, Jack had no appetite for public speaking as a
schoolboy. I think this is another reason why Jack's career – his
development and his victories in the face of challenge – should be an
inspiration to young men who have had years of perplexity and self-
doubt before deciding who they are and who they want to become.

While I was watching the debates and was hoping and praying for
Jack at every point or *riposte* he made, I found myself wondering about
Richard Nixon's mother, who was watching and listening somewhere
and was just as involved emotionally as I was. From everything I had
heard she was a fine woman and devoted mother – who had suffered
the tragic loss of a child – and was firm in the faith and principles of her
Quakerism. Of course she had the same love and hopes for her son as
I had for mine; and, as I saw Jack doing so extremely well, my sym-
pathies were also with her.

The evening of Election Day we were all at Hyannis Port waiting for
the returns to come in. Bobby's house had been converted into election
headquarters, so that's where the action was. It looked and often
sounded like chaos – teletype machines clattering, telephones ringing,
television sets going, typewriters clicking, and people walking around
with pencils and pieces of paper in their hands and talking with other
people earnestly about something that was happening in one place or
another and what that might mean. There were lots of people. The
whole top echelon of the campaign staff; the expert analysts such as
Lou Harris; newspaper reporters, photographers, stenographers, telephone operators, and many others. Bobby was in the middle of it all.
Jack was in and out. Teddy, Sarge, Peter and Steve, and the girls, the
cousins and friends, were doing whatever was helpful. Everybody was
working and not interfering with anybody else. There wasn't very
much kidding or very much gaiety. The race was very close, and there
was great tension in the air. One or two people came over to our house
now and then for a sandwich or a drink or a change of scene. Jack
would come in to tell his father about a new development. And Joe
and I would be wandering in and out of Bobby's house. We had very
little conversation that evening.

Bobby was tense. He was trying to get the latest exact figures and to
project from them how the counts in critical districts were likely to
develop. I didn't want to interrupt his train of thought. I went over to
see Jackie a couple of times at her house because she was rather alone

there, out of the mêlée because she was in the eighth month of preg-
nancy. Jack was deeply preoccupied.

I was moving around a lot. For me, movement and activity have
always been necessities in times of stress. People have asked me if I
prayed. I'm sure I did, even though it was a little late for that after
the polls had closed. But I pray instinctively – instead of talking to
myself, or burdening others – it's my natural reaction.

I couldn't bear to think that Jack would lose. In spite of the un-
certainties, the figures that shifted back and forth all that evening and
into the night I kept thinking, he'll win, of course he will. Finally late
that night, after the tide seemed to have swung in his favour, I went to
bed in order to be rested enough to be somewhat prepared for the
outcome, whatever it would be.

I'm sure everyone who was there has a store of special memories.

Eunice:

> It was very long. Everybody would be walking back and forth from
> house to house. Jack was over at our father's house a lot, and back
> to Bobby's to see what was on there, and now and then over to his
> house to check there and to sit and rest a while.
>
> There were a lot of people and a lot of discussing of votes in each
> state. We were behind in Illinois, and everybody was waiting for
> Chicago, Chicago. The West Coast came in late – the time zone – and
> of course is terrifically important. Sometime early the next morning –
> there were a few hours' sleep in there for most people, but we were
> still walking around – I ran into Jack and asked him if he had won
> and he said, we don't know yet, we haven't heard from California –
> or maybe it was still Chicago – so it's not over yet. And made some
> funny remark. He had his walking-stick and was going for a walk
> on the beach.
>
> No one ever felt we were going to lose, I think everybody managed
> to – we never thought we weren't going to win. There was a general
> air of confidence. Of course you're never sure of anything. But we
> always thought we were going to win everything, actually. Trying
> very hard and usually winning.

I think the outcome must have been decided sometime towards day-
break because it was around 4.30 – as I learned later – that the Secret
Service men closed in around our adjoining properties and particularly
around Jack's house, taking over the protection of the presumed
President-elect.

Pat (in a letter, much later):

> I remember that around 3 a.m., when it looked good for Jack – later reversed, but reversed again – we all went into the kitchen for something to eat. Jack left later by the kitchen door and I can see him now, crossing into Bobby's back lawn in the dark, walking to his own house, and the Secret Service closing in right behind him. A couple of us said (hardly able to believe it): 'Good night, Mr President.'

Later that morning, when it was clear that Jack was indeed the President-elect, it was, of course, essential that he address the nation through the press and television. Arrangements had been made at the US Armory in Hyannis. Cars assembled to carry Jack, his family and his staff members there.

Pat remembers:

> We all got into the caravan of cars in the circle in front of the house – everybody but Dad, who was on the front porch, back a little in the shadows, looking very happy. He never wanted even to imply any credit to himself for Jack's successes, and he had decided to stay at home out of the range of photographers and reporters. Jack suddenly realized what was happening. He got out of the car, went back up to the porch, and told Dad to come along and hear his speech. Jack insisted on it. And finally he talked Daddy into getting into our car.

> At the Armory, Jack's audience consisted of the press, TV crews, and a small crowd of townspeople. The Hyannis public school stands directly across the street. For reasons hard to understand, the school authorities didn't choose to let classes out so the children could see and hear the newly elected President of the United States. Cape Codders are noted for reserve and taciturnity, and it is said that 'summer people' never are quite accepted by the year-around native residents. But Jack had been coming there since he was about eight years old; and in these unusual circumstances I would have thought they could have made an exception, but they didn't.

Towards the end of perhaps the busiest, most exciting months of our lives we closed the house for the winter and made the annual migration to Palm Beach.

We had Thanksgiving at Palm Beach and, needless to say, it was a day of very special thanksgiving. Jack and Jackie and Caroline couldn't be with us because by then the new baby was due to arrive at almost any time and Jackie remained near her own doctor and hospital in

Washington. John Fitzgerald Kennedy Jr was born early in the morning of November 25, to the great relief and joy of all, especially Jack, who adored Caroline but also wanted a son.

I know I was in residence and functioning by December 1 because that is the date of a note I wrote from there to Ethel, who saved it and thinks it belongs in this book:

> Dear Ethel,
>
> While I was there, I talked quite a bit to the children separately about Thanksgiving and also about Mass.
>
> Joe [Joseph Patrick Kennedy III, Ethel's and Bobby's eldest son] seemed to know quite a little about it.
>
> I think in the future it might be well to review history and current events with him so that he may remember facts in that way. You might ask him questions like who the President of France is; what holidays are national holidays or church holidays, or both; the name of the Queen of England, etc.
>
> This will give you an idea of our discussions.
>
> Love,
G'Ma

Jack stayed on in Washington through early December, busily occupied in selecting his Cabinet and other high officials for his Administration. Yet he also found time too to pay attention to Caroline and visit Jackie and baby John two or three times a day. The baby had been delivered by Caesarean operation, which of course meant that Jackie's recovery from childbirth took longer than usual. However, by December 9 she was well enough to travel and he brought her and the baby and Caroline and a nurse and nursemaid aboard his plane, the *Caroline*, to stay with us during the Christmas and New Year's holidays and until we all went back north for the Inauguration. He was at the house for a long weekend, then had to return to Washington, then came back, and was back and forth several times (with flocks of Secret Service men and swarms of journalists) during the next four or five weeks.

I have an extraordinarily vivid memory, which is of Jack visiting the White House on an official courtesy call and to be advised by President Eisenhower about current important matters of state. The retiring President met the new one at the White House steps. They shook hands, smiled, stood together and chatted a minute or so for the photographers, and then President Eisenhower – looking, I thought, rather like a kindly uncle turning over the keys to the manor to a bright and well-favoured nephew – escorted Jack inside.

It was then at last, in that one small episode seen on television, that I realized fully that Jack was going to be the President.

This may seem strange. But Joe, who was somewhere else, saw the same news programme and told me later he had had exactly the same reaction. The almost impossible dream had come true.

During the intervals with us at Palm Beach, Jack was almost as busy as in Washington, meeting and talking with all sorts of people, putting his government together, working on his Inaugural Address, issuing announcements and answering questions at daily press conferences. Often he conducted the latter almost any place around the house or grounds, but if it were a formal conference with a large group from various media it would most likely be held on the spacious patio at the front of the house – where so often, in earlier, quieter times we had enjoyed dining *al fresco* at a few small tables and staying on, with a few guests and the household help, to watch a film. One of these big conferences took place late in December at the time of Senator William Fulbright's visit. He was chairman of the Senate's Foreign Relations Committee, and there had been a lot of speculation that he might be the new Secretary of State. I have some diary notes:

After a game of golf, Jack and Senator Fulbright came in through the back door, showered, and then went out to the patio, which was bright with klieg lights and full of cameramen and reporters, about fifty of them. The camera people kept moving around and the reporters asked a lot of questions which Jack and Fulbright, looking showered and spick and span, answered with poise and good humour. Ann Gargan was visiting us. She and I stayed in the upper balcony, hidden in the dark, and watched.

I had met Fulbright earlier in the day, found him charming, relaxed, easy to talk to, and very interesting. Mrs Fulbright joined us for dinner. Looks refined, conservative, middle-aged, greying hair; simple and intelligent. Liked her, as she was pleasant and natural and contributed to the conversation without intruding, which after all is the proper role for a wife, I believe. Men have had the experience and the knowledge and people want to know what they think, and not the opinions of their wives.

(I was referring to matters of state, in which the men have the knowledge. Generally speaking, I think it is very broadening, for husbands as well as wives, for wives to participate in conversations.)

There was a continual stream of guests, all of them notables of some degree, which kept me in a state of hyper-activity. I'm sure I went around much of the time covered with notes from myself to myself. It was a hectic time for the help. They all bore up bravely and cheerfully, showing initiative and gallantry under fire. Evelyn recalls some episodes:

One day Mr Johnson, who was going to be Mr Jack's Vice-President, and Mr Sam Rayburn and several others were coming. Mr Johnson and Mr Rayburn would be in the house, that was an understanding already made, but the question became, which rooms?

We were working on this the day before, and Mrs Jack didn't want Caroline and her nursemaid moved upstairs next to the baby and his nurse – she wanted Caroline down next to her, in an adjoining room in that suite. But we had already discussed and decided the only way was to put Rayburn in Mrs Kennedy's room and put Mr Johnson in the next one – she insisted he go in the next one and share the bath with the nurse and the baby – and you know how that would have been. The other alternative was to move Caroline and the nurse up to the adjoining bath with the other nurse and the baby, but she didn't want that.

The next morning when I came to work everything was in a furore. I said, 'What's going on?' The cook, Matilda, said, '*The Johnsons are at the airport and they'll be here for breakfast!*' Not he, but the Johnsons. So I said, 'Well, all right, you take care of breakfast, and I'll see what I can do.'

Well, after quite a few other complications we finally did get everyone arranged, or rearranged, and Mr Jack said to me, 'Oh, that's fine. Good. Good, and thank you, Evelyn, very much.'

But then guess what happened? Senator Mike Mansfield flew down later that day to join in the meetings with the others, and Jack invited him to spend the night at the house.

There was no place to put him except in one of those small rooms in the back: the area the architect designed as servants' quarters in the early days when people at Palm Beach used to have a lot of live-in help. He didn't mind at all. They're nice rooms. But the layout of the house is confusing to someone who doesn't know it. And after the meetings, when he came back into the house late that night, and one of the Secret Service boys showed him the way through the back entrance and through to the back stairway, he went on up from there – quietly and in the dark, not wanting to disturb anybody – and opened the first door on his left, which he remembered was the one to his room. He lit a match to find the light switch and at the same moment heard a woman's tense voice calling, 'Who's there?' And he was startled to see Mrs Kennedy's Swedish masseuse sitting up in bed with the covers drawn up around her and a frightened look on her face.

I'm sure he didn't wait to reply, 'I am Senator Mansfield of Montana, a trusted friend of the next President of the United States of America and Majority Leader of the Senate during his Administration.'

As I heard the story next day, he said something apologetic and got out of there as fast as he could, barking his shins on the way, around the corner and into the room next door, which was his room. I expect that's one of the first events of the Kennedy administration that Senator Mansfield has always remembered.

The house was in a state of happy chaos. Here are a couple of other diary notes of mine that will help demonstrate both the happiness and the chaos:

January 4, 1961: The photographer from *Harper's Bazaar*, Avedon, has been here to take pictures of Jackie. Also with him two young women, one of whom I heard later was the sister of Leonard Bernstein, the young conductor of the New York Philharmonic. Kenneth, the famous hairdresser from New York, came down and cut Jackie's hair the previous day and then came over that morning to set it, before the photographs. The furniture in the living-room was all moved around and a mammoth white screen was hung from the ceiling to the floor for a backdrop. Jackie told me later that Kenneth was not going to charge her for coming here but probably would charge her later when he goes to Washington for the Inauguration. Then a fitter from Cassini, the dressmaker, appeared carrying long boxes containing Jackie's dresses, most of which were not yet finished but were advanced enough for photos.

She is still convalescing and rested in between. She looks marvellous, as her figure is much better than previously, I believe.

Jack came in – freshly shaven, handsome, well groomed, poised. The next thing I knew Caroline was romping about all dressed up in an adorable white organdy dress and a pink ribbon in her hair. She had been outside with her nurse awaiting the call for pictures. The most precious addition was yet to come: John F. Jr, who looked infinitely adorable as he lay cuddled in his mother's arms being photographed. As it was rather a cool day I worried that he would get cold, because his head was exposed for a long time in the living-room which has no heat and which may be draughty, although the photographer's big screen probably cut off a lot of the draught.

It seemed that the house was full of dressmakers and photographers and assistants. A lot of milling around.

LeMoyne Billings is here. I heard Jack say to him afterwards, 'Well, that was certainly a morning wasted.'

January 5, 1961: I was going to make an appointment for myself with the hairdresser downtown when Joe told me that Kenneth was here again, and Avedon and the same screen and same personnel appeared all over again, much to my surprise as no one told me they were coming.

Jackie and Jack have the bedroom downstairs in the extreme corner of the house, which is Jack's old room. She has to rest. She is reading all those books from the Library of Congress on the White House. She has just written a very good article, 'How To Bring Up A Child To Be Happy'. One thing which she suggested was the merit of learning a piece of poetry for the mother's birthday present, or drawing a picture no matter how crude. Both ideas stimulate the child and encourage its interest and please the mother and they are simple pleasures which can be developed in any home.

Well, anyway, I dashed downstairs, found Kenneth in Jackie's room just setting her hair on mammoth-sized rollers. He said for me to shampoo my hair upstairs, and then he would set it. Which he proceeded to do. It looked very well until I played golf in the afternoon. Meanwhile I had to sit under the drier in the guest room, next door to where Jack and Lem were staying; so while I sat, the maid packed Jack's clothes, LeMoyne dashed in and out opening doors, and Kenneth dashed in to see if I was dry.

After my hair had been set and combed out, I had to walk back through the living-room in my long blue bathrobe. I nodded to one of the photographer's assistants and warned her about the loose neckline on Jackie's half-finished velvet dress. I looked out the window to the front lawn and saw someone was swinging Caroline, of which I disapproved, as I thought she would be too tired for the photographers. Then I took a quick look at John F. Jr, wrapped in blankets and awaiting his turn to be photographed. And I caught a glimpse of the Secret Service men on the beach outside on the ocean-front.

Boxes are piled galore in the back part of the house, presents for Jackie and the baby, mostly for the baby, and everything had to be opened first and examined by the Secret Service. None very expensive but all appreciated as sincere tokens.

If I go into the study, Jack probably is in there in conference. If I want to go out the front door to the street the door is locked behind me almost before I get out. There are policemen and Secret Service men there, and often a crowd of fifty to a hundred people gathered in hopes of seeing Jack.

The back door is also always locked now. None of this makes too much difference to me except I am a bit confounded as to where I should enter and exit. If I go out my front door there are people there and having their pictures taken. Last night I went out the back way through the help's dining-room, and there was a hairdresser from the town delving into a bowl of salad. Evidently she had waited quite a while to do somebody's hair and was hungry, and the salad bowl was on the maids' table and they had disappeared to their respective duties. I was dumbfounded, and she was doubly so at seeing me, and me exiting through the servants' quarters. She just threw up her hands and I gave a laugh and she gave a laugh and out I went.

Not long afterwards, Jack and Jackie and their family went back to their house in Georgetown. Bobby and Ethel lived about half an hour away in McLean, Virginia. The rest of us, when we assembled at the scene a few days before Inauguration Day, which was January 20, lived in Georgetown in several houses which were rented at the prevailing rate of $1000 per house for five days. Joe and I had Teddy and Joan and Ann Gargan with us at our house.

The afternoon before the Inauguration it began to snow. And it snowed and snowed and turned into one of the worst snowstorms in the history of Washington. By evening traffic was hopelessly snarled, cars were sliding and struggling through the drifts, and many were stalled, immobilized and abandoned.

Pat and Peter and some of their friends in the entertainment world, especially Roger Edens, the brilliant director, had worked long and hard to organize a pre-Inaugural variety show – a Gala – and some celebrated performers, including Sir Laurence Olivier, Alan King, Helen Traubel, Leonard Bernstein, Ella Fitzgerald, Sidney Poitier, Ethel Merman and many others, would be contributing their names and services to honour the new President. Obviously Joe and I wanted to be there and should somehow manage to go despite the incredible weather. I have a vision of Joe and me and Ann Gargan (Teddy and Joan were off in another car) in a big, powerful, official car being driven through the black January night and enveloped in great, white, fluffy snowflakes, which were quite beautiful but limited visibility to a few yards and progress to a few miles an hour. In the front seat, with the driver, was a man with a snow-shovel. Every now and then, when the drifts and the churned-up snow-slush had us in jeopardy, he would put on his gloves, hunch his coat collar up, seize the shovel and go out and extricate us. I was so bemused by the situation and preoccupied with wondering whether we would actually get to our destination that I didn't learn his name or anything else about him. Yet in my memory he remains one of the heroes of the evening.

The Gala was excellent, though a bit disjointed because half the performers had been stuck or delayed in the snow and arrived at random times and the show had to be rearranged according to the order of their coming, with a lot of *ad lib* inventiveness to fill the gaps. But nearly every performer arrived sooner or later, in the best traditions of showbusiness.

The show continued until early morning and Jack and his father stayed through the final number. I left around midnight, knowing I would be getting up for early Mass and that the day was sure to be a long one and I wanted to get some rest. An after-theatre party had been arranged by Joe at one of the Washington restaurants. Jack felt he ought to attend, with the result that he couldn't have been home in bed for some sleep until after 4 a.m. Not the amount of sleep I would have recommended for him to be bright and alert on his Inauguration Day.

By daylight that morning the storm was spent, or nearly so, but had left a thick blanket of snow and a combination of cold, wet wind. Our rented house was only half a mile or so from the nearest Catholic church, and since I am accustomed to walking, except when the weather is really impossible, I decided to walk to Mass, though one look outside showed me that the sidewalks were buried and I would have to trudge up the middle of the street. I put on galoshes and a heavy coat and thick gloves and a couple of woollen scarves, including one tied over and around my head, babushka-style, and took off to church.

As I approached I noticed a great many policemen outside, police cars, and other unmarked cars occupied by anonymous-looking men whom I automatically thought of as Secret Service agents. Suddenly it occurred to me that Jack must be coming there for Mass.

I asked one of the policemen if President-elect Kennedy was expected, and he gave me a kindly but guarded look and said he didn't know, maybe so. I went inside and sat near the rear in a side aisle. A few minutes later Jack came in and sat in one of the middle aisles towards the front.

I hadn't suggested to him that he go to Mass that morning. Jackie wasn't with him, because she was still convalescing from the birth of John Jr. I realized that he was there of his own volition: that he wanted to start his Presidency by offering his mind and heart, and expressing his hopes and fears, to Almighty God and asking His blessing as he began his great duties. He didn't know I was there and I didn't want to go and sit with him, bundled up as I was in my scarves and in my galoshes. I just followed the Mass and, from a distance, looked at him very happily.

Nor did I come to him after Mass, because I knew there would be photographers ready to pop pictures of any personal encounter and I wanted no picture taken of him with me in my regalia. However, since I had already come ploughing through the snow and it was an hour later and I had many things to do that morning to get ready for the ceremonies, I thought it would be good if I could get a ride back to the house. I went over to one of the Secret Service men and said, 'I am Mrs Kennedy, the President's mother. Could you have someone come with a car and pick me up and take me to where I'm staying?' He nodded. But no car came. Evidently he thought I was either an impostor or demented – because I certainly didn't look like a President's mother.

After waiting a while, I walked home. It was no hardship, accustomed as I had been to New England winters, although I would rather have had a ride.

The rest of that day is somewhat blurred in my memory because so much was happening, all of it so grand and colourful and exciting with one stupendous scene following another. My emotions were deeply involved because it all centred on my son. It was overwhelming. The scenes need no description here – they were photographed and written about endlessly. What I can add are some personal notes and thoughts, and some details that may be interesting or amusing.

I have already described Jack's steadfast aversion to hats. There had been a long tradition going back more than a century that the men involved in the Inaugural ceremonies, except for the military, wear some version of the top hat. General Eisenhower, for his two inaugurations, wore a black homburg. For his inaugural, Jack changed back to the top hat. Whether because of his respect for history and for the dignity of the event and the degree of formality it implied, or influenced by Jackie's sense of style and decorum, it was part of the costume of the day. The assortment of top hats that turned up was extraordinary.

As for Jack, I later saw photographs of him in which he was wearing or waving his own top hat, and I have fleeting memories of scenes in which he actually kept it on his head for a while, but nearly all the time he either carried it at his side, or stuck it under a chair, or turned it over to somebody to take care of until the next unwelcome moments when it would be necessary to put it back on.

In the inaugural seating arrangements at the Capitol Plaza, Jack and Jackie were of course front and centre with President and Mrs Eisenhower and flanked by the Nixons and Johnsons, the two Vice-Presidential couples, and surrounded by the leaders of the Court, the Congress, the military services, and the diplomatic corps. Although Joe and I and our niece Ann Gargan were in the front row of the Kennedy-Johnson side, we were at the end, and since the photographers were focusing on the middle we were left out of everything except the panoramic pictures. I have never seen one in which I am recognizable, in fact some friends asked me later where I had been during the ceremonies. I have always afterwards wished I had a picture of me with my son when he was being inaugurated President. Joe and I were close enough that we could have exchanged some words with our son in the minutes after he came down the Capitol steps, under escort of notables and took his place. But we didn't do that. We stood and applauded him, as everyone else did, and resumed our seats, and then we gave each other a squeeze of the hand and sat down with no need or desire for words because everything was understood in this moment.

My mother, who was in her mid-nineties, was living with my brother Tom's family, and was too frail for the trip from Boston to Washington. Her eyesight had begun to fail but she could see well enough to watch television; and I knew what a thrill and satisfaction it must be for her as she saw her grandson with his right hand upraised, his left resting on the Fitzgerald family Bible (sent at Jack's request) which contains the records of her and my father's marriage and forebears and descendants. One of the few sad thoughts I had during that day was that my father had not lived long enough to rejoice with her and with us. How immeasurably pleased he would have been.

Joe had been a little apprehensive about the Inaugural Address, not because he doubted Jack's ability to create and deliver one that would be memorable, but because he had so admired the speech Jack had given only a fortnight earlier to a joint session of the Massachusetts legislature, dealing with the same basic ideas he was bringing to the Presidency, that he wondered if Jack could equal his own eloquence on the same themes so soon afterwards, speaking to the Nation. I remember their conversation after the Massachusetts speech, with Jack back in Florida and his father complimenting him and saying it was so good he should have saved it for the Inaugural Address; or, since he hadn't done so, that he might well incorporate some of the best parts of it in the Inaugural, because the time was short and Jack would have to have a truly excellent speech ready. And Jack said, 'Yes, Dad, I will have,' and nodded. His father said, 'Well, I hope you're working on a good one, because it should be good – it should be your best.' Jack had said, 'Yes, Dad.' His father took his word for it and didn't ask to see a draft, nor did Jack volunteer to show him; and this, I suppose, was mainly because he kept on revising and polishing it and, so I have heard, was still at it the morning of the Inauguration. Hence when he stepped to the rostrum neither his father nor I had more than a general idea of what he would be saying.

Because the Massachusetts speech, on which the Inaugural Address was based, was delivered to a state audience it is not as widely remembered in the nation as it deserves to be. Next to the Inaugural Address, it is my favourite among Jack's speeches.

THE YEARS AHEAD

Speech to the Massachusetts State Legislature,
January 9, 1961

I have welcomed the opportunity to address this historic body and, through you, the people of Massachusetts, to whom I am so deeply indebted for a lifetime of friendship and trust. For fourteen years I have placed my confidence in the voters of this state, and they have generously responded by placing their confidence in me.

Now, on the Friday after next, I am to assume new and broader responsibilities. But I am not here to bid farewell to Massachusetts. For forty-three years, whether I was in London, Washington, the South Pacific or elsewhere, this has been my home; and, God willing, wherever I serve, it will always remain my home.

It was here my grandparents were born; it is here I hope my grandchildren will be born.

I speak neither from false provincial pride nor artful political flattery. For no man about to enter high public office in this country can ever be unmindful of the contributions this state has made to our national greatness. Its leaders have shaped our destiny since long before the great Republic was born. Its principles have guided our footsteps in times of crisis as well as calm. Its democratic institutions, including this historic body, have served as beacon lights for other nations as well as your sister states. For what Pericles said of the Athenians has long been true of this Commonwealth: 'We do not imitate, but are a model to others.'

I have been engaged in the task of constructing an Administration. It has been a long and deliberate process. Some have counselled greater speed. Others have counselled more expedient tests. But I have been guided by the standard John Winthrop set before his shipmates on the flagship *Arbella* 331 years ago, as they, too, faced the task of building a government on a new and perilous frontier. 'We must always consider,' he said, 'that we shall be as a city upon a hill – the eyes of all people are upon us.'

Today, the eyes of all people are truly upon us, and our governments, in every branch, at every level, national, state and local, must be as a city upon a hill, constructed and inhabited by men aware of their grave trust and their great responsibilities.

History will not judge our endeavours, and a government cannot be selected merely on the basis of colour or creed or even party affiliation. Neither will competence and loyalty and stature, while essential to the utmost, suffice in times such as these.

For of those to whom much is given, much is required. And when at some future date the high court of history sits in judgment on each of us, recording whether in our brief span of service we fulfilled our responsibilities to the state, our success or failure, in whatever office we hold, will be measured by the answers to four questions:

First, were we truly men of courage, with the courage to stand up to one's enemies, and the courage to stand up, when necessary, to one's associates, the courage to resist public pressure as well as private greed?

Second, were we truly men of judgment, with perceptive judgment of the future as well as the past, of our own mistakes as well as the mistakes of others, with enough wisdom to know what we did not know, and enough candour to admit it?

Third, were we truly men of integrity, men who never ran out on either the principles in which we believed or the people who believed in us, men whom neither financial gain nor political ambition could ever divert from the fulfilment of our sacred trust?

Finally, were we truly men of dedication, with an honour mortgaged to no single individual or group, and compromised by no private obligation or aim, but devoted solely to serving the public good and the national interest?

Courage, judgment, integrity, dedication – these are the historic qualities of the Bay Colony and the Bay State which, with God's help, this son of Massachusetts hopes will characterize our government's conduct in the four stormy years that lie ahead.

As we all know now, Jack's was one of the great Inaugural Addresses in the history of the Republic. Several people reported that when it was over they saw tears glistening in Joe's eyes. Perhaps so. I had been rapt in my own feelings. I was proud, thankful and humble that I, among the millions of American women of my generation, was the mother of the new President – this confident young leader in whom so many had put their trust. I thought to myself: What a glorious opportunity he has to mould his country and to influence the whole world. I found myself thinking of those words of St Luke I had often recited to him: 'Of those to whom much is given, much is required.' I said to myself, drawing on Cardinal Newman's words, 'He will do good, he will do God's work.'

I felt that Joe and I had given our country a young President whose words, manner, ideas, character, everything about him bespoke future greatness.

After the ceremonies Jack and Jackie, and Lyndon and Lady Bird Johnson, went into the Capitol to the old Supreme Court Chamber – a most handsome room that had been refitted for such occasions as this – where they were the guests of honour at a luncheon given by the Joint Congressional Inaugural Committee. The guest list was, of course, limited to 'official' personages, so Joe and I were not there. Instead, Joe and I, and Jackie's family, and various relatives and friends lunched together at the White House, and afterwards went out to the reviewing stand to watch the Inaugural Parade.

A few personal notes about that:

The weather continued bitter cold and in fact became worse. The reviewing stand was roofed and enclosed on three sides, but of course was open across most of the front – ample space for the frigid breezes to sweep in. If we, bundled in our coats, were chilled, I hated to think of what must be happening to the marchers: the boys from the service academies, the bandsmen and fife and drum corpsmen, the patriotic and fraternal societies, all those hundreds of groups from near and far. But at least they could keep moving and thus work up a little warmth. Worse off were the thousands of spectators lining the streets – especially those who had been lucky enough, they had thought, to have seats in the stands – whose blood must have been slowly congealing. Nevertheless, the parade went on as planned, about three and a half hours, and every unit that came along stepped smartly, looked lively, performed whatever stunts or formations they had practised, and looked as cheerful as a day in May. Even most of the spectators along the way and in the stands stayed on, risking frostbite. In all, it was a triumph of mind over matter and, I thought, an extraordinary testimonial to the enthusiasm – the warmth, so to speak – that Jack inspired in them.

Jack had given the Inaugural Address not only hatless – which I suppose could be considered a seemly gesture of respect to the occasion – but also overcoatless, which struck many people as being far beyond the call of duty or any need to demonstrate 'vigour' and dauntlessness. However, since the speech lasted only fourteen minutes it was unlikely he would freeze. Later, during the parade, he was again without an overcoat most of the time. He would slip it on now and then, wear it for five or ten minutes, then off it would come again. I think this was a quite unconscious response to his feeling of excitement. I was reminded of that evening back in 1952 when the returns from the Senate election were coming in and he kept taking off his jacket, then putting it on a bit later, sometimes with the sleeves inside out.

I don't know what the reasons might be, but extremes of heat and cold didn't seem to bother him as much as they do most people. As he stood there in the frigid wind, with no hat, no overcoat, reviewing the great parade, I thought of that boy who in late fall, when the weather was really getting cold, would start out of the house in thin trousers and no sweater; and if I intercepted him and suggested a sweater or jacket he would look back with that disarming smile and say, 'Yes, Mother, I'll do that later' – and be on his way.

Bobby was in the reviewing stand as Attorney-General. Jack wanted him in that office, their father thought it was a perfect idea. Bobby had resisted for weeks because he feared it would be misunderstood and criticized as nepotism (and criticized it was), but had submitted to the arguments of his brother and father. In any case, I found myself in the position of being the mother of both the President and the Attorney-General which I found rather overwhelming.

That night there was the Inaugural Ball. In fact, there were five Balls at different locations. The big one, at the Armory, had a throng of about a thousand people, including Joe and me, other members of the family and good friends waiting for Jack and Jackie in the Presidential box at one end of that great arena. Everyone turned and applauded as they arrived and took their places and smiled out at the crowd, and everyone was smiling back at them: there was such a feeling of admiration and warmth that one could almost literally feel a wave of love and pleasure.

Jackie looked perfectly beautiful, and Jack had never looked more handsome. During the gruelling months of the campaign and pre-inaugural, tired and often exhausted as he was, he had somehow put on ten or fifteen extra pounds. I thought of how I used to save the steak juice and any extra portions for him, and stuff him with custards and other healthy desserts; and of how he used to drink rich milk-shakes at school and college, hoping to fill out – and now despite all the stress and labour that should theoretically have worn him down he had instead been built up. The life of Presidential candidate, President-elect, now President apparently agreed with him very well. He had lost that lean, Lincolnesque look I had liked, but had gained something I liked better: he looked entirely healthy.

Joe wore the white tie and tails he had seldom worn since the Ambassadorship, and had found to his satisfaction that they still fitted quite well, nearly twenty years later. I had saved the gown I wore when I had been presented at Court and was pleased to find I had not changed in any dimension and I could wear it without alteration; and I did so, in confidence, because it was a classic, timeless design and thus as much 'in style' as when Molyneux had made it for me more than twenty years earlier. There were many compliments about it that evening. It is now part of the Smithsonian collection of gowns worn by American women during significant times or special events in history.

After the Ball, Joe and I returned to our quarters in Georgetown. Jack and Jackie, the President and First Lady, went home to the White House.

We left the next day. We didn't stop for a visit or farewells at the White House. We knew that Jack would be immersing himself in his new duties and obligations; and that Jackie, too, would have a lot to do and think about, and we didn't want to take up any of their time. And so, quietly and happily, we returned to Florida.

18

'A great tradition can be inherited but greatness itself must be won.'

WINSTON CHURCHILL

'I am a man and therefore whatever concerns mankind is my concern.'

TERENCE, ca 150 BC

' "The exercise of vital powers along lines of excellence in a life affording them scope" is an old Greek definition of happiness. It is a conception permeated with energy of life . . . It led along many an untried way.'

EDITH HAMILTON

Joe was so determined to avoid any appearance of being Jack's Grey Eminence that he did not set foot in the White House except once during the rest of that year, and even then only for part of a day and evening and at the personal insistence of Jack and Jackie. There is a memorandum to him from his secretary, in advance of the date, which has a couple of charming and evocative little touches:

> Mr Kennedy:
> Tish Baldridge called to confirm the following: Jackie is most anxious to have you visit all the grandchildren at the White House down by the duck pond. All the children will have had their naps, and she is bringing Caroline in from Glen Ora.
> President JFK would be delighted if you would lunch with him.
> They also confirm dinner with Robert and President Jack for 7.30. Jackie asks if she could possibly sit quietly in the corner – and be included for dinner.

If the world were as logical a place as one would hope, Joe's reluctance to be seen in Washington in those times seems illogical. After all, both the US mails and the telephone system still functioned and anything his father wanted to say to Jack could be said more conveniently by those means than if he lived in Washington, near the White House. And in fact there was a lively correspondence between the President and his father, and they talked by telephone several times a week and sometimes several times a day; though mostly the calls were about personal or family matters, or matters of information about something or somebody that Jack knew his father could provide. There was also, now and then, advice that Jack solicited, or his father felt was really worth offering about matters of state. But if we had taken a house in Washington (there had been rumours, totally unfounded, that we would) each time Joe went to the White House to see his grandchildren there would have been speculative news reports that he had gone to give Jack advice about how to run the Government. So his absence from the scene was probably necessary.

But I suffered no such strictures. Indeed I suppose my absence would have been a cause for comment, as his presence would have been. I would appear lacking in family devotion and preoccupied with the frivolous life of a Palm Beach dowager. In any case I was lucky enough (an unforeseen additional blessing of motherhood) to be at the White House now and then.

When I was there I often used to walk on the lawn at the White House pausing occasionally to peek at Jack at his desk in his study, which was located in a bright sunny corner on the ground floor. On two sides it has long window-doors. He could look out and see Caroline, and later baby John, playing close by; and when he had a few minutes he could go out and join them.

I believe Mrs Paul Mellon, encouraged by Jackie, donated the large and lovely rose-garden. Jack could see this from his windows, too, and would go outside when he felt like a breath of air and stroll among the scented plants. Wherever we lived we had always had gardens: from zinnias and marigolds and the hardiest annual backyard garden flowers at Beals Street, to the tropical exotics at Palm Beach and the fine roses and old-fashioned beds of colourful mixed annuals at Hyannis Port (the source of those bouquets that Ethel mentioned as one of her first memories of us). Jack took both pride and interest in the rose-garden. He wanted to know the varieties. He also had ideas about the juxta-position of colours, and if there were yellow leaves or other signs of distress he wanted to know what ought to be done and who would take care of it. I must say I was a bit surprised, for I never had heard nor seen him demonstrate any interest in such things at home.

When I visited the White House I stayed the first few times in 'The

Queen's Room' but then later on usually in 'The Lincoln Room'. Each had its interesting and attractive qualities, along with a few disadvantages. Both are suites of sitting-room, bedroom and bath. In the Queen's room there is – or was when I was there – a four-poster canopied bed done in lovely chintz and taffeta, with the other furniture and the drapes mostly in chintz also: everything in harmonious colours and designs, and comfortable and feminine. The ideas carried through also, in a somewhat more formal way, into the sitting-room or reception-room, which gave this room a sense of spacious ease and comfort along with just the right degree of elegance. As I recall, all this was largely Jackie's doing. The sitting-room also had a quite good looking convertible couch, or day-bed, which in need could be folded out to accommodate a child or nursemaid or extra family guest.

On the other hand, it gets very little morning sun, and since I am an early riser that was not to my liking. Further, the view from the windows is of Pennsylvania Avenue, a most noble name with many historic associations but, I'm sorry to say, visually rather drab.

The Lincoln room – which I dare say is just the same now as it was then and had been – received a lot more sun but even so always seemed a bit damp, probably because the ceilings were so high it was difficult to heat; while also, in the warm weather, it was not easy to get air because the windows were so long and heavy they were hard to raise or lower. The furniture is dark, austere and rather massive, in the style of those mid-nineteenth-century times. I remember, for instance, the bed being so high that I, being short, had first to mount a bedside stool that was there for the purpose, and from there levitate up on to the bed, and that it was something of an adventure every time. The dressing-tables included what apparently were some of the first electric lights ever installed. This wouldn't matter to a man but did for a woman; so every time I wanted to put on my make-up for the evening and inspect my coiffure and decide on a necklace or brooch and the usual folderols I would do so in the bathroom, where the lighting was modern twentieth-century.

But I preferred the Lincoln room for my own reasons, which mainly involved the view. Any time I looked out of those long and heavy windows I could see the Washington Monument; simple, straight, pointing directly to the sky. I could see also the children's playground down below just beyond the rose-garden and I often watched them and some of their little playmates on the swings and slides; or, in the winter, watched as Jackie drove them around that part of the grounds in a sleigh pulled by Caroline's pony Macaroni. (A sweet sight. Joe and I had done that – sleigh and horse and jingle bells – so often.) Then, too, in any season – away from the rose-garden and the children's play area but still in view – there was the frequent drama of the Presidential helicopters. One of Jack's innovations was to have distinguished visitors, such as heads of foreign governments, met by protocol officers at the Washington airport and then transferred to helicopters and flown directly to the White House grounds. An honour guard would be drawn up there in smart formation and full dress uniforms. Passing through this corridor of splendid-looking young men, the visitor would come to the front entrance of the White House where Jack would be waiting on the steps to greet him.

The first time the drama was put on it turned into something of a comedy, because the strong air currents from the helicopter blades blew off a lot of the hats of the honour guard and there was a scramble of guardsmen chasing hats and trying to get back into line. From then on they were held at a discreet distance until the machine landed, and everything went as it was supposed to; always an impressive and exciting scene.

As I mentioned, the Lincoln room is actually a bedroom and sitting-room suite. I spent a good deal of time in the sitting-room reading the papers, taking breakfast and often other meals – Jack and Jackie had so much official entertaining to do and I certainly did not want to intrude – and writing notes and cards to friends and relations who, I knew, would treasure a personal communication from the White House.

Of course I was at family meals when the White House schedule of the day allowed simple, informal family meals to occur. And if I happened to be there at the time of a State Dinner of formal entertainment I would always be included if I wished to be. Apparently this raised a matter of official protocol which I had never even thought about until I began doing this book.

'Protocol' is on the face of things an affront to our democratic-republican ideals that all people are created equal. Yet at an official function, or even a private one where dignitaries are present, there has to be some order of precedence in entering, leaving and seating and so forth; otherwise there would be confusion and embarrassment; and thus protocol is, so it seems to me, just an extension of such a useful amenity as putting place-cards at a luncheon or dining or bridge table – it makes life really far more simple for everyone involved.

People in official positions soon learn to take the whole thing for granted. There are staff assistants who know who is coming to an official luncheon or state banquet, let us say, and who communicate with other assistants or secretaries who pass on to you the necessary information, such as that Mrs Joseph P. Kennedy is to be escorted to dinner by the Ambassador from Someplace and in the order of procedure will follow HRH the Crown Prince of Something; and on the scene there will be somebody to introduce the Ambassador and point out the Crown Prince in case you haven't met them, as probably you haven't. I was so used to all this, from our time at the Embassy in London, and from much else I have related, that I simply followed the instructions and didn't bother to wonder about my exact rank in protocol as 'The President's Mother'. And I believe that the protocol people had to burrow back through the archives to find precedents and decide what to do about me because not many mothers of Presidents had been alive when their sons took office and fewer still had been at formal White House functions. There really were no firm precedents. But they finally decided they would have to give me some position because I was or might be there. I have now inquired and discovered where I belonged: where the mother of a President belongs – at least until they change the rules:

She belongs behind the President and the First Lady, behind the Vice-President and his wife, behind the Justices of the Supreme Court and their wives, behind the Speaker of the House and his wife, but ahead of all the members of the Senate and House, the Cabinet, the military establishment, the diplomatic corps, and all the rest, and their respective wives.

Twice, when Jackie had to be elsewhere, Jack asked me to substitute for her as his official hostess at state dinners. One was that for President and Señora Arosmena of Ecuador. The other was for Emperor Haile Selassie of Ethiopia. On those occasions, escorted by my son, the President, I was automatically advanced to first in precedence. Needless to say, I felt aglow with honour and pride and excitement – along with feeling slightly like Cinderella, knowing that my high and glamorous position would vanish with the end of the party and I would be reduced in rank from First Lady to mother-in-law of the First Lady.

Incidentally, the Emperor and I discovered that not only were we contemporaries, but had birthdays within a day of each other. We decided that sometime we must arrange to celebrate our birthdays together. And actually – unlike most such socially inspired spontaneous great ideas – we later did. But since it did come later I will leave that episode for then.

Another rather odd matter of official manners: when your son is President, how do you address him and how do you refer to him in conversations with others, and under what circumstances would you change from one mode of nomenclature to another?

Obviously this is not a common problem but it was one that Joe and I suddenly found ourselves encountering; as did his brothers and sisters and relatives and friends and associates, in some degree. The dignity of the office is such that there is an automatic mental shifting of gears, so to speak, and people who had been on first name, nickname terms with him felt constrained to address him as 'Mr President' and mention him even in conversations among themselves as 'The President'. (Dave Powers says that even when they were splashing around together in the White House pool and Dave was entertaining him with his endless supply of jokes and anecdotes, it was still the same: it was 'Mr President'.) For the family, however, there were a few complications which were resolved – more or less – as follows.

Whenever we were with him in any official or public setting we addressed him as 'Mr President' just as everyone else was supposed to do. In a conversation with anyone in such a setting we spoke of him as 'the President' or 'President Kennedy'. (Bobby would do the same, by the way, at Cabinet meetings.) We would do this also with members of his staff and official family and leaders of Congress and other dignitaries, public and private – except that if the person happened to be an old and good friend there would be a tendency to say 'President Jack'.

When it was just the family, or family and very close friends, he was still 'Jack' or any nickname someone had liked to give him. There was an additional complication about that. Pat clarifies it as much as it can be – that is, not completely:

All of us, the sisters and brothers, usually had called him 'Johnny'. It's rather interesting, the affectionate diminutive among ourselves – it was Johnny, Bobby, Teddy, Eunie, Patty, Jeanie. Our parents didn't do that except, for some reason, they did do it a lot with Bobby and Teddy. I can remember Dad sometimes referring to 'Johnny'. But almost always – with both him and Mother – it was 'Jack'. As we all grew older, I suppose 'Jack' seemed an older name and more appropriate and we began calling him that. Except that still, a lot of the time, we would call him 'Johnny'. Then later we loved calling him 'Mr President' and referring to him among ourselves as 'The President' – because we all thought it was so marvellous that he was the President. And so it could be that depending on circumstances and the mood we might call him 'Johnny' or 'Jack' or 'Mr President' the same day, or for that matter all in the same hour.

I'm sure he couldn't have cared less except in so far as nomenclature might affect the honour of the Presidency as an institution. He did care about that. Otherwise he took it all in stride, with his usual humour and modesty.

One reason for my bringing up this topic is that all of us, and I too – I who used to whack him on the breeches when he was a naughty little boy – became so used to referring to him in public as the President or as President Kennedy that I still do now and then even in family and personal correspondence in my diary.

One hears about the burdens of the Presidency.

It seemed to me that – most of the time – Jack enjoyed his Presidency enormously. I think the challenges of the office excited him, and that he was exhilarated by the opportunities it could give him truly and effectively to do what he could for his country. He thrived in eloquence, wisdom, poise and confidence and – to my special satisfaction – in physical health. I believe he had not since earliest childhood been so robust as he was in those last three years; a factor that made his death not only so tragic but so ironic.

But of course there were burdens, and are and always will be so long as the country and the office exist. They can be terrible; and of course Jack was fully sensitive to them. But by the time he was President he had developed such poise, self-control, self-discipline that he could not be overwhelmed and bore his trials with the same determination and grace as he had borne his illnesses. I was an inadvertent witness to this quality on the very day of the first crisis of his Presidency:

April 19, 1961; The White House: Phoned Joe, who said Jack had been on the phone with him much of the day, also Bobby. I asked him how he was feeling and he said 'dying' – result of trying to bring up Jack's morale after the Cuban débâcle.

That night, anyway, Jack and Jackie and I went to dinner at Greek Embassy as previously arranged. Many people outside the Embassy. Greek Ambassador came down steps to meet the President, much as we had come outside to meet the King when he came to London Embassy. Many photographs. I wore pink chiffon dress made by Greek designer, Dresses. Jackie in white satin sheath of Cassini. Hairdresser had come to White House before the dinner to give combing out.

After dinner, Jackie and I chatted with women awhile. Then joined the men for a short time as Jack wanted to leave. Throughout dinner and evening, and way there and back, he had seemed his usual self, quite composed, gave no hint of worries until back at The White House when he said 'good night' to me in car and rushed to his office.

Jackie walked upstairs with me and said he'd been so upset all day. Had practically been in tears, felt he had been misinformed by CIA and others. I felt so sorry for him. Jackie so sympathetic and said she had stayed with him until he had lain down that afternoon for a short nap. Said she had never seen him so depressed except once at time of his operation . . .

It happened that I was present, on the sidelines, at the first great triumph of his Presidency. This came soon, only about ten weeks later, in early June of that year, in Paris and then Vienna at the time of his meetings with President de Gaulle and Chairman Khrushchev.

When I say 'happened' I mean it literally since a US President is not under obligation to have his mother nearby while consulting with other heads of states. Yet ever since the late 'twenties and early 'thirties, from the time he was about twelve years old, I had been going to Paris in the spring almost every year, the war years of course excepted. I went because I love the city especially at that season, and because I wanted to look at the spring collections at the fashion houses and pick out a few things that I felt becoming, and thought Joe would like, to wear on special occasions during the season ahead. Usually I would go over around the middle of May and, since it takes several fittings for a dress to be perfect, would stay on through early June.

Jack knew from boyhood that this was part of my yearly schedule, which I would not like to change, especially as I was now the mother of the President and would be making appearances at the White House and diplomatic receptions and would want to look my best. So there it was. He and I would be in Paris during part of the state visit, and it would have made a poor impression if he ignored his mother. So the State Department had to find some way to involve me in the festivities, even though I would not be officially part of the Presidential party.

I almost missed seeing Jack and Jackie's arrival at Orly airport. Inasmuch as I was unofficial it was explained to me that there seemed to be no way to work me into the official reception committee – headed by President and Mme de Gaulle, which would be driving to Orly in a fleet of cars. I asked if I could go along, unofficially, and sit and wait in one of the cars so I could see and hear the welcome and reception of my son. This was permitted. But the concession apparently upset the precision of the French official logic, because at the airport I was invited to the pavilion where the others had assembled.

General and Mme de Gaulle arrived and I was presented to them. I sat on the presidential divan a few minutes with Mme de Gaulle and we exchanged the usual pleasantries about the impressive ceremonies attending Jack's arrival, and my excitement and pleasure at his being in Paris, and about children.

It was a beautiful morning. At about 10 a.m. – on time – the gleaming, graceful form of Air Force One glided down from the sky and taxied to the mark at the end of a long red carpet. Jack came down the steps first and was greeted by De Gaulle and a delegation of other high officials. As the honour guard saluted, they strode to the pavilion followed by Jackie and the Presidential group. Jack made a short, eloquent speech expressing his appreciation and his pleasure at being in France. Then he and Jackie circulated among the welcoming party, being introduced and exchanging greetings with those they knew. I thought he looked a little surprised when he spotted me, but he gave me a big grin. Yet I expect he wasn't very surprised, even when three chairs were brought forward and I was asked to sit with Mme de Gaulle and Jackie while the photographers and television crews clicked and popped and whirred away at us together.

On the way from the airport, as soon as we entered Paris we found the streets lined with throngs of people – shopkeepers, factory workers, housewives, people of all sorts including a great many children waving little American flags; nearly all of them looking very friendly and rather excited. I will always remember those thousands and thousands of faces full of welcome and those miles and miles of smiles. Apparently – so I was told – there had been few times, if any, when the Parisians had demonstrated such a spontaneous friendly interest in visitors from abroad. I rode in a car with Mrs Gavin, the wife of our ambassador to France, and with Mme Alphand, the wife of France's ambassador to the United States.

That evening there was a dinner for a hundred and fifty at Versailles, which with its furnishings and courtyards and sweeping balustrades and fabulous fountains and perfect grounds is undoubtedly the most beautiful and most impressive of all great palaces in the world. The banquet was in the Hall of Mirrors; which again was an extraordinary tribute to Jack and Jackie – and Franco-American friendship – for it is very rare in these times that it is used for state entertainments. I knew in advance that I would be invited to this grand event so I had prepared myself with a new evening gown, which of course was French. Jackie, in her new role as a leader of American fashion, had been buying all her clothes from American designers (winning the adoration of the American fashion industry) but tactfully this time broke her rule by having a gown designed and made for her by a French designer, Givenchy. (It wasn't built in a day, needless to say. It was a trans-Atlantic enterprise, with final fittings at the White House.) She looked absolutely stunning that evening – and never less than marvellous during the whole visit – and with her French maiden name, her command of the country's language and familiarity with its customs and civilization and appreciation for all the French virtues from *couture* to *cuisine* to *courage* to *culture* she was, it seemed, adopted by the French people almost instantly as an exquisite expatriate daughter. Her own excitement at being in France, the country she loved most next to her own, seemed to add to her beauty, and the more beautiful she became, the more enthusiastic the French became.

It has been said that success in any milieu involves a combination of the right person at the right place at the right time. Jackie was the woman; Paris was the place; spring was the time. She was indeed a *succès fou*, a 'fiery success'. Jack was delighted, both with her and for her. And he took delighted account of the phenomenon by saying at an event the next day: 'I think I should introduce myself – I am the man who accompanied Jacqueline Kennedy to Paris.'

Despite the glamour and beauty of those dinners of state, I found myself wondering, once again, what useful purpose such events really serve. They cost the treasury a lot of money. They require a great amount of planning and effort, attention to fine details. But it has always seemed to me they are rather a waste of time for the statesmen involved, both hosts and guests, for they have important matters on their minds and yet must spend hours chatting away with the wives of state functionaries and listening to speeches.

At least speeches are shorter than they used to be. Years ago my father was speaking some place, my mother was sitting in the audience and the person next to her didn't know who she was, and when the speech ended she turned and said something like, 'Well, what do you think about him?' The person said: 'He's OK. But he talks too long.' We used to tease my father a little about that.

Between ceremonials, however, President Kennedy and President de Gaulle did have a series of long, private, friendly and very frank talks – cumulatively about eight hours, I understand – ranging over all the mutual concerns of the two nations. The informal young President and the monolithic old President evidently got along very well together;

each liked and admired the other; they found a great deal to agree about and established a rapport that would enable them to deal with points of difference amicably and productively.

Apparently I had behaved myself reasonably well, because I was allowed to go on to Vienna, where Jack would be holding meetings with Chairman Khrushchev of the USSR.

I have diary entries written in Vienna:

June 3 & 4, 1961: Here in Austria again after about fifty years. The last time was with my father and sister Agnes. Father was Mayor of Boston and we came with the Boston Chamber of Commerce to visit different European cities.

I had remembered, though vaguely, the magnificent palace of Schoenbrunn, and the art galleries. But what had stayed in my mind most was remembrance of the thrill I had when I went on a small steamer one night down the Danube and waltzed joyfully as the orchestra played the Blue Danube waltz. I wonder to myself as I write this if the young man with whom I waltzed has ever come back, and if he too has remembered the night in 1911 when, young and gay and carefree, we danced the hours away. Nowhere do the waltzes sound quite the same as when they are played here, and no matter how often they are played one does not tire of them. The thought crosses my mind every night when I listen to the little three-piece orchestra in this small hotel.

I have had so little opportunity to speak German in later years that I am no longer fluent, but it is fun to try it again now. The two Austrian government officials between whom I sat at the big state dinner given in honour of Jack and Khrushchev did not speak English – so at last, at least for once, I found my German very useful.

Met Mrs Khrushchev for the first time at the evening (first evening) reception at the Schoenbrunn Palace. She has a very pleasant, welcoming smile when she meets people and it is quite disarming. Figure looked strong, sturdy, capable of hard physical exertion. Wears her hair drawn straight back. No make-up. After introduction, she told me immediately she knew a lot about me as she read an article about me in McCall's magazine, which surprised me.

The following day I saw her again at the concert given by the Vienna Philharmonic Orchestra. Karajan conducted. The Russian violinist Oistrakh played and was superb. Afterwards he and his wife came up to the box and were received by Mrs Khrushchev. She wore a plain dark grey tailored suit.

During the stay in Vienna I chatted with her several times. The diary continues:

I had hoped Mrs Khrushchev might speak German. But she spoke English. We discussed our children, etc., always a safe subject. Her daughter-in-law was with her. An engineer who knows English expressions connected with engineering but otherwise no English, French nor German. Mrs Khrushchev does not smoke, nor does her daughter-in-law, nor do they drink vodka. This was brought to light during a good-natured discussion of our respective daughters-in-law. I powdered my nose and she watched me and said, 'I must learn your beauty secrets.'

Mrs Khrushchev was one of the special surprises and delights of that trip.

Her English was quite good, and I learned later that the reason was she had been a schoolteacher for many years and had been teaching English to others. Further, the fact that she was official and I was not made me all the more surprised that she had read an article about me, in an American magazine at that. She had little or no prior notice that I would be in Vienna – because I hadn't known, myself, until I asked Jack in Paris and he dutifully agreed, 'Yes, Mother.' Whereas I had known well in advance that if the Kennedy–Khrushchev talks took place in Vienna as scheduled, she would be there as her husband's hostess. Yet I had not bothered to read up about her and felt the more ashamed of myself for not having equal foresight. The Russians like folk-sayings, so if anyone in Russia happens to read these words I hope it will be understood as a compliment when I say I thought Mrs Khrushchev showed she was 'really on the ball'.[1] It occurred to me that if through some chance of history, we had lived in the same American town and knew each other, and if I had suddenly been called away somewhere else and really needed a reliable friend to come in and look after my children, she was the sort of woman I would have depended on.

Sturdy, capable, earthy – yes; but also she had a certain finesse, she had charm, she was congenial, and she was well-informed. She impressed me. In my lifetime I have met quite a number of great ladies. I suppose that Queen Elizabeth the Queen Mother of England would

[1] Incidentally, I realize that I should be saying 'USSR' and 'Soviet citizen' instead of 'Russia' and 'Russian'—especially as the Khrushchevs were from the Ukraine—but my ear is not accustomed to the nomenclature. So I would want to assure those readers in the USSR, supposing there are some, that when I say 'Russia' I am using a term of convenience for me and practically all 'Americans', as they call us, though properly we are 'USA citizens'.

be at the top of my list, almost anyone's list, of women in public life who have managed the rather delicate balance of being themselves, being natural and unaffected and open and womanly, being charming and considerate, while also using their minds, their education, and their intuitive as well as intellectual comprehensions in a responsible way. If I stopped to make a list I suppose it would contain a few dozen such women; but Mrs Khrushchev would be on it and somewhere near the top.

Later on when people asked me about meeting the Khrushchevs, I would often work in the facts that Mrs Khrushchev had learned English and had read up on me, whereas her daughter-in-law had not; and I would add, 'This shows that although some daughters-in-law are smarter than their mothers-in-law, there are some mothers-in-law who are smarter than their daughters-in-law.' People's expressions would become interested. But I thought it better to leave them in suspense.

Ethel says: 'Well, we're not going to put that to the test, I hope. Which one is she talking about?'

One other thought about Mrs Khrushchev. Her husband was the leading communist of the time and my husband was one of the leading capitalists. Yet she and I understood each other and got along very well.

I had begun collecting autographs as a girl. Later, as the children arrived and grew and Joe became increasingly prominent, I would ask various leading personages – such as President Hoover and President Roosevelt – to autograph copies of their books, and I would pass those out to the children at Christmas or birthdays as souvenirs of the times and as a way to encourage their interest in current history. When Jack became President I decided to continue with the custom but in a special way, by getting autographed books by people who were outstanding in many fields – the arts and sciences as well as government – during the years of his Presidency. Such a collection would be particularly treasured by Caroline and John Jr when they grew up. I had accumulated quite a few, in a gamut from Sean O'Casey to the Duchess of Windsor and including some chiefs of government, such as Prime Minister Macmillan and Prime Minister Nehru. I was rather surprised to find that Generalísimo Franco had not written a book, and even more surprised that by that time, 1961, neither had Chancellor Adenauer. However, Adenauer's office had copies of his speeches, some of which they bound in book-form, and he autographed that and sent it to me.

On inquiry, it turned out that Premier Khrushchev had not written a book either.

But, of course, there had been many photographs taken of him and Jack together during the Vienna meeting. And so as the next best alternative I decided to send some of those to him and ask him to sign them; then I would have Jack do the same, and probably return one to Premier and Mrs Khrushchev and distribute the others among our family.

Premier Khrushchev signed the photographs and returned them to me and I sent them on to Jack with a note about my plan.

I received the following letter from him:

Dear Mother,

If you are going to contact the heads of state, it might be a good idea to consult me or the State Department first, as your gesture might lead to international complications.

Love,
Jack

To which I replied:

Dear Jack,

I am so glad you warned me about contacting the heads of state, as I was just about to write to Castro.

Love,
Mother

Of course, I would not have done so. But Jack and I used to joke that I might have.

Joe and I spent most of that summer on the Riviera. After he went back to Hyannis Port I stayed on in France for some weeks more, partly because I wanted to see the fall fashion collections in Paris and also because I realized that with Jack and Bobby in high office and so much attention in the media about our family, our enclave at Hyannis Port would be a tourist attraction right through the months of fine fall weather at the Cape. The scene had been noisy enough with the children and grandchildren, without tourist traffic. I had always needed times of peace and quiet and by then had reached a stage in life when I needed them more; so I thought it behoved me to stay away until near Thanksgiving, which I did.

Meanwhile the telephone and postal systems had continued to work quite well. And meanwhile, too, all through the year, despite the dramas that occurred, our family life went on. I won't suggest that it went on altogether normally because, naturally, it was complicated by the official positions of Jack and Bobby – and Sarge, as Director of the

Peace Corps – and Jackie and Ethel and Eunice as their wives; and further by the fact that Teddy was preparing to run for Jack's old Senate seat from Massachusetts, and that in Joan he had a strikingly beautiful wife who caused heads to turn wherever she went; and that Pat was married to Peter, a movie and TV star; and that all of us, as a family, consequently were under continual public scrutiny, which does not make for an altogether placid existence. But the public and private portions of our lives merged in a seamless way, really. To give at least a general sense of what it was like for us in that first year of Jack's Presidency, I shall again make use of a chronological sample of the family correspondence, with explanatory notes as needed.

January 24, 1961
Palm Beach

Mrs John F. Kennedy
The White House
Washington, DC
Dear Jackie,

I have enclosed a few items for Jack's diet. I tried to get a few ideas from Dr Travel that were constructive. There are copies enclosed in case you want to leave one at the other house.

Just discovered *Never On Sunday* is on the condemned list.

With love,
Affectionately,
G.Ma

February 23, 1961
The White House

Dear Grandma,

We went to the White House after having dinner at Daddy's office. We had lots of fun. I wish you had been with us. We saw lots of rooms.

Love,
Kathleen, Joe, Bobby, David,
Michael, Courtney

These were six of Bobby's children, and the office was the Attorney General's. It must have been a picnic in more ways than one.

March, 1961
Boston

Dear Dad,

Frankie is keeping me on the go day and night. I think that the reaction has been quite good except for a few cynical old pros. I have found some old Irish stories that Grampa used to tell which have really helped out during the activities of St Patrick's Day.

Enclosed is a comment from the Worcester paper after we were up there last week . . . Everything else is going well.

Love,
Ted

Frank Morrissey was a widely experienced Massachusetts political figure who had helped Jack in his campaign and who had been enlisted now to help Teddy in his first bid for elective office. As the newspaper clipping shows, there was still some testing and decision-making to do as to whether this should be for the Governorship or the Senate. Extracts from the article, by John F. Battles in the Worcester *Telegram*, follow:

> One of Central Massachusetts's most astute politicians says 'Ted Kennedy will run for governor next year!' This Democratic leader made his private prediction at the Emerald Club's big St Patrick's Day party at the Auditorium where young Kennedy was the featured speaker – a smash, by the way . . . He says the only thing that can stop Ted Kennedy from running for governor is if he decides instead to run for US senator . . . Hardly a day or night goes by that doesn't see the handsome, personable brother of the President speaking before some group somewhere in the Bay State . . . Those who came in contact with him at the Auditorium were struck by the warmth he generates . . .

April 13, 1961

Dear Dad,

Thanks so much for shipping Smiths, Shrivers and Charlie Bartlett all the way to New York. It was a great luxury to ride on the *Caroline* during the campaign but to ride in it now without any 'Cause' was just too marvellous – really too much. We had to keep our seat-belts on the whole way and Jean retired immediately to the bedroom . . . she says from fear. It didn't stop the rest of us from enjoying a very good dinner and toasts galore to you, the biggest hearted leader on The New Frontier.

Love,
Eunice

July 13, 1961
Beverley Hills

Dearest Mother and Daddy,

Well, it finally arrived. Five and a half pounds, red hair and the longest fingers I have ever seen. So maybe she'll have Dad's brains too! She was born Sunday the 2nd and we had the christening last Saturday as Bobby was out that weekend. He's the godfather . . . Talked to Jack today and he asked me to hostess the end of the month as Jackie can't be there . . . should be fun. I will then go to the Cape and leave there August 7th, arriving the 8th at Nice, where I will see you . . .

Love + xxx
Patricia

'She' was Robin, the only grandchild until then to have inherited Joe's colouring. Later on there would be another, Teddy's and Joan's third child, Patrick. But only those two out of all the grandchildren, which rather surprises me.

July 22, 1961
Hyannis Port

(Cablegram to me)

GRANDMA THE GOATS ARE NOT ENJOYING EATING IN YOUR DINING ROOM HALF AS MUCH SINCE THE GOOD TABLE IS GONE. HAPPY BIRTH-DAY. ALL THE GRANDCHILDREN.

The dining-room table is a beautiful old piece which had begun to show signs of wear and tear, so I had sent it out for repairs. Knowing there would be a lot of small grandchildren, and playmates, around that summer, I thought it just as well not to have it brought back to the house until I returned.

July 25, 1961
The White House

Dear Dad,

Many thanks for your letter. I must say Macmillan has an even tougher time with the British press than we do with ours. It is difficult to understand Lord Beaverbrook . . .

Things seem to be going reasonably well here. I will call you this weekend.

Love,
Jack

Late July, 1961
Aboard airliner

Dear Mother and Dad,

Am on the first leg of the trip to Latin America, which in the last few days has really shaped up very well . . .

Recently saw Dr Sidney Farber who is the head of the Children's

Hospital and Jimmy Fund and really well regarded, and he said he would help out preparing some position papers on medical care and some other programmes.

Visited the Kennedy Home in Brighton . . . the Catholic Guidance Centre where we gave the gym . . . the Mass. General to see the progress in the Kennedy Laboratories. So you can see we have been keeping busy in your absence.

Eddie McCormack told Hal Clancy last week that he definitely was going to run for the US Senate. He said that he doubted whether I would, because about a week before at a luncheon in Washington the Attorney General congratulated him on his brief on the school desegregation cases and said some nice words about him. When I heard this I ran down brother Bob, and he said what's so bad about that and he would say some nice things about me, too . . .

Jack is in good shape in spite of the fact that I cleared his clock in backgammon, taking 7 out of 9 games from him . . . The final game we played he said he would never play again unless he licked me and a good thing for all of us he did.

Eunice had a birthday party and is still trying to figure out why the dining-room table has disappeared, since Bobby Shriver doesn't dance on it this year.

Caroline still is looking for Grampa and asking her father where Grampa git his ice-cream and why can't he do as well.

Joan and Kara send their love.

The *Marlin* is still afloat and everyone is fine.

Love
Ted

July 26, 1961
Hyannis Port

Dear Mother and Dad,

This summer is passing like no other summer. The weather has been great, the children are all fine and the help is fantastic. Jack is feeling the best he has felt in six months. We went out in the *Marlin* yesterday over to Cotuit and he swam like mad and is in fantastically good humour and so is Jackie. We are all told to build air raid shelters but otherwise he has no startling news!

Pat comes next Saturday with her children. She will stay one week and then leaves for Europe and cruising, heading in your direction.

Teddy calls Joan 4 or 5 times a week and is having a great time in SA.

Tommy is working the grey pony so that he is going much more smoothly.

All is great – for today.

Love & hugs,
Eunice

July 28, 1961
The White House

Dear Grandpa,

Caroline dictated this letter. In case you don't understand Snapdragon Swallow, she never says her name now. This week it is Lilac Birdie and last week Daffodil Horse. People are rather surprised when they ask her name . . .

She says your birthday is in September and she will give you a tie and a red dog.

All love,
Jackie

Caroline's letter follows:

Dear Grandpa,

You know what Stephen did to me? He wiggled me back and forth. He didn't knock me down but he wiggled me and I didn't like it.

Give my love to Grandma and Grandma and Anne and Peppy's down there so give him this letter. When the whirly-birds came in he was fast asleep.

It was raining today rainy rainy. I think it was quite a storm. I'm sick and tired of this weather.

Next week I'll be Snapdragon Swallow.

Early August, 1961
Hyannis Port

Dearest Mother and Daddy,

Everything is going splendidly at the Cape. It is just like a health camp – tennis, golf, water-skiing everyday. Stephen told me he wants to live here forever and so do we all. Jackie is talking of staying here till October . . . Jack is in splendid form . . . swimming last weekend and seems very relaxed and cheerful . . . Pat arrives tonight for a week . . . Bobby and Ethel are going to Africa next week for 2 days for Independence day on the Ivory Coast . . . The Secret Service men spend most of their day entertaining the children and driving the motor-boat. So see what you are missing . . . How's the Riviera??

Love & xxx
Jean

Ambassador and Mrs   August 21, 1961
Joseph P. Kennedy.   Hyannis Port
Villa Vista Bella
Cap d'Antibes
France

Dear Gramma and Grampa,

Things were supposed to simmer down here at the Cape with all the troops moving out scattered all over Poland and Jugoslavia. Tho' we really miss the contingent in the south of France an awful lot and it is sad you're so very far away, when I think of Gramma's 'tummy' and what's going on here maybe 3600 miles is about the right distance.

I think roughly the whole attitude of the Secret Service down here is about the same as Casey Jones when he said so determinedly, 'We're gonna reach 'Frisco but we'll all be dead.'. . .

The tales about the Secret Service are endless: sitting and slurping their popsicles with the children every afternoon at 2.45 when the Dairy Maid Milk Bar truck drives in – or this very afternoon when one who has never heard of Metrecal but should have simply wrapped his arms about the mast of the senior and refused to budge during the 2 hour sail returning from Great Island in the teeth of a Nor'-easter . . . Of course the children kept shouting to him that seniors hardly ever tip over – only when there's a storm or something like if the centreboard hits the bottom too hard or if water comes rushing in (you couldn't see the gunrail the entire afternoon for all the water that was pouring in) . . .

Thank you for the wonderful time you gave all of us at Bella Vista . . . Those fantastic meals and that relaxation which you cooked up in the Waring blender . . . Hugs to all of you . . .

Kisses & love,
Ethel

Several notes on this. Eunice and Jean, escorted by Lem Billings, had gone touring in Poland and Jugoslavia and places between. The contingent in the south of France was Joe and I. Ethel and Bobby had visited us there. The blended 'relaxation' was a rum cocktail, Joe's favourite.

Joe was seventy-three that September 6. Jean, who was still travelling in Jugoslavia with Lem, sent him a cable:

HEPPY NIRSKEY LOVE
FUMSKY JEANSKY LENNSKY

Birthdays always were gala events in our family, and for Joe's in particular the children were inspired to all sorts of inventive lengths: theatricals written, costumed and performed by themselves; musical numbers in which they set lyrics about him to the tunes of popular songs; and much doggerel versifying. The humour was always full of 'inside jokes' which don't translate well without extended footnotes, which I want to avoid since nothing kills a joke like having it explained. Anyway, as an example of the literary form, here is the poetic master-piece Jean sent to her father for his birthday:

> There once was a gruff old bear
> Who summertimes left his lair.
>   While he was away
>   Do you think we would say
> What went on in that very chair?

> He summer'd in Juan-les-Pins
> With Gramma and Huxy and Ann.
>   He thought he would get us
>   Thru Frank's funny lettahs
> Shall we tell him, gang, shall we?
>   Un - unh.

> Do you 'spose he got word of the rumour
> of mistaking Houphet for Nkrumah?
>   No, I think that old Daddy
>   Was checking that caddy,
> No wonder he's in such a good humour.

> Daddy says when we travel – Behave.
> To watch it or people will rave
>   But does he tell a fella
>   About Isabella
> I'd say he had a close shave.

Grampa likes it when we don't spend,
To Bergdorf's we've put an end.
    Do you 'spose in October
    When Tom Walsh[1] comes over
He'll come on business or just as a friend?

Daddy we had a great time in Hyannis
And only dreamt of living like Landis
    So here's to dear Pappy
    Have a real happy, happy –
For you Vivas, Hurrahs and Hossanah.

                            September 19, 1961
                            Paris
Jo Dearest,
        How can I have all this – and you –
        And still have Heaven, too!
                    Love to all,
                    Rosa

                            November 20, 1961
                            Hyannis Port
Dear Ethel,
    I think it would be a good idea if the children learned to bring in their bicycles at night, as it really is a pity to have them outside in the dampness.
    It would be quite easy to make them do this by just forbidding them to ride the following day after not putting their bicycles away the night before.
                    Much love,
                    G. Ma

The next month both Joe and I were at the Palm Beach house as usual and making our preparations for Christmas. My niece Ann Gargan, younger daughter of my sister Agnes, was staying with us at the time. She had been in training to be a nun, in one of the orders that specialize in the care of the sick, and was nearing the time for her vows when she herself developed symptoms of multiple sclerosis, a disabling disease, and hence had to give up her plans to be a nursing nun. That had been

[1] Tom Walsh works at the Kennedy office in New York, where he has been in charge of monitoring the personal finances of family members. In that assignment, a delicate one, he has somehow always remained a friend indeed.

in 1959, and since then she had been living much of the time with us, while undergoing medical treatment, which was extraordinarily successful: by late 1961 practically all signs of nerve impairment were gone and she could take part in life fully, including sports. Joe was as pleased about this as I was. Ann was the youngest of the Gargan children and thus so to speak our youngest daughter, and Joe had made a special pet of her. And of course she adored him. He liked to play golf early in the morning, whereas I preferred the mid-afternoon, so Ann was often his golfing companion.

In Teddy's book *The Fruitful Bough*, Ann wrote:

. . . Uncle Joe always wanted to keep life interesting and moving – maybe he kept on the move too much. On the morning of December 19, 1961, we were on the move again. We generally played golf about 8.30 but Jack was down in Palm Beach and was leaving for Washington that morning. Uncle Joe rode to the airport with him. I followed in another car, so that I could bring Caroline and 'Grandpa' back home from the airport. We dropped Caroline off at home and went directly to the Palm Beach Country Club to play nine holes. Being later than usual, the front nine was crowded. So we played the back nine. We finished the sixteenth, and as Uncle Joe picked up his ball, he said he felt rather faint. But he told me to tee-off the seventeenth, as there were people waiting behind us. I did. He was sitting on the bench. I asked if he wanted his ball teed up. He said no – he would just walk along.

So we started out. His balance was all off. I asked his caddy to run and get a golf cart. With some difficulty, Uncle Joe asked if we had got Caroline home all right. I assured him we had. This seemed to ease his mind. The golf cart arrived. I got the car and we drove home. Upon reaching the house, he felt better. He was delighted to find Jackie and Caroline waiting to have a swim with him. No one made him happier than his grandchildren. He went upstairs right away to change for his swim. I persuaded him to rest . . . He fell fast asleep, then awoke about five minutes later, coughing and unable to speak, or to move on the right side . . .

That morning I had been at Mass as usual. Then I had a few errands to do, so I was home a bit later than ordinarily I would have been; which didn't bother me because I had kissed Jack goodbye and knew that Joe and Ann would be going with him to the airport and then would be playing golf. Perhaps it was around 11.30 that I arrived back at the house. Ann came to me and, looking rather worried, but not too worried, told me that Uncle Joe was not feeling well at all and she had managed to get him to take a nap. None of it registered much on me at the time. After all, everyone feels giddy or weak or otherwise indisposed from time to time – and, if there is some place to lie down, in that case one sensibly lies down, rests, naps, waits for Nature to take the healing course it usually does. It barely occurred to me there could be anything seriously wrong with him. True enough, he was seventy-three, yet he had always been enormously vital and active and vigorous and alert and such a strong central presence in all our lives that in my own mind, I suppose, I had thought of him just going on and on to some indeterminate time, getting older but meanwhile immune to any serious physical impairments.

And so, when Ann told me about his not feeling well on the golf course – this temporary 'spell', as I supposed – and that he was upstairs resting – I was concerned but not alarmed, and went on ahead with my usual schedule at that time of the day. Until Ann soon came down to tell me this did not seem to be just a temporary upset but needed the attention of a doctor; who was called and came out quickly, and after examining Joe sent for an ambulance in which he was taken to St Mary's Hospital, about 15 minutes from our house, on the other side of Lake Worth.

I of course followed to St Mary's, and while the medical examinations were going on – a number of doctors involved – I was most of the time in the hospital chapel, praying, praying.

After the examination the doctors told us that he had had a blood clot and partial haemorrhage in one of the arteries of his brain – a 'stroke' – and his chances of living were problematical; and that, if he lived, his chances of being restored to anything near his customary level of activities were not good.

Jack was still on his way back to the White House when his father was taken ill, and had barely arrived at his office when it was realized how seriously ill he was or might be. Meanwhile Bobby had been notified – he in turn was the one who called Jack – and a few hours later, that same afternoon, Jack was back in Palm Beach on Air Force One bringing Bobby and Jean with him. Eunice was some place else and couldn't get on that plane, but came down on a commercial flight that afternoon or evening. Pat came in from California, and Teddy down from Boston.

In other words Joe was not expected to live; though no one then, or in the next days, wanted to tell me.

That was December 19. By the 24th, Christmas Eve, which for so many years had been such a time of joyous expectation in our house, he had developed pneumonia and had such difficulty in breathing that the doctors had to make an incision in his throat and insert a tube through which he could receive oxygen.

He survived the crisis, began to gain and a few weeks later was off the 'critical' list and strong enough to be brought home. From that time on, Ann entered into a life of devotional care that could not possibly have been more complete had she taken her vows. Her Uncle Joe had done everything possible for her during her illness and recuperation; she now dedicated herself wholeheartedly and single-mindedly to helping him. He needed nursing care around the clock, so of course she couldn't do it all and there were other nurses and assistants, but it was Ann who interviewed and hired them and remained in charge. This was a wonderful comfort for Joe, for he loved and trusted her as if she were one of his own daughters. And of course I loved and trusted her, too, and knowing that she had been well trained in nursing I was sure I could count on her to do or cause to be done everything that could help him towards recovery; needless to say, her presence was a tremendous help for me.

The blood clot and neurological damage had left him unable to speak and with almost complete paralysis of his right arm and leg. His mind, however – his comprehension of things said and seen and sensed and in short of all the life around him – apparently had suffered little or no impairment. By springtime his general physical condition had improved to such a degree that his doctors said he was ready to begin the long, laborious process of exercises and other therapies through which, hopefully, he might regain the powers of speech and movement. Accordingly we – Ann and I, and Joe on a stretcher, and half a plane-load of medical personnel and special equipment – flew to New York, where Joe entered Dr Howard Rusk's Rehabilitation Institute. There his personal, full-time attending physician was one of Dr Rusk's most trusted assistants, Dr Henry Betts, a brilliant young man who subsequently became head of a similar Rehabilitation Institute in Chicago. Dr Betts was in charge of Joe's case at the New York Institute and later on attended him also at Hyannis Port and other places. At Teddy's request he contributed some memories of that period to *The Fruitful Bough*:

> The most pervading characteristic he exhibited was that of a gigantic and natural commanding presence. At no time was he a pitiful or passive invalid. There was no question for even a second of who was the dominant force when he was around. With his eyes, facial expression, and strong left hand, he could convey any reaction from tremendous disdain to the most poignant and feeling expression of affection and appreciation. He had an uncanny comprehension and

was able to convey appropriately his understanding of the most subtle aspects of life around him. He noticed the most meticulous details of the manner in which the staff performed their duties and always expressed his evaluation, either positive or negative, leaving no doubt as to his opinion . . . his displeasure at lack of perfection . . . his satisfaction with a job well done.

For probably the first time in his life, he was dependent on the planning of another individual. This was not an easy adjustment to make . . . He vacillated from complete cooperation and appreciation of my efforts to total dissatisfaction . . . [But soon] there was never the slightest problem between the two of us.

He showed gigantic strength of character, not only in adapting to [his] limits but also in the great drive he showed in working towards recovery. There was a difficulty in maintaining himself as the symbol of strength and the family leader in such a relatively passive state, but he did it by just his presence, and the indefinable qualities still so evident in him, that convey strength and leadership in all great men . . .

Mr Kennedy learned to walk quite soon and put tremendous effort into this with great satisfaction. The First Lady visited him several times during these sessions. He was particularly happy when she came, did unusually well and seemed encouraged about his progress . . .

The greatest pleasure in his leisure time was, of course, his family. In the evenings, Mrs Kennedy would come [to the Institute] for a quiet dinner, then both would sit peacefully and watch television until it was time for bed. He was always especially relaxed with his wife and, even though he could say no words, they seemed to communicate completely.

Probably the most moving moment during his stay in New York was when the President visited. Dr Rusk had suggested he demonstrate the walking he had just learned to do, which he could manage then only between two parallel bars with assistance.

Mr Kennedy refused to agree to this, but greeted the President in the little house assigned to him [on the Institute grounds]. After the visit, the President wheeled his father to the garden and indicated that he must leave. Mr Kennedy anchored his progress in the chair with his good and very strong left foot, locked the chair and indicated that he wanted to stand, which he had previously not been able to do alone. Some assistance was offered, but he shunned it angrily.

Then, with incredible effort, he forced himself to an erect, dignified and normal-appearing standing position. He then fixed the President with his piercing eyes and extended his left hand to say goodbye. The President, obviously moved, quickly turned and disappeared to the street and out of sight. We could hear loud applause and shouts, then the roar of motor-cycles. Until their din was entirely gone, Mr Kennedy stood, his eyes fixed straight ahead to where his son had disappeared. He sat down then and was slowly wheeled away into the garden . . .

When we were in Hyannis Port [Dr Betts remembers] he seemed the most happy and the pleasures there were simple. He loved to go to movies [in our little theatre and projection room, which I have described], to be in a boat, and he revelled in the company of his many grandchildren, to whom he was extremely gentle and affectionate. He often went for [automobile] rides, always stopping to greet familiar faces . . . He loved to sit quietly, even alone, and watch the sea from his chair, strategically placed for the view.

On weekends, the President usually arrived and, as soon as we knew his jet had landed at a nearby air force base, Mr Kennedy would go to the centre of the front porch, in any weather, and await the arrival of the helicopter . . . The number one helicopter always landed directly in front of him. Right after greeting his wife and children, the President would stride, with his energy echoed by the tremendous roar and force of the jet helicopters, to pay homage to his father, who seemed to dominate it all. These were touching moments; even more so when the President departed, when Mr Kennedy would be left with his thoughts as the helicopters disappeared into the Cape Cod fog. He sometimes cried, but even that somehow never destroyed the image of strength he projected . . .

Joe had always disliked self-pity on the part of anyone for any reason, and overt displays of grief made him uncomfortable. He used to tell the children, and later the grandchildren, that tears accomplished nothing and instead of thinking about a hurtful present they should think about better times tomorrow, and how to bring those about.

His secretary for several years before his stroke was Diane Winter, who wrote in *The Fruitful Bough*:

Despite . . . tragedy, Mr Kennedy was unshakably positive and optimistic about the future. I remember hearing him clap his hands in steady rhythm to accentuate the admonition, said in mock sternness to his grandchildren, 'No – crying – in – this – house! No – crying – in – this – house!'

25　At the opening of the
John F. Kennedy Center for the Performing Arts
in Washington, DC

Our Grandchildren

26 *Above* Excited arrivals
Below 1957. Bobby Shriver, Bobby Kennedy Jr, Joe Kennedy II,
Maria Shriver, Christopher Lawford, Kathleen Kennedy, David
Kennedy, Courtney Kennedy with Grandpa and Grandma

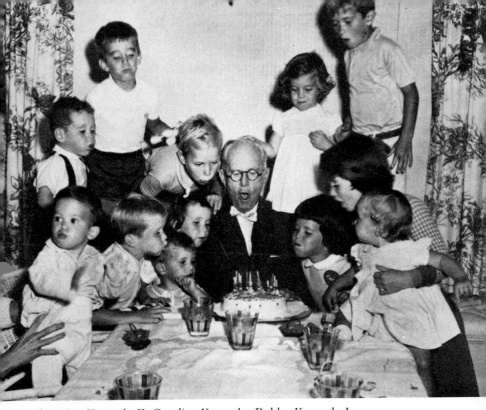

27 *Above* Joe Kennedy II, Caroline Kennedy, Bobby Kennedy Jr.
Seated, l. to r., are Timmy Shriver, David Kennedy, Michael
Kennedy, Courtney Kennedy, Joe, Maria Shriver, Kathleen Kennedy
holding Kerry Kennedy
Below Caroline Kennedy and Grandpa
Jackie took this picture of Joe with John in the White House grounds, 1961
Joe's birthday, 1960. Standing are Stephen Smith, Jr, Bobby Shriver,

Joe and I

28 *Above* Relaxing on an autumn day in the 1940's

At the Hialeah racecourse

Left One of the last pictur us together

His tears afterwards were of course entirely involuntary and un-controllable – a side-effect, I suppose, of the neurological damage – but anyway there they were, from time to time, and made his situation all the more heart-breaking for those who loved him.

Joe's stroke not only was severe but had occurred in a part of the brain that was inaccessible to surgery, so the major hope for him, as Dr Betts had indicated, was a retraining process in which the intact parts of his nervous system would take over the functions of the damaged parts. This required not only courage and determination, which he always had had and still had in abundance and applied to his problem of recovery, but also a sheer long time spent in repetitious and laborious exercises for the benefit of a daily or weekly almost imperceptible gain. And of course this was completely against his nature. He was, in Dr Bett's term, 'massively frustrated'. And it was so contrary to everything about him that I had known – known for some fifty-five years by then – that I think I underwent a certain degree of emotional paralysis for a time. I find that one of the very few diary notes I took was in mid-summer of 1962 and was this:

Joe's illness. The grief when I see him cry and the pity when I see one who was so strong and independent lie helpless in bed, saying 'no, no, no.' Sometimes when he means 'yes.'

Little by very little, with good care and his indomitable will, and sup-ported by prayer and by the love and encouragement which surrounded him, he came back as far as it was possible physically for him to come. He was able to stand, with the aid of a cane, and with the cane, and someone's arm for balance on the other side, to walk some few steps. He had been an athlete, had loved exercise. We built an enclosed swim-ming pool at Hyannis Port, heated and with the sprays and bubblers and other fixtures of a health spa (and enclosed and heated the pool we had at Palm Beach) so that with the muscles still under his command he could swim every day, which kept him in trim and was part of his therapy. Going up or down stairs, even with assistance, remained beyond possibility, hence elevators were installed at both houses. Mainly – aside from the considerable time every day he would have to rest in bed – he was confined to his wheelchair, or favourite easy chairs at our houses, or a chair on a boat; in any case, to a chair, because standing for more than a few minutes was a great strain on his strength. His speech improved somewhat but the few words he acquired were slurred and hard for others to understand. I'm sure this embarrassed him, and after awhile he settled back on the two words he could say with some distinctness, 'yes' and 'no', and sometimes would not even try those, and rely wholly on the expressive language of his face and good left arm and hand. The learned skills gained and faded, came back and increased and then went again, for physiological and psychological reasons that were beyond my knowledge and probably beyond that of the medical specialists.

He and I had always talked with each other a lot; that was not so much because we were verbal people (though I suppose we were, comparatively) as because there was just always so much to talk about. Yet, in so many ways, we had understood each other with no need for words: a gesture, an expression, a look, a nod, a cue or, as I believed possible, that harmonious meeting of minds that is empathy, the unspoken understanding. In his distressed condition I couldn't count on it but most of the time it was still there. In the midst of his tragedy this was one blessing.

In any case, as he made progress, minute and sometimes evanescent though it was, and as his general health became fairly stabilized, he could again take part in life. The limits of his participation were of course severe, but the margin that was left to him was enough to give him many enjoyments and satisfactions and interests and quite enough to make life worth living. He came to family meals, occupying his usual position at the head of the table and followed the conversation attentively and, so far as possible for anyone who was speechless, took part in it. As always, his was the dominant personality, and as always he could silence anyone or the group with that special 'look'. He was amused by the family banter that went on (though he couldn't speak he could laugh; and that marvellous grin of his was intact) and was as receptive as ever to any badinage or *infra dig* humour that they might direct at him. For instance, there was a series of 'souvenir pillows' (this had started before his illness, but continued) printed with one of his characteristic expletives such as *Applesauce!* or admonitions such as *You're dipping into your capital!* Or familiar sayings such as *You have just made a political contribution* – an 'inside joke' that in this case deserves explanation. He had given them trust funds but the income was still administered by his business office. When one of them was involved in a campaign and needed funds a tithe was levied on the others, which they would hear about in a letter from him beginning 'You have just made a political contribution . . .'

And so it was with everyone: everyone trying to give him the support and reassurance that he had always given us.

Evelyn Jones was with us during some of those times, and remembers:

When I'd be going by near his chair I'd always talk to him as if he were just the same, and he was the boss and he was the king of the ship, and that's all there was to it and just the same. My husband Tom and I had bought a place. I took pictures of it and showed them to him. He was so interested. Once in a while he'd put his good hand on your arm as if he were trying to say thank you. Which of course you knew. And one of his smiles when you fixed him up in his chair was worth all the money in the world – you couldn't pay for it. He knew that you knew he was handicapped and yet was still Mr Kennedy; and that was it.

One thing I insisted on doing, though the girl working with me used to get a little upset once in a while. When Mr Kennedy was quite ill he would often change his mind. So I had a place set for him in the dining-room, I had a tray set in the butler's pantry to take into the library, and if they were eating out on the patio I had a place set for him there. Because if he thought he wanted to eat in the library by himself, by the time I was serving he might be out on the patio – and I would *not* not have had a place for that man for the world. The other girl said, why don't you wait and find out? I said it would be too late. And I said just don't fret about it because if he suddenly decides he wants to go some place to eat there's going to be a place for him. And he's not going to find somebody in his place. It would break his heart to find somebody sitting in his place. So you did these things for him and you did them because you loved him.

Mrs Kennedy was wonderful with him. They all were. They did anything and everything they could think of to do for him, in any and every way, all the details. Mrs Kennedy went over the linens with me after he became ill and she ordered new linens. She said, 'Because I want him to have the best.' And Mrs Shriver said one day, 'You know, I think the fact that Daddy still dresses and has his clothes come from Sulka's just the same as if he were well is *important*.' And he felt so too, because he'd come down the elevator to the library and would be dressed so nicely and would be so proud and everyone would be complimenting him. They were passing TL's around the place but in those days especially for him. Often they'd come to the table and say, 'I've got a TL for you.' And then they'd tell him something that someone else had said to them about him that was a compliment . . .

And so, fairly soon, sooner than one could reasonably expect at the time of his attack, we were able to resume in a general way the annual pattern of our lives: spring, summer and fall in Hyannis Port, winter in

Palm Beach, with intervals in New York. Joe, with Ann and the medical
staff, and with emergency medical equipment aboard, would make
these trips in the *Caroline*. Usually I would leave about a fortnight
earlier, to get the houses opened and everything in readiness; and to do
some personal shopping and perhaps see a few old friends; and also,
in that interval, to go out to Wisconsin to see Rosemary.

When we were in New York, there were always friends and distinguished former associates who wanted to see him to pay their
respects, wish him good progress and, I suppose, by their attention,
reassure him that he was still a very important person. One day, for
instance, General Douglas MacArthur came to the apartment. I have a
diary note:

> I was amazed at his diction, wonderful command of English and
> felicity of expression. He stayed about half an hour and talked all
> the time, which was wonderful as Joe does not talk, but during the
> General's remarks nodded his head in assent occasionally.

Another time we were invited to lunch with former President
Herbert Hoover at his apartment in the Waldorf Towers. A diary note:

> It was wonderful to see the delight on both faces when they met.
> Though of different political allegiances they were old friends. And I
> remembered Joe saying once that Mr Hoover was one of the few
> people in the world who really did enlighten him with knowledge
> and experience and wisdom. I had met him a couple of times and
> found him rather withdrawn and aloof, but on this day he was
> amiable, seemed in a very expansive mood, talked a great deal and
> seemed anxious to put us at our ease and make our visit a happy one.
> But he had been very sick himself. His nurse, whom he had had for
> a long time, was near to help him if he needed anything and she
> sat with us at luncheon. He obviously was frail. Moreover he was
> very deaf.
>
> So here was Joe, who cannot speak, and Mr Hoover, who cannot
> hear, trying to communicate. The two men, friends, both with great
> achievements to remember; each aware of his own and the other's
> crippling infirmities now, trying to make the best of it. And so
> poignant, inexpressibly sad, when each of them from time to time
> through the meal wept silently.

As I have said, I expect that these occasional weeping spells were
associated with the neurological damage he had suffered; but I think
also they were a manifestation of the 'massive frustration' that Dr

Betts mentioned. André Malraux once wrote: 'Man is not made for defeat. He may be vanquished but not destroyed.' Malraux meant Man as *Homo sapiens* but there seldom if ever could have been a better example than Joe. He absolutely, resolutely and even furiously refused to accept any idea of defeat and he could barely tolerate the idea of having been temporarily vanquished. A few of my diary notes of the time:

> Joe wants and tries to do things like he did in the past. I keep thinking what a pity that such a superior person dedicated to goodness and efficiency should be so crippled – through no fault of his own . . .
>
> . . . It was so sad and nerve-racking to see him try to tell me something which I could not understand, or complain about something which I could not fathom. He is still very vital and vigorous about expressing his wishes and gets cross and impatient if we cannot understand him . . . Sometimes he uses his left arm or leg to push or whack the nurses . . .
>
> . . . The nurses work only eight hours at a time and sometimes I do not think they coordinate very well. For instance, one says that Joe has slept well, while the night nurse has told me his breathing was irregular or heavy. Then the first one says, 'The night nurse is new and is not accustomed to his breathing.' Often one goes on vacation or says she has to take a few days off, and then the substitute doesn't know the routine or perhaps even how to work the wheelchair properly . . . One night, a nurse got him into the elevator and then didn't know how to operate the release pedal on the chair, so the chair was too extended and the elevator door could not close. Also, once they did get down, she had difficulty getting the chair out of the elevator. And so Joe sat for five or six minutes bursting with rage . . .
>
> Naturally, all these times fill me with annoyance and sadness for his sake, and with frustrations because I can do so little about them . . .

Nevertheless, it was because of this tremendous determination – this power of sheer will, I think – that he was able to keep going, within the limits of the human frame, and to take part in such a number of aspects of the life towards which he had worked. In New York we continued to go to the theatre and to concerts and to dine out: dinner usually at La Caravelle, which he had helped found and where the manager, Robert Meuzin, and the head waiters knew his table and our tastes and could arrange everything gracefully. And he continued to go to his New York office – not long at a time, perhaps an hour or two, a few times a week – to look over the books and operations with Stephen Smith who was running the office.

Sometimes on these journeys or stop-overs he and I would go to Washington and spend a few days in the White House. This was another rather strange blessing: for by then not even the most cynical persons could suppose that Jack was being directed by his father; and so at last Joe could feel free to visit and take a father's pride and pleasure in the fact his son was the President. Whenever he was there, Jack made sure to be with him several times a day, give him the news of government and, in the most respectful and tactful way, solicit his advice, so far as he could give it.

And of course Bobby and Ethel. They would come to the White House for dinner or, if everything seemed propitious, Joe and I, and Ann and perhaps the night nurse, and Jack and Jackie, would converge at their house in the countryside near Washington; probably be joined there by Eunice and Sarge, who lived in the same area; and perhaps by Pat and Peter, and Jean and Steve, and Teddy and Joan, if they happened to be around at the time. We seldom lacked a quorum.

The year that Teddy ran for the Senate was also the first year of Joe's illness; and of course this put Teddy under extra pressure, not only because he loved and revered his father and was worried about him but because he knew that his father had very much wanted him to make the race and naturally wanted him to win. Teddy would have worked extremely hard in any case. But if there is anything beyond 'going all out' that's where Teddy went because he knew how much a victory would mean to his father.

It was quite a memorable campaign and attracted much national attention in the various media, for it had intrinsic elements of drama. The first, obviously, was that if Teddy won, our family would have the Presidency, the Attorney Generalship and a Senate seat at the same time, which was entirely unprecedented and really would be amazing. But also the contest involved a collision of some of the strongest political forces in the state, and some of the best-known names in US politics – with a lot of evocative political history in the background. Teddy's opponent for the Democratic endorsement, at the state convention, was Eddie McCormack who not only was Attorney General of Massachusetts but was the nephew and protégé of John W. McCormack, the Speaker of the US House of Representatives, who of course was backing him with all the influence at his command. (The Fitzgeralds, Kennedys and McCormacks had had many encounters in

Boston and Massachusetts political life: usually as friends, sometimes as foes, sometimes friendly-enemies.) The prospective, and actual, winner on the Republican side was George Cabot Lodge whom Jack had defeated for the Senate in 1952, and great-grandson of the same Henry Cabot Lodge who had defeated my father for the Senate in 1916. Making matters even more interesting, there was an independent candidate, Stuart Hughes, professor of history at Harvard, grandson of Chief Justice Charles Evans Hughes (whose house, by the way, we had rented when we moved down from Boston to Riverdale) who had run against Woodrow Wilson for the Presidency in that election of 1916 and who, in one of the most famous turn-overs in American politics, had gone to sleep on election night believing he had been elected, but had awakened to find that Wilson had instead.

A considerable confrontation, to be sure.

I was involved very little in that campaign, for I felt that Joe needed me, and I wanted to be with him. Furthermore, Teddy apparently was feeling a bit oppressed by this time at being the 'kid brother' in the family and was out to show that he could win on his own merits as a candidate. He made this well known in the family. Jack was very pleased with him and also rather amused. Teddy recalls:

> He knew that when I was running in Massachusetts I told the voters I wanted to be judged on my own, and not on the family name. So in a speech he made in 1963, he said, 'Teddy wants to be judged on his own; so he is thinking of changing his name . . . from Teddy Kennedy to Teddy Roosevelt.'

As I recall, I did go on radio or television a couple of times, gave some interviews about Teddy, helped Joan with a few special contacts such as my friends in the French-Canadian communities, and also played the piano several times at meetings; really only a 'stunt' because despite my lessons and years of playing in the circle of friends and family I was only an amateur, whereas she was accomplished enough to be a concert pianist. Joan had been out a few times before, on the road here and there, with Teddy and the others when Jack was running, but this was her first time as the wife of a candidate – a special and difficult and delicate role for anyone, as I have said earlier. Like Jackie, Joan is a rather private, reserved and shy person for whom the public appearances, with the receiving lines and hand-shaking and motor-cades and speech-making and interviews and all the rest, would not be at all easy. In fact, all this could be almost crushingly difficult at times; we women in our family had plenty of reason to know, having done such a lot to set the pattern. But again like Jackie, Joan with her radiant beauty and soft shyness proved herself to be made of iron when the needs were put upon her. She was a great campaigner. And at this point in my story, I think it can be understood – in all dimensions – that this is a great compliment.

Teddy won in the state convention against Eddie McCormack, who however refused to accept that decision and took the matter to the state primaries, where Teddy won in the popular vote by a very big margin. This left him eyeball-to-eyeball, so to speak, with George Lodge, the Republican nominee, in the general election, with Stuart Hughes, the Independent, in nominal contention.

Meanwhile a great many of the people – local 'Kennedy secretaries' and others, sometimes the younger relatives or even descendants of those who had helped in the early campaigns – had rallied to Teddy's cause, or were on their way or said they would be ready whenever needed. Members of the family, and of Jack's circle of assistants and friends, were on the scene from time to time. Bobby came up from Washington, as did Ted Sorenson. Polly and her group arranged teas and receptions. Joey Gargan was there doing numerous jobs. Steve Smith spent most of that spring-summer-fall in Boston coordinating the campaign. So again it was a matter of loyalty, of organizational effort with attention to all details, of devoted family participation and guidance – and, needless to say, of a hard-working and intelligent and attractive candidate.

Teddy won over George Lodge by 285,000 votes, and had a majority over Lodge and Hughes together of 235,000 votes. As soon as he could be certain of his victory Teddy called his father. Joe couldn't speak, so there could be no conversation, but he listened as Ted told him the news and all about everything he knew his father would want to know. Joe smiled and smiled, delightedly, which in Evelyn's true perception 'was worth all the money in the world – you couldn't pay for it . . .'

Not long ago, in going through files for this book, I came across an article about Joe that appeared in the September 7, 1957, issue of the *Saturday Evening Post* in which he was quoted as predicting that someday one of our sons would be President, another would be Attorney General, and another would be a US Senator – all this simultaneously. I suppose I had seen the article when it came out and perhaps had read this forecast, but if so I had put it out of my mind because it seemed such an implausible idea. Nevertheless, it had happened; and once again, but even more so, I was amazed at and grateful for Joe's almost preternatural ability to judge people and events and discern the shape of the future.

I must say also that when Teddy was elected, when all three of our surviving sons were in positions of leadership and great responsibility in the nation's government, then I – looking back over all the years to when they had been children, little boys on their way to youth and manhood, those impressionable years when 'the twig is bent' – I thought to myself that I must have done something right.

And so we entered a golden time. It was shadowed by Joe's illness; yet, as I have said, he was still able to enjoy a good many of the pleasures of life; and his spirit was comforted by the manifest affection that surrounded him – surrounded would be a literal term when the grandchildren were visiting – and above all by the accomplishment of the grand design he had for his sons, and by their love and respect for him.

He delighted in hearing from the grandchildren and received reams of mail from them, sometimes in their own scrawls if they were old enough to write, otherwise dictated to their mothers (who I dare say were egging them on to have a few words for Grandpa). From this large trove, here are a few samples.

February 5, 1962
The White House

Dear Grandpa,

We rode on the sleigh and there was no snow – but there was no snow – but there was some and we ried all the morning.

Macaroni tried to get in front and he tried to kick Buster too and we rode on the leadline . . .

Daddy is sitting with Mummy and me and not John a bad squeaky boy who tries to spit in his mother's Coca-Cola and who has a very bad temper.

I hope to meet you soon. Antoni lives in London but he's here now and he likes you and he wants you to be his Grandpa.

I love you so much. Twenty hundred yards I love you.

From Caroline
(as told to her mother)

September 25, 1962
Peace Corps
Office of the Director
Washington

Dear Grandpa,

I hope you are feeling better. And I hope that I will be comeing up to see you soon. And I whant to tell you what I have to do evry week. I have to do reading and writing and Arithmetic. Some day I am going to get sick of school work too. Oh! I ment to tell you. I've been in school for two weeks . . . I'm in the third grade. And I am working very hard . . . I hope you will feel better.

Your loving child
Bob Sargent Shriver

1962; undated
The White House

Dear Grandpa,

Come back to the White House and throw all the horses out of the President's office.

With all our love,
Jack – Jackie – John –
Caroline
(dictated to her mother)

(undated)
Washington

Dear Grampa and Granma,

I will be at the cape in a week. how are you feeling? I have a giant turtle. I will see you soon.

Bobby
Robert Francis Kennedy Jr

April 6, 1963
Rockville, Maryland

Dear Grandpa and Grandma,

My sister Maria made her first confession on Thursday. Now she wants to go to confession every minut, hour, and day. Plus go to communion. Whitch she will do on April 28, 1963. Whitch is my birthday. She is looking forward to this day very much. She sends her love to you and Grandma.

I am now an Altar boy and I serve Mass. I have a partner . . . He is a nut. Because he makes mistaks when we serve. He is so nutty. Well Good by now I hope I will see you soon. Your loving child.

Bobby Sargent Shriver

And of course the children and their spouses wrote him often, always keeping him informed of what was going on, what they were doing or about to do out there in the wide world he could no longer reach. Here, for instance, is one from Jackie, from the White House, in 1962:

Dearest Grandpa –

You were taking a nap when I left. I am off to Italy with Caroline for 2 weeks – to stay with Lee and Stas. We will send you lots of postcards and pictures and miss you very much. We will see you soon when we get home and bring you some marvellous present . . .

Please put the picture of Jack and me and Caroline and John right by your favourite chair where Eunice will see it – and nail it down so she can't take it away and put Timmy there instead.

I love you –
Jackie

A characteristic scene – from that sweet, golden, short time we had together – a scene that seldom varied much and I remember so well, would be when Jack and the Presidential party would come up to the Cape for summer weekends. Dr Betts has mentioned this, but I can supply some details and from another viewpoint, and from another point in time. These are diary notes that I made in 1964, when it was all over and I was trying to remember what it had been like when . . .

Jack was here with all the excitement of the helicopters arriving on Friday evenings in front of our house. The Secret Service would set up a telephone in front of the porch an hour or two in advance, in order to keep track of the exact time of arrival, because there could be a change of a few minutes to half an hour. The children would gather in the driveways – fifteen or twenty or thirty of them with their friends. The dogs would be there barking, the maids would stand a bit in the background, and probably a few close friends would also have gathered. The firetrucks were at the end of the driveway. The voice of the Secret Service man could be heard discussing the time and the weather conditions for landings.

Then at a distance we could hear the sound of the motors. Joe would be wheeled out on the porch with a robe over his knees. A wave of excitement would sweep over the group as we watched the first helicopter approach, then slow down, then balance itself gracefully, expertly, precisely to land exactly on the small yard in front of Joe's chair where he was waiting on the porch. The door of the helicopter would open, officers would step out, then the President.

Caroline and John would run and jump into his arms. He would lean over ever so affectionately and hug and embrace them. I always realized he was a little wary as to how he bent, so as not to hurt his back; and, of course, he never lifted them up into his arms. But the casual onlooker would never have detected any difficulty.

Then Bobby's children would run to him, or the Shrivers' or

Lawfords' or Smiths' or Teddy and Joan's – whoever was there. They would all be laughing, joking, about the sunburns or the races won or lost.

Jack then would come up on to the front porch where his father was sitting so proudly in his wheelchair. They would embrace, say a few words; then Jack would come and hug me too and let me kiss him on the cheek. And Jack would always have a big, all-embracing smile.

Then, after a few minutes, everyone would separate, going to their own various houses but to come together later, for dinner, at our house and perhaps – depending on how many people were on hand – at one of the other houses.

The Presidential yacht – the *Honey Fitz* – usually was anchored here during those summers. Often the next day Jack would go out in it with some of the family, friends and staff. Joe usually would go out in the family cruiser, the *Marlin*, and one or two of the boys would take turns being with him. Jackie and some of the other girls did a lot of water-skiing, pulled by a speedboat. Sunday, after Mass, was more of the same, mixed in with golf and tennis and other sports and lively conversation.

Then on Monday morning the same scene, the same excitement, as the helicopters took off for the airport and the trip back to Washington.

Jack's administration had its rough times, as all of them do, and more than its share of crises, especially in the earlier part, beginning with the Cuban débâcle. But as he settled into the Presidency and learned his way, it seemed that he gained increasing confidence and momentum and that soon he proceeded from triumph to triumph. Among the most remarkable had been those that June, on official travels that took him to Germany, Ireland, England and Italy. I wished that I could go along, as all four countries have special associations for me, and I thought in particular I might be helpful in Germany as Chancellor Adenauer spoke very little English and my German might at last come in handy.

Alas, it was not to be. First because Joe was not feeling very well and I hesitated to leave him; also because Jack had already invited Eunice and Jean, and Jackie's sister, Lee, for most of the trip and I really felt it would be unfair to the poor boy to have his mother along too – otherwise I might have hitched my way to Germany as I had to Austria in 1961.

However, Jack seemed to get along quite well without my linguistic assistance: he had tremendous and enthusiastic crowds everywhere he went in West Germany; and this was the time, too, when he went to

West Berlin and was greeted by perhaps the biggest crowds ever seen, more than a million people, and gave that famous speech that closed with the words: 'All free men, wherever they may live, are citizens of Berlin, and therefore as a free man, I take pride in the words *Ich bin ein Berliner!*'

He flew then to Ireland. Not really for matters of state – Irish-American relations couldn't have been more cordial – but as a brief, sentimental journey to the land of his ancestors. Jack delighted in his Irish heritage. And, perhaps, took a more than ordinary interest in it because of stories he had heard from his grandparents, handed down to them by their parents, about the miserable conditions under which the immigrants of the 1840s and '50s had arrived in Boston, and the poverty and social disdain they suffered there as 'muckers' and the like, a condition from which they could rise only by hard work, belief and ingenuity. Jack believed fully, devoutly, in America as a land of opportunity. He took to heart the ideal of America as a land of liberty and the words inscribed on the pedestal of the Statue of Liberty: 'Give me your tired, your poor, your huddled masses yearning to breathe free . . .' For some years he had been making notes for a book he intended to write, someday, about the migrations of the many national, ethnic, political and religious groups to this country, the problems they fled and those they had to face, the processes of their assimilation here: the title he had in mind was *A Nation of Immigrants*. And so I'm sure his heart was in it fully when he spoke on the quayside at New Ross and said: 'When my great-grandfather left here to become a cooper in East Boston he carried nothing with him except two things, a strong religious faith and a strong desire for liberty. I am glad to say that all of his great-grandchildren have valued that inheritance.'

The people of Ireland already felt a proud affinity for him as one of their own. But when they saw him in person and heard him speak and sensed his special feeling for them, they went all but berserk with joy. The whole island – as those with him told me later – appeared to be a tumult of admiration and celebration.

Later on, after he was gone from this life, Sybil Connolly, the Irish designer, who was there at the time, mentioned a certain remark she heard and I asked her to write it out for me. This was her note:

I promised you that I would send you the remark made by the then Dutch Ambassador to Ireland, commenting on the visit of President Kennedy there in the spring of 1963.

On the fantastic reception which the President received and the way the Irish people took him to their hearts, he said: 'It is the conquering Alexander returning to his people.' And there is a ring of truth in this.

I wish that you could see for yourself, over the hearth of almost every cottage in Ireland – a picture of the Sacred Heart, of the Blessed Virgin, and of President Kennedy – it is extremely moving.

Jack loved poetry. I think Jackie broadened his taste in that, as in painting and as in much else. But there remained a special place in his heart and mind for that delicate, dew-drenched and musical poetry that seems characteristic of Ireland. Among the Irish poems he cherished most was one that was recited for him by the Irish Ambassador, Thomas Kiernan, in honor of John Jr, when John was still a baby:

> We wish to the new child
> A heart that can be beguiled by a flower
> That the wind lifts as it passes
> Over the grasses after a summer shower,
> A heart that can recognize
> Without aid of the eyes
> The gifts that life holds for the wise.
> When the storms break for him,
> May the trees shake for him their blossoms down.
> In the night that he is troubled
> May a friend wake for him
> So that his time be doubled,
> And at the end of all loving and love,
> May the Man Above
> Give him a crown.

Jack, I am told, was so moved that he found it difficult to speak. But then said, 'I wish it had been written for me.'

I think that in a way it was.

He went to England for talks with Prime Minister Macmillan. But this too was in part a sentimental journey, for on the way he went privately, with Jean and Lee, and accompanied by the Duke and Duchess of Devonshire, to Chatsworth, to visit Kick's grave. They prayed by the graveside and left a bunch of fresh-picked Irish roses at the headstone.

In Italy, his last stop, he conferred not only with the leaders of government but with the newly crowned Pope Paul VI at the Vatican. The Pope told him he remembered our family very well from the time, twenty-five years earlier, we had come to the coronation of Pope Pius XII and then Pius had confirmed little Teddy in the Church in a private ceremony. Pope Paul sent his greetings to all of us, with special ones for Teddy.

Then he was back in Washington, and cleared his desk enough that he was able to come up and have the long Fourth of July weekend with us, and tell us about his rather fabulous experiences. From then on, he was with us for most of the summer and fall weekends.

The last of these visits was on Sunday, October 20, 1963. Kenny O'Donnell and Dave Powers have described the Monday morning departure:

> Ambassador Kennedy was on the porch in his wheelchair. The President went to him, put his arm around the old man's shoulder and kissed him on the forehead. He started to the helicopter, turned, looked at his father for a moment and went back and kissed him a second time . . . It almost seemed as if the President had the feeling that he was seeing his father for the last time.
>
> When the President was inside the helicopter waiting for the take-off, he looked out at the figure in the wheelchair and his eyes filled with tears.
>
> 'He's the one who made all of this possible,' the President said to Dave sadly, 'and look at him now.'

Jack had to be in Texas several days during mid-November, to smooth some political problems in the Democratic party there, and would be taking Jackie with him. But then they planned to come back, with Caroline and John, for the annual family reunion and Thanksgiving at Hyannis Port.

I remember that Friday, November 22, began as one of those perfect late autumn days at the Cape. At that time of year the air is crisp but not cold, just cool enough to make some warmth from fireplaces most welcome even if not entirely needed, and it has such freshness from the sea that one's spirits are lifted up. There is a special quality to the light then, too: it is golden, pure, making everything stand out in clear relief and with a peculiar and lovely luminosity – every white clapboard house and every tree and autumn-coloured leaf or bare branch, every bayberry and sumac and wild beach rose with its red pips and valiant remaining blossoms, seems to come to special life, as if to assert its qualities and beauties and reasons for being just before the frosts and snows. Many of the garden flowers are still in bloom, too: the asters and chrysanthemums and calendulas and dark-eyed susans and marigolds and other old-fashioned reliables that we always planted abundantly in our gardens and that made such a show of colour through the fall. By then, also, the tourists and 'summer people' had gone and the village, though not deserted, was somnolent. And so on that beautiful morning, after I had been to Mass and we had had breakfast, Joe and I went for a ride in the station-wagon, simply enjoying the weather and the scenery and the serenity; then went back to the house; then I went over to the golf course. As I have said, usually I liked to play in the afternoons, but at this season on the Cape the afternoons become short and dusk soon falls, and my eyesight was becoming poor, so I played in the mornings: played the usual nine holes, then came back to have lunch with Joe.

After lunch, Joe had his nap as usual. I was feeling rather tired and went to my room to lie down for a while. Soon, however, I heard Ann's radio set blaring so loudly in her room down the hall that I got up and went to tell her please to tune it down, or better yet just turn it off. Ann said the volume was up because she had just heard from one of the help, who had been listening to a favourite programme that was interrupted by a news bulletin, that along the route in Dallas someone had taken some shots at the President and he had been wounded.

I had a mixture of reactions. Worry about Jack, of course, instinctively. But then a rejection of the idea that it could be something terribly serious because, after all, he had been through so much, from the time he was in danger of death from scarlet fever as a little child to the time he nearly died from his back operation, and so many things in between – all those illnesses and misfortunes of health that I have mentioned in this narrative and more besides – all those things his little brother Bobby summed up jokingly in saying that if a mosquito bit Jack the mosquito would die – so that almost automatically I had in the back of my mind the thought, Jack is having some more hard luck, another problem about his health but he'll surmount it. Further, I had trained myself through the years not to become too visibly upset at bad news, even very bad news, because I had a strong notion that if I broke down, caved in, wept, everybody else in the household would and therefore I had to hold myself together.

I went back to my room and paced the floor, trying to think that Jack was going to be all right; that soon the news would come that he had not been wounded badly. After a while I went back to Ann's room and found that the news was worse. My heart sank. But I still couldn't realize that what seemed to be happening was really happening. Then, a few minutes later, Bobby telephoned from Washington and said Jack was in an extremely serious condition and was not expected to live. And then, soon, the news came through that Jack was gone.

At any such time of shock and grief I suppose that most people fall back for some support on familiar patterns of behaviour that can be followed automatically. In our household, many long years before, Joe and I had adopted as a general principle that if there was bad news to be faced it should be given in the mornings, not late in the day, for otherwise there would be a sleepless night which would only make the debility worse. Hence I made a spontaneous decision that Joe should not be told of the tragedy when he awakened from his nap, and that if it were at all possible he should not know of it until the following morning. This would also allow time for his physician, then Dr Boles, to come down to the Cape from Boston, and for Teddy and Eunice to come up from Washington, as they had called and said they wanted to do, with Bobby staying in Washington to take care of Jackie and supervising all the things that would need to be done there: Bobby making arrangements, even to getting Pat on the first flight from California; Sarge, Jean, Steve, also in Washington, helping in all ways. I told Ann and the nurses that Mr Kennedy was not to be informed of anything until those who would arrive had arrived and we could decide how and when he would be told.

They all, the household staff and everyone, entered into a conspiracy of kindness. Shocked and grief-ridden though they were, they acted their parts superbly well. For example, Joe was in the habit of looking at television after his nap, or else of seeing a movie in our basement projection room. The TV screen was filled with news of the tragedy, so Ann worked on him to see a movie that day instead. He agreed. But he lost interest in the film after a while and wanted to come back up to see his TV programme. We had two or three sets but none worked, Ann having unplugged them and stuffed the cords out of sight. He was irritated, but then he seemed to accept this as one of those coincidental freakish defects of modern technology and contented himself as much as he could by reading a magazine. Now and then, one or another or several of us would go into his room to chat about something, almost anything that would have been an ordinary thing to talk about. Joey Gargan heard the news and hurried down from Boston to help in any way he could – one way being to enter into these apparently casual and rather aimless conversations during which everyone was inwardly anguished except his Uncle Joe, who may have suspected something was wrong but didn't know. Ann was supposed to have left that day to visit her sister Mary Jo and Dick Clasby and their family, who lived in Detroit at that time. Joe realized this, but Ann explained by telling him that Wilbert Marsh, the gardener and caretaker of our Hyannis Port place of whom Joe was very fond (he was the brother of Evelyn Jones, who has contributed some memories here) had been in an accident and she wanted to stay back to be sure everything was all right with him. Joe accepted this well-meant fabrication.

Meanwhile, as that afternoon wore on, I spent much time in our front yard or on our beach, and walked and walked and walked, and prayed and prayed and prayed, and wondered why it had happened to Jack. He had everything to live for: a lovely and talented wife, a perfect partner for him, and two beautiful little children whom he adored. He had made such a great and glorious success of his life and of his Presidency, and at last, for the first time since early childhood, he had become really healthy. Everything – the culmination of all his efforts, abilities, dedication to good and to the future – lay boundlessly before him. Everything was gone. And I wondered why.

I heard and read later that most of the nation, and even much of the world, was in a state of suspended animation after the tragedy: some mixture of incredulity, outrage, shock and immense grief, and that this was true wherever the news came and among all groups and ages, but especially among the young, because so many young people looked to Jack as a hero and model for their lives. A friend of mine – this was one instance – told me later that his young son, a boy then of about thirteen, came home from school looking taut and almost ashen and went at once to his room. And when the father, knowing the news and knowing how the boy, Kevin, had idolized Jack, went up and touched him on the shoulder and started to try to say something that would make it bearable, the boy began sobbing 'It's not fair! . . . It's not fair! . . . It's just *not fair* . . .'

I walked on the beach and I thought, 'Why?'

In the afternoon the day had turned quite cold and the fogs and mists had begun coming in, as often happens there at that time of year, and on one of my trips to the house I had bundled up in warm clothing. I think I put on the same tacky but warm coat I had worn through the snows when I went to Mass the morning of Jack's Inauguration. It was then, or somewhere around that time, about four in the afternoon, that someone came out to tell me President Johnson was calling us on the radio-telephone from Air Force One, on the way back to Washington. It was I who took the call, of course.

When I had picked up the receiver and said hello, I heard his voice, full of recognizable anguish saying, 'Mrs Kennedy, I wish to God there was something I could do.' I don't remember what I said, but I thanked him for calling with his sympathy; then I heard Lady Bird's voice. She and I had done some campaigning together in 1960, and had liked each other. I had found her to be not only attractive, well-groomed and composed in spite of a native reticence to be in public life, but also a person of intelligence, warmth, understanding and also certainly not lacking in a certain straightforward eloquence. She said a few words first – I don't remember – and then, 'We must all realize how fortunate the country was to have your son as long as it did.' And I said, 'Thank you, Lady Bird.' And that's all either of us could think of or felt like saying just then.

I went back to the yard and the beach.

My reaction to grief takes in part the form of nervous activity. I have to keep moving, walking, pulling away at things, praying to myself while I move, and making up my mind that I am not going to be defeated by tragedy. Because there are the living still to work for, while mourning for the dead.

Dr Boles arrived. There were many telephone calls, some useful in one way or another, all of them so wonderfully well-meant. Dr Boles went to check on Joe's general condition, on the acceptable grounds that he would be leaving for Florida soon after Thanksgiving and this was therefore a routine check-up. Dr Boles told us that Joe could, physically, withstand the emotional shock, though he agreed it would be better if it came not that evening but in the morning. Joey had come down. Ted and Eunice arrived together and went in, as casually as they could manage, to see their father. Perhaps Joe was surprised by this conjunction but there was no reason to be very surprised: after all, he was due for a check-up from Dr Boles. Joey did work in Boston and had a weekend and vacation and holiday house at Hyannis Port. Ted and Eunice travelled a lot because of their numerous public interests and responsibilities, and therefore might drop in on us most anytime.

After dinner – Joe having a tray in his room, which was not unusual, I having a cup of broth or something in mine, the others having something downstairs – we all assembled, as casually as possible, in Joe's room and chatted there for a while until he was ready for sleep.

It was decided among us, with Ted really deciding to take it on himself, that he should be the one to tell his father that next morning.

I went to the morning devotions at the beautiful little church, St Francis Xavier's, in Hyannis – where all four sons in their time had served as altar boys – and stayed on for the first Mass of the day, to which Ted and Eunice came. I had called the pastor the night before and asked him to say this Mass for Jack. It was one of the first things I had thought of to do. There were reporters and photographers, some of whom even tried to talk to me within the church, but I could do nothing but ignore them.

After Mass we went home to breakfast. And, as usual, after breakfast Joe went back to his room for a while for a rest. It was very soon then that Ted – with Eunice, Ann, the doctor, a nurse, perhaps one or two others; not I, for I couldn't stand it – went in and told him, as gently yet as straight-out as he possibly could, what had happened and that Jack had passed away.

As I heard from them afterwards, Joe not only took the tragic news bravely but seemed to want to comfort them.

The doctor had already given him a sedative, and soon he went back to sleep.

The doctor said that it would be feasible for Joe to go to the funeral in Washington that Monday, but he rejected the idea. One of his old friends, Father John Cavanaugh, the former president of Notre Dame University, came to stay at the house for a while for such aid and comfort as he could give. The two of them sat together and watched the ceremonies on television.

It was far easier for me to travel and I felt I should be there. And I was. I did not walk with the others in the procession from the White House to the Cathedral because I felt queasy, quite unwell, that morning. Nor did I take Communion at the Cathedral, as some others did, because I had already been to an early Mass and had received it then. I was at the graveside in Arlington, of course, for the final ceremonies. Afterwards, with the others, I went to the White House to help express our family's appreciation to the numerous heads of state, other dignitaries and many friends who had travelled from far places to pay respects; among those friends, the Duke and Duchess of Devonshire.

Then, that evening, I came back to Hyannis Port to be with Joe.

19

'For I have promises to keep
And miles to go before I sleep
And miles to go before I sleep'
ROBERT FROST

'I know the one thing Joe would never want is that we should feel sad
and gloomy about life without him. Instead he'd laugh with that
wonderful twinkle shining out of his Irish eyes and say, 'Gee, can't you
all learn to get along without me.'
KATHLEEN, IN JACK'S BOOK, *As We Remember Joe*

We in the family reacted to our common grief in our own ways. But
we could all be reasonably steady because of the faith, hope and love
we shared. And because we knew quite well what Jack would want
from us: he would want courage, he would want as many smiles as we
could manage, and he would want his death to be an affirmation of life.
He would want us to think of him with love, but to live for the living;
and to cherish such happiness as we could find and give, and any bit of
light and hope and example of fortitude that might help us and others.
We all realized this, and it needed no discussion, and we all did our best.

Everyone knows the bravery and dignity with which Jackie conducted herself during those ceremonies. Afterwards, at the White
House, she had received the many eminent visitors from abroad; and
did so not only with composure but with some appropriate word or
gesture of thanks for each of them. As General de Gaulle remarked,
'She gave an example to the whole world of how to behave.'

Thanksgiving was three days later. I think it was well understood –
with only a few words passed around in confirmation – that we would
go ahead with it as usual at Hyannis Port. And so during Tuesday
and Wednesday the children and in-laws and cousins and grandchildren
began arriving. We didn't know whether Jackie would come. After
everything she had been through in Dallas and Washington it would

have been entirely understandable if she had wanted a time of seclusion. But on Wednesday evening she too arrived, bringing Caroline and John. And on Thursday we had the Thanksgiving celebrations, with every one of us hiding the grief that gnawed at us and doing our best to make it a day of peace and kindnesses and optimism and good-humour and of thankfulness for the blessings that were still left to us.

Not long ago Jackie was thinking back to that time – and to times of hard misfortune or tragedy that came later on – and she said:

> Something so incredible about them is their gallantry. You can be sitting down to dinner with them and so many sad things have happened to each, and – God! – maybe even some sad thing has happened that day, and you can see that each one is aware of the other's suffering. And so they can sit down at the table in a rather sad frame of mind. Then each one will begin to start to make this conscious effort to be gay or funny or to lift each other's spirits; and you find that it's infectious, that everybody's doing it. They all bounce off each other.
>
> They all have a humour that's my favourite kind. It's a little bit irreverent, a little bit self-mocking, a little sense of the ridiculous, and in times of sadness a wildly wicked humour of irreverence. I don't mean they're laughing when they shouldn't be. But to make a real effort to use the light touch when everybody's sad – I think it is wonderful.
>
> They have been such a great help to me. My natural tendency is to be rather introverted and solitary and to retreat into myself and brood too much. But they bring out the best. No one sits and wallows in self-pity. It's just so gallant that it really makes you proud. And you think, look at these people and the effort they are making, and you think that's a lesson you want to take with you.

Early that December, as we had through so many years, Joe and I went back to the Palm Beach house. We had Christmas there in the usual way – the big tree and all the trimmings – and some of the children and grandchildren were able to be there. They all came for visits that winter and spring as often as they could, to cheer our lives.

There was much for me to do, especially during those first few months. Many thousands of letters of sympathy and condolence came to us: far more than I could possibly reply to personally, so most had to be taken over by the girls, or near relatives, or people in the New York or Washington offices who knew our minds and would know what to say. However, there were hundreds from personal friends and others whom I felt ought to hear directly from us; and, of course, that was up to me, since it was impossible for Joe.

His general health seemed about the same as before, and his spirit was firm. But whereas, when the President came to visit he had often been able to move around somewhat in a walker, or even with a cane and some help, soon after Jack's passing he seldom tried this and spent most of the rest of his days chairbound.

There are some lines from Tennyson's 'Ulysses' which Jack had especially liked:

> I am a part of all that I have met:
> Yet all experience is an arch wherethrough
> Gleams that untravelled world, whose margin fades
> For ever and for ever when I move.
> How dull it is to pause, to make an end,
> To rust unburnished, not to shine in use!
> As tho' to breathe were life.
> Life piled on life were all too little.

And I thought sometimes to myself how aptly and how sadly more than ever those words could apply to Joe, whose horizons always had been limitations and now seemed doomed mainly, 'To rust unburnished, not to shine in use,' whereas we others had the solace of being able to move about and do things useful to Jack's memory and ideals.

There were so many memorials for Jack that even we in the family were surprised – as well as deeply appreciative – for bereaved as we felt, we could not have anticipated the sense of bereavement that was felt apparently by most Americans and indeed by such vast numbers of people all over the world. I was often invited to take part in the programme and ceremonies; and when I could, I did.

The first major one, as I remember, that I felt I could and should and really wanted to attend was in January, in Boston, when Cardinal Cushing offered a solemn high Mass for Jack at Holy Cross Cathedral and Erich Leinsdorf conducted the Boston Symphony Orchestra in Mozart's *Requiem in D Minor*.

Boston, Jack's birthplace and associated with so many memories of him and such intimate, almost infinite memories of our family . . . The Cardinal, who married Jack, who had given benediction at his Inauguration and now so recently had buried him, and who was such a very dear family friend . . . the Boston Symphony, with all it had meant to Joe and me when we were courting and as young-marrieds . . . the beauty of the Mass, of the Cathedral, and of the music and the special poignancy that Mozart had died leaving it an unfinished work . . . all these elements together had a nearly overpowering effect. I managed to keep a grip on myself and show outward composure, but with difficulty.

The next month I went north again, to New York, to attend a benefit dinner for the Joseph P. Kennedy Jr Foundation for Mental Retardation. Eunice had organized it. Bobby and Ted were there also. President Johnson was the speaker. In the course of an eloquent address, in which he pledged his Administration to continue the government's support for work in mental retardation, initiated by Jack, he also paid what I'm sure was a deeply felt tribute to Jack as a man and a statesman, and to our family, saying: 'Our generation is proud and blessed to have known the Kennedys.'

Soon afterwards, the Johnsons had to come to Florida for a Democratic fund-raising dinner in Miami. I have a diary note:

February 27, 1964: President and Mrs Johnson stopped at Palm Beach to see Joe, on their way to Miami. He had mentioned the possibility of coming here to Bobby, and the hour was arranged. Strange to say, I was a little excited as well as sad. About an hour before their arrival they called up from Air Force One to see if I was going to be home. In that case, Lady Bird would come over with him. They arrived about 4.45, saw Joe in the study. The President told his plans for the Miami meeting. I showed Mrs Johnson our living-room, with the beamed ceilings and old Spanish tiles which are characteristic of the early Palm Beach houses built by the architect Meisner. Then we joined the men for a glass of orange juice. Pierre Salinger, the press secretary who used to work for Jack, was with the President; also a military aide in uniform. After about twenty minutes they departed. There were a few people outside on the street who applauded them, and they waved back.

Easter came early that year and Jean said she would come down to Palm Beach with Steve and their children to stay two weeks and see about her father if I wanted her to, as ceremonies had been arranged for Jack in Paris by the city government – one of the principal avenues to be renamed for him – and I was invited to be there. And so I did go. This was late March and early April.

An entry in my diary:

First, I went to Boston to see my mother before going abroad, spent the night there, and was glad of it. I put my head in her room in the morning and I saw a shaft of light directly across her face. It crept in through a space between the wall and the curtain. I do not know why the nurses do not do something about such things. The same way when I came to lunch with her one day and found her scrambled eggs cold on a cold plate. The same principle as nurses and governesses with the children. I always used to walk up the beach in the summer to see that a new governess was not flirting with the swimming instructor while the children sat around in wet bathing suits. Or I would go to the children's dances and walk around to see how they were dancing, a very easy thing to do in the summertime when you could stand outside and look through the windows. Also, I was always present during the children's meals. Perhaps the cook gave them the same soup every night because she did not have enough imagination, or did not want to bother giving them a different soup. Or a different dessert. The nurse would not want to complain about it because she would not want to get in wrong with the cook. So it was a good idea for me, as a mother, to keep an eye on all these things, which I tried to do.

Mother 98 now. I have tried to see her every few months. Sight and hearing are failing and I think she knows nothing about Jack's passing. I have not mentioned. When I see her she is quiet, sitting always in the same chair, and weeping a little when she sees me.

In Paris:

Arrived in Paris at midnight, their time, and unpacked my bags to be ready for the ceremony in the morning. Ambassador Bohlen met me at the plane and explained all details. In the morning about 9.30 stopped at the ambassadorial residence for coffee, then drove to the site of ceremony, on the Seine, where Ambassador Bohlen and André Malraux, the French Minister of Culture, escorted me. The President of the Parisian city council, Aubertin, made some brief but eloquent remarks renaming the Quai de Passy to Avenue du President Kennedy. It is a beautiful street, going along the right bank, and had many memories for me; many more now . . . In numerous French towns and villages, streets are being renamed for Jack. And also in other countries.

At the Paris ceremony the people looked grim and sympathetic. As they do everyplace if I go out and am recognized. My old acquaintance M. Zembrzoski, manager at the Ritz, said he really dreaded to see me because his grief was so deep and he would not know what to say.

Much as I appreciate these sentiments they make it more difficult for me, because of the constant reminders.

Loel and Gloria Guinness are friends of our family. They have a house down the coast from us in Florida, and also (among other places, for they move around a lot) a house in Normandy where they spend the spring. Knowing I would be in France in that season, they had invited me to drop in on them. After my time in Paris, I wanted to get away from people who wished to commiserate with me. Since the Guinnesses are always lively and cheerful, I went off to see them.

Later they were recalling that visit for my book, and Gloria said:

It was the coldest Easter I have ever known in my life. We wanted to send a car and driver to Paris to bring her because, you know, with the train there is a big waiting-room, the confusion, the luggage. But she said, 'Thank you, don't bother at all, I would prefer to take the train.' Then some hours later she arrived at our station in Normandy and Loel went with a car and driver and got her and her luggage and she arrived at our house.

Now, staying with us at the house, where my niece was seventeen and my son was twenty-six – Freddie Brisson was there too – the first thing Rose Kennedy did when she arrived, she said, 'How can I find out what time is Mass and where?'

She found out there was a Mass at 7 o'clock in the morning every day in different churches, which would take turns. Now, this woman never, but never, once in the three or four days she was there, talked about pessimism, about tragedy or that she was in mourning.

She supped with the young people, talked with them, made them laugh, found out that my niece was a heretic who didn't like to go to church so she dragged her to church right away and said it doesn't make any difference if you don't believe – you come with me because I don't want to be alone. So then the girl began to go to church again because she likes it. She is still going to church in Mexico, where she lives.

My husband had terrible backaches in those days, and the day before she left we were sitting and suddenly she said, 'You know, Loel, what you should do is try these pads that one sticks on the back. Because you know Jack had this terrible problem with his back, and I told him about those plasters and they helped him.' At that moment she cried. Then recovered immediately and said terribly sorry and she dried her tears and changed the conversation. And that is the only time in the years I have known Rose Kennedy I have ever seen her cry, and I think it was only because, I think, thinking of her boy as a young boy being hurt, that was what made her cry. We were good friends and from then on we became the greatest friends.

I should add a note of explanation about the 'plasters'. They are thin but strong adhesive bandages made of an elastic fabric that can be applied across the back to give extra support. I had suggested to Jack that he try them, and he took a supply along on that last trip of his to Europe. And when he came back and – that July 4 weekend – helicoptered on to the front lawn at Hyannis Port and after greeting the children, then his father and coming to me, he said, 'Mother, those plasters of yours really helped, and I only wish I had known about them sooner.' To my mind this was an example of his demeanour and attitude in so many ways: he was open to advice, and when it worked he was open in his thanks.

Back home in the US there was much to do and think about: memorials, dedications, ceremonials; grand projects conceived in Jack's honour, particularly the Kennedy Center for the Performing Arts, in Washington, and the John F. Kennedy Memorial Library in Cambridge, near the Harvard campus.

It has become customary, in modern times, for American Presidents to collect speeches, state papers, correspondence and multitudinous documents of their administrations and put them in archives so they can be accessible to historians and other scholars and students. Jack had chosen the place he wanted for his library, on property owned by Harvard but on the other side of the Charles River; overlooking the river and with a view of the main campus. He planned to spend a great deal of his time there after his Presidency was finished. Assuming that he was elected to a second term, he would still, when he left the White House, be only fifty-two years old, with many years ahead in which to apply his experience, energy and talents to the good of the nation and of the world; and this location would give him access to the tremendous intellectual facilities and personnel of the Boston area, with its distinguished universities and colleges, and also to the minds of the thousands of students whom he could hope to inspire and inform and encourage towards the ideals he held. The library, as he envisioned it, would have been of fairly modest proportions: big enough for a few offices and reading rooms, for the archives, and for books about or relevant to his Presidency – including the history of it that he intended to write himself.

After his death the idea seemed to grow spontaneously that it should be much enlarged to include all the other facilities, programmes and staff to make it a major centre for the study of political science and statecraft. As well as a library, it would become a School of Government and, especially through its adjunct Institute of Politics, would 'seek to further one of President Kennedy's deepest concerns – increasing the understanding and co-operation between the scholarly community and the political world – conceiving politics not only as the search for public power but also as its use for public purposes: in short, the whole of government.' There would also be a room for the personal memorabilia of his life, such as the childhood letters, some of which have been quoted here; the coconut shell on which he wrote the message that the natives took to the nearest Allied base after the PT boat episode and resulted in his rescue with his surviving crew members; and a few thousand other items. (Dave Powers is curator of that collection.) And the archives would be broadened to include family and other materials that could shed light on his life. The materials for this book will eventually go there.

This much bigger enterprise needed a great deal of money. Hence fund-raising committees came into being all across the country. It also needed enabling legislation on the part of several government bodies, in the first instance by the Massachusetts legislature. One of the things I did after returning from France was to give testimony to the joint legislative committee in whose purview this fell, explaining why – with Jack's boyhood interests, and his adult career – a centre of this sort would be such an appropriate memorial to him and why I felt he would have appreciated it so much.

Others in the family were out doing the same sort of thing – making appearances, giving talks, helping to raise funds, helping to make plans, doing affirmative things – and I'm sure it was a helpful catharsis for them, especially for Jackie, who had every reason to be in a state of deep depression after everything that had been happening to her, all so quickly. Her sister Lee, to whom always she was extremely devoted, stayed with her for a time but then of course had to return to her home and husband and children in London. Fortunately, Jackie enjoyed the company of her sisters-in-law, and they all rallied to her with love and affection and with all the time they could find free from their husbands, families and other responsibilities. Jean, who had the smallest family and was also the nearest in age, was probably her closest companion – especially after Jackie moved with the children from Washington to New York, where Jean and Steve and their family live. Jackie and Jean went around the country a lot, looking at libraries and cultural centres, and at drawings and scale-models, talking with architects, trying to plan what should be done in memory of their husband and brother. And surely this was good for both of them and all of us.

Early that summer, on June 19, there was very nearly another tragedy within our family. Ted and another young Senator, Birch Bayh of Indiana and Mrs Bayh, and Ed Moss, a close friend and aide of Ted's, were due at a meeting in central Massachusetts and had taken a charter flight – through a foggy night – and the plane crashed during the approach to the landing field. The pilot was killed; later Ed Moss died. Senator and Mrs Bayh were bruised and cut and had some fractures, and were hospitalized, but escaped without long-range serious effects. Ted was very badly injured. As we learned later, he had sent all the others ahead in the first ambulance that arrived – while he lay stretched out on the ground with no more than first aid – and waited for the second one to take him to the emergency ward. Once in the hospital, it was touch and go for a while as to whether he would live; and after that, if he lived, whether he would be able to walk and lead a normal life again, since several of his vertebrae were fractured and there was a possibility his spinal cord had been damaged.

He was bedfast for many months – several months in traction – but with his rugged constitution he was able to progress to a wheelchair, to crutches, and finally to walk and run and even engage in sports; although for years afterwards, until fairly recently, he had to wear a back brace. He seems to be in perfect health now.

Meanwhile, during his convalescence, he was soon able to take care of the important business of his Senate office by telephone, mail and courier, in the same way Jack had done while recovering from his back operations. And again like Jack, who had used the months while he was laid up to write *Profiles In Courage*, Ted turned his incapacity to constructive use by collecting and editing, and writing introductions to, the essays about his father that became *The Fruitful Bough*.

Here are a few diary entries made during the early summer of 1964, following Ted's accident:

Ted is in the hospital, and Joan is with him most of the time. And if she can't be there, Jean or Pat try to go up. I have not been yet. The day I was planning to go, Teddy was supposed to make a speech in Philadelphia at a memorial for Jack and I substituted for him. Then, the next time I planned to go turned out to be the day of dear Mary Moore's funeral.

I try to keep myself very busy all the time, as it is the only way I can keep normal and not think too much about the way things were for us before. I read and study French continually although at times think it is foolish, as in Paris everyone at the hotel and at the couture speaks English and I know few French people socially. I am reading a lot of books on art, and especially the Seminars issued by the Metropolitan Museum. We go around here to the different houses of the family for dinner and often there are guests, many of them friends of Jack's. Once at our house we gathered around the piano, Joan played and we sang songs, but then hit on one of Jack's old favourites. I looked over at Jackie, her eyes were filled, and then my eyes filled and then everybody began to dissolve in tears and Joan just closed the piano. We have not tried that again.

President and Mrs Johnson have called to tell us how sorry they felt to hear of Ted's accident and to wish him full recovery. Spoke highly of him – as also have often heard of Bobby. During these six months since Jack's tragedy they have seemed most thoughtful and solicitous about our family. Have called us a number of times and also have called Jackie often. They seem anxious to do whatever they can to assuage our grief. I have written them several times, thanked them, and told the President how much these attentions have meant, particularly to Joe: a boost to his morale.

Bobby is here, but seems to be distracted by the confusion and uncertainty surrounding his own plans. He feels that he should do nothing to prevent his being chosen by President Johnson to run as Vice-President, although he thinks it unlikely that will happen. Sometimes he talks about going abroad for a year to write a book or just to get away from it all.

Bobby had been very close to Jack; had felt united with him. Not so much, of course, in the earlier years because there were eight years between them and that is a big gap when children in a family are young. But then in maturity the difference lessens and soon they discover one another as equals and contemporaries with the same interests. And so it was with Jack and Bobby. Bobby had worked in the 1946 Congressional campaign, had managed the first Senate campaign, had managed the Presidential campaign, had been in Jack's Cabinet and at his right hand through every problem that arose during the Presidency. And as brothers they shared a million ties of loyalty, sentiment, memory; and thus could not have been more closely united in thought and deed. No wonder, then, that Bobby at first acted as if he had been cut adrift and did not know quite what to try to do with himself in the years ahead. However, automatically and instinctively and very deeply he wanted to do what Jack would have wanted of him, which in the first and urgent priority of things would be to help Jackie and the two children.

It was, for example, he who met Air Force One when it arrived back from Dallas that night of the assassination with Jack in his coffin and Jackie in her bloodstained suit and who took charge of everything and stayed in charge, acting for the family and for himself and for her. Bobby stayed with Jackie through most of the waking hours of those next days; was with her during John Jr's birthday party; went out with her then to Arlington at midnight to pray at Jack's grave and leave a little personal bouquet of beloved flowers there. Stayed on in support or nearby until she was on the plane with Caroline and John Jr to fly up to us on Thanksgiving Eve.

Bobby, whose life had been so much involved with Jack's, did not himself come up for Thanksgiving. It was something he could not quite do. He had reached a state, I suppose, of almost insupportable emotional shock. He and Ethel and their older children went down to Florida for a few days, where I dare say he too walked the beach and thought, and thought, as Jack had done when he heard of Joe Jr's death.

In any event, during those next months – and indeed for the next years – Bobby was a main pillar of strength in Jackie's life: adviser, protector, confidant and good, cheerful companion whenever he was needed. Ted, of course, did everything he could for her too, but he was younger than she, whereas Bobby was four years older and thus suited by age as well as temperament to be in the role of a protective older brother. She had no really close male kin of her own. Her father was dead. There was a much younger half-brother, only a boy. So it was natural and fitting that she should turn to Bobby in this time of sorrow and reconstruction in her life.

We were at Hyannis Port when Teddy's aeroplane accident happened. Jean had tuned in the 11.00 news: just then a bulletin came through. She ran across the lane and told Bobby. The two of them, without disturbing their father and me at the big house, began driving and arrived at the hospital around four in the morning. After assuring himself that his brother was still alive and might pull through, Bobby found Mrs Moss, whose husband was dying, and spent a long time walking and talking with her to give her any comfort he could.

He went back to check on Ted, who was encumbered with all the tubes and tents and medical paraphernalia of the desperately ill, but who was able to summon a small smile and in a muffled voice say, 'Is it true that you are ruthless?' It was a typical Kennedy brotherly joke, and I expect that at that moment Bobby felt things were really going to be all right for Ted.

Ted was up for re-election that year. The earlier win, which I have described, had been to fill the unexpired portion of the Senate term Jack had won in 1958. Obviously, campaigning in person was out of the question for him but he had a very able and devoted staff. Through them he was able to direct the campaign from his hospital bed. I made a few appearances for him to help out. But it was Joan who was the star of that campaign. She was all over the state, doing all the chatting and speaking and hand-shaking and all the rest that a hard-working candidate must do, and which came to her not in the least naturally but which she performed tirelessly and superbly. A lot of others, too, were certainly doing something right, because Teddy was re-elected with more than 75 per cent of the votes.

It became apparent, as that summer of 1964 went on, that President Johnson preferred to have someone other than Bobby on the ticket with him for Vice-President. I suppose that was a natural reaction on his part, not involving unfriendly feelings necessarily, but rather that if he were elected to his own term of office he would want to start afresh on his own, without the continual reminder of Jack's brilliant Presidency which Bobby's presence in White House councils and events and as presiding officer in the Senate inevitably would bring. I was disappointed for Bobby because I knew he wanted the nomination. But I felt that the Johnsons had behaved towards us with decency and tact and kindness and genuine sympathy and good-will in a situation that, difficult as it was for us, was difficult for them also. There were people who had been on Jack's staff who resented Mr Johnson – perhaps some within the family who did – but I never felt that way. I liked him, admired him for his qualities and I could understand his position. And I certainly could sympathize also with Lady Bird who has her own wonderful qualities – because I felt that almost any woman who followed Jackie as First Lady at the White House would enter with a disadvantage.

In any case Bobby then had to decide; and, having made the basic judgment that he wanted to stay in public life, that he had 'promises to keep', he decided to run for the Senate in the New York State elections. He won the Democratic nomination without too much trouble – just a great deal of organization and effort, to which he was well accustomed – but the general election was something else indeed, for his opponent was the Republican incumbent Kenneth Keating, a distinguished man in record and appearance, with his silvery hair and fine features, and with a polished platform manner and well-demonstrated appeal to voters.

Although by this time Bobby knew all the ins and outs and behind-the-scenes techniques of politics, he had never himself run for public office, never been a candidate in a way that would oblige him to come through to the general public as a personality. And he was not overly-endowed by nature and temperament for that different role. It hadn't been his style and he had never had reason until then to develop it. He took on the challenge but not entirely happily and not easily. (But I remembered that Jack too had been ill at ease at first meeting strangers and asking for their votes. I recall the story that at the very beginning of the 1946 Congressional campaign, Joe happened to be standing chatting with some friends on a corner in South Boston when suddenly Jack appeared across the street and started introducing himself to people who came along. Joe looked on in pleased amazement and commented: 'I never would have thought he had it in him!')

By the time of Bobby's debut as a candidate I was, to say the least, an experienced speaker and campaigner. So I was in this campaign quite a bit. Previous campaigns had shown that I could attract an audience. Also, I realized Bobby could stand a little coaching, and further that if he and I were on the platform together I could make him feel somewhat more at ease. I had a special utility also, as his mother, in meeting the charge that he was a 'political carpet-bagger', an out-of-stater who had no business running in New York State. We had a little routine worked out about this, originating in a meeting at the auditorium of the Riverdale school. He brought up the charge that he was an outlander, then turned to me and said, 'Tell them, Mother.' Which I would do, chapter and verse, about moving from Brookline to Riverdale and Bronxville when Bobby was only two years old, and this was home to us for the next fourteen years; and then even afterwards we always had a residence in New York City, and that the city had always remained the headquarters for my husband's business interests, and Bobby and all the others had gone for some years to schools in New York, and so forth – and what more identification with the state could anyone want? All of which seemed to soothe people's fears that Bobby, as Senator from New York, might not have the state's interests fully at heart.

On request, Polly Fitzgerald and several of her loyal helpers came down from Boston to organize the teas, receptions and handle a few thousand details. I asked her – for this book – to write me some recollections:

There was one incident in Bobby's Senate Campaign I'll always remember. He was such a reluctant candidate in those days – still bereft after Jack's death the year before.

There were telephone calls to us, 'Tell Bob he's got to look at the people when he meets them!' Or 'Tell Bob to smile – he looks as if he hates campaigning!' I used to wish the people could know the real Bobby. One night we had a reception in a hotel in New York City. You were there with him. The plan was for you to say a few words and then introduce him. His speech, which was being typed at headquarters, had not been delivered to the hotel – and we were all a little frantic.

You were on the platform speaking. He turned to me and said, 'What will I talk about?' I said to him, just go out with your mother and talk and be yourself – it will be better than any speech.

He did just that. You kidded him and he relaxed – he teased you – you both chatted about politics as you knew them through your father when you were young. You talked with him about his childhood. You were superb. And he was so warm. The people loved it and I always felt that evening was the turning-point in him as a campaigner.

Bobby won the election by more than 700,000 votes.

Teddy had been discharged from the hospital in mid-December.

And so, when Congress reconvened that next January of 1965 there were two Kennedy brothers present in the US Senate for roll-call.

A little later *Time* did a long article about the two of them and the extraordinary circumstances that had brought them to the Senate at the same time; and they were shown on the cover of the magazine, facing each other in quarter-profile with the Capitol dome in the background. We had the cover glassed and framed and their father indicated he wanted it put up on the wall, in his bedroom at the Palm Beach house, directly opposite his bed, so it would be in his view every time he was in bed but awake. Facing it, hanging above his headboard, he wanted a portrait – a soft pastel, charming and true – of Caroline at the age of three or four. The bed is gone now, a few things in the room have been changed, but the two pictures still hang in the same place.

During the next two or three years there were no profound changes in our lives. Bob and Ted had their important and time-consuming duties in the Senate. Sarge was appointed Ambassador to France, so he and Eunice and their family were there; and, as I suppose is generally known, making a great success of the ambassadorial mission. Pat and Peter were separated and then finally divorced, which of course was a source of unhappiness for them, their children and within the family, for many reasons; yet evidently there had been a serious incompatibility for some time, so when the break came it was not too surprising to us. She and the other daughters and daughters-in-law had their children to attend to (and no matter how much help there may be in a house, the mother's attention is always needed). And we all had much to do that could be constructive and affirmative and encouraging, and healing, about the memorials for the family members who were no longer present; and, in their memory, try to bring the fullest measure of meaning to the lives of others.

Joe's condition was about the same as it had been. Times of crisis when it seemed he might be nearing the end. Then recoveries when he felt so well that he was determined to stand on his feet and take a few steps. Mostly a slow, gruelling process of attrition and gradual wearing out, yet with a spirit never less than valiant.

Ever since his stroke we had needed a strong man to help with him because he would need to be lifted in and out of the car, boat, bath or other situations in which a woman's attentions would have been insufficient or inappropriate; the same man would also drive for him, pilot the *Marlin*, help with the nursing care such as turning him in bed (Joe still weighed about 180 pounds, so that wasn't easy) and in general do what needed to be done. There had been several, in series, but the last one – a strapping young fellow named John Ryan, 6 ft 2 ins or so, and with a gentle, cheerful, witty and optimistic outlook – came in 1966, stayed through the time of my husband's death in 1969, then stayed on to help me until 1973 when he left, with my blessing and affection, to find a lifetime career for himself, for he was then still only in his very early thirties. I asked him to give some of his memories and he has done so:

I had heard through a friend that the family would be needing an aide for Mr Kennedy, because the one they had was leaving to go to law school. I had an interview with Ann Gargan – she hired anyone who had anything to do with her uncle – and got the job. So one day, with Frank Saunders, the fellow who was driving for Mrs Kennedy and the family at the time, I went up to Boston to meet Mr Kennedy, because he'd had a relapse and was in the New England Baptist Hospital. That was *the* hospital for the family. Jack had spent most of his recovery there after the war. Teddy did most of his convalescing there after the airplane accident. And so forth. Most of them had been in there, and I think some of the children were born there. Never mind about 'Baptist'; they wanted good medical care and this was one of the very best hospitals in Boston. Mr Kennedy was in bed and Frank said to him, 'Mr Ambassador, this is John Ryan and when you get out of here, sir, he'll be working for you.' The Ambassador looked up at me, and Frank said, 'He's a big one, isn't he?' The Ambassador smiled a little bit.

Frank and I drove back to Hyannis Port and went to the house to report in to Ann Gargan. She said that since the time I had been hired the doctors had told her it didn't look as if the Ambassador was going to live much longer, and of course in that case there was no job. A day or so after that I was introduced to Mrs Kennedy: 'John Ryan, who has come to work for the Ambassador.' I said, 'But I have been let go, because I guess I won't be needed.' She said: 'I don't believe that the Ambassador is going to die in the hospital and I believe that he will come back – he'll be back here in Hyannis Port. So why don't you just stay around? If you want to get another job, go ahead, but I would like to have you here.' I said: 'Well, if I'm going to be on the payroll I want to be doing something useful.' There are always a lot of odd jobs to do around the compound, so I kept busy enough. Then just a few weeks later, around December 1, the Ambassador came home from the hospital.

Knowing him – as I came to know him during the three years after that – I would say it was because of determination that he came home. The man had such power in him, such a will to live. He had been a strong man all his life and I really believe that he just had that *will* to live. And that every time he seemed to be dying he was thinking at the doctors, 'I don't care what your prognosis is, and the hell with you, I'm going to *do* it.' There were several times he would have these drastic seizures and become unconscious – out for an hour or hour and a half at a time, totally out. The nurse would have started cardiac massage, I would start the oxygen. The priest would be called: he'd come and give him the last rites. And then he'd wake up. And want to go out on the boat. Just as if nothing had happened. And we would try saying, 'Sir, why don't you just rest now and we'll go out tomorrow?' But he really wanted to go, he felt like going. We'd go, and he'd be all right.'

I remember such episodes, and one in particular when he seemed so near the end that we called the children in Washington to say they should hurry home at once. We weren't able to reach them easily because, as it happened, they had gone up to New York to attend a big political dinner. By the time we could talk with them their father had recovered from the attack and was sleeping soundly. Next day he was alert, had a good colour and was expecting to go for his usual morning drive in the car.

John Ryan continues:

A great many people outside the family and staff thought, just assumed, that by this time he must be sort of a 'vegetable' but that was wrong. Mentally he was active. Mrs Kennedy made sure that he got the *New York Times* and the Boston papers every day, and *Time*, *Life* and *Look* every week. He couldn't hold them or manage them well all the time because he had only the one good hand, but when he'd finished a page he'd signal, and you'd turn the page; and he'd go right through a whole magazine. He loved sports: so now and then we'd go off to some baseball or football game. We would discuss players and strategies, I giving my opinions and he with a Yes or No or a whole range of comments he could get across with his facial expressions and his gestures. He didn't like pills or shots, in fact he didn't like medication, because he didn't want to be dependent on medicines, or on people for that matter; he wanted to do for himself as much as he possibly could. Like in the mornings in the swimming pool. Because of the buoyancy of the water Ann Gargan could be the one to help him in. We had bars all around the side of the pool then and he'd go along the bars. He'd move his right leg along and he'd take his left leg and kind of give a little kick or hop with it and move himself along. To him it would be a bad morning – and it was an exceptional morning – if he got only half or three-quarters of the way around and was too tired and had to come out. Then he'd be mad at himself because he didn't have enough energy. We'd tell him it was really great but he never accepted our compliments unless he went the complete way. Then it was fine.

He didn't like having to be helped but he was the type of person who appreciated things. He would do little things that expressed his gratitude. On several occasions riding with him in the elevator, he'd just . . . I'd be alone with him in the elevator riding downstairs . . . and he would just take my hand, and kiss it. As his expression of gratitude. In other words, he wanted to let you know that he knew what was happening . . . Mrs Kennedy was there, basically, all the time. She was there with him and around him.

'Basically' is an apt word for it. I was there most of the time; and when I was, I saw him often through the day and evening. We always had breakfast, lunch and dinner together. I would talk to him, tell him news of the family or of friends or other matters I thought would be

interesting to him. Sometimes I would read to him from letters I had
received, or newspaper items I had clipped out, or passages that had
struck me in some book I might be browsing in for my continuing
education and as a help for insomnia. Often, after dinner, we would
look at television together until his bedtime, which was quite early
because he tired easily.

I had luncheon and dinner invitations rather often, and also there
were a few traditional social events – the big charity balls at Palm Beach
–that were organized for good causes and to which everyone sub-
scribed and turned out in finery and fine spirits. It was a way to see old
friends; the atmosphere was always rather exciting; I enjoyed it; so I
went to them, perhaps three or four a winter season. None of this,
however, interfered with my times with Joe. If I had a luncheon or
dinner engagement I would tell my hostess I might be a bit late; and,
since Joe lunched punctually at noon and dined punctually at 6.00, I
could have a light meal with him and still usually arrive in time for
another light meal there. The galas and concerts and such seldom began
before eight in the evening, and by that time he was in bed. He always
knew my plans because I always told him. He was interested. There
was never any sign from him of anything but approval. He did not want
me to be tied to his sick-bed; he did want me to have some life of my
own, and to enjoy life. The circumstances had changed drastically, but
we still had the same complete understanding that we had had during
more than fifty years of marriage. One thing, though, that from the
beginning of his illness I did – or let's say refrained from doing – was
that when one of these events required wearing something fancy, as
would be the case with the charity balls, I always waited to dress until
after dinner and after he was in his room in bed. As I say, there was
nothing of subterfuge: it was simply that I thought the sight would
remind him of the irretrievable past and that it would be kinder if I
dressed and then went on my way.

With Ann in charge, with an efficient and devoted nursing staff, and
stalwarts such as John Ryan on hand, and with excellent doctors who
would always respond quickly in any emergency, I felt that I could be
away from time to time for periods of days or weeks. There were things
that were needful and that I wanted to do. I wanted to visit Rosemary
every few months. I wanted to encourage and participate in the programme for the mentally retarded that we had established as living
memorials to her, and the numerous other good works in various other
fields that also had been developed by the Joseph P. Kennedy Jr
Foundation. I wanted to take part in and help to move along the

memorials to Jack – the library, the cultural centre, so many others. For instance, towards the end of 1964 and in early 1965 I was abroad several times to lend my presence and a few words to an exhibit of photographs, documents and memorabilia of Jack's life and Presidency. It went to England, France, Germany, a number of countries, and each time I tried to be there, at least briefly, and it was inspiring to see and sense the great interest, the deep affection and admiration, that was shown by such vast numbers of people of so many nations about Jack.

So, in those years there were many demands, opportunities, reasons to be active. And the more so, naturally enough, in 1968 when Bobby decided to run for the Democratic nomination for the Presidency.

His father didn't want him in that race; but, in his condition, was not able to explain to Bobby why it was not a good idea at that time.

I had profound misgivings of my own about it. I felt that Bobby had so many responsibilities to his family, and within our general family; and that he was still young enough – at the age of forty-three – for there to be later opportunities for him to try for the Presidency; and that meanwhile he shouldn't take the burdens of the nation on his shoulders and instead should try to relax a little bit.

Polly Fitzgerald has recalled:

> In December 1967 I was in Washington for a meeting. I called Bobby the day I was leaving and he said that he too was going to Boston and would go on my flight so we could have a visit. We had a very philosophical talk all the way home and at one point he spoke of you and said, 'My mother says I'm too serious and that I should do more things that I'd like to do – have more fun, and not always do what I think I should do or must do.'

But Bobby, once having made up his mind about the right course for him, balancing everything together – everything, I dare say, from his childhood through all that had happened to this time, in his full maturity – was not going to be deflected from what he believed he 'should do or must do'. People have talked about the streak of 'romanticism' in Jack: 'Camelot' and all that. But Bobby, for all his supposed ruthlessness – such a grotesquely mistaken term for him as he really was – was easily as much a romantic idealist. I use that expression in the way *I* mean, and that is that with faith and effort it is humanly possible to do great good in the world. I have mentioned Tennyson's 'Ulysses' as one of Jack's favourite poems, from which he liked to recite, and among the lines he liked best – and which I'm sure Bobby took as one of his inspirations – were these:

> Come, my friends,
> 'Tis not too late to seek a newer world.
> Push off, and sitting well in order smite
> The sounding furrows: For my purpose holds
> To sail beyond the sunset, and the baths
> Of all the western stars, until I die.
> It may be that the gulfs will wash us down;
> It may be we shall touch the happy isles,
> And see the great Achilles, whom we knew.
> Though much is taken, much abides; and though
> We are not now that strength which in old days
> Moved earth and heaven; that which we are, we are.
> One equal temper of heroic hearts,
> Made weak by time and Fate, but strong in will
> To strive, to seek, to find, and not to yield.

And so once again 'the troops rallied': the loyal cadres that Bobby and Ted and Jack himself, and Steve and others, had built all over the country. Polly Fitzgerald came out again, accompanied by some of those same wonderful selfless women who had helped set up the 'Kennedy teas' during Jack's campaigns. And I, of course, prepared to take to the road again to help wherever and however I could. I was seventy-seven then, and it seemed to surprise people that I should be out stumping for my son, leading the demanding life entailed by a big campaign. It didn't seem at all odd to me: by then it had come to seem perfectly natural.

I find that people who have not been in politics are often curious about some of the 'how-to' aspects of campaigning. 'How to shake hands with a thousand people without having your right hand become sore.' 'How to stand in a receiving line for two or three hours without having your back begin to sag.' As for the hand-shaking: I was lucky in being a woman and in that my audiences were largely women, for women usually do not press one's hand very hard. Most men, shaking hands with a woman, do not either, whereas it seems to be part of the male mentality that a man is not fully a man unless he has a firm handshake with another man. Thus it is not unusual that a male candidate, after a hard day's campaigning – I know this has happened with Jack, Bob and Ted – might end the evening with his right hand soaking in a basin of warm water spiked with some analgesic, muscle-relaxing medication.

As for being on one's feet for hours at a time, there is nothing so unusual about that – sales people, production-line workers, postal employees, many others are obliged to be – but there is a difference: in a receiving line one has no chance to move around and keep the blood circulating and the muscles and bones and tendons functioning more or less normally. Instead, one is fairly much rooted to the spot. I found that thin, sponge-rubber footpads – the kind available in any drugstore and sold by the millions – were helpful; they were part of my sixty-item list of campaign necessities. But more important, I learned, if it's a long reception, is to have a heavy and preferably upholstered chair or couch directly behind you, its back to you so that you can lean on it or halfway sit on the edge. With a little practice at this, you can look as if you're practically standing. And, of course, people are kind. They realize you may be a little tired; so if you seem to be perched just a bit to relieve your aching back and feet they understand.

In a national campaign, one should try not to be in a receiving line with local candidates, or for that matter even state candidates unless that is necessity, because the people in line include so many of their personal friends or close associates who want to stop and chat with them, thus delaying everyone else behind and adding an extra hour or so – like traffic backing up on a busy highway when one car has a blow-out – and that could be an hour one really couldn't spare in a hard campaign because one had an appointment to be someplace else just then.

It is bad politics – and basic bad manners – to keep an audience waiting, and the speaker who does so begins with an initial disadvantage that he has to overcome before he can get his message across. Hence when meetings are closely scheduled, ways have to be devised to disengage the candidate or speaker from one place in time to get to the next place. Yet in almost any receiving line there will be people who want to stop and chat; others who want to stand with you while a friend with a flash camera focuses and takes aim and snaps some pictures including the proverbial 'just one more, please.' And at the end of the meeting, while you are on your way out, there are likely to be those who come up to you to have a personal discussion about something.

Now, all this is not only pleasant in its way but also useful, for the essence of campaign politics is to establish personal rapport with the voters, so one must be tactful, patient, cooperative and make sure that no one's feelings are hurt. But this takes some planning. I remember an evening, for instance, early in Jack's campaign for the Presidency, when he was outside in the car after a meeting and feeling irritated with Jackie because she was still inside the hall or vestibule in conversation with people. I said to him, the girl can't just rush away from people; it would make a very bad impression. You ought to have an aide of some sort with her and primed in these situations to say, excuse me, Mrs Kennedy, but your husband is waiting for you, or, you have another engagement and I'm afraid you'll be late if you don't leave now. Jack agreed and from then on it was done that way; though I don't know why I had to be the one to remind him, for this is only sensible. What it takes is an aide or two whom one can trust to be watchful, discreet, tactful and to have briefed himself, and you, as to who's who in the line or the audience or, later, in the aisles or vestibule; and who would have the sense of pace and time and circumstance to know when to come up and say, in the nicest way, Mrs Kennedy, I'm afraid we're going to be late. This takes talent, insight, charm, intuition and a sense of the proportion of things. Polly Fitzgerald, Dave Powers, Frank Morrissey are among those whom I remember with special gratitude because they could always keep things moving, always nicely. Because, in anything, there is only a certain amount of time.

I was almost never on the same platform at the same time with Bob during that 1968 campaign. He had hesitated a considerable while before going into the primaries. Not because he was by inclination indecisive but because he valued good advice and the two inestimably valuable sources of advice were no longer available. Jack was gone; their father incapable of speech and by this time clearly declining. Thus Bobby came into those primaries late, not until mid-March. There was a lot of time to make up.

He had become a fine speaker, an iridescent personality, a national figure of great stature in his own right and could attract huge audiences. I, for my part, could by then count on having audiences of considerable size. So the best idea was that we should go our own ways – and needless to say, others in the family and scores of loyal friends – and cover as much ground and contact as many people as possible in the time available. The only advice I gave him was about a few personal details. I heard some of his speeches and realized he was lapsing into the family habit of talking too rapidly, so I would send him a note about that. I noticed also that he was letting his hair grow awfully long, perhaps because he was racing around the country so fast with so much on his mind that he didn't think about getting to a barber shop. Anyway, I began to hear comments such as 'Why the dickens doesn't he get a haircut?' and I told him. And he got a haircut.

I made an absent-minded mistake myself in that campaign. Perhaps I made several but this one landed in the newspapers. Bobby had just won in Indiana, and as usual there were interviews – always interviews; I must have been interviewed a few thousand times in the course of my life – and a reporter commented that the Indiana campaign had cost a lot of money, and it must be nice to know the Kennedys could afford it; something to that effect.

I heard such comments so many times during the years, ranging from the complete malice of reports that Jack had won in West Virginia because Kennedy agents were out buying votes (investigated and found to be without a grain of truth) to the slightly funny cartoon showing Jack with his father, and Joe saying to him, 'Don't worry, son. If you lose the election I'll buy you a country.' All this struck me as unfair, for although Joe did contribute substantially to the financing of the campaigns, the amounts were almost trifling compared to those he gave to schools, charities, medical research and so forth. And further, the secret of the Kennedy successes in politics was not money but meticulous planning and organization, tremendous effort, and the enthusiasm and devotion of family and friends. Apparently my irritation had reached a flash-point, because I was quoted as saying: 'It's our money and we're free to spend it any way we please. It's part of this campaign business. If you have money, you spend it to win . . .'

I may have said that, or something like it if not necessarily in those words, but what I'm sure I went on to say – and what was not in the report – was that some people with money spend it collecting art, some spend it on big yachts or on 'show place' mansions or on elaborate entertainments. People spend according to their interests; and if we were interested in political life and wanted to spend money in it, what was wrong with that? In fact, wasn't it far healthier for the whole political process if my husband put up some of his own cash than if his sons had to solicit contributions from various rich men and organizations to which they then would be under obligation?

This seemed to me a sensible line of reasoning, and in fact it still does. But it violated one of the rules of American politics, which is that if a candidate comes from a wealthy or well-to-do family, the less said about that the better. As I realized anew the next morning when I saw the newspapers with headlines and reportage inferring that Bobby was a 'spoiled rich kid' whose father was ready to pour his fortune into getting him the nomination. I had made a mistake – the subject of money was never to be discussed.

The boys at first were leary about calling me – afraid, I suppose, that I would be so annoyed with myself that I would be irritable with them too. Finally, later in the day, Steve Smith did call and said, 'Well, Gramma, I guess we'd better not mention anything about money from now on.' Then Teddy called and suggested, 'Why don't you just laugh it off – just joke about it,' which I thought was a good idea. At the next meeting there were reporters trying to draw me out some more on the subject. I had a reply: 'I have been informed by the campaign managers that if I mention money again I will be sent home on the next airplane, so if you don't mind . . .' That was quoted. And a bit later on, at a $100-a-plate campaign-fund-raising dinner in Boston, where I was to speak, Teddy introduced me and said with a grin, 'Mother thinks that when we run these campaigns we spend our own money, so I think it's nice for her to be here tonight and see whose money –' gesturing around the room at those $100-dinners – 'we are really spending.' That was quoted too, and so the small furore I had created faded away.

During Jack's candidacy in 1960 a main purpose of my talks for him had been to show that he was not too young for the Presidency: this because of lifelong interest in history and government, his family background and his long and varied experience in matters of political science. For Bobby, in 1968, a main purpose was to dispose of the peculiar image of 'ruthlessness' that had somehow become associated with him, and I tried to do this by pointing out that he had many difficult assignments in government and had fulfilled them successfully because of his willingness to commit himself with a whole heart, with all his great energy and determination, and with high moral probity: that the word for him was not 'ruthless' but 'dedicated'. And other words would be 'devoted' and 'zestful' and 'compassionate' and 'idealistic' and 'courageous'. And perhaps above all, 'kind' – for it was true of him that often his heart ruled his intellect. He was open and honourable and selfless.

As his mother, I suppose my testimony can be considered biased. I would like now, therefore, to quote some passages from the book that Pat did about him, *That Shining Hour*.

Averell Harriman:

Robert F. Kennedy was one of the most gallant men I have ever known. He was fearless. He faced facts squarely. It was impossible for him not to tell the truth as he saw it. I think that is why some people thought he was ruthless. At times the truth is ruthless. He supported the causes he believed in regardless of the enemies he knew that he would make. But few men have won the deep respect and affection of so many. Negroes and other minorities knew that he had accepted their cause as his own.

If he had been elected President, he would have been a great President . . . He understood the problems of our time . . .

Sandy Vanocur:

Bobby was the most vulnerable human being I have ever known. He was also the most outraged. I now believe that the two go together, and that it was his sense of outrage that made him so vulnerable. He was outraged that there was poverty, sickness, war and evil and all he asked was that we respond to all that is wrong in this world . . . He was a conscience in our midst and now we have come to understand how little some people wish to understand conscience . . . But there is simply no sense in being a Kennedy if you do not keep asking yourself and others to try to do better. He kept telling us this or that was unacceptable. And ultimately, this is what so many people could not abide and that which so many of us cherished, that he only asked that we try to do better, that we try to love each other a little more. He asked only that we try to be more than we are.

Dame Margot Fonteyn:

He was a man of great compassion and intelligence. He loved people but not in any muddle-minded or sentimental way. He was as intolerant of fools as anyone. Clearly his family took first place in his life. This alone represented a considerable number of people with whom he was constantly in touch; and this gave him his strength. Then there were his many friends. He never spoke of them superficially but seemed always to know what they were doing and to be concerned about their problems.

Then there were just people. He really cared about millions of people: about children, young people, poor people, American people, and people all over the world . . . Somehow he found time for everyone. Compassion for people was the motivation of all his life.

Benno Schmidt (financier, lifelong Republican; and the topic here, Bedford-Stuyvesant, is a grievously depressed area in New York City):

I was surprised and slightly curious when I arrived at my office on December 8, 1966, to find a note that Senator Robert Kennedy wanted me to call him in Washington. I had never met nor even seen Senator Kennedy at that time. I returned the call and he said he would like to see me . . . 'today, if possible.' 'I will be in my office all day,' I answered, perhaps a bit curtly. 'Good,' he replied very gently. 'I would like to fly up on the four o'clock shuttle, if I may. This should get me to your office slightly before six, and I will try to be through in time not to disrupt your dinner. Thank you so much . . .' Where, I thought, was the arrogance I had heard about?

He arrived on schedule, and I liked him enormously from the time he set foot in the office. After very brief initial amenities, he outlined with simple eloquence and great persuasiveness his programme for Bedford-Stuyvesant and concluded by asking me to serve as a director.

Commencing with that first meeting . . . I was to be increasingly aware of how incredibly inaccurate the widespread impressions of Bob were, both as a person and a politician. He was a man of enormous compassion, the highest principles, essentially shy and somewhat reticent, with one of the greatest senses of humour I have ever encountered (usually with himself the victim of the joke). He was great fun to work with. He not only accepted but he sought views which differed from his own, and one of the wonderful things about working with him was the extent to which one could differ with him and part company feeling so clearly that friendship had not been touched . . .

Harold Macmillan:

My relations with Bobby were certainly a case of friendship at first sight . . . Bobby's magic was inherent in his character. It was part of him; inherited, not acquired. Nor was it always connected with a happy mood. For he could be angry; especially angry with selfishness and folly, and with the wicked neglect of pressing and urgent cries for help going out both from his own country and from all the world. He could be savage as well as smiling. For what he felt, he felt deeply, even passionately. But he had taught himself to acquire a trained mind to serve his generous heart . . . He had reached an intellectual as well as moral maturity.

Arthur Schlesinger, Jr:

It was obvious, first of all, that he had a direct, fresh and unconventional intelligence of a high order. He had, in addition, what Eliot somewhere calls an 'experiencing nature' – that is, exceptional powers of curiosity and sympathy which enabled him to see problems from the viewpoint of the other fellow and which in time led to his extraordinary identification with the outcasts, victims and casualties of our society. One had always supposed him to be tough and courageous. But the readiness and warmth of his friendship made it impossible ever after to accept the then prevalent theory of him as an unyielding man . . . one was increasingly impressed by his rare gentleness and consideration and increasingly enchanted by his wonderful, wry, sardonic humour.

For a long time these remained private qualities. What was exciting in the last decade was to watch Bobby, almost in spite of himself, become a public man and to see how, somewhat to his embarrassment, he became the vital hope for so many millions of Americans . . . For a shy man, he eventually achieved a remarkable rapport with his audiences. I will never forget whistle-stopping with him through the Central Valley of California at the end of May 1968. It was a clear, sunny, joyous day. Great crowds streamed out to see him – the weatherbeaten faces of old farmers, rapt Mexican-Americans, ardent young men and women, excited boys and girls. He beguiled and exhorted his hearers with a marvellous mixture of banter and intensity – kidding them, kidding himself, then talking with great seriousness about poverty or racial injustice or the war in Vietnam.

He was always growing and would never have stopped. He had become the voice of American reason and conscience . . . His powers as leader, thinker and orator seemed to be coming into rich maturity all at once. Some who become public men repress and destroy their private personalities. In Bobby's case, the public face became a faithful expression of the private face; at last, one felt, people were beginning to understand what Robert Kennedy was really like.

No one offered a greater promise of superb public service for our country.

Theodore Sorensen:

That Bob Kennedy was regarded as a ruthless 'hater' by those who did not know him was a bitter irony bordering on absurdity. For I never knew a man with more capacity for love.

He truly loved his fellow men . . . and could be deeply, visibly moved by both individual and mass demonstrations of human goodwill and generosity. He truly loved his country, while simultaneously trying to improve it, and was willing to serve it in any post . . . provided it offered him an opportunity to make a genuine contribution to this nation's advancement.

Above all, he loved his family – openly, unashamedly and uncritically – and it was this love which seemed to many of us outside the family to illuminate his life and to enrich his spirit more than anything else. His love for his brother Jack was special and fierce . . . After the President's death, he showed it by showering affection upon Jackie, Caroline and John. Like many others whom he rallied after the Dallas tragedy, I will always remember how deeply moved and greatly helped I was by his visit to my White House office a few days later, still wearing sun-glasses to conceal his puffed and reddened eyes, but there to talk about our future instead of the past.

His love for his father was redoubled, not strained, by the latter's tragic illness that might have discouraged a less determined son. Bob's campaign schedule for May 9, 1968, was incredibly heavy and hectic . . . before a four-week Western trip for the Nebraska, Oregon and California primaries. Yet he insisted on adding in the middle of that schedule a flight to the Cape for a farewell lunch with his father . . . At lunch, I saw Bob – as I had so many times before – tell his father how the campaign was coming, how much the old warhorse's advice and assistance were needed, where the campaign trail had been and was headed . . . On the plane returning to Washington, he fell fast asleep in his seat, content that his exhausting effort had made possible this brief and not easy visit that sadly turned out to be his last.

His love for his mother shone through on that same visit. Her strength renewed his, her concern for his well-being warmed him. I chose not to remind either of an evening many years earlier when Mrs Kennedy vowed to us both that she would campaign once more for Jack in 1964 but never for Bob. They had teased each other about it that night, and when I asked him the reason (she had simply said to him, 'You know why.') he told me it was because he had not kept his clothes neat as a teen-ager. Whatever the reason, he was in 1968 lovingly grateful that she had relented . . .

If Ted Sorensen says Bobby said that to him it must be true. But it must have involved some 'inside' family humour, because Bobby had been comparatively well organized – for a teen-ager – whereas Lem Billings has told how he and Jack had the messiest room at the Choate school, and Jack's teen–age inclinations had been much the same at home.

In any case, having made a number of appearances for Bobby in the eastern and mid-western states, I did go out to help in those western primaries, especially the one in California, which of course has become one of the crucial factors in a national nomination.

Having then done what I could I wanted to get home again to check on things there. So on election day I flew back to Hyannis Port to await the returns on radio and TV. It seemed to be a close race at first, as we had expected, with Bobby ahead, then behind, pulling ahead again. But by eleven that night, eastern time, he was ahead substantially and it seemed nearly certain he was the winner. Feeling thankful but also a bit tired after my travels, I went to bed.

The next morning I awakened around 6.00 as usual, in time for

Poem for Grandpa

Love Caroline   Christmas 1967

Once there lived a little blue mouse

Who wasn't scared of cats

He lived in a tiny shocking pink house

With his friend the sparrow, Ignatz.

They went on long walks and had long talks
In mostly the month of May.
They would picnic by a laughing brook
And spend a pleasant day.

The only thing they didn't have
For which they used to pray
Was someone as nice as Grandpa
Who they missed more every day.

To Grandma with love

Above Caroline's poem to Grandpa

Below Bobby's and Ethel's children have given me a Spiritual Bouquet. They have recited Rosaries and gone to Mass for our intentions. A loving and deeply appreciated tribute

Dearest Gramma,

We offer you this small gift as a token of our love and gratitude for all the happiness you and Grampa gave us

 Spiritual Bouquet

250   Masses
250   Communions
250   Rosaries
100   Acts of Reparation
1000   Aspirations

With the promise of continued prayer and all our love

Kathleen   Courtney & MAX
Joe   Kerry
Michael
David   Chris K

My Work for Handicapped Children

Opposite The Canadian Association for Retarded Children presented me with the International Award of Merit for Distinguished Service to the Mentally Handicapped

Visiting retarded children in Canada

This page The late King Gustaf of Sweden received me at Drottningholm Castle, 1966
Below Visiting Rickomberyn, a home and school for handicapped children in Sweden

At an outing for handicapped children at Niagara Falls in 1969 I accepted a Girl Scout calendar from Liz Scotland

The New Generation

32 Me and my 28 grandchildren

early Mass, and turned on the television for news of the final results and instead heard that Bob was being taken to the hospital.

Again, I couldn't believe – my mind somehow would not allow me to think – that it could be anything really serious. There had been an accident of some sort, perhaps during a victory celebration. I went on dressing, listening distractedly; then Ann came in, saying he had been shot.

It seemed impossible that the same kind of disaster could befall our family twice in five years. If I had read anything of the sort in fiction I would have put it aside as incredible. I still wanted to go to Mass – urgently wanted to go to Mass – though Ann told me the phones had been ringing and reporters and photographers would be at the church.

On the way out of the house we met our pastor, Monsignor Thomson, who had heard the news and had come up from Hyannis. He rode back down to the church with me. I really don't remember what was said or much of what I was thinking, except that I was praying. *Lord have mercy!* And thinking, *Oh, Bobby, Bobby, Bobby.*

Later that morning Pat called from California, and Eunice from Paris, and both seemed optimistic that Bob would recover. But the news reports became worse. Teddy called to say it was only a matter of time. I kept busy in my room, sorting, rearranging, doing anything to keep busy, because I had to keep moving. And I prayed. And I wondered. I still couldn't believe it although I knew it was so.

The next morning, Thursday, June 6, Bobby passed away.

I went in and told Joe, and we sat together a while. His eyes were wet but he was calm – there was no breakdown. We held hands. I felt that, as always, we gave each other strength.

The funeral plane arrived from California that evening, and Bobby lay in state at St Patrick's Cathedral in New York, where great throngs came to pay their respects. I have read that there were a hundred thousand people that night and through the next day and night.

At the service, on Saturday, Ted delivered the eulogy and did so, in some of the most demanding minutes of his life or that could ever be, with dignity, simplicity, and eloquence and grace. His three brothers were gone. His father would go soon, as he knew. And he was a credit to all of them.

His summary of Bobby's character was perfect in truth: '. . . a good and decent man, who saw wrong and tried to right it, saw suffering and tried to heal it, saw war and tried to stop it.'

And of Bobby's idealistic aims:

Some men see things as they are and say 'Why?'
I dream things that never were and say, 'Why not?'

BOBBY

Bobby had a consuming passion to do what he thought was right and the will and the vigour to pursue that goal regardless of physical fatigue or difficulties.

The seventh child in a large family, he had to listen for years to kudos about his two brilliant, older brothers, so when his turn came, he had to work extra hard to make his record equal theirs. Handicapped by a small stature, he had to face insurmountable odds when trying to win his letter in football at college, but he made it.

He received his baptism in politics when he helped his brother, Jack, who was the candidate for the Senate in Massachusetts, the old political stronghold of the Kennedy family. However, he himself won his Senate seat in New York where he had spent his youthful years before enlisting in the Navy.

In government service, he espoused tough assignments, the criminal segment, the gangster element, and he had an unflagging zeal for trying to correct some of the inequalities of life among the disadvantaged, the handicapped, the aged. The Vietnam War he viewed as a tragic episode in our history. In all his endeavours, he was indifferent to either fatigue or adverse criticism.

He considered these goals as the right ones for him and for mankind, and he pursued them nights as well as days, travelled to Watts and Bedford Stuyvesant as well as to Africa and Vietnam, ate and slept wherever his destiny led him.

He adored with a passionate devotion Ethel and his little children with whom he laughed and played in his happiest moments. On his holidays, they always accompanied him – whether it was climbing mountains, ski-ing on the snowy slopes, or shooting the rapids on river boats. Even when I advised Ethel and him to be free – to be relaxed – to be concerned with only their own personal comfort, he never wanted to spare himself these added responsibilities.

He accepted life's challenges and he welcomed the opportunities for work which opened before him. He rejoiced in life's gifts and laughed and sang and played, too, with zest and enthusiasm. He was a deeply religious man, a fact for which his father and I were very grateful.

How sad are our hearts when we realize that we shall never see Bobby again, with his tousled, windblown hair, his big, affectionate smile, carrying one child piggy-back and leading another by the hand – his dog close behind. What joy he brought us. What an aching void he has left behind, which nothing in the world can ever fill. We admired him, we loved him, and our lives are indeed bleak without him.

A devoted husband, a beloved son, an adored brother, I know that I shall not look upon his like again.

There were some comments later in the press about my 'composure' and 'self-possession' and 'bravery', and it was remarked that from time to time I gave a wave of the hand to people who had gathered in the cities and towns and hamlets – some even on rooftops – to watch the funeral train pass. I don't know now whether the waving was a good idea or not. Apparently there were those who thought it inappropriate. But I did this, and encouraged the children and grandchildren to do so as most of them did, because I felt that if people cared enough to come out and pay their respects we ought at least to give them some sign of appreciation. As for my being composed – I had to be. If I had broken down in grief I would only have added to the misery of the others and possibly could have set off a chain reaction of tearfulness. But in fact it was not just I who set an example. They all set it for one another. Young Joe II, who adored his father and who was barely seventeen, went through the cars where various elder friends, official dignitaries, and colleagues and staff assistants of Bobby's and some of the press were riding and introduced himself and thanked them on behalf of the family for being with us.

Ethel was most admirable of all. She and Bobby loved each other deeply – they loved being together, sharing everything; they had a perfect life. Much as I would grieve for Bobby and miss him, I knew she would miss him even more: not only for all they meant to each other but as the father of her ten children, with the eleventh to come posthumously a few months later. I knew how difficult it was going to be for her to raise that big family without the guiding role and influence that Bobby would have provided. And, of course, she realized this too, fully and keenly. Yet she did not give way: she was calm and she was stalwart, and I was very proud of her.

After Bobby's death there were so many messages of sympathy, from all over the country and most of the world, from people of every station in life, that – until such time as they could be acknowledged individually, which would take months – I felt I ought to do something to express our gratitude. Accordingly I went on television on a national broadcast. This is the substance of my message:

> May I extend my sincere thanks to all of you who offered your prayers, affection and condolences . . . We know that this tribute came from your hearts and our hearts responded with deep appreciation . . .
>
> We cannot always understand the ways of Almighty God. The crosses which He sends us, the sacrifices which He demands of us . . . But we accept with faith and resignation His Holy Will with no looking back to what might have been and we are at peace. We have courage, we are undaunted and steadfast and we shall carry on the principles for which Bobby stood . . .
>
> We know his heart's hopes and so we shall honour him, not with useless mourning and vain regrets but with firm resolutions . . . Acting now to relieve the hungry, working now to aid the disadvantaged for whom he felt so deeply and for whom he worked long hours.
>
> And in our thoughts of him and in our prayers we shall remember Ethel. And their little children, with whom he laughed and played. May they remember their father not only as one who gaily shared their childhood sports and triumphs but also as one who pledged his heart, soul and strength to the betterment of humanity, and to the spiritual enrichment and honour of our great country.

After Bobby's death, Joe's condition declined until by the fall of that year he was approaching helplessness, not even able to feed himself the greater part of the time, suffering all the annoyances and discomforts and indignities of hopeless infirmity. With his remarkable physical stamina and his remarkable will, he stayed on until November 18, 1969. Then, surrounded by those who remained of his family, and quite peacefully, he passed away. I was kneeling by his bedside, holding his hand. Next to Almighty God, I had loved him – do love him – with all my heart, all my soul, all my mind. But I felt now that it was God's blessing that took him.

With the deaths of his brothers and then the death of his father, Ted was the only surviving male member of our immediate family. Ninth and last child, youngest son, it was now up to him to be 'the head of the family'. And he responded magnificently.

20

'In perfect honour, perfect truth,
And gentleness to all mankind,
You trod the golden paths of youth,
Then left the world and youth behind.

Ah, no! 'tis we who fade and fail –
And you, from Time's slow torments free,
Shall pass from strength to strength and scale
The steeps of immortality.'

The lines are from John Buchan's '*Fratri Dilectissimo*' (Dearest Brother) and I found them a few years ago and transcribed them in my notebook in which I keep favourite quotations; for, to me, they signified my lost children.

From the same author, in another book, *Pilgrim's Way*, I drew other words and adapted them and made them my motto:

I know not age, or weariness or defeat

So my life went on with both an overwhelming sense of loss and a determination to remember with dearest love, yet to meet the future with my head into the wind.

I'd thought, during this period, a good deal about Jacqueline.

I think that all of us felt that after a suitable time of mourning, and such time as it might take her to mend her spirits and be able to participate fully again in life, Jackie should marry. Woman, no less than man, is not meant to live alone; and certainly not Jackie, who was still so young and lovely and with such a sensitive and warm-hearted nature. And, of course, there were Caroline and John Jr to consider. No one could take Jack's place, but a man in their lives would be good for them.

After a while, when she did feel like going out to the theatre and some of the events in New York City, and having a few dinner parties at her apartment, and needed escorts, the men were either members of the family – Bobby particularly at that time – or close family friends and associates, men such as Arthur Schlesinger Jr, Kenneth Galbraith and William Walton, the artist. Since nearly all of them were married, however, the number of 'eligibles' was small. As she went out more, it grew rather larger, as we in the family noticed with interest and approval.

I had known Aristotle Onassis for some years. I used to see him here and there when I was travelling in Europe: we would be at some of the same parties and receptions, and be having lunch or dinner at some of the same restaurants, so we would chat a bit about this or that and became friendly acquaintances. Once or twice, as I recall, during his travels he stopped in to visit us for a day or evening at Hyannis Port. I have a memory of him one summer day on our front porch sitting rather scrunched up in one of our tall fan-back white wicker chairs. Others of us were in other white wicker chairs, and still others were seated, reclining or sprawled out on cushions that were somewhat the worse from summer sun and wet and fogs and hard use from grand-children. The white paint on the wicker was beginning to flake, as it always does. Everything was pleasant, attractive, practical, but far from elegant. And knowing of Onassis's fabulous wealth and style of life – islands, yachts and villas with retinues of servants – I wondered if he might find it a bit strange to be in such an informal environment as ours. If so, he showed no sign of it. He was quietly companionable, easy to talk with, intelligent, with a sense of humour and a fund of good anecdotes to tell.

I liked him. He was pleasant, interesting and, to take a Greek term, charismatic.

Even so, when Jean called me one morning in October 1968 and said Jackie was going to marry him – and would be calling me later in the day to tell me about it – I was completely surprised. In fact I was rather stunned. And then perplexed. I thought of the difference in their ages. I thought of the difference in religion, he being Greek Orthodox; and the fact that he had been divorced; and I wondered whether this could be a valid marriage in the eyes of the Church. I thought of Caroline and John Jr and whether they could learn to accept Onassis in the role of stepfather so that he could give them the guidance that children need from a man. There were many things on my mind – my thoughts were awhirl – but I began trying to sort them out, give the various factors some order of priority.

And, with contemplation, it seemed to me the first basic fact was that

Jackie deserved a full life, a happy future. Jack had been gone five years, thus she had had plenty of time to think things over; and she was not a person who would jump rashly into anything as important as this, so she must have her own very good reasons.

I decided I ought to put my doubts aside and give Jackie all the emotional support I could in what, as I realized, was bound to be a time of stress for her in the weeks and months and more that lay ahead. When she called I told her to make her plans as she chose to do, and to go ahead with them with my loving good wishes. I was reassured when during our talk she said she had consulted Cardinal Cushing and he had given his benediction.[1] She seemed relieved by my attitude and afterwards, when she saw Ted, told him she was greatly cheered by my congratulations and my confidence in her.

The wedding would be in Greece. Jackie invited me but I felt that I shouldn't be that far away because of my husband's declining health. Pat and Jean, the girls nearest Jackie in age, did go to represent our family, and our regard for Jackie in every circumstance.

Jackie recently was remembering that time and said:

When I married Ari, she of all people was the one who encouraged me. Who said, 'He's a good man.' And 'Don't worry, dear.' She's been extraordinarily generous. Here I was, I was married to her son and I have his children, but she was the one who was saying, if this is what you think is best, go ahead. It wouldn't surprise anyone who has really known her; but anyway, how extraordinarily generous that woman is in spirit. I always called her 'Belle Mère' – I still call her that.

She comes and visits us. It's wonderful for Caroline and John. And Ari adores her. The first Easter after we were married she came to spend a few days with us in the Caribbean. That next summer she stopped over in Greece. She was on her way to Ethiopia to have a joint birthday celebration with Haile Selassie. Then, after Grandpa died late that year – I was there in the room with the others when he died – she was feeling sort of shaky. She came and spent New Year's with us.

If I ever feel sorry for myself, which is a most fatal thing, I think of her. I've seen her cry just twice, a little bit. Once was at Hyannis Port, when I came into her room: and her husband was ill, and Jack

---

[1] Cardinal Cushing also spoke out for her, through the press, with this statement: 'My advice to people is to stop criticizing this poor woman. She has had an enormous amount of sadness in her life and she deserves whatever happiness she can find.'

was gone, and Bobby had been killed . . . and . . . the other time was on the ship after her husband died, and we were standing on deck at the rail together, and we were talking about something . . . just something that reminded her. And her voice began to sort of break and she had to stop. Then she took my hand and squeezed it and said, 'Nobody's ever going to have to feel sorry for me. Nobody's ever going to feel sorry for me,' and she put her chin up. And I thought, God, what a thoroughbred.

I have a diary note dated February of that new year, 1970, when I was back home:

Jackie sent me an album of photos taken while I was in Greece and wrote amusing captions under them. One on the Acropolis – where I went with Ari and an historian – shows me in a black midi with cock feathers and she wrote 'Me like Circe.' Another of me going to church the following Sunday and she captioned it 'Demure like Heidi with a kerchief on her head.'

Along with the album she sent a letter which quite overwhelmed me, with her really heart-warming expressions of the pleasure all of them shared in my visit at New Year's. And how utterly unexpected was life's chain of events – that she and I, after all our experiences together, should now start to share new experiences in an extremely different environment and atmosphere and it all happened so unexpectedly.

I am thrilled by her assurances of welcome because this way I shall always be able to contact Caroline and John, and to know that all enjoy having me with them, including Ari and his relatives. And New Year's was possibly a little less foreign to the children because I was there.

Jackie has often quoted the words in the Biblical Book of Ruth in which Ruth declares to her mother-in-law Naomi: 'Whither thou goest, I will go.' And I too feel that the bonds of loving understanding between Jackie and me are just as strong as those between Ruth and Naomi. I am certain that very few mothers-in-law ever have received a letter such as Jackie wrote to me.

I asked Jackie if I could include it in this book. She said, 'Of course you may use it. Of course, anything you want to use that involves me in any way is fine with me.'

Letter from Mrs Onassis, dated June, 1973:
I had just had the premature Caesarean birth with John – I nearly

lost him – as I had lost our first little girl – and he was in an incubator for days – with the same lung affliction Patrick, my Patrick, later died of. I had a close shave myself – I had to be wheeled in a wheelchair to John's christening. Though I stood up for a few moments, I had to be wheeled back. There was a tradition that the First Lady always showed the incoming first lady around the White House. I was pregnant and told not to move. I asked Tish Baldridge to say to Mr Eisenhower's secretary that if it was a tradition I should adhere to, could I come now (this was about November 15), as doctors were forbidding me to move to insure that I wouldn't lose my baby again. I really just wanted to see which rooms would be ours and the children's rooms when we moved in.

Then I had John prematurely – and Mrs Eisenhower asked me to come the day I left the hospital – I knew I wasn't up to it. But Jack said I should go. I asked that there be a wheelchair there – because I couldn't walk very far without it troubling me.

When I arrived, there was no wheelchair. I was given the full tour – including all those stairs – all the things Miss Hennessey had told me were fatal – and to pose for photographers. I went back to our house in Georgetown – quite ill – took the baby and nurse to Florida.

And John wasn't doing so well. There was, thank God, a brilliant paediatrician in Palm Beach – who really saved his life – as he was going downhill then because he was premature.

I was ill and recuperating in the room I shared with dear Jack. The house was so crowded – he was writing his inaugural speech in the room – I remember the yellow pages being strewn all around the room – and when he left I would get up and try to keep them all together under some weight on the desk.

Then Pierre Salinger or someone would come in the room and have conferences with Jack – so I would go sit in the bathroom 'til it was all over – every day. I didn't come to meals – couldn't hold any food down.

Then reporters, especially Laura Bergquist at *Look*, wanted to do an interview with me about which First Lady I admired most.

I knew which one I admired most. But the day she came I was too sick to see her, so I asked Jack to give the interview for me and he did, which was nice of him. So they expected me to say Dolly Madison or Mrs Roosevelt – but I said Mrs Truman – and I still mean it – because she kept her family together in the White House – she brought a teen-age daughter there – a difficult time for any child – and she kept her unspoiled and she kept her husband and child close – she kept a family together – under the bright hot heat of the limelight that suddenly hits a President – she kept her own values as before. That is what I wanted to do more than anything. Keep my family together in the White House – I didn't want to go into coal-mines (Mrs Roosevelt) or be a symbol of elegance (Dolly Madison) – I just wanted to save some normal life for Jack and the children and me – and even if lots of beautiful things happened there later – because I felt that that great house – the President's house – should stand for – in every field – what Jack always stood for – excellence – my first fight was to fight for a sane and normal life for my babies and their father.

That month – December – when I left the hospital – till inauguration – with all the confusion that you so well describe. I don't know if you remember – the day Jack left for Washington for the Inauguration – he was going to leave in the *Caroline* and I was going to take a commercial plane – I had been in my room for days – not getting out of bed – all the details were getting too much.

Back to Washington – Inaugural Gala – Inauguration – I guess I was just in physical and nervous exhaustion – because the month after the baby's birth had been the opposite of recuperation – and then Dr Travell came in and told Jack she was so worried about me – so he either flew to Washington commercially and sent me back on the *Caroline* – or went on the *Caroline* and sent it back to take me – Dr Travell told him I couldn't be up to facing all the barrage of going and arriving on a commercial plane – there is a picture of me waving goodbye (in a hat!) at the Palm Beach airport – these were almost the first really long steps I had taken (since the White House Tour with Mrs Eisenhower).

In Washington there were a couple of days in our house in Georgetown – I had to stay in bed – I missed all the gala things I would so have loved to share with Jack – Grandpa gave a party at Paul Young's Chinese restaurant – Jean and Steve gave a party with a big marquee – a tent in their garden – with everyone who was going to be in the New Frontier – I had to stay in bed and couldn't go to any of these. I went to the Inaugural Gala with Jack – (that wonderful picture of Grandpa taking off his tailcoat along with his overcoat!) – but I had to go home in the first intermission.

I couldn't even go to Mass with Jack Inauguration morning. We went to the Inauguration and the parade – but I had to leave in the middle. Jack went to the dinner before the ball and I couldn't go to any of the lunches or receptions before – he picked me up about 10.30 at the White House – I had been in bed all afternoon after the parade.

I went to the first Ball with Jack and the Johnsons and I so wanted to do the whole round of that wonderful evening with him – but suddenly in the car – there just wasn't any strength left – so he dropped me back at the White House and he went to the other four balls alone.

Then I had to stay in bed for a week – I remember the next morning Jack brought President Truman by to see me.

Jack was so happy – I always wished I could have participated more in those first shining hours with him – but at least I thought – I had given him our John, the son he longed for so much – it was a week before they would let me get out of bed – and I spent that week reading all these books I had had sent to me from the Library of Congress – about the history of the White House – because I knew what I wanted to do there – and I knew – as you had told me – that you had to hit the ground running and start out with a great beginning.

Then I had David Finley – Chairman at the Fine Arts Committee – come to see me – he was an old friend of my mother and stepfather's – he was slightly ill at ease to be received by me in bed – but I knew without his support I could do nothing – (Jack had told me that I mustn't try to tamper with the White House – so had Clark Clifford – because look at the criticism the Truman balcony had brought to Truman – but I thought they were wrong – and that if one did it with the backing of scholars, Republicans, Henry DuPont at Winterhur – the greatest museum of Americana – it would be something to be proud of) – so I wasn't idle.

And I had Caroline's cat – Tom Kitten – an old grey Tom cat I adored in the room with me – (I was in the Queen's Room then – as our rooms at the other end of the hall were being repainted) – then Jack would come in and start sneezing – so we realized it was his asthma – and poor Tom Kitten got relegated to the basement.

Anyway – I don't think I disgraced Jack in that time – as when there is an occasion one rises to it – but as I said earlier in this endless letter – it wasn't all Kenneth's and Cassini's.

Jack had so much suffering in all his life – so did you – the period I have spoken of was not a happy time in my life that it looks in all the pictures.

There was a human strain behind it – and you, who are so brave – will never overdo the emphasis on that – but I just thought you should know the background – your house was in turmoil – and I never let you know what was happening to me.

So I don't think it's too bad to show a little bit of strain – and then your gallant spirit makes light of it – heaven knows – you must have been under so much more strain – but you musn't toss it all off as a joke – it wasn't.

Jack was so wise – he always had a sense of what was correct – he hated hats – but he didn't want a lot of businessmen's Homburg hats at his Inauguration – he wanted it to be done the way it should be done – and he chose what was traditional – he respected the office of the Presidency so much – he who cared so little for clothes or appurtenances – I was so touched when he told me that – that he had chosen the formal traditional way – he wasn't especially at home in those clothes – but he wouldn't demean the day by having everyone in business suits and Homburg hats.

My favourite (no, one of my favourite) pictures of him – is standing in the doorway at the White House that day – in his cutaway – holding his top hat – so happy.

I remember – at our wedding – he was going to rent a cutaway – and Grandpa told him he was crazy – and he should get one made – he looked so shining in it and he wore it at his Inauguration.

The time of his funeral – Teddy didn't have one – and Provy (my adored maid from the Dominican Republic) – let it out the night before – so Teddy could get into it – (I don't know where it is now – but it must be still slightly expanded from the beautiful day when Jack wore it.)

Now I want to say some things about Ted. My thoughts turn to a time recently when Eunice and I were invited to lunch with the editors of this book and someone proposed the question to us: 'Would you rather be a Senator or the mother of a Senator?' Eunice with alacrity said she'd rather be a Senator. Very well, each to one's own. But I began to think about my answer, and later I wrote a note to myself:

I would much rather be known as the mother of a great son than the author of a great book or the painter of a great masterpiece.

He is like his brothers were in many ways, yet different from them, just as they differed from each other: each of them a unique personality; each child a product of the fascinating and mysterious equation of 'nature and nurture'. As for nurture, I suppose his position in the family had some bearing. Being the last child and a robust, handsome little boy, I expect that in our family, he received the most affection from the most people at the earliest age, and that this helps to account for his cheerful and outgoing character, his expectation of liking people and of being liked. In a rather old-fashioned but good term, he always had a 'sunny disposition'.

Further, quite considerably more than the other three boys, he had the wonderful advantage of having sustained attention and influence from his father. He was not quite nine years old when his father resigned the Ambassadorship and went into semi-retirement. True, it was only semi, for Joe remained active both in business and in public affairs, as I have related here earlier. True, Teddy would soon be in boarding-school. But during the school holidays, during the long summer vacations at Hyannis Port, Joe was at home with the family and also, at last, he could take time to go to any event, school or otherwise, in which his young son Teddy was involved. It was not a qualitative matter, because as anyone who reads this book will realize, Joe was very closely concerned with all of them. But it was a quantitative difference of large order. Joe spent a great deal more time with Teddy than with the other boys. And of course that counted.

In conversations for this book Ted discussed various influences, as he saw them, that his father and I had in the family's life, and his own life in particular. The paragraphs preceding are entirely my own opinions. Those that follow are entirely his:

Mom and Dad's characteristics balanced remarkably well. He was a motivating, dominating, powerful force with very high expectations – especially for his sons. She had the softness and gentleness and understanding that made his standards livable and reachable. From him you felt powerful demands on you. From her you felt compassion, encouragement and support.

That was more true with the boys than with the girls, because my father pretty much took charge of the education and activities of the sons and she did the same with the daughters. She asked a lot from them; then my father would be the mellowing factor.

Of course, it wasn't that well defined, because my father was kind-hearted and understanding and my mother could be quite exacting. She wanted excellence. She always strove for it herself. Even now, when I visit her, I'll find her listening to those French records. Or walking up and down the lawn reading that notebook of hers with all the quotations she's clipped from someplace and scotch-taped in. She still sends me copies of them. And all those little drills – how to use 'I' and 'me' – which she'll bring out even now if she hears you make a grammatical slip.

And when you're out for a walk with her, she might say: 'How would you describe the shutters on that house?' Or 'How would you describe the change of light on those trees?' Or 'How would you describe the different colours of the grass?' Every little walk with Mother is an educational experience.

Another of Ted's advantages, in my opinion, is that he had three older brothers to take as his models, and to strive to please. I have mentioned earlier that his faith in them was so great that, at the age of seven or eight, he would jump off the cliff at Eden Roc down to the water while Joe Jr and perhaps Jack would be yelling at him to make the effort, ready to save him in case he was stunned on impact and sank. He has some other memories of that era – when our home was still in Bronxville – that seem to me rather amazing and which probably added strength to his character and even more admiration for his brothers:

> I remember their teaching me how to ride my bicycle, and coaching me how to jump off the garage roof with a parachute. And then Bobby had a pig. He was interested in making money, to supplement his allowance, and somebody had convinced him there was money in raising pigs, so he had bought a shoat and had it in a pen and was feeding it up – it was a medium-size pig by then. One day it got loose. Bobby must have been away from the house at the time, because I remember Joe and Jack chasing the pig around the lawn. Pigs are very hard to catch, but they finally got it, and I thought that was really great. Bronxville is a respectable place and we lived in a nice neighbourhood and what the neighbours thought must have been something. This was probably about the same year that they got an alligator and put it in our swimming pool down in Florida to surprise us.

Yes, and it was about that time that both of them went off to boarding-school.

I won't guess who among the brothers might most have resembled whom, but I expect there was a special bond between Jack and Teddy if only for one reason. With our large family, and the spread in ages, it occurred to me when Jean was born to nominate the eldest, Joe Jr – who was old enough let's say to be her uncle – as her godfather. He was honoured. Thus, from some odd inspiration, in this case mine, traditions can be born. For when Teddy arrived there was a letter from Jack, a very sweet letter asking if he could be the godfather of the new baby. And he was. Thus Teddy, as he grew old enough to understand and appreciate the ideas involved – and Joe Jr being gone – could see Jack in that extra dimension, not only as the admired elder brother but as the godparent whose words, ideas, inspirations, examples, attitudes – really, everything about Jack – were bound to be respected.

The two surviving older brothers both had their influences, as Ted was recalling in conversation:

> When I was young I had two different types of relationship with my brothers. I suppose the relationship with Jack in the early years was more as an older friend than as a brother. You know, there were fourteen years between us. And he was not going to be too interested for a while in me. Not, say, when I was six and he was twenty. Or I was ten and he was twenty-four. Or when he was a Congressman and I was fourteen.
>
> I did more things with Bobby. He kept track of me more when I was in the lower school at Milton – sixth, seventh, eighth grades, along in there – because he had gone to the same school and knew about it and because he was that much closer in age. He was only seven years older than I was. That put him out of reach in any possible sense as a contemporary in those years – for instance he would be seventeen when I was ten – but it did mean that he could be my big brother.
>
> I think it was when I was around tenth-eleventh grade in school when Jack – he was always interested but he began to take a more direct personal interest, and he would give me encouragement about school. He could look at the lighter sides of situations, which made things look not so grim as the headmaster might have reported.
>
> He was almost a combination of father and brother, but as a brother would be, he was more approachable and better able to look at the lighter side of difficulties.

I expect that Jack may have been remembering certain problems that he had had at Choate. From which he had survived and had managed.

Obviously this is not the place, nor would there be the space, to describe Teddy's development from kid brother to statesman. But there are a few points I do want to mention. After Jack's and Bobby's deaths he made it his responsibility to work towards the goals that had been most important to them. Jack had proposed abolishing the discriminatory parts of our immigration laws. But it was Ted who guided the bill through the Senate. He took over Bobby's interest in the poor and the hungry and expanded it into the international field with the war victims in Biafra and the refugees in Bangladesh. Bobby had campaigned to end this country's military involvement in Vietnam. Ted was one of the most effective leaders in mobilizing the Congressional and public sentiment that finally brought that about. It wasn't a matter simply of following their footsteps, however: he brought his own judgment and skills to bear and developed his own themes and programmes in such fields as defence policy, better health care, arms control, reform of the Selective Service, and voting rights for 18-, 19- and 20-year-olds.

What few people would have any way of knowing, however, was that at the same time he was doing everything needful, everything generous and thoughtful on my behalf and on behalf of Jackie and Ethel and their children. With Jackie's two and Ethel's eleven there were thirteen children for whom he was *in loco parentis*; and with his own three, that made sixteen for whom he felt a close responsibility. He was at the hospital with Ethel when the last baby was born, and again when she was ready to come home, and when they left the hospital he was the one who carried the baby. There were all sorts of responsibilities, most of them simply implicit in the role that devolved on him as the only surviving son, and he took them wholly and cheerfully and carried them along, busy as he was. With his extraordinary thoughtfulness and understanding, Ted has been a loving, guiding influence for all the grandchildren. No one outside the family can ever know how much his efforts have meant in the shaping of their lives.

All of which made it especially ironic when he was accused of being 'irresponsible' in the aftermath of his tragic accident in July 1969 at Chappaquiddick.

The Edgartown Regatta weekend is always one of the gala times at the Cape, with people coming in from all directions and mixing into all sorts of festivities besides those having to do directly with the race. My children have participated in it for many years. I knew that Ted was flying up from Washington to Martha's Vineyard on Friday the 18th to skipper Jack's old boat, the *Victura*, in a race that afternoon, with Joey Gargan to crew for him. I knew also, probably from Joey – since it was his idea and he was the host, organizer and chef – that after the race they would be going to a cottage Joey had rented in the area for a 'cook-out' with some of the men and women who had worked with Bobby during his Presidential campaign. It was a typical scene familiar to me since girlhood. Politics is built on personal loyalties, and the people who work so hard with such devotion in a campaign need the gesture of personal thanks and appreciation that a get-together of this sort provides.

One of the girls invited was Mary Jo Kopechne. She had been one of Bobby's most trusted staff assistants in Washington and during that 1968 campaign for the Presidency. She and most of the others had been guests at Hyannis Port the previous summer for a cook-out and a sailboat race. She had high intelligence, strong moral fibre, and was a loyal, hardworking and wonderful young woman. Ethel knew her well, of course, as did several of the other girls in the family.

Hearing from him after that fateful night, Ted, who had never been on Chappaquiddick Island before, took a wrong turn on the road and drove over a narrow, unlit bridge that had no guard rails of any sort. Ted did not see the turn the bridge took, and plunged into the water upside down and Mary Jo was drowned.

Ted nearly drowned too, and he was badly bruised and shaken. He had managed to get out of the car. He swam back to it and dived down repeatedly trying to find and extricate Mary Jo – if she was still inside; for in the blackness and swirling tidal currents he couldn't be sure what had happened to her. He went back to the cottage for help from Joey and his friend Paul Markham. The three of them, working together, finally had to give up. Then Ted swam across to Edgartown, but the accident was not reported until later that morning.

Ted returned to Hyannis Port that afternoon. He was so unlike himself it was hard to believe he was my son. His usual positive attitude had vanished. He was disturbed, confused and deeply distracted and sick with grief over the death of the young woman. Oddly, but significantly, it hadn't occurred to him to have a medical exam to check on his physical injuries. We called Dr Robert Watt, who practises in Hyannis and has been our family doctor at the Cape for many years. Dr Watt's report showed that, along with various minor injuries, he had wrenched his back – which had still not fully healed after his aeroplane accident – and this caused muscle spasm and pain. Further, there was evidence – 'a big spongy swelling' – that he must have struck his head against the windshield or metal frame with very hard impact as the car turned turtle over the side of the bridge and that this could have been enough to knock him out of his wits for a while. Dr Watt's report notes that '. . . a temporary loss of consciousness and retrograde amnesia' and 'impairment of judgment and confused behaviour are symptoms consistent with an injury of the character sustained by the patient.'

But from my own impressions of him during the days directly following, it seems clear to me that his actions and ideas in the aftermath were those of a person in a state of shock. His own near death from drowning, the physical trauma and pain, the exhaustion as he dived repeatedly against the strong tidal current trying to find his passenger and get her out of the car, the despair and emotional turmoil, the blow on his head – surely these terrible events surpassed the limits of human endurance. I was crushed and shocked too, even in the wake of all the tragedies which preceded this one, as was the rest of the family. The impact was on all of us. What made the sorrow all the more vivid was the fact that he had always associated these trips to the Edgartown Regatta as events of relaxation and joy.

In the days after the accident, I watched, as did my daughters, with apprehension as Ted tried to recover from this terrible shock. With Dr Watt's good care, and his own natural resiliency and reserves of strength, he started to pull himself back together. I have a diary note: 'Ted improved every day.' A good many friends came to show support and friendship even though he really needed peace and rest.

At the end of the week, after he had appeared in court to answer the charge of leaving the accident, he went on television to address the voters of Massachusetts, to explain what had happened, to admit the seriousness of his actions, and to accept full responsibility for the tragedy. In view of his plea of guilty, and the unwarranted but ugly and destructive gossip that was being spread about the accident, he said he had to decide whether it was proper for him to remain in public life. I thought he spoke well and truly from his heart. The public response – over 100,000 telegrams and letters – the opinion polls, editorial comment, and more or less the whole spectrum of means for judging public sentiment without actually going to the lengths of a general referendum – was quite favourable and helped persuade him that the criticism could be overcome, that he could still be an effective voice for his constituents, and he should therefore stay on in the Senate and in public life.

There is not a great deal on this earth that one can do to relieve grief except to let the bereaved know that one does understand, care and feel; and to try to add to hope and faith, in any possible way. There is a quote I remember which says that '. . . in this way, we turn our heartaches into constructive efforts and lighten the sorrows of others.' I think letters help. I wrote to Mr and Mrs Kopechne, trying to say that I, having suffered the loss of one of my own daughters, could realize what a suffering this was for them; and how badly I felt that my son was in any way involved in their loss; and that my sympathy and prayers were with them. Later when I was in New York and learned they also were there, I asked them over to the apartment and we talked together about the joys and sorrows and strangenesses that life brings to all of us.

I remember reading sometime later an opinion by one of the political commentators that 'Chappaquiddick drove the iron into Ted Kennedy's soul'. That would be mainly wrong because there was plenty of iron there already; but I would agree that if there was any tendency to waver under stress, this dire event became a strong reinforcement to his will; and if there were any traces left of the juvenile 'kid brother syndrome' they were washed away forever in the waters of that black night.

By the time of the primaries for the 1972 Presidential nominations, the opinion polls showed that Ted was one of the 'most admired' men in the US and that among both party leaders and voters around the nation he was at or near the top as the choice for the Democratic nomination.

I did not want him to run. No one who really cared about him wanted him to – the family and the old friends and the close members of his staff; I'm sure it was practically unanimous. Even strangers would approach me and say, 'Don't let him, Mrs Kennedy.' The reason was altogether too obvious in view of what had happened in our family and I won't say more except that there seemed to be a certain number of crazy people wandering around. I could not bear another such loss. And there were all those sixteen children, Jack's and Bobby's and his own, for whom he had a responsibility and who needed him.

There was a great deal of pressure on him, from many leaders and supporters of the Democratic Party, to run for the Presidential nomination. Then, as much or even more pressure to get him on the ticket for the Vice-Presidency, as I was in a position to deduce since he spent most of the Convention time at Hyannis Port with the family, doing a lot of sailing, especially with the children.

Now, it may seem strange, but he and I never had anything remotely like a full and direct discussion and examination of the situation. No sitting down together on the davenport in the living-room and, 'Teddy, what I think is . . .' and 'Well, Mother, this is how I feel . . .' We wouldn't do that. It would be, for us, clumsy and would go against the grain of our relationship, which doesn't need that sort of dialogue for us to understand each other. He knew I didn't want him on the ticket in either place that year, and it soon became clear to me that he had no intention of seeking or taking either one.

Some day, perhaps, Ted may decide to seek the Presidency. When the time and circumstances are right, I would like to see him President, because I know he would be a credit to that high office and do wonderful things for the country. But as for the immediate future, the same considerations that persuaded my family against his running in 1972 still hold. Most of the grandchildren are still young and still need him.

And there are still too many risks, as anyone who reads the daily newspapers knows well. Ted, of course, will decide for himself, just as his brothers did. But if someone were to ask me whether I thought he should run for President in 1976, I would say: 'I hope not.'

Meanwhile, during these past few years, my life has been so full that I must schedule my time carefully in order to accomplish a large portion of the things I want to do. I keep going from early morning to fairly late at night (except for a nap after lunch) but nevertheless find that I am often sorely pressed for time. People seem surprised that I keep going as I do, appearing at various events and on television and so forth, and manage to hold my own.

I believe in keeping interested, growing and learning. Sedentary people are apt to have sluggish minds: a sluggish mind is apt to be reflected in flabbiness of body and in a dullness of expression that invites no interest and gets none. Vivacity, intelligence, curiosity, receptivity to ideas, true interest in other people have special relevance as one gets on in years.

I try to take my own advice. I am busy with many projects for the mentally retarded. Eunice is the one who is really in charge, for the family, of the large range of on-going programmes created by the Joseph P. Kennedy Jr Foundation, but I serve in any useful way I can. For instance, when I accept invitations to appear on commercially sponsored television shows – David Frost's and Dinah Shore's are recent instances – it is always with the proviso that I can take part of the time to describe the great need for programmes to aid the mentally handicapped, discuss some of the programmes that have come into existence, and encourage people to take an interest and to make contributions to expand the work. In other words I am really there to deliver a commercial for my favourite cause. If I get a fee for these appearances, I turn the cheques over to the Foundation.

As for politics, I dare say I have long since acquired a conditioned reflex. When Sarge accepted the 1972 Democratic Vice-Presidential nomination I felt the same old excitement and volunteered to help in any way I could. I was quite busy with several things at the time – particularly, this book – so they took it easy on me, but I did go out a few times that summer/autumn to make appearances and some short speeches on behalf of the McGovern–Shriver ticket. There was one rather notable time at Madison Square Garden; people jammed to the rafters. There was great enthusiasm for the candidates and a prolonged welcome for me. It was quite inspiring.

Meanwhile I respond to politics, to the demands and opportunities of public life and service. Evidently I have acquired a certain status – I wouldn't know how to describe it, except perhaps as a position of 'respect' – and there is no point in having that advantage unless one uses it for good causes. I don't take to the stump, I don't head up committees, I don't join demonstrations, I don't do any of those things and I don't assert my ideas and hopes in didactic ways.

Teddy says:

> Mother is especially good in a one-to-one relationship, and that's because she not only cares about people in general but as individuals. She and I might be out walking together in the dusk at Hyannis Port and a car full of people, usually parents and children, would pull up, lost, and ask directions to the Kennedy compound. Tourists, citizens, people from all over. I used to accuse her of always looking at the licence plate first to see if it was from a state with a Presidential primary. But that was entirely a joke, because invariably she would not only give them directions but point out one or two sights of special interest. Now, most of these people probably had seen her at some time on television when she was all dressed up in one of her Paris creations, so that probably would be their idea of her, which didn't match at all with this woman who was walking down Scudder Avenue or one of those roads in flat heels, a sweater and skirt, maybe a scarf, probably a golf cap, probably with a pair of dark glasses she still had on because the evening sun had bothered her eyes. But they would start recognizing her voice and way of speaking; and ask her, is it . . . ? and she would say, yes it is . . . and they would smile, and thank her, and drive off in a state of complete captivation and rapture. All right. That's part of Mother.
>
> Then there is another aspect which is her one-to-one relationship with people in government. I can talk with Mother in the political sense about how to get a bill passed or a government programme going, for instance, for the mentally retarded because I know she has been so interested in that. I could tell her what we were doing, working with the key figures in the House and Senate, and she'd make the suggestion, 'Well, I wonder if I'd write to them and tell them how interested our family is, and how interested I personally am . . . because of Rosemary and our experience . . .' And then she writes an absolutely beautiful letter. She really takes the time. These are personal letters. And they really have a tremendous impact on the committee members, the key men on Appropriations Committee and so forth. They have been exposed to testimony from all directions, yapped at by interest groups and disagreeing experts with reputations and positions to guard, and here comes a letter from

someone they know of, and respect, who cares because of personal experience, and who has studied and thought about it from that point of view. This is what I mean by person to person. But everything is in there.

She has lived that way, with the idea, 'If it's worth doing, it's worth doing well.' She communicates that; raising children, meeting people, writing to Congressmen, she exemplifies it, and this is political in the fine sense.

I was at dinner at a friend's house where Jimmy Stewart, the actor, was another of the guests and as I recall was sitting across the table from me. The conversation had taken a solemn and slightly morbid turn, which caused me to remark: 'But I'm sure God wants us to be happy and take pleasure in life. He doesn't want us to be sad.' Jimmy Stewart looked at me as if he had discovered a miracle and said, 'Mrs Kennedy, that is one of the most inspiring statements I ever heard.' I remember the incident because of his rather thunderstruck reaction and the fact that all I said was something I have always believed.

I see no reason still to doubt it. God made the world and made us to live in it for a while. We owe Him infinite thanks and obligations and duties, but surely among them is to appreciate the delights of life: the beauties of nature, the manifold varieties of the places and people of this earth, the pleasures of good company, the grace of laughter, the scent of a flower, the infinite satisfactions of true love – all those joys that are there to reach out for and claim as our own as human beings created by God's Will and endowed, by His wisdom, with capacities to enjoy this life in which He has put us as part of His design. Birds sing after a storm; why shouldn't people feel as free to delight in whatever sunlight remains to them? If more people were more thankful for what they have instead of mournful for what they have not, much good would come to the world. Pessimism feeds on itself. So does optimism.

In some aspects of living I want and need stability and certainty. I have found that a daily schedule, with regular hours assigned to certain activities in a customary pattern not only enables me to accomplish much more than I could otherwise but lends structural support to living: because there it is, you know what you will be doing or at least intend to do the next day. In fact I seem to be rather famous or notorious, or at least well known, within the family for budgeting time. Teddy has said:

We all know how difficult it can be to get Mother to change her schedule or programmes. It can be a monumental kind of movement.

Although in the day to day course of events I like predictabilities, I couldn't stand spending my life that way all the time. I would hate having to be rigid. Life is too full of things waiting to be seen. When I was a girl I used to pause and stare at the windows of steamship or travel agencies, with their displays of posters, and wonder what it would be like to *be* there: actually to *be* in Rome and Paris and London and St Petersburg and Constantinople and Athens and Cairo and Addis Ababa and Tokyo and Hong Kong and Shanghai and all those other imagined places.

I have never recovered from that wanderlust. I have seen much of the world now, but there is much more that I wish to see.

In short, I want to keep refreshing my mind and senses for as long as I live with new places and fresh experiences in them.

I feel much the same way about people. There are those I love dearly and whose welcome could never, never wear out. There are friends whom I cherish and want to see often; and, of course, friends whom I don't see often, because of geography or other complications, but still cherish. But except for those to whom one is attached by kinship or other bonds of old or deeply shared experience, I prefer to see a variety of people, because everyone is different and one enjoys people for different reasons.

I would dislike spending all my time with people who are tremendously serious all the time, who take up one cause after another. And I would be bored to distraction and worse if I ever had to spend a great deal of time with people who think the good life consists of luncheons and teas and golf games and bridge parties. One of the advantages of the Ambassadorship was just that: a variety of people whom one met, or was even obliged for official reasons to entertain at the Residence, but almost invariably interesting people with something to say. Yet I should add that I have found that nearly everyone, if drawn out a little and given an opportunity, will have something interesting or even remarkable to say.

And so, I have liked to travel. And I have liked to be with various people.

I suppose that, at least so far, the apotheosis of the idea – when I travelled to some of the most interesting places and was with some of the most interesting people in the shortest period of time – came in the summer of 1970. Late that June I flew to Switzerland and spent about two weeks in the Alpine resort and spa of Bergenstock, near Lake Lucerne; then, much refreshed, I flew to Greece to visit Jackie and Ari; and from there to Ethiopia to visit the Emperor. I took some diary notes and when I was back at Hyannis Port in August I wrote them up. These are excerpts, which I trust may be interesting:

Took the plane to Athens where I was met by Mr Kindel of the Embassy and his wife who kindly accompanied me in an airport car to the location of Ari's seaplane. There I met Mr and Mrs Emil Mosbacher. He – known as 'Bus' – is the great yachtsman, defender of the America's Cup, and presently is the State Department's Chief of Protocol. We were joined by Franklin Roosevelt Jr and his wife. We would be flying for about an hour to Ari's island, Skorpios, where his yacht the *Christina* was anchored, and there would be a cruise through some of the Greek islands.

All the others sensibly fastened their seat-belts but I left mine loose. We landed at Skorpios with a tremendous bump and I, in my loose belt, flew into the air and came down on my back a little strongly. Then more bumps, and though they were milder, by the end of three or four bumps I was really rather lame in my back. Which taught me the lesson that I must secure my seat-belt firmly in the future.

I had been on the *Christina* several times before – in the Caribbean and over there – and the life was as I remembered, really quite casual. All the guests did just about as they wanted. The Roosevelts and Mosbachers usually would take one of the smaller boats and a picnic lunch and go off investigating some of the little islands and the little nooks and corners of Skorpios, and would find a pretty cove and have their lunch and would swim in the azure water and bask in the hot sunshine. Lee and Stas Radziwill were there too, with their children, who are close contemporaries of Caroline and John Jr. The boy, Tony, is practically John's age and they are great pals. The girl is younger than Caroline, but Caroline is affectionate with her. Maria and Timmy Shriver were there too, and both are near Caroline's age. So they all played merrily together on the beach and went swimming and diving and snorkeling and fishing.

Maria is regarded as quite a beauty, with her regular features, rather piercing blue eyes, and, for a young girl of twelve, showing promise of having quite a good figure, now that she has lost weight. Years ago when I was young there was no discussion of weight, we just lost it automatically when we grew older and fell in love with a beau and wanted to be thin.

Caroline is of course a beautiful child too. She resembles Jack a great deal. She looks at you like Jack used to. Listens, thinks and feels out the situation in her mind, then goes on to act but with certain reservations unspoken.

But to get back to the adults, FDR Jr and I reminisced about the old days . . . when my husband was such a close colleague of his father and campaigned for him . . . when Franklin Jr visited us at Palm Beach and went campaigning for Jack in West Virginia . . . time had passed, much had happened . . .

Ari's main headquarters are in Athens, so he is there generally through the week and then joins Jackie and the guests at Skorpios on weekends. Hence I saw little of him this time. But when I did he was very congenial, considerate, a perfect host. And Jackie of course is a perfect hostess. It seems to be a good marriage.

In the evenings we would leave the yacht and go up the high hill – some in cars, some walking – to the house there at the top, to have a leisurely dinner. Food would be sent up from the yacht. We had delicious *hors d'œuvres* as we sat outside on the main terrace. Then go inside and dine at the long table in the spacious dining-room, simply and comfortably furnished. Clustering near the fire-place if it was a cool evening. Or strolling outside, exclaiming over the beauty of the moon on the sea and the neighbouring islands. It was quite lovely. At about eleven we would start down the hill again, most of us walking because it was only six or seven minutes when going downhill. Then a few minutes' boat ride back to the *Christina* and a sound sleep.

Left Skorpios July 20 and I went to Mass in Athens, dined alone in my hotel room and went to bed until about 1.30 a.m. Then I arose, took the plane at 2.30 in the morning. But photographers were every place around the plane. I was going Economy Class, finally went to sleep and thought I was safe from interruptions until I would arrive in Addis Ababa but the plane stopped at the other main city, Asmara, and Bus Mosbacher or someone had sent word I would be on that flight, so there was a group from the US Consulate waiting for me. They greeted me and brought me flowers. It was 8.30 in the morning and I had had very little sleep – dozing or half-asleep for a few hours – and my dress was all wrinkled and my hair was disorderly, so I was not very glad to see them. However, I appreciated the trouble they had gone to and they were charming to do it.

I arrived then at Addis Ababa, and was met by the Emperor's representative, whose name I was told was pronounced 'Martha' which was simple enough, and by the US Ambassador Hall and his wife, and was brought to the Emperor's guest-house. I unpacked and rested for much of the rest of that day.

This adventure had begun years earlier, during Jack's Presidency, when the Emperor paid a visit of state to the US and – as I have mentioned – Jackie was indisposed and Jack asked me to substitute for her as his official hostess at the White House. I had read that his birthday is July 23, and since mine is July 22 I brought this up in the course of the chatter one engages in to take the stiffness out of these official events. One remark led to another, and the Emperor declared that since we were practically twins we must celebrate our birthdays together sometime, and invited me to Ethiopia. This is the kind of opportunity that, for me, is impossible to resist: everything I had ever heard about Ethiopia, the name itself, made it seem fascinating. I had found the Emperor to be congenial. So I had kept the thought in the back of my mind ever since; and with the approach of my eightieth birthday I decided to take him up on his invitation.

Another reason to go at that time was that Jean would be in East Africa that summer with her two young sons, on safari to see the wild game, and on their way back from Kenya they would be stopping in Ethiopia at the same time I would be there; so I thought it would be fun to see them there and share an interesting experience. Further, in Jack's honour and memory, the Emperor – through his own charitable foundation, the His Imperial Majesty Haile Selassie I Foundation (to which we later contributed through one of our family foundations) – had built a new library for the university, The John F. Kennedy Library, and this would be ready for dedication.

Sarge, with all his contacts in the world of diplomacy, took a helpful interest in the plans, and in conversation with the Ethiopian Ambassador found out that whereas I would be eighty on my birthday Haile Selassie would be only seventy eight. I had somehow got it into my mind that he and I were born the same year. I felt some chagrin to learn he was younger than I. But not enough to interfere with the trip.

From my diary:

The State Guest House is a large and comfortable house at the end of a long garden with many flowers, trees and shrubs that were strange to me but most of them colourful and attractive. Everything well kept. No elevator but a wide and easy flight of stairs up to my room, and a large and well-appointed bathroom/dressing-room, most welcome to me.

I relaxed most of that first day, not only from the fatigue I felt from the long flight and lack of proper sleep but because of an advance cable from Dr Hansford, the State Department's regional medical adviser, with 'advice regarding health precautions' which included this: 'Altitude of Guest House 8500 feet. Necessitating slower pace of activity, good cardio-vascular reserve.'

High altitude never really has bothered me. I have mentioned a flight over the Andes many years ago before the era of pressurized cabins, when others in the plane were sucking oxygen tubes while I was trying to scrape frost off my window so I could have a view of the majestic snow-covered peaks. However, I preferred not to tempt fate that first day, not before I had been to my birthday party at the Imperial Palace and also had the chance to see something of the city and the country.

The Emperor put his car, a dark red Cadillac, at my disposal, and after Jean and the two boys arrived the next day, as scheduled, we did a lot of sight-seeing in it; mostly she and I, as the boys would be much more interested in such features of palace life as the large enclosure full of lions. The Emperor traces his genealogy to an alliance between the Queen of Sheba and King Solomon, as related in the Old Testament of the Bible. Hence one of the principal among his numerous titles is that of 'Lion of Judah'. Hence the lion as a symbol of his throne and the tradition of keeping a lot of lions in the enclosed park of the royal palace. Indeed I was told that the tamer ones used to be allowed to roam free in the grounds or even in the palace itself. Although I could sympathize with the lions, I was personally relieved that was no longer the case.

When we were out for drive in the Emperor's car, it was a very odd sensation to see how people along the boulevards or on the roads – probably knowing nothing at all about who was in the car but recognizing it as the royal vehicle – would stop in their tracks and bow reverently as it passed. Another disconcertment: the middle of the back seat had been elevated several inches, because the Emperor is small, not much taller than I, and when he rode this would enable his subjects to view him. But Jean is several inches taller than I, so when she sat next to me, perched on this special throne, she truly looked down on me and I felt like a midget. I may have detected a smirk on her face.

We thought the Ethiopian people were good-looking and many of the women quite beautiful, with large luminous eyes and almost classic features; well-built, poised, erect, confident, with pleasant and friendly smiles and white teeth that seemed to glisten in contrast to their dark brown skin. Among the aristocracy and governing class they seem to dress in European fashion, often in the latest styles, but I can see enough of that elsewhere and I was most struck and pleased at the sight of average women moving along the streets with such natural grace and dignity clad in immaculate white cloth, draped in something between a toga and a sari, and with the hems and borders done in three or four inches of embroidery in beautiful colours and designs.

I had rested and aroused and refreshed myself enough by the afternoon to go to the palace to be received by H.I.M. He sat at the end of a table at the end of a long room. I approached, stopping to make a deep curtsey, and he greeted me in the kindest way and we spoke for a few minutes about mutual memories; then I took my leave.

The next day was my birthday, and the Emperor gave a luncheon in my honour at the palace; or, more precisely, at the modern new palace, since the much older and slightly crumbling but more traditionally palatial one is still used also. We lunched at a long table in a quite pleasant dining-room, with the Emperor, naturally, at the head of the table:

I was on the Emperor's right. He said he preferred speaking French, as we had in Washington.

Jean was there, and the American Ambassador Hall and Mrs Hall, but otherwise the guest list of perhaps twenty-five or thirty was made up of Ethiopians, evidently of high rank – including the Emperor's grandson, the then heir-presumptive to the throne; his father, the late Duke of Harrar, having lost his life in the aftermath of an attempted *coup d'état* against the Emperor.

The Emperor was cordial to me. We chatted about this and that. He had two small dogs with him, as apparently he almost always has: the mother and one of her male offspring. The male dog was much bigger than his mother, which led to a few humorous exchanges inasmuch as my sons all have been considerably taller than I am. However, I would not describe this as a festive occasion. The women were more or less grouped together, except for Jean and Mrs Hall and me, and there was a certain air of constraint. I had heard that the family and nobility and officials were deeply in awe of H.I.M. He has great dignity and sits unusually straight. Afterwards Jean said that the little dogs and I seemed to be the only ones that were not afraid of the Emperor.

The next day, the birthday of the Emperor, there was a dinner for hundreds of people in the tremendous banquet hall of the Old

Palace. Again I was at the Emperor's right, with his sister and sister-in-law opposite on the left. One of the former Ethiopian Ambassadors to Washington sat between Jean and me. Interesting to see the combination of protocol and convenience in a different setting. But the most noticeable thing, for me, about the Emperor's birthday 'party' was the solemnity. No one spoke loudly, nearly in whispers: and few people spoke at all. There were no toasts to H.I.M.'s health and happiness, so far as I recall, no humorous attempts, no slightest word directed to or about the Head of the State – the sort of thing we would do in America, and I dare say would happen in most countries of the western world.

During the next couple of days, Jean and I had the opportunity to see a good deal of the countryside – and it is magically beautiful, with its flowering vegetation and lush green hills and valleys with mingled clouds and mists and sunshine and thin and brilliant air; and to see many places in Addis Ababa, such as the rehabilitation centre where the girls are handicapped by nature or accident in one way or another – including blindness, a common affliction in many countries in that part of the world – and are being taught to have useful lives by weaving summer silks and other fabrics and especially rugs, which are done mostly in tones of beige and brown and are quite attractive. Of course also, since Ethiopia is one of the oldest Christianized countries in the world, it was quite fascinating to visit some of the ancient churches and religious sites, and to see the Coptic version of the Mass celebrated. The Emperor is, without mistake, the official head of the Ethiopian Coptic church as well as of the state, but nevertheless allows a great degree of religious tolerance in the country. For instance, one afternoon I visited the Church of Our Saviour, a Roman Catholic Church under the direction of the Order of the Christian Brothers. I remembered that my husband, early in his boyhood, had gone to a school in East Boston where he was taught by the Christian Brothers. And that later on, an 'anonymous American' had given a big amount of money to Catholic charities with a stipulation that some of it be devoted to this school in Ethiopia. From what I saw, my general hopes for the ecumenical movement were reinforced.

I arrived back at Hyannis Port in early August, having been gone five or six weeks, and travelled 25,000 miles or so. Surely, whatever the distance, travel is one of the essences of life and of vitality. Moving, seeking, learning, enjoying being alive.

I continue to make rather extensive trips – to France, Greece, other places on the Continent – three or four times a year, and also travel a lot in the US on personal and charitable matters. But so far as possible, I prefer to keep my time free during the summer months, because that is when the children come to Hyannis Port, bringing their children, and this is a time of family reunion. Of course, since all the adults and for that matter the older grandchildren are always busy with many things in many places, there is a continual ebb and flow, but they all get there at some point, and they try to coordinate so that as many as possible can be there together at the same time.

The summer of 1972 was especially hectic because of Sarge's Vice-Presidential candidacy, which meant that he and Eunice had to be on the go most of the time. And so was Ted, because he was out campaigning all over the country for the national ticket, and also for state and local ones; so he was in and out from time to time, as was Joan. And, of course, Steve Smith was active behind the scenes, supplying his cool sagacity to any political situation involving members of the family. Ethel and Jean were there most often, but they too had their projects that took time and travel, one in particular being the now-annual RFK Celebrity Tennis Tournament which raises money for young and disadvantaged blacks, Chicanos, Puerto Ricans and Indians, to which Bobby was so devoted. Pat alternates most of the time these days between Paris (where she raised money for the McGovern/Shriver ticket and electioneered among the hundreds of thousands of American absentee voters living in western Europe) and California, with various way-stations such as New York, but she too was in Hyannis Port for a couple of weeks. Somehow, despite all the comings and goings of that unusually busy summer it happened – partly by planning but mostly by lucky coincidence – that for about forty-eight hours all 28 grandchildren were in Hyannis Port at the same time. Such a thing had never happened before and the odds would I daresay be very long indeed against its happening again, so I did what was obviously the thing to do: I hired a photographer, managed – with intricate complications and manoeuvres, and imprecations and persuasions, such as I can leave easily to the imagination – to corral all of them and had their picture taken with me.

When Jackie remarried, some wondered whether she would keep the house she and Jack had at Hyannis Port. But she soon said she was going to, because it meant so much to her and such a great deal to Caroline and John Jr and she wanted them always to be able to come back to it. And, save for some intervals, that is the way it has worked out. Jackie was talking about all this – in her house, towards the end of a recent summer – and about what Hyannis Port and the family times there have meant to her, and do mean to her and the two children, and said:

We spent the first four summers of our marriage, most of those summer months, with them at Hyannis Port. We didn't have our own house here until Caroline was born, or what I mean to say is that's when we moved into it, because Mr Kennedy especially, Grandpa, wanted to keep everyone together here. I fought against it, I thought it was too close, I wanted to be away from the compound. He had this house for us before we lived in it after Caroline was born.

But now I am glad. I was reading about some Harvard or some university study of what it is that makes for happy families. Especially what would count most in this nuclear age of uncertainty. There were many factors of course, interlocking, but one of the important, at or close to the top, would be a situation in which a number of families know each other well and have ideas and values they share and the children can play at one another's houses and sometimes would be invited and welcomed for meals. That could happen in a village, or a neighbourhood or a small town anywhere, and it's kind of what happens here with the cousins. They're separated more or less most of the year, they live in different cities or different areas of big cities, but they all know each other; and this is the place where most of them would get together, and I think that's awfully important for them.

The first two summers after I married Ari I wasn't here with the children; though they were here at times for visits. Then I came back with them this year for about half the summer.

And sometimes I think that time heals things . . . and you forget certain things . . . I mean I can't remember Jack's voice exactly any more . . . but I still can't stand to look at pictures of him and I don't have any around here except in the childrens' rooms . . . and when I came back everything just hit me, because this was the only house where we really lived, where we had our children, where every little pickle jar I had found in some little country lane on the Cape . . . and nothing's changed since we were in it . . . and all of the memories came before my eyes.

So anyway, after I looked around and unpacked and all that the first thing I did was walk over to see her. And we were sitting and talking about a lot of things, and I said, 'It really hits, doesn't it?' . . . something like that . . . and that evening she called me and said would I like to take a little walk around 9.30 or 10.00 because she didn't want me to be here and alone and be sad. And I thought: 'That woman who has so many reasons to be sad – for her to be thinking about calling me up;' it shows you what else she's like. Then the next morning she called and asked me to come and swim with her at such and such a time and . . . you know, as if she's sort of taking care of me because she thinks I'm in this house by myself with too many memories. So that's what she's like really.

And I found myself becoming so happy here. The children are happy, and the cousins are here, and all the grandchildren adore her. She's their grandmother and they love her, they're touched by her, they're amused by her and they respect her. And she does something so clever with them: she sees them in little groups . . . like she'll ask my two over for a little lunch or she'll ask herself here for lunch, or she'll see all the Lawfords or see the three teen-age girls, or the two little boys who will be interested in fishing, or the college and pre-college ones – and talk with all of them on the level of what interests them – instead of in some great mass scene where they're all tangled little bodies.

She has the food they like, which is the same food she gave to her children . . . creamed chicken and Boston Cream Pie and apple jelly and . . . in all the years I've known her she's always had the same kind of food, which is the most wonderful, best food there is in the world, sort of American home cooking food . . . always the apple jelly and the carrot and celery sticks and the wonderful roast chicken and the acorn squash and the ice-cream and cake and all those things that are so good and children love. I think you always like to know that all the best kinds of things are at your grandmother's house.

I don't know. Sometimes I'm not sure what I should talk with them about, because so many years have passed, times change, ideas change as the generations come along, and it is hard to keep up with what they are thinking and what the 'in thing' may be that season. But the daughters and daughters-in-law tell me just to keep going in the same ways I did in raising my own children.

Pat says:

I think she had a great influence on the way we brought up our children. (I don't know whether she'd appreciate credit for that or not – maybe not all twenty-eight of them.) But even in little things – like I keep my own card index on my four, due to her example. And her interest in historical places and history in general . . . and conversation at the table about events . . . I've always tried to do something like that too. I have maps in my dining-room – countries, states, capitals and all that. I think she influenced us a lot that way, the girls and the boys too. And the idea of public life. My children are very much interested, which I think is marvellous. Of course they have heard so much about politics, campaigns; they've lived through so much of it that it seems natural, but most of it comes down to them through us from Mother and of course from Daddy.

Ethel says:

I've never met a woman who is so constantly thinking about how to get others to think. I mean, it's really extraordinary. Certainly it's because of her that our children, for instance at the dining table and in the car pools, would have something to say about current events. Instead of all that same stuff children usually talk about, that spinach stuff. It makes the conversation so much more interesting. I get it into them with some of the newspaper clippings and maps and all that – but which I never would have thought about on my own, really. I think to some extent we've all taken over some of those things she did.

And then too it was really at Grandma's very strong suggestion that we began to separate the family at supper hour into two or three groups. Otherwise you'd just have been trying to spoon pabulum into baby Rory and not paying much attention to Kathleen's or Joe's or the others' problems.

Several of the grandchildren – on sufficient encouragement from fathers or mothers, aunts, uncles, others – have given their own opinions about life as it is these days in our family, and about me, and about Hyannis Port and indeed about quite a number of matters that may be interesting to others as they have been to me. 'For everything there is a season,' and they of course were speaking from the season of life they had reached. That would have been eleven and getting close to twelve for John Jr. Some of what he has said – and what others have said in other 'oral histories' that follow in the next pages – may make me beam a bit, some may make me blush a bit. But never mind, this is what was said:

John Jr:

She really likes me to learn a lot. And every time you go over there she asks you all about math and history and languages, or who were the Pilgrims and when they came and asks you who everyone is. And like do you know this and do you know that. And she talks about the church and talks about learning things, and she tries to teach you things. She talks a lot, but it's interesting what she talks about. Sometimes she talks about my father and she'll maybe tell a story about how bad he was when he was little, or when she was little and some of the bad things she did. She laughs and then you laugh. Every time we go she tells a few of the same stories. Most of the things are pretty funny.

She has very good food. She has really good Boston Cream Pie. She has millions of cakes all of the time and she has good custard.

I'd like to come back here every year. I love it.

Caroline:

She wants everybody to be as happy as they can and stuff like that. If she can do anything about it, I mean if they can be happier because of something she can do, then she does it.

She makes such an effort over everybody. She wants everybody to have a chance.

I saw her in New York when she was on the David Frost show – I was in the audience. The people sitting behind me thought she was terrible. They were a little bit older than me, and they said she was dead-to-the-world and so on because she was saying everybody should get out and work and help everybody else because she did it for the retarded. They didn't like being told they should go out and work. But I thought she was really good.

Grandmothers don't have to get mad at you for a lot of things like mothers do, but Grandma only gets mad at stuff you do that's not nice to other people – if you're rude or mean or something. Even then she does it nicely. She doesn't get really mad – she just says something in a way that you can see that it wasn't nice to somebody else.

She's always trying to bring out the best things. If she sees some picture of me she'll say things like, 'You should always remember to stand with your hands away from your sides because it makes you look thinner.' Or like I shouldn't put my teeth over my lip because it might give me buck teeth. She really goes out of her way to see if you have anything that could help you and then she encourages you to develop it. I like to draw and paint and write verses. It's pretty bad, it's really pathetic, but now and then when I write to her I send a verse, and she'll write back something like, 'We know you're not only an artist, but also a poet.' She always put a CM at the bottom, for 'Child of Mary' because that's a Sacred Heart thing and I used to go to Sacred Heart.

I guess all grandmothers are supposed to be good, and I could say something like that: 'All grandmothers are good but Grandma is the best' – but that would sound really stupid. It would be really gross.

But she is good. I know that if I ever really needed her for anything, she'd always be there.

I cheerfully admit to bias in the matter but I do think that Caroline shows a lot of talent in her verses, not only in her ability to handle rhyme and metre but in her observations and her wit. For Christmas 1971 she sent me a poem about her little brother. She had illuminated each verse with a water-colour drawing in the margin, so that it was as much a painting as a poem.

JOHN

He paints his bathroom walls in the middle of the night,
He comes into my room and unscrews every light,
Swinging on a door smeared with Crazy Foam
Singing to himself, 'Consider Yourself at Home.'[1]
At four in the morning you can find him making glue
In the back hall near his guinea-pig zoo.
He is trying to grow sea monkeys in his toothbrush glass,
You can see it on his teeth which bear a coating like grass.
He comes spitting in my room jabbing left and right
Shouting OK Caroline ready for a fight.
He is trying to blow us up with his chemistry set,
He has killed all the plants but we've escaped as yet.
He loves my mother's linen sheets and hates his own percale.
He can imitate the sounds of the humpback whale.
I love him not just because I oughter
But also because blood runs thicker than water.

> Signed: For Grandma
> Merry Christmas, 1971
> Lots of love,
> Caroline

In September of 1972 Caroline went off to boarding-school at

---

[1] Jackie has supplied an explanatory note: This is a song from *Oliver*, which was John's school show that year. He was in the cast as a member of Fagan's gang of pickpockets and thieves.

Concord Academy. I was on one of my excursions to Paris just at that time. I wrote her a letter from there. Recently she sent it back to me for use in this book, with a note saying, 'You have to use it even if there's no room because it's so good and it's so "you" and it made such a difference . . .' Therefore:

September 22, 1972
Paris

Dearest Caroline,

This is just a little note to tell you I am thinking about you and hoping all goes well and that you are not too lonely, etc. The first few weeks in a new environment are always the most difficult ones so do not be too discouraged, but meet the challenge with determination and the realization that this new school is your particular commitment this year, and that you are going to make it a happy year and a successful one. Life is really so wonderful for you all, dearest Caroline, because you have new and exciting experiences constantly under such pleasant circumstances. Learn all you can about Concord and New England, the part of the world which your dear father cherished so deeply and to which he referred nostalgically in several of his speeches.

Have fun, too, because I know God has given us many opportunities to be gay and happy and we should enjoy them to the utmost.

When you pass the Concord Library, the Concord High School or the Catholic Church, think of me almost seventy years ago driving my horse and carriage to the library in the summer, searching the Louisa Alcott books – studying my Latin (the *Aeneid*) in high school – going to Mass at the Catholic Church; and if you are near say a little prayer for me, as I pray for you here in Paris – that all may go well.

I am sure you will be happy as I was, my dear grand-daughter.

My deepest affection and love and hugs and come to Hyannis whenever possible.

Grandma

I had a note recently from Maria Shriver, Eunice's daughter:

Dear Grandma,

When I was little I used to yell every time I had to go to the dentist's. My mother mentioned this to you, and you wrote me a letter about it. Mother had me keep the letter and re-read it every time before I was to see the dentist, so I would be more courageous,

It really did help. I still didn't like going to the dentist, but I stopped yelling.

Since I have practically memorized it by this time I am returning it to you, because I think it belongs in your book.

> Love,
> Maria

In that case, here it is:

> October 15, 1965

Dear Maria,

Your mother just told me how nervous and upset you were at the dentist's office. I was so surprised, dear Maria, because I always think of you as being very brave about everything . . .

Usually in this family, we try not to complain and try to co-operate with the doctors and the dentists. You know Uncle Jack had a pain in his back so severe he never could lift his children up in the air those last few years, but he never said, 'I feel terrible,' or 'I cannot stand this backache.' He just let the doctors do their best to help him.

Your mother and all our children had such good dental care and co-operated so well that now everyone speaks of the Kennedy smile and the Kennedy teeth. They even ask what kind of vitamins I used to give the children. All of them had to wear braces on their teeth for years . . .

So, dear Maria, the next time you go to the dentist, say a little prayer, smile, and make up your mind that no one is going to say that you are a baby but rather they will say that you are a courageous girl, willing and eager to help your mother and the doctor do what they think is best for you.

> Much love,
> Affectionately,
> G.Ma

PS. Be an example to the younger ones. If you squeal, they will squeal. If you say it is OK, they will say OK.

> Love again,
> G.Ma

Bobby's and Ethel's children are the eldest among the 28; in fact, among them the span runs from eldest to youngest grandchild. Kathleen – known in the family as Cathy – is the eldest grand-daughter. She is a wonderful girl: highly intelligent, interested in public service –

she has worked, for instance, among the Indians – and has decidedly a mind of her own. Which means, naturally, that she and I do not agree about some things that I consider important. But that's all right. I defend her right to disagree, and besides I think that as she gets older she will come more to my way of thinking. Be that as it may, here is a segment of 'oral history' from her viewpoint.

Kathleen:

I arrived in Paris with this friend of mine and we had our backpacks on because we had this great idea we'd bicycle through the Loire Valley. It was raining in Paris and we really had no place to stay, and so Anne said why don't you call your grandmother? Because we knew she was in Paris and she always stayed at the Ritz. So we trekked over to the Ritz, after marching about fifteen blocks because we got off at the wrong subway station. We asked for her at the Ritz and the man at the desk said in low tones of regret that Mrs Kennedy is not staying here this year, she's at the Plaza Athéné. So we arrived over there.

First of all, they'd hardly let us in the door, because I had blue jeans on that hadn't been washed, as usual, and the backpack and a floppy hat and sort of half of a raincoat, and did not look like the material you would want. But we got through to her from the lobby phone and she was totally surprised because she didn't know we were going to be in Paris then; and we went up, and she could hardly believe it when these two dirty kids arrived in her hotel room. But she was terrific. She sort of gasped and said well, ah, go over and do this and sit down and didn't know exactly what to do with us. (Like she'll say, 'When my children were growing up we all liked nice clothes. You don't like those sort of clothes. What can I give you?') She always wants to help out but she doesn't know exactly how to do it. So she was terrific, you know. She gave us a big tea and suggested we might want to use her bathroom to bathe and clean up and make ourselves more comfortable.

She wanted to get us a room at her hotel, but we didn't think we'd fit in too well in the long run. We began making telephone calls and reached some friends and they told us about a good cheap place on the other side of town. She was very nervous about that. So we all went down and she asked at the concierge desk about it, and of course they had never heard of it at all and they were totally disdainful about it. Grandma said she wondered if it was all right for boys to stay there – but not girls? She took us over to the Left Bank in a taxi, and with her long Dior gown on walked into this half-way shabby hotel and interviewed the concierge there. 'Will these girls be safe?' 'Is there a shower?' And trying out her French. Because that's what the man at this hotel spoke. But she was terrific about it, and she was keeping her sense of humour throughout. Anne and I stayed there the next few days while we were in Paris.

She always tries to keep that sense of humour going. She wants to know what's going on and is really interested. And always wants to ask questions, making sure we're learning. Like we're going by a landmark building like Notre Dame or Les Invalides or the Louvre and it's 'Do you know the differences among the Doric, Ionic and Corinthian columns?' And seems a little surprised when you do. And then this thing of saying a little plaintively, can I give you a Dior dress. 'I don't know, Kathleen, what exactly do you *like*?'

Well, in all frankness, I do find that I am often puzzled by the young. In my generation there was nothing wrong with looking one's best. And that was one of the things that men of few or moderate means worked towards: to be able to put themselves and their wives and children in good attractive clothing, and with a lot of enterprise and luck, in the very best clothing. And in my time it was considered a great advantage and privilege to be able to go to college: something exceptional and really to be appreciated. Then, not long ago, there was a period of students burning the colleges down. And what's the point of that? When I was young, sobriety or at least strict temperance were considered normal and virtuous. And any idea of a 'drug culture' among the young would have been too incredible and simply beyond imagination.

However, one of the benefits of a long life is that one learns there are not so many things to be didactic about. I am sure of certain truths – which I will come to shortly – but the more that knowledge and understanding increase in this changing world, the more humble I become, realizing how quickly some of the 'established truths' can fade. I try to keep an open mind. Furthermore, honey is more attractive than vinegar if one is trying to get a message across to some busy bees.

Kathleen:

There's that thing about grandmothers and the grandchildren always get along and the parents have to be the disciplinarians, and I can see how it could be partly true. She'll write these Mummy and Eunice and Jean and Pat and Joan letters suggesting they tell us where to put the bicycles and what to do with the dogs and so forth, but with the grandchildren – well, she still wants to teach us but she still wants to side with us, in a lot of ways.

And she has this amazing ability to sort of step outside herself for a while and realize that though you're this proper person and you like to speak French and to do everything properly, on the other hand now and then in the 1970s being proper can be slightly absurd. But always *knowing*. It always strikes you when somebody has a sense of humour about themselves, especially older people. You think they've grown wise because they're older. Not realizing that the sense of humour goes with it, and if they didn't have that they wouldn't have become wise. And that's one of the best things about her.

Well, it is pleasant to be credited with a quality that one had always assumed about oneself, even though it may have been hidden from time to time from public or even private view by the overburden and what I might call the avalanches of events. But as for being such a 'proper' person, I have never thought of myself that way and I think I can refute the charge with one recent incident that landed me in the Palm Beach newspaper as a hitchhiker.

I had stopped in at Mrs Wrightman's house because she was giving a luncheon honouring my friend Mary Lasker, but I had to leave early because there was something else I had scheduled, and John Ryan was supposed to come and pick me up in the car. But there was a misunderstanding about the time, or somebody's watch was wrong, so after waiting for him on the porch I walked down the long driveway to wait for him at the road. He still didn't come, so I started walking home. But it is quite a long distance, and it was a hot day, so I decided the sensible thing was to try to get a ride with one of the passing motorists. I raised my thumb in the way I had seen hitchhikers do. I was well dressed in a white suit, with a good scarf and hat, and I was sure I looked respectable and I thought I looked attractive. I was therefore rather mortified when car after car went by, at least a dozen of them, until finally a man did stop and I got in.

Lest there be any misinterpretation of my motives, I told him who I was and what the problem was. He looked a bit amazed and very kindly drove me to my front door. As it happened, later that afternoon I was in the Bonwit Teller shop and saw him with his wife helping her pick a few things, so I went over to thank him again and introduce myself to her and also to tell her how it happened that I had been riding with her husband. She said he had already told her. We all smiled and I shook hands and that was the end of the story except that a day or two later the press got hold of it and it became a feature article with a cartoon drawing of me and words to the effect that 'Rose Kennedy, although now in her eighties, has taken up hitchhiking . . .'

Most of my grandchildren are still too young to be thinking much about what they want from life except the next allowance time and the penny candies they are going to load up on at the News Shop. Or being allowed to crew in races. And dolls and footballs. Cowboys and cowgirls and explorers and Indians. Ice-cream sodas and going to the movies. Dreams of glory and Boston Cream Pies.

Even the older ones are still too young to know what they really want.

I don't and will not try to impose my ideas and values on them (not that it would do any good if I did try) and I don't pry into their lives. I don't have the opportunity to see them often enough in a directly personal, relaxed and conversational way to know what they are doing most of the time, or what they are thinking about most things. I don't know whether they go to Church with any regularity – Cathy, I think, does more or less; more than some of the others – and although we do sometimes have religious discussions I often find that their ideas about the Church, about Faith, about God are groping, tentative, sceptical and thus, to me, rather hard to understand. When I have talked with them about Holy Week they were interested, but there was little knowledge about it even among those who had attended Catholic schools and even though some had been to the Holy Land. And the idea of going to Church because it's Lent didn't seem to occur to some of them. But of course the Church has changed too. The ancient rule of no meat on Fridays – which my father, in public life, had to be so careful about at official luncheons and banquets – and the rule of fasting after midnight before taking Communion (now it's only one hour) and such things as those, which were based on the idea of self-sacrifice, have been changed. So, in my lifetime, life has changed on every level. I dare say that in any such period of time it often has and that at the present pace of events in the modern world the rate of change will accelerate and become even rather more dizzying than it has been.

And so, in this world of change, in which it is very easy for anyone to become temporarily confused, I think naturally of my grandchildren, and perhaps the great-grandchildren that I may be lucky enough to see, and of those even beyond that generation, and I wonder what I can say that will be meaningful.

The best I can do is to give them ideas and a few special hopes. And again calling on the insights of others past and present for the useful extra perspectives.

I hope they will realize where they came from and how they happen to be where they are. They came – on the Kennedy-Fitzgerald side – from ancestors who were quite poor and disadvantaged through no fault of their own, but who had the imagination, the resolve, the intelligence and the energy to seek a newer, better world for themselves and their families; and the willingness to work as hard as they had to, and suffer whatever had to be suffered, and to look to the future and plan for whatever could be planned and to seize gratefully on any piece of good luck that came their way; or if none came, look for it, look for opportunity. In a short time, just a few generations, these beleaguered Irish immigrants had produced a family to whom the world looked in admiration, including a President of the United States. It was really quite an amazing story. They are the continuing part of it and I hope they will try always to be worthy of it.

I hope they will realize and remember that the United States of America was one of the few places – perhaps almost the only place – in the world where this family saga could have happened. I hope they will always feel a deep sense of gratitude towards this country, and deep pride in it, and deep obligation to 'preserve, protect and defend' it. If they choose to take the means of political life and public office, so much the better, for this has been so much a part of the family tradition and it would please me to think of it being continued. But there are other careers, other ways and means, full-time or part-time or spare-time as the case may be and circumstances may permit: but everyone should do something for the common good, the 'common weal'.

I hope they will have courage. And my definition of the term would be similar to that given by Socrates:

We are capable at the same time of taking risks and of estimating them beforehand. Others are brave out of ignorance. When they stop to think they begin to fear. But the man who most truly can be accounted brave is he who most knows the meaning of what is sweet in life and of what is terrible, then goes out undeterred to meet what is to come.

I hope they will have strength to bear the inevitable difficulties and disappointments and griefs of life. Bear them with dignity and without self-pity. Knowing that tragedies befall everyone, and that although one may seem singled out for special sorrows that is not really so; that worse things have happened many times to many others in the world, and that it is not tears but determination that makes pain bearable.

I hope they will comprehend that the span of any life is short and all the days and hours are precious. I hope they will live life fully while they are alive, in all the dimensions of both its duties and its beauties. Here are some lines from Cardinal Newman:

> God has created me to do Him some definite service. He has committed some work to me which he has not committed to another. I have my mission. I have a part in a great work; I am a link in the chain, a bond of connection between persons. He has not created me for naught. I shall do good. I shall do His work.

Very often I am asked about what people like to call my 'philosophy of life'. When it is put that way it always seems to me to be a rather formidable expression, and one too profound to respond to in simple terms. All the same, like everyone else, I am sure, I do have certain principles and values which have always loomed large in my approach to life and the problems we all face in living it to the best of our abilities. Now, as I approach my eighty-fourth year – it seems even older when I see it in print – I find it interesting to reflect on what has made my life, even with its moments of pain, such an essentially happy one.

I have come to the conclusion that the most important element in human life is faith.

If God were to take away all His blessings: health, physical fitness, wealth, intelligence and leave me but one gift, I would ask for faith – for with faith in Him, in His goodness, mercy, love for me and belief in everlasting life, I believe I could suffer the loss of my other gifts, etc., and still be happy – trustful, leaving all to His Inscrutable Providence. When I start my day with a prayer of consecration to Him, with complete trust and confidence, I am perfectly relaxed and happy regardless of what accident of fate befalls me because I know it is part of His Divine Plan and He will take care of me and my dear ones.

For me, faith means the continuing awareness of the existence of God, not in some far-off and unrelated manner, but as an object of a spiritual experience in which I am personally involved. I am referring only to the fact that I am as confident of God's existence as I am of my own, and I see Him as Lord and Saviour relating lovingly to all who are created by His hand. He reveals himself in his Word and for Catholics especially He reveals himself also in his Church, and both of these must be experienced in faith to comprehend the riches they enfold.

We must guard against the thought that faith is merely credulity, that we can simply talk or reason ourselves into possessing it; the truth is that just as it centres upon God, so too it comes from Him to those who seek it. Nor should we think of faith either as something we are born into, a kind of family legacy in the spiritual realm. Although we teach our children very early in life what we call the truths of faith, each one of them at some time in their development as human beings must pray for the gift of faith, must personally accept the gift of faith and cherish it as their own.

Having begun this book with a favourite and most meaningful passage from the Old Testament, I want to bring it to a close with a timeless passage from the New Testament. My conviction is that the instrument for conveying in purest form the purest truths of this religion is the Roman Catholic Church. But I do not urge my church beliefs on anyone. What is the point? There are many truths, and we share all the great truths. This is from St Paul's first letter to the Corinthians:

If I speak with the tongues of men and of angels, and have not charity, I am become as sounding brass, or a tinkling cymbal.

And if I should have prophecy and should know all mysteries, and all knowledge, and if I should have all faith, so that I could remove mountains, and have not charity, I am nothing . . .

Charity is patient, is kind; charity envieth not, dealeth not perversely; is not puffed up;

Is not ambitious, seeketh not her own, is not provoked to anger, thinketh no evil;

Rejoiceth not in iniquity, but rejoiceth with the truth;

Beareth all things, believeth all things, hopeth all things, endureth all things.

Charity never faileth . . .

When I was a child, I spoke as a child, I understood as a child, I thought as a child. But when I became a man, I put away the things of a child.

We see now through a glass in a dark manner, but then face to face. Now I know in part; but then I shall know even as I am known. And now there remain faith, hope, and charity, these three; but the greatest of these is charity.

INDEX OF PERSONS

INDEX OF PERSONS